For the Record

A DOCUMENTARY HISTORY

OF AMERICA

For the Record

A DOCUMENTARY HISTORY OF AMERICA

SECOND EDITION

VOLUME 1

From Contact through Reconstruction

DAVID E. SHI AND HOLLY A. MAYER

W · W · NORTON & COMPANY   NEW Y

Copyright © 2004, 1999 by W. W. Norton & Company, Inc.
Printed in the United States of America
Second Edition

Composition by PennSet.
Manufacturing by Maple-Vail.
Book design by Jack Meserole.

Library of Congress Cataloging-in-Publication Data
Shi, David E.
    For the record : a documentary history of America / David E. Shi and Holly A. Mayer.—
2nd ed.
      p.   cm.
    Includes bibliographical references.
    Contents: v. 1. From contact through Reconstruction — v. 2. From Reconstruction
through contemporary times.
    ISBN 0-393-92444-0 (v. 1). — ISBN 0-393-92445-9 (v. 2)
    1. United States—History—Sources. I. Mayer, Holly A. (Holly Ann), 1956–   II. Title.
E173.S487   2003
973—dc21   2003048715

W. W. Norton & Company has been independent since its founding in 1923, when William Warder Norton and Mary D. Herter Norton first published lectures delivered at the People's Institute, the adult education division of New York City's Cooper Union. The Nortons soon expanded their program beyond the Institute, publishing books by celebrated academics from America and abroad. By mid-century, the two major pillars of Norton's publishing program—trade books and college texts—were firmly established. In the 1950s, the Norton family transferred control of the company to its employees, and today—with a staff of four hundred and a comparable number of trade, college, and professional titles published each year—W. W. Norton & Company stands as the largest and oldest publishing house owned wholly by its employees.

W. W. Norton & Company, Inc., 500 Fifth Avenue, New York, N.Y. 10110
www.wwnorton.com
W. W. Norton & Company Ltd., Castle House, 75/76 Wells Street, London W1T 3QT

2 3 4 5 6 7 8 9 0

DAVID E. SHI is professor of history and president of Furman University in Greenville, South Carolina. He is a specialist in cultural history and is the author most recently of *Facing Facts: Realism in American Thought and Culture.*

HOLLY A. MAYER is an associate professor of history at Duquesne University in Pittsburgh, Pennsylvania. Her primary field is Early America, and she is the author of *Belonging to the Army: Camp Followers and Community during the American Revolution.*

For George Tindall

For our students

CONTENTS

CHAPTER 3 ❧ COLONIAL WAYS OF LIFE   46

INTERPRETING VISUAL SOURCES:
COLONIAL ARCHITECTURE   82

CHAPTER 4 ⌒ THE IMPERIAL PERSPECTIVE   94

CHAPTER 5 ⌒ FROM EMPIRE TO INDEPENDENCE   123

CHAPTER 9 ⤫ THE EARLY REPUBLIC   248

CHAPTER 10 ⤫ NATIONALISM AND SECTIONALISM   285

CHAPTER 11 ~ THE JACKSONIAN IMPULSE 317

CHAPTER 12 ~ THE DYNAMICS OF GROWTH 351

CHAPTER 13 ~ AN AMERICAN RENAISSANCE: RELIGION, ROMANTICISM, AND REFORM 383

CHAPTER 14 ⤜ MANIFEST DESTINY   412

CHAPTER 15 ⤜ THE OLD SOUTH   454

CHAPTER 16 ❧ THE CRISIS OF UNION   483

CHAPTER 17 ❧ THE WAR OF THE UNION   525

INTERPRETING VISUAL SOURCES: PICTURING THE CIVIL WAR   562

CHAPTER **18** ᥬ RECONSTRUCTION: NORTH AND SOUTH   573

PREFACE FOR INSTRUCTORS

"The historian, essentially, wants more documents than he can really use."
　　　　　　　　　　　　　　　　　　　　　　—Henry James, Jr.

For the Record: A Documentary History of America is a collection of primary sources intended to supplement textbooks in American history survey courses. This collection may also serve as a convenient reference work for both teachers and students of history. It provides a comprehensive yet diverse array of documents that have shaped the American experience. We know from our own experiences in the classroom that students can benefit greatly from studying the original sources that historians have used to craft their interpretations of the past. And students can use such sources to develop their own perspectives on the past.

In selecting these documents, we sought to represent the wide spectrum of historical developments by striking a balance among political, diplomatic, economic, social, and cultural perspectives. As work has often defined the lives of Americans, we have also added some more perspectives on labor and laborers in this revised edition. In general, we have tried to provide entire documents or substantial portions rather than brief snippets, which so often are pedagogically unsound and intellectually unsatisfying. We also incorporated some documents that provide comparative views on certain events and issues. We have edited several of these documents to eliminate extraneous material and make them more accessible to the reader. Ellipses and asterisks indicate where passages or portions have been omitted. In a few cases, we have also modernized spelling and punctuation, taking care not to change the meaning of the original selection.

Chapter introductions set the stage for the accompanying selections by describing each historical period and highlighting its key issues and actors. Each document in turn is introduced by a headnote that places it in the context of the period and suggests its significance. And each document is followed by a list of review questions to stimulate reflections about the material.

One of the unique features of *For the Record* is its recognition that visual artifacts are also important primary sources for the historian. Each volume contains two special sections intended to help students learn how to analyze and interpret visual sources. The four visual features include the following:

- *Colonial Architecture* explores the relationship between form and function by comparing the designs of colonial homes from three different regions.
- *Picturing the Civil War* explores the Civil War as the first "total war" represented through the camera lens of Mathew Brady and his associates.
- *Photography and Progressive Reform* explores the Progressive era through the famous and controversial photos of the immigrant reformer Jacob Riis.
- *Vietnam War Photographs* explores the relationship between media coverage and propaganda during America's longest war and period of greatest social turmoil.

Taken as a whole, *For the Record* reveals the diversity of sources that contribute to our understanding of American history. In the process, it exposes students to important public documents and powerful personal accounts of events and experiences. The result is a more textured and comprehensive understanding of the ways in which we recreate and understand the past.

In compiling *For the Record*, we have benefited from the talents and advice of the editorial and marketing staff at W. W. Norton. Steve Forman and Jon Durbin shepherded us through the first edition with great insight and considerable forbearance, and now Steve Forman has done it again with this second edition. Accolades also go to copyeditor Claire McCabe, who, with the able assistance of Sarah England, did a splendid job of shaping up the final product.

WHERE TO BEGIN

This checklist contains a series of questions that can be used to analyze most of the documents in this reader.

✔ What type of document is it?

✔ Why does the document exist? What motives prompted the author to write the material down in this form?

✔ Who wrote this document?

✔ Who or what is left out of the document—women, children, other minorities, members of the majority?

✔ In addition to the main subject, what other kinds of information can be obtained from the document?

✔ How do the subjects of the document relate to what we know about broader society?

✔ What was the meaning of the document in its own time? What is its meaning for the reader today?

✔ What does the document tell us about change in society?

For the Record

A DOCUMENTARY HISTORY

OF AMERICA

1 ✺ THE COLLISION OF CULTURES

One day life was as it had always been. And then came the following day, when vessels like no others hove into view, and in so doing hewed a new horizon for the islanders. These vessels, resembling small islands with "trees" covered in cloth rather than leaves, carried light-skinned beings wrapped in cloth and metal. Were these men? The islanders were perhaps more curious than fearful as they contemplated the correct response to these newcomers. Should the islanders fete them, fight them, or flee them? They would try all three.

When Christopher Columbus sailed into view of the island he named San Salvador in October 1492, he was greeted by inhabitants he promptly and erroneously called Indians because of his preconceived notions of the world. He was not the only one to operate under cultural concepts that undermined first—and second, and third, and subsequent—contact. Preconceptions operated on both sides while eastern and western Atlantic peoples tried to make sense of each other from within their own frames of reference. As a result, when Columbus and ensuing explorers landed on the other islands of the Caribbean and then the shores of the landmass that blocked their passage to the Pacific, they would encounter hospitality and hostility from the natives who perceived both opportunity and threat in these contacts.

During those first few years of mutual discovery, some seventy-five million people inhabited the continents later known as the Americas. The ancestors of these aborigines had themselves migrated from Asia thousands of years earlier. Over the centuries, these peoples had created richly diverse civilizations. Some of these "Indian" societies had formed highly complex cultural, political, and economic organizations. They had conceptualized intricate cosmologies, built magnificent cities, and established mighty dominions based on agriculture and trade. The most powerful native empire at the time of Spanish exploration was that of the Aztecs. Other cultures, practicing different beliefs, operated as nomadic tribes, relying on hunting, fishing, and gathering for their subsistence. Yet as strong as *they all were in their own sense of self, community, and the world, none of them was prepared to deal with the impact of the European invasion.*

The Europeans who crossed the Atlantic came from different empires or king-doms and spoke various languages, but their home cultures were not dissimilar. Thus there were similarities as well as differences in how they viewed and treated the natives. These Europeans may have had mixed motives for exploring and ex-ploiting the New World, but they all carried with them powerful biological, cul-tural, and technological weapons. They sowed germs, wielded the cross, and fired guns. Many did so while seeking gold, spices, and other precious commodities. Others, both Catholics and Protestants, saw the Native Americans as potential converts to the Christian faith. The Catholic Church in Rome had long before ap-proved the use of military force as a means of controlling people who rejected the proclaimed teachings of Jesus Christ. In the New World, Spanish authorities were required to read a statement (the requerimento*) to the Indians, inviting them to embrace Christianity. If they did not, the Spanish were then allowed to subjugate them by force. Variations on this precedent were practiced in other areas of the New World by the expansionistic and evangelistic Europeans.*

The people on each side of this cultural divide viewed the other through the prisms of their own ethnocentrism. Such views led some individuals to repudiate negotiations based on commonalities and instead go to war over their differences. Furthermore, ethnocentrism caused both sides to over and underestimate the ca-pabilities of the other as they clashed over such ideological concerns as govern-mental and religious doctrines and fought over such material matters as mineral resources and territory. Yet despite the inherent ethnocentrism of everyone in-volved, not all thought contact should be a synonym for conflict. There were indi-viduals among the Europeans and aborigines who sought to understand, if not appreciate, other peoples. Humanity as well as inhumanity was inherent to cul-tural contact.

CHRISTOPHER COLUMBUS

FROM A Letter to Luis de Santangel, Keeper of the Privy Purse (1493)

Christopher Columbus (1451–1506) tacked in and around various islands in the Caribbean as he gathered goods, foodstuffs, and information in the waning months of 1492. Then, without having reached the rich Oriental lands that had been his goal, but sure that they would be readily found on a succeeding voyage, he turned his ships east. During the voyage home, Columbus sat down to record his adventures and impressions of the New World in various letters to his supporters. He wrote one such letter to Luis de Santangel, an official of the royal court. Santangel had not only been instrumental in persuading Ferdinand and Isabella, the Spanish monarchs, to support the expedition, but he had believed strongly enough in the endeavor to raise much of the necessary funding himself.

From Bernard Quaritch, ed., *The Spanish Letter of Columbus to Luis de Sant'angel.* (London, 1893), pp. 10–18. [Editorial insertions that appear in square brackets are from the Quaritch edition—*Ed.*]

Sir: As I know that you will have pleasure from the great victory which our Lord hath given me in the voyage, I write you this, by which you shall know that in thirty-three days I passed over to the Indies with the fleet which the most illustrious King and Queen, our Lords, gave me; where I found very many islands peopled with inhabitants beyond number. And, of them all, I have taken possession for their Highnesses. . . .

*   *   *

Espanola is a marvel; the mountains and hills, and plains, and fields, and the soil, so beautiful and rich for planting and sowing, for breeding cattle of all sorts, for building of towns and villages. There could be no believing, without seeing, such harbors as are here, as well as the many and great rivers, and excellent waters, most of which contain gold. . . .

*   *   *

The people of this island, and of all the others I have seen, or not seen, all go naked, men and women, just as their mothers bring them forth; although some women cover a single place with the leaf of a plant, or a cotton something they make for that purpose. They have no iron or steel, nor any weapons; nor are they fit thereunto; not because they are not a well-formed people and of a fair stature, but that they are wondrously timorous. They have no other weapons than the stems of reeds in their seeding state, on the end of which they fix little sharpened stakes. Even these, they dare not use; for many times has it happened that I sent two or three men ashore to some village to parley, and countless numbers of them sallied forth, but as soon as they saw those approach, they fled away. . . .

*   *   *

It is true that since they have become more assured, and are losing that terror, they are artless and generous with what they have, to such a degr as no one would believe but him who had seen it. Of anything they gave, if it be asked for, they never say no, but do rather invite the person to accept it, and show as much lovingness as though they would give their hearts. . . .

*   *   *

I gave gratuitously a thousand useful things that I carried, in order that they may conceive affection, and furthermore may become Christians; for they are inclined to the love and service of their Highnesses and . . . they strive to combine in giving us things which they have in abundance, and of which we are in need. And they knew no sect, nor idolatry; save that they all believe that power and goodness are in the sky, and in such opinion, they received me at every place where I landed, after they had lost their terror. And this comes not because they are ignorant; on the contrary, they are men of very subtle wit, who navigate all those seas, and who give a marvelously good account of everything, but because they never saw men wearing clothes nor the like of our ships.

And as soon as I arrived in the Indies, in the first island that I found, I took some of them by force, to the intent that they should learn [our speech] and give me information of what there was in those parts. And so it was, that very soon they understood [us] and we them, what by speech or by signs; and those [Indians] have been of much service. To this day I carry them [with me] who are still of the opinion that I come from Heaven. . . . In all those islands, I saw not much diversity in the looks of the people, nor in their manners and language; but they all understand each other, which is a thing of singular advantage for what I hope their Highnesses will decide upon, for converting them to our holy faith, unto which they are now well disposed. . . .

*   *   *

It seems to me that in all those islands, the men are content with a single wife; and to their chief or king they give as many as twenty. The women, it appears to me, do more work than the men. Nor have I been able to learn whether they held personal property, for it seemed to me that whatever one had, they all took share of, especially of eatable things. Down to the present, I have not found in those islands any monstrous men, as many expected, but on the contrary all the people are very comely; nor are they black like those in Guinea, but have flowing hair. . . . Thus I have not found, nor had any information of monsters, except of an island which is here the second in approach to the Indies, which is inhabited by a people whom, in all the islands, they regard as very ferocious, who eat human flesh. These have many canoes with which they run through all the islands of India, and plunder and take as much as they can. They are no more ill-shapen than the others, but have the custom of wearing their hair long, like women; and they use bows and arrows of the same reed stems, with a point of wood at the top, for lack of iron they have not. Amongst those other tribes who are excessively cowardly, these are ferocious; but I hold them nothing more than the others. . . .

*   *   *

This is enough; and [thanks to] Eternal God our Lord who gives, to all those who walk His way, victory over things which seem impossible, and this was signally one such, for although men have talked or written of those lands, it was all by conjecture, without confirmation from eyesight, amounting only to this much that the hearers for the most part listened and judged that there was more fable in it than anything actual, however trifling. Since thus our Redeemer has given to our most illustrious King and Queen, and to their famous kingdoms, this victory in so high a matter, Christendom should have rejoicing therein and make great festivals, and give solemn thanks to the Holy Trinity for the great exaltation they shall have by the conversion of so many people to our holy faith; and next for the temporal benefit which will bring hither refreshment and profit, not only to Spain, but to all Christians. This briefly, in accordance with the facts. Dated, on the caravel, off the Canary Islands, the 15th February of the year 1493.

At your command,
THE ADMIRAL

REVIEW QUESTIONS

1. Was Columbus writing just to Santangel or to a wider audience?
2. What was he suggesting the Spanish do with these newly found lands and peoples? Why?
3. What was more important to Columbus, faith or fortune?
4. Would the natives be a threat to any Spanish plans? Why or why not?

HERNANDO CORTÉS

FROM A Letter Describing the Natives (1519)

Hernando Cortés (1485–1547) and his contingent of conquistadores landed at Veracruz, on the mainland of what is now called Mexico, in April 1519. Cortés started the march inland toward the Aztec metropolis, Tenochtitlán, about which he had heard such enticing accounts. He met with many native peoples on the way, some of whom, though wary, readily supported the Europeans as a means to countering Aztec power. Cortés was as fascinated by the natives as they were by him, but his interest, unlike theirs, was tinged with revulsion rather than fear. His distaste for certain native religious practices, however, did not prevent him from dealing with the Indians diplomatically when and where he could. Such diplomacy generally included pronouncements that both the land and people now belonged to Spain (as in the requerimiento, which stated that if the natives resisted, they could be subjugated by force and enslaved), and promises that the Spanish would enlighten the natives with Christianity and European civilization in return for their allegiance, labor, and resources. When his speeches did not result in the natives accepting subjugation quickly and quietly, Cortés readily resorted to swords.

From *Five Letters of Cortés to the Emperor* by Hernando Cortés, trans. J. Bayard Morris. Translation copyright © 1969 by J. Bayard Morris. Reprinted by W. W. Norton & Company. [Modern paragraph structure has been added to this selection—*Ed.*]

*   *   *

The natives who inhabit the island of Cozumel and the land of Yucatán from its northern point to where we are now settled, are of middle height, and well proportioned, except that in our district they disfigure their faces in various ways, some piercing their ears and introducing large and extremely ugly ornaments, others the lower part of the nose and upper lip in which they insert large circular stones having the appearance of mirrors, others still piercing the thick underlip right through to the teeth and hanging therefrom round stones or pieces of gold so heavy that they drag the lip down, giving an extraordinarily repulsive appearance. They wear as clothes a kind of highly coloured shawl, the men wear breech cloths, and on the top half of the body cloaks finely worked and pain' after the fashion of Moorish draperies. The common women wear highly coloured robes reaching from the waist to the feet and others which cover only the breast, all the rest of the body being uncovered; but the women of high rank wear bodices of fine cotton, very loose fitting, cut and embroidered after the vestment worn by our bishops and abbots.

Their food is composed of maize and such cereals as are to be found on the other Islands. . . . In addition they have whatever they can obtain by fishing or hunting; and they also breed large numbers of hens similar to those of the mainland which are as big as peacocks.

There are a few large towns very passably laid out. The houses in those parts which can obtain stone are of rough masonry and mortar, the rooms being low and small. . . . In addition they have their mosques, temples and walks, all of very fair size, and in them are the idols which they worship whether of stone, clay or wood. . . . These private mosques where they exist are the largest, finest, and most elaborately built buildings of any that there are in the town, and as such they keep them very much bedecked with strings of feathers, gaily painted cloths and all matter of finery. And always on the day before they are to begin some important enterprise they burn incense in these temples, and sometimes even sacrifice their own persons, some cutting out their tongues, others their ears, still others slicing their bodies with knives in order to offer to their idols the blood which flows from their wounds; sometimes sprinkling the whole of the temple with blood and throwing it up in the air, and many other fashions of sacrifice they use, so that no important task is undertaken without previous sacrifice having been made.

One very horrible and abominable custom they have which should certainly be punished and which we have seen in no other part, and that is that whenever they wish to beg anything of their idols, in order that their petition may find more acceptance, they take large numbers of boys and girls and even of grown men and women and tear out their heart and bowels while still alive, burning them in the presence of those idols, and offering the smoke of such burning as a pleasant sacrifice. Some of us have actually seen this done and they say it is the most terrible and frightful thing that they have ever seen. Yet the Indians perform this ceremony so frequently that . . . there is no year passes in which they do not thus kill and sacrifice fifty souls in every such temple, and the practice is general from the island of Cozumel to the region in which we have now settled. . . .

Your Majesties may therefore perceive whether it is not their duty to prevent such loss and evil, and certainly it will be pleasing to God if by means of and under the protection of your royal Majesties these people are introduced into and instructed in the holy Catholic Faith, and the devotion, trust and hope which they now have in their idols turned so as to repose in the divine power of the true God; for it is certain that if they should serve God with that same faith, fervour and diligence they would work many miracles. . . .

*   *   *

[As Cortés marched from Vera Cruz to Tenochtitlán, he delivered the *requiremiento* to the natives and picked them up as vassals or allies. While on the march his forces entered and "pacified" the town of Cholula.]

During the three days I was there they provided us with very indifferent food which grew worse each day, and the nobles and chief men of the city hardly ever came to speak with me. And being somewhat perplexed by this I learnt through the agency of my interpreter . . . that a girl of the city had told her that a large force of Montezuma's men had assembled nearby, and that the citizens themselves, having removed their wives, and children and clothes, intended to attack us suddenly and not leave any of us alive. . . . On the strength of such evidence and the signs of preparation that I perceived, I determined to surprise rather than be surprised, and sending for some nobles of the city I told them I wished to speak with them and assembled them all in a certain room; and meantime I ordered that our men should be on the alert and that at the sound of a musket shot they should fall upon a large number of Indians who were either close to or actually inside our quarters. So it was done; for having got the nobles into the room I left them, leapt on my horse and ordered the musket to be fired, and upon which we fell upon the Indians in such a fashion that within two hours more than three thousand of them lay dead. . . .

*　　*　　*

REVIEW QUESTIONS

1. What does Cortés's description of the mainlanders and Columbus's description of the islanders reveal about native cultures and the European evaluation of them?
2. Did Cortés display any understanding of Indian customs and practices? Of what did he approve and disapprove?
3. In most instances, did the *conquistadores* seem to prefer diplomacy or military action when dealing with native populations?

AZTEC ACCOUNTS

The Siege of Tenochtitlán (Sixteenth Century)

After the Spanish seized Montezuma, his treasure, and Tenochtitlán, Cortés left the city to take care of other matters. During his absence in the spring of 1520, Spanish soldiers massacred Aztecs celebrating a fiesta in honor of their war-god Huitzilopochtli. The Aztecs retaliated, drove the Spanish from the city, and probably killed Montezuma for betraying them (though some accused the Spanish of his murder). Even Cortés, returning with more troops, could not immediately retake the Aztec capital. While Cortés regrouped, the Aztecs celebrated their victory, elected a new king, and set out to return to life as they had known it before the Spanish arrived. That, however, was not to be.

From Miguel Leon-Portilla, ed., *The Broken Spears: The Aztec Account of the Conquest of Mexico* (Boston: Beacon Press, 1962) pp. 92–94, 96–97, 99, 105–107, 109, 111–12, 116–17, 124. [Editorial insertions appear in square brackets—*Ed.*]

While the Spaniards were in Tlaxcala, a great plague broke out here in Tenochtitlan. It began to spread during the thirteenth month [30 September–19 October] and lasted for seventy days, striking everywhere in the city and killing a vast number of our people. Sores erupted on our faces, our breasts, our bellies; we were covered with agonizing sores from head to foot.

The illness was so dreadful that no one could walk or move. The sick were so utterly helpless that they could only lie on their beds like corpses, unable to move their limbs or even their heads. They could not lie face down or roll from one side to the other. If they did move their bodies, they screamed with pain.

A great many died from this plague, and others died of hunger. They could ne search for food, and everyone else was too sick to care for them, so they starved to death in their beds.

Some people came down with a milder form of the disease; they suffered less than the others and made a good recovery. But they could not escape entirely. Their looks were ravaged, for wherever a sore broke out, it gouged an ugly pockmark in the skin. And a few of the survivors were left completely blind.

The first cases were reported in Cuatlan. By the time the danger was recognized, the plague was so well established that nothing could halt it, and eventually it spread all the way to Chalco. . . .

*   *   *

And now the Spaniards came back again. They marched here by way of Tezcoco, set up headquarters in Tlacopan and then divided their forces. . . .

The first battle began outside Tlatelolco, either at the ash pits or at the place called the Point of the Alders, and then shifted to Nonohualco. Our warriors put the enemy to flight and not a single Aztec was killed. The Spaniards tried a second advance but our warriors attacked them from their boats, loosing such a storm of arrows that the Spaniards were forced to retreat again.

Cortes, however, set out for Acachinanco and reached his goal. He moved his headquarters there, just outside the city. Heavy fighting ensued, but the Aztecs could not dislodge him.

*   *   *

[Cortes then brought up vessels he had built in Tlaxcala with European sails, rigging, and ironwork.] . . .

The Spaniards now decided to attack Tenochtitlan and destroy its people. The cannons were mounted in the ships, the sails were raised and the fleet moved out onto the lake.

When the ships approached the Zoquiapan quarter, the common people were terrified at the sight. They gathered their children into the canoes and fled helter-skelter across the lake, moaning with fear and paddling as swiftly as they could. They left all their possessions behind them and

abandoned their little farms without looking back.

Our enemies seized all our possessions. They gathered up everything they could find and loaded it into the ships in great bundles. They stole our cloaks and blankets, our battle dress, our tabors and drums, and carried them all away. The Tlatelolcas followed and attacked the Spaniards from their boats but could not save any of the plunder.

When the Spaniards reached Xoloco, near the entrance to Tenochtitlan, they found that the Indians had built a wall across the road to block their progress. They destroyed it with four shots from the largest cannon. The first shot did little harm, but the second split it and the third opened a great hole. With the fourth shot, the wall lay in ruins on the ground.

Two of the brigantines, both with cannons mounted in their bows, attacked a flotilla of our shielded canoes. The cannons were fired into the thick of the flotilla, wherever the canoes were crowded closest together. Many of our warriors were killed outright; others drowned because they were too crippled by their wounds to swim away. The water was red with the blood of the dead and dying. Those who were hit by the steel arrows were also doomed; they died instantly and sank to the bottom of the lake.

*   *   *

When the Aztecs discovered that the shots from the arquebuses and cannons always flew in a straight line, they no longer ran away in the line of fire. They ran to the right or left or in zigzags, not in front of the guns. If they saw that a cannon was about to be fired and they could not escape by running, they threw themselves to the ground and lay flat until the shot had passed over them. The warriors also took cover among the houses, darting into the spaces between them. The road was suddenly as empty as if it passed through a desert. . . .

*   *   *

Then the Spaniards brought forward the largest cannon and set it up on the sacrificial stone. The priests of Huitzilopochtli immediately began to beat their great ritual drums from the top of the pyramid. The deep throbbing of the drums resounded over the city, calling the warriors to defend the shrine of their god. But two of the Spanish soldiers climbed the stairway to the temple platform, cut the priests down with their swords and pitched them headlong over the brink.

The great captains and warriors who had been fighting from their canoes now returned and landed. The canoes were paddled by the younger warriors and the recruits. As soon as the warriors landed, they ran through the streets, hunting the enemy and shouting: "Mexicanos, come find them!"

The Spaniards, seeing that an attack was imminent, tightened their ranks and clenched the hilts of their swords. The next moment, all was noise and confusion. The Aztecs charged into the plaza from every direction, and the air was black with arrows and gunsmoke.

The battle was so furious that both sides had to pull back. The Aztecs withdrew to Xoloco to catch their breath and dress their wounds, while the Spaniards retreated to their camp in Acachinanco, abandoning the cannon they had set up on the sacrificial stone. Later the warriors dragged this cannon to the edge of the canal and toppled it in. It sank at a place called the Stone Toad.

*   *   *

[The Spanish attacked again after filling in the canal that intersected the causeway into the city.]

When the canal had been filled up, the Spaniards marched over it. They advanced cautiously, with their standard-bearer in the lead, and they beat their drums and played their chirimías as they came. The Tlaxcaltecas and the other allies followed close behind. The Tlaxcaltecas held their heads high and pounded their breasts with their hands, hoping to frighten us with their arrogance and courage. They sang songs as they marched, but the Aztecs were also singing. It was as if both sides were challenging each other with their songs. They sang whatever they happened to remember and the music strengthened their hearts.

The Aztec warriors hid when the enemy reached solid ground. They crouched down to make themselves as small as possible and waited for the signal, the shout that told them it was the moment to stand up and attack. Suddenly they heard it: "Mexicanos, now is the time!"

The captain Hecatzin leaped up and raced toward the Spaniards, shouting: "Warriors of Tlatelolco, now is the time! Who are these barbarians? Let them come ahead!" He attacked one of the Spaniards and knocked him to the ground, but the Spaniard also managed to knock Hecatzin down. The captain got up and clubbed the Spaniard again, and other warriors rushed forward to drag him away.

Then all the Aztecs sprang up and charged into battle. The Spaniards were so astonished that they blundered here and there like drunkards; they ran through the streets with the warriors in pursuit. This was when the taking of captives began. A great many of the allies from Tlaxcala, Acolhuacan, Chalco and Xochimilco were overpowered by the Aztecs, and there was a great harvesting of prisoners, a great reaping of victims to be sacrificed.

The Spaniards and their allies waded into the lake because the road had become too slippery for them. The mud was so slick that they sprawled and floundered and could not stand up to fight. The Aztecs seized them as captives and dragged them across the mud.

The Spanish standard was taken and carried off during this encounter. The warriors from Tlatelolco captured it in the place known today as San Martin, but they were scornful of their prize and considered it of little importance.

Some of the Spaniards were able to escape with their lives. They retreated in the direction of Culhuacan, on the edge of the canal, and gathered there to recover their strength.

*   *   *

The Aztecs took their prisoners to Yacacolco, hurrying them along the road under the strictest guard. Some of the captives were weeping, some were keening, and others were beating their palms against their mouths.

When they arrived in Yacacolco, they lined up in long rows. One by one forced to climb to the temple platform, where they were sacrificed by the priests. The Spaniards went first, then their allies, and all were put to death.

As soon as the sacrifices were finished, the Aztecs ranged the Spaniards' heads in rows on pikes. They also lined up their horses' heads. They placed the horses' heads at the bottom and the heads of the Spaniards above, and arranged them all so that the faces were toward the sun. However, they did not display any of the allies' heads. All told, fifty-three Spaniards and four horses were sacrificed there in Yacacolco.

The fighting continued in many different places. At one point, the allies from Xochimilco surrounded us in their canoes, and the toll of the dead and captured was heavy on both sides.

* * *

The Spanish blockade caused great anguish in the city. The people were tormented by hunger, and many starved to death. There was no fresh water to drink, only stagnant water and the brine of the lake, and many people died of dysentery.

The only food was lizards, swallows, corncobs and the salt grasses of the lake. The people also ate water lilies and the seeds of the colorin, and chewed on deerhides and pieces of leather. They roasted and seared and scorched whatever they could find and then ate it. They ate the bitterest weeds and even dirt.

Nothing can compare with the horrors of that siege and the agonies of the starving. We were so weakened by hunger that, little by little, the enemy forced us to retreat. Little by little they forced us to the wall.

* * *

During this time, the Spaniards mounted a wooden catapult on the temple platform to fling stones at the Indians. While it was being set up, the Indians who had gathered in Amaxac came out to stare at it. They pointed at the machine and asked each other what it could be. When the Spaniards had finished their preparations and were ready to shoot it at the crowd, they wound it up until the wooden beams stood erect. Then they released it like a great sling.

But the stone did not fall among the Indians. It flew over their heads and crashed into a corner of the market place. This seemed to cause an argument among the Spaniards: they gestured toward the Indians and shouted at each other. But still they could not aim the machine correctly. It threw out its stones in every direction.

Finally the Indians were able to see how it worked: it had a sling inside it, worked by a heavy rope. The Indians named it "the wooden sling."

The Spaniards and Tlaxcaltecas retreated again, marching back to Yacacolco and Tecpancaltitlan in closed ranks. Their leader was directing the campaign against us from his headquarters in Acocolecan.

* * *

Our warriors rallied to defend the city. Their spirits and courage were high; not one of them showed any fear or behaved like a woman. They cried: "Mexicanos, come here and join us! Who are these savages? A mere rabble from the south!" They did not move in a direct line; they moved in a zigzag course, never in a straight line.

The Spanish soldiers often disguised themselves so that they would not be recognized. They wore cloaks like those of the Aztecs and put on the same battle dress and adornments, hoping to deceive our warriors into thinking they were not Spaniards.

Whenever the Aztecs saw the enemy notching their arrows, they either dispersed or flattened themselves on the ground. The warriors of Tlatelolco were very alert; they were very cautious and vigilant, and watched intently to see where the shots were coming from.

But step by step the Spaniards gained more ground and captured more houses. They forced us backward along the Amaxac road with their spears and shields.

* * *

At nightfall it began to rain, but it was more like a heavy dew than a rain. Suddenly the omen appeared, blazing like a great bonfire in the sky. It wheeled in enormous spirals like a whirlwind and gave off a shower of sparks and red-hot coals, some great and some little. It also made loud noises, rumbling and hissing like a metal tube placed over a fire. It circled the wall nearest the lakeshore and then hovered for a while above Coyonacazco. From there it moved out into the middle of the lake, where it suddenly disappeared. No one cried out when this omen came into view: the people knew what it meant and they watched it in silence.

Nothing whatever occurred on the following day. Our warriors and the Spanish soldiers merely waited in their positions. Cortes kept a constant watch, standing under a many-colored canopy on the roof of the lord Aztautzin's house, which is near Amaxac. His officers stood around him, talking among themselves.

*　　*　　*

The Aztec leaders gathered in Tolmayecan to discuss what they should do. Cuauhtemoc [the new king] and the other nobles tried to determine how much tribute they would have to pay and how best to surrender to the strangers. Then the nobles put Cuauhtemoc into a war canoe, with only three men to accompany him: a captain named Teputztitloloc, a servant named Iaztachimal and a boatman named Cenyautl. When the people saw their chief departing, they wept and cried out: "Our youngest prince is leaving us! He is going to surrender to the Spaniards! He is going to surrender to the 'gods'!"

The Spaniards came out to meet him. They took him by the hand, led him up to the rooftop and brought him into the presence of Cortes. The Captain stared at him for a moment and then patted him on the head. Then he gestured toward a chair and the two leaders sat down side by side.

The Spaniards began to shoot off their cannons, but they were not trying to hit anyone. They merely loaded and fired, and the cannonballs flew over the Indians' heads. . . .

*　　*　　*

Once again the Spaniards started killing and a great many Indians died. The flight from the city began and with this the war came to an end. The people cried: "We have suffered enough! Let us leave the city! Let us go live on weeds!" Some fled across the lake, others along the causeways, and even then there were many killings. The Spaniards were angry because our warriors still carried their shields and *macanas* [flattened club edged with shards of obsidian].

. . . [The Spaniards also demanded and searched for gold.] . . .

*　　*　　*

The siege of Tenochtitlan, according to the histories, paintings and chronicles, lasted exactly eighty days. Thirty thousand men from the kingdom of Tezcoco were killed during this time, of the more than 200,000 who fought on the side of the Spaniards. Of the Aztecs, more than 240,000 were killed. Almost all of the nobility perished: there remained alive only a few lords and knights and the little children.

*　　*　　*

REVIEW QUESTIONS

1. What tactics did the Spanish employ in their attacks against the Aztecs? What do those tactics reveal about the conquistadores?
2. What tactics did the Aztecs use to defend themselves and their city from the invaders? What do such actions reveal about these natives?
3. Various factors contributed to the defeat of the Aztec people and the destruction of their society. What were some of those factors as revealed here? Which do you believe were most significant? Why?

RODRIGO DE ALBORNOZ

Report to Charles V (15 December 1525)

When Tenochtitlán fell in August 1521, Cortés faced the interrelated problems of re-
warding his soldiers and converting the Indians to European culture, while controlling
both groups. His solution, despite his severe criticism of the system as it was practiced
in the West Indies, was to continue the encomienda *(a system in which Spanish offi-*
cials, encomenderas, *were to control and care for Indians while the natives, in turn,*
were to provide tribute via goods or labor) in Mexico. Due to Cortés's earlier criti-
cisms, as well as those of others, Charles V had already ordered that the encomienda
not be instituted in New Spain, but he was too late. Cortés explained his refusal to
follow orders by stating that he would not allow the abuses practiced in the islands to
occur on the mainland. He also argued that servitude to the Spanish was better than
the slavery the Indians had suffered under their native masters. Furthermore, the en-
comienda *ensured prosperity and security. As the natives had no money with which*
to pay tribute, the empire could benefit only from their labor. The Spanish troops had
to be supported by that labor or they could not remain in the country to hold it for
their emperor. As officials on both sides of the Atlantic debated the issue, Cortés left
Mexico to counter another conquistadore's actions in Honduras (1524–26). He left
four treasury officers in charge of the government. They, in turn, immediately divided
into two factions: Alonso de Estrada and Rodrigo de Albornoz against Peralmíndez
Chirinos and Gonzalo de Salazar. The latter faction eventually gained full control of
the colony's government and exploited the encomienda *system for their own and*
their followers' benefit. Albornoz wrote the emperor to protest the extremes to which
his foes exploited the system, yet argued in support of the system itself.

From Lesley Byrd Simpson, *The Encomienda in New Spain: The Beginning of Spanish Mexico*
(Berkeley and Los Angeles: University of California Press, 1966) pp. 205–13. [Editorial insertions appear in square brackets—*Ed.*]

[Albornoz wrote about Cortés's Honduras expedition, complained about the other faction, asked for
more friars, and commented on some positive
changes among the natives due to their association
with the Europeans before he presented his argument for the encomienda.] . . .

*   *   *

If your Caesarean Majesty should order the Indians to be given in perpetuity, either in encomienda
or of their own free will, or in any way which your

Majesty may be pleased to order, it will be for the
good of your service that those to whom Indians
are given, either in perpetuity or for a period, be
obliged to sow a certain quantity of land with
Spanish wheat, so that the people who are here and
those who are coming will settle and take root and
decide to remain in this land, which is as fertile as
Spain and resembles it. There is wheat already
growing here where the Indians plant it. And let
them [the settlers] plant a certain number of vines
and trees and grains and vegetables of Spain. And

let it be obligatory upon each to plant them within a year or a year and a half after being granted his Indians, and [to raise] a certain number of cows and sheep and mares, and to keep a horse and arms according to the number of Indians he has, and [to do this] in the sight of, and at the discretion of, the governor and officers of your Majesty. Thus, since the land is so fertile and so like Spain, they will cultivate it and the people will remain in it, Christians as well as Indians, and your Majesty will receive a much greater tribute from it, and the people will not be so ready, as they are now, to leave it and go back to Spain, and to strip the Indians because they have no security in their possession. This is the cause of the ruin of your Majesty's islands and of the increase and settlement of those of Portugal, for the Portuguese are great colonizers. . . .

As your Caesarean Majesty has learned, and as those of your high council have learned, the Indians of these parts are very intelligent and peaceful and accustomed to work, and are as used to paying tribute to Montezuma and their overlords as are the farmers of Castile. Since they are already living in the way and manner of the latter, and since your Majesty has ordered us to bring this about as the best and surest means for the increase of your revenue, I have attempted to encourage them to continue in their adoption of the manners and customs of the vassals of Castile. And, although several [Spaniards] have interfered with me, moved by their private interests, as your Majesty must know, I came to an understanding with the cacique of Zacatula, which is on the coast of the South Sea where two Spanish ships are being built; and I sent an officer of mine to him . . . and we agreed on what he was to contribute to your Majesty every four months. It was that he should give two cups of gold and two bars, and maize and cacao beans, which are like almonds and which they use here for money and for their beverage. When the four months were up he came with it at the very time he had agreed upon. And in the same manner we reached an agreement with the lords of Zascatecla [sic] and with those of this city of Temixtitán [Mexico] about ordinary tributes. And thus the same would have been done with all the provinces

and towns of this New Spain if we had not been interfered with by some persons known to your Majesty.

[Albornoz will have all the natives paying tribute within the year if he is allowed to carry out his plan. He begs the King to send to New Spain a competent person as governor.]

And your Majesty may believe that if, for this purpose and for the relief of the country, since God has disposed of Hernán Cortés [there was a widely-believed rumor that Cortés was dead], you do not send a governor who will be of age, authority, and wisdom, and free from cupidity, and one who will believe that he is coming only to serve your Majesty, this country will be ruined and nothing will ever be done for the good of your Majesty's service. . . .

In this country, as your Majesty knows, there have been, with licenses procured there [at Court], expeditions into provinces and tribes to take slaves, on the pretext that they have refused to render obedience to your Majesty. These licenses were procured by delegates who have gone there [to Court] in the name of this country, although they generally go only to do what is in the interest of those in power. Your Majesty has ordered that demands first be made of the Indians before a notary, with the help of interpreters who were to give them to understand that they were to come under the dominion of your Majesty, and that if they refused to do so they would be captured and made slaves. If, most Catholic Lord, in this case all the precautions had been taken which they gave your Majesty to understand [would be taken] and which are fitting for the service of God and your Majesty . . . it would be very well and proper; but . . . it should not have been done with tricks and frauds, or for the sake of robbing them or making them slaves, but by inducing them with words and practices to adopt our Faith and the service of your Majesty.

As I have learned, it has often happened that when the Indians of some province went to offer their obedience, and in peace, the Christians fell upon them and made those who were following understand that they did not wish to be frie but to kill them. They did not wish the I offer them obedience, so that they might rob them and make them slaves. Thus great havoc has been wrought and will be wrought in this country, and its people ruined, together with those who might have come under the dominion of your Majesty, unless you order the remedy immediately.

In no wise should this [slave-taking] be allowed without great cause, for it is a heavy charge on one's conscience. Your Majesty gave permission to the people of this country to buy from the Indians the slaves they had among themselves, but much abomination and cruelty is also practiced against them. Your Majesty was given to understand that the Spaniards would buy them, but they are rarely bought. The Christian demands gold of the cacique, and if he says he has none, or if he has it and gives it to him, he is required to give a hundred or two slaves besides. And if perhaps the cacique has not so many, for the sake of obeying he gives others of his vassals who are not slaves. And the Christian, in order to content his employer, forces them to say they are slaves, although they are not. If their cacique demands it of them they will suffer death rather than admit they are not slaves, for they are very obedient to their lords. Thus great harm will come to the land if your Majesty does not order this remedied. . . .

And in order that your Majesty may provide for the good of your service I shall tell the advantages and disadvantages which there seem to be in this business. The advantage which there is in the said slaves is that, if there are many of them in the power of the Christians, more gangs of slaves will be sent to the mines, and more gold and silver and other metals will be produced, and the revenues and fifths of your Majesty will be increased, and the Christians will establish more plantations with them. And, since they are in the power of the Christians, they, and especially their children, will become Christians, and some of the Christians will teach them in the Faith, although few of us do as much as we should.

The harm, Catholic Majesty, that is done the Indians by making them slaves and branding so many is that the greatest service and aid that the Indian lords have for settling and cultivating the land and for paying tribute to the Christians by whom they are held in encomienda, is in having slaves. . . . In the second place, since the Christians demand of them much more [tribute] than they can give, in order to satisfy the Christians, with ten slaves that they send them, they send six others who are not, and sometimes these are branded as slaves, because they themselves say they are slaves just to satisfy their lords. In the third place, when the caciques have not enough vassals [to give as slaves] they bring some of their own children and sell them to one another, for some of the Indians have from ten to twenty wives, especially the chiefs, and it happens that one man will have twenty or thirty children, and it seems that they use them in their commerce, just as the Christians use animals. In the fourth place, the Indians make slaves of one another for very slight matters: some are purchased from their parents for ten or twelve measures of grain; another is purchased from his father for seven or eight blankets, which they use for clothing; another, because he was fed while a child for half a year or a year. And thus for very slight reasons and in jest they make slaves of one another . . .

Moreover, if great moderation and care are not exercised, the slaves will diminish daily, although the land is well peopled, because the slaves taken in the cold provinces and brought to the mines in the hot country die and diminish from the labor as well as from the heat, and the same holds true for those brought from the hot country to the cold, although not so much. . . .

Some, Caesarean Majesty, who have been in these parts and had experience here, say that the reason for their destruction and diminution is that they [the Spaniards], great or humble, have no care for anything but to get rich and make enough money to go back to Spain. Thus they exploit the country and take what they can and flay the Indians, and when they think they are going to get a great deal more out of them, there is no more, and they are finished. . . .

The Indians, most <u>Puissant</u> Lord, as your Majesty has been informed many times, are many and able, strong, of great stature and fond of war, and so intelligent that they need only to be drilled and to have arms in the manner of the Christians. Being so quickwitted, they are becoming used to them, and they see that horses and Christians die from a blow or a lance-thrust like themselves, whereas they formerly thought they were immortal, and two or three hundred would fly from one or two on horseback. So now it happens that an Indian will make a stand against a Christian on foot, a thing which they would not have done before, and ten or twelve Indians will attack a horseman on one side, and as many more on the other, and seize him by the legs. Then seeing how the Christians fight and arm themselves, they do the same and secretly try to collect arms and swords. And they can make pikes with the gold they give the Christians, because in the quarrels which the Christians have among themselves . . . they have used the Indians against one another. This is a bad thing and worthy of rigorous punishment by your Majesty. Besides, they teach the Indians to fight, so that one day when they have the opportunity or the equipment they will not leave a single Christian [alive]. . . .

Moreover, in order that this country may be perpetuated it seems to those who have had experience here that your Majesty should see to its settlement and grant privileges to those who are here and to those who are to come. They hold that your Majesty, in order to perpetuate the land and to be served more loyally than heretofore, should not fail to give Indians to those to whom you have granted Indians in perpetuity, because those who have governed here, even for three days, give Indians, and thus they are better obeyed than if they were lords of the land. And, since they give them without your Majesty's authority, they seek present rewards rather than their duty. . . .

If in any of your domains, Caesarean Majesty, it was ever necessary to prescribe the manner of life of your subjects and vassals, here it is even more necessary, for, since the land is rich in food and in gold and silver mines, and since everyone becomes swollen with the desire to spend and possess, by the end of a year and a half he who is a miner, or a farmer, or a swineherd, no longer wishes to be so, but wishes to be given Indians, and so he tries to spend everything he has on ornaments and silks, and the same holds for his wife, if he has one. And in the same fashion the other mechanics cease from pursuing their trades and incur excessive expense and do not work or extract gold or silver from the mines, thinking that the Indians . . . will serve them and support their families and their gentility and mine gold for them. . . . I have heard many times from those who have been a long time in these islands that in the days when silks and brocades were not brought in, the people were busy in the mines, and the best man in the land enjoyed going to them, and the least had six or seven thousand pesos in bars and was trying to send them to Castile to his family or relatives. But now that all are gentlemen and will not apply themselves to gold mining, although there is the best equipment for it that was ever in any land yet discovered, because of the many slaves and the numerous population, the one who ought to have most in this country is in debt, and thus everything is ruined and daily is getting worse. . . . I certify to your Majesty that the wives of mechanics and public women wear more silks than does the wife of a gentleman in Castile, and thus all are poor and ruined, and they destroy the poor Indians, who are the best servants in the world. . . .

REVIEW QUESTIONS

1. What abuses did Albornoz see in the application of the *requerimiento* and *encomienda*? What did he say were some of the results of those abuses?
2. Why did he recommend that the *encomienda* system be rectified rather than eliminated?
3. How did he believe it should be corrected?

THOMAS HARRIOT AND JOHN WHITE

FROM *A Briefe and true report of the new found land of Virginia* (1590)

In April of 1585 an expedition organized by Sir Walter Raleigh, but commanded by Sir Richard Grenville, left England to sail across the Atlantic and establish a colony in the New World. By July the explorer-colonists had secured a foothold on Roanoke Island in the newly named Virginia territory. With the expedition were two professional observers: Thomas Harriot and John White. While Harriot identified and described the new discoveries—whether flora, fauna, or human—in words, White recorded them in detailed drawings and paintings. After this first attempt at colonization failed in 1586, White, under Raleigh's aegis, would organize and lead another

THE TOWN OF SECOTA

group of people to attempt settlement again in 1587. In the meantime the printer-publisher Theodor de Bry set to work typesetting Harriot's words and engraving White's drawings for the book A Briefe *and* true report of the new found land of Virginia. *Published in 1590, it served to publicize the wonders of the New World—with particular attention paid to the Indian village of Secoton, which lay across the sound from Roanoke.*

From Paul Hulton, *America, 1585: The Complete Drawings of John White* (Chapel Hill: University of North Carolina Press, 1984), p. 126.

The Towne of Secota

Their townes that are not inclosed with poles aire commonlye fayrer. Then suche as are inclosed, as appereth in this figure which liuelye expresseth the towne of Secotam. For the howses are Scattered heer and ther, and they haue gardein expressed by the letter E. wherin groweth Tobacco which the inhabitants call Vppowoc. They haue also groaues wherin thei take deer, and fields vherin they sowe their corne. In their corne fields they builde as yt weare a scaffolde wher on they sett a cottage like to a rownde chaire, signiffied by F. wherin they place one to watche. For there are suche nomber of fowles, and beasts, that vnless they keepe the better watche, they would soone deuoure all their corne. For which cause the watcheman maketh continual cryes and noyse. The Sowe their corne with a certaine distance noted by H. other wise one stalke would choke the growthe of another and the corne would not come vnto his rypeurs G. For the leaues therof are large, like vnto the leaues of great reedes. They haue also aseuerall broade plotte C. whear they meete with their neighbours, to celebrate their cheefe solemne feastes as the 18. picture doth declare: and a place D. whear after they haue ended their feaste they make merrie togither. Ouer against this place they haue a rownd plott B. wher they assemble themselves to make their solemne prayers. Not far from which place ther is a lardge buildinge A. wherin are the tombes of their kings and princes, as will appere by the 22. figure likewise they haue garden notted bey the letter I. wherin they vse to sowe pompions. Also a place marked with K. wherin the make a fyre att their solemne feasts, and hard without the towne a riuer L. from whence they fetche their water. This people therfore voyde of all coutousnes lyue cherfullye and att their harts ease. Butt they solemnise their feasts in the nigt, and therfore they keepe verye great fyres to auodye darkenes, ant to testifie their loye.

REVIEW QUESTIONS

1. The description was reproduced in the original language and spelling (except that the old English β was converted to modern s). What does this example of sixteenth-century English tell you about the language and the culture which used it?

2. What does the engraving reveal about the artist's talent and the engraver's skill and tools?

3. How may people's imaginations and perceptions of the New World have been shaped by such publicists?

4. What kind of crops did the Indians cultivate?

5. What were some of the activities described and illustrated by Harriot and White?

6. Why did these two observers particularly mark these activities? How were such products or activities significant to an understanding of native life or to European plans?

7. Did Harriot and White provide idealistic or realistic portrayals of Indian culture? Why or why not?

2 ✦ ENGLAND AND ITS COLONIES

As the Old World pushed some peoples out, the New World pulled them over the Atlantic. Over the course of the seventeenth century, English colonists shipped out for a number of reasons, including those of economics, politics, and religion. Their motives were reflected in where they settled and how they sowed, nurtured, and defended their cuttings from that hardy oak called English civilization. In the course of transplantation, the colonists took with them certain shared attitudes and behaviors; but they also carried with them localized variations depending on where in England they came from and why they decided to emigrate. Further modification or deviation occurred as the offshoots took root in new soils, were nurtured by new fertilizers, and not only survived but thrived due to grafts from aborigine, African, and other European cultures. Thus, although the colonies had much in common as they developed, they also differed, in their religious, political, and social establishments.

The English colonists compared themselves to and defined themselves against native peoples, including the Powhatans, Pequots, and Mohawks, and immigrant groups, such as the Dutch and African. Coming in contact with those cultures made many colonists more aware and more defensive of their own. While adopting what they deemed useful from the other cultures, they simultaneously established their own identity—or identities—through their interactions with these groups and with English settlers in other colonies. Thus these colonists proclaimed their English identity, while developing regional—New England, Virginian, and Carolinian, for instance—and ethnic or racial ones. Cultural interchange differed in kind and amount, since colonists in some areas had more contact with diverse groups than the colonists in others. Intent on implementing their own version of civilization, however, the English colonists —as well as other European colonists—attempted to control this cultural interchange wherever, whenever, and however it happened by imposing their own legal and social principles.

Controlling intercultural exchanges was but one of the complex tasks inherent to colonization; commanding the colonists themselves was another. Military, political, social, and religious leaders found it difficult to impose order in the colonies. From the first, the often dreadful demands of survival challenged the colonists' plans and attempts to create properly regulated and cohesive societies; although the need to survive caused some people to work together, it led others to struggle and strive for their own ends at the expense of others. While the vastness of the land and the different peoples that inhabited it frightened some settlers into huddling their houses close together and accepting strict regulation for protection, others embraced the wilderness for the implied freedom it promised from nosy neighbors and government's rules. Then, as settlement proceeded, other factors, such as the growing diversity of religions and immigrants, complicated social transplantation. Whereas many colonists had hoped to reconstruct traditional social structures and mores, they found that circumstances sometimes demanded new constructions or adaptations. Each colony addressed such problems in different ways: some rooted out those who did not conform to their religious and social prescripts, while others attempted limited toleration and even inclusion. Such reactions, and the results they produced, illuminate both the initial challenges inherent to colonization as well as the developing nature of the different colonial societies.

CAPTAIN JOHN SMITH

FROM Smith's *The Generall Historie* (1624)

The Virginia Company, after receiving its charter from King James I in 1606, moved quickly to plant a colony within the territory granted to it. Within a year approximately 100 men—called adventurers—encompassing artisans, soldiers, gentlemen, as well as a few farmers, sailed across the Atlantic Ocean and in May 1607 established a plantation—a term which meant settlement to them—and fort on a river off the Chesapeake Bay. They named both the river and their small settlement after their monarch.

The adventurers had hoped to find readily-exploitable natural resources and natives to serve as laborers, but such expectations did not, literally, bear fruit. As they struggled with the reality of the land and its indigenous people, the colonists discovered just how ill-prepared they actually were. Captain John Smith, who was admitted to the governing council in June 1607 and then elected its president in the fall of 1608, strove to correct the settlers' deficiencies, subordinate the natives, and make the colony a profitable operation. His actions ensured the survival of the colony, but his *authoritarian leadership alienated many of its people. Due to his enemies' efforts, company reorganization, and a wound he suffered when some gunpowder exploded, Smith quit the colony in the fall of 1609.*

From John Lankford, ed., *Captain John Smith's America: Selections from His Writings* (New York: Harper Torchbooks, 1967) pp. 81–83. [Editorial insertions appear in square brackets—Ed.]

[In the fall of 1608 Captain Christopher Newport took some of the men on an expedition up and down the peninsula to find mineral resources and to open trade relations with native inhabitants.]

*   *   *

Trade they would not, and find their corn we could not; for they had hid[den] it in the woods: and being thus deluded, we arrived at Jamestown, half sick, all complaining, and tired with toil, famine, and discontent, to have only but discovered our gilded hopes, and such fruitless certainties, as Captain Smith foretold us. . . .

No sooner were we landed, but the President dispersed so many as were able, some for glass, others for tar, pitch, and soap ashes, leaving them with the fort to the Council's oversight.

But 30 of us he conducted down the river some 5 miles from Jamestown, to learn to make clapboard, cut down trees, and [to make] lye in [the] woods. Amongst the rest he had chosen Gabriel Beadle, and John Russell, the only two gallants of this last supply, and both proper gentlemen. Strange were these pleasures to their conditions; yet lodging, eating, and drinking, working or playing, they but doing as the President did himself. All these things were carried so pleasantly as within a week they became masters: making it their delight to hear the trees thunder as they fell; but the axes so oft blistered their tender fingers, that many times every third blow had a loud oath to drown the echo; for remedy of which sin, the President devised how to have every man's oaths numbered, and at night for every oath to have a can of water poured down his sleeve, with which every offender was so washed (himself and all) that a man should scarce hear an oath in a week. . . .

By this, let no man think that the President and these gentlemen spent their times as common wood haggers [cutters] at felling of trees, or such other like labors; or that they were pressed to it as hirelings, or common slaves; for what they did, after they were but once a little inured, it seemed and some conceited it, only as a pleasure and recreation: yet 30 or 40 of such voluntary gentlemen would do more in a day than 100 of the rest that must be pressed to it by compulsion; but twenty good workmen had been better than them all.

Master Scrivener, Captain Waldo, and Captain Winne at the fort, every one in like manner carefully regarded their charge. The President returning from amongst the woods, seeing the time consumed and no provision gotten, (and the ship lay idle at a great charge and did nothing) presently embarked himself in the discovery barge, giving order to the Council to send Lieutenant Percy after him with the next barge that arrived at the fort; two barges he had himself and 18 men, but arriving at *Chickahominy*, that dogged nation was too well acquainted with our wants, refusing to trade, with as much scorn and insolency as they could express. The President perceiving it was Powhatan's policy to starve us, told them he came not so much for their corn, as to revenge his imprisonment [December 1607], and the death of his men murdered by them; and so landing his men and ready to charge them, they immediately fled: and presently after sent their ambassadors with corn, fish, fowl, and what they had to make their peace; (their corn being that year but bad) they complained extremely of their own wants, yet fraughted our boats with a hundred bushels of corn, and in like manner Lieutenant Percy's that not long after arrived, and having done the best they could to content us, we parted good friends, and returned to Jamestown.

Though this much contented the company (that feared nothing more than starving), yet some so envied his good success, that they rather desired to hazard a starving, than his pains should prove so much more effectual than theirs. Some projects there were invented by Newport and Ratcliffe [the former president], not only to have deposed him, but to have kept him out of the fort . . . but their horns were so much too short to effect it, as they themselves more narrowly escaped a greater mischief.

All this time our old tavern made as much of all them that had either money or ware as could be desired: by this time they were become so perfect on all sides (I mean the soldiers, sailors, and savages) as there was ten times more care to maintain their damnable and private trade, than to provide for the colony things that were necessary. Neither was it a small policy in Newport and the mariners to report in England we had such plenty, and bring us so many men without victuals, when they had so many private factors [business agents] in the fort, that within six or seven weeks, of two or three hundred axes, chisels, hoes, and pick-axes, scarce[ly] twenty could be found: and for pike-heads, shot, powder, or anything they could steal from their fellows, [which] was vendible; they knew as well (and as secretly) how to convey them to trade with the savages for furs, baskets, *mussaneeks*, young beasts, or such like commodities, as exchange them with the sailors for butter, cheese, beef, pork, aqua vitae, beer, biscuit, oatmeal, and oil: and then feign all was sent them from their friends. And though Virginia afforded no furs for the store, yet one master in one voyage hath got so many by this indirect means, as he confessed to have sold in England for £30.

Those are the saint-seeming worthies of Virginia (that have notwithstanding all this, meat, drink, and wages); but now they begin to grow weary, their trade being both perceived and prevented.

None hath been in Virginia, that hath observed anything, [who] knows not this to be true: and yet the loss, the scorn, the misery, and shame, was the poor officers', gentlemen's, and careless governors', who were all thus bought and sold; the adventurers cozened, and the action overthrown by their false excuses, informations, and directions. By this let all men judge, how this business could prosper, being thus abused by such pilfering occasions. And had not Captain Newport cried *peccavi* [admitted his mistake], the President would have discharged the ship, and caused him to have stayed one year in Virginia, to learn to speak of his own experience.

Master Scrivener was sent with the barges and pinnace to *Werowocómoco*, where he found the savages more ready to fight than trade: but his vigilancy was such as prevented their projects, and by the means of Namontack, [he] got three or four hogsheads of corn; and as much *puccoon*, which is a red root, which then was esteemed an excellent dye.

Captain Newport being dispatched [December 1608], with the trials [samples] of pitch, tar, glass, frankincense, soap ashes; with that clapboard and wainscot that could be provided met with Master Scrivener at Point Comfort, and so returned [to] England. We remaining were about two hundred.

*   *   *

REVIEW QUESTIONS

1. How did each group, native and newcomer, act toward the other? What impact did that have on the colonists' settlement?
2. What kind of work did Smith have the men do? Were they productive?
3. What undermined Smith's efforts to secure and stabilize the colony?

RICHARD FRETHORNE

An Indentured Servant's Letter Home (1623)

Despite deteriorating relations with the natives, often miserable environmental conditions, and a high mortality rate, Englishmen—along with some Englishwomen and, after 1619, some Africans—continued to colonize Virginia by planting more settlements. Although the later colonists were still fundamentally adventurers, more and more of them came prepared to seek their fortune through agriculture, specifically the cultivation of tobacco. Tobacco was a labor-intensive crop, thus success and profit depended upon the acquisition and utilization of enough workers. Although Virginia planters would eventually come to rely on slaves, for most of the seventeenth century they turned to indentured laborers: colonists who contracted to work for a master for a specified number of years in return for passage to America along with room and board and other benefits as noted in the contract. Thousands of men and women accepted that challenge of hard work in the hope of future reward, only to realize once they were in America that they were not willing or able to work quite so hard in such conditions. Richard Frethorne was one of them. He was an indentured servant working at Martin's Hundred, a plantation a few miles away from Jamestown, a year after the 1622 Indian attack that left hundreds dead there and in the surrounding area. This was also a year before the royal government took over the struggling colony.

From "An Indentured Servant's Letter," in *Major Problems in the History of American Workers,* Eileen Boris and Nelson Lichtenstein (Lexington, MA: D.C. Heath, 1991) pp. 34–36. Copyright © 1991 by Houghton Mifflin Company. [The spelling in the selection has been modernized. Editorial insertions that appear in square brackets are from the Boris and Lichtenstein edition.—*Ed.*]

Loving and kind father and mother:
My most humble duty remembered to you, hoping in God of your good health, as I myself am at the making hereof. This is to let you understand that I your child am in a most heavy case by reason of the nature of the country, [which] is such that it causeth much sickness, [such] as the scurvy and the bloody flux and diverse other diseases, which maketh the body very poor and weak. And when we are sick there is nothing to comfort for us; for since I came out of the ship I never ate anything but peas, and loblollie (that is, water gruel). As for deer or venison I never saw any since I came into this land. There is indeed some fowl, but we are not allowed to go and get it, but must work hard both early and late for a mess of water gruel and a mouthful of bread and beef. A mouthful of bread for a penny loaf must serve for four men which is most pitiful. [You would be grieved] if you did know as much as [I do], when people cry out day and night— Oh! that they were in England without their limbs—and would not care to lose any limb to be in England again, yea, though they beg from door to door. For we live in fear of the enemy [Powhatan Indians] every hour, yet we have had a combat with them on the Sunday before Shrovetide [Monday before Ash Wednesday], and we took

two alive and made slaves of them. But it was by policy, for we are in great danger; for our plantation is very weak by reason of the death and sickness of our company. For we came but twenty for the merchants, and they are half dead just; and we look very hour when two more should go. Yet there came some four other men yet to live with us, of which there is but one alive; and our Lieutenant is dead, and [also] his father and his brother. And there was some five or six of the last year's twenty, of which there is but three left, so that we are fain to get other men to plant with us; and yet we are but 32 to fight against 3000 if they should come. And the nighest help that we have is ten miles of us, and when the rogues overcame this place [the] last [time] they slew 80 persons. How then shall we do, for we lie even in their teeth? . . .

And I have nothing to comfort me, nor there is nothing to be gotten here but sickness and death, except [in the event] that one had money to lay out in some things for profit. But I have nothing at all—no, not a shirt to my back but two rags (2), nor no clothes but one poor suit, nor but one pair of shoes, but one pair of stockings, but one cap, [and] but two bands. My cloak is stolen by one of my own fellows, and to his dying hour [he] would not tell me what he did with it; but some of my fellows saw him have butter and beef out of a ship, which my cloak, I doubt [not], paid for. So that I have not a penny, nor a penny worth, to help me to either spice or sugar or strong waters, without the which one cannot live here. For as strong beer in England doth fatten and strengthen them, so water here doth wash and weaken these here [and] only keeps [their] life and soul together. But I am not half a quarter so strong as I was in England, and all is for want of victuals; for I do protest unto you that I have eaten more in [one] day at home than I have allowed me here for a week. You have given more than my day's allowance to a beggar at the door; and if Mr. Jackson had not relieved me, I should be in a poor case. But he like a father and she like a loving mother doth still help me.

For when we go up to Jamestown (that is 10 miles of us) there lie all the ships that come to land, and there they must deliver their goods. And when we went up to town, as it may be, on Monday at noon, and come there by night, [and] then load the next day by noon, and go home in the afternoon, and unload, and then away again in the night, and [we would] be up about midnight. Then if it rained or blowed never so hard, we must lie in the boat on the water and have nothing but a little bread. . . . But that Goodman Jackson pitied me and made me a cabin to lie in always when I [would] come up, and he would give me some poor jacks [fish] [to take] home with me, which comforted me more than peas or water gruel. Oh, they be very godly folks, and love me very well, and will do anything for me. And he much marvelled that you would send me a servant to the Company; he saith I had been better knocked on the head. And indeed so I find it now, to my great grief and misery; and [I] saith that if you love me you will redeem me suddenly, for which I do entreat and beg. And if you cannot get the merchants to redeem me for some little money, then for God's sake get a gathering or entreat some good folks to lay out some little sum of money in meal and cheese and butter and beef. . . . But for God's sake send beef and cheese and butter, or the more of one sort and none of another. But if you send cheese, it must be very old cheese; and . . . you must have a care how you pack it in barrels; and you must put cooper's chips between every cheese, or else the heat of the hold will rot them. And look whatsoever you send me—be it never so much—look, what[ever] I make of it, I will deal truly with you. I will send it over and beg the profit to redeem me; and if I die before it come, I have entreated Goodman Jackson to send you the worth of it, who hath promised he will. If you send, you must direct your letters to Goodman Jackson, at Jamestown, a gunsmith. (You must set down his freight, because there be more of his name there.) Good father, do not forget me, but have mercy and pity. . . . I pray you to remember my love to all my friends and kindred. I hope all my brothers and sisters are in good health, and as for my part I have set down my resolution that certainly will be; that is, that the answer of this letter will be life or death to me. Therefore, good father, send as soon as you can; and if you send me anything let this be the mark.

    ROT

                            Richard Frethorne,
                             Martin's Hundred

REVIEW QUESTIONS

1. What sense of community did Frethorne note in this early settlement?
2. Although Frethorne worked primarily at the Martin's Hundred plantation, what other task did this company servant commonly have to perform?
3. What were Frethorne's major complaints?
4. What did Frethorne want of his parents?

NATHANIEL BACON

FROM Bacon's *Manifesto* (1676)

Later colonists in Virginia echoed Frethorne's complaints as they struggled with the hardships of settlement. They also started to grumble about how some colonists who had managed to establish themselves earlier were limiting the opportunities of others by amassing the best lands and controlling the government. By the 1670s most new immigrants and servants just freed from their indentures found that they could not afford lands in the settled areas, so they had to push on to the frontier. As they pushed out, the Native Americans pushed back. These issues led to a split between the colonists: those who supported Governor William Berkeley's Indian policies and defended his administration against those who favored Nathaniel Bacon's ideas. Bacon's Rebellion (1676), which was ultimately a battle over who was to rule the settlement, showed that Indian actions could pose not only external threats, but also internal ones. In the latter case, their actions produced violent schisms within settler communities. Bacon was a recent immigrant to Virginia and a young man still in his twenties when he challenged Governor Berkeley's authority. Representing the small farmers of the frontier who had been battling the natives, Bacon called for the extermination of the Indians so as to secure the territory. When Berkeley appeared to be more interested in subduing the frontiersmen, Bacon and his supporters marched against the government in Jamestown to force the issue. Having been declared a rebel, pardoned, and then condemned again, Bacon rebutted the charges against him and other rebels in a public declaration that outlined their motivation and purpose.

From Warren M. Billings, ed., *The Old Dominion in the Seventeenth Century: A Documentary History of Virginia, 1606–1689.* (Chapel Hill: University of North Carolina Press, 1975), pp. 277–79. As taken from the *Virginia Magazine of History and Biography*, I (1893):55–58.

... [I]f there bee as sure there is, a just God to appeal too, if Religion and Justice be a sanctuary here, If to plead the cause of the oppressed, If sincerely to aime at his Majesties Honour and the Publick good without any reservation or by Interest, If to stand in the Gap after soe much blood of our dear Brethren bought and sold, If after the losse of a great part of his Majesties Colony deserted and dispeopled, freely with our lives and estates to indeavor to save the remaynders bee Treason God Almighty Judge and lett guilty dye, But since wee cannot in our hearts find one single spott of Rebellion or Treason or that wee have in any manner aimed at subverting the setled Government or attempting of the Person of any either magistrate or private man not with standing the severall Reproaches and Threats of some who for sinister ends were disaffected to us and censured our ino[cent][1] and honest designes, and since all people in all places where wee have yet bin can attest our civill quiet peaseable behaviour farre different from that of Rebellion and tumultuous persons let Trueth be bold and all the world know the real Foundations of pretended giult, Wee appeale to the Country itselfe what and of what nature their Oppressions have bin or by what Caball and mistery the designes of many of those whom wee call great men have bin transacted and caryed on, but let us trace these men in Authority and Favour to whose hands the dispensation of the Countries wealth has been commited; let us observe the sudden Rise of their Estates composed with the Quality in which they first entered this Country Or the Reputation they have held here amongst wise and discerning men, And lett us see wither their extractions and Education have not bin vile, And by what pretence of learning and vertue they could soe soon into Imployments of so great Trust and consequence, let us consider their sudden advancement and let us also consider wither any Publick work for our safety and defence or for the Advancement and propogation of Trade, liberall Arts or sciences is here Extant in any [way]

---

[1]Further editorial insertions that appear in square brackets are from Billings' edition.

adaquate to our vast chardg, now let us compare these things togit[her] and see what spounges have suckt up the Publique Treasure and wither it hath not bin privately contrived away by unworthy Favourites and juggling Parasites whose tottering Fortunes have bin repaired and supported at the Publique chardg, now if it be so Judg what greater giult can bee then to offer to pry into these and to unriddle the misterious wiles of a powerfull Cabal let all people Judge what can be of more dangerous Import then to suspect the soe long Safe proceedings of Some of our Grandees and wither People may with safety open their Eyes in soe nice a Concerne.

Another main article of our Giult is our open and manifest aversion of all, not onely the Foreign but the protected and Darling Indians, this wee are informed is Rebellion of a deep dye For that both the Governour and Councell are by Colonell Coales Assertion bound to defend the Queen and Appamatocks with their blood Now whereas we doe declare and can prove that they have bin for these Many years enemies to the King and Country, Robbers and Theeves and Invaders of his Majesties' Right and our Interest and Estates, but yet have by persons in Authority bin defended and protected even against His Majesties loyall Subjects and that in soe high a nature that even the Complaints and oaths of his Majesties Most loyall Subjects in a lawfull Manner proffered by them against those barborous Outlawes have bin by the right honourable Governour rejected and the Delinquents from his presence dismissed not only with pardon and indemnitye but with all incouragement and favour, ...

Another main article of our Giult is our Design not only to ruine and extirpate all Indians in Generall but all Manner of Trade and Commerce with them, Judge who can be innocent that strike at this tender Eye of Interest; Since the Right honourable the Governour hath bin pleased by his Commission to warrant this trade who dare oppose it, or opposing it can be innocent, Although Plantations be deserted, the blood of our dear Brethren Split, ...

Another Article of our Giult is To Assert all those neighbour Indians as well as others to be outlawed, wholly unqualified for the benefitt and Protection of the law, For that the law does reciprocally protect and punish, and that all people offending must either in person or Estate make equivalent satisfaction or Restitution according to the manner and merit of the Offences Debts or Trespasses; Now since the Indians cannot according to the tenure and forme of any law to us known be prosecuted, Seised or Complained against, Their Persons being difficulty distinguished or known, Their many nations languages, and their subterfuges such as makes them incapeable to make us Restitution or satisfaction would it not be very giulty to say They have bin unjustly defended and protected these many years.

If it should be said that the very foundation of all these disasters the Grant of the Beaver trade to the Right Honourable Governour was illegall and not granteable by any power here present as being a monopoly, were not this to deserve the name of Rebell and Traytor.

Judge therefore all wise and unprejudiced men who may or can faithfully or truely with an honest heart attempt the country's good, their vindication and libertie without the aspersion of Traitor and Rebell, since as soe doing they must of necessity gall such tender and dear concernes, But to manifest Sincerity and loyalty to the World, and how much wee abhorre those bitter names, may all the world know that we doe unanimously desire to represent our sad and heavy grievances to his most sacred Majesty as our Refuge and Sanctuary, where wee doe well know that all our Causes will be impartially heard and Equall Justice administred to all men.

REVIEW QUESTIONS

1. Whom did Bacon think should judge whether or not he and his followers had engaged in rebellion and treason?
2. Whom did he believe should bear the guilt for the colony's problems? Why?
3. How did he argue that the protection of the Indians under the law is unjust? Was it a valid argument

FROM The Maryland Toleration Act (1649)

Joint-stock companies established the Virginia and Massachusetts Bay colonies under royal charters. These companies undertook settlement as business ventures, although in the latter case of Massachusetts profit was almost immediately made secondary to piety. The settlement of Maryland, like that of Massachusetts, also had a religious basis; but that basis was established by a "Papist"—the term used by hostile English Protestants—proprietor instead of a Puritan company. Cecilius Calvert, the second Lord Baltimore, hoped to make his colony into a refuge for Roman Catholics; however, from its very planting in 1634, not all the settlers in Maryland were Catholic. Calvert was willing to accept all Christians in his colony, but his acceptance was not echoed or acted upon by all of the other colonists. As a result, the Maryland proprietor had to make a rather bold move for that era: he passed the Toleration Act of 1649. The act would be revoked by a Puritan parliamentary commission in 1654, but restored by 1656. Later, as a result of the revolt of the Protestant Associators in 1689 and the 1692 establishment of the Church of England in the colony, Catholics would face active discrimination, but a precedent had been set for tolerance.

From Browne, William H., ed., *The Archives of Maryland*, vol. 1 (Baltimore: Maryland Historical Society, 1883), pp. 244–47.

*   *   *

And whereas the enforcing of the conscience in matters of Religion hath frequently fallen out to be a dangerous Consequence in those common-wealths where it hath been practiced, and for the more quiet and peaceable government of this Province, and the better to preserve mutual Love and amity among the Inhabitants thereof: Be it Therefore . . . enacted . . . that no person or persons whatsoever within this Province . . . professing to believe in Jesus Christ, shall from henceforth be any ways troubled, molested or discountenanced for or in respect of his or her religion nor in the free exercise thereof within this Province or the Islands thereunto belonging nor any way compelled to the belief or exercise of any other Religion against his or her consent, so as they be not unfaithful to the Lord Proprietary, or molest or conspire against the civil government established or to be established in this Province under him or his heirs.

And that all and every person and persons that shall presume Contrary to this Act and the true intent and meaning thereof, directly or indirectly, either in person or estate willfully to wrong, disturb, trouble, or molest any person whatsoever within this Province professing to believe in Jesus Christ for or in respect of his or her religion or the free exercise thereof in this Province . . . shall be compelled to pay triple damages to the party so wronged or molested. . . . Or if the party so offending as aforesaid shall refuse or be unable to recompense the party so wronged, or to satisfy such fine or forfeiture, then such Offender shall be severely punished by public whipping and imprisonment during the pleasure of the Lord proprietary. . . .

*   *   *

REVIEW QUESTIONS

1. Why did the proprietor promote tolerance?
2. To which faiths did this toleration for differing religious practices extend?
3. What were the penalties for prejudicial actions?
4. Why do you think they were so harsh?

WILLIAM BYRD II

FROM *The History of the Dividing Line Betwixt Virginia and North Carolina* (1728)

An excess of religious sentiment was not evident in North Carolina, nor apparently, according to William Byrd II, was that of the good husbandry and industry that supposedly marked the English yeoman. Byrd was an erudite Virginia landholder and official, who in 1728 headed the Virginia commission that, along with the North Carolina team, surveyed the disputed boundary line between the two colonies. The conscientious and ambitious Byrd duly reported not only the commission's findings but his own. His observations are marked by scathing sarcasm and insightful ironies—which are as revealing of him as they are of segments of North Carolina society. Byrd deplored waste in any degree or kind—whether in land, livestock, time, or people. While he accepted calamity as God's will, he certainly believed that prosperity could be the result of man's will. That determination, and the ability to use it for profit, marked for him the difference between the lower and upper ranks of humanity.

From Wright, Louis B., ed., *The Prose Works of William Byrd* (Cambridge: Harvard University Press, 1966), pp. 158–62, 168–69. [Editorial insertions appear in square brackets—*Ed.*]

[March] 10. The Sabbath happened very opportunely to give some ease to our jaded people, who rested religiously from every work but that of cooking the kettle. We observed very few cornfields in our walks and those very small, which seemed the stranger to us because we could see no other tokens of husbandry or improvement. But upon further inquiry we were given to understand people only made corn for themselves and not for their stocks, which know very well how to get their own living. Both cattle and hogs ramble into the neighboring marshes and swamps, where they maintain themselves the whole winter long and are not fetched home till the spring. Thus these indolent wretches during one half of the year lose the advantage of the milk of their cattle, as well as their dung, and many of the poor creatures perish in the mire, into the bargain, by this ill management. Some who pique themselves more upon industry than their neighbors will now and then, in compliment to their cattle, cut down a tree whose limbs are loaded with the moss aforementioned. The trouble would be too great to climb the tree in order to gather this provender, but the shortest way (which in this country is always counted the best) is to fell it, just like the lazy Indians, who do the same by such trees as bear fruit and so make one harvest for all. By this bad husbandry milk is so scarce in the winter season that were a big-bellied woman to long for it she would tax her longing. . . .

The only business here is raising of hogs, which is managed with the least trouble and affords the diet they are most fond of. The truth of it is, the inhabitants of North Carolina devour so much swine's flesh that it fills them full of gross humors.

*   *   *

[March 11] We had encamped so early that we found time in the evening to walk near half a mile into the woods. There we came upon a family of mulattoes that called themselves free, though by the shyness of the master of the house, who took care to keep least in sight, their freedom seemed a little doubtful. It is certain many slaves shelter themselves in this obscure part of the world, nor will any of their righteous neighbors discover them. On the contrary, they find their account in settling such fugitives on some out-of-the-way corner of their land to raise stocks for a mean and inconsiderable share, well knowing their condition makes it necessary for them to submit to any terms. Nor were these worthy borderers content to shelter runaway slaves, but debtors and criminals have often met with the like indulgence. But if the government of North Carolina have encouraged this unneighborly policy in order to increase their people, it is no more than what ancient Rome did before them, which was made a city of refuge for all debtors and fugitives and from that wretched beginning grew up in time to be mistress of a great part of the world. And, considering how Fortune delights in bringing great things out of small, who knows but Carolina may, one time or other, come to be the seat of some other great empire?

*   *   *

[March] 14. Before nine of the clock this morning the provisions, bedding, and other necessaries were made up into packs for the men to carry on their shoulders into the Dismal [Swamp]. They were victualed for eight days at full allowance, nobody doubting but that would be abundantly sufficient to carry them through that inhospitable place; nor indeed was it possible for the poor fellows to stagger under more. As it was, their loads weighed from sixty to seventy pounds, in just proportion to the strength of those who were to bear them. . . . Besides this luggage at their backs, they were obliged to measure the distance, mark the trees, and clear the way for the surveyors every step they went. It was really a pleasure to see with how much cheerfulness they undertook and with how much spirit they went through all this drudgery. . . .

*   *   *

[March 15] While the surveyors were thus painfully employed, the commissioners . . . marched in good order along the east side of the Dismal and passed the long bridge that lies over the south branch of Elizabeth River. At the end of eighteen miles we reached Timothy Ivy's plantation, where we pitched our tent for the first time and were furnished with everything the place afforded. We perceived the happy effects of industry in this family, in which every one looked tidy and clean and carried in their countenances the cheerful marks of plenty. We saw no drones there, which are but too common, alas, in that part of the world. Though, in truth, the distemper of laziness seizes the men oftener much than the women. These last spin, weave, and knit, all with their own hands, while their husbands, depending on the bounty of the climate, are slothful in everything but getting of children, and in that only instance make themselves useful members of an infant colony.

There is but little wool in that province, though cotton grows very kindly and, so far south, is seldom nipped by the frost. The good women mix this with their wool for their outer garments; though, for want of fulling, that kind of manufacture is open and sleazy. Flax likewise thrives there extremely, being perhaps as fine as any in the world, and I question not might with a little care and pains be brought to rival that of Egypt; and yet the men are here so intolerably lazy they seldom take the trouble to propagate it.

[March 16] We passed by no less than two Quaker meetinghouses, one of which had an awkward ornament on the west end of it that seemed to ape a steeple. I must own I expected no such piece of foppery from a sect of so much outside simplicity. That persuasion prevails much in the lower end of Nansemond County [in southeast Virginia], for want of ministers to pilot the people a decenter way to Heaven. . . . 'Tis a wonder no popish missionaries are sent from Maryland to labor in this neglected vineyard, who we know have zeal enough to traverse sea and land on the meritorious errand of making converts. Nor is it less strange that some wolf in sheep's clothing arrives not from New England to lead astray a flock that has no shepherd. People uninstructed in any religion are ready to embrace the first that offers. 'Tis natural for helpless man to adore his Maker in some form or other, and were there any exception to this rule, I should suspect it to be among the Hottentots of the Cape of Good Hope and of North Carolina.

[March 17] For want of men in holy orders, both the members of the council and justices of the peace are empowered by the laws of that country to marry all those who will not take one another's word; but, for the ceremony of christening their children, they trust that to chance. If a parson come in their way, they will crave a cast of his office, as they call it; else they are content their offspring should remain as arrant pagans as themselves. They account it among their greatest advantages that they are not priest-ridden, not remembering that the clergy is rarely guilty of bestriding such as have the misfortune to be poor. One thing may be said for the inhabitants of that province, that they are not troubled with any religious fumes and have the least superstition of any people living. They do not know Sunday from any other day, any more than Robinson Crusoe did, which would give them a great advantage were they given to be industrious. But they keep so many Sabbaths every week that their disregard of the seventh day has no manner of cruelty in it, either to servants or cattle.

*　　*　　*

[March] 24. This being Sunday, we had a numerous congregation, which flocked to our quarters from all the adjacent country. The news that our surveyors were come out of the Dismal increased the number very much, because it would give them an opportunity of guessing, at least, whereabouts the line would cut, whereby they might form some judgment whether they belonged to Virginia or Carolina. Those who had taken up land within the disputed bounds were in great pain lest it should be found to lie in Virginia; because this being done contrary to an express order of that government, the patentees [landholders via patents] had great reason to fear they should in that case have lost their land. But their apprehensions were now at an end when they understood that all the territory which had been controverted was like to be left in Carolina.

*　　*　　*

[March 25] Surely there is no place in the world where the inhabitants live with less labor than in North Carolina. It approaches nearer to the description of Lubberland [mythical land of ease and plenty] than any other, by the great felicity of the climate, the easiness of raising provisions, and the slothfulness of the people. Indian corn is of so great increase that a little pains will subsist a very large family with bread, and then they may have meat without any pains at all, . . . The men, for their parts, just like the Indians, impose all the work upon the poor women. They make their wives rise out of their beds early in the morning, at the same time that they lie and snore till the sun has risen one-third of his course and dispersed all the unwholesome damps. Then, after stretching

and yawning for half an hour, they light their pipes, and, under the protection of a cloud of smoke, venture out into the open air; though if it happen to be never so little cold they quickly return shivering into the chimney corner. When the weather is mild, they stand leaning with both their arms upon the cornfield fence and gravely consider whether they had best go and take a small heat at the hoe but generally find reasons to put it off till another time. Thus they loiter away their lives, . . . and at the winding up of the year scarcely have bread to eat. To speak the truth, 'tis a thorough aversion to labor that makes people file off to North Carolina, where plenty and a warm sun confirm them in their disposition to laziness for their whole lives. . . .

*　　*　　*

[March 27] A citizen here is counted extravagant if he has ambition enough to aspire to a brick chimney. Justice herself is but indifferently lodged, the courthouse having much of the air of a common tobacco house. I believe this is the only metropolis in the Christian or Mahometan world where there is neither church, chapel, mosque, synagogue, or any other place of public worship of any sect or religion whatsoever. What little devotion there may happen to be is much more private than their vices. The people seem easy without a minister as long as they are exempted from paying him. Sometimes the Society for Propagating the Gospel has had the charity to send over missionaries to this country; but unfortunately, the priest has been too lewd for the people, or, which oftener happens, they too lewd for the priest. For these reasons these reverend gentlemen have always left their flocks as arrant heathen as they found them. Thus much, however, may be said for the inhabitants of Edenton, that not a soul has the least taint of hypocrisy or superstition, acting very frankly and aboveboard in all their exercises.

Provisions here are extremely cheap and extremely good, so that people may live plentifully at a trifling expense. Nothing is dear but law, physic, and strong drink, which are all bad in their kind, and the last they get with so much difficulty that they are never guilty of the sin of suffering it to sour upon their hands. . . . They are rarely guilty of flattering or making any court to their governors but treat them with all the excesses of freedom and familiarity. They are of opinion their rulers would be apt to grow insolent if they grew rich, and for that reason take care to keep them poorer and more dependent, if possible, than the saints in New England used to do their governors. . . .

REVIEW QUESTIONS

1. How does this account indicate that there was some truth to the tales and publications that circulated through England and Europe extolling America as a land of plenty?
2. Why did Byrd see that as something both to commend and condemn?
3. What were some of the behaviors exhibited by the Carolinians that seemed to incense Byrd? Did he draw any conclusions as to why these settlers acted as they did?
4. Was religion part of the problem or the solution to the evils he believed were besetting North Carolina? Why?

JOHN WINTHROP

FROM General Observations AND Model of Christian Charity (1629–30)

The Puritans, like the Pilgrims, felt impelled to emigrate to escape religious persecution. Puritans were dissenters who strove to "purify" the Anglican Church of the vestiges of Catholicism and reform it through a stronger application of Calvinism. Condemned and harassed by crown and church officials, some decided to move to the New World. There they planned to establish, as their governor John Winthrop phrased it, a "city upon a hill" that was to set a shining example of piety and community for the rest of the world. Instead of pursuing property and profit, the Puritans were on a mission—though they certainly prayed that peace and prosperity would attend their piety. In 1629, as Winthrop, the forty-one-year-old Suffolk county squire, prepared to lead the first contingent of Puritans to the Massachusetts Bay colony, he listed some of the reasons why he was emigrating and why others should too. Then in 1630 while aboard the Arbella, *as the colonists struggled with homesickness, seasickness, and fear of the unknown, he both chastised and encouraged them by reminding them that they were engaged in a labor of love and that their endeavors would be judged.*

From John Winthrop, *Winthrop Papers*, vol. II, 1623–1630 (Massachusetts Historical Society, 1931), pp. 114–15, 282, 292–95. [Editorial insertions appear in square brackets—*Ed.*]

General Observations, 1629

1. It wilbe a service to the Churche of great Consequence to carrye the Gospell into those partes of the world, and to rayse a bullwarke against the kingdom of Antichrist which the Jesuites labour to reare vp in all places of the worlde.

2. All other Churches of Europe are brought to desolation, and it cannot be, but the like Judgment is comminge vpon vs: and who knows, but that God hathe provided this place, to be a refuge for manye, whom he meanes to save out of the general destruction?

3. This land growes wearye of her Inhabitantes, so as man which is the most pretious of all Creatures, is heere more vile and base, then the earthe they treade vpon: so as children neighbours and freindes (especi[ally] if they be poore) are rated the greatest burdens, which if things were right, would be the cheifest earthly bless[ings].

4. We are growne to that height of Intemperance in all excesse of Ryot, as no mans estate all most will suffice to keepe sayle with his equalls: and he that fayles in it, must liue in scorn and contempt: hence it comes, that all artes and trades are carried in that deceiptful and vnrighteous course, as it is allmost imposs[ible] for a good and vpright man to maintaine his charge and liue comfortably in any of them.

5. The fountains of learninge and Relig[ion] are so corrupted, as (besides the vnsupport[able] chardge of their educat[ion] most Children, even the best wittes and of fayrest hopes, are perverted corrupted and vttrly overthrowne by the multitude of evill examples and the licentious government of those seminaryes.

6. The whole earthe is the Lordes garden: and he hathe given it to the sons of men to be tilld and improved by them: why then should we stand striving heere for places of habitation etc. (many men spending as muche labor and cost to recover or keepe sometyme an Acre or 2 of lande, as would procure him many C [hundred] acres as good or better in another place) and in the mene tyme suffere whole countrys as fruitfull and convenient for the vse of man, to lye waste without any improvement?

7. What can be a better worke and more honorable and worthy [a Christian then to helpe] rayse and supporte a partic[ular] Churche while it is in the infancye, and to ioine our forces with suche a Companye of faithfull people, as by a tymely assistance maye growe strong and prosper, and for want of it may be putt to great hazard, if not wholly ruined?

8. If suche as are knowne to be godly and liue in wealthe and prosperitye heere, shall forsake all this to ioine themselves to this Churche, and to runne the hazard with them of a harde and meane condition, it wilbe an example of great vse, bothe for removinge the schandale of worldly and sinister respectes to give more life to the Faithe of Godes people in their prayers for the plantation, and allso to incourage others to ioyne the more willingly in it.

*   *   *

Christian Charitie. A Modell Hereof [1630]

God Almightie in his most holy and wise providence hath soe disposed of the Condicion of man-kinde, as in all times some must be rich some poore, some highe and eminent in power and dignitie; others meane and in subieccion.

*   *   *

It rests now to make some applicacion of this discourse by the present designe which gaue the occasion of writeing of it. Herein are 4 things to be propounded: first the persons, 2ly, the worke, 3ly, the end, 4ly the meanes.

I. For the persons, wee are a Company professiong our selues fellow members of Christ, In which respect only though wee were absent from eache other many miles, and had our imploymentes as farre distant, yet wee ought to account our selues knitt together by this bond of loue, and liue in the exercise of it, . . .

2ly. For the worke wee haue in hand, it is by a mutuall consent through a speciall overruleing providence, and a more then an ordinary approbation of the Churches of Christ to seeke out a place of Cohabitation and Consorteshipp vnder a due forme of Government both ciuill and ecclesiasticall. In such cases as this the care of the publique must oversway all private respects, by which not onely conscience, but meare Ciuill pollicy doth binde vs; for it is a true rule that perticular estates cannott subsist in the ruine of the publique.

3ly. The end is to improue our liues to doe more seruice to the Lord the comforte and encrease of the body of christe whereof wee are members that our selues and posterity may be the better preserued from the Common corrupcions of this euill world to serue the Lord and worke out our Salvacion vnder the power and purity of his holy Ordinances.

4ly. For the meanes whereby this must bee effected, they are 2fold, a Conformity with the worke and end wee aime at, these wee see are extraordinary, therefore wee must not content our selues with vsuall ordinary meanes whatsoever wee did or ought to haue done when wee liued in England, the same must wee doe and more allsoe where we goe: That which the most in theire Churches maineteine as a truthe in profession onely, wee must bring into familiar and constant practise, . . . neither must wee think that the lord will beare with such faileings at our hands as hee dothe from those among whome wee haue liued, and that for 3 Reasons.

I. In regard of the more neare bond of mariage, betweene him and vs, wherein he hath taken vs to be his after a most strickt and peculiar manner which will make him the more Jealous of our loue and obedience soe he tells the people of Israell, you onely haue I knowne of all the families of the Earthe therefore will I punishe you for your Transgressions.

2ly, because the lord will be sanctified in them that come neare him. Wee know that there were many that corrupted the seruice of the Lord some setting vpp Alters before his owne, others offering both strange fire and strange Sacrifices allsoe; yet there came noe fire from heaven, or other sudden Judgement vpon them as did vpon Nadab and Abihu whoe yet wee may thinke did not sinne presumptuously.

3ly When God giues a speciall Commission he lookes to haue it strictly obserued in every Article, when hee gaue Saule a Commission to destroy Amaleck hee indented with him vpon certaine Articles and because hee failed in one of the least, and that vpon a faire pretence, it lost him the kingdome, which should haue beene his reward, if hee had obserued his Commission: Thus stands the cause between God and vs, wee are entered into Covenant with him for this worke, wee haue taken out a Commission, the Lord hath giuen vs leaue to drawe our owne Articles, . . . wee haue herevpon besought him of favour and blessing: Now if the Lord shall please to heare vs, and bring vs in peace to the place wee desire, then hath hee ratified this Covenant and sealed our Commission, [and] will expect a strickt performance of the Articles contained in it, but if we shall neglect the observacion of these Articles which are the ends wee haue propounded, and dissembling with our God, shall fall to embrace this present world and prosecute our carnall intencions, seekeing great things for our selues and our posterity, the Lord will surely breake out in wrathe against vs be revenged of such a periured people and make vs knowe the price of the breache of such a Covenant.

Now the onely way to avoyde this shipwracke and to provide for our posterity is to followe the Counsell of Micah, to doe Justly, to loue mercy, to walke humbly with our God, for this end, wee must be knitt together in this worke as one man, must entertaine each other in brotherly Affection, wee must be willing to abridge our selues of our superfluities, for the supply of others necessities, wee must vphold a familiar Commerce together in all meekenes, gentlenes, patience and liberality, wee must delight in eache other, make others Condicions our owne, reioyce together, mourne together, labour, and suffer together, allwayes haueing before . . . Commission and

Community in the worke, our Community as members of the same body, soe shall wee keepe the vnitie of the spirit in the bond of peace, the Lord will be our God and delight to dwell among vs, as his owne people and will commaund a blessing vpon vs in all our wayes, soe that wee shall see much more of his wisdome power goodnes and truthe then formerly wee haue beene acquainted with, wee shall finde that the God of Israell is among vs, when tenn of vs shall be able to resist a thousand of our enemies, when hee shall make vs a prayse and glory, that men shall say of succeeding plantacions: the lord make it like that of New England: for wee must Consider that wee shall be as a Citty vpon a Hill, the eies of all people are vppon vs; soe that if wee shall deale falsely with our god in this worke wee haue vndertaken and soe cause him to withdrawe his present help from vs, wee shall be made a story and a by-word through the world, wee shall open the mouthes of enemies to speake euill of the wayes of god and all professours for Gods sake; wee shall shame the faces of many of gods worthy seruants, and cause theire prayers to be turned into Cursses vpon vs til wee be consumed out of the good land whether wee are goeing: And to shutt vpp this discourse with that exhortacion of Moses that faithfull seruant of the Lord in his last farewell to Israell Deut. 30. Beloued there is now sett before vs life, and good, deathe and euill in that wee are Commaunded this day to loue the Lord our God, and to loue one another to walke in his wayes and to keepe his Commaundements and his Ordinance, and his lawes, and the Articles of our Covenant with him that wee may

liue and be multiplyed, and that the Lord our God may blesse vs in the land whether wee goe to possesse it: But if our heartes shall turne away soe that wee will not obey, but shall be seduced and worshipp other Gods our pleasures, and proffitts, and serue them; it is propounded vnto vs this day, wee shall surely perishe out of the good Land whether wee passe over this vast Sea to possesse it;

Therefore lett vs choose life,
that wee, and our Seede,
may liue; by obeying his
voyce, and cleaueing to him,
for hee is our life, and
our prosperity.

REVIEW QUESTIONS

1. Did Winthrop focus on what pushed the Puritans out of England or what was pulling them to the New World when promoting emigration in 1629? How does this selection compare with his 1630 address?
2. How did dissent from the English establishment and consensus among themselves affect the movement of Puritans to the New World and the establishment of their city upon a hill?
3. Why did Winthrop think that the Puritans were a special people? And, why did he believe that they had to be especially careful in their new endeavor?
4. How might the Puritans' creation and interpretation of a covenant have affected the relationships between church and state and people?

The Massachusetts Bay Colony Case against Anne Hutchinson (1637)

tans' struggle to practice their own religion freely did not extend to tolera-
e who questioned church policies, as Anne Hutchinson, the intelligent,
-six-year-old wife of a prosperous merchant, discovered. In 1637

Hutchinson faced prosecution for practices and beliefs deemed threatening to the stability of church and commonwealth. The ministers and magistrates did not think her weekly meetings unseemly when she began them in 1635, but revised their opinions as her audience, interpretation, and instruction of scripture changed. Hutchinson attacked some doctrinal premises, such as blaming Eve—and, correspondingly, women—for Original Sin, while denouncing some ministers for not properly teaching Puritan dogma. She also revealed that she had an inclination to mysticism. For her antinomianism (beliefs against the law) the magistrates exiled Hutchinson. She then moved with her family into what became Rhode Island, helping found Portsmouth there, and then on to Long Island where she and most of her children were later slain by Indians.

From Thomas Hutchinson, *History of the Colony and Province of Massachusetts Bay*, vol. II, 1767 (Cambridge: Harvard University Press, 1936), pp. 366–84.

Mr. Winthrop, governor. Mrs. Hutchinson, you are called here as one of those that have troubled the peace of the commonwealth and the churches here; you are known to be a woman that hath had a great share in the promoting and divulging of those opinions that are causes of this trouble, and to be nearly joined not only in affinity and affection with some of those the court had taken notice of and passed censure upon. But you have spoken divers things as we have been informed very prejudicial to the honour of the churches and ministers thereof, and you have maintained a meeting and an assembly in your house that hath been condemned by the general assembly as a thing not tolerable nor comely in the sight of God nor fitting for your sex; and notwithstanding that was cried down, you have continued the same. Therefore we have thought good to send for you to understand how things are. . . .

*   *   *

Mrs. Hutchinson. What have I said or done?

Gov. Why for your doings, this you did harbour and countenance those that are parties in this faction that you have heard of.

Mrs. H. That's matter of conscience, Sir.

Gov. Your conscience you must keep, or it must be kept for you. . . .

*   *   *

Gov. Why do you keep such a meeting at your house as you do every week upon a set day?

Mrs. H. It is lawful for me so to do, as it is all your practices; and can you find a warrant for yourself and condemn me for the same thing? . . .

Gov. For this, that you appeal to our practice you need no confutation. If your meeting had answered to the former it had not been offensive, but I will say that there was no meeting of women alone. But your meeting is of another sort, for there are sometimes men among you.

Mrs. H. There was never any man with us.

Gov. Well, admit there was no man at your meeting and that you was sorry for it, there is no warrant for your doings; and by what warrant do you continue such a course?

Mrs. H. I conceive there is a clear rule in Titus, that the elder women should instruct the younger; and then I must have a time wherein I must do it.

Gov. All this I grant you, I grant you a time for it; but what is this to the purpose that you, Mrs. Hutchinson, must call a company together from their callings to come to be taught of you?

Mrs. H. Will it please you to answer me this and to give me a rule, for then I will willingly submit to any truth? If any come to my house to be instructed in the ways of God, what rule have I to put them away?

Gov. But suppose that a hundred men come unto you to be instructed, will you forbear to instruct them?

Mrs. H. As far as I conceive I cross a rule in it.

Gov. Very well and do you not so here?

Mrs. H. No Sir, for my ground is they are men.

Gov. Men and women all is one for that, but suppose that a man should come and say, "Mrs. Hutchinson, I hear that you are a woman that God hath given his grace unto and you have knowledge in the word of God. I pray instruct me a little." Ought you not to instruct this man?

Mrs. H. I think I may.—Do you think it not lawful for me to teach women, and why do you call me to teach the court?

Gov. We do not call you to teach the court but to lay open yourself.

Mr. Dudley, dep. gov. Here hath been much spoken concerning Mrs. Hutchinson's meetings and among other answers she saith that men come not there. I would ask you this one question then, whether never any man was at your meeting?

Gov. There are two meetings kept at their house.

Dep. Gov. How; is there two meetings?

Mrs. H. Ey Sir, I shall not equivocate, there is a meeting of men and women, and there is a meeting only for women.

Dep. Gov. Are they both constant?

Mrs. H. No, but upon occasions they are deferred.

Mr. Endicot. Who teaches in the men's meetings, none but men? Do not women sometimes?

Mrs. H. Never as I heard, not one. . . .

Dep. Gov. Now it appears by this woman's meeting that Mrs. Hutchinson hath so forestalled the minds of many by their resort to her meeting that now she hath a potent party in the country. Now if all these things have endangered us as from that foundation, and if she in particular hath disparaged all our ministers in the land that they have preached a covenant of works, . . . why this is not to be suffered. And therefore being driven to the foundation, and it being found that Mrs. Hutchinson is she that hath depraved all the ministers and hath been the cause of what is fallen out, why we must take away the foundation and the building will fall.

Mrs. H. I pray, Sir, prove it that I said they preached nothing but a covenant of works.

Dep. Gov. Nothing but a covenant of works? Why, a Jesuit may preach truth sometimes.

Mrs. H. Did I ever say they preached a covenant of works, then?

Dep. Gov. If they do not preach a covenant of grace clearly, then they preach a covenant of works.

Mrs. H. No Sir, one may preach a covenant of grace more clearly than another, so I said.

Dep. Gov. We are not upon that now, but upon position.

Mrs. H. Prove this then, Sir, that you say I said.

Dep. Gov. When they do preach a covenant of works, do they preach truth?

Mrs. H. Yes Sir, but when they preach a covenant of works for salvation, that is not truth.

Dep. Gov. I do but ask you this: when the ministers do preach a covenant of works, do they preach a way of salvation?

Mrs. H. I did not come hither to answer to questions of that sort.

Dep. Gov. Because you will deny the thing.

Mrs. H. Ey, but that is to be proved first.

Dep. Gov. I will make it plain that you did say that the ministers did preach a covenant of works.

Mrs. H. I deny that.

Dep. Gov. And that you said they were not able ministers of the new testament. . . .

Mrs. H. If ever I spake that, I proved it by God's word.

Court. Very well, very well. . . .

Mrs. H. If you please to give me leave, I shall give you the ground of what I know to be true. Being much troubled to see the falseness of the constitution of the church of England, I had like to have turned separatist; whereupon I kept a day of solemn humiliation and pondering of the thing; this scripture was brought unto me—he that denies Jesus Christ to be come in the flesh is antichrist—This I considered of, and in considering found that the papists did not deny him to be come in the flesh, nor we did not deny him—who then was antichrist? Was the Turk antichrist only? The Lord knows that I could not open scripture; he must by his prophetical office open it unto me. So after that, being unsatisfied in the thing, the Lord was pleased to bring this scripture out of the Hebrews. He that denies the testament denies the testator, and in this did open unto me and give me to see that those which did not teach the new covenant had the spirit of antichrist, and upon this he did discover the ministry unto me and ever since. I bless the Lord, he hath let me see which was the clear ministry and which the wrong. Since that time I confess I have been more choice, and he hath let me to distinguish between the voice of my beloved and the voice of Moses, the voice of John Baptist and the voice of antichrist, for all those voices are spoken of in scripture. Now if you do condemn me for speaking what in my conscience I know to be truth, I must commit myself unto the Lord.

Mr. Nowell. How do you know that that was the spirit?

Mrs. H. How did Abraham know that it was God that bid him offer his son, being a breach of the sixth commandment?

Dep. Gov. By an immediate voice.

Mrs. H. So to me by an immediate revelation.

Dep. Gov. How! an immediate revelation.

Mrs. H. By the voice of his own spirit to my soul. I will give you another scripture, Jer. 46. 27, 28—out of which the Lord shewed me what he would do for me and the rest of his servants.—But after he was pleased to reveal himself to me, I did presently like Abraham run to Hagar. And after that, he did let me see the atheism of my own heart, for which I begged of the Lord that it might not remain in my heart; and being thus, he did shew me this (a twelvemonth after) which I told you of before. Ever since that time I have been confident of what he hath revealed unto me. . . . You see this scripture fulfilled this day, and therefore I desire you that as you tender the Lord and the church and commonwealth to consider and look what you do. You have power over my body, but the Lord Jesus hath power over my body and soul; and assure yourselves thus much, you do as much as in you lies to put the Lord Jesus Christ from you; and if you go on in this course you begin, you will bring a curse upon you and your posterity, and the mouth of the Lord hath spoken it.

Dep. Gov. What is the scripture she brings?

Mr. Stoughton. Behold I turn away from you.

Mrs. H. But now having seen him which is invisible, I fear not what man can do unto me.

Gov. Daniel was delivered by miracle. Do you think to be deliver'd so too?

Mrs. H. I do here speak it before the court. I look that the Lord should deliver me by his providence.

Mr. Harlakenden. I may read scripture and the most glorious hypocrite may read them and yet go down to hell.

Mrs. H. It may be so. . . .

Mr. Endicot. I would have a word or two with leave of that which hath thus far been revealed to the court. I have heard of many revelations of Mr. Hutchinson's, but they were reports, but Mrs. Hutchinson I see doth maintain some by this discourse; and I think it is a special providence of God to hear what she hath said. Now there is a revelation you see which she doth expect as a miracle. She saith she now suffers, and let us do what we will she shall be delivered by a miracle. I hope the court takes notice of the vanity of it and heat of her spirit.

REVIEW QUESTIONS

1. What were the charges brought against Anne Hutchinson?
2. What do you suppose were the most serious: those having to do with faith or with practices? Why?
3. How did Hutchinson respond to the various accusations? What did she say gave her the authority to interpret scripture?
4. What was the court's response to her answer?
5. Which side had the stronger case? Why?

JOHANNES MEGAPOLENSIS

A Short Account of the Mohawk Indians (1644)

Before the Pilgrims and Puritans cleared their first farms in New England, the Dutch were planting trading posts and villages on Manhattan, Long Island, and up the Hudson River. Although they were primarily interested in trading with the natives, Dutch colonists also studied the Indians with an eye to converting them. One such person was the minister Johannes Megapolensis. This Dutch minister arrived in New Netherland in 1642. As he set about to save native souls in the area near present-day Albany in 1643, he recorded his observations about the land and its people. He compiled these into an account he then sent back home in 1644 both to satisfy and further fuel the curiosity (and thus perhaps the emigration) of the people there. Megapolensis remained up river for another five years and then moved down to minister in Manhattan.

J. Franklin Jameson, ed., *Narratives of New Netherland, 1609–1664* (1909; New York: Barnes and Noble, 1946), pp. 168ff. [Editorial insertions appear in square brackets—*Ed.*]

The country here is in general like that in Germany. The land is good, and fruitful in everything which supplies human needs, except clothes, linen, woollen, stockings, shoes, etc., which are all dear here. The country is very mountainous, partly soil, partly rocks, and with elevations so exceeding high that they appear to almost touch the clouds. Thereon grow the finest fir trees the eye ever saw. There are also in this country oaks, alders, beeches, elms, willows, etc. In the forests, and here and there along the water side, and on the islands, there grows an abundance of chestnuts, plums, hazel nuts, large walnuts of several sorts, and of as good a taste as in the Netherlands, but they have a somewhat harder shell. The ground on the hills is covered with bushes of bilberries or blueberries; the ground in the flat land near the rivers is covered with strawberries, which grow here so plentifully in the fields, that one can lie down and eat them. Grapevines also grow here naturally in great abundance along the roads, paths, and creeks, and wherever you may turn you find them. . . . If people would cultivate the vines they might have as good wine here as they have in Germany or France. I had myself last harvest a boat-load of grapes and pressed them. As long as the wine was new it tasted better than any French or Rhenish Must, . . . In the forests is great plenty of deer, which in autumn and early winter are as fat as any Holland cow can be. I have had them with fat more than two fingers thick on the ribs, so that they were nothing else than almost clear fat, and could hardly be eaten. There are also many turkies, as large as in Holland, but in some years less than in others. The year before I came here, there were so many turkies and deer that they came to feed by the houses and hog pens, and were taken by the Indians in such numbers that a deer was sold to the Dutch for a loaf of bread, or a knife, or even for a tobacco pipe; but now one commonly has to give for a good deer six or seven guilders. In the forests here there are also many partridges, heathhens and pigeons that fly together in thousands, and sometimes ten, twenty, thirty and even forty and fifty are killed at one shot. We have here, too, a great number of all kinds of fowl, swans, geese, ducks, widgeons, teal, brant, which sport upon the river in thousands in the spring of the year, and again in the autumn fly away in flocks, so that in the morning and evening any one may stand ready with his gun before his house and shoot them as they fly past. . . .

. . . In this ground there appears to be a singular strength and capacity for bearing crops, for a farmer here told me that he had raised fine wheat on one and the same piece of land eleven years successively without ever breaking it up or letting it lie fallow. . . . Through this land runs an excellent river, about 500 or 600 paces wide. . . . In this river is a great plenty of all kinds of fish— pike, eels, perch, lampreys, suckers, cat fish, sun fish, shad, bass, etc. In the spring, in May, the perch are so plenty, that one man with a hook and line will catch in one hour as many as ten or twelve can eat. . . .

As for the temperature in this country, and the seasons of the year, the summers are pretty hot, so that for the most of the time we are obliged to go in just our shirts, and the winters are very cold. The summer continues long, even until All Saints' Day; but when the winter does begin, just as it commonly does in December, it freezes so hard in one night that the ice will bear a man. . . .

The inhabitants of this country are of two kinds: first Christians—at least so called; second, Indians. Of the Christians I shall say nothing; my design is to speak of the Indians only. . . . The principal nation of all the savages and Indians hereabouts with which we have the most intercourse, is the Mahakuaas [Mohawks], which have laid all the other Indians near us under contribution. This nation has a very difficult language, and it costs me great pains to learn it, so as to be able to speak and preach in it fluently. There is no Christian here who understands the language thoroughly; those who have lived here long can use a kind of jargon just sufficient to carry on trade with it, but they do not understand the fundamentals of the language. . . .

The people and Indians here in this country are like us Dutchmen in body and stature; some of them have well formed features, bodies and limbs; they all have black hair and eyes, but their skin is yellow. In summer they go naked, having only their private parts covered with a patch. The children and young folks to ten, twelve and fourteen years of age go stark naked. In winter, they hang about them simply an undressed deer or bear or panther skin; or they take some beaver and otter skins, wild cat, raccoon, martin, otter, mink, squirrel or such like skins, which are plenty in this country, and sew some of them to others, until it is a square piece, and that is then a garment for them; or they buy of us Dutchmen two and a half ells of duffel, and that they hang simply about them, just as it was torn off, without sewing it, and walk away with it. They look at themselves constantly, and think they are very fine. They make themselves stockings and also shoes of deer skin, or they take leaves of their corn, and plait them together and use them for shoes. The women, as well as the men, go with their heads bare. . . .

They generally live without marriage; and if any of them have wives, the marriage continues no longer than seems good to one of the parties, and then they separate, and each takes another partner. I have seen those who had parted, and afterwards lived a long time with others, leave these again, seek their former partners, and again be one pair. And, though they have wives, yet they will not leave off whoring; and if they can sleep with another man's wife, they think it a brave thing. The women are exceedingly addicted to whoring; they will lie with a man for the value of one, two, or three *schillings*, and our Dutchmen run after them very much.

The women, when they have been delivered, go about immediately afterwards, and be it ever so cold, they wash themselves and the young child in the river or the snow. They will not lie down (for they say that if they did they would soon die), but keep going about. They are obliged to cut wood, to travel three or four leagues with the child; in short, they walk, they stand, they work, as if they had not lain in, and we cannot see that they suffer any injury by it; and we sometimes try to persuade our wives to lie-in so, and that the way of lying-in in Holland is a mere fiddle-faddle. The men have great authority over their concubines, so that if they do anything which does not please and raises their passion, they take an axe and knock them in the head, and there is an end of it. The women are obliged to prepare the land, to mow, to plant, and do everything; the men do nothing, but hunt, fish, and make war upon their enemies. They are very cruel towards their enemies in time of war; for they first bite off the nails of the fingers of their captives, and cut off some joints, and sometimes even whole fingers; after that, the captives are forced to sing and dance before them stark naked; and finally, they roast their prisoners dead before a slow fire for some days, and then eat them up. The common people eat the arms, buttocks and trunk, but the chiefs eat the head and the heart.

Our Mahakas carry on great wars against the Indians of Canada, on the River Saint Lawrence, and take many captives, . . . They spare all the children from ten to twelve years old, and all the women whom they take in war, unless the women are very old, and then they kill them too. Though they are so very cruel to their enemies, they are very friendly to us, and we have no dread of them. We go with them into the woods, we meet with each other, sometimes at an hour or two's walk from any houses, and think no more about it than as if we met with a Christian. . . . Their bread is Indian corn beaten to pieces between two stones, of which they make a cake, and bake it in the ashes: their other victuals are venison, turkies, hares, bears, wild cats, their own dogs, etc. The fish they cook just as they get them out of the water without cleansing; also the entrails of deer with all their contents, which they cook a little; and if the intestines are then too tough, they take one end in their mouth, and the other in their hand, and between hand and mouth they separate and eat them. So they do commonly with the flesh, for they carve a little piece and lay it on the fire, as long as one would need to walk from his house to church, then it is done; and then they bite into it so that the blood runs along their mouths. . . . It is natural to them to have no beards; not one in an hundred has any hair about his mouth.

They have also naturally a very high opinion of themselves; they say, *Ihy Othkon*, ("I am the Devil")

by which they mean that they are superior folks. In order to praise themselves and their people, whenever we tell them they are very expert at catching deer, or doing this and that, they say, *Tkoschs ko, aguweechon Kajingahaga kouaane Jountuckcha Othkon*; that is, "Really all the Mohawks are very cunning devils." They make their houses of the bark of trees, very close and warm, and kindle their fire in the middle of them. They also make of the peeling and bark of trees, canoes or small boats, which will carry four, five and six persons. . . . Their weapons in war were formerly a bow and arrow, with a stone axe and mallet; but now they get from our people guns, swords, iron axes and mallets. Their money consists of certain little bones, made of shells or cockles, which are found on the seabeach; a hole is drilled through the middle of the little bones, and these they string upon thread, or they make of them belts as broad as a hand, or broader, and hang them on their necks, or around their bodies. They have also several holes in their ears, and there they likewise hang some. They value these little bones as highly as many Christians do gold, silver and pearls; but they do not like our money, and esteem it no better than iron. . . .

They are entire strangers to all religion, but they have a *Tharonhijouaagon*, (whom they also otherwise call *Athzoockkuatoriaho*,) that is, a Genius, whom they esteem in the place of God; but they do not serve him or make offerings to him. They worship and present offerings to the Devil, whom they call *Otskon*, or *Aireskuoni*. If they have any bad luck in war, they catch a bear, which they cut in pieces, and roast, and that they offer up to their *Aireskuoni*, saying in substance, the following words: "Oh! great and mighty Aireskuoni, we confess that we have offended against thee, inasmuch as we have not killed and eaten our captive enemies;—forgive us this. We promise that we will kill and eat all the captives we shall hereafter take as certainly as we have killed, and now eat this bear." Also when the weather is very hot, and there comes a cooling breeze, they cry out directly, *Asoronusi, asoronusi, Otskon aworouhsi reinnuha*; that is, "I thank thee, I thank thee, devil, I thank thee, little uncle!" If they are sick, or have a pain or soreness anywhere in their limbs, and I ask them what ails them they say that the Devil sits in their body, or in the sore places, and bites them there; so that they attribute to the Devil at once the accidents which befall them; they have otherwise no religion. When we pray they laugh at us. Some of them despise it entirely; and some, when we tell them what we do when we pray, stand astonished. When we deliver a sermon, sometimes ten or twelve of them, more or less, will attend, each having a long tobacco pipe, made by himself, in his mouth, and will stand awhile and look, and afterwards ask me what I am doing and what I want, that stand there alone and make so many words, while none of the rest may speak. I tell them that I am admonishing the Christians, that they must not steal, nor commit lewdness, nor get drunk, nor commit murder, and that they too ought not to do these things; and that I intend in process of time to preach the same to them and come to them in their own country and castles (about three days' journey from here, further inland), when I am acquainted with their language. . . .

The other day an old woman came to our house, and told my people that her forefathers had told her "that *Tharonhij-Jagon*, that is God, once went walking with his brother, and a dispute arose between them, and God killed his brother." I suppose this fable took its rise from Cain and Abel. They have a droll theory of the Creation, for they think that a pregnant woman fell down from heaven, and that a tortoise, (tortoises are plenty and large here, in this country, two, three and four feet long, some with two heads, very mischievous and addicted to biting) took this pregnant woman on its back, because every place was covered with water; and that the woman sat upon the tortoise, groped with her hands in the water, and scraped together some of the earth, whence it finally happened that the earth was raised above the water. They think that there are more worlds than one, and that we came from another world. . . .

The government among them consists of the oldest, the most intelligent, the most eloquent and most warlike men. These commonly resolve, and then the young and warlike men execute. But if the common people do not approve of the resolution, it is left entirely to the judgment of the mob. The chiefs are generally the poorest among them, for instead of their receiving from the common people as among Christians, they are obliged to give to the mob; especially when any one is killed in war, they give great presents to the next of kin of the deceased; and if they take any prisoners they present them to that family of which one has been killed, and the prisoner is then adopted by the family into the place of the deceased person. There is no punishment here for murder and other villainies, but every one is his own avenger. The friends of the deceased revenge themselves upon the murder until peace is made by presents to the next of kin. But although they are so cruel, and live without laws or any punishments for evil doers, yet there are not half so many villainies or murders committed amongst them as amongst Christians; so that I oftentimes think with astonishment upon all the murders committed in the Fatherland, notwithstanding their severe laws and heavy penalties. These Indians, though they live without laws, or fear of punishment, do not (at least, they very seldom) kill people, unless it may be in great passion, or a hand-to-hand fight. Wherefore we go wholly unconcerned along with the Indians and meet each other an hour's walk off in the woods, without doing any harm to one another.

REVIEW QUESTIONS

1. How did Dutch colonization have an impact on the environment, and the environment an impact on Dutch settlement?
2. In describing the Indians, what did Megapolensis reveal about the Dutch? What did he reveal about himself?
3. How would you analyze native social, economic, and administrative structures based on this account?
4. How does this account illuminate the possibility that morality and ethics may be socially relative rather than absolute?

WILLIAM PENN

FROM *Some Account of the Province of Pennsilvania* (1681)

William Penn echoed Megapolensis's praise of the richness of the land in the mid-Atlantic region in the tracts he published to promote his colony of Pennsylvania. This William Penn was the son of Admiral Sir William Penn, a man knighted by Charles II as a reward for having assisted him in regaining his crown. William Penn the junior (1644–1718), however, was eventually imprisoned for appearing to subvert the power of that crown by promoting the Quaker religion. As religious persecution continued in England and in Europe, the younger Penn looked more and more to America as the only place where he could establish a colony that would be a refuge for his religious compatriots and a model of Christian liberty. With that in mind, after his father's death, he asked the king to give him a grant of land in lieu of the payment still owed on the crown's debt to his father. Charles II, with due consideration of the advantages of the exchange, granted Penn the charter to Pennsylvania in 1681. Penn immediately set about to promote his colony in England and Europe, especially Germany, by writing various pamphlets, including the following one.

From Albert Cook Myers, ed., *Narratives of Early Pennsylvania, West New Jersey, and Delaware, 1630–1707* (1912; New York: Barnes and Noble, 1967), pp. 202, 207–211. [Editorial insertions appear in square brackets—*Ed.*]

Since (by the good providence of God) a Country in America is fallen to my lot, I thought it not less my Duty than my honest Interest to give some publick notice of it to the World, that those of our own, or other Nations, that are inclin'd to Transport themselves or Families beyond the Seas, may find another Country added to their choice, . . .

*   *   *

I. *Something of the Place*

. . . I shall say little in its praise, to excite desires in any, whatever I could truly write as to the Soil, Air and Water: This shall satisfie me, that by the Blessing of God, and the honesty and industry of Man, it may be a good and fruitful Land.

For Navigation it is said to have two conveniencies; the one by lying Ninescore miles upon Delaware River; that is to say, about three-score and ten miles, before we come to the Falls [now Trenton, New Jersey]. . . . The other convenience is through Chesapeak-Bay.

For Timber and other Wood there is variety for the use of man.

For Fowl, Fish, and Wild-Deer, they are reported to be plentiful in those Parts. Our English Provision is likewise now to be had there at reasonable Rates. The Commodities that the Country is thought to be capable of, are Silk, Flax, Hemp, Wine, Sider, Woad, Madder, Liquorish, Tobacco,

Potashes, and Iron, and it does actually produce Hides, Tallow, Pipe-staves, Beef, Pork, Sheep, Wool, Corn, as Wheat, Barly, Ry, and also Furs, as your Peltree, Mincks, Racoons, Martins, and such like; store of Furs, which is to be found among the Indians, that are profitable Commodities in Europe.

The way of trading in those Countries is thus: they send to the Southern Plantations Corn, Beef, Pork, Fish and Pipe-staves, and take their Growth and bring for England, and return with English Goods to their own Country. Their Furs they bring for England, and either sell them here, or carry them out again to other parts of Europe, where they will yield a better price: And for those that will follow Merchandize and Navigation there is conveniency, and Timber sufficient for Shipping.

II. *The Constitutions*

For the Constitutions of the Country, the Patent shows, first, That the People and Governour have a Legislative Power, so that no Law can be made, nor Money raised, but by the Peoples Consent.

2dly. That the Rights and Freedoms of England (the best and largest in Europe) shall be in force there.

3dly. That making no Law against Allegiance (which should we, 'twere by the Law of England void of it self that moment) we may Enact what Laws we please for the good prosperity and security of the said Province.

4thly. That so soon as any are ingaged with me, we shall begin a Scheam or Draught together, such as shall give ample Testimony of my sincere Inclinations to encourage Planters, and settle a free, just and industrious Colony there.

III. *The Conditions*

My Conditions will relate to three sorts of People: 1st. Those that will buy: 2dly. Those that take up Land upon Rent: 3dly. Servants. To the first, the Shares I sell shall be certain as to number of Acres; that is to say, every one shall contain Five thousand Acres, free from any Indian incum-

brance, the price a hundred pounds, and for the Quit-Rent but one English shilling or the value of it yearly for a hundred Acres; and the said Quit-Rent not to begin to be paid till 1684. To the second sort, that take up Land upon Rent, they shall have liberty so to do, paying yearly one peny per Acre, not exceeding Two hundred Acres. To the third sort, to wit, Servants that are carried over, Fifty Acres shall be allowed to the Master for every Head, and Fifty Acres to every Servant when their time is expired. . . .

The Divident may be thus; if the persons concern'd please, a Tract of Land shall be survey'd; say Fifty thousand Acres to a hundred Adventurers; in which some of the best shall be set out for Towns or Cities; and there shall be so much Ground allotted to each in those Towns as may maintain some Cattel and produce some Corn; then the remainder of the fifty thousand Acres shall be shar'd among the said Adventurers. . . .

IV. *These persons that providence seems to have most fitted for Plantations are,*

1st. Industrious Husbandmen and Day-Labourers, that are hardly able (with extreme Labour) to maintain their Families and portion their Children.

2dly. Laborious Handicrafts, especially Carpenters, Masons, Smiths, Weavers, Taylors, Tanners, Shoemakers, Shipwrights, etc. where they may be spared or are low in the World: And as they shall want no encouragement, so their Labour is worth more there than here, and there provision cheaper.

3dly. A Plantation seems a fit place for those Ingenious Spirits that being low in the World, are much clogg'd and oppress'd about a Lively-hood, for the means of subsisting being easie there, they may have time and opportunity to gratify their inclinations, and thereby improve Science and help Nurseries of people.

4thly. A fourth sort of men to whom a Plantation would be proper, takes in those that are younger Brothers of small Inheritances; yet because they would live in sight of their Kindred in some proportion to their Quality, and can't do it without a labour that looks like Farming, their condition is too strait for them; and if married, their Children are often too numerous for the Estate, and are frequently bred up to no Trades, but are a kind of Hangers on or Retainers to the elder Brothers Table and Charity: which is a mischief, as in it self to be lamented, so here to be remedied; For Land they have for next to nothing, which with moderate Labour produces plenty of all things necessary for Life, and such an increase as by Traffique may supply them with all conveniencies.

Lastly, There are another sort of persons, not only fit for, but necessary in Plantations, and that is, Men of universal Spirits, that have an eye to the Good of Posterity, and that both understand and delight to promote good Discipline and just Government among a plain and well intending people; such persons may find Room in Colonies for their good Counsel and Contrivance, who are shut out from being of much use or service to great Nations under settl'd Customs: These men deserve much esteem, and would be harken'd to. . . .

V. *The Journey and its Appurtenances, and what is to be done there at first coming*

Next let us see, What is fit for the Journey and Place, when there, and also what may be the Charge of the Voyage, and what is to be expected and done there at first. That such as incline to go, may not be to seek here, or brought under any disappointments there. The Goods fit to take with them for use, or sell for profit, are all sorts of Apparel and Utensils for Husbandry and Building and Household Stuff. And because I know how much People are apt to fancy things beyond what they are, and that Immaginations are great flatterers of the minds of Men; To the end that none may delude themselves, with an expectation of an Immediate Amendment of their Conditions, so soon as

it shall please God they Arrive there; I would have them understand, That they must look for a Winter before a Summer comes; and they must be willing to be two or three years without some of the conveniences they enjoy at home; And yet I must needs say that America is another thing then it was at the first Plantation of Virginia and New-England: For there is better Accommodation, and English Provisions are to be had at easier rates: However, I am inclin'd to set down particulars, as near as those inform me, that know the Place, and have been Planters both in that and in the Neighbouring Colonys.

1st. The passage will come for Masters and Mistresses at most to 6 Pounds a Head, for Servants Five Pounds a Head, and for Children under Seven years of Age Fifty Shillings, except they Suck, then nothing.

Next being by the mercy of God, safely Arrived in September or October, two Men may clear as much Ground by Spring (when they set the Corn of that Country) as will bring in that time twelve month Forty Barrels, which amounts to two Hundred Bushels, which makes Twenty Five quarters of Corn. So that the first year they must buy Corn, which is usually very plentiful. They may so soon as they come, buy Cows, more or less, as they want, or are able, which are to be had at easy rates. For Swine, they are plentiful and cheap; these will quickly Increase to a Stock. So that after the first year, what with the Poorer sort, sometimes labouring to others, and the more able Fishing, Fowling, and sometime Buying; They may do very well, till their own Stocks are sufficient to supply them, and their Families, which will quickly be and to spare, if they follow the English Husbandry, as they do in New-England, and New-York; and get Winter Fodder for their Stock.

*   *   *

REVIEW QUESTIONS

1. How does Penn's account compare to Megapolensis's description of New Netherland and

Frethorne's letter presented earlier? How do you account for the differences among the three accounts?

2. What did Penn reveal about a developing intercolonial trade?

3. Why did he note the political organization or precepts of the colony? What kind of government was to be instituted there?

4. Whom did Penn think would benefit most by moving to the New World? Why?

5. How does Penn's dream or sense of mission compare to Winthrop's?

3   COLONIAL WAYS OF LIFE

Colonization was both a destructive and constructive act. While immigrants and Native Americans often sought to purge themselves of undesirable elements, whether of the Old World or New, they also experimented with and embraced new ideas and different ways of doing things. Cultural transference—ideas, methods, and products transmitted from one side of the Atlantic to the other or from one group of people to another—was thus neither complete nor unilateral. This was especially true for the colonists. In the process of establishing their interpretations of European civilization in the new settlements, the colonists laid the foundations for an American civilization: they constructed what they believed to be intellectually desirable and environmentally necessary social, cultural, and institutional structures within the frontier that was America.

A variety of factors influenced the formation of colonial society and culture, including the beliefs and social ranks of the immigrants, the people who came as leaders and those who became ones, the need or desire for laborers (both free and unfree), the impact of the land and its peoples upon newcomers, and their impact on the same. The colonists did not always recognize changes as they occurred; but when they did, reactions ranged from satisfied acceptance to dismay, denial, or determined rejection. Yet, whether fully conscious of it or not, the colonists felt a freedom to experiment with ideas, both those imported and domestic. This experimentation occurred in the public domain of government, the public and private spheres of gender relations, and in the spiritual realm of religion.

Colonization meant hard work and hard times for everyone, but the tasks and rewards differed according to one's rank, religion, region, and race. Most colonists of the seventeenth and early eighteenth centuries, in accord with their contemporaries across the ocean, believed that social hierarchy, strict legal codes, and uniform religious beliefs and practices were essential to public order. This appeared to be especially true in early New England when civil and religious authorities collaborated to impose order in the wilderness. Religious equality among the saints was not supposed to translate into social equality. People were expected to act according to their place, and that place was proscribed by birth, worth, gender, and age.

The colonists faced both internal and external threats to their societies. Nonconformists represented the former while Indians represented the latter kind of menace. Native Americans attacked and tried to eliminate the threat that the immigrant groups posed to their persons, property, and cultures. Some of the settlers taken prisoner over the course of the numerous raids died in captivity, others decided that they preferred the Indian way of life and stayed (such rejection was a feared and despised rebuttal to a vaunted European superiority), while still others were eventually released or managed to escape. A few of those who returned, as they embraced even more fervently their society's beliefs and lifestyles, narrated accounts that served not only as cautionary tales to prove that the natives were enemies, but as allegories to describe the struggle between good and evil, civilization and barbarism, on the cultural frontier.

The struggle to survive and prosper did affect traditional gender relations to a certain degree, and to a lesser extent gender perceptions, but it did not radically change them. Indeed, there are indications that as the colonists became more secure in the American provinces the more likely they were to insist upon maintaining separate roles or spheres for men and women. Some women chafed at these strictures, but they generally did not (or could not) rebel against them. For most people, the issue of greatest importance to gender relations was marriage to a good wife or provident husband.

In the eighteenth century, colonial culture—the developing Anglo- or Euro-American civilization—was affected by two major cultural movements: the Enlightenment and the Great Awakening. Although there were some European Enlightenment philosophers who advocated radical social change, most provincials tended to adopt more moderate interpretations; but they not only professed these new ideas, they acted upon them. The emphasis on reason during the Enlightenment caused some people to question their religious beliefs and practices, but it also gave ministers, and others, new ways to answer those questions as well as counter the challenges raised by life in an increasingly complex and consumerist society. Ultimately, however, the Great Awakening focused not on the human ability to reason—an ability that varied from person to person—as the way to understand and command the natural order, but on revelation—a most democratic gift embraced by many Americans—as the route by which to comprehend God's design.

Many colonists credited God's design for the creation and expansion of Euro-American culture (without acknowledging the African element), but some also recognized that it was due to human design—and human accident. With some divinely inspired and others not, the colonists created a new, amalgam culture within the British empire.

ANNE BRADSTREET

A Woman's Reflections (Seventeenth Century)

Anne Dudley Bradstreet (c. 1612/13–1672) married Simon Bradstreet in 1628 and migrated to Massachusetts with him and her family, the Dudleys, in 1630. Both her father, Thomas Dudley, and her husband became governors of the colony. This extremely talented woman, who was well-educated and encouraged by her family, wrote some of the most sophisticated poetry that is still in existence from the seventeenth century. She composed these pieces even as she raised a family and helped build a community in the wilderness. Bradstreet published a book of formal poetry, The Tenth Muse, *in 1650, but also wrote lyrical poetry that was published after her death. Much of the latter relates to her family, showing her great love for her parents, spouse, and eight children.*

From Joseph R. McElrath, Jr. and Allan P. Robb, eds., *The Complete Works of Anne Bradstreet* (Boston: Twayne Publishers, 1981), pp. 7, 165–67, 180.

In the prologue to *The Tenth Muse* (1650)

*   *   *

I am obnoxious to each carping tongue,
Who sayes, my hand a needle better fits,
A Poets Pen, all scorne, I should thus wrong;
For such despight they cast on female wits:
If what I doe prove well, it wo'nt advance,
They'l say its stolne, or else, it was by chance.

*   *   *

From *Several Poems* (posthumous publication, 1678)

To the Memory of my dear and ever honoured Father Thomas Dudley Esq; Who deceased, July 31, 1653. and of his Age, 77.

*   *   *

Well known and lov'd, where ere he liv'd, by
   most

Both in his native, and in foreign coast,
These to the world his merits could make
   known,
So needs no Testimonial from his own;
But now or never I must pay my Sum;
While others tell his worth, I'le not be dumb:
One of thy Founders, him *New-England* know,
Who staid thy feeble sides when thou wast low,
Who spent his state, his strength, & years with
   care
That After-comers in them might have share.
True Patriot of this little Commonweal,
Who is't can tax thee ought, but for thy zeal?
Truths friend thou wert, to errors still a foe,
Which caus'd Apostates to maligne so.
Thy love to true Religion e're shall shine,
My Fathers God, be God of me and mine.

*   *   *

No ostentation seen in all his wayes,
As in the mean ones, of our foolish dayes,
Which all they have, and more still set to view,
Their greatness may be judg'd by what they shew.
His thoughts were more sublime, his actions
   wise,

Such vanityes he justly did despise.
Nor wonder 'twas, low things ne'r much did
  move
For he a Mansion had, prepar'd above,
For which he sigh'd and pray'd & long'd full
  sore
He might be cloath'd upon, for evermore.

*   *   *

An Epitaph

On my dear and ever honoured Mother Mrs.
Dorothy Dudley, Who deceased Decemb. 27. 1643.
and of her age, 61.

Here lyes,
A worthy Matron of unspotted life,
A loving Mother and obedient wife,
A friendly Neighbor, pitiful to poor,
Whom oft she fed, and clothed with her store:
To Servants wisely aweful, but yet kind,
And as they did, so they reward did find:
A true Instructer of her Family,
The which she ordered with dexterity.
The publick meetings ever did frequent,
And in her Closet constant hours she spent:
Religious in all her words and wayes,
Preparing still for death, till end of dayes:
Of all her Children, Children, liv'd to see,
Then dying, left a blessed memory.

To my Dear and loving Husband

If ever two were one, then surely we.
If ever man were lov'd by wife, then thee;
If ever wife was happy in a man,
Compare with me ye women if you can.
I prize thy love more then whole Mines of gold,
Or all the riches that the East doth hold.
My love is such that Rivers cannot quench,
Nor ought but love from thee, give recompence.
Thy love is such I can no way repay,
The heavens reward thee manifold I pray.
Then while we live, in love lets so persever,
That when we live no more, we may live ever.

REVIEW QUESTIONS

1. Did Bradstreet believe her work would ever be given full credit? Why or why not?
2. Why did she define her father as a patriot? How did she turn his enemies' criticisms into praise of him?
3. How did he epitomize the Puritan magistrate and father? How did Bradstreet's mother exemplify the ideal Puritan woman?
4. How do Bradstreet's poems contradict the image of Puritans as sour, pragmatic people?

FROM Connecticut's "Blue Laws" (1672)

Connecticut tried to prevent the development of resistance to authority—whether so-cial or religious—by passing a series of very strict statutes that came to be known as blue laws (a term later used to describe laws that prohibited certain activities on Sundays), including the ones here, in 1672. Such laws could not be, nor were, gener-ally enforced with the severity prescribed, but they were used to impose order. The display of proper respect to God, one's neighbors, and one's family was deemed absolutely necessary to the success of this Christian commonwealth.

From George Brinley, ed., *The Laws of Connecticut* (Hartford, 1865), pp. 9–10. [Editorial insertions appear in square brackets—*Ed.*]

1. If any man or woman, after legal conviction, shall have or worship any other God but the Lord God, he shall be put to death. (Deuteronomy 13.6. Exodus 22.20.)

2. If any person within this colony shall blaspheme the name of God, the Father, Son, or Holy Ghost, with direct, express, presumptuous, or high-handed blasphemy, or shall curse in the like manner, he shall be put to death. (Leviticus 24.15, 16.)

3. If any man or woman be a witch, that is, has or consults with a familiar spirit, they shall be put to death. (Exodus 22.18. Leviticus 20.27. Deuteronomy 18.10, 11.)

4. If any person shall commit any willful murder, committed upon malice, hatred, or cruelty, not in a man's just and necessary defense, nor by casualty [accident] against his will, he shall be put to death. (Exodus 21.12, 13, 14. Numbers 35.30, 31.)

5. If any person shall slay another through guile, either by poisoning or other such devilish practices, he shall be put to death. (Exodus 21.12, 13, 14. Numbers 35.30, 31.)

*   *   *

10. If any man steals a man or mankind and sells him, or if he be found in his hand, he shall be put to death. (Exodus 21.16.)

11. If any person rise up by false witness wittingly and of purpose to take away any man's life, he or she shall be put to death. (Deuteronomy 19.16, 18, 19.)

*   *   *

14. If any child or children above sixteen years old, and of sufficient understanding, shall curse or smite their natural father or mother, he or they shall be put to death, unless it can be sufficiently testified that the parents have been very unchristianly negligent in the education of such children, or so provoked them by extreme and cruel correction that they have been forced thereunto to preserve themselves from death or maiming. (Exodus 21.17. Leviticus 20.9. Exodus 21.15.)

15. If any man have a stubborn or rebellious son, of sufficient understanding and years, viz. sixteen years of age, which will not obey the voice of his father, or the voice of his mother, and that when they have chastened him, he will not harken unto them; then may his father or mother, being his natural parents, lay hold on him, and bring him to the magistrates assembled in court, and testify unto them that their son is stubborn and rebellious, and will not obey their voice and chastisement, but lives in sundry notorious crimes, such a son shall be put to death. (Deuteronomy 21.20, 21.)

REVIEW QUESTIONS

1. Where did the writers of these statutes find precedents for them?
2. If the order of these statutes is deemed significant, what kind of rebelliousness was thought to be the most pernicious? Why would that be the case?
3. Why was extreme disrespect and disobedience to one's parents considered to be a criminal act?

MARY ROWLANDSON

FROM A Captivity Narrative (1676)

During Metacomet's or, using the colonists' name for that leader of the Wampanoags, King Philip's War (1675–78), bands of Indians attacked numerous frontier settlements. After the 10 February 1676 attack on Lancaster, Massachusetts, the warriors led away a group of captives, among whom was Mary Rowlandson. She was the wife of the minister Joseph Rowlandson and the mother of four children. Rowlandson remained a captive until ransomed in May for the £20 raised by the women of Boston. Her account, published a few years after her ordeal, stands as one of the premier examples of a distinctive form of colonial literature: the captivity narrative.

From Mary Rowlandson, *The Narrative of the Captivity and Restoration of Mrs. Mary Rowlandson,* (Cambridge, MA: Samuel Greer, 1682; Lancaster, MA: John Wilson & Son, 1903), pp. 1–11, 15–17, 19, 22–24, 30–31, 43–44, 46, 48–50, 53–55, 59, 64, 72. [Spelling and punctuation modernized—*Ed.*]

On the tenth of *February* 167[6]. Came the *Indians* with great numbers upon *Lancaster.* Their first coming was about Sunrising; bearing the noise of some Guns, we looked out; several Houses were burning, and the Smoke ascending to Heaven. There were five persons taken in one house, the Father, and the Mother and a sucking Child they knockt on the head; the other two they took and carried away alive. Their were two others, who being out of their Garison upon some occasion were set upon; one was knockt on the head, the other escaped: Another their was who running aroug was shot and wounded, and fell down; he begged of them his life, promising them Money (as they told me) but they would not hearken to him but knockt him in head, and stript him naked, and split open his Bowels. . . .

At length they came and beset our own house, and quickly it was the dolefullest day that ever mine eyes saw. The House stood upon the edg of a hill; some of the *Indians* got behind the hill, others into the Barn, and others behind any thing that could shelter them; from all which places they shot against the House, so that the Bullets seemed to f[l]y like hail; and quickly they wounded one man among us, then another, and then a third, About two hours (according to my observation, in that amazing time) they had been about the house before they prevailed to fire it (which they did with Flax and Hemp, which they brought out of the Barn, . . . they fired it once and one ventured out and quenched it, but they quickly fired it again, and that took. . . . Then I took my Children (and one of my sisters, hers) to go forth and leave the house: but as soon as we came to the dore and appeared, the *Indians* shot so thick that the bulletts rattled against the House, as if one had taken an handfull of stones and threw them, so that we were fain to give back. . . . But out we must go, the fire increasing, and coming along behiad us, roaring, and the *Indians* gaping before us with their Guns, Spears and Hatchets to devour us. No sooner were we out of the House, but my Brother in Law (being before wounded, in defending the house, in or near the throat) fell down dead, whereat the *Indians* scornfully shouted, and hallowed, and were presently upon him, stripping off his cloaths, the bulletts flying thick, one went through my side, and the same (as would seem) through the bowels and hand of my dear Child in my arms. One of my elder Sisters Children, named *William*, had then his Leg broken, which the *Indians* perceiving, they knockt him on head. Thus were we butchered by those merciless Heathen, standing amazed, with the blood running down to our heels. . . .

*   *   *

The first Remove

Now away we must go with those Barbarous Creatures, with our bodies wounded and bleeding, and our hearts no less than our bodies. About a mile we went that night, up upon a hill within sight of the Town where they intended to lodge, . . . To add to the dolefulness of the former day, and the dismalness of the present night: my thoughts ran up on my losses and sad bereaved condition. . . .

*   *   *

The second Remove

But now, the next morning, I must turn my back upon the Town, and travel with them into the vast and desolate Wilderness, I knew not whither. It is not my tongue, or pen can express the sorrows of my heart, and bitterness of my spirit, that I had at this departure: but God was with me, in a wonderfull manner, carrying me along, and bearing up my spirit, that it did not quite fail. One of the Indians carried my poor wounded Babe upon a horse, it went moaning all along, I shall dy, I shall dy. I went on foot after it, with sorrow that cannot be express. At length I took it off the horse, and carried it in my armes till my strength failed, and I fell down with it: Then they set me upon a horse with my wounded Child in my lap, and there being no furniture upon the horse back; as we were going down a steep hill, we both fell over the horses head, at which they like inhumane creatures laught, and rejoyced to see it, though I thought we should there have ended our dayes, as overcome with so many difficulties. But the Lord renewed my strength still,

and carried me along, that I might see more of his Power; yea, so much that I could never have thought of, had I not experienced it.

*   *   *

The third Remove

The morning being come, they prepared to go on their way. One of the Indians got up upon a horse, and they set me up behind him, with my poor sick Babe in my lap. A very wearisome and tedious day I had of it; what with my own wound, and my Childs being so exceeding sick, and in a lamentable condition with her wound. It may be easily judged what a poor feeble condition we were in, there being not the least crumb of refreshing that came within either of our mouths, from *Wednesday* night to *Saturday* night, except only a little cold water. This day in the afternoon, about an hour by Sun, we came to the place where they intended, *viz.* an *Indian* Town, called *Wenimesset*, Norward of *Quabaug*. When we were come, Oh the number of Pagans (now merciless enemies) that there came about me, . . . The next day was the Sabbath: I then remembered how careless I had been of Gods holy time how many Sabbaths I had lost and mispent, and how evily I had walked in Gods sight: which lay so closs unto my spirit, that it was easie for me to see how righteous it was with God to cut off the threed of my life, and cast me out of his presence for ever. . . . I sat much alone with a poor wounded Child in my lap, which moaned night and day, having nothing to revive the body, or cheer the spirits of her, but instead of that, sometimes one *Indian* would come and tell me one hour, that your Master will knock your Child in the head, and then a second, and then a third, your Master will quickly knock your Child in the head.

This was the comfort I had from them, . . . Thus nine dayes I sat upon my knees, with my Babe in my lap, till my flesh was raw again; my Child being even ready to depart this sorrowfull world, they bade me carry it out to another Wigwam (I suppose because they would not be troubled with such spectacles) Whither I went with a very heavy heart, and down I sat with the picture of death on my lap. About two houres in the night, my sweet Babe, like a Lambe departed this life, on *Feb. 18, 167[6]*. It being about *six yeares*, and *five months* old. . . . I have thought since of the wonderfull goodness of God to me, in preserving me in the use of my reason and senses, in that distressed time, that I did not use wicked and violent means to end my own miserable life. . . .

Now the lad, began to talk of removing from this place, some one way, and some another. There were now besides my self nine, *English* Captives in this place (all of them Children, except one Woman) I got an opportunity to go and take my leave of them; they belng to go one way, and I another, I asked them whether they were earnest with God for deliverance, they told me, they did as they were able, and it was some comfort to me, that the Lord stirred up *Children to look to him*. . . .

The fourth Remove

And now I must part with that little Company I had. Here I parted from my Daughter *Mary*, (whom I never saw again till I saw her in *Doroester* [Dorchester], returned from Captivity, and from four little Cousins and Neighbours, some of which I never saw afterward: the Lord only knows the end of them. Amongst them also was that poor Woman before mentioned, who came to a sad end, as some of the company told me in my travel: She having much grief upon her Spirit, about her miserable condition, being so near her time, she would be often asking the *Indians* to let her go home; they not being willing to that, and yet vexed with her importunity, gathered a great company together about her, and stript her naked, and set her in the midst of them; and when they had sung and danced about her (in their hellish manner) as long as they pleased, they knockt her on head, and the child in her arms with her: when they had done that, they made a fire and put them both into it, and told the other Children that were with them, that if they attempted to go home, they would serve them in like manner: The Children said, she did not shed one tear, but prayed all the while. . . .

*   *   *

The fifth Remove

The occasion (as I thought) of their moving at this time, was, the English *Army it being near and following them*: For they went, as if they had gone for their lives, for some considerable way, and then they made a stop, and chose some of their stoutest men, and sent them back to hold the *English* Army in play whilst the rest escaped: . . .

The first week of my being among them, I hardly ate any thing; the second week, I found my stomach grow very faint for want of something; and yet it was very hard to get down their filthy trash: but the third week, though I could think how formerly my stomach would turn against this or that, and I could starve and dy before I could eat such things, yet they were sweet and savoury to my taste. . . .

*   *   *

The eighth Remove

On the morrow morning we must go over the River, *i.e. Connecticot*, to meet with King *Philip*, two *Cannoos* full, they had carried over, the next turn i my self was to go; but as my foot was upon the *Cannoo* to step in, there was a sudden out-cry among them, and i must step back; and instead of going over the River, i must go four or five miles up the River farther Northward. Some of the *Indians* ran one way, and some another. The cause of this rout was, as i thought, their espying some *English Scouts*, who were thereabout. In this travel up the River; about noon the Company made a stop, and sate down; some to eat, and others to rest them. As I sate amongst them, musing of things past, my Son *Joseph* unexpectedly came to me: we asked of each others welfare, bemoaning our dolefull condition, and the change that had come upon uss. . . . We travelled on till night; and in the morning, we must go over the River to *Philip*'s Crew. When I was in the Cannoo, I could not but be amazed at the numerous crew of Pagans that were on the Bank on the other side. When I came ashore, they gathered all about me, I sitting alone in the midst: I observed they asked one another questions, and laughed, and rejoyced over their Gains and Victories. Then my heart began to fail: and I fell a weeping which was the first time to my remembrance, that I wept before them. . . . There one of them asked me, why I wept, I could hardly tell what to say: yet I answered, they would kill me: No, said he, none will hurt you. Then came one of them and gave me two spoonfulls of Meal to comfort me, and another gave me half a pint of Pease; which was more worth than many Bushels at another time. Then I went to see King *Philip*, he bade me come in and sit down, and asked me whether I would smoke it (a usual Complement now adayes amongst Saints and Sinners) but this no way suited me. For though I had formerly used Tobacco, yet I had left it ever since I was first taken. It *seems to be a Bait, the Devil layes to make men loose their precious time*: I remember with shame, how formerly, when I had taken two or three pipes, I was presently ready for another, such a bewitching thing it is: But I thank God, he has now given me power over it; surely there are many who may be better imployed than to ly sucking a stinking Tobacco-pipe.

*   *   *

The twelfth Remove

. . . This morning i asked my master whither he would sell me to my Husband; he answered me *Nux*, which did much rejoyce my spirit. My mistriss, before we went, was gone to the burial of a *Papoos*, and returning, she found me sitting and reading in my Bible; she snatched it hastily out of my hand, and threw it out of doors; I ran out and catcht it up, and put it into my pocket, and never let her see it afterward. Then they pack'd up their things to be gone, and gave me my load: I complained it was too heavy whereupon she gave me a slap in the face, and bade me go; I lif[t]ed up my heart to God, hoping the Redemption was not far

off: and the rather because their insolency grew worse and worse.

But the thoughts of my going homeward for *so we bent our courses much cheared my Spirit, and made my burden seem light, and almost nothing at all.* . . .

*   *   *

The sixteenth Remove

We began this Remove with wading over Baquag *River: the water was up to the knees, and the stream very swift, and so cold that I thought it would have cut me in sunder.* i was so weak and feeble, that I reeled as I went along, and thought there I must end my dayes at last, after my bearing and getting thorough so many difficulties; the *Indians* stood laughing to see me staggering along: but in my distress the Lord gave me experience of the truth, and goodness of that promise, Isai. 43.2. *When thou passest thorough the Waters, I will be with thee, and through the Rivers, they shall not overflow thee.* Then I sat down to put on my stockins and shoos, with the teares running down mine eyes, and many sorrowfull thoughts in my heart, but I gat up to go along with them. Quickly there came up to us an *Indian*, who informed them, that I must go to *Wachusit* to my master, for there was a Letter come from the Council to the *Saggamores*, about redeeming the Captives, and that there would be another in fourteen dayes, and that I must be there ready. My heart was so heavy before that I could scarce speak or go in the path; and yet now so light, that I could run. My strength seemed to come again, and recruit my feeble knees, and aking heart: . . .

*   *   *

The nineteenth Remove

They said, when we went out, that we must travel to Wachuset *this day.* But a bitter weary day I had of it, travelling now three dayes together, without resting any day between. . . .

*　　*　　*

Then came Tom *and* Peter, *with the second Letter from the Council, about the Captives.* Though they were *Indians,* i gat them by the hand, and burst out into tears; my heart was so full that I could not speak to them; but recovering my self, I asked them how my husband did, & all my friends and acquain[t]ances they said, *They are all very well but melancohly* They brought me two Biskets, and a pound of Tobacco. . . . When the Letter was come, the *Saggamores* met to consult about the Captives, and called me to them to enquire how much my husband would give to redeem me, when I came I sate down among them, as I was wont to do, as their manner is: *Then they bade me stand up, and said, they were the General Court. They bid me speak what I thought he would give,* Now knowing that all we had was destroyed by the *Indians.* I was in a great strait: I thought if I should speak of but a little, it would be slighted, and hinder the matter; if of a great sum, I knew not where it would be procured: yet at a venture, I said *Twenty pounds,* yet desired them to take less; but they would not hear of that, but sent that message to *Boston,* that for *Twenty pounds* I should be redeemed. . . .

*　　*　　*

The twentieth Remove

It was their usual manner to remove, when they had done any mischief, lest they should be found out: and so they did at this time. We went about three or four miles, and there they built a great *Wigwam,* big enough to hold an hundred *Indians,* which they did in preparation to a great day of Dancing. . . . The *Indians* now began to come from all quarters, against their merry dancing day. Among some of them came one *Goodwife Kettle:* I told her my heart was so heavy that it was ready to break: so is mine too said she, but yet said, I hope we shall hear some good news shortly. I could hear how

earnestly my Sister desired to see me, & I as earnestly desired to see her: and yet neither of us could get an opportunity. My Daughter was also now about a mile off, and I had not seen her in nine or ten weeks, as I had not seen my Sister since our first taking. I earnestly desired them to let me go and see them: yea, I intreated, begged, and perswaded them, but to let me see my Daughter; and yet so hard hearted were they, that they would not suffer it. They made use of their tyrannical power whilst they had it; but through the Lords wonderfull mercy, their time was now but short.

*　　*　　*

On *Tuesday morning* they called their *General Court* (as they call it) to consult and determine, whether I should go home or no: And they all as one man did seemingly consent to it, that I should go home; except *Philip,* who would not come among them.

*　　*　　*

. . . I may well say as his Psal. 107.12. *Oh give thanks unto the Lord for he is good, for his mercy endureth for ever.* Let the Redeemed of the Lord say so, whom he hath redeemed from the hand of the Enemy, especially that I should come away in the midst of so many hundreds of Enemies quietly and peacably, and not a Dog moving his tongue. So I took my leave of them, and in coming along my heart melted into tears, more then all the while I was with them, and I was almost swallowed up with the thoughts that ever I should go home again. . . .

*　　*　　*

Before I knew what affliction meant, I was ready sometimes to wish for it. When I lived in prosperity; having the comforts of the World about me, my relations by me, my Heart chearfull: and taking little care for any thing; and yet seeing many, whom I preferred before my self, under many tryals and afflictions, in sickness, weakness, poverty, losses, crosses, and cares of the World, I should be sometimes jealous least I should have my portion in this life, and that Scripture would come to my mind,

Heb. 12.6. *For whom the Lord loveth he chasteneth, and scourgeth every Son whom he receivith.* But now I see the Lord had his time to scourge and chasten me. The portion of some is to have their afflictions by drops, now one drop and then another; but the dregs of the Cup, the Wine of astonishment: like a sweeping rain that leaveth no food, did the Lord prepare to be my portion Affliction I wanted, and affliction I had, full measure (I thought) pressed down and running over; yet I see, when God calls a Person to any shing, and through never so many difficulties, yet he is fully able to carry them through and make them see, and say they have been gainers thereby. And I hope I can say in some measure, As *David* did, *It is good for me that I have been afflicted*: The Lord hath shewed me the vanity of these outward things. That they are the *Vanity of vanities, and vexation of spirit*; that they are but a shadow, a blast, a bubble, and things of no continuance. That we must rely on God himself, and our whole dependance must be upon him. If trouble from smaller matters begin to arise in me, I have something at hand to check myself with, and say, why am I troubled? It was but the other day that if I had had the world, I would have given it for my freedom, or to have been a Servant to a Christian.

I have learned to look beyond present and smaller troubles, and to be quieted under them, as *Moses* said, *Exod.* 14.13. *Stand still and see the salvation of the Lord.*

REVIEW QUESTIONS

1. How did the Native Americans treat their captives? Was what they expected of their captives very different from what they expected of themselves?
2. What did Rowlandson's observations—especially those that surprised her—reveal about native lifestyles and the colonists' lives and prejudices?
3. Rowlandson was most vulnerable at the very beginning of her captivity when she was suffering from shock. How did she start to recover? What did she say supported her through all her afflictions?
4. How did she explain this episode in her life to herself and others?
5. What does this story reveal when analyzed as a Puritan sermon? What does it reveal when interpreted as a frontier epic?

COTTON MATHER

FROM Accounts of the Salem Witchcraft Trials (1693)

Cotton Mather (1639–1728), a respected minister in Boston, straddled both the seventeenth and eighteenth centuries. By birth,—as the son and grandson of Puritan divines—education, and profession, he was primarily a man of the earlier century, but as a profoundly curious intellectual, he proved himself ready to consider and adopt some new ideas. Mather's belief in witchcraft and fear of the devil's work in New England reveal his seventeenth-century mental map, but his embrace of a new and controversial medical procedure shows how he adapted—both consciously and unconsciously—that map to a new age.

A communal hysteria over witchcraft engulfed Salem and Andover, Massachusetts, in 1692 and 1693. Historians able to focus a more objective, wide-angle lens on the phenomena have shown how the accusations and trials reveal that these were communities experiencing various crises: problems of growth, gender, generations, and antagonistic groups. As a contemporary observer, however, Mather interpreted the personal and community antagonisms and actions as evidence of Satan's work and New England's fall from grace.

From Cotton Mather, *Cotton Mather on Witchcraft: Being the Wonders of the Invisible World First Published at Boston in Octr. 1692 and now Reprinted, with Additional Matter. . . .* (1693; New York: Dorset Press, 1991), pp. 113–20, 170–71.

The Tryal of Susanna Martin at the Court of Oyer and Terminer, Held by Adjournment at Salem, June 29, 1692

SUSANNA MARTIN, pleading *Not Guilty* to the Indictment of *Witchcraft*, brought in against her, there were produced the Evidences of many Persons very sensibly and grievously Bewitched; who all complained of the Prisoner at the Bar, as the Person whom they believed the cause of their Miseries. And now, as well as in the other Trials, there was an extraordinary Endeavour by *Witchcrafts*, with Cruel and frequent Fits, to hinder the poor Sufferers from giving in their Complaints, which the Court was forced with much Patience to obtain, by much waiting and watching for it.

2. There was now also an account given of what passed at her first Examination before the Magistrates. The Cast of her *Eye*, then striking the afflicted People to the Ground, whether they saw that Cast or no; there were these among other Passages between the Magistrates and the Examinate.

Magistrate. Pray, what ails these People?

Martin. I don't know.

Magistrate. But what do you think ails them?

Martin. I don't desire to spend my Judgment upon it.

Magistrate. Don't you think they are bewitch'd?

Martin. No, I do not think they are.

Magistrate. Tell us your Thoughts about them then.

Martin. No, my thoughts are my own, when they are in, but when they are out they are anothers. Their Master——

Magistrate. Their Master? who do you think is their Master?

Martin. If they be dealing in the Black Art, you may know as well as I.

Magistrate. Well, what have you done towards this?

Martin. Nothing at all.

Magistrate. Why, 'tis you or your Appearance.

Martin. I cannot help it.

Magistrate. Is it not *your* Master? How comes your Appearance to hurt these?

Martin. How do I know? He that appeared in the Shape of *Samuel,* a glorified Saint, may appear in any ones Shape.

It was then also noted in her, as in others like her, that if the Afflicted went to approach her, they were flung down to the Ground. And, when she was asked the reason of it, she said, *I cannot tell; it may be, the Devil bears me more Malice than another.*

*   *   *

4. *John Atkinson* testifi'd, That he exchanged a Cow with a Son of *Susanna Martin's,* whereat she muttered, and was unwilling he should have it. Going to receive this Cow, tho he Hamstring'd her, and Halter'd her, she, of a Tame Creature, grew so mad, that they could scarce get her along. She broke all the Ropes that were fastned unto her, and though she were ty'd fast unto a Tree, yet she made her escape, and gave them such further trouble, as they could ascribe to no cause but Witchcraft.

*   *   *

6. *Robert Downer* testified, That this Prisoner being some Years ago prosecuted at Court for a Witch, he then said unto her, *He believed she was a Witch.* Whereat she being dissatisfied, said, *That some She-Devil would shortly fetch him away!*

Which words were heard by others, as well as himself. The Night following, as he lay in his Bed, there came in at the Window, the likeness of a *Cat*, which flew upon him, took fast hold of his Throat, lay on him a considerable while, and almost killed him. At length he remembered what *Susanna Martin* had threatned the Day before; and with much striving he cried out, *Avoid, thou She-Devil! In the Name of God the Father, the Son, and the Holy Ghost, Avoid!* Whereupon it left him, leap'd on the Floor, and flew out at the Window.

And there also came in several Testimonies, that before ever *Downer* spoke a word of this Accident, *Susanna Martin* and her Family had related, *How this* Downer *had been handled!*

7. *John Kembal* testified, that *Susanna Martin*, upon a Causeless Disgust, had threatned him, about a certain Cow of his, *That she should never do him any more Good:* and it came to pass accordingly. For soon after the Cow was found stark dead on the dry Ground, without any Distemper to be discerned upon her. Upon which he was followed with a strange Death upon more of his Cattle, whereof he lost in one Spring to the value of Thirty Pounds. . . .

*   *   *

12. But besides all of these Evidences, there was a most wonderful Account of one *Joseph Ring*, produced on this occasion. This Man has been strangely carried about by *Dæmons*, from one *Witch-meeting* to another, for near two years together; and for one quarter of this time, they have made him, and keep him Dumb, tho' he is now again able to speak. . . .

. . . this poor Man would be visited with unknown shapes . . . which would force him away with them, unto unknown Places, where he saw Meetings, Feastings, Dancings; . . . When he was brought until these hellish Meetings, one of the first Things they still did unto him, was to give him a knock on the Back, whereupon he was ever as if bound with Chains, uncapable of stirring out of the place, till they should release him. He related, that there often came to him a Man, who presented him a *Book*, whereto he would have him set his Hand; promising to him, that he should then have even what he would; and presenting him with all the delectable Things, Persons, and Places, that he could imagin. But he refusing to subscribe, the business would end with dreadful Shapes, Noises and Screeches, which almost scared him out of his Wits. Once with the Book, there was a Pen offered him, and an Ink-horn with Liquor in it, that seemed like Blood: But he never toucht it.

This Man did now affirm, That he saw the Prisoner at several of those hellish Randezvouzes. Note, this Woman was one of the most impudent, scurrilous, wicked Creatures in the World; and she did now throughout her whole Tryal, discover her self to be such an one. Yet when she was asked, what she had to say for her self? Her chief Plea was, *That she had lead a most virtuous and holy Life.*

*   *   *

Here were in *Salem, June* 10, 1692, about 40 persons that were afflicted with horrible torments by *Evil Spirits*, and the afflicted have accused 60 or 70 as Witches, for that they have *Spectral appearances* of them, tho the Persons are absent when they are tormented. When these Witches were Tryed, several of them confessed a contract with the Devil, by signing his Book, and did express much sorrow for the same, declaring also their *Confederate Witches*, and said the Tempters of them desired 'em to sign the *Devils Book*, who tormented them till they did it. There were at the time of *Examinations*, before many hundreds of Witnesses, strange Pranks play'd; such as the taking Pins out of the Clothes of the afflicted, and thrusting them into their flesh, many of which were taken out again by the *Judges* own hands. Thorns also in like kind were thrust into their flesh; the accusers were sometimes *struck dumb, deaf, blind,* and sometimes lay as if they were dead for a while, and all foreseen and declared by the afflicted just before 't was done. Of the afflicted there were two Girls, about 12 *or* 13 years of age, who saw all that was done, and were therefore called the *Visionary Girls*; they would say, *Now he, or she, or they, are going to bite* or *pinch the Indian*; and all there present in Court saw the visible marks on the *Indians* arms; they would also cry out, *Now look, look, they are going to bind such an ones Legs*, and all present saw the same person spoken of, fall with her Legs twisted in an extraordinary manner; Now say they, we shall all fall, and immediately 7 or 8 of the afflicted fell down, with *terrible shrieks and Out-crys*: at the time when one of the Witches was *sentenc'd, and pinnion'd* with a Cord, at the same time was the afflicted *Indian* Servant going home, (being about 2 or 3 miles out of town,) and had both his Wrists at the same instant bound about with a like Cord, in the same manner as she was when she was sentenc'd, but with that violence, that the Cord entred into his flesh, not to be untied, nor hardly cut—Many *Murders* are suppos'd to be in this way committed; for these Girls, and others of the afflicted, say, *they see Coffins, and bodies in Shrowds*, rising up, and looking on the accused, crying, *Vengeance, Vengeance on the Murderers*—Many other strange things were transacted before the Court in the time of their Examination; and especially one thing which I had like to have forgot, which is this, One of the accus'd, whilst the rest were under Examination, was drawn up by a Rope to the Roof of the house where he was, and would have been choak'd in all probability, had not the Rope been presently cut; the Rope hung at the Roof by some *invisible tye*, for there was no hole where it went up; but after it was cut the *remainder* of it was found in the Chamber just above, lying by the very place where it hung down.

In *December* 1692, the Court sate again at *Salem* in *New-England*, and cleared about 40 persons suspected for Witches, and Condemned three. The Evidence against these three was the same as formerly, so the Warrant for their Execution was sent, and the *Graves digged* for the said three, and for about five more that had been Condemned at *Salem* formerly, but were Reprieved by the Governour.

*   *   *

REVIEW QUESTIONS

1. Why was Susanna Martin accused of witchcraft? What was the evidence presented against her?
2. How did she defend herself?
3. Who were the chief accusers in many of the cases brought before the Salem court? What kind of proof did they proffer?
4. Did most accusations result in convictions?

COTTON MATHER

FROM A Letter about Smallpox Inoculation (1723)

Mather, reflecting his own and his culture's traditional beliefs, thought that smallpox was a scourge "which the Holy and Righteous God has inflicted on a Sinful World." When an epidemic hit Boston in 1721, the ministers led prayers for redemption from sin and disease, while the magistrates enforced public health measures such as quarantining suspect ships and infected citizens. Then Mather, impressed by inoculation accounts coming out of Europe, and remembering an earlier story his slave told him about inoculation as a common practice in Africa, tried to convert Boston's physicians to the new practice. Affected by the Scientific Revolution and the Enlightenment, Mather took the tenet that God helps those who help themselves to mean that human reason and resources could and should solve profound problems, including smallpox epidemics. He finally arranged for Dr. Zabdiel Boylston (1679–1766) to begin administering the procedure late that June. But not all Bostonians were willing to accept this new practice without a battle—which turned out to be a long one. Mather was still defending the practice in 1723 when he addressed this letter to his friend Dr. James Jurin on 21 May.

From Kenneth Silverman, comp., *Selected Letters of Cotton Mather* (Baton Rouge: Louisiana State University Press, 1971), pp. 360–67. Reprinted by permission of Louisiana State University Press from *Selected Letters of Cotton Mather*, compiled with commentary by Kenneth Silverman. Copyright © 1971 by Louisiana State University Press. [Editorial insertions that appear in square brackets are from the Silverman edition unless noted otherwise—*Ed.*]

The Case of the Small pox Inoculated, further cleared

Sir,

. . . The perpetual (and sometimes very strangely periodical) visits which this destructive malady is ever making to all the commercial parts of the earth, and even unto them that are afar off upon the sea, do hold mankind in a continual bondage, through the fear of being once in their life seized with it, yea, of having their life extinguished by it. . . . The apprehensions of dying a very terrible death, after a burning for many days, . . . or at best of having many weary nights roll away under the uneasy circumstances of loins filled with a loathsome disease and recovering with boils, and scars, and wounds, not quickly to be forgotten, hold the children of men in the terrors of death, until the fiery trial be over with them.

[Mather mentions that previously it has been impossible to cure the disease.]

One would have thought, when the compassion of Heaven had made unto a miserable world a discovery of an *unfailing method*, not only to redeem our lives from the destruction threatened by this common enemy of mankind, but also to prevent the uneasy circumstances which make the most that outlive it profess that thousands of pounds would not hire them again to undergo

them, I say, one could not but think that the children of men should have agreed in the most solemn thanksgivings to a gracious God, and most thankfully have accepted the offered favor. But now to find that people should be generally under the energy of an unaccountable aversion from coming into this method of safety; yea, that they should with a rage that reaches up to Heaven, malign and revile those that only propose it unto them, and not only wish the death of those that come into it, but also actually seek the death of the friends that only show them how to save their lives from a formidable adversary! [But goodness always meets with opposition.]

The manner wherein the opposition has been usually carried on has been so satanic, that he must be very blind who sees not the evident original of it. The railing, the lying, the fury, the bloody malice, and even the subordination of perjury, with attempts of assassination, which has distinguished it, have been such as hardly have ever been equalled on any occasion; . . .

But, if there be anything of argument that has ever been produced against this method of safety, I pray let us be apprised of it. [All of the objections have been mere superstitions]

*   *   *

One sort of objections against the method of managing and governing the smallpox in the way of inoculation, has been fetched from conscience; and it has been the cry of a multitude that they *can't see through it* how one can with a good conscience bring a sickness on himself, until it shall please the God of our life to send it upon him.

Now and then persons of serious piety become the opposers of it from a real scruple of conscience concerning the practise. And as these, for the most part, express their dissent with modesty, sobriety, humility, and without censuring of those that are otherwise minded, so we ought ever to treat them with the respects of brethren. But it has been somewhat remarkable and equally ridiculous that the most fierce opposers of the practise have commonly been such as have most cast off the restraints of conscience in other matters, and in their way of talking upon this also, show that conscience has very little [awe?] upon them. With a mouth full of cursing and the language of fiends, at the moment, they vow *they would not be guilty of such a wickedness for all the world!* I have known some good people that have opposed the practise brought over to it by this, as the first of their motives: they were ashamed of their company. [Many who oppose the inoculation are the worst sort of people.] However, let us hear what may be said in opposition. Verily, nothing but what may be said against all the preventing physic in the world. It is urged that it is unlawful to prevent our falling into a greater, and even a deadly, sickness by using a remedy which will throw us into a lesser, and more gentle turn of illness, and such a one as will not ordinarily endanger the life of him that uses it. This is a thing that must be affirmed by all that hold it unlawful to seek a deliverance from the danger of a deadly smallpox in the gentle way of inoculation. But they who affirm this, understand not what they say, nor whereof they affirm. . . . Certainly, never till now was that rule contested, of two evils, choose the least. How commonly do people in health use emetics and cathartics too, under the operation whereof ten thousand more have lost their lives, than ever there have under the smallpox inoculated?

Yea, how many millions have only in learning to smoke tobacco (and this perhaps only to qualify themselves for the pleasure of an exercise which their health is little enough consulted in) procured unto themselves much more sickness, and of a more dangerous tendency too, than is undergone by the most of them that undergo the smallpox inoculated?

It is a hundred to one but the objector may have been chargeable at some time or other with one or both of these things. But he would be angry if you should charge them as crimes upon him.

*   *   *

. . . I beseech you, what is there in the Word of the blessed God (which proscribes and limits the whole duty of man) that forbids the use of this medicine any more than an antidote against the plague? It is rather plain that the Sixth Commandment requires him to use it; and I always thought the Word of the blessed God had instructed us that for our physic as well as for our food, every creature of God is good, and nothing to be refused if it be received with thanksgiving.

*   *   *

If there be anything unlawful in the medicine it must arise from the way of its operation. But let us examine this. [Argues that it would not be called unlawful if it caused vomiting or raised a sweat.]

But then suppose the medicine work in the way of what we may call a despumation, and raise a ferment with pustules, that we may call a sort of smallpox, and is indeed so much of it as forever to secure from any further arrest from that grievous distemper? Where is the Word of God that forbids this despumation, when it may be made with expectation of safety and success? Tho' the medicine be a *variolous quittor* applied unto an incision [i.e., applying smallpox pus into the incision—*Ed.*], I say again, where is the use of it forbidden unto us, any more than the rest that the *Microcosmus Medicus* advises of? This, at last, is the very case! Here is the medicine! He takes a medicine that operates with the symptoms of that smallpox that ordinarily kills nobody, and prevents his ever falling into that smallpox that kills us by millions, and prevents also the distresses which many that are not killed yet commonly meet withal. What shall we say? The Word of God has allowed medicines that operate in all other ways except that of despumation? Profane caviller! *Add not unto His Word, lest He reprove thee, and thou be found a liar.* [It is true that a few die under the inoculation, but some people die from having a tooth drawn.]

In short, I have never seen any Scripture brought against this practise but what has been brought with as foolish and faulty a violation of the Third Commandment, as it would be to bring that Scripture against blood-letting: *He that sheds man's blood, by man shall his blood be shed.*

But I am now drawn to make some remark upon another sort of objections against the method of saving our lives from the horrible pit, and this they pretend is fetched from nature. They allege, *'tis a dangerous practise.*

Now to confute this allegation, there can be no answer comparable to that of constant experience; and by this it is abundantly answered, and so victoriously, that it is amazing there should be heard the least sibilations of it any more.

[Many foolish physicians argue against the inoculation.]

Now this is what I maintain, that constant experience has declared for this practise that it is a safe and sure method. . . .

The constant experience to which I make my first appeal shall be fetched from foreign countries. [Mentions the success of the inoculation in the Levant and in Africa.]

But then, my own country, if I may call it so, or that where I was born and bred, and in the tents whereof I am a sojourner, shall be what I will with yet more assurance appeal unto.

When I first addressed the physicians of Boston (as the smallpox was entering the city, two years ago) with the account which Timonius and Pylarinus [physicians who described the process of inoculation in early eighteenth-century Turkey— *Ed.*] gave of this practise, one word (of the feminine gender!) let fall in that account caused some to foretell that the physicians would never come into it, but would set themselves to decry it with all their might. I will not mention the reason given for this prediction, because I am far from casting a blemish on that honorable profession from the humors of some that are got into it. But this I will say, the prediction was accomplished unto admiration. And how far they can comfort themselves in seeing above a thousand of their neighbors within a few months killed before their eyes, when they knew a method that in ordinary way would have saved them, *they know better than I!*

*   *   *

There are two towns contiguous to Boston. The smallpox entered the town to the northward, where the people were poisoned with outcries against the inoculation. There they died by the scores; they died in shoals; the place was an Aceldama. The smallpox entered the town to the southward, and of the first fourteen or fifteen men that were taken with it, about eleven died. But the survivors, after the example of their wiser pastors, coming at once into the inoculation, there died *not one man* after it. One would think here was an experiment enough to instruct a country; yea, to instruct a nation. [Cites some individual cases.]

Upon the whole, one that shall have the effontery to utter an intimation that it is confessed, as many die under the smallpox inoculated as there do of the smallpox taken in the common way, ought certainly to have the penance of a very long silence imposed on him. Instead of insinuating so vile a falsehood, it may, for ought anything that I have ever yet met withal, be very truly declared, *it yet remains to be proved, that of the many hundreds and thousands that have been under the smallpox inoculated, there was ever any one person who miscarried, that the operation was regularly used upon.* There never was a more successful operation brought into the world! And the reception which it has among those that should be wiser, administers to Heaven too much cause of that complaint, *wherefore is a price put into the hands of the fools, that have no heart unto it?*

If your physicians will discourage the practise, they will do well to examine their hearts, what principles they act upon, and consider how they can answer to God for the loss of so many hundreds of thousands of lives, as would have been saved if *they* had not hindered it? . . .

As for the other vehement opposers of this practise, if they are not so possessed that all talking to them would be only to argue with a whirlwind! I would ask them whether it be not a bold presumption in them to make that a sin which God, the Judge of all, has never made a sin, but really commanded and enjoined and required as a duty? And I would ask them whether they can count it a trusting in God, and not a tempting of Him, to depend on Him for the prolongation of their lives, while they neglect the duty of doing what they can in the use of means that He has kindly shown them for it.

I would also ask them whether it be not a most criminal ingratitude unto the God of Health, when He has acquainted us with a most invaluable method for the saving of our lives from so great a death, to treat it with neglect, and contempt, and multiply abuses on them who thankfully and in a spirit of obedience to Him, embrace His blessings?

I would finally ask them whether they have no dread at all of being accessory to the innumerable deaths which may be, in part, owing to their boisterous opposition unto the method of safety?

For my part, I cannot lay aside my sentiments that the sense of the fascination with which the great adversary of mankind makes these unhappy men his instruments of helping the curse to devour the earth, and those who dwell therein to be desolate, so that anon, few, few men, to what might

have been, shall be left, may call them to walk humbly all their days, that ever they should be *so left of God!*

In the meantime, we that cry with a loud voice to them, *Do yourselves no harm,* and show them how to keep themselves from the paths of the destroyer, are conscious of nothing but of a pity for mankind under the rebukes of God, a concern to see the madness of the people, a desire to have our neighbors *do well,* and a solicitude for a better state of the world. And all the obloquies and outrages we suffer for our charity, we shall entertain as persecutions for a good cause, which will not want its recompenses.

* * *

REVIEW QUESTIONS

1. What was one of the first things Mather thought the people should do upon being offered a chance to be inoculated? Whom did Mather think should be inoculated?
2. What were some of the objections that Mather noted some people voicing? How did he answer them?
3. What were the strengths and weaknesses of his case?
4. How does this letter indicate both continuity and change—in terms of ideas and leadership—in New England?

JONATHAN EDWARDS

Some Thoughts Concerning the Present Revival of Religion (1743)

Jonathan Edwards (1703–1758), a Congregationalist minister in New England, was a vigorous intellectual who studied Enlightenment philosophy but preferred the rich, challenging Calvinist theology of the earlier Puritan church. Edwards believed that people had fallen away from the demanding faith, with its emphasis on God's grace, that was so essential to their salvation. With that in mind, the great theologian began a revival in his Northampton, Massachusetts church in the 1730s that became part of the general revival movement called the Great Awakening. As critics supporting order and orthodoxy increased their attacks against the movement, Edwards emerged as one of its strongest champions.

From Jonathan Edwards, *Some Thoughts Concerning the Present Revival of Religion in New England* in *The Works of President Edwards*, vol. 6 (1817; New York: Burt Franklin, 1968) pp. 31–36, 44–49, 54–57.

Part I, Sect. IV.

The Nature of the Work in general.

Whatever imprudences there have been, and whatever sinful irregularities; whatever vehemence of the passions, and heats of the imagination, transports, and ecstasies: whatever error in judgment, and indiscreet zeal; and whatever outcries, faintings, and agitations of body; yet, it is manifest and notorious, that there has been of late a very uncommon influence upon the minds of a very great part of the inhabitants of *New England*, attended with the best effects. There has been a great increase of seriousness, and sober consideration of eternal things; a disposition to hearken to what is said of such things, with attention and affection; a disposition to treat matters of religion with solemnity, and as of great importance; to make these things the subject of conversation; to hear the word of God preached, and to take all opportunities in order to it; to attend on the public worship of God, and all external duties of religion, in a more solemn and decent manner; so that there is a remarkable and general alteration in the face of *New England* in these respects. Multitudes in all parts of the land, of vain, thoughtless, regardless persons, are quite changed, and become serious and considerate. There is a vast increase of concern for the salvation of the precious soul, and of that inquiry, *What shall I do to be saved?* The

hearts of multitudes have been greatly taken off from the things of the world, its profits, pleasures, and honours. Multitudes in all parts have had their consciences awakened, and have been made sensible of the pernicious nature and consequences of sin, and what a dreadful thing it is to be under guilt and the displeasure of God, and to live without peace and reconciliation with him. They have also been awakened to a sense of the shortness and uncertainty of life, and the reality of another world and future judgment, and of the necessity of an interest in Christ. They are more afraid of sin, more careful and inquisitive that they may know what is contrary to the mind and will of God, that they may avoid it, and what he requires of them, that they may do it, more careful to guard against temptations, more watchful over their own hearts, earnestly desirous of knowing, and of being diligent in the use of the means that God has appointed in his word, in order to salvation. Many very stupid, senseless sinners, and persons of a vain mind, have been greatly awakened.

There is a strange alteration almost all over *New England* amongst young people: by a powerful invisible influence on their minds, they have been brought to forsake, in a general way, as it were at once, those things of which they were extremely fond, and in which they seemed to place the happiness of their lives, and which nothing before could induce them to forsake; as their frolicking, vain company-keeping, night-walking, their mirth and jollity, their impure language, and lewd songs. In vain did ministers preach against those things before, in vain were laws made to restrain them, and in vain was all the vigilance of magistrates and civil officers; but now they have almost every where dropt them as it were of themselves. And there is great alteration amongst old and young as to drinking, tavern-haunting, prophane speaking, and extravagance in apparel. Many notoriously vicious persons have been reformed, and become externally quite new creatures. Some that are wealthy, and of a fashionable, gay education; some great beaux and fine ladies, that seemed to have their minds swallowed up with nothing but the vain shews and pleasures of the world, have been wonderfully altered, have relinquished these vanities, and are become serious, mortified, and humble in their conversation. It is astonishing to see the alteration there is in some towns, where before there was but little appearance of religion, or any thing but vice and vanity. And now they are transformed into another sort of people; their former vain, worldly, and vicious conversation and dispositions seem to be forsaken, and they are, as it were, gone over to a new world. Their thoughts, their talk, and their concern, affections and inquiries, are now about the favour of God, an interest in Christ, a renewed sanctified heart, and a spiritual blessedness, acceptance, and happiness in a future world.

Now, through the greater part of *New England*, the holy Bible is in much greater esteem and use than before. The great things contained in it are much more regarded, as things of the greatest consequence, and are much more the subjects of meditation and conversation; and other books of piety that have long been of established reputation, as the most excellent, and most tending to promote true godliness, have been abundantly more in use. The Lord's day is more religiously and strictly observed. And much has been lately done at making up differences, confessing faults one to another, and making restitution: probably more within two years, than was done in thirty years before. . . . And many have been deeply affected with a sense of their own ignorance and blindness, and exceeding helplessness, and so of their extreme need of the divine pity and help.

Multitudes in *New England* have lately been brought to a new and great conviction of the truth and certainty of the things of the gospel; to a firm persuasion that Christ Jesus is the son of God, and the great and only Saviour of the world; and that the great doctrines of the gospel touching reconciliation by his blood, and acceptance in his righteousness, and eternal life and salvation through him, are matters of undoubted truth. . . . And not only do these effects appear in new converts, but great numbers of those who were formerly esteemed the most sober and pious people, have, under the influence of this work, been greatly quickened, and their hearts renewed with greater degrees of light, renewed repentance and humiliation, and more lively exercises of faith, love and joy in the Lord. . . . And now, instead of meetings at taverns and drinking-houses, and of young people in frolics and vain company, the country is full of meetings of all sorts and ages of persons—young and old, men, women and little children—to read and pray, and sing praises, and to converse of the things of God and another world. In very many places the main of the conversation in all companies turns on religion, and things of a spiritual nature. . . . And there has been this alteration abiding on multitudes all over the land, for a year and a half, without any appearance of a disposition to return to former vice and vanity.

And, under the influences of this work, there have been many of the remains of those wretched people and dregs of mankind, the poor *Indians*, that seemed to be next to a state of brutality, and with whom, till now, it seemed to be to little more purpose to use endeavours for their instruction and awakening, than with the beasts. Their minds have now been strangely opened to receive instruction, and been deeply affected with the concerns of their precious souls; they have reformed their lives, and forsaken their former stupid, barbarous and brutish way of living; . . . And many of the poor *Negroes* also have been in like manner wrought upon and changed. Very many little children have been remarkably enlightened, and their hearts wonderfully affected and enlarged, and their mouths opened, expressing themselves in a manner far beyond their years, and to the just as-tonishment of those who have heard them. . . .

The divine power of this work has marvellously appeared in some instances I have been acquainted with; in supporting and fortifying the heart under great trials, such as the death of children, and ex-treme pain of body; and in wonderfully maintain-ing the serenity, calmness and joy of the soul, in an immoveable rest in God, and sweet resignation to him. And some under the blessed influences of this work have, in a calm, bright and joyful frame of mind, been carried through the valley of the shadow of death.

And now let us consider;——Is it not strange that in a Christian country, and such a land of light as this is, there are many at a loss to conclude whose work this is, whether the work of God or the work of the devil? Is it not a shame to *New England* that such a work should be much doubted of here? . . . We have a rule near at hand, a sacred book that God himself has put into our hands, with clear and infallible marks, sufficient to resolve us in things of this nature; which book I think we must reject, not only in some particular passages, but in the substance of it, if we reject such a work as has now been described, as not being the work of God. The whole tenor of the gospel proves it; all the notion of religion that the scripture gives us confirms it.

I suppose there is scarcely a minister in this land, but from sabbath to sabbath is used to pray that God would pour out his Spirit, and work a reformation and revival of religion in the country, and turn us from our intemperance, profaneness, uncleanness, worldliness and other sins; and we have kept from year to year, days of public fasting and prayer to God, to acknowledge our backslid-ings, and humble ourselves for our sins, and to seek of God forgiveness and reformation: And now when so great and extensive a reformation is so suddenly and wonderfully accomplished, in those very things that we have sought to God for, shall we not acknowledge it? or, do it with great cold-ness, caution and reserve, and scarcely take any no-tice of it in our public prayers and praises, or mention it but slightly and cursorily, and in such a

manner as carries an appearance as though we would contrive to say as little of it as ever we could, and were glad to pass from it? And that because the work is attended with a mixture of error, impru-dences, darkness and sin; because some persons are carried away with impressions, and are indiscreet, and too censorious with their zeal; and because there are high transports of religious affections; and some effects on their bodies of which we do not understand the reason.

*   *   *

Sect. VI.

This Work is very Glorious.

Now if such things are enthusiasm, and the fruits of a distempered brain, let my brain be evermore possessed of that happy distemper! If this be dis-traction, I pray God that the world of mankind may be all seized with this benign, meek, benefi-cent, beatifical, glorious distraction! . . . The great affections and high transports, that others have lately been under, are in general of the same kind with those in the instance that has been given, though not to so high a degree, and many of them not so pure and unmixed, and so well regulated. I have had opportunity to observe many instances here and elsewhere; and though there are some instances of great affections in which there has been a great mixture of nature with grace, and in some, a sad degenerating of religious affections; yet there is that uniformity observable, which makes it easy to be seen, that in general it is the same spirit from whence the work in all parts of the land has originated. And what notions have they of religion, that reject what has been described, as not true religion! . . .

Those who are waiting for the fruits, in order to determine whether this be the work of God or no, would do well to consider, what they are waiting for: Whether it be not to have this wonderful reli-gious influence, and then to see how they will be-have themselves? That is, to have grace subside, and the actings of it in a great measure to cease, and to have persons grow cold and dead; and then to see whether, after that, they will behave themselves with that exactness and brightness of conversation, that is to be expected of lively Christians, or those that are in the vigorous exercises of grace. There are many that will not be satisfied with any exactness or laboriousness in religion now, while persons have their minds much moved, and their affections are high; for they lay it to their flash of affection, and heat of zeal, as they call it; they are waiting to see whether they will carry themselves as well when these affections are over; that is, they are waiting to have persons sicken and lose their strength, that they may see whether they will then behave themselves like healthy strong men. I would desire that they would also consider, whether they be not waiting for more than is reasonably to be expected, supposing this to be really a great work of God, and much more than has been found in former great out-pourings of the Spirit of God, that have been universally acknowledged in the Christian church? Do not they expect fewer instances of apostacy and evidences of hypocrisy in professors, than were after that great out-pouring of the Spirit in the apostles' days, or that which was in the time of the reformation? And do not they stand prepared to make a mighty argument of it against this work, if there should be *half* so many? And, they would do well to consider how *long* they will wait to see the good fruit of this work, before they will determine in favour of it. Is not their waiting unlimited? The visible fruit that is to be expected of a pouring out of the Spirit of God on a country, is a visible reformation in that country. What reformation has lately been brought to pass in *New England*, by this work, has been before observed. And has it not continued long enough already, to give reasonable satisfaction? If God cannot work on the hearts of a people after such a manner, as reasonably to expect it should be acknowledged in a year and a half, or two years' time; yet surely it is unreasonable that our expectations and demands should be unlimited, and our waiting without any bounds.

As there is the clearest evidence, from what has been observed, that this is the work of God; so it is evident that it is a very great and wonderful, and exceeding glorious work.—This is certain, that it is a great and wonderful event, a strange revolution, an unexpected, surprising overturning of things, suddenly brought to pass; such as never has been seen in *New England*, and scarce ever has been heard of in any land. Who that saw the state of things in *New England* a few years ago, would have thought that in so short a time there would be such a change? . . .

Such a work is, in its nature and kind, the most glorious of any work of God whatsoever, and is always so spoken of in scripture. It is the work of redemption (the great end of all the other works of God, and of which the work of creation was but a shadow) in the event, success, and end of it: It is the work of new creation, which is infinitely more glorious than the old. . . .

This work is very glorious both in its *nature*, and in its *degree* and *circumstances*. It will appear very glorious, if we consider the unworthiness of the people who are the subjects of it; what obligations God has laid us under by the special privileges we have enjoyed for our souls' good, and the great things God did for us at our first settlement in the land; how he has followed us with his goodness to this day, and how we have abused his goodness; how long we have been revolting more and more, (as all confess,) and how very corrupt we were become at last; in how great a degree we had forsaken the fountain of living waters; how obstinate we have been under all manner of means that God has used to reclaim us; how often we have mocked God with hypocritical pretences of humiliation, as in our annual days of public fasting, and other things, while, instead of reforming, we only grew worse and worse; and how dead a time it was every where before this work began. If we consider these things, we shall be most stupidly ungrateful, if we do not acknowledge God's visiting us as he has done, as an instance of the glorious triumph of free and sovereign grace.

The work is very glorious, if we consider the *extent* of it; being in this respect vastly beyond any that ever was known in *New England*. There has formerly sometimes been a remarkable awakening and success of the means of grace, in some particular congregations; and this used to be much noticed, and acknowledged to be glorious, though the towns and congregations round about continued dead: But now God has brought to pass a new thing, he has wrought a great work, which has extended from one end of the land to the other, besides what has been wrought in other *British* colonies in *America.*

The work is very glorious in the great *numbers* that have, to appearance, been turned from sin to God, and so, delivered from a wretched captivity to sin and Satan, saved from everlasting burnings, and made heirs of eternal glory. . . .

The work has been very glorious and wonderful in many *circumstances* and events of it, wherein God has in an uncommon manner made his hand visible and his power conspicuous; as in the extraordinary degrees of awakening, and the suddenness of conversions in innumerable instances. How common a thing has it been for a great part of a congregation to be at once moved by a mighty invisible power? and for six, eight, or ten souls to be converted to God (to all appearance) in an exercise, in whom the visible change still continues? How great an alteration has been made in some towns, yea, some populous towns, the change still abiding? And how many very vicious persons have been wrought upon, so as to become visibly new creatures? God has also made his hand very visible, and his work glorious, in the multitudes of little children that have been wrought upon. I suppose there have been some hundreds of instances of this nature of late, any one of which formerly would have been looked upon so remarkable, as to be worthy to be recorded, and published through the land. The work is very glorious in its influences and effects on many who have been very ignorant and barbarous, as I before observed of the *Indians* and *Negroes.*

The work is also exceeding glorious in the high attainments of Christians, in the extraordinary degrees of light, love and spiritual joy, that God has bestowed upon great multitudes. In this respect also, the land in all parts has abounded with such instances, any one of which, if they had happened formerly, would have been thought worthy to be noticed by God's people throughout the *British* dominions. The *New-Jerusalem* in this respect has begun to come down from heaven, and perhaps never were more of the prelibations of heaven's glory given upon earth.

*   *   *

Part II, Sect. II.

The Latter-Day Glory, is probably to begin in America.

It is not unlikely that this work of God's Spirit, so extraordinary and wonderful, is the dawning, or at least, a prelude of that glorious work of God, so often foretold in scripture, which, in the progress and issue of it, shall renew the world of mankind. If we consider how long since the things foretold as what should precede this great event, have been accomplished; and how long this event has been expected by the church of God, and thought to be nigh by the most eminent men of God, in the church; and withal consider what the state of things now is, and has for a considerable time been, in the church of God, and the world of mankind; we cannot reasonably think otherwise, than that the beginning of this great work of God must be near. And there are many things that make it probable that this work will begin in *America.*—It is signified that it shall begin in some very remote part of the world, with which other parts have no communication but by navigation, in Isa. lx. 9. *Surely the isles shall wait for me, and the ships of* Tarshish *first, to bring my sons from far.* It is exceeding manifest that this chapter is a prophecy of the prosperity of the church, in its most glorious state on earth, in the latter days; and I cannot think that any thing else can be here intended but *America* by the isles that are far off, from whence the first-born sons of that glorious day shall be brought. . . .

God has made as it were two worlds here below, two great habitable continents, far separated one from the other: The latter is as it were now but newly created; it has been, till of late, wholly the possession of *Satan*, the church of God having never been in it, as it has been in the other continent, from the beginning of the world. This new world is probably now discovered, that the new and most glorious state of God's church on earth might commence there; that God might in it begin a new world in a spiritual respect, when he creates the *new heavens* and *new earth*.

God has already put that honour upon the other continent, that Christ was born there literally, and there made the *purchase of redemption*. So, as Providence observes a kind of equal distribution of things, it is not unlikely that the great spiritual birth of Christ, and the most glorious *application of redemption*, is to begin in this. . . .

*   *   *

The old continent has been the source and original of mankind, in several respects. The first parents of mankind dwelt there; and there dwelt *Noah* and his sons; there the second *Adam* was born, and crucified and raised again: And it is probable that, in some measure to balance these things, the most glorious renovation of the world shall originate from the new continent, and the church of God in that respect be from hence. And so it is probable that will come to pass in spirituals, which has taken place in temporals, with respect to *America*; that whereas, till of late, the world was supplied with its silver, and gold, and earthly treasures from the old continent, now it is supplied chiefly from the new; so the course of things in spiritual respects will be in like manner turned.—And it is worthy to be noted, that *America* was discovered about the time

of the reformation, or but little before: Which reformation was the first thing that God did towards the glorious renovation of the world, after it had sunk into the depths of darkness and ruin, under the great antichristian apostacy. So that, as soon as this new world stands forth in view, God presently goes about doing some great thing in order to make way for the introduction of the church's latter-day glory—which is to have its first seat in, and is to take its rise from that new world.

*   *   *

REVIEW QUESTIONS

1. According to Edwards, what was New England like before the Great Awakening? After? What do his descriptions reveal about colonial society? What do they reveal about him?
2. While he noted that all sorts of people were affected by the Awakening, whom did he indicate were most affected by it? Why do you suppose this concerned both proponents and opponents of the movement?
3. How did Edwards answer critics who believed that the dissension and disorder of the Awakening may be a manifestation of the devil's, rather than God's, work?
4. Did Edwards champion the Awakening as a democratic as well as a providential process?
5. How did Edwards interpret the Awakening as a sign of the possible destiny of America? Did his argument reflect earlier ideas about America or foreshadow later ones? Explain.

BENJAMIN FRANKLIN

The Way to Wealth (1757)

Benjamin Franklin (1706–1790) was the epitome of the self-made man. Born into a large artisan family in Boston, his father apprenticed him at the age of twelve to his brother James, a printer. At the age of seventeen, Franklin ran away from his brother in Boston and traveled to Philadelphia where he first worked for another printer, and then set up his own shop. Industrious and shrewd, Franklin prospered. He became the editor and publisher of the Pennsylvania Gazette *in 1729 and started publishing* Poor Richard's Almanack, *an annual best-seller, in 1732. Franklin did so well that he was able to retire from the greater part of his printing business—namely as editor and publisher of the* Pennsylvania Gazette—*while still in his forties (1748). He then had ample time to devote to other interests, which included science and politics. He continued, however, to publish* Poor Richard's Almanack *until 1757. In its final edition, Franklin, in his persona of "Richard Saunders" (i.e., "Poor Richard"), made up a story about an old man who advised some people on work and financial matters at a vendue (public sale). Delighted by the old man's use of Poor Richard's principles (which Franklin admitted reflected sayings in general use at the time), Franklin, as Saunders, ended the piece by saying he intended to follow his own advice and recommended that his readers do the same.*

From Benjamin Franklin, *Benjamin Franklin: The Autobiography and Other Writings*, ed. Kenneth Silverman (New York: Penguin Books, 1986) pp. 215–25.

*   *   *

. . . I stopt my Horse lately where a great Number of People were collected at a Vendue of Merchant Goods. The Hour of Sale not being come, they were conversing on the Badness of the Times, and one of the Company call'd to a plain clean old Man, with white Locks, *Pray, Father* Abraham, *what think you of the Times? Won't these heavy Taxes quite ruin the Country? How shall we be ever able to pay them? What would you advise us to?*— Father *Abraham* stood up, and reply'd, If you'd have my Advice, I'll give it you in short, for a *Word to the Wise is enough,* and *many Words won't fill a Bushel,* as *Poor Richard says.* They join'd in desiring him to speak his Mind, and gathering round him, he proceeded as follows;

"Friends, says he, and Neighbours, the Taxes are indeed very heavy, and if those laid on by the Government were the only Ones we had to pay, we might more easily discharge them; but we have many others, and much more grievous to some of us. We are taxed twice as much by our *Idleness,* three times as much by our *Pride,* and four times as much by our *Folly,* and from these Taxes the Commissioners cannot ease or deliver us by allowing an Abatement. However let us hearken to good Advice, and something may be done for us; *God helps them that help themselves,* as *Poor Richard* says, in his Almanack of 1733.

It would be thought a hard Government that should tax its People one tenth Part of their *Time,* to be employed in its Service. But *Idleness* taxes many of us much more, if we reckon all that is spent in absolute *Sloth*, or doing of nothing, with that which is spent in idle Employments or Amusements, that amount to nothing. . . . If Time be of all Things the most precious, *wasting Time must be*, as *Poor Richard* says, *the greatest Prodigality*, since, as he elsewhere tells us, *Lost Time is never found again*; and what we call *Time-enough, always proves little enough:* Let us then be up and be doing, and doing to the Purpose; so by Diligence shall we do more with less Perplexity. *Sloth makes all Things difficult, but Industry all easy*, as *Poor Richard* says; and *He that riseth late, must trot all Day, and shall scarce overtake his Business at Night. While Laziness travels so slowly, that Poverty soon overtakes him*, as we read in *Poor Richard*, who adds, *Drive thy Business, let not that drive thee*; and *Early to Bed, and early to rise, makes a Man healthy, wealthy and wise.*

So what signifies *wishing* and *hoping* for better Times. We may make these Times better if we bestir ourselves. *Industry need not wish*, as *Poor Richard* says, and *He that lives upon Hope will die fasting. There are no Gains, without Pains*; then *Help Hands, for I have no Lands*, or if I have, they are smartly taxed. And, as *Poor Richard* likewise observes, *He that hath a Trade hath an Estate*, and *He that hath a Calling hath an Office of Profit and Honour*; but then the *Trade* must be worked at, and the *Calling* well followed, or neither the *Estate*, nor the *Office*, will enable us to pay our Taxes.—If we are industrious we shall never starve; for, as *Poor Richard* says, *At the working Man's House* Hunger *looks in, but dares not enter*. Nor will the Bailiff nor the Constable enter, for *Industry pays Debts, while Despair encreaseth them*, says *Poor Richard*. . . . If you were a Servant, would you not be ashamed that a good Master should catch you idle? Are you then your own Master, *be ashamed to catch yourself idle*, as *Poor Dick* says. When there is so much to be done for yourself, your Family, your Country, and your gracious King, be up by Peep of Day; *Let not the Sun look down and say, Inglorious here he lies*. . . .

Methinks I hear some of you say, *Must a Man afford himself no Leisure?*— I will tell thee, my Friend, what *Poor Richard* says, *Employ thy Time well if thou meanest to gain Leisure*; and, *since thou art not sure of a Minute, throw not away an Hour*. Leisure, is Time for doing something useful; this Leisure the diligent Man will obtain, but the lazy Man never; so that, as *Poor Richard* says, a *Life of Leisure and a Life of Laziness are two Things*. . . .

But with our Industry, we must likewise be *steady, settled* and *careful*, and oversee our own Affairs *with our own Eyes*, and not trust too much to others; for, as *Poor Richard* says, . . . *Keep thy Shop, and thy Shop will keep thee*; and again, *If you would have your Business done, go; If not, send*. . . .

And again, *The Eye of a Master will do more Work than both his Hands*; and again, *Want of Care does us more Damage than Want of Knowledge*; and again, *Not to oversee Workmen, is to leave them your Purse open*. Trusting too much to others Care is the Ruin of many; for, as the *Almanack* says, *In the Affairs of this World, Men are saved, not by Faith, but by the Want of it*; but a Man's own Care is profitable; for, saith *Poor Dick*, *Learning is to the Studious*, and *Riches to the Careful*, as well as *Power to the Bold*, and *Heaven to the Virtuous*. And farther, *If you would have a faithful Servant, and one that you like, serve yourself*. And again, he adviseth to Circumspection and Care, even in the smallest Matters, because sometimes *a little Neglect may breed great Mischief*; adding, *For want of a Nail the Shoe was lost; for want of a Shoe the Horse was lost; and for want of a Horse the Rider was lost*, being overtaken and slain by the Enemy, all for want of Care about a Horse-shoe Nail.

So much for Industry, my Friends, and Attention to one's own Business; but to these we must add *Frugality*, if we would make our *Industry* more certainly successful. A Man may, if he knows not how to save as he gets, *keep his Nose all his Life to the Grindstone*, and die not worth a *Groat* at last. . . .

If you would be wealthy, says he, in another Almanack, *think of Saving as well as of Getting: The Indies have not made Spain rich, because her* Outgoes *are greater than her* Incomes. Away then with your expensive Follies, and you will not have so much Cause to complain of hard Times, heavy Taxes, and chargeable Families; for, as *Poor Dick* says,

> *Women and Wine, Game and Deceit,*
> *Make the Wealth small, and the Wants great.*

And farther, *What maintains one Vice, would bring up two Children.* You may think perhaps, That a *little* Tea, or a *little* Punch now and then, Diet a *little* more costly, Clothes a *little* finer, and a *little* Entertainment now and then, can be no *great* Matter; but remember what *Poor Richard* says, . . . *Beware of* little *Expences; a small Leak will sink a great Ship*; and again, *Who Dainties love, shall Beggars prove*; and moreover, *Fools make Feasts, and wise Men eat them.*

Here you are all got together at this Vendue of *Fineries* and *Knicknacks.* You call them *Goods*, but if you do not take Care, they will prove *Evils* to some of you. You expect they will be sold *cheap*, and perhaps they may for less than they cost; but if you have no Occasion for them, they must be *dear* to you. Remember what *Poor Richard* says, *Buy what thou hast no Need of, and ere long thou shalt sell thy Necessaries.* And again, *At a great Pennyworth pause a while:* He means, that perhaps the Cheapness is *apparent* only, and not *real*; or the Bargain, by straitning thee in thy Business, may do thee more Harm than Good. . . . Many a one, for the Sake of Finery on the Back, have gone with a hungry Belly, and half starved their Families; *Silks and Sattins, Scarlet and Velvets*, as *Poor Richard* says, *put out the Kitchen Fire.* These are not the *Necessaries* of Life; they can scarcely be called the *Conveniencies*, and yet only because they look pretty, how many *want* to *have* them. The *artificial* Wants of Mankind thus become more numerous than the *natural*; and, as *Poor Dick* says, *For one* poor *Person, there are an hundred* indigent. By these, and other Extravagancies, the Genteel are reduced to Poverty, and forced to borrow of those whom they formerly despised, but who through *Industry* and *Frugality* have maintained their Standing; in which Case it appears plainly, that a *Ploughman on his Legs is higher than a Gentleman on his Knees,* as *Poor Richard* says. . . . *If you would*

know the Value of Money, go and try to borrow some; for, *he that goes a borrowing goes a sorrowing*; and indeed so does he that lends to such People, when he goes *to get it in again* . . .

*   *   *

But what Madness must it be to *run in Debt* for these Superfluities! We are offered, by the Terms of this Vendue, *Six Months Credit*; and that perhaps has induced some of us to attend it, because we cannot spare the ready Money, and hope now to be fine without it. But, ah, think what you do when you run in Debt; *You give to another Power over your Liberty.* If you cannot pay at the Time, you will be ashamed to see your Creditor; you will be in Fear when you speak to him; you will make poor pitiful sneaking Excuses, and by Degrees come to lose your Veracity, and sink into base downright lying; for, as *Poor Richard* says, *The second Vice is Lying, the first is running in Debt.* And again, to the same Purpose, *Lying rides upon Debt's Back.* Whereas a freeborn Englishman ought not to be ashamed or afraid to see or speak to any Man living. But Poverty often deprives a Man of all Spirit and Virtue: *'Tis hard for an empty Bag to stand upright*, as *Poor Richard* truly says. What would you think of that Prince, or that Government, who should issue an Edict forbidding you to dress like a Gentleman or a Gentlewoman, on Pain of Imprisonment or Servitude? Would you not say, that you are free, have a Right to dress as you please, and that such an Edict would be a Breach of your Privileges, and such a Government tyrannical? And yet you are about to put yourself under that Tyranny when you run in Debt for such Dress! Your Creditor has Authority at his Pleasure to deprive you of your Liberty, by confining you in Goal for Life, or to sell you for a Servant, if you should not be able to pay him! When you have got your Bargain, you may, perhaps, think little of Payment; but *Creditors, Poor Richard* tells us, *have better Memories than Debtors*; and in another Place says, *Creditors are a superstitious Sect, great Observers of set Days and Times.* The Day comes round before you are aware, and the Demand is made before you are prepared to satisfy it. Or if you bear your Debt in Mind, the Term which at first seemed so long, will, as it lessens, appear extreamly short. *Time* will seem to have added Wings to his Heels as well as Shoulders. *Those have a short Lent,* saith *Poor Richard, who owe Money to be paid at Easter.* Then since, as he says, *The Borrower is a Slave to the Lender, and the Debtor to the Creditor,* disdain the Chain, preserve your Freedom; and maintain your Independency: Be *industrious* and *free*; be *frugal* and *free.* . . .

This Doctrine, my Friends, is *Reason* and *Wisdom*; but after all, do not depend too much upon your own *Industry,* and *Frugality,* and *Prudence,* though excellent Things, for they may all be blasted without the Blessing of Heaven; and therefore ask that Blessing humbly, and be not uncharitable to those that at present seem to want it, but comfort and help them. Remember *Job* suffered, and was afterwards prosperous.

And now to conclude, *Experience keeps a dear School, but Fools will learn in no other, and scarce in that*; for it is true, *we may give Advice, but we cannot give Conduct,* as *Poor Richard* says: However, remember this, *They that won't be counselled, can't be helped,* as *Poor Richard* says: And farther, That *if you will not hear Reason, she'll surely rap your Knuckles.*

Thus the old Gentleman ended his Harangue. The People heard it, and approved the Doctrine, and immediately practised the contrary, just as if it had been a common Sermon; for the Vendue opened, and they began to buy extravagantly, notwithstanding all his Cautions, and their own Fear of Taxes. . . .

REVIEW QUESTIONS

1. What did Franklin believe was the key to making money? He provided plenty of aphorisms to make that point. Of those, which do you believe provided the best advice? Why?
2. What did Franklin say about holding on to money? What do you believe was the most pertinent piece of that advice? Why?
3. What does this story, and the advice in it, reveal about colonial society? About Franklin?

OLAUDAH EQUIANO

FROM An African Narrative (1791)

While there was land aplenty in America, the key to the American dream of prosperity was labor: one's own and others'. The primary labor group was the family, but added to those laborers tied by marriage and birth were those tied by wages ("free" laborers), contracts (indentured servants), and coercion (slaves). Although Indian and African slavery had been part of the colonization process in the Americas since the conquistadores, the importation and use of African slaves in the English mainland colonies did not commence in earnest until the late seventeenth century. The exploitation of enslaved Africans and their descendants then increased tremendously in the eighteenth century, especially in the southern colonies, although slaves were found in every colony.

First African and then European traders carried Olaudah Equiano (1745– 1797), an Ibo of Nigeria, into the trap of trans-Atlantic slavery when he was a boy of eleven. Slavery as an institution was not new to Equiano; his father had slaves, but he found that the Euro-American concept of slavery was different from the African one. Equiano survived the passage from Africa to the colonies and was bought by a Virginia planter, and shortly thereafter, by an English naval officer. He served on warships during the Seven Years' War and then, as the property of a Quaker merchant, participated in the trade between the West Indies and the southern colonies. Equiano bought his freedom in 1766 and supported himself as a sailor. His life did not parallel the lives of most of those enslaved, for he learned to read and write and gained his own liberty. Greatly influenced by evangelical ministers who preached the equality of souls, he used his freedom and education to work for the abolition of slavery.

From Olaudah Equiano, *The Interesting Narrative of the Life of Olaudah Equiano, Written by Himself,* ed. Robert J. Allison (Boston: Bedford Books of St. Martin's Press, 1995) pp. 53–59.

*   *   *

The first object which saluted my eyes when I arrived on the coast, was the sea, and a slave ship, which was then riding at anchor, and waiting for its cargo. These filled me with astonishment, which was soon converted into terror, when I was carried on board. I was immediately handled, and tossed up to see if I were sound, by some of the crew; and I was now persuaded that I had gotten into a world of bad spirits, and that they were going to kill me. Their complexions, too, differing so much from ours, their long hair, and the language they spoke (which was very different from any I had ever heard), united to confirm me in this belief. Indeed, such were the horrors of my views and fears at the moment, that, if ten thousand worlds had been my own, I would have freely parted with them all to have exchanged my condition with that of the meanest slave in my own country. When I looked round the ship too, and saw a large furnace of copper boiling, and a multitude of black people of every description chained together, every one of their countenances expressing dejection and sorrow, I no longer doubted of my fate; and, quite overpowered with horror and anguish, I fell motionless on the deck and fainted. When I recovered a little, I found some black people about me, who I believed were some of those who had brought me on board, and had been receiving their pay;

they talked to me in order to cheer me, but all in vain. . . .

I now saw myself deprived of all chance of returning to my native country, or even the least glimpse of hope of gaining the shore, which I now considered as friendly; and I even wished for my former slavery in preference to my present situation, which was filled with horrors of every kind, still heightened by my ignorance of what I was to undergo. I was not long suffered to indulge my grief; I was soon put down under the decks, and there I received such a salutation in my nostrils as I had never experienced in my life: so that, with the loathsomeness of the stench, and crying together, I became so sick and low that I was not able to eat, nor had I the least desire to taste anything. I now wished for the last friend, death, to relieve me; but soon, to my grief, two of the white men offered me eatables; and, on my refusing to eat, one of them held me fast by the hands, and laid me across, I think, the windlass, and tied my feet, while the other flogged me severely. . . .

In a little time after, amongst the poor chained men, I found some of my own nation, which in a small degree gave ease to my mind. I inquired of these what was to be done with us? They gave me to understand, we were to be carried to these white people's country to work for them. I then was a little revived, and thought, if it were no worse than working, my situation was not so desperate; but still I feared I should be put to death, the white people looked and acted, as I thought, in so savage a manner; for I had never seen among any people such instances of brutal cruelty; and this not only shown towards us blacks, but also to some of the whites themselves. One white man in particular I saw, when we were permitted to be on deck, flogged so unmercifully with a large rope near the foremast, that he died in consequence of it; and they tossed him over the side as they would have done a brute. This made me fear these people the more; and I expected nothing less than to be treated in the same manner. . . .

*   *   *

At last, when the ship we were in, had got in all her cargo, they made ready with many fearful noises, and we were all put under deck, so that we could not see how they managed the vessel. But this disappointment was the least of my sorrow. The stench of the hold while we were on the coast was so intolerably loathsome, that it was dangerous to remain there for any time, and some of us had been permitted to stay on the deck for the fresh air; but now that the whole ship's cargo were confined together, it became absolutely pestilential. The closeness of the place, and the heat of the climate, added to the number in the ship, which was so crowded that each had scarcely room to turn himself, almost suffocated us. This produced copious perspirations, so that the air soon became unfit for respiration, from a variety of loathsome smells, and brought on a sickness among the slaves, of which many died—thus falling victims to the improvident avarice, as I may call it, of their purchasers. This wretched situation was again aggravated by the galling of the chains, now became insupportable, and the filth of the necessary tubs, into which the children often fell, and were almost suffocated. The shrieks of the women, and the groans of the dying, rendered the whole a scene of horror almost inconceivable. Happily perhaps, for myself, I was soon reduced so low here that it was thought necessary to keep me almost always on deck; and from my extreme youth I was not put in fetters. In this situation I expected every hour to

share the fate of my companions, some of whom were almost daily brought upon deck at the point of death, which I began to hope would soon put an end to my miseries. . . .

*   *   *

One day, when we had a smooth sea and moderate wind, two of my wearied countrymen who were chained together (I was near them at the time), preferring death to such a life of misery, somehow made through the nettings and jumped into the sea; immediately, another quite dejected fellow, who, on account of his illness, was suffered to be out of irons, also followed their example; and I believe many more would very soon have done the same, if they had not been prevented by the ship's crew, who were instantly alarmed. Those of us that were the most active, were in a moment put down under the deck; and there was such a noise and confusion amongst the people of the ship as I never heard before, to stop her, and get the boat out to go after the slaves. However, two of the wretches were drowned, but they got the other, and afterwards flogged him unmercifully, for thus attempting to prefer death to slavery. In this manner we continued to undergo more hardships than I can now relate, hardships which are inseparable from this accursed trade. Many a time we were near suffocation from the want of fresh air, which we were often without for whole days together. This, and the stench of the necessary tubs, carried off many.

*   *   *

At last we came in sight of the island of Barbadoes, at which the whites on board gave a great shout, and made many signs of joy to us. We did not know what to think of this; but as the vessel drew nearer, we plainly saw the harbor, and other ships of different kinds and sizes, and we soon anchored amongst them, off Bridgetown. Many merchants and planters now came on board, though it was in the evening. They put us in separate parcels, and examined us attentively. They also made us jump, and pointed to the land, signifying we were to go there. We thought by this, we should be eaten by these ugly men, as they appeared to us; and, when soon after we were all put down under the deck again, there was much dread and trembling among us, and nothing but bitter cries to be heard all the night from these apprehensions, insomuch, that at last the white people got some old slaves from the land to pacify us. They told us we were not to be eaten, but to work, and were soon to go on land, where we should see many of our country people. This report eased us much. And sure enough, soon after we were landed, there came to us Africans of all languages.

We were conducted immediately to the merchant's yard, where we were all pent up together, like so many sheep in a fold, without regard to sex or age. . . .

We were not many days in the merchant's custody, before we were sold after their usual manner, which is this: On a signal given (as the beat of a drum), the buyers rush at once into the yard where the slaves are confined, and make choice of that parcel they like best. The noise and clamor with which this is attended, and the eagerness visible in the countenances of the buyers, serve not a little to increase the apprehension of terrified Africans, who may well be supposed to consider them as the ministers of that destruction to which they think themselves devoted. In this manner, without scruple, are relations and friends separated, most of them never to see each other again.

*   *   *

I stayed in this island for a few days, I believe it could not be above a fortnight, when I, and some few more slaves that were not saleable amongst the rest, from very much fretting, were shipped off in a sloop for North America. On the passage we were better treated than when we were coming from Africa, and we had plenty of rice and fat pork. We were landed up a river a good way from the sea, about Virginia county, where we saw few or none of our native Africans, and not one soul who could talk to me. I was a few weeks weeding grass and gathering stones in a plantation; and at last all my companions were distributed different ways, and only myself was left. I was now exceedingly miserable, and thought myself worse off than any of the rest of my companions, for they could talk to each other, but I had no person to speak to that I could understand. In this state, I was constantly grieving and pining, and wishing for death rather than anything else.

REVIEW QUESTIONS

1. What did Equiano reveal about the "middle passage"?
2. How did the slave trade operate in the West Indies?
3. What seemed to disturb Equiano more: brutality or isolation?
4. Is such a response significant to an understanding of enslavement?

NEWSPAPERS

Ads for Runaway Servants and Slaves
(1733–1772)

Both slavery and freedom thrived in colonial America. Desire for the latter meant that people constantly sought opportunities to escape the former. As the number of indentured servants and slaves rose, so too did the number of runaways. Many such runaways, or fugitives, were soon caught, or they voluntarily returned to their masters. If they did not do so, and if the owners believed the expense and effort (and indeed the servants or slaves) worthwhile, then they published advertisements in the provincial newspapers. These ads often provided physical descriptions of the runaways, accounts of what kind of work these laborers performed, and why their masters believed they ran away. Such observations can reveal much about the society and individuals, specifically about masters and servants, and about the differences in such working relationships over time and place.

From Lathan A. Windley, comp., *Runaway Slave Advertisements: A Documentary History from the 1730s to 1790*, vol. 2, Maryland (Westport, CT: Greenwood Press, 1983), pp. 22–23, 26–27, 41–42, 93–94; and vol. 3, South Carolina, pp. 6–7, 81, 158–59, 220. Billy G. Smith and Richard Wojtowicz, eds., *Blacks Who Stole Themselves: Advertisements for Runaways in the Pennsylvania Gazette, 1728–1790* (Philadelphia: University of Pennsylvania Press, 1989), pp. 54–55. [Editorial insertions appear in square brackets—*Ed.*]

South-Carolina Gazette (Whitemarsh), April 28 to May 5, 1733.

RUN away three Weeks ago, a Negro Man named Hampshire, belonging to Mrs. Elizabeth Bampfield. Whoever will bring the said Negro to his Mistress, shall have 40 s. Reward, and if taken out of the Town, any reasonable Charge as the Law allows. The aforesaid Negro is to be sold, as is another young Fellow named Stafford, who has been bred a Butcher, and a Negro Woman that is a very good Cook, Washer, and understanding any Sort of Houshold [sic] Work. Enquire of

Elizabeth Bampfield.

South-Carolina Gazette (Whitemarsh), May 26 to June 2, 1733.

Run away the 14th of last month, a Mustee Wench, that may be taken for an Indian, about 20 Years of Age, speaks good English, and can do anything about House, as spinning, carding, needlework &c. [S]he is a short, well sett, fat Wench, and may be taken to be a Free Wench, and has her Tongue at Pleasure, and her Back will shew the Marks of her former Misdeeds. Whoever will bring the said Wench to James Mackewn, at Stono, shall have 5 l. Reward.

South-Carolina Gazette (Timothy), February 22 to February 29, 1748.

RUN-away on the 20th Inst. from Silas Parvin, at Cobausey in New-Jersey, a very lusty Negro Man named Sampson, aged about 58 Years, and has some mixture of Indian Blood in him, he is Hip shot and goes very Lame. He has taken with him a Boy about 12 or 14 Years of Age named Sam, who was born of an Indian Woman, and looks much like an Indian only his Hair. They were both well Cloathed, only the Boy is barefoot, they have taken with them a gun and Ammunition, and two Ruggs. They both talk Indian very well, and it is likely have dress'd themselves in an Indian Dress, and gone towards Carolina. Whoever secures the said Slaves so that their Master may have them again, or delivers them to Thomas Shute in Charles-Town, shall have THIRTY POUNDS Reward, from the said Shute or

Silas Parvin.

Annapolis *Maryland Gazette*, March 20, 1755.
TEN PISTOLES REWARD.
Kent County, Maryland, March 19, 1755.

WHEREAS there were several Advertisements, (some of which were printed, and others of the same Signification written), dispers'd through this Province, describing, and offering a Reward of Two Pistoles, &c. for taking up a Servant Man, named James Francis, and a Mulatto Man Slave call'd Toby, both belonging to the Subscriber, and ran away on the 11th Instant: And whereas it has been discover'd since the Publishing of the said Advertisements, that they carried with them many more Things than is therein described, I do hereby again and farther give Notice, that the white Man, James Francis, is aged about 21 Years, his Stature near five Feet and an half, slender bodied, with a smooth Face, almost beardless, born in England, and bred a Farmer. The Mulatto is a lusty, well-set Country born Slave, with a great Nose, wide Nostrils, full mouth'd, many Pimples in his Face, very slow in Speech, he is a tolerable good Cooper and House-Carpenter, and no doubt will endeavour to pass for a Free-Man: Each hath a Felt Hat, Country Cloth Vest and Breeches, and Yarn Stockings; one of them has a light colour'd loose Coat of Whitney or Duffel: the white Man a dark close bodied Coat, a striped short Vest of Everlasting, another of blue Fearnothing, with other Cloaths. The Slave has also many other more valuable Garments; they took with them likewise a Gun, Powder and Shot, and are suppos'd either to cross, or go down the Bay in a Pettiauger.

Whoever brings the said Servant and Slave to the Subscriber on the Mouth of Chester River, or to Thomas Ringgold at Chester-Town, shall have for a Reward Ten Pistoles, and all reasonable Charges in taking and securing the said Servant and Slave, paid by

James Ringgold.

THAT this Slave shou'd ran away and attempt getting his Liberty, is very alarming, as he has been always too kindly used, if any Thing, by his Master, and one in whom his Master has put great Confidence, and depended on him to overlook the rest of his Slaves, and he had no kind of Provocation to go off. It seems to be the Interest, at least of every Gentleman that has Slaves, to be active in the beginning of these Attempts, for whilst we have the French such near Neighbours, we shall not have the least Security in that kind of Property. I should be greatly obliged to any Gentleman that shall hear of these Fellows, to endeavour to get certain Intelligence which Way they have taken, and to inform me of it by Express, and also to employ some active Person or Persons immediately to take their Track and pursue them and secure them, and I will

thankfully acknowledge the Favour, and immediately answer the Expence attending it.

Thomas Ringgold.

Annapolis *Maryland Gazette*, November 11, 1756.

RAN away on the 10th of October last, from the Subscriber, living near George-Town on Rock-Creek, in Frederick County, a Mulatto Woman Slave, named Kate, who formerly belonged to Mr. Benjamin Lane in Anne-Arundel County, and bought of him last June; she is a pert pallavering Wench, of a middle Size, about 30 Years old. She took with her a small Black Horse, branded on the near Buttock with a large S: And as she is pretty well dressed may sometimes pass for a free Woman where she is not known to be otherwise. It is supposed she is secreted by a Mulatto Slave called Jemmy (a Carpenter by Trade), belonging to Mr. Thomas Sprigg, on West-River, with the Assistance and Contrivance of some other Slaves in the neighbourhood where she was bought, who (it seems she has bragg'd) had promised to conceal her whenever she would run away from me. I understand she has been a great Rambler, and is well known in Calvert and Anne-Arundel Counties, besides other Parts of the Country. She may indulge herself a little in visiting her old Acquaintance; but it is most probable she will spend the greater Part of her Time with or near wherever the aforesaid Mulatto Slave of Mr. Sprigg's may be at Work.

Whoever brings the said Wench to the Subscriber, shall have Two Pistoles for their Trouble, besides a good Reward if they discover the Persons that harbour her, so that they may be brought to Justice.

HENRY THRELKELD.

South-Carolina Gazette (Timothy), October 13, 1757.

RUN AWAY from the Subscriber, at Wando, a negro woman named KATE, about 32 years old, of a yellowish complexion, hollow jaw'd, a pouting look, all her upper fore-teeth gone, and speaks good English, formerly belong'd to Mrs. L'Escott, and afterwards to Paul Villepontoux, of whom she was purchased. She is well known in Charles-Town, and it's supposed has changed her name and is harboured there (as she formerly was for 23 months together); and 'tis probable she will get into some of the negro washing-houses or kitchens, to be employ'd in them, and say she belongs to Mr. Villepontoux aforesaid. She is 7 months gone with child; and carried with her, her son Billy (a squat well-set boy about 13 years of age, who is apt to stutter when spoke smartly to), and her daughter Alce [sic?] (a girl about 5 years old, with a mark in her forehead and another somewhere about her breast, occasioned by accidental burns, and silver drops in her ears. She will no doubt change her dress, but had on when she went away, a blue jacket (the sleeves scolloped) and petticoat. As this inhuman creature, when she went away, left myself extreme ill in one bed, her mistress in another, and two of my children, not one able to help the other, she must be conscious of some very atrocious crime: I therefore humbly request every friend and acquaintance I have, in town and country, to use their utmost endeavours, in taking and delivering the said wench and children to me, or to the warden of the work-house; hereby promising a reward of 10 1. for so doing, and 20 1. to whoever will prove where she is harboured or employed.

STEPHEN HARTLEY

Annapolis *Maryland Gazette*, August 20, 1761. Fairfax County (Virginia) August 11, 1761.

RAN away from a Plantation of the Subscriber's, on Dogue-Run in Fairfax, on Sunday the 9th Instant, the following Negroes, viz.

Peres, 35 or 40 Years of Age, a well-set Fellow, of about 5 Feet 8 Inches high, yellowish Complexion, with a very full round Face, and full black Beard, his Speech is something slow and broken, but not in so great a Degree as to render him remarkable. He had on when he went away, a dark colour'd Cloth Coat, a white Linen Waist-coat, white Breeches and white Stockings.

Jack, 30 Years (or thereabouts) old, a slim, black, well made Fellow, of near 6 Feet high, a small Face, with Cuts down each Cheek, being his Country Marks, his Feet are large (or long) for he requires a great Shoe. The Clothing he went off in cannot be well ascertained, but it is thought in his common working Dress, such as Cotton Waistcoat (of which he had a new One) and Breeches, and Osnabrig Shirt.

Neptune, aged 25 or 30, well-set, and of about 5 Feet 8 or 9 Inches high, thin jaw'd, his Teeth stragling and fil'd sharp, his Back, if rightly remember'd, has many small Marks or Dots running from both Shoulders down to his Waistband, and his Head was close shaved: Had on a Cotton Waistcoat, black or dark colour'd Breeches, and an Osnabrig Shirt.

Cupid, 23 or 25 Years old, a black well made Fellow, 5 Feet 8 or 9 Inches high, round and full faced, with broad Teeth before, the Skin of his Face is coarse, and inclined to be pimpley, he has no other distinguishable Mark that can be recollected; he carried with him his common working Cloaths, and an old Osnabrigs Coat made Frockwise.

The two last of these Negroes were bought from an African Ship in August 1759, and talk very broken and unintelligible English; the second one, Jack, is Countryman to those, and speaks pretty good English, having been several Years in the Country. The other, Peres, speaks much better than either, indeed has little of his Country Dialect left, and is esteemed a sensible judicious Negro.

As they went off without the least Suspicion, Provocation, or Difference with any Body, or the least angry Word or Abuse from their Overseers, 'tis supposed they will hardly lurk about in the Neighbourhood, but steer some direct Course (which cannot even be guessed at) in Hopes of an Escape: Or, perhaps, as the Negro Peres has lived many Years about Williamsburg, and King-William County, and Jack in Middlesex, they may possibly bend their Course to one of those Places.

Whoever apprehends the said Negroes, so that the Subscriber may readily get them, shall have, if taken up in this County, Forty Shillings Reward, beside what the Law allows; and if at any greater Distance, or out of the Colony, a proportionable Recompence paid them, by

GEORGE WASHINGTON.

Pennsylvania Gazette, April 29, 1762

New-York, Printing-Office, in Beaver-Street, April 17, 1762.

Run away, on Monday the 12th Instant, from the Subscriber, a Mulattoe Servant Man, named CHARLES, and known by the Name of CHARLES ROBERTS, or GERMAN. He is a likely well set Fellow, 28 or 30 Years of Age, about 5 Feet 6 Inches high, and has had the Small-Pox. He has a Variety of Clothes, some of them very good, affects to dress very neat and genteel, and generally wears a Wig. He took with him two or three Coats or Suits, viz. A dark brown, or Chocolate coloured Cloth Coat, pretty much worn; a dun, or Dove coloured Cloth, or fine Frize, but little worn; and a light blue grey Summer coat, of Grogram, Camblet, or some such Stuff; a Straw coloured Waistcoat, edged with a Silver Cord, almost new; and several other Waistcoats, Breeches, and Pairs of Stockings; a blue Great coat, and a Fiddle. His Behaviour is excessively complaisant, obsequious and insinuating; he speaks good English, smoothly and plausibly, and generally with a Cringe and a Smile; he is extremely artful, and ready at inventing specious Pretences to conceal villainous Actions or Designs. He plays on the Fiddle, can read and write tolerably well, and understands a little of Arithmetick and Accounts. I have Reason to believe some evil minded Persons in town have encouraged, and been Accomplices with him in villainous Designs; and it is probable he will contrive the most specious Forgeries to give him the Appearance of being a Free Man: I have already been informed of a Writing he has shewn for that Purpose, by which he has imposed upon many People; who may all be easily satisfied that he has no legal Claim to Freedom, even from Slavery, nor any Pretence to it but by the very Law by which he is my Servant for 40 Years, as the Records of the Superior Court at New Haven will Witness. At that Place, where the former Owner of the said Slave lived, he was guilty of a Variety of Crimes and Felonies, for which he was several Times publickly whipped, and only escaped the Gallows by want of Prosecution. When he became my Servant, I intended to have shipped him to the West Indies, and sold him there; and kept him in Prison till I should get an Opportunity; but on his earnest Request, solemn Promises of his good Behaviour, and seeming Penitence, I took him into my Family upon Trial, where for some Time he behaved well, and was very serviceable to me. Deceived by his seeming Reformation, I placed some Confidence in him, which he has villainously abused; having embezzled Money sent by him to pay for Goods, borrowed Money, and taken up Goods in my Name unknown to me, and also on his own Account, pretending to be a Freeman. By this villainous Proceeding I suppose he has collected a considerable Sum of Money, and am also apprehensive that he has been an Accomplice in some of the late Robberies committed in and near this City. Whoever will take up the said Servant, and bring him to me, or secure him in some of His Majesty's Goals, so that I may get him again, if taken up in the City of New-York, shall have Five Pounds Reward, and a greater, if taken up at a greater Distance. Any Persons who take him up, are desired to be careful to carry him before the next Magistrate, and have him well searched, leaving all the Money and Goods found upon him, except the necessary Clothes he has on, in the Hands of the said Magistrate; and to be very watchful against an Escape, or being deceived by him, for he is one of the most artful of Villains.

JOHN HOLT.

South-Carolina Gazette (Timothy), August 7 to August 14, 1762.

FIVE POUNDS REWARD,

RUN away about 12 days ago, a negro girl named MARY, about 20 years old, well known in Charles-Town, and has been entertained in several houses at needle-work, &c. to whom she has past herself for free. Whoever will apprehend the said negro girl, and deliver her to the warden of the work-house, or to the subscriber, shall receive five pounds currency reward, besides all reasonable charges, and thirty pounds reward to any person who will inform me of her being harboured by a white person, on conviction of the offender, or five pounds to a negro: She has on a blue negro cloth habit, and a strip'd jacket under, with a coat of the same; she is artful and speaks good English, but fast, and stutters a little; by pretending to be free may endeaver to get on board some vessel, as she has a mother that lives at Winyah; or may make for John's or James-Island where she has a father and brother: She is said to have changed her name, and says she belongs to Mrs. Matthews. All persons are hereby forbid to carry off or harbour the said slave, as they may depend on being prosecuted by

JOHN-PAUL GRIMKE.

N.B. If the said negro wench will return home, she shall be forgiven.

Annapolis *Maryland Gazette*, July 16, 1772.
TEN POUNDS REWARD.
July 6, 1772.

RAN away from the Subscribers, living near Soldiers Delight, in Baltimore County, Maryland, a dark Mulatto Slave, who goes by the Name of CHARLES HARDING, but formerly by the Name of DICK; about 30 Years of Age, 5 Feet 7 Inches high, large Nose, hollow eyed, low Forehead, has upwards of Forty Scars on his Head of different Sizes, well made, has a small Scar on the upper Part of his Nose on the left Side, a small Scar on the right Side his under Lip, close knee'd, his Shins bend forwards, some Scars on the small of his legs occasioned by wearing of irons, a large Scar on the Outside of his left Leg occasioned by a Burn, a Scar on one of his Thumbs, he has been unmercifully whipped from his Neck to his Knees, which he says was by his former Master, is a Carpenter and Joiner by Trade, and can paint, which he learned of Lewis Allmorn, of Nanceman County in Virginia, who sold him to Edward Voss, a Bricklayer by Trade, and worked in sundry Parts of Virginia, and when the said Slave ran away from him, lived in King and Queen County near Rapahannah, got by Water to Philadelphia, and from thence travelled through Lancaster and York Counties to Hanover-Town, and worked there about a Year, and from thence into Baltimore County near Baltimore-Town, where he continued, from about the Year 1765 to the Year 1772, as a free Man, and since he left his former Masters in Virginia, has learnt to read and write, and to play on the Violin; it is possible he may forge a Pass and change his Name, as he has done before: Took with him a Castor Hat, a Suit of white Russia Drab Cloaths, a blue Cloth Coat, red striped Jacket, a new redish brown Broad-Cloth Jacket much too large for him, new darkish coloured Cotton Velvet Breeches with large old fashioned Pocket Flaps, Shirts, Stockings and Shoes of different Sorts, and large plated Buckles. Whoever secures the above Slave in any jail, so that his Masters get him again, shall receive Five Pounds, and if 50 Miles from Home Seven Pounds Ten Shillings, and if 100 Miles the above Reward, and reasonable Charges if brought Home, paid by

SAMUEL OWINGS, jun.
ALEXANDER WELLS.

REVIEW QUESTIONS

1. What kind of physical characteristics were mentioned in the ads? Why may these have been deemed significant enough to mention? What do they reveal about the composition of slave society?

2. What kind of work did the slaves noted in these ads perform? What does this indicate about the slave labor force?

3. Do these advertisements state or suggest why the slaves may have run away? What may have been some of these reasons?

4. What do the notices reveal about the masters who submitted them?

5. What do these pieces suggest about colonial-American slavery in general?

INTERPRETING VISUAL SOURCES: COLONIAL ARCHITECTURE

The foundations of American culture can be found in the country's dirt as well as its documents. Postholes at archaeological sites reveal where colonists shouldered into place the heavy pieces of timber that sat upright at each corner of a building and carried the beams that held the walls, floors, and roofs. By connecting these "dots" in the soil, an observer can determine the size and design of the early wooden structures that sheltered the European settlers in their New World. As settlement proceeded, some provincials turned to more durable building materials such as stone and brick. Their desire for more permanent and sometimes more comfortable or grander buildings has benefited later generations, for even when time, nature, or man finally destroyed the superstructures, more of the foundations remained for study. In addition to these remains, some buildings have survived into the present—and their walls speak to historians.

Material remains are another form of historical documentation. While most historians concentrate on deciphering the written evidence of the past, some dig into the physical artifacts. Writings themselves can be interpreted as material artifacts: one need only take the time to look at the paper, ink, and even formation of the letters. When examined in their original forms, written sources physically manifest the past in the way they look, feel, and smell. Some people like to examine physical remnants because such things help them picture the worlds that the words describe. Material artifacts, which include clothing and jewelry, pottery and porcelain, glass and silver, needlework and furniture, as well as art and architecture, are especially helpful when one tries to visualize cultures that existed prior to photographic records.

As with written sources, one must be as aware of what is not present as well as what still exists. Material artifacts that have been carefully preserved generally reflect what people have deemed to be of value. Such items serve to illuminate elite lifestyles and epochal events, but one may be left wondering about the "common" folk and everyday life. Fortunately, some physical remains, including archi-

tectural elements, have been uncovered that reveal such aspects of the colonial world.

Architecture, the design and construction of buildings, may be studied as a form of art when people deem its products creative works of style and beauty. Whether or not certain buildings are called art, however, the study of architecture can help explain the past, just as an examination of the past—the context in which buildings were erected—can illuminate their construction and function. Architecture can reveal not only a society's aesthetic "taste" and sophistication in building skills, but its environmental, economic, and social constraints. Buildings, for instance, whether for domestic or public use, may show when exigency outweighed artistic sensibilities in a society, as well as when plush pockets and exaggerated interpretations of aesthetic models led some people to ignore necessity and comfort in favor of fancy.

Being pragmatic people in need of shelter, and generally being people without the time or money to engage in architectural fancies, exaggeration did not often surface in early colonial architecture. Immediate necessity as well as economic and material constraints often determined the style and substance of peoples' homes. They were not the only factors, however, that influenced colonial building designs. Early American architecture also reveals the colonists' origins as well as their adaptation to their new environment, their economic and social ranks, and even the personalities of both individuals (for example, Thomas Jefferson as revealed by Monticello) and their societies (as seen in church architecture).

Early American architecture reflected the colonists' origins both in time and place. Seventeenth-century colonists from England, seeking to reproduce at least part of their Old World in the New, built homes in a medieval or late Gothic style. In these generally simple timber-framed structures, the primary—and often only—room was the hall. The hall, found in both grand and simple medieval dwellings, served all purposes. People cooked and ate, worked and slept in that room: it was just a matter of moving the furniture about as needed for each function. The French, Dutch, and Swedish settlers of the period also tended to replicate their versions of the late medieval style of architecture. Spanish colonial architecture, on the other hand, reflected the fact that the Renaissance hit Spain earlier than northern Europe: by the seventeenth century, the officials of imperial Spain tended to build public edifices in the Baroque style.

While many settlers in the eighteenth-century English colonies continued to build homes that reflected the medieval tradition, others, especially those conversant with new cultural trends in the mother country and with the economic resources to pursue them, preferred to build homes in the Renaissance style that came to be known as Georgian. Even as some Italian and Spanish architects tweaked the constraints of classical architecture with the color and ornamentation that defined the Baroque style, English and French architects generally preferred to remain within the restraints of the classical Roman form as they tried to impose formality, symmetry, and order upon their physical world.

Although the colonists used the architectural forms of the Old World to pro-tect themselves from the New World's environment, ultimately the climates and natural resources of that New World did affect the styles and materials of their buildings. Timber-framed houses were the norm on both sides of the Atlantic, but not all English construction techniques and materials worked or weathered well in the American climate, thus colonists rejected some, such as wattle-and-daub walls and thatched roofs, in favor of others, namely clapboard siding and shingled roofs. Furthermore, as substantial deposits of lime for mortar and clay for bricks were found, wealthier colonists chose brick and stone construction for their homes.

Almost all of the early colonial immigrants, whether of high or low social rank, with great or little economic resources, began their lives in America in very humble shelters: they made do with cabins, cottages, and even the dome- or long-house-shaped wigwams found among Native Americans of the eastern woodlands culture. Over time, however, houses reflected the growing stratification and so-phistication of American society. Some people pushed out walls or raised roofs to add rooms, while others built totally new homes based on the new architectural ideas coming out of Europe.

Architecture is, of course, only part of the picture. Furnishings and furniture —in kind, amount, and placement—further illuminate the physical dimensions of the past, as do the garden, farm, and even town layouts that have managed to survive into the present era.

Shelter in the Seventeenth Century

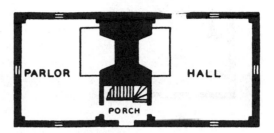

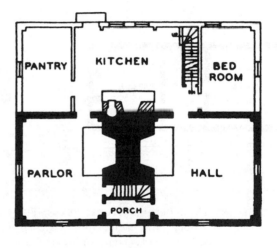

SEVENTEENTH-CENTURY HOUSE PLANS: NEW ENGLAND (PHILIP WHITE)
Hugh Morrison, *Early American Architecture: From the First Colonial Settlements to the National Period* (New York: Oxford University Press, 1952), p. 21.

The simplest homes in colonial America were one-room structures, yet even within that constraint, there were a considerable number of variations. Some houses had but one story, while others had two. In the latter case, some had a ladder and others a staircase leading to the sleeping loft above. The placement of doors, the number and size of windows, and the size of the chimney all differed according to the resources of the builders and the climate against which they were protecting themselves. New Englanders, concerned about heat retention, preferred massive fireplaces and off-set doors. Southerners, however, favored doors set opposite each other that would let cooling air breeze through their homes.

Shelter in the Seventeenth Century

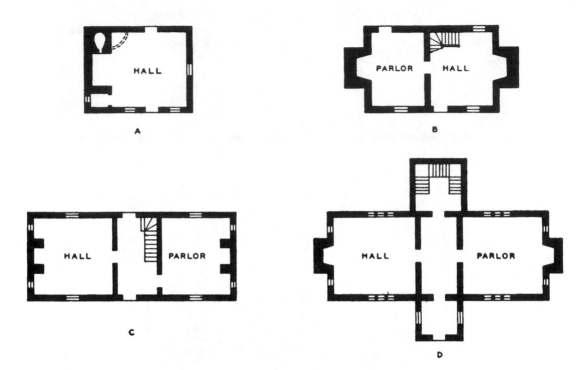

SEVENTEENTH-CENTURY HOUSE PLANS: THE CHESAPEAKE (PHILIP WHITE)
Hugh Morrison, *Early American Architecture: From the First Colonial Settlements to the National Period* (New York: Oxford University Press, 1952), p. 141.

While one-room houses were common structures throughout the colonies (and in later western settlements), provincial Americans often added to them as soon as they could. There were distinct regional variations to these additions. New Englanders, for instance, tended to build around the chimney so as to keep the heated stonework within their houses. Then, in adding kitchens and other rooms to the back of a house under a "lean-to" roof, New Englanders created the distinctive "saltbox" style of architecture. The early southern colonists, on the other hand, generally liked to foster cross-ventilation by adding central halls and chimneys at opposite ends of their buildings.

Shelter in the Seventeenth Century:
Parson Joseph Capen House,
Massachusetts, 1683

PARSON JOSEPH CAPEN HOUSE, TOPSFIELD, MASSACHUSETTS, 1683

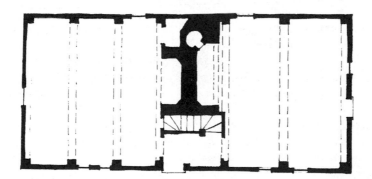

FLOOR PLAN OF PARSON CAPEN HOUSE
Leland M. Roth, *A Concise History of American Architecture* (New York: Harper & Row, 1980), p. 15. Photography courtesy New York Public Library, Astor, Lenox and Tilden Foundations, New York.

The Parson Capen house stands as a fine example of early New England architecture. The people of Topsfield, Massachusetts, built the house for the Reverend Joseph Capen in 1683. As appropriate in a church-going community, they set it next to the town's common and close to the meetinghouse. Covered in clapboards and shingles and with the upper stories overhanging the lower, the house boasts a large hall and parlor on either side of the chimney. Inside the entrance porch (called a hall today) is a steep staircase leading to the second-floor rooms.

Eighteenth-Century Developments: Typical Plans of New England Georgian Homes (Philip White)

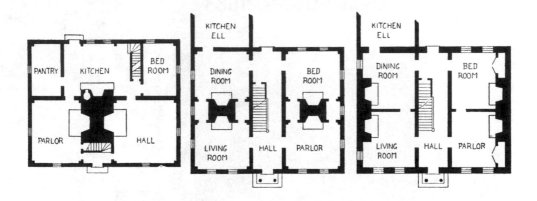

NEW ENGLAND GEORGIAN HOUSE PLANS
Hugh Morrison, *Early American Architecture: From the First Colonial Settlements to the National Period* (New York: Oxford University Press, 1952), p. 474.

Even though some Americans continued to build and live in houses of the older styles, more and more of them, especially in the elite and middling ranks of society, preferred to construct homes that reflected the new style of architecture that reigned supreme in Georgian England. As England established its empire and attempted to mold the modern era, its architects and their patrons reached back to antiquity for ideas and ornaments. The Georgian house plan was based upon their interpretation of classical architectural designs: an interpretation that resulted in an interior symmetrical organization around a central hall and an exterior symmetrical placement of windows and doors. Such houses were strongly cubical or rectangular in appearance.

There were variations in Georgian houses that reflected the time in which they were built, the economic resources of the builders, and the regional resources the architects had at their disposal. Whereas Georgian architecture in the South tended to be confined to the mansions of the gentry, it was seen in middle-class as well as elite dwellings in the mid-Atlantic and New England regions. Although there were some stone or brick Georgian homes in New England, frame construction and clapboard continued to dominate building there. Furthermore, many early Georgian homes in New England still incorporated some old design elements. At the beginning of the eighteenth century, many New England homes were built on plans that were, at least for the interior layout of the ground floor, similar to the old lean-to design. Builders soon abandoned that plan for the central hall design, but still tended to place chimneys within the house. As brick and stone construction became more common, chimneys were moved to the exterior walls.

Eighteenth-Century Developments, New England:
The Lindens, Massachusetts, 1754

THE LINDENS, DANVERS, MASSACHUSETTS, 1754. RE-ERECTED IN WASHINGTON, D.C., IN 1937 (ARTHUR C. HASKELL, HABS)

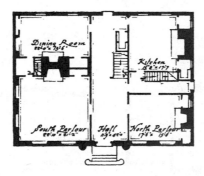

FLOOR PLAN OF THE LINDENS (*GREAT GEORGIAN HOUSES*, *II*)
Hugh Morrison, *Early American Architecture: From the First Colonial Settlements to the National Period* (New York: Oxford University Press, 1952), p. 490.

Robert Hooper, a wealthy merchant from Marblehead, built The Lindens in Danvers, Massachusetts, in 1754 (it was dismantled, moved, and reerected in Washington, DC, in 1937). A fine example of colonial Georgian architecture, especially its great entrance hall, its interior plan shows how an individual could vary the formal Georgian design. The home's exterior was in keeping with New England predilections: three of the walls were clapboard while the fourth, the front, was faced with wood that was sanded and painted in a faux stone finish.

Eighteenth-Century Developments, Middle Colonies: Mount Pleasant, Pennsylvania, 1761–62

MOUNT PLEASANT, PENNSYLVANIA, 1761–62 (WAYNE ANDREWS)

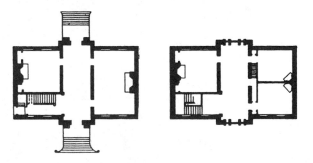

FLOOR PLANS, MOUNT PLEASANT (PHILIP WHITE)
Hugh Morrison, *Early American Architecture: From the First Colonial Settlements to the National Period* (New York: Oxford University Press, 1952), pp. 526–27.

The Scotsman John Macpherson, who had amassed a fortune at sea, built Mount Pleasant near Philadelphia, Pennsylvania, between 1761 and 1762. In this formal house with elegant woodwork, the stairway was placed in a small hall off to one side instead of in the center hall. Underneath the stairway a small corridor linked the dining room to an outside door, which in turn led to the kitchen. Outside, the masonry walls were surfaced with stucco while the window lintels were made of stone.

Eighteenth-Century Developments, Southern Colonies: Westover, Virginia, 1730s

WESTOVER, VIRGINIA

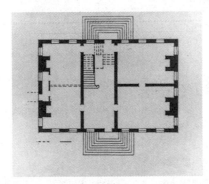

FLOOR PLAN OF MAIN HOUSE, WESTOVER, VIRGINIA
Thomas Tileston Waterman, *The Mansions of Virginia*, 1706–1776 (New York: Bonanza Books, 1945), pp. 152, 164.

William Byrd II, a member of the Virginia gentry, probably built Westover on the James River northwest of Williamsburg in the early 1730s. There is the possibility that it was built over the site of an earlier structure, for the kitchen wing (which was originally a separate dependency but was connected to the main house by a brick passage in 1901) on the west flank of the main building is older than the manor house. While true symmetry was maintained on the outside, the hall on the inside was placed off center. Instead of having four equally sized rooms, as found in the more common plans, Byrd, perhaps in a quest to make the rooms better fit a variety of needs, put smaller rooms on the western side of the house. He built Westover out of brick, put in superb stone doorways, and roofed his home with slate.

Eighteenth-Century Developments,
For Folks of More Modest Means:
Letitia Street House, Pennsylvania, 1703–15

LETITIA STREET HOUSE, PHILADELPHIA, 1703–15 (PHILADELPHIA MUSEUM OF ART)

PLAN OF FIRST FLOOR, LETITIA STREET HOUSE (THOMAS T. WATERMAN, *THE DWELLINGS OF COLONIAL AMERICA*, UNIVERSITY OF NORTH CAROLINA PRESS)
Hugh Morrison, *Early American Architecture: From the First Colonial Settlements to the National Period* (New York: Oxford University Press, 1952), pp. 515–16.

Although Georgian architectural design especially marked the homes of the elite in the eighteenth century, the humble abodes of other colonists also incorporated elements of that style. The Letitia Street House, for example, was far more modest—as was appropriate to the city home of an artisan or small merchant—in dimensions and ornamentation than the manors described above. Built sometime between 1703 and 1715 on the Philadelphia street for which it is named, it was moved to Fairmount Park in 1883. The house shows the Georgian influence in its exterior, but its interior plan appears to be based on an older, Swedish design: back room smaller than the front room, and corner fireplaces backed against one another and sharing an internal chimney.

REVIEW QUESTIONS

1. What were some of the regional variations in seventeenth-century colonial architecture?
2. What do those variations reveal about the respective climates and/or cultures?
3. How did Georgian architecture differ from the earlier seventeenth-century styles?
4. Were there regional variations to Georgian architecture? If so, were they as distinct as some of the variations seen in seventeenth-century architecture?
5. How does colonial architecture illustrate the development of an American culture?

4 ∾ THE IMPERIAL PERSPECTIVE

Hail Britannia! English subjects at home and abroad gloried in the growth of their dominion as the colonization of North America contributed to the rise of the first British Empire. The crown did not have to do much to foster trans-Atlantic enterprises, nor did it, initially, attempt to regulate them closely. As the colonies expanded in trade, territories, and peoples, however, royal ministers tried to tighten their control and administer the colonies more effectively to ensure that benefits accrued to the empire as a whole and the government in particular. At times this strategy strained relations between those at the center of the empire and those at its periphery.

As succeeding monarchs, ministers, and members of Parliament tried to consolidate and strengthen the machinery of empire, they faced challenges from colonists who began to hold slightly different views on the form and function of that empire. Through such challenges, the colonists sought redress, not rebellion. Most colonists, at least those of English origin, deemed themselves loyal subjects even when they were anxious about or angered by the crown's colonial administrators and policies. These subjects, many of whom by the end of the seventeenth century were born in America, accepted that they were provincials within the empire, but they refused to accept that as such they might have little power or recourse over legislation that directly affected them. They countered, overtly and covertly, any measures that they believed would hinder their survival and endanger their prosperity. These provincials insisted vehemently, and at times violently, that the privileges they believed to have been granted them by English birth, charter, or previous colonial practices be recognized. They did not see themselves as revolutionaries in their recalcitrance: they were merely insisting that the power and liberties acquired by the people over time—from the Magna Carta through the English Revolution of 1649 to the Glorious Revolution of 1688—be applied to them as well.

Although diversions at home, such as civil war, regicide, and revolution, sometimes led the British ministry to neglect colonial affairs, the government did want the colonies bound to the empire by law as well as culture. It established regulations for trade, issued orders, and sent over officials, if not always armed troops, to secure its territories. Colonial wars, in turn, strained the sinews of empire at the same time they stimulated them: conflicts against the natives as well as against other European powers sometimes led to hostilities between different interest groups within the colonies as well as between colonists and mother country. In the latter case, the desires of an empire that wished to encourage trade with the Indians and minimize the expenses of security in the New World occasionally clashed with the expansionist wishes of the settlers.

Native tribes, England, France, and Spain all jockeyed for power and position in North America in a series of armed conflicts that culminated in what the colonists called the French and Indian War and what the English at home called the Seven Years' War. Joint action with, and subordination to, the British army, as well as the necessity to acquiese with the results of British diplomacy over the course of some of these wars began to make some colonists question the notion that colonial needs and British desires could always be met concurrently. Slowly, though certainly not surely, the provincials also began to recognize that closer ties needed to be forged between their colonies based on common interests. They were still loyal subjects, but they wanted to strengthen their power within the empire to make sure that it met their needs.

THE RESTORATION GOVERNMENT OF CHARLES II

FROM The Navigation Act of 1660

Empire is both a political and economic construct. The first British empire was built upon the concept of mercantilism—that the economic interests of the nation have priority over those of all other groups and areas and thus the periphery, or provinces, must profit the mother country. Acting upon such a doctrine, the British government enacted a series of Navigation Acts over the course of the second half of the seventeenth century. The first was passed by the Parliament of Oliver Cromwell's Commonwealth in 1651. When the monarchy was restored in 1660, the new Parliament, to ensure the legality as well as continuation of the mercantile system that had been established, renewed the earlier legislation and added to it. The Navigation Act

*of 1660 further defined how trade among the mother country, colonies, and foreign
lands was to be conducted.*

From Danby Pickering, ed., *The Statutes at Large from the Magna Charta*, 46 vols. (Cambridge: J. Bertham, 1762–1807), 7:452ff.

For the increase of shipping and encouragement of the navigation of this nation, wherein, under the good providence and protection of God, the wealth, safety, and strength of this kingdom is so much concerned; be it enacted by the King's most excellent majesty, and by the lords and commons in this present parliament assembled, and by the authority thereof, That from and after the first day of *December* 1660, and from thenceforward, no goods or commodities whatsoever shall be imported into or exported out of any lands, islands, plantations or territories to his Majesty belonging or in his possession . . . in Asia, Africa, or America, in any other ship or ships, vessel or vessels whatsoever, but in such ships or vessels as do truly and without fraud belong only to the people of England or Ireland . . . and whereof the master and three fourths of the mariners at least are *English*; under the penalty of the forfeiture and loss of all the goods and commodities which shall be imported into or exported out of any of the aforesaid places in any other ship or vessel. . . .

II. And be it enacted, That no alien or person not born within the allegiance of our sovereign lord the King, his heirs and successors . . . shall from and after the first day of *February*, 1661, exercise the trade of a merchant or factor in any of the said places; upon the pain of forfeiture and loss of all his goods and chattels. . . .

III. And it is further enacted, That no goods or commodities whatsoever, of the growth, production or manufacture of Africa, Asia, or America, or any part thereof . . . be imported into England, Ireland, or Wales . . . in any other ship or ships, vessel or vessels whatsoever, but in such as do truly and without fraud belong only to the people of England, Ireland or Wales. . . .

*   *   *

XVIII. And be it further enacted, That from and after the first day of *April*, 1661, no sugars, tobacco, cotton-wool, indigos, ginger, fustick, or other dying wood, of the growth, production or manufacture of any *English* plantations in America, Asia, or Africa, shall be shipped, carried, conveyed or transported from any of the said *English* plantations to any land . . . other than to such *English* plantations as do belong to his Majesty. . . .

REVIEW QUESTIONS

1. Why did Parliament want to organize and maintain control over maritime trade?
2. What was Parliament's purpose in restricting shipment into and out of English possessions to vessels owned by subjects?
3. How was Article III a further restriction upon shipment? How might this have affected colonial trade?
4. What restrictions applied to the enumerated goods? Why was trade in these products restricted?

COTTON MATHER

FROM *The Declaration of the Gentlemen, Merchants*
and Inhabitants of Boston, and
the Country Adjacent (18 April 1689)

The crown appointed officers to execute the orders and legislation passed for the regulation of the colonies. Such officers and orders were not always well received, as the troubled relationship between Sir Edmund Andros and the inhabitants of Massachusetts illustrates. Although both the colonists and Andros noted, with somewhat different interpretations, how Indian affairs contributed to their difficult situation, the antagonists tended to concentrate on the possession and practice of power within the Dominion of New England. Part of Andros's problem, at least in the eyes of these northern colonists, was that he served the wrong kind of king: one ignorant of his responsibilities to his people. Both king and servant were deposed, actions that were soon justified in mother country and colonies by referring to the philosopher John Locke's treatises on civil government. Although confirmation did not arrive until May, reports of William of Orange's successful invasion and overthrow of James II had reached Boston by March 1689. The town's response came in the form of an uprising on 18 April. Citizens of Massachusetts had long been upset with the establishment of the Dominion of New England, and the administration of Sir Edmond Andros in particular, so they took this opportunity to rebel against this system and servant of the Stuart king. Cotton Mather penned a declaration and summary of grievances that was used to justify the revolt.

From Charles M. Andrews, ed., *Narratives of the Insurrections, 1675–1690* (New York: Charles Scribner's Sons, 1915), pp. 175–82.

§ I. We have seen more than a decad of Years rolled away since the English World had the Discovery of an horrid Popish Plot, wherein the bloody Devotoes of Rome had in their Design and Prospect no less than the Extinction of the Protestant Religion: which mighty Work they called the utter subduing of a Pestilent Heresy; wherein (they said) there never were such Hopes of Success since the Death of Queen Mary, as now in our Days. And we were of all Men the most insensible, if we should apprehend a Countrey so remarkable for the true Profession and pure Exercise of the Protestant Religion as New-England is, wholly unconcerned in the Infamous Plot. To crush and break a Countrey so entirely and signally made up of Reformed Churches, and at length to involve it in the miseries of an utter Extirpation, must needs carry even a Supererogation of Merit with it among such as were intoxicated with a Bigotry inspired into them by the great Scarlet Whore.

§ II. To get us within the reach of the Desolation desired for us, it was no improper thing that we should first have our Charter vacated, . . . without a fair leave to answer for our selves, concerning the Crimes falsly laid to our Charge, we were put under a President and Council, without any liberty for an Assembly, which the other American Plantations have, by a Commission from his Majesty.

§ III. The Commission was as Illegal for the Form of it, as the Way of obtaining it was Malicious and Unreasonable: yet we made no Resistance thereunto as we could easily have done; but chose to give all Mankind a Demonstration of our being a People sufficiently dutiful and loyal to our King: and this with yet more Satisfaction, because we took Pains to make our selves believe as much as ever we could of the Whedle then offer'd unto us; That his Magesty's Desire was no other then the happy Encrease and Advance of these Provinces by their more immediate Dependance on the Crown of England. And we were convinced of it by the Courses immediately taken to damp and spoyl our Trade; . . .

§ IV. In little more than half a Year we saw this Commission superseded by another yet more absolute and Arbitrary, with which Sir Edmond Andross arrived as our Governour: who besides his Power, with the Advice and Consent of his Council, to make Laws and raise Taxes as he pleased, had also Authority by himself to Muster and Imploy all Persons residing in the Territory as occasion shall serve; and to transfer such Forces to any English Plantation in America, as occasion shall require. And several Companies of Souldiers were now brought from Europe, to support what was to be imposed upon us, not without repeated Menaces that some hundreds more were intended for us.

§ V. The Government was no sooner in these Hands, but Care was taken to load Preferments principally upon such Men as were Strangers to and Haters of the People. . . . And his far-fetch'd Instruments that were growing rich among us, would gravely inform us, that it was not for his Majesties Interest that we should thrive. But of all our Oppressors we were chiefly squeez'd by a Crew of abject Persons fetched from New York, to be the Tools of the Adversary, standing at our right Hand; by these were extraordinary and intollerable Fees extorted from every one upon all Occasions, without any Rules but those of their own insatiable Avarice and Beggary; and even the probate of a Will must now cost as many Pounds perhaps as it did Shillings heretofore; . . .

§ VI. It was now plainly affirmed, both by some in open Council, and by the same in private Converse, that the People in New-England were all Slaves, and the only difference between them and Slaves is their not being bought and sold; and it was a Maxim delivered in open Court unto us by one of the Council, that we must not think the Priviledges of English men would follow us to the End of the World: Accordingly we have been treated with multiplied Contradictions to Magna Charta, the Rights of which we laid claim unto. Persons who did but peaceably object against the raising of Taxes without an Assembly, have been for it fined, some twenty, some thirty, and others fifty Pounds. Packt and pickt Juries have been very common things among us, . . . Without a Verdict, yea, without a Jury sometimes have People been fined most unrighteously; and some not of the meanest Quality have been kept in long and close Imprisonment without any the least Information appearing against them, or an Habeas Corpus allowed unto them. In short, when our Oppressors have been a little out of Money, 'twas but pretending some Offence to be enquired into, and the most innocent of Men were continually put into no small Expence to answer the Demands of the Officers, who must have Mony of them, or a Prison for them, tho none could accuse them of any Misdemeanour.

*   *   *

§VIII. Because these Things could not make us miserable fast enough, there was a notable Discovery made of we know not what flaw in all our Titles to our Lands; and tho, besides our purchase of them from the Natives, and besides our actual peaceable unquestioned Possession of them for near threescore Years, and besides the Promise of K. Charles II. in his Proclamation sent over to us in the Year 1683, That no Man here shall receive any Prejudice in his Free-hold or Estate, . . . Yet we were every day told, That no Man was owner of a Foot of Land in all the Colony. Accordingly, Writs of Intrusion began every where to be served on People, that after all their Sweat and their Cost upon their formerly purchased Lands, thought themselves Freeholders of what they had. And the Governor caused the Lands pertaining to these and those particular Men, to be measured out for his Creatures to take possession of; and the Right Owners, for pulling up the Stakes, have passed through Molestations enough to tire all the Patience in the World. They are more than a few, that were by Terrors driven to take Patents for their Lands at excessive rates, to save them from the next that might petition for them: and we fear that the forcing of the People at the Eastward hereunto, gave too much Rise to the late unhappy Invasion made by the Indians on them. . . .

§ IX. All the Council were not ingaged in these ill Actions, but those of them which were true Lovers of their Country were seldom admitted to, and seldomer consulted at the Debates which produced these unrighteous Things: . . .

*   *   *

§ XI. We have been quiet hitherto, and so still we should have been, had not the Great God at this time laid us under a double engagement to do something for our Security: . . . For first, we are informed that the rest of the English America is alarmed with just and great Fears, that they may be attaqu'd by the French, who have lately ('tis said) already treated many of the English with worse then Turkish Cruelties; and while we are in equal Danger of being surprised by them, it is high time we should be better guarded, than we are like to be while the Government remains in the hands by which it hath been held of late. Moreover, we have understood, (though the Governour has taken all imaginable care to keep us all ignorant thereof) that the Almighty God hath been pleased to pros-

per the noble Undertaking of the Prince of Orange, to preserve the three Kingdoms from the horrible brinks of Popery and Slavery, and to bring to a condign Punishment those worst of Men, by whom English Liberties have been destroy'd; in compliance with which glorious Action we ought surely to follow the Patterns which the Nobility, Gentry and Commonalty in several parts of those Kingdoms have set before us, though they therein chiefly proposed to prevent what we already endure.

§ XII. We do therefore seize upon the Persons of those few ill Men which have been (next to our Sins) the grand Authors of our Miseries; resolving to secure them, for what Justice, Orders from his Highness with the English Parliament shall direct, lest, ere we are aware, we find (what we may fear, being on all sides in Danger) our selves to be by them given away to a Foreign Power, before such Orders can reach unto us; for which Orders we now humbly wait. In the mean time firmly believing, that we have endeavoured nothing but what meer Duty to God and our Country calls for at our Hands: We commit our Enterprise unto the Blessing of Him, who hears the cry of the Oppressed, and advise all our Neighbours, for whom we have thus ventured our selves, to joyn with us in Prayers and all just Actions, for the Defence of the Land.

REVIEW QUESTIONS

1. Was the declaration a valid summary of just grievances or just bitter criticisms?
2. How does Mather attempt to give the revolt a nobler cause than simply that of the overthrow of an unpopular administration?
3. What did Andros and his appointees do that so upset the citizens of Massachusetts?
4. What were the reasons given for taking action at this particular time?

SIR EDMUND ANDROS

FROM A Report on the Administration of the Dominion of New England (1690)

Governor Andros's duty was to implement and administer a new, centralized system incorporating multiple colonies that was supposed to benefit the empire both in terms of security and trade. Andros, as an experienced soldier and administrator, had the professional qualifications for the job, but due to his imperious nature, perhaps not the personal ones. After the revolt, and upon his return to England, Andros laid his defense of his actions before the Lords of Trade.

From Charles M. Andrews, ed., *Narratives of the Insurrections, 1675–1690* (New York: Charles Scribner's Sons, 1915), pp. 229–36. [Editorial insertions appear in square brackets—*Ed.*]

To the Right Hon'ble the Lords of the Committee for Trade and Plantations

The State of New England under the Government of Sr Edmond Andros

That in the yeare 1686 Sir Edmond Andros was by comission under the Greate Seale of England appoynted to succeed the President Dudley and Councill in the government of the Massachusetts Colloy, the Provinces of Hampshire and Maine and the Narragansett Country, to w'ch was annexed the Collonyes of Rhoad Island New Plymouth and the County of Cornwall.

In the yeare 1687 the Collony of Connecticott was also annexed and in the yeare 1688 he received a new Commission for all New England includeing the Province of New Yorke and East and West Jersey, with particuler order and directions to assert and protect the Five warlike Nations or Cantons of Indians, lying West from Albany above the heads of our rivers as far or beyond Maryland *vizt* Maquaes, Oneydes, Onondages, Caeujes, and Sennekes, as the Kings subjects upon whom the French had made severall incursions, and to demand the set-

ting at liberty severall of them surprized and deteyned by the French, and reparation for sundry goods taken from severall Christians His Majesties subjects in the lawfull prosecution of their trade.

*   *   *

The severall Provinces and Collonys in New England being soe united, the revenue continued and setled in those parts, for the support of the government, amounted to about twelve thousand pounds *per annum* and all places were well and quietly setled and in good posture.

The Church of England being unprovided of a place for theyr publique woship, he did, by advice of the Councill, borrow the new meeting house in Boston, at such times as the same was unused, untill they could provide otherwise; and accordingly on Sundays went in between eleven and twelve in the morning, and in the afternoone about fower; but understanding it gave offence, hastned the building of a Church, w'ch was effected at the charge of those of the Church of England, where the Chaplaine of the Souldiers performed divine service and preaching.

He was always ready to give grants of vacant

lands and confirme defective titles as authorized (the late Corporation not haveing passed or conveyed any pursuant to the directions in their Charter) but not above twenty have passed the seal in the time of his government.

Courts of Judicature were setled in the severall parts, soe as might be most convenient for the ease and benefitt of the subject, and Judges appoynted to hold the Terms and goe the Circuite throughout the Dominion, to administer justice in the best manner and forme, and according to the lawes Customes and statutes of the realme of England, and some peculiar locall prudentiall laws of the Country, not repugnant therto; and fees regulated for all officers.

That particular care was taken for the due observance of the severall Acts made for the encouragement of navigation and regulateing the plantation trade, whereby the lawfull trade and His Majestys revenue of Customs was considerably increased.

The Indians throughout the goverm't continued in good order and subjection untill, towards the latter end of the yeare 1688, by some unadvised proceedings of the Inhabitants in the Eastern parts of New England, the late rupture with the Indians there commenced, severall being taken and some killed, when Sir Edmond Andros was at New Yorke more than three hundred miles distant from that place; . . . by advice of the Councill he went with [the forces] in person and by the settlement of severall garrisons, frequent partyes, marches and pursuits after the enemy, sometimes above one hundred miles into the desart further than any Christian settlement, in w'ch the officers and souldiers of the standing forces always imployed, takeing and destroying their forts and settlem'ts, corne, provision, ammunicion and canooes, dispersed and reduced them to the uttermost wants and necessitys, and soe secured the Countrey, . . .

About the latter end of March 1688 Sir Edmond Andros returned for Boston, leaving the garrisons and souldiers in the Easterne parts in good condition, and sufficiently furnished with provisions and all stores and implyments of warr and vessells for defence of the coast and fishery.

On the 18th of Aprill 1689 severall of His Ma'ties Councill in New England haveing combined and conspired togeather with those who were Magistrates and officers in the late Charter Government annually chosen by the people, and severall other persons, to subvert and overthrow the government, and in stead thereof to introduce their former Comonwealth; and haveing by their false reports and aspersions gott to their assistance the greatest part of the people, whereof appeared in arms at Boston under the comand of those who were Officers in the sayd former popular goverment, to the number of about two thousand horse and foote; which strange and sudden appearance being wholly a surprize to Sir Edmond Andros, as knowing noe cause or occasion for the same, but understanding that severall of the Councill were at the Councill Chamber where (it being the Ordinary Councill day) they were to meet, and some particularly by him sent for from distant parts also there, he and those with him went thither. And tho' (as he passed) the streets were full of armed men, yett none offered him or those that were with him the least rudeness or incivillity, but on the contrary usuall respect; but when he came to the Councill Chamber he found severall of the sayd former popular Majestrates and other cheife persons then present, with those of the Councill, who had noe suitable regard to him, nor the peace and quiet of the Countrey, but instead of giveing any assistance to support the Goverment, made him a prisoner and also imprisoned some members of the Councill and other officers, who in pursuance of their respective dutyes and stations attended on him, and kept them for the space of ten months under severe and close confinement untill by His Ma'ties comand they were sent for England to answer what might be objected them, Where, after summons given to the pretended Agents of New England and their twice appearance at the Councill Board, nothing being objected by them or others, they were discharged. In the time of his confinement being denyed the liberty of discourse or conversation with any person, his own servants to attend him, or any communication or correspondence with any by letters, he hath noe particular knowledge of their further proceedings, but hath heard and understands:—

That soone after the confinem't of his person, the Confederates [took the] fort and Castle from the Officers that had the comand of them, whom they also imprisoned and dispersed the few souldiers belonging to the two standing Companyes then there, as they did the rest, when they recalled the forces imployed against the Indians Eastward (which two Companys are upon His Ma'ties establishment in England,) in w'ch service halfe a company of the standing forces at New Yorke being also imployed, the officers were surprised and brought prisoners to Boston, and the souldiers dispersed, as the remaining part of them at New Yorke were afterwards upon the revolucion there. The other company was, and remained, at Fort Albany and are both upon establishment to be payd out of His Ma'ties revenue there. And the Confederates at Boston possessed themselves of all His Ma'ties stores, armes ammunicion and other implements of warr, and disabled His Ma'ties man of war the *Rose* frigatt by secureing the Comander and bringing her sayles on shoare; and at the same time haveing imprisoned the secretary and some other officers, they broke open the Sec'rys Office and seized and conveyed away all records papers and wrightings.

*   *   *

By the encouragem't and perswasion of those of the Massachusetts the severall other provinces and collonys in New England as far as New Yorke have disunited themselves, and set up their former seperate Charter, or popular governments without Charter, and by that meanes the whole revenue of the Crowne continued and setled in the severall parts for the support of the Goverment is lost and destroyed.

The usuall time for election of new Majestrates at Boston comeing on in the begining of May 1689, great controversie arose about the setling of Civill Goverment; some being for a new election, and others that the Majestrates chosen and sworne in 1686 before the alteracion should reassume; the latter of w'ch was concluded on by them and the

pretended representatives of the severall townes of the Massachusetts, and assumed by the sd Majestrates accordingly, and thereupon the old Charter Goverment, tho' vacated in Westminster Hall, was reassumed without any regard to the Crowne of England, and they revived and confirmed their former laws contrary and repugnant to the laws and statutes of England, setled their Courts of Judicature, and appoynted new officers, and have presumed to try and judge all cases civill and criminall, and to pass sentence of death on severall of Their Ma'ties subjects, some of whom they have caused to be executed.

Alltho in the revenue continued on the Crowne for support of the goverment dureing his time, the country pay'd but the old establisht rate of a penny in the pound *per Annum* as given and practised for about fifty yeares past, the present Administrators have of their own authority, for not above six months, raysed and exacted from the people of the Massachusetts Collony seven rates and a half.

Since this insurrection and alteracion in New England they doe tollerate an unlimited irregular trade, contrary to the severall acts of Plantations, Trade and Navigacion, now as little regarded as in the time of their former Charter Goverment; they esteeming noe laws to be binding on them but what are made by themselves, nor admit English laws to be pleaded there, or appeales to His Ma'tie. And many shipps and vessells have since arrived from Scotland, Holland, Newfoundland, and other places prohibitted, they haveing imprisoned His Ma'ties Collector, Surveyor and searcher, and displaced other Customhouse officers.

That they sent to Albany to treat with the Indians in those parts, particularly with the Five Nations, Maquaes etc. and invited them to Boston; which is of ill and dangerouse consequence, by makeing the sayd Indians particularly acquainted with the disunion and seperate goverments, and shewing them the countrey and disorders therof, as far as Boston, giveing thereby the greatest advantage to the French of gaining or subdueing the sayd Indians and attempting Fort Albany (the most advanced frontier into the country and great mart of the beaver and peltry trade) and of infesting other parts.

The forces raysed and sent out by them the last summer, notwithstanding the great encouragem't they promised of eight pounds per head for every Indian should be killed, besides their pay, proved neither effectuall to suppresse the enemy or secure the country from further damage and murthers; and upon the winters approaching the forces were recalled and the country left exposed to the enemy, who have already over runn and destroyed soe great a part therof. And now by the assistance of the French of Canada may probably proceed further into the heart of the country, being soe devided and out of order unless it shall please His Ma'tie by his owne authority to redress the same, and put a stop to the French and Indians, and thereby prevent the ruine or loss of that whole dominion of New England and consequently of Their Maj'ties other American Plantacions; . . .

REVIEW QUESTIONS

1. What were Andros's answers to some of the charges that had been laid against him in the colonists' declaration?
2. Whose account—Mather's or Andros's—do you tend to believe? Why?
3. For what actions in particular did Andros condemn the colonists?
4. How would such condemnations bolster his position before the crown and gain him advocates among the Lords of Trade?

PROTESTANT ASSOCIATORS

The Declaration of the Reasons and Motives for the Present Appearing in Arms of Their Majesties Protestant Subjects in the Province of Maryland (1689)

From the 1660s on, Maryland suffered due to bad management by Governor Charles Calvert (who became third Lord Baltimore and the proprietor of the province in 1675), depressed tobacco prices, and the discontent of the majority of the smaller landowners and those without land. These people complained about their heavy taxes, limited franchise, and the actions of the deputy governor, William Joseph, who was administering the colony while Calvert was away. They also worried about how the accession of James II and the possibility of a Catholic line of succession might further empower the Calvert clique. Discontent erupted into rebellion in the summer of 1689 when the colonists believed they were under attack at home—there were reports of an Indian uprising on the frontier—and might be from abroad as well. They heard not only about the Glorious Revolution in England, but also that the proprietor had not yet proclaimed allegiance to the new monarchs. That news, plus rumors of war with France, led some colonists to fear that the proprietary faction might hand over the colony to France. A planter and politician named John Coode then gathered hundreds of men together to march on St. Mary's, the capital. The Protestant Associators, as the insurgents called themselves, also issued a declaration in July (sent to the Lords of Trade) listing their charges against the proprietary government. When the rebels got to St. Mary's, Joseph and the council surrendered, the Protestant Associators took control of the government. They remained in power from August 1689 to April 1692 when the crown sent a royal governor to take over.

Charles M. Andrews, ed. *Narratives of the Insurrections, 1675–1690* (New York: Charles Scribner's Sons, 1915) pp. 305–14.

[F]orasmuch as (by the Plots, Contrivances, Insinuations, Remonstrances, and Subscriptions, carried on, suggested, extorted, and obtained by the Lord Baltemore, his Deputies, Representatives, and Officers here) the Injustice and Tyranny under which we groan is palliated, and most if not all the Particulars of our Grievances shrouded from the Eye of Observation and the Hand of Redress, We thought fit for general Satisfaction, and particularly to undeceive those that may have a sinister Account of our Proceedings, to Publish this Declaration of the Reason and Motives inducing us thereunto.

His Lordship's Right and Title to the Government is by Virtue of a Charter to his Father Cecilius, from King Charles the First, of Blessed Memory. How his present Lordship has managed the Powers and Authorities given and granted in the same, We could Mourn and Lament only in silence, would our Duty to God, our Allegiance to his Vicegerent, and the Care and Welfare of our Selves and Posterity, permit us.

In the First Place, In the said Charter, is a Reservation of the Faith and Allegeance due to the Crown of England (the Province and Inhabitants being immediately subject thereunto) but how little that is manifested, is too obvious to all unbiassed Persons that ever had any thing to do here; The very name and owning of that Soveraign Power is sometimes Crime enough to incur the Frowns of our Superiors, and to render our Persons obnoxious and suspected to be Ill Affected to the Government.

The Ill Usage and Affronts to the King's Officers belonging to the Customs here, were a sufficient Argument of this; . . .

Allegeance here, by these Persons under whom We Suffer, is little talk'd of, other then what they would have done and sworn to his Lordship, the Lord Proprietary; for it was very lately owned by the President himself, openly enough in the Upper House of Assembly, That Fidelity to his Lordship was Allegeance, and that the denial of the one was the same thing with refusal or denial of the other. In that very Oath of Fidelity that was then imposed under the Penalty and Threats of Banishment, there is not so much as the least word or intimation of any Duty, Faith, or Allegeance to be reserved to Our Soveraign Lord the King of England.

How the *Jus Regale* is improved here, and made the Prerogative of his Lordship, is too sensibly felt by us all in that absolute Authority exercised over us, and by the greatest part of the Inhabitants in the Seizure of their persons, Forfeiture and Loss of their Goods, Chattels, Freeholds and Inheritances.

In the next place, Churches and Chappels (which by the said Charter should be Built and Consecrated according to the Ecclesiastical Laws of the Kingdom of England) to our great Regret and Discouragement of our Religion are erected and converted to the use of Popish Idolatry and Superstition. Jesuits and Seminary Priests are the only Incumbents (for which there is a Supply provided by sending our Popish Youth to be Educated at St. Omers [in France]) as also the chief Advisers and Councellors in Affairs of Government, and the

Richest and most Fertile Land set apart for their Use and Maintenance, while other Lands that are piously intended, and given for the Maintenance of the Protestant Ministry, become Escheat, and are taken as Forfeit, the Ministers themselves discouraged, and no care taken for their Subsistance.

The Power to Enact Laws is another branch of his Lordship's Authority; but how well that has been Executed and Circumstanced is too notorious. . . . [His Lordship not only diminished representation by allowing only two, rather than four, delegates from each county, he also nullified laws passed by the Assembly.] . . .

*   *   *

How Fatal, and of what Pernicious Consequence, that Unlimited and Arbitrary pretended Authority may be to the Inhabitants, is too apparent, but by considering, That by the same Reason, all the rest of our Laws, whereby our Liberty and Property subsists, are subject to the same Arbitrary Disposition, and if timely Remedy be not had, must stand or fall according to his Lordship's Good Will and Pleasure.

Nor is this Nullifying and Suspending Power the only Grievance that doth perplex and burthen us, in relation to Laws; but these Laws that are of a certain and unquestioned acceptation are executed and countenanced, as they are more or less agreeable to the good liking of our Governours in particular; One very good Law provides, That Orphan Children should be disposed of to Persons of the same Religion with that of their deceased Parents. In direct opposition to which, several Children of Protestants have been committed to the Tutelage of Papists, and brought up in the Romish Superstition. We could instance in a Young Woman, that has been lately forced, by Order of Council, from her Husband, committed to the Custody of a Papist and brought up in his Religion. 'Tis endless to enumerate the particulars of this nature, while on the contrary those Laws that enhance the Grandeur and Income of his said Lordship are severely Imposed and Executed; especially one that against all Sense, Equity, Reason, and Law Punishes all Speeches, Practices and Attempts relating to his Lordship and Government that shall be thought Mutinous and Seditious by the Judges of the Provincial Court, with either Whipping, Branding, Boreing through the Tongue, Fine, Imprisonment, Banishment, or Death; all or either of the said Punishments, at the Discretion of the said Judges; who have given a very recent and remarkable Proof of their Authority in each particular Punishment aforesaid, upon several of the good People of this Province, while the rest are in the same danger to have their Words and Actions liable to the Constructions and Punishment of the said Judges, and their Lives and Fortunes to the Mercy of their Arbitrary Fancies, Opinions, and Sentences.

To these Grievances are added,

Excessive Officers Fees, and that too under Execution, directly against the Law made and provided to redress the same; wherein there is no probability of a Legal Remedy, the Officers themselves that are Parties and culpable being Judges.

The like Excessive Fees imposed upon and extorted from Masters and Owners of Vessels Trading into this Province, without any Law to Justifie the same, and directly against the plain Words of the Charter, that say, there shall be no Imposition or Assessment without the Consent of the Freemen in the Assembly: To the great Obstruction of Trade, and Prejudice of the Inhabitants.

The like excessive Fees Imposed upon and extorted from the Owners of Vessels that are Built here, or do really belong to the Inhabitants; contrary to an Act of Assembly, made and provided for the same: Wherein, Moderate and Reasonable Fees are assertained, for the Promoting and Encouragement of Shipping and Navigation amongst our selves.

The frequent Pressing of Men, Horses, Boats, Provisions, and other Necessaries, in time of Peace; and often to gratifie private Designs and Occasions, to the great Burthen and Regret of the Inhabitants, contrary to Law and several Acts of Assembly in that Case made and provided.

The Seizing and Apprehending of Protestants in their Houses, with Armed Force consisting of Papists, and that in time of Peace; their hurrying them away to Prisons without Warrant or Cause of Commitment, there kept and Confined with Popish Guards, a long time without Trial.

Not only private but publick Outrages and Murthers committed and done by Papists upon Protestants without any Redress, but rather connived at and Tollerated by the chief in Authority; and indeed it were in vain to desire or expect any help or measures from them, being Papists and Guided by the Counsels and Instigations of the Jesuits, either in these or any other Grievances or Oppression. And yet these are the Men that are our Chief Judges, at the Common Law, in Chancery, of the Probat of Wills, and the Affairs of Administration, in the Upper House of Assembly, and the Chief Military Officers and Commanders of our Forces; being still the same Individual Persons, in all these particular Qualifications and Places.

These and many more, even Infinite Pressures and Calamities, we have hitherto with Patience lain under and submitted too; hoping that the same Hand of Providence, that hath sustained us under them, would at length in due time release us; and now at length, For as much as it has pleased Almighty God, by means of the great Prudence and Conduct of the best of Princes, Our most gracious King William, to put a Check to the great Innundation of Slavery and Popery, that had like to overwhelm Their Majesties Protestant Subjects in all their Territories and Dominions (of which none have suffered more, or are in greater Danger than our selves) we hope[d] and expected in our particular Stations and Qualifications, a proportionable Share of so great a Blessing. But to our great Grief and Consternation, upon the first News of the great Overture and happy Change in England, we found our selves surrounded with Strong and Violent Endeavours from our Governours here, being the Lord Baltemore's Deputies and Representatives, to defeat us of the same.

We still find all the means used by these very Persons and their Agents, Jesuits, Priests, and lay Papists, that Art or Malice can suggest, to divert the Obedience and Loyalty of the Inhabitants from Their Most Sacred Majesties, to that heighth of Impudence, that solemn Masses and Prayers are used

(as we have very good Information) in their Chappels and Oratories, for the prosperous Success of the Popish Forces in Ireland, and the French Designs against England, whereby they would involve us in the same Crime of Disloyalty with themselves, and render us Obnoxious to the Insupportable Displeasure of Their Majesties.

We every where hear, not only Publick Protestation against Their Majesties Right and Possession of the Crown of England, but their most Illustrious Persons villified and aspers'd with the worst and most Traiterous Expressions of Obloquy and Detraction.

We are every day threatned with the Loss of our Lives, Liberties, and Estates, of which we have great Reason to think our selves in Imminent Danger, by the Practices and Machinations that are on foot to betray us to the French, Northern, and other Indians, of which some have been dealt withal, and others Invited to Assist in our Destruction; well remembring the Incursion and Inrode of the said Northern Indians, in the Year 1681, who were conducted into the Heart of the Province by French Jesuits, and lay sore upon us, while the Representatives of the Country, then in the Assembly, were severely press'd upon by our Superiors, to yield them an Unlimited and Tiranical Power in the Affairs of the Militia. As so great a Piece of Villany cannot be the Result but of the worst of Principles; so we should with the greatest Difficulties believe it to be true, if Undeniable Evidence and Circumstances did not convince us.

*   *   *

But above all, with Due and Mature Deliberation, we have reflected upon that vast Gratitude and Duty incumbent likewise upon us, To our Soveraign Lord and Lady, the King and Queen's most Excellent Majesties, in which, as it would not be safe for us, so it will not suffer us to be Silent, in so great and General a Jubile, withal considering and looking upon our selves Discharged, Dissolved, and Free from all manner of Duty, Obligation, or Fidelity, to the Deputies, Governors, or Chief Magistrates here, as such: They having Departed from their Allegiance (upon which alone our said Duty and Fidelity to them depends) and by their Complices and Agents aforesaid endeavoured the Destruction of our Religion, Lives, Liberties, and Properties, all which they are bound to Protect.

These are the Reasons, Motives, and Considerations, which we do Declare, have induced us to take up Arms, to Preserve, Vindicate, and Assert the Sovereign Dominion, and Right, of King William and Queen Mary to this Province: To Defend the Protestant Religion among us, and to Protect and Shelter the Inhabitants from all manner of Violence, Oppression, and Destruction, that is Plotted and Designed against them; which we do Solemnly Declare and Protest, we have no Designs or Intentions whatsoever.

For the more Effectuate Accomplishments of which, We will take due Care that a Free and full Assembly be Called, and Convened with all Possible Expedition, by whom we may likewise have our Condition and Circumstances and our most Dutifull Addresses represented and rendered to Their Majesties: From whose great Wisdom, Justice, and especial Care of the Protestant Religion, We may Reasonably and Comfortably hope to be Delivered from our present Calamities, and for the Future be secured under a Just and Legal Administration,

from being evermore subjected to the Yoke of Arbitrary Government, Tyrany and Popery.

*   *   *

REVIEW QUESTIONS

1. The Protestant Associators claimed there was a crisis—indeed, there was more than one—over allegiance in the colony. What were the problems as they described them? Where did they say they stood in this crisis? Was that an attempt to show themselves as better Englishmen than those in the proprietary camp?
2. How does this piece reflect upon the exercise of religious toleration in Maryland? Consider the language of the Associators, the accusations they levied against the proprietary faction, and the Maryland Toleration Act (1649) (excerpted in Chapter 2).
3. Are the Associators' concerns about their rights connected to concerns about their property? Explain.
4. Why did the English government represent liberty and justice to the Associators?

JOHN LOCKE

FROM *The Second Treatise on Civil Government* (1689)

The philosopher John Locke (1632–1704), a supporter of the Glorious Revolution that deposed King James II, enthroned William and Mary, and established the supremacy of Parliament, attacked the divine right of kings in his first treatise on civil government. In his second treatise, the one excerpted here, he promulgated the idea that government rests in the will of the people, thus those people have the right to challenge and change their rulers and government. The colonists readily accepted Locke's theory, but it would be a later generation of provincials who would apply this revolutionary concept.

From John Locke, *The Second Treatise of Civil Government,* ed. John W. Gough (Oxford: Basil Blackwell, 1946), pp. 4, 15, 48–50, 66–72, 107–109, 118–19.

Of the State of Nature

To understand political power aright, and derive it from its original, we must consider what estate all men are naturally in, and that is, a state of perfect freedom to order their actions, and dispose of their possessions and persons as they think fit, within the bounds of the law of Nature, without asking leave or depending upon the will of any other man.

A state also of equality, wherein all the power and jurisdiction, is reciprocal, no one having more than another, there being nothing more evident than that creatures of the same species and rank, promiscuously born to all the same advantages of Nature, and the use of the same faculties, should also be equal one amongst another, without subordination or subjection, unless the lord and master of them all should, by any manifest declaration of his will, set one above another, and confer on him, by an evident and clear appointment, an undoubted right to dominion and sovereignty. . . .

Of Property

*   *   *

God, who hath given the world to men in common, hath also given them reason to make use of it to the best advantage of life and convenience. The earth and all that is therein is given to men for the support and comfort of their being. And though all the fruits it naturally produces, and beasts it feeds, belong to mankind in common, as they are produced by the spontaneous hand of Nature, and nobody has originally a private dominion exclusive of the rest of mankind in any of them, as they are thus in their natural state, yet being given for the use of men, there must of necessity be a means to appropriate them some way or other before they can be of any use, or at all beneficial, to any particular men. The fruit or venison which nourishes the wild Indian, who knows no enclosure, and is still a tenant in common, must be his, and so his—i.e., a part of him, that another can no longer have any right to it before it can do him any good for the support of his life.

Though the earth and all inferior creatures be common to all men, yet every man has a "property" in his own "person." This nobody has any right to but himself. The "labor" of his body and the "work" of his hands, we may say, are properly his. Whatsoever, then, he removes out of the state that Nature hath provided and left it in, he hath mixed his labor with it, and joined to it something that is his own, and thereby makes it his property. It being by him removed from the common state Nature placed it in, it hath by this labor something annexed to it that excludes the common right of other men. For this "labor" being the unquestionable property of the laborer, no man but he can have a right to what that is once joined to, at least where there is enough, and as good left in common for others. . . .

Of the Beginning of Political Societies

Men being, as has been said, by nature all free, equal, and independent, no one can be put out of this estate and subjected to the political power of another without his own consent, which is done by agreeing with other men, to join and unite a community for their comfortable, safe, and peaceable living, one amongst another, in a secure enjoyment of their properties, and a greater security against any that are not of it. This any number of men may do, because it injures not the freedom of the rest; they are left, as they were, in the liberty of the state of Nature. When any number of men have so consented to make one community or government, they are thereby presently incorporated, and make one body politic, wherein the majority have a right to act and conclude the rest.

For, when any number of men have, by the consent of every individual, made a community, they have thereby made that community one body, with a power to act as one body, which is only by the will and determination of the majority. . . .

And thus every man, by consenting with others to make one body politic under one government, puts himself under an obligation to everyone of that society to submit to the determination of the majority, and to be concluded by it; or else this original compact, whereby he with others incorporates into one society, would signify nothing, and be no compact if he be left free and under no other ties than he was in before in the state of Nature. . . .

Whosoever, therefore, out of a state of Nature unite into a community, must be understood to give up all the power necessary to the ends for which they unite into society to the majority of the community, unless they expressly agreed in any number greater than the majority. And this is done by barely agreeing to unite into one political society, which is all the compact that is, or needs be, between the individuals that enter into or make up a commonwealth. And thus, that which begins and actually constitutes any political society is nothing but the consent of any number of freemen capable of majority, to unite and incorporate into such a society. And this is that, and that only, which did or could give beginning to any lawful government in the world. . . .

Of the Extent of the Legislative Power

The great end of men's entering into society being the enjoyment of their properties in peace and safety, and the great instrument and means of that being the laws established in that society, the first and fundamental positive law of all commonwealths is the establishing of the legislative power, as the first and fundamental natural law which is to govern even the legislative. Itself is the preserva-

tion of the society and (as far as will consist with the public good) of every person in it. This legislative is not only the supreme power of the commonwealth, but sacred and unalterable in the hands where the community have once placed it. Nor can any edict of anybody else, in what form soever conceived, or by what power soever backed, have the force and obligation of a law which has not its sanction from that legislative which the public has chosen and appointed; for without this the law could not have that which is absolutely necessary to its being a law, the consent of the society, over whom nobody can have a power to make laws but by their own consent and by authority received from them; and therefore all the obedience, which by the most solemn ties anyone can be obliged to pay, ultimately terminates in this supreme power, and is directed by those laws which it enacts. Nor can any oaths to any foreign power whatsoever, or any domestic subordinate power, discharge any member of the society from his obedience to the legislative, acting pursuant to their trust, nor oblige him to any obedience contrary to the laws so enacted or farther than they do allow, it being ridiculous to imagine one can be tied ultimately to obey any power in the society which is not the supreme.

Though the legislative, whether placed in one or more, whether it be always in being or only by intervals, though it be the supreme power in every commonwealth, yet, first, it is not, nor can possibly be, absolutely arbitrary over the lives and fortunes of the people. For it being but the joint power of every member of the society given up to that person or assembly which is legislator, it can be no more than those persons had in a state of Nature before they entered into society, and gave it up to the community. For nobody can transfer to another more power than he has in himself, and nobody has an absolute arbitrary power over himself, or over any other, to destroy his own life, or take away the life or property of another. A man, as has been proved, cannot subject himself to the arbitrary power of another; and having, in the state of Nature, no arbitrary power over the life, liberty, or possession of another, but only so much as the law of Nature gave him for the preservation of himself and the rest of mankind, this is all he does, or can give up to the commonwealth, and by it to the legislative power, so that the legislative can have no more than this. Their power in the utmost bounds of it is limited to the public good of the society. It is a power that has no other end but preservation, and therefore can never have a right to destroy, enslave, or designedly to impoverish the subjects; the obligations of the law of Nature cease not in society, but only in many cases are drawn closer, and have, by human laws, known penalties annexed to them to enforce their observation. Thus the law of Nature stands as an eternal rule to all men, legislators as well as others. The rules that they make for other mens' actions must, as well as their own and other men's actions, be comfortable to the law of Nature—i.e., to the will of God, of which that is a declaration, and the fundamental law of Nature being the preservation of mankind, no human sanction can be good or valid against it.

Secondly, the legislative or supreme authority cannot assume to itself a power to rule by extemporary arbitrary decrees, but is bound to dispense justice and decide the rights of the subject by promulgated standing laws, and known authorized judges. For the law of Nature being unwritten, and so nowhere to be found but in the minds of men, they who, through passion or interest, shall miscite or misapply it, cannot so easily be convinced of their mistake where there is no established judge; and so it serves not as it ought, to determine the rights and fence the properties of those that live under it, especially where everyone is judge, interpreter, and executioner of it too, and that in his own case; and he that has right on his side, having ordinarily but his own single strength, hath not force enough to defend himself from injuries or punish delinquents. To avoid these inconveniences which disorder men's properties in the state of Nature, men unite into societies that they may have the united strength of the whole society to secure and defend their properties, and may have standing rules to bound it by which everyone may know what is his. To this end it is that men give up all their natural power to the society they enter into,

and the community put the legislative power into such hands as they think fit, with this trust, that they shall be governed by declared laws, or else their peace, quiet, and property will still be at the same uncertainty as it was in the state of Nature.

Absolute arbitrary power, or governing without settled standing laws, can neither of them consist with the ends of society and government, which men would not quit the freedom of the state of Nature for, and tie themselves up under, were it not to preserve their lives, liberties, and fortunes, and by stated rules of right and property to secure their peace and quiet. It cannot be supposed that they should intend, had they a power so to do, to give anyone or more an absolute arbitrary power over their persons and estates, and put a force into the magistrate's hand to execute his unlimited will arbitrarily upon them; this were to put themselves into a worse condition than the state of Nature, wherein they had a liberty to defend their right against the injuries of others, and were upon equal terms of force to maintain it, whether invaded by a single man or many in combination. . . . And, therefore, whatever form the commonwealth is under, the ruling power ought to govern by declared and received laws, and not by extemporary dictates and undetermined resolutions, for then mankind will be in a far worse condition than in the state of Nature if they shall have armed one or a few men with the joint power of a multitude, to force them to obey at pleasure the exorbitant and unlimited decrees of their sudden thoughts, or unrestrained, and till that moment, unknown wills, without having any measures set down which may guide and justify their actions. For all the power the government has, being only for the good of the society, as it ought not to be arbitrary and at pleasure, so it ought to be exercised by established and promulgated laws, that both the people may know their duty, and be safe and secure within the limits of the law, and the rulers, too, kept within their due bounds, and not be tempted by the power they have in their hands to employ it to purposes, and by such measures as they would not have known, and own not willingly.

Thirdly, the supreme power cannot take from any man any part of his property without his own consent. For the preservation of property being the end of government, and that for which men enter into society, it necessarily supposes and requires that the people should have property, without which they must be supposed to lose that by entering into society which was the end for which they entered into it; too gross an absurdity for any man to own. Men, therefore, in society having property, they have such a right to the goods, which by the law of the community are theirs, that nobody has a right to take them, or any part of them, from them without their own consent; without this they have no property at all. . . . Hence it is a mistake to think that the supreme or legislative power of any commonwealth can do what it will, and dispose of the estates of the subject arbitrarily, or take any part of them at pleasure. This is not much to be feared in governments where the legislative consists wholly or in part in assemblies which are variable, whose members upon the dissolution of the assembly are subjects under the common laws of their country, equally with the rest. But in governments where the legislative is in one lasting assembly, always in being, or in one man as in absolute monarchies, there is danger still, that they will think themselves to have a distinct interest from the rest of the community, and so will be apt to increase their own riches and power by taking what they think fit from the people. For a man's property is not at all secure, though there be good and equitable laws to set the bounds of it between him and his fellow-subjects, if he who commands those subjects have power to take from any private man what part he pleases of his property, and use and dispose of it as he thinks good.

*   *   *

It is true governments cannot be supported without great charge, and it is fit everyone who enjoys his share of the protection should pay out of his estate his proportion for the maintenance of it. But still it must be with his own consent—i.e., the consent of the majority, giving it either by themselves or their representatives chosen by them; for if anyone shall claim a power to lay and levy taxes on the people by his own authority, and without such

consent of the people, he thereby invades the fundamental law of property, and subverts the end of government. For what property have I in that which another may by right take when he pleases to himself?

Fourthly, the legislative cannot transfer the power of making laws to any other hands, for it being but a delegated power from the people, they who have it cannot pass it over to others. The people alone can appoint the form of the commonwealth, which is by constituting the legislative, and appointing in whose hands that shall be. And when the people have said, "We will submit, and be governed by laws made by such men, and in such forms," nobody else can say other men shall make laws for them; nor can they be bound by any laws but such as are enacted by those whom they have chosen and authorized to make laws for them.

These are the bounds which the trust that is put in them by the society and the law of God and Nature have set to the legislative power of every commonwealth, in all forms of government. First, they are to govern by promulgated established laws, not to be varied in particular cases, but to have one rule for rich and poor, for the favorite at Court, and the countryman at plow. Secondly, these laws also ought to be designed for no other end ultimately but the good of the people. Thirdly, they must not raise taxes on the property of the people without the consent of the people given by themselves or their deputies. And this properly concerns only such governments where the legislative is always in being, or at least where the people have not reserved any part of the legislative to deputies, to be from time to time chosen by themselves. Fourthly, legislative neither must nor can transfer the power of making laws to anybody else, or place it anywhere but where the people have.

Of the Dissolution of Government

*   *   *

The reason why men enter into society is the preservation of their property; and the end while they choose and authorize a legislative is that there may be laws made, and rules set, as guards and fences to the properties of all the society, to limit the power and moderate the dominion of every part and member of the society. For since it can never be supposed to be the will of the society that the legislative should have a power to destroy that which everyone designs to secure by entering into society, and for which the people submitted themselves to legislators of their own making: whenever the legislators endeavor to take away and destroy the property of the people, or to reduce them to slavery under arbitrary power, they put themselves into a state of war with the people, who are thereupon absolved from any farther obedience, and are left to the common refuge which God hath provided for all men against force and violence. Whensoever, therefore, the legislative shall transgress this fundamental rule of society, and either by ambition, fear, folly, or corruption, endeavor to grasp themselves, or put into the hands of any other, an absolute power over the lives, liberties, and estates of the people, by this breach of trust they forfeit the power the people had put into their hands for quite contrary ends, and it devolves to the people, who have a right to resume their original liberty, and by the establishment of a new legislative (such as they shall think fit), provide for their own safety and security, which is the end for which they are in society.

What I have said here concerning the legislative in general holds true also concerning the supreme executor, who having a double trust put in him, both to have a part in the legislative and the supreme execution of the law, acts against both, when he goes about to set up his own arbitrary will as the law of the society. He acts also contrary to his trust when he employs the force, treasure, and offices of the society to corrupt the representatives and gain them to his purposes, when he openly pre-engages the electors, and prescribes, to their choice, such whom he has, by solicitation, threats, promises, or otherwise, won to his designs, and employs them to bring in such who have promised beforehand what to vote and what to enact. Thus to regulate candidates and electors, and new model

the ways of election, what is it but to cut up the government by the roots, and poison the very fountain of public security? For the people having reserved to themselves the choice of their representatives as the fence to their properties, could do it for no other end but that they might always be freely chosen, and so chosen, freely act and advise as the necessity of the commonwealth and the public good should, upon examination and mature debate, be judged to require. This, those who give their votes before they hear the debate, and have weighed the reasons on all sides, are not capable of doing. To prepare such an assembly as this, and endeavor to set up the declared abettors of his own will, for the true representatives of the people, and the law-makers of the society, is certainly as great a breach of trust, and as perfect a declaration of a design to subvert the government, as is possible to be met with. To which, if one shall add rewards and punishments visibly employed to the same end, and all the arts of perverted law made use of to take off and destroy all that stand in the way of such a design, and will not comply and consent to betray the liberties of their country, it will be past doubt what is doing. . . .

Here it is like the common question will be made: Who shall be judge whether the prince or legislative act contrary to their trust? This, perhaps, ill-affected and factious men may spread amongst the people, when the prince only makes use of his due prerogative. To this I reply, The people shall be judge; for who shall be judge whether his trustee or deputy acts well and according to the trust reposed in him, but he who deputes him and must, by having deputed him, have still a power to discard him when he fails in his trust? If this be reasonable in particular cases of private men, why should it be otherwise in that of the greatest moment, where the welfare of millions is concerned and also where the evil, if not prevented, is greater, and the redress very difficult, dear, and dangerous?

But, farther, this question, Who shall be judge? cannot mean that there is no judge at all. For where there is no judicature on earth to decide controversies amongst men, God in heaven is judge.

He alone, it is true, is judge of the right. But every man is judge for himself, as in all other cases so in this, . . .

If a controversy arise betwixt a prince and some of the people in a matter where the law is silent or doubtful, and the thing be of great consequence, I should think the proper umpire in such a case should be the body of the people. For in such cases where the prince hath a trust reposed in him, and is dispensed from the common, ordinary rules of the law, there, if any men find themselves aggrieved, and think the prince acts contrary to, or beyond that trust, who so proper to judge as the body of the people (who at first lodged that trust in him) how far they meant it should extend? But if the prince, or whoever they be in the administration, decline that way of determination, the appeal then lies nowhere but to Heaven. Force between either persons who have no known superior on earth, or which permits no appeal to a judge on earth, being properly a state of war, wherein the appeal lies only to Heaven; and in that state the injured party must judge for himself when he will think fit to make use of that appeal and put himself upon it.

To conclude. The power that every individual gave the society when he entered into it can never revert to the individuals again, as long as the society lasts, but will always remain in the community; because without this there can be no community— no commonwealth, which is contrary to the original agreement; so also when the society hath placed the legislative in any assembly of men, to continue in them and their successors, with direction and authority for providing such successors, the legislative can never revert to the people whilst that government lasts; because, having provided a legislative with power to continue forever, they have given up their political power to the legislative, and cannot resume it. But if they have set limits to the duration of their legislative, and made this supreme power in any person or assembly only temporary; or else when, by the miscarriages of those in authority, it is forfeited; upon the forfeiture of their rulers, or at the determination of the time set, it reverts to the society, and the people have a right to act as supreme, and continue the legislative in themselves or place it in a new form, or new hands, as they think good.

REVIEW QUESTIONS

1. According to Locke, what is accorded all humans in a state of nature?
2. Why or how is property a basis for political society?
3. When people in a state of nature unite to form a political society, is creation an act of consensus or conflict?
4. If such a society rests upon majority rule, then what kind of government is established? What are the limits of this government?
5. What are legitimate reasons for dissolving a government?

THE ALBANY CONGRESS

FROM *The Albany Plan of Union* (1754)

Throughout the colonial period British settlers, French colonists, and Native Americans were constantly in conflict with each other as they tried to expand and/or secure their territories. Advances spurred attacks that sometimes led to war. In many cases this border warfare was limited by the time, territory, and people involved. In 1754, however, a border skirmish near the Forks of the Ohio escalated into what the British colonists called the French and Indian War. Lieutenant Colonel George Washington's Virginia troops and Indian allies attacked a French detachment on 28 May. French forces then issued out from Fort Duquesne to return the favor—defeating Washington at Fort Necessity on 4 July. While Virginia conducted that military venture, delegates from seven northern colonies met at Albany, New York, to consult on defense matters and reestablish friendly relations with the Iroquois. They managed the latter to a limited degree by 9 July. The former became more complicated when the delegates decided to create a plan of union for all the colonies to ensure better common defenses and to secure the frontier as they expanded. Benjamin Franklin had advocated such a union, and it was primarily from his plan that the delegates chose to work (though they did incorporate ideas from other plans submitted). The final product was ultimately ignored or rejected by the imperial as well as colonial governments, but it served as an example and basis for later plans of union.

Stephen L. Schechter, ed., *Roots of the Republic: American Founding Documents Interpreted* (Madison, WI: Madison House Publishers, 1990), pp. 114–17. Used by permission. [Editorial insertions that appear in square brackets are from Schechter's edition—*Ed.*]

Plan of a proposed Union of the Several Colonies of Massachusetts Bay, New Hampshire, Connecticut, Rhode Island, New York, New Jersey, Pensilvania, Maryland, North Carolina, and South Carolina, for their mutual defence & Security & for the Extending the British Settlements in North America.

That humble application be made for an act of the Parliament of Great Britain by virtue of which one General Government may be formed in America including all the said Colonies within & under which Government each Colony may retain it present constitution except in the Perticulars wherein a Change may be directed by the said act as Hereafter follows.—

That the said General Government be administered by a President General to be appointed & supported by the Crown, & a Grand Council to be chosen by the Representatives of the People of the several Colonies met in their respective Assemblies.

That within —— Months after the passing of such act, the House of Representatives in the several Assemblies that happens to be sitting within that time or that shall be exspecially for that purpose convened may & Shall chuse Members for the Grand Council in the following proportions that is to say.

Massachusetts Bay	7
New Hampshire	2
Connecticut	5
Rhode Island	2

New York	4
New Jersey	3
Pensilvania	6
Maryland	4
Virginia	7
North Carolina	4
South Carolina	4
	48

Who shall meet for the first time at the City of Philadelphia in Pensilvania being called by the President General as soon as conveniently may be after his Appointment.

That there shall be a new Election of members for the Grand Council every three Years, & on the Death or resignation of any Member, his place shall be Supplyed by a new choice at the next sitting of the Assembly of the Colony he represented.

That after the first three years when the proportion of Money arising out of each Colony, to the General Treasury can be known, the Number of Members to be chosen for each Colony shall from time to time in all Ensuing Elections be regulated by that proportion yet so as that the Number to be chosen by any one Province be not more than Seven nor less than two.

That the Grand Council shall meet once in every year and oftener if occasion require at such time & place as they shall adjourn to at the last preceding meeting or as they shall be called to meet at by the President General on any Emergency he having first obtained in Writing the consent of Seven of the Members to such Call, & sent due & timely notice to the whole.

That the Grand Council have power to chuse their Speaker & shall neither be dissolved, prorogued, nor continue Sitting longer than Six Weeks at one time, without the[ir] own consent or the Special Command of the Crown.

That the Members of the Grand Council shall be allowed for their Service ten Shillings Sterling per diem during their Sessions and Journey to & from the place of meeting; twenty Miles to be reckoned a Days Journey.

That the assent of the President General be requisite to all Acts of the Grand Council, & that it be his Office & duty to cause them to be Carried into Execution.

That the President General with the advice of the Grand Council hold or direct all Indian Treaties in which the General Interest or Welfare of the Colonies may be concerned, & to make Peace or declare War with Indian Nations. That they make such Laws as they judge necessary for regulating all Indian Trade. That they make all purchases from Indians for the Crown, of Lands now not within the bounds of particular Colonies or that Shall not be within their Bounds when some of them are reduced to more Convenient Dimensions. That they make New Settlements on such Purchases by Granting Lands in the Kings name reserving a Quit Rent to the Crown for the use of the General Treasury. That they make Laws for Regulating & Governing such new Settlements till the Crown shall think fit to form them into particular Governments. That they may raise & pay Soldiers, and build Forts for the Defence of any of the Colonies, & equip Vessels of force to guard the Coast and protect the Trade on the Ocean Lakes or great Rivers, but they shall not impress men in any Colony without the consent of its Legislature— That for these Purposes they have power to make Laws, & lay, & levy such General Dutys Imposts or Taxes as to themselves appear most equal & just considering the ability & other Circumstances of the Inhabitants in the Several Colonies, & such as may be collected with the least Inconvenience to the People, rather discorageing Luxury, than loading Industry with unnecessary Burthens—that they may appoint a general Treasurer, and a perticular Treasurer in each Government when necessary and from time to time may order the Sums in the Treasuries of each Government into the General Treasury, or draw on them for special Payments as they find most convenient, Yet no money to Issue but by joint orders of the President General and Grand Council except where Sums have been appropriated to perticular purposes, and the President General is previously impowered by an Act to draw for Such Sums—That the General Accounts shall be yearly settled & reported to the Several Assemblies.—that a Quorum of the Grand

Counsil, impowered to Act with the President General do consist of Twenty Five Members among who there shall be one or more from a Majority of the Colonies.—That the Laws made by them for the purposes aforesaid shall not be repugnant but as near as may be agreeable to the Laws of England and shall be transmitted to the King in Council for approbation as soon as may be after their passing and if not disapproved within three years after presentation to remain in force.—That in case of the Death of the President General the Speaker of the Grand Council for the time being shall Succeed and be vested with the same power and authorities & continue till the Kings pleasure be known.

That all Military Commission Officers whether for Land or Sea Service to act under this General Constitution Shall be nominated by the President General, but the approbation of the Grand Council is to be obtained before they receive their Commissions And all civil Officers are to be nominated by the Grand Council, and to receive the President Generals approbation before they officiate But in case of Vacancy by Death or removal of any Officer civil or Military under this Constitution, the Governor of the Provinces in which such Vacancy happens may appoint till the Pleasure of the President General and Grand Council be known.—That the perticular Military as well as civil Establishments in each Colony remain in their present State, this General Constitution notwithstanding; and that on Sudden Emergenceys any Colony may defend itself, and lay the Accounts of Expence Thence arisen before the President General and Grand Council, who may allow and order payment of the same as far as they judge such Accounts just and reasonable.

REVIEW QUESTIONS

1. What was to be the imperial government's relationship with the newly formed "General Government"? What would define the relationship between this government and those of the individual colonies?
2. How did the delegates propose to organize this government?
3. What were to be the main duties of the General Government?
4. What power would enable this government to carry out these duties?

HENRY BOUQUET

FROM A Report on the Expedition to Fort Duquesne (1758)

When the colonists, via the Albany Congress, did not establish a common defense, and the French did not withdraw from the Ohio Country, the British government decided to act in defense of its imperial interests. General Edward Braddock was sent to push out the French; but he was killed in battle and his force of British regulars and provincial troops defeated near Fort Duquesne in 1755. After the dismal campaigns of 1756 and 1757, William Pitt, the king's chief minister, made a number of changes in leadership and strategy for the war in America. One of those changes was the appointment of Brigadier General John Forbes to command a new expedition against

Fort Duquesne. Forbes, a Scot, was a fine officer with much experience who was suf-
fering from a debilitating disease. Even so, he set to work building a road and a series
of fortifications across western Pennsylvania. With those established, he could move
in to take the French fort and secure the area. Aiding him in the planning
and execution of the mission was his field commander, Colonel Henry Bouquet.

S. K. Stevens, Donald H. Kent, and Autumn L. Leonard, eds., *The Papers of Henry Bouquet*, vol. II (Harrisburg: The Pennsylvania Historical and Museum Commission, 1951),
pp. 396–99.

[Bouquet to Forbes, Fort Bedford at Raystown, 20 August 1758: The officers sent to cut out the road west of there have done well.] These gentlemen deserve much praise for having surmounted all these obstacles in so short a time; and what gives me much satisfaction—they have kept their troops in a good humor. Every one is contented, and believes himself immortalized by having worked to open this route.

They are going so rapidly that they oblige me to have the post of Loyalhanna occupied before your arrival. Fortunately, Major Grant [James Grant, second-in-command of the Highlanders] has arrived, and I can entrust this mission to him. He has gracefully sacrificed his dislike to serve under provincial officers for the good of the service; and as there is no one more energetic, and at the same time receptive to advice, than Colonel Burd [James Burd, Colonel Commandant of the 2nd Battalion, Pennsylvania Regiment], I shall send him with him. They will have all the Americans (they are too few to be divided), 400 Highlanders, 400 of Washington's, and 400 of the Second Battalion of Pennsylvania. These 1500 men will begin by making entrenchments for their camp, as protection against a surprise attack. Then they will go to work building storehouses for our provisions, and will shield them by a fort built of stockades or logs; and this fort may, if necessary, be reinforced by another exterior line, and the interval of fifteen to eighteen feet filled with earth from the ditch. For the present they will make only the interior enclosure. They will keep advanced posts all around them, which will be relieved every day, and which will lay in ambush along the approaches, changing their location often. They will also send out parties of some strength to reconnoiter, etc.

While they are working at this post, Colonel Armstrong [John Armstrong of 1st Battalion, Pennsylvania Regiment] with 400 men of his battalion, and the two companies of workmen from Virginia and one company from the Lower Counties [Delaware], will improve the road, build a redoubt at Edmund's Swamp, and cut the road from Kickeny Pawlins, in order to go and join them, leaving detachments at the redoubt which is at the head of the gap, at Edmund's Swamp, and at Kickeny Pawlins. The first division of the artillery will march Tuesday or Wednesday with

2	12-pounders and their ammunition . . .23	wagons
2	6-pounders with ditto 2	
8	cohorns 1	
108	barrels of powder 9	
72	cases of shot 6	
24	reams of cartridge paper, thread, etc. .1	

In all 42

The horses will come back here, and after they have rested, the second division will march. I shall have forage carried along the route, and have good care taken of the horses. There is little grass on the mountain, but a prodigious quantity of locust which will be cut, and which is more nourishing than grass.

We shall not lack for pasturage here, and we shall find it in abundance, they say, at Loyalhanna.

There is already plenty of provisions at Kickeny Pawlins with forty cattle, and I shall easily supply all the food necessary with pack horses.

I hope that this arrangement is in conformity with your ideas. I take a great deal on myself, but I have carefully considered all the circumstances and do not believe that there are any risks attached.

Your idea to have paths opened for flanking parties is excellent, and I shall have it carried out at once. I have always drawn up the troops and had them march in double file, and I have found by experience that seven columns in this order have penetrated the densest thickets, and at a drum signal they have spread out and formed line of battle in two minutes, holding a very long front—with light troops and cavalry off to the side keeping up a continual fire, and the same all along the line. In all the encounters in the field or in the woods, I notice that the enemy—especially the Indians—attack our flanks first and try to surround us. This will be impossible for them through this plan; we should outflank them every time, and if they detach parties to turn our position, they must encounter our light troops advanced at least 200 paces; but more about it at meeting.

I can assure you that, whatever our fate, you will never experience the indignities suffered by General Abercromby [Montcalm's French forces beat back Major General James Abercromby's combined British and provincial forces at Fort Carillon, Ticonderoga, on 8 July 1758] through the laxness of his provincials. I have established harmony between the different corps which will prevent any accident of that nature, and by holding the balance even, encouraging these, and restraining the overbearing spirit of the others, chiefly of your countrymen, I can truly assure you that you will find no fault other than ignorance and inexperience, which I cannot remedy—but they are loyal and will not abandon you. . . .

You render the most important service to our colonies by the treaty [the fourth Easton Council] which you have so wisely appointed. I hope that you will be able to prevail on the plenipotentiaries to carry to it plans suitable to the critical circumstances in which we find ourselves; and that, for once in their lives, they will forget their jealousies and their petty provincial interests, for the general

good of their fatherland. The inactivity of the Indians will be the first advantage we shall receive from it, and if you should accomplish nothing more, I believe that on this occasion you do them a service more important than a victory.

Tomorrow I shall arrange with Hoops the dispatch of his cattle. I do not know if I have informed you of my opinion on that subject. This is to send 1500 cattle to Loyalhanna where they will be slaughtered in September. We shall build smoke houses there, to smoke all this salt beef, which will give us a supply of provisions for 4000 men for four months, barring accidents, and we shall have nothing to provide and transport but flour. Hoops must have salt sent without delay.

Forage is another article which will require many wagons. Hoops says that almost all those which are in service can no longer be used, or would take so long on the way that they could not be depended on, aside from the expense and the quantity of forage they consume. There remains only one decision to take in my opinion, which is to dismiss all the wagons in bad condition and hire new ones. That is the difficulty: to count on the good will of the inhabitants of Pennsylvania or on the press warrants of the magistrates would be folly, and we should die of hunger. You have no more regular troops to use for that purpose, but there are about 300 provincials between Shippensburg, Carlisle, and the east side of Susquehanna, not counting the 200 men at Fort Augusta. These fine gentlemen will not impress anyone, unless you give them a leader who will make them step. I think that Sir John [Sir John St. Clair, quartermaster of the regular forces] would be very suitable for that expedition, and that if you would terrorize the entire province and would find for you, between Philadelphia, Lancaster, Berks County, and York, 300 wagons which might bring us in a single trip about three months' supply of flour at a fixed price per hundredweight delivered at Raystown, supplying their own forage, Fifteen shillings per hundredweight from Carlisle would perhaps not be too much.

Sickness has weakened the army so much that I do not see how you can furnish the necessary escorts nor guard the communication, without employing for this the 300 men below here. I know that the whole province will cry murder, but if that measure is necessary for the success of the expedition, their unfounded complaints will not stop you.

The minister Bay [Andrew Bay, chaplain to the 3rd Battalion, Pennsylvania Regiment] who can be of greater service by procuring wagons than by preaching, will promise you a hundred from York, but he does not want to undertake it until after sowing-time. We have two months' supply of flour, and if we can depend on him, there would be time; but the other way is more certain, because in one day of bargaining you could snatch 200 wagons at Philadelphia and load them there. The Sheriff of Lancaster will get 100 in his county, which would make your number. . . .

Captain [James] Sinclair is busy ransacking all the storehouses; as many of the things were sent without a list, it is necessary to examine everything. When that is done, I shall send him to you, unless you would prefer to send an order to his parent, who will have nothing to do here for some time; and he might go back to continue the road from Loyalhanna, after obtaining wagons, and placing stores of forage along the way.

I just received a report from one of our officers who is returning from the fort. I am having it copied to send to you, and I learn that another officer, detached with the same orders, will arrive tomorrow. They have reconnoitered the place from two different sides, and it seems that with five or six hundred Frenchmen there are a great number of Indians, many cattle, and many sheep. The savages are of little consequence, when one is forewarned, and I believe that it is in your power to render them completely useless.

*   *   *

REVIEW QUESTIONS

1. Was Bouquet's evaluation of the provincials' contributions to the expedition positive or negative? Did his comments appear to reflect the general perceptions of the British military? Explain.
2. What did Bouquet think about the Native Americans? Did this affect his planning?
3. What does this account reveal about the nature of warfare in this conflict?

TESSECUMME AND SIMEON ECUYER

FROM Speeches at Fort Pitt (1763)

While General John Forbes's army moved slowly westward, his emissaries met with some of the Indians from the area. Both the diplomatic and military campaigns ended successfully, first with the Treaty of Easton (by which the Delaware and Shawnee Indians promised to quit attacking English settlers), and then with the taking of Fort Duquesne (soon renamed Fort Pitt). The treaty that officially ended the war between France and England was signed in February 1763, but that did not mean that peace immediately reigned in the backcountry. The British, colonists, and Native Americans (both those who had been allies and those who had been enemies) had to establish new postwar relationships, but problems quickly arose due to the expectations of all involved. One result was the Ottawa rebellion led by Pontiac which erupted in May 1763 and soon included other tribes. Tessecumme of the Delaware stated his people's position and hopes in a speech at Fort Pitt on 26 July 1763 while Captain Simeon Ecuyer of the Royal American Regiment, commanding at Fort Pitt, gave the British response on 27 July.

From Louis M. Waddell, ed., *The Papers of Henry Bouquet*, vol. VI (Harrisburg: The Pennsylvania Historical and Museum Commission, 1994), pp. 333–37. [Punctuation has not been modernized—*Ed.*]

. . . Tessecumme, then taking out a large Belt, spoke

*   *   *

Brothers; listen now with attention to what I am going to say.

As it has been alway's your desire that we should hold fast by the Chain of Friendship; I now assure you, that we have alway's done it & do it still & we hope you do the same, it is now in your Power to continue it.

Brother's,

On your first coming to this place, we were the first Nation you contracted a Friendship with; after this, you extended, a Belt of Friendship across this Country, the End of which reach'd those Nations over, the Lakes Towards the Sun Setting, then as we were Situated in the centre between you /of this Country/ you requested that we would hold fast by the middle of this Belt; this we assure you we have done, & with both hand's, have held it close to our Hearts; but now I see both ends let loose & we are now, the only people to hold this Belt up, by the middle Brother's let us be Strong on both sides, & take Pity of our Warriors, Women & Children, let us be sincere, & Speak from our Hearts, & be honest in everything that passes now between us; I now take this Friendship Belt, & lay it in the Fort where we request you will Assist us, in preserving it. Brother's don't imagine that what I have said comes from my lips only; I do assure you it comes from the bottom of our Hearts,

& we make no doubt but this will give you the same pleasure if you are as sincere as we really are.

Brother

You sent us word that you were so firmly Seated here that you were not to be removed; Brothers you have Town's & places of your own; you know this is our Country; & that your having Possession of it must be offensive to all Nations therefore it would be proper, that you were in your own Country where our Friendship might always remain Undisturbed.

Brother's

some Time ago you desired that we would go out of your way that you might Pass, to those Nations, that have disturbed the Chain of Friendship; you yourselves are the people that have done it. In the first place by coming with large Armies into our Country & building Strong Forts, we were then the first people that Met you, having no Mistrust of your design and nothing but Good in our Hearts towards you; agreed to every thing you desired; at the same time requested of you in the Strongest Terms not to extend your Forts any further than this Post. Notwithstanding this you cross'd the Lakes, & what pass'd between the Nations living that way and you, we are unacquainted with, but you see they have Slipped their Hand's from their Friendship with you, & as you have desired to know who Struck you, we take this opportunity to make you Sensible of it. which I believe you can't help Thinking this is True; so you have no Body else to blame, but yourselves; for what has happened.

Gave a large Belt. 10 row's

Brothers

We have endevoured to Stop all Parties we saw going against you some we were able to prevail with, other's we were not, who we suppose will prosecute the War against you. our reason for not comiing two days ago to speak with you, was that we riceived this String of Wampum which I have now in my hand from all the Nations over the Lakes. the following is what they said upon it.

Grandfather's the Delawares.

By this String, we inform you, that we intend in a Short time to pass in a very great Body; thro' your Country on our way to the Forks of Ohio: Grandfather's, you know us to be a foolish people, we are determined to stop at nothing, and as we expect to be very hungry, we will seize and eat up every thing that comes in our way. Brother here is their Wampum you have heard what they design; If you go quietly Home, to your Wise Men this is the furthest the will go. if not you see what will be the Consequence, so we desire that you do Remove off.

A String.

Brother's

We have now delivered every thing we have to say   consider and when you have a mind to answer us, fire a Gun & we will come over to hear you, we hope when this is done to be able each of us to rise up and go to our respective Homes.

*   *   *

Answer: The Comanding Officer to his
Brothers the Delawares

July 27th 1763

Brothers

You must be certain of our Sincerity towards you, as we have never broke our treaties with you or any other Indians Nations Since our first com-ing into this Country; Therefore observe what I will inform you now. In your Speech Yesterday to me, you complain that we have taken your Country, & build Strong Forts; Now Brothers, these Forts was to protect you & your trade, which you have been often told. With regard to your Lands, we have taken none only such parts as our Enemies the French did Possess. You Suffered them first to settle in the Heart of your Country without molestation, and why would you pretend to turn us out of it now; who have always been friendly and Kind to you.

Brothers

For these reasons I now tell you, that I will not abandon this Post; I have Warriors; Provisions, and Ammunitions plenty to defend it three Years against all the Indians in the Woods, and we shall never abandon it as long as a white Men Lives in America. I despise the Ottawas, and I am very much Surprise at our Brothers Delawares for proposing us to leave this Place and to go Home. This is our Home, You have attaked us without reason or provacation, you have Murdered & plundered our Warriors and Traders you have took off our Horses & Cattles, and at the Same time you tell us, your Hearts are good towards your Brothers the English; how can I have faith on you and believe that you are Sincere. Therefore now Brothers, I will advise you to go Home to your Towns, and take care of your Wymen and Children, when we have occasion for you to Speak to you we shall send for you.

If your Chiefs at any time have anything to Say to us, they must go for the present, to Bedford where they will meet our Great Men & George Croghan, they will be well used, and I will give them Letters & Copies of the Speeches I receive from you.

If any one should apear near the Fort, or fire upon my Warriors, I shall not only return the fire but shall throw shells about and fire Canons at them with hundred and twenty balls in each, therefore Keep off I dont want to hurt you

S: ECUYER; Captⁿ Comand^t

REVIEW QUESTIONS

1. What did Tessecumme mean when he said that his people were the only ones holding the belt? Whom did he blame for this new war that had erupted in the backcountry? Why?

2. What did he believe would end it?

3. What was the British interpretation of events?

4. What was the commander's response to Tessecumme's solution? The Indian response came when warriors attacked British forces at Bushy Run on the 5th and 6th of August.

5 ∽ FROM EMPIRE TO INDEPENDENCE

"'Tis time to part." Thomas Paine declaimed this as a matter of common sense in January 1776. But was it? How and why did so many colonists arrive at this decision? Just a dozen years earlier they had been celebrating their good fortune in belonging to the British empire. Even James Otis, who was labeled an incendiary by Lieutenant Governor Thomas Hutchinson in 1766, was still praising the British government in 1764. He wrote, "I believe there is not one man in an hundred (except in Canada) who does not think himself under the best national civil constitution in the world. . . . Their affection and reverence for their mother country is unquestionable. They yield the most chearful and ready obedience to her laws, particularly to the power of that august body the parliament of Great-Britain, the supreme legislative of the kingdom and in dominions." The events of 1765 changed his mind, as they did the sentiments of others. Insanity felled this early champion of colonists' rights by the end of the 1760s, but numerous others carried on the fight. And a fight it was, for not all the colonists rejected the mother country. Neighbors turned against neighbors as some people, who had lived through the same events and faced the same demands as those who turned rebel, continued to be loyal to those ties.

Loyalists abhorred the escalation of protest into rebellion. Many had advocated reform and resisted ministerial and parliamentary edicts throughout the 1760s and into the 1770s. But every imperial action from the Sugar Act to the Tea Act begat increasingly radical colonial reaction. Colonists were confronted time and time again with the need to make decisions as to how far they were willing to go in protesting British policy. Some consciously, and others rather unconsciously, ended up choosing revolutionary resistance. Over the same time, growing numbers of their fellow colonists reached personal political precipices over which they would not or could not jump. Whether in 1766 or 1776, when they had to choose between rebellion or supporting the sovereignty of king and Parliament, many conservative colonists chose the latter course, and then found themselves condemned as Tories while their opponents retained the name Whig, and later Patriot, for themselves.

Colonists resisted British policies for various reasons, both materialistic and nonmaterialistic, and in numerous ways. Initially their protests seemed to be grounded in economics, but in time constitutional issues (which were instrumental in the move to revolution) assumed greater importance. The colonists presented their grievances by way of petitions, boycotts, speeches, and ultimately spectacles, such as the Boston Tea Party. By the time the latter occurred in December 1773, and certainly after Parliament's punishing response the following spring, most colonists were taking a stand: some actively promoted rebellion, some advocated a self-interested or disinterested neutrality, while others profusely professed loyalty to the king and his government.

By 1774 the initiative had clearly shifted from the imperial government to the colonies. Members of Parliament, responding to the growing dissent across the Atlantic, began to concentrate on coercive tactics to bring the colonists in line, while colonists debated the possibility of creating a new system of government within—or perhaps outside of—the British empire. The radicals, some of whom had begun to call themselves Americans as well as Virginians, Pennsylvanians, and so on, sent delegates to a continental congress, which in turn considered a plan of union, endorsed the Suffolk Resolves, and adopted a Declaration of American Rights along with the Continental Association. That declaration served as an ideological defense while the association became an economic offense. The conflict continued to escalate. As the Pilgrims had removed themselves from the Church of England to escape the corruption they had perceived there, so by 1775 through 1776 did some Americans propose to remove themselves from the perceived corruption of the British government. These colonists, over a period of twelve years, had moved from agitation for reform to resistance against government acts and officials and on to a rebellion against the crown and a revolution in government.

STAMP ACT CONGRESS

FROM Declaration of Rights and Grievances of the Colonies (1765)

The king's chief minister in 1765, George Grenville, was determined to have the colonies help defray the costs of the vast empire of which they were a part. Among the various solutions he proposed, and which were enacted by Parliament, was a stamp duty. Starting in November of that year the colonists were to buy and affix stamps to all sorts of printed matter. These stamps did not represent postage fees, nor were they to help regulate trade; they were to be used simply as a way to raise money for the government from within the colonies. Although the Stamp Act was easily passed in Parliament, its implementation in the colonies was another matter altogether. In the midst of riots and other mob actions, the representative bodies of various colonial governments, such as the House of Burgesses in Virginia, met and drew up resolutions that not only denounced the act but established the constitutional argument for denying Parliament's right to tax the colonies. To send a stronger message across the Atlantic, nine of the colonies also acted in concert: their representatives met that October in New York City in what became known as the Stamp Act Congress. These delegates issued resolutions and petitions to both the king and the two houses of Parliament establishing the colonial position. The combination of both economic and ideological interests can be seen in the resolutions passed by the Stamp Act Congress in October 1765.

From *Journal of the First Congress of the American Colonies in Opposition to the Tyrannical Acts of the British Parliament, 1775* (New York, 1845), pp. 27–29.

The members of this Congress, sincerely devoted with the warmest sentiments of affection and duty to His Majesty's person and Government, inviolably attached to the present happy establishment of the Protestant succession, and with minds deeply impressed by a sense of the present and impending misfortunes of the British colonies on this continent; having considered as maturely as time will permit the circumstances of the said colonies, esteem it our indispensable duty to make the following declarations of our humble opinion respecting the most essential rights and liberties of the colonists, and of the grievances under which they labour, by reason of several late Acts of Parliament.

I. That His Majesty's subjects in these colonies owe the same allegiance to the Crown of Great Britain that is owing from his subjects born within the realm, and all due subordination to that august body the Parliament of Great Britain.

II. That His Majesty's liege subjects in these colonies are intitled to all the inherent rights and liberties of his natural born subjects within the kingdom of Great Britain.

III. That it is inseparably essential to the freedom of a people, and the undoubted right of

Englishmen, that no taxes be imposed on them but with their own consent, given personally or by their representatives.

IV. That the people of these colonies are not, and from their local circumstances cannot be, represented in the House of Commons in Great Britain.

V. That the only representatives of the people of these colonies are persons chosen therein by themselves, and that no taxes ever have been, or can be constitutionally imposed on them, but by their respective legislatures.

VI. That all supplies to the Crown being free gifts of the people, it is unreasonable and inconsistent with the principles and spirit of the British Constitution, for the people of Great Britain to grant to His Majesty the property of the colonists.

VII. That trial by jury is the inherent and invaluable right of every British subject in these colonies.

VIII. That the late Act of Parliament, entitled *An Act for granting and applying certain stamp duties, and other duties, in the British colonies and plantations in America, etc.*, by imposing taxes on the inhabitants of these colonies; and the said Act, and several other Acts, by extending the jurisdiction of the courts of Admiralty beyond its ancient limits, have a manifest tendency to subvert the rights and liberties of the colonists.

IX. That the duties imposed by several late Acts of Parliament, from the peculiar circumstances of these colonies, will be extremely burthensome and grievous; and from the scarcity of specie, the payment of them absolutely impracticable.

X. That as the profits of the trade of these colonies ultimately center in Great Britain, to pay for the manufactures which they are obliged to take from thence, they eventually contribute very largely to all supplies granted there to the Crown.

XI. That the restrictions imposed by several late Acts of Parliament on the trade of these colonies will render them unable to purchase the manufactures of Great Britain.

XII. That the increase, prosperity, and happiness of these colonies depend on the full and free enjoyments of their rights and liberties, and an intercourse with Great Britain mutually affectionate and advantageous.

XIII. That it is the right of the British subjects in these colonies to petition the King or either House of Parliament.

Lastly, That it is the indispensable duty of these colonies to the best of sovereigns, to the mother country, and to themselves, to endeavour by a loyal and dutiful address to His Majesty, and humble applications to both Houses of Parliament, to procure the repeal of the Act for granting and applying certain stamp duties, of all clauses of any other Acts of Parliament, whereby the jurisdiction of the Admiralty is extended as aforesaid, and of the other late Acts for the restriction of American commerce.

REVIEW QUESTIONS

1. Did the members of the congress deny the authority of Parliament over the colonies?
2. What did they deem to be at issue here: their duties to the government or their rights as English subjects?
3. What were their grievances?
4. Did they appear more concerned about the constitutional issues raised by this act or the possible economic repercussions? Why?

JOHN DICKINSON

FROM *Letters from a Farmer in Pennsylvania* (1767–68)

In 1767 John Dickinson, a well-educated and wealthy lawyer in his thirties, began writing the popular essays which in the following year were collected and published together as Letters from a Farmer in Pennsylvania. *Dickinson was no radical (as a member of the Second Continental Congress, he abstained in the vote for independence), but he was determined to protect his fellow colonists' rights to life, liberty, and property. In a moderate, reasonable tone, Dickinson articulated the American position against the Townshend Acts. Before he died, Charles Townshend, as Chancellor of the Exchequer, had pushed the acts through in his determination to raise money in America that could be used not only to help defray the costs of the troops in the colonies but to pay the royal officials there so that they would be independent of popular control. Dickinson outlined a reasonable program of protest but, unfortunately for the moderates in the colonies, it was doomed when expectations on both sides of the Atlantic were not met.*

From *Empire and Nation: Letters from a Farmer in Pennsylvania, John Dickinson, Letters from the Federal Farmer, Richard Henry Lee*, intro. Forrest McDonald (Englewood Cliffs, NJ: Prentice-Hall, Inc., 1962), pp. 7–20. [Editorial insertions appear in square brackets—*Ed.*]

Letter II

My dear Countrymen,

There is another late act of parliament, which appears to me to be unconstitutional, and as destructive to the liberty of these colonies, as that mentioned in my last letter; that is, the act for granting the duties on paper, glass, etc.

The parliament unquestionably possesses a legal authority to *regulate* the trade of *Great Britain*, and all her colonies. Such an authority is essential to the relation between a mother country and her colonies; and necessary for the common good of all. He who considers these provinces as states distinct from the *British Empire*, has very slender notions of *justice*, or of their *interests*. We are but parts of a *whole*; and therefore there must exist a power somewhere, to preside, and preserve the connection in due order. This power is lodged in the parliament; and we are as much dependent on *Great Britain*, as a perfectly free people can be on another.

I have looked over *every statute* relating to these colonies, from their first settlement to this time; and I find every one of them founded on this principle, till the *Stamp Act* administration. *All before*, are calculated to regulate trade, and preserve or promote a mutually beneficial intercourse between the several constituent parts of the empire; and though many of them imposed duties on trade, yet those duties were always imposed *with design* to restrain the commerce of one part, that was injurious to another, and thus to promote the general welfare. . . . Never did the *British* parliament, till the period above mentioned, think of imposing duties in *America* FOR THE PURPOSE OF RAISING A REVENUE. . . .

*   *   *

This I call an innovation: and a most dangerous innovation. It may perhaps be objected, that *Great Britain* has a right to lay what duties she pleases upon her exports, and it makes no difference to us, whether they are paid here or there.

To this I answer. These colonies require many things for their use, which the laws of *Great Britain* prohibit them from getting any where but from her. Such are paper and glass.

That we may legally be bound to pay any *general* duties on these commodities, relative to the regulation of trade, is granted; but we being *obliged by her laws* to take them from *Great Britain*, any *special* duties imposed on their exportation *to us only, with intention to raise a revenue from us only*, are as much *taxes* upon us, as those imposed by the *Stamp Act*.

What is the difference in *substance* and *right*, whether the same sum is raised upon us by the rates mentioned in the *Stamp Act*, on the *use* of paper, or by these duties, on the *importation* of it. It is only the edition of a former book, shifting a sentence from the end to the *beginning*.

*   *   *

. . . [T]he *Stamp Act* was said to be a law THAT WOULD EXECUTE ITSELF. For the very same reason, the last act of parliament, if it is granted to have any force here, WILL EXECUTE ITSELF, and will be attended with the very same consequences to *American* liberty.

Some persons perhaps may say that this act lays us under no necessity to pay the duties imposed because we may ourselves manufacture the articles on which they are laid; . . .

*   *   *

. . . But can any man, acquainted with *America*, believe this possible? I am told there are but two or three *Glass-Houses* on this continent, and but very few *Paper-Mills*; . . . This continent is a country of planters, farmers, and fishermen; not of manufacturers. . . .

Inexpressible therefore must be our distresses in evading the late acts, by the disuse of *British* paper and glass. Nor will this be the extent of our misfortune, if we admit the legality of that act.

Great Britain has prohibited the manufacturing *iron* and *steel* in these colonies, without any objection being made to her *right* of doing it. The *like* right she must have to prohibit any other manu-

facture among us. Thus she is possessed of an undisputed *precedent* on that point. This authority, she will say, is founded on the *original intention* of settling these colonies; that is, that she should manufacture for them, and that they should supply her with materials. . . .

*   *   *

Here then, my dear countrymen, ROUSE yourselves, and behold the ruin hanging over your heads. If you ONCE admit, that *Great Britain* may lay duties upon her exportations to us, *for the purpose of levying money on us only*, she then will have nothing to do, but to lay those duties on the articles which she prohibits us to manufacture—and the tragedy of *American* liberty is finished. . . . if *Great Britain* can order us to come to her for necessaries we want, and can order us to pay what taxes she pleases before we take them away, or when we land them here, we are as abject slaves as *France* and *Poland* can show in wooden shoes and with uncombed hair.[1]

*   *   *

. . . [T]he single question is, whether the parliament can legally impose duties to be paid *by the people of these colonies only*, FOR THE SOLE PURPOSE OF RAISING A REVENUE, *on commodities which she obliges us to take from her alone*, or, in other words, whether the parliament can legally take money out of our pockets, without our consent. If they can, our boasted liberty is but

> *Vox et praeterea nihil.*
> A sound and nothing else.

Letter III
My dear Countrymen,

*   *   *

. . . [T]he meaning of [these letters] is, to convince the people of these colonies that they are at this

---

[1] Dickinson remarked in a footnote that French peasants wore wooden shoes and that Polish vassals had uncombable matted hair.

moment exposed to the most imminent dangers; and to persuade them immediately, vigorously, and unanimously, to exert themselves in the most firm, but most peaceable manner, for obtaining relief.

The cause of *liberty* is a cause of too much dignity to be sullied by turbulence and tumult. It ought to be maintained in a manner suitable to her nature. Those who engage in it, should breathe a sedate, yet fervent spirit, animating them to actions of prudence, justice, modesty, bravery, humanity and magnanimity.

*   *   *

I hope, my dear countrymen, that you will, in every colony, be upon your guard against those who may at any time endeavor to stir you up, under pretenses of patriotism, to any measures disrespectful to our Sovereign, and our mother country. Hot, rash, disorderly proceedings, injure the reputation of the people as to wisdom, valor, and virtue, without procuring them the least benefit. . . .

Every government at some time or other falls into wrong measures. These may proceed from mistake or passion. But every such measure does not dissolve the obligation between the governors and the governed. The mistake may be corrected; the passion may subside. It is the duty of the governed to endeavor to rectify the mistake, and to appease the passion. They have not at first any other right, than to represent their grievances, and to pray for redress, unless an emergency is so pressing as not to allow time for receiving an answer to their applications, which rarely happens. If their applications are disregarded, then that kind of *opposition* becomes justifiable which can be made without breaking the laws or disturbing the public peace. . . .

If at length it becomes UNDOUBTED that an inveterate resolution is formed to annihilate the liberties of the governed, the *English* history affords frequent examples of resistance by force. What particular circumstances will in any future case justify such resistance can never be ascertained till they happen. Perhaps it may be allowable to say generally, that it never can be justifiable until the people

are FULLY CONVINCED that any further submission will be destructive to their happiness.

When the appeal is made to the sword, highly probable is it, that the punishment will exceed the offense; and the calamities attending on war outweigh those proceeding it. . . .

To these reflections on this subject, it remains to be added, and ought for ever to be remembered, that resistance, in the case of colonies against their mother country, is extremely different from the resistance of a people against their prince. A nation may change their king, or race of kings, and, retaining their ancient form of government, be gainers by changing. Thus *Great Britain*, under the illustrious house of *Brunswick* [Hanover], a house that seems to flourish for the happiness of mankind, has found a felicity unknown in the reigns of the *Stuarts*. But if once we are separated from our mother country, what new form of government shall we adopt, or where shall we find another *Britain* to supply our loss? Torn from the body, to which we are united by religion, liberty, laws, affections, relation, language and commerce, we must bleed at every vein.

In truth—the prosperity of these provinces is founded in their dependence on *Great Britain*; and when she returns to her "old good humor, and her old good nature," as Lord *Clarendon* expresses it, I hope they will always think it their duty and interest, as it most certainly will be, to promote her welfare by all the means in their power.

We cannot act with too much caution in our disputes. Anger produces anger; and differences, that might be accommodated by kind and respectful behavior, may, by imprudence, be enlarged to an incurable rage. . . .

The constitutional modes of obtaining relief are those which I wish to see pursued on the present occasion; that is, by petitions of our assemblies, or where they are not permitted to meet, of the people, to the powers that can afford us relief.

We have an excellent prince, in whose good dispositions toward us we may confide. We have a generous, sensible and humane nation, to whom we may apply. They may be deceived. They may, by artful men, be provoked to anger against us. I cannot believe they will be cruel and unjust; or that their anger will be implacable. Let us behave like dutiful children who have received unmerited blows from a beloved parent. Let us complain to our parent; but let our complaints speak at the same time the language of affliction and veneration.

If, however, it shall happen, by an unfortunate course of affairs, that our applications . . . prove ineffectual, let us then take *another step*, by withholding from *Great Britain* all the advantages she has been used to receive from us. . . . Let us all be united with one spirit, in one cause. . . .

REVIEW QUESTIONS

1. Why did Dickinson believe the Townshend duties to be unconstitutional?
2. How did he argue that the taxes on certain enumerated goods such as glass and paper were particularly pernicious? In forming his argument did he condemn the actor (Parliament) as well as the act?
3. Why did he, an author who was trying to persuade people to exert themselves vigorously against encroachments on their liberty, condemn those who more violently stirred up the populace?
4. Why did he want protest to be reasonable and limited? Was that a reasonable desire?

SAMUEL SEABURY

A View of the Controversy between Great Britain and her Colonies (1774)

The Reverend Samuel Seabury (1729–1796), an Anglican minister in Westchester, New York, wrote a critique of the First Continental Congress under the pseudonym, "A Westchester Farmer." A King's College student by the name of Alexander Hamilton responded with a pamphlet titled A Full Vindication of the Measures of the Congress *(New York, 1774). Seabury answered with another vigorous attack in* A View of the Controversy between Great Britain and her Colonies *(New York, 1774), which is excerpted below. In late 1775, after pamphlet battles had given way to armed ones, revolutionaries confined Seabury to New Haven, Connecticut, for a time. He then served as a chaplain to a loyalist unit. When the war ended, Seabury remained in the United States. He became the first bishop of the American Episcopal Church.*

From Leslie F. S. Upton, ed., *Revolutionary Versus Loyalist: The First American Civil War, 1774–1784* (Waltham, MA: Blaisdell Publishing Co., 1968), pp. 24–34.

I wish you had explicitly declared to the public your ideas of the *natural rights of mankind*. Man in a *state of nature* may be considered as perfectly free from all restraints of law and government: And then the *weak* must submit to the *strong*. From such a state, I confess, I have a violent aversion. I think the form of government we lately enjoyed a much more eligible state to live in: And cannot help regretting our having *lost* it, by the *equity, wisdom,* and *authority* of the Congress, who have introduced in the room of it, confusion and violence; where all must submit to the power of a mob.

You have taken some pains to prove what would readily have been granted you—that *liberty* is a very *good* thing, and *slavery* a very *bad* thing. But then I must think that liberty under a *King, Lords* and *Commons* is as good as liberty under a republican Congress: And that slavery under a republican Congress is as bad, at least, as slavery under a *King, Lords* and *Commons*: And upon the whole, that *liberty* under the supreme authority and protection of Great-Britain, is infinitely preferable to *slavery* under an American Congress. I will also agree with you, "that Americans are entitled to freedom." I will go further: I will own and acknowledge that not only *Americans,* but *Africans, Europeans, Asiaticks,* all men, of all countries and degrees, of all sizes and complexions, have a right to as much freedom as is consistent with security of civil society: And I hope you will not think me "an enemy to the *natural* rights of mankind" because I cannot wish them more. We must however remember, that more liberty may, without inconvenience, be allowed to individuals in a small government, than can be admitted of in a large empire.

But when you assert that "since then, Americans have not by any act of theirs impowered the British Parliament to make laws for them, it follows they can have no just authority to do it" you advance a position subversive of that dependence which all colonies must, from their very nature, have on the Mother Country. By the British Parliament, I suppose you mean the supreme legislative authority, the King, Lords, and Commons, because

no other authority in England has a right to make laws to bind the kingdom, and consequently no authority to make laws to bind the colonies. In this sense I shall understand, and use the phrase *British Parliament.*

Now the dependence of the colonies on the Mother Country has ever been acknowledged. It is an impropriety of speech to talk of an independent colony. The words *independency* and *colony,* convey contradictory ideas: much like *killing* and *sparing.* As soon as a colony becomes independent on its parent state it ceases to be any longer a colony; just as when you *kill* a sheep, you cease to *spare* him. The British colonies make a part of the British empire. As parts of the body they must be subject to the general laws of the body. To talk of a colony independent of the Mother Country, is no better sense than to talk of a limb independent of the body to which it belongs.

In every government there must be a supreme, absolute authority lodged somewhere. In arbitrary governments this power is in the monarch; in aristocratical governments, in the nobles; in democratical governments in the people; or the deputies of their electing. Our own government being a mixture of all these kinds, the supreme authority is vested in the King, Nobles and People, in the King, House of Lords, and House of Commons elected by the people. This supreme authority extends as far as the British dominions extend. . . .

Legislation is not an inherent right in the colonies. Many colonies have been established, and subsisted long without it. The Roman colonies had no legislative authority. It was not till the later period of their republic that the privileges of Roman citizens, among which that of voting in the assemblies of the people at Rome was a principal one, were extended to the inhabitants of Italy. All the laws of the empire were enacted at Rome. Neither their colonies, nor conquered countries had anything to do with legislation.

The position that we are bound by no laws to which we have not consented, either by ourselves, or our representatives, is a novel position, unsupported by any authoritative record of the British Constitution, ancient or modern. It is republican in its very nature, and tends to the utter subversion of the English monarchy.

This position has arisen from an artful change of terms. To say that an Englishman is not bound by any laws, but those to which the representatives of the nation have given their consent, is to say what is true: But to say that an Englishman is bound by no laws but those to which *he* hath consented in person, or by *his* representative, is saying what never was true, and never can be true. A great part of the people in England have no vote in the choice of representatives, and therefore are governed by laws to which they never consented either by *themselves* or by *their* representatives.

The right of colonists to exercise a legislative power, is no natural right. They derive it not from nature, but from the indulgence or grant of the parent state, whose subjects they were when the colony was settled, and by whose permission and assistance they made the settlement.

Upon supposition that every English colony enjoyed a legislative power independent of the parliament; and that the parliament has no just authority to make laws to bind them, this absurdity will follow—that there is no power in the British empire, which has authority to make laws for the whole empire; i.e. we have an empire, without government; or which amounts to the same thing, we have a government which has no supreme power. . . .

To talk of being liege subjects to King GEORGE, while we disavow the authority of Parliament is another piece of whiggish nonsense. I love my King as well as any whig in America or England either, and am as ready to yield him all lawful submission: But while I submit to the King, I submit to the authority of the laws of the state, whose guardian the King is. The difference between a good and bad subject, is only this, that the one obeys, the other transgresses the law. The difference between a loyal subject and a rebel, is, that the one yields obedience to, and faithfully supports the supreme authority of the state, and the other endeavours to overthrow it. If we obey the laws of the King, we obey the laws of the Parliament. If we

disown the authority of the Parliament, we disown the authority of the King. . . .

*   *   *

If it be said, that admitting the foregoing reasoning and authorities, yet the right of taxation will not follow, let it be considered, that in every government, *legislation* and *taxation*, or the right of raising a revenue, must be conjoined. If you divide them, you weaken, and finally destroy the government; for no government can long subsist without power to raise the supplies necessary for its defence and administration. It has been proved, that the supreme authority of the British empire extends over all the dominions that compose the empire. The power, or right of the British Parliament to raise such a revenue as is necessary for the defence and support of the British government, in all parts of the British dominion, is therefore incontestable. For if no government can subsist without a power to raise the revenues necessary for its support, then, in fact, no government can extend any further than its power of raising such a revenue extends. If therefore the British Parliament has no power to raise a revenue in the colonies, it has no government over the colonies, i.e., no government can support itself. . . . Government implies, not only a power of making and enforcing *laws*, but defence and protection. Now protection implies tribute. Those that share in the protection of any government, are in reason and duty, bound to maintain and support the government that protects them: . . .

There are but two objections that can reasonably be made to what has been said upon this subject. The first is, that if the British Parliament has a right to make laws to bind the whole empire, our assemblies become useless. But a little consideration will remove this difficulty.

Our assemblies, from the very nature of things, can have but a legated, subordinate, and local authority of legislation. Their power of making laws in conjunction with the other branches of the legislature, cannot extend beyond the limits of the province to which they belong. Their authority must be subordinate to the supreme authority of the nation, or there is *imperium in imperio*: two sovereign authorities in the same state; which is a contradiction. Every thing that relates to the internal policy and government of the province which they represent comes properly before them; whether they be matters of law or revenue. But all laws relative to the empire in general or to all the colonies conjunctively, or which regulates the trade of any particular colony, in order to make it compatible with the general good of the whole empire, must be left to the parliament. There is no other authority which has a *right* to make such regulations, or *weight* sufficient to carry them into execution.

Our Assemblies are also the true, proper, legal guardians of our *rights, privileges* and *liberties.* If any laws of the British parliament are thought oppressive; or if, in the administration of the British government, any unnecessary or unreasonable burthen be laid upon us, *they* are the proper persons to seek for redress: And they are the most likely to succeed, they have the legal and constitutional means in their hands. They are the *real* not the *pretended* representatives of the people. They are bodies known to and acknowledged by the public laws of the empire. Their representations will be attended to, and their remonstrances heard. . . .

*   *   *

The other objection to what has been said upon the legislative authority of the British Parliament, is this: That if the Parliament have authority to make laws to bind the whole empire;—to regulate the trade of the whole empire;—and to raise a revenue upon the whole empire; then we have nothing that we can call our own:—By the same authority that they can take a penny, they can take a pound, or all we have got.

Let it be considered, that no scheme of human policy can be so contrived and guarded, but that something must be left to the integrity, prudence, and wisdom of those who govern. We are apt to think, and I believe justly, that the British constitu-

tion is the best scheme of government now subsisting: the rights and liberties of the people are better secured by it, than by any other system now subsisting. And yet we find that the rights and liberties of Englishmen may be infringed by wicked and ambitious men. This will ever be the case, even after human sagacity has exerted its utmost ability. This is, however, no argument, that we should not secure ourselves as well as we can. It is rather an argument, that we should use our utmost endeavour to guard against the attempts of ambition or avarice.

A great part of the people in England, a considerable number of people in this province, are bound by laws, and taxed without their consent, or the consent of their representatives: for representatives they have none, unless the absurd position of a *virtual* representation be admitted. These people may object to the present mode of government. They may say, that they have nothing that they can call their own. That if they may be taxed a penny without their consent, they may be taxed a pound; and so on. You will think it a sufficient security to these people, that the representatives of the nation or province cannot hurt *them*, without hurting themselves; because, they cannot tax *them*, without taxing themselves. This security however may not be so effectual as at first may be imagined. The rich are never taxed so much in proportion to their estates as the poor: And even an equal proportion of that tax which a rich man can easily pay, may be a heavy burthen to a poor man. But the same security that these people have against being ruined by the representatives of the nation, or province where they live; the same security have we against being ruined by the British Parliament. They cannot hurt us without hurting themselves. The principal profits of our trade center in England. If they lay unnecessary or oppressive burthens on it; or any ways restrain it, so as to injure us, they will soon feel the effect, and very readily remove the cause. If this security is thought insufficient, let us endeavour to obtain a more effectual one. Let it however be remembered, that this security has been thought, and felt sufficient till within a short period; and very probably, a prudent management, and a temperate conduct on our part, would have made it permanently effectual.

But the colonies have become so considerable by the increase of their inhabitants and commerce, and by the improvement of their lands, that they seem incapable of being governed in the same lax and precarious manner as formerly. They are arrived to that mature state of manhood which requires a different, and more exact policy of ruling, than was necessary in their infancy and childhood. They want, and are entitled to, a fixed determinate constitution of their own. A constitution which shall unite them firmly with Great Britain, and with one another;—which shall mark out the line of British supremacy, and colonial dependence, giving on the one hand full force to the supreme authority of the nation over all its dominions and on the other, securing effectually the rights, liberty, and property of the colonists.—This is an event devoutly to be wished, by all good men; and which all ought to labour to obtain by all prudent, and probable means. Without obtaining this, it is idle to talk of obtaining a redress of the grievances complained of. They naturally, they necessarily result from the relation which we at present stand in to Great Britain. . . .

* * *

I will here, Sir, venture to deliver my sentiments upon the line that ought to be drawn between the supremacy of Great-Britain, and the dependency of the Colonies. And I shall do it with the more boldness, because I know it to be agreeable to the opinions of many of the warmest advocates for America both in England and in the colonies, in the time of the Stamp Act.—I imagine that if all internal taxation be vested in our own legislatures, and the right of regulating trade by duties, bounties, &c be left in the power of the Parliament; and also the right of enacting all general laws for the good of all the colonies, that we shall have all the security for our rights, liberties and property, which human policy can give us: The dependence of the colonies on the Mother Country will be fixed on a firm foundation; the sovereign authority

of Parliament, over all the dominions of the empire will be established, and the mother-country and all her colonies will be knit together, in ONE GRAND, FIRM, AND COMPACT BODY. . . .

* * *

Now what concessions can Great Britain make, that would satisfy you and your party? She has it not in her power to make any—were she even desirous of doing it, and willing to sacrifice her own honour and dignity, to gratify your humours. She has no choice but to declare the colonies independent states, or to try the force of arms, in order to bring them to a sense of their duty. This is the wretched state to which your adored Congress have reduced us, and to which they deserve the *curse* of every inhabitant of America. No alternative is left us, but either to renounce *their* measures, or to plunge head-long into rebellion and civil war. . . .

* * *

You affect on every occasion to display "the omnipotency and all-sufficiency" of those colonies which have entered into *the* solemn league and covenant against Great-Britain. You mention the considerable numbers of their men—400,000, I think your *Generalissimo* rates them at their valour, and bloody disposition in the cause of liberty. I wish you had told us what resources the colonies have, to pay, cloath, arm, feed these considerable numbers:—who are to levy the taxes necessary to defray the expense of these articles. Whether that is to be the business of the next congress.

On the other hand you always speak of Great-Britain, as of some pitiful state just sinking into obscurity. . . . Do you think, Sir, that Great Britain is like an old, wrinkled, withered, wornout hag, whom every jackanapes that truants along the streets may insult with impunity?—You will find her a vigorous matron, just approaching a green old age; and with spirit and strength sufficient to chastise her undutiful and rebellious children. Your measures have as yet produced none of the effects you look for: Great Britain is not as yet intimidated. She has already a considerable fleet and army in America: More ships and troops are expected in the spring: Every appearance indicates a design in her to support her claim with vigour. . . .

Consider, Sir, is it right to risk the valuable blessings of property, liberty and life, to the single chance of war? Of the worst kind of war—a civil war? a civil war founded on rebellion. Without ever attempting the peaceable mode of accommodation? Without ever asking a redress of our complaints, from the only power on earth who can redress them? When disputes happen between nations independent of each other, they first attempt to settle them by their ambassadors; they seldom run hastily to war, till they have tried what can be done by treaty and mediation. I would make many more concessions to a parent, than were justly due to him, rather than engage with him in a duel. But we are rushing into a war with our parent state, without offering the least concession; without even deigning to propose an accommodation. You, Sir, have employed your pen, and exerted your abilities, in vindicating and recommending measures which you know must, if persisted in, have a direct

tendency to produce and accelerate the dreadful event.

REVIEW QUESTIONS

1. What do you think of Seabury's comparing the contradiction of independency versus colony to that of killing versus sparing? What about his analogy that the British colonies are to the British empire what limbs are to the body? Consider also his example of the Roman empire. Do these comparisons help support the logic of his argument?
2. What do you believe was the strongest part of his argument? Why?
3. How did Seabury propose to resolve the problems between the colonies and the mother country?
4. Why did he believe that the Continental Congress was driving everyone into war?

LIEUTENANT COLONEL FRANCIS SMITH

FROM Report to Governor Gage (22 April 1775)

Although the Revolution began and ended in a barrage of words, military actions were a fundamental part of it: from the quartering of British troops in the colonies to the Boston Massacre; from the march on Concord to the siege at Yorktown. British soldiers and Massachusetts militiamen opened the war phase of the Revolution with an exchange of shots at Lexington and Concord in 1775.

That spring there were two governments in Massachusetts: the extralegal (the British would say illegal) Provincial Congress that held sway outside of Boston and that of the military governor, General Thomas Gage, within Boston. Although reviled as the instrument of imperial tyranny by the revolutionaries, Gage practiced considerable restraint in administering affairs in the town. The result was criticism from British troops and loyalists and rebuke from the home government. The king and his ministers wanted action: they especially wanted Gage to seize the leaders of the Provincial Congress. Gage saw that as too provocative an action given the temper of the colony and instead decided to go ahead with his own plans to seize or destroy the military stores—not private property—at Concord and thus weaken the provincial forces and display the strength of his own. Gage gave the portly and slow-moving Lieutenant Colonel Francis Smith of the Tenth Infantry command of the expedition on 18 April and then chose Major John Pitcairn of the Second Marines Regiment to act as second in command, probably in the hopes that Pitcairn would guarantee the expedition's speed and propriety in dealing with inhabitants and their property. Upon his return to Boston, Smith submitted his official written account to Gage.

From Massachusetts Historical Society, *Proceedings*, 1876, p. 350ff.

Sir,—In obedience to your Excellency's commands, I marched on the evening of the 18th inst. with the corps of grenadiers and light infantry for Concord, to execute your Excellency's orders with respect to destroying all ammunition, artillery, tents, &c, collected there, which was effected, having knocked off the trunnions of three pieces of iron ordnance, some new gun-carriages, a great number of carriage-wheels burnt, a considerable quantity of flour, some gun-powder and musket-balls, with other small articles thrown into the river. Notwithstanding we marched with the utmost expedition and secrecy, we found the country had intelligence or strong suspicion of our coming, and fired many signal guns, and rung the alarm bells repeatedly; and were informed, when at Concord, that some cannon had been taken out of the town that day, that others, with some stores, had been carried three days before, which prevented our having an opportunity of destroying so much as might have been expected at our first setting off.

I think it proper to observe, that when I had got some miles on the march from Boston, I detached six light infantry companies to march with all expedition to seize the two bridges on different roads beyond Concord. On these companies' arrival at Lexington, I understand, from the report of Major Pitcairn, who was with them, and from many officers, that they found on a green close to the road a body of the country people drawn up in military order, with arms and accoutrements, and, as appeared after, loaded; and that they had posted some men in a dwelling and Meeting-house. Our troops advanced towards them, without any intention of injuring them, further than to inquire the reason of their being thus assembled, and, if not satisfactory, to have secured their arms; but they in confusion went off, principally to the left, only one of them fired before he went off, and three or four more jumped over a wall and fired from behind it among the soldiers; on which the troops returned it, and killed several of them. They likewise fired on the soldiers from the Meeting and dwelling-houses. . . .

Rather earlier than this, on the road a countryman from behind a wall had snapped his piece at Lieutenants Adair and Sutherland, but it flashed and did not go off. After this we saw some in the woods, but marched on to Concord without anything further happening. While at Concord we saw vast numbers assembling in many parts; at one of the bridges they marched down, with a very considerable body, on the light infantry posted there. On their coming pretty near, one of our men fired on them, which they returned; on which an action ensued, and some few were killed and wounded. In this affair, it appears that, after the bridge was quitted, they scalped and otherwise ill-treated one or two of the men who were either killed or severely wounded. . . .

On our leaving Concord to return to Boston, they began to fire on us from behind the walls, ditches, trees, &c., which, as we marched, increased to a very great degree, and continued without intermission of five minutes altogether, for, I believe, upwards of eighteen miles; so that I can't think but it must have been a preconcerted scheme in them, to attack the King's troops the first favorable opportunity that offered, otherwise, I think they could not, in so short a time from our marching out, have raised such a numerous body, and for so great a space of ground. Notwithstanding the enemy's numbers, they did not make one gallant attempt during so long an action, though our men were so very much fatigued, but kept under cover.

REVIEW QUESTIONS

1. Did Smith act properly in carrying out his mission? Why or why not?
2. Did he complete his mission? Why or why not?
3. What did he offer as proof to his claim that the colonists started the various fights on the 19th?

THE MASSACHUSETTS PROVINCIAL CONGRESS

American Account of the Battle of Lexington (26 April 1775)

The Massachusetts Provincial Congress undermined Gage's civil and military powers when it established itself as the people's elected governing body and asserted its control over the militia. The Provincial Congress demonstrated its power when on 30 March, while at Concord, its members resolved to alert the military forces of the province so that whenever Gage's army moved out of Boston it could be opposed. Their precautions were generally effective, including their move out of Concord. The Provincial Congress then met at Watertown, near the troops at Cambridge, and reflected upon what had just occurred and what needed to be done next. The delegates knew that they had to disseminate an official account of the 19 April events and justify the call to arms in the escalating conflict.

From Hezekiah Niles, ed., *Principles and Acts of the Revolution* (Baltimore, 1822), pp. 434–35.

The Provincial Congress at Watertown, Massachusetts, 26 April 1775

Friends and fellow subjects—Hostilities are at length commenced in this colony by the troops under the command of general Gage, and it being of the greatest importance, that an early, true, and authentic account of this inhuman proceeding should be known to you, the congress of this colony have transmitted the same, and from want of a session of the hon. continental congress, think it proper to address you on the alarming occasion.

By the clearest depositions relative to this transaction, it will appear that on the night preceding the nineteenth of April instant, a body of the king's troops, under the command of colonel Smith, were secretly landed at Cambridge, with an apparent design to take or destroy the military and other stores, provided for the defence of this colony, and deposited at Concord—that some inhabitants of the colony, on the night aforesaid, whilst travelling peaceably on the road, between Boston and Concord, were seized and greatly abused by armed men, who appeared to be officers of general Gage's army; that the town of Lexington, by these means, was alarmed, and a company of the inhabitants mustered on the occasion—that the regular troops on their way to Concord, marched into the said town of Lexington, and the said company, on their approach, began to disperse—that, not-withstanding this, the regulars rushed on with great violence and first began hostilities, by firing on said Lexington company, whereby they killed eight, and wounded several others—that the regulars continued their fire, until those of said company, who were neither killed nor wounded, had made their escape—that colonel Smith, with the detachment then marched to Concord, where a number of provincials were again fired on by the troops, two of them killed and several wounded, before the provincials fired on them and provincials were again fired on by the troops, produced an engagement that lasted through the day, in which many of the provincials and more of the regular troops were killed and wounded.

To give a particular account of the ravages of the troops, as they retreated from Concord to Charlestown, would be very difficult if not impracticable; let it suffice to say, that a great number of the houses on the road were plundered and rendered unfit for use, several were burnt, women in child-bed were driven by the soldiery naked into the streets, old men peaceably in their houses were shot dead, and such scenes exhibited as would disgrace the annals of the most uncivilized nation.

These, brethren, are marks of ministerial vengeance against this colony, for refusing, with her sister colonies, a submission to slavery; but they have not yet detached us from our royal sovereign. We profess to be his loyal and dutiful subjects, and so hardly dealt with as we have been, are still ready, with our lives and fortunes, to defend his person, family, crown and dignity. Nevertheless, to the persecution and tyranny of his cruel ministry we will not tamely submit—appealing to Heaven for the justice of our cause, we determine to die or be free. . . .

By order,
Joseph Warren, President.

REVIEW QUESTIONS

1. What was the theme of the American account?
2. Compare this account to Smith's report. Were there any similarities or points upon which both sides agreed? What were the differences?
3. Which account do you believe to be the most accurate? Why?

THOMAS PAINE

FROM *Common Sense* (1776)

Once the first shots had been exchanged, the American reformers and radicals had to decide if they were indeed rebels (as King George had declared them) and, even more importantly, revolutionaries. Thomas Paine (1737–1809) played a major role in effecting their transformation. Paine arrived in Philadelphia in November 1774 with a history of misfortune both in work and marriage. The New World, however, offered him a fresh start, and he soon established himself as a political revolutionary. In Jan-

uary 1776, he published Common Sense, *which immediately became, using today's term, a best-seller. Hundreds of thousands of copies were sold. Americans read and debated the pamphlet: some denounced the sentiments it expressed while others embraced and acted upon them. In* Common Sense, *Paine not only provided clear, material arguments for separation, he articulated the revolutionaries' sense of mission: to be free at home and to serve as an example to the world.*

From Merrill Jensen, ed., *Tracts of the American Revolution, 1763–1776* (New York: The Bobbs-Merrill Co., Inc., 1967), pp. 418–27, 431–38, 441–46.

Thoughts, on the present State of American Affairs

*   *   *

Volumes have been written on the subject of the struggle between England and America. Men of all ranks have embarked in the controversy, from different motives, and with various designs; but all have been ineffectual, and the period of debate is closed. Arms as the last resource decide the contest; the appeal was the choice of the King, and the Continent has accepted the challenge.

*   *   *

The Sun never shined on a cause of greater worth. 'Tis not the affair of a City, a County, a Province or a Kingdom; but of a Continent—of at least one eighth part of the habitable Globe. 'Tis not the concern of a day, a year, or an age; posterity are virtually involved in the contest, and will be more or less affected even to the end of time by the proceedings now. Now is the seed time of Continental union, faith, and honour. The least fracture now, will be like a name engraved with the point of a pin on the tender rind of a young oak; the wound will enlarge with the tree, and posterity read it in full grown characters.

By referring the matter from argument to arms, a new era for politics is struck—a new method of thinking hath arisen. All plans, proposals, &c. prior to the 19th of April, i.e. to the commencement of hostilities, are like the almanacks of the last year; which tho' proper then, are superceded and useless now. Whatever was advanced by the advocates on either side of the question then, terminated in one and the same point, viz. a union with Great-Britain; the only difference between the parties, was the method of effecting it; the one proposing force, the other friendship; but it hath so far happened that the first hath failed, and the second hath withdrawn her influence.

As much hath been said of the advantages of reconciliation, which like an agreeable dream, hath passed away and left us as we were, it is but right, that we should examine the contrary side of the argument, and enquire into some of the many material injuries which these Colonies sustain, and always will sustain, by being connected with and dependant on Great-Britain. To examine that connection and dependance on the principles of nature and common sense, to see what we have to trust to if separated, and what we are to expect if dependant.

I have heard it asserted by some, that as America hath flourished under her former connection with Great-Britain, that the same connection is necessary towards her future happiness and will always have the same effect—Nothing can be more fallacious than this kind of argument: . . . America would have flourished as much, and probably much more had no European power taken any notice of her. The commerce by which she hath enriched herself are the necessaries of life, and will always have a market while eating is the custom of Europe.

But she has protected us say some. That she hath engrossed us is true, and defended the Continent at our expence as well as her own is admitted; and she would have defended Turkey

from the same motive viz. the sake of trade and dominion.

Alas! we have been long led away by ancient
prejudices and made large sacrifices to superstition. We have boasted the protection of Great
Britain, without considering, that her motive was
interest not *attachment*; that she did not protect us
from *our enemies* on *our account*, but from *her
enemies* on *her own account*, from those who had
no quarrel with us on any *other account*, and who
will always be our enemies on the *same account*.
Let Britain wave her pretensions to the Continent,
or the Continent throw off the dependance, and
we should be at peace with France and Spain
were they at war with Britain. The miseries of
Hanover last war ought to warn us against connections.

It hath lately been asserted in parliament, that
the Colonies have no relation to each other but
through the Parent Country, *i.e.* that Pennsylvania
and the Jerseys and so on for the rest, are sister
Colonies by the way of England; this is certainly a
very roundabout way of proving relationship, but
it is the nearest and only true way of proving en-
mity (or enemyship, if I may so call it.) France and
Spain never were, nor perhaps ever will be our enemies as *Americans* but as our being the *subjects of
Great Britain*.

But Britain is the parent country say some.
Then the more shame upon her conduct. Even
brutes do not devour their young, nor savages
make war upon their families; wherefore the assertion if true, turns to her reproach; but it happens
not to be true, or only partly so, and the phrase,
parent or *mother country*, hath been jesuitically
adopted by the King and his parasites, with a low
papistical design of gaining an unfair bias on the
credulous weakness of our minds. Europe and not
England is the parent country of America. This
new World hath been the asylum for the persecuted lovers of civil and religious liberty from *every
part* of Europe. Hither have they fled, not from the
tender embraces of the mother, but from the cruelty of the monster; and it is so far true of England,
that the same tyranny which drove the first emigrants from home, pursues their descendants still.

*   *   *

Much hath been said of the united strength of
Britain and the Colonies, that in conjunction they
might bid defiance to the world: But this is mere
presumption, the fate of war is uncertain, neither
do the expressions mean any thing, for this Continent would never suffer itself to be drained of inhabitants, to support the British Arms in either
Asia, Africa, or Europe.

Besides, what have we to do with setting the
world at defiance? Our plan is commerce, and that
well attended to, will secure us the peace and
friendship of all Europe, because it is the interest
of all Europe to have America a free port. Her trade
will always be a protection, and her barrenness of
gold and silver will secure her from invaders.

I challenge the warmest advocate for reconciliation, to shew, a single advantage that this Continent can reap, by being connected with Great
Britain. I repeat the challenge, not a single advantage is derived. Our corn will fetch its price in any
market in Europe and our imported goods must be
paid for buy them where we will.

But the injuries and disadvantages we sustain by
that connection, are without number, and our duty
to mankind at large, as well as to ourselves, instruct
us to renounce the alliance: because any submission
to, or dependance on Great Britain, tends directly
to involve this Continent in European wars and
quarrels. As Europe is our market for trade, we
ought to form no political connection with any part
of it. 'Tis the true interest of America, to steer clear
of European contentions, which she never can do,
while by her dependance on Britain, she is made the
make-weight in the scale of British politics.

Europe is too thickly planted with Kingdoms,
to be long at peace, and whenever a war breaks out
between England and any foreign power, the trade
of America goes to ruin, *because of her connection
with Britain*. The next war may not turn out like
the last, and should it not, the advocates for reconciliation now, will be wishing for separation then,
because neutrality in that case, would be a safer
convoy than a man of war. Every thing that is right
or reasonable pleads for separation. The blood of

the slain, the weeping voice of nature cries. 'TIS TIME TO PART. Even the distance at which the Almighty hath placed England and America, is a strong and natural proof, that the authority of the one over the other, was never the design of Heaven. The time likewise at which the Continent was discovered, adds weight to the argument, and the manner in which it was peopled encreases the force of it. The Reformation was preceded by the discovery of America as if the Almighty graciously meant to open a sanctuary to the persecuted in future years, when home should afford neither friendship nor safety.

The authority of Great Britain over this Continent is a form of Government which sooner or later must have an end: . . .

Though I would carefully avoid giving unnecessary offence, yet I am inclined to believe, that all those who espouse the doctrine of reconciliation, may be included within the following descriptions. Interested men who are not to be trusted, weak men who cannot see, prejudiced men who will not see, and a certain set of moderate men who think better of the European world than it deserves; and this last class, by an ill-judged deliberation, will be the cause of more calamities to this Continent, than all the other three.

It is the good fortune of many to live distant from the scene of present sorrow; the evil is not sufficiently brought to their doors to make them feel the precariousness with which all American property is possessed. But let our imaginations transport us for a few moments to Boston; that seat of wretchedness will teach us wisdom, and instruct us for ever to renounce a power in whom we can have no trust. The inhabitants of that unfortunate city who but a few months ago were in ease and affluence, have now no other alternative than to stay and starve, or turn out to beg. Endangered by the fire of their friends if they continue within the city, and plundered by government if they leave it. In their present condition they are prisoners without the hope of redemption, and in a general attack for their relief, they would be exposed to the fury of both armies.

Men of passive tempers look somewhat lightly over the offences of Britain, and still hoping for the best, are apt to call out: *Come, come, we shall be friends again for all this.* But examine the passions and feelings of mankind: bring the doctrine of reconciliation to the touchstone of nature, and then tell me, whether you can hereafter love, honour, and faithfully serve the power that hath carried fire and sword into your land? . . .

. . . 'Tis not in the power of England or of Europe to conquer America, if she doth not conquer herself by delay and timidity. The present winter is worth an age if rightly employed, but if lost or neglected, the whole Continent will partake of the misfortune; and there is no punishment which that man doth not deserve, be he who, or what, or where he will, that may be the means of sacrificing a season so precious and useful.

*   *   *

Every quiet method for peace hath been ineffectual. Our prayers have been rejected with disdain; and hath tended to convince us that nothing flatters vanity or confirms obstinacy in Kings more than repeated petitioning—and nothing hath contributed more, than that very measure, to make the Kings of Europe absolute. Witness Denmark and Sweden. Wherefore, since nothing but blows will do, for God's sake let us come to a final separation, and not leave the next generation to be cutting throats under the violated unmeaning names of parent and child.

To say they will never attempt it again is idle and visionary, we thought so at the repeal of the stamp-act, yet a year or two undeceived us; as well may we suppose that nations which have been once defeated will never renew the quarrel.

As to government matters 'tis not in the power of Britain to do this Continent justice: the business of it will soon be too weighty and intricate to be managed with any tolerable degree of convenience, by a power so distant from us, and so very ignorant of us; for if they cannot conquer us, they cannot govern us. To be always running three or four thousand miles with a tale or a petition, waiting four or five months for an answer, which when obtained requires five or six more to explain it in, will in a few years be looked upon as folly and childishness—There was a time when it was proper, and there is a proper time for it to cease.

Small islands not capable of protecting themselves are the proper objects for government to take under their care: but there is something very absurd, in supposing a Continent to be perpetually governed by an island. In no instance hath nature made the satellite larger than its primary planet, and as England and America with respect to each other reverse the common order of nature, it is evident they belong to different systems. England to Europe: America to itself.

*   *   *

If there is any true cause of fear respecting independance, it is because no plan is yet laid down. . . .

. . . Let a Continental Conference be held in the following manner, and for the following purpose.

A Committee of twenty six members of Congress, viz.. Two for each Colony. Two Members from each House of Assembly, or Provincial Convention; and five Representatives of the people at large, to be chosen in the capital city or town of each Province, for, and in behalf of the whole Province, by as many qualified voters as shall think proper to attend from all parts of the Province for that purpose: or if more convenient, the Representatives may be chosen in two or three of the most populous parts thereof. In this conference thus assembled, will be united the two grand principles of business, *knowledge* and *power*. The Members of Congress, Assemblies, or Conventions, by having had experience in national concerns, will be able and useful counsellors, and the whole, by being impowered by the people, will have a truly legal authority.

The conferring members being met, let their business be to frame a Continental Charter, or Charter of the United Colonies; (answering, to what is called the Magna Charta of England) fixing the number and manner of choosing Members of Congress, Members of Assembly, with their date of sitting, and drawing the line of business and jurisdiction between them: Always remembering, that our strength is Continental not Provincial. Secur-

ing freedom and property to all men, and above all things, the free exercise of religion, according to the dictates of conscience; with such other matters as is necessary for a charter to contain. Immediately after which, the said conference to dissolve, and the bodies which shall be chosen conformable to the said charter, to be the Legislators and Governors of this Continent, for the time being: Whose peace and happiness, may GOD preserve. AMEN.

*   *   *

But where say some is the King of America? I'll tell you friend, he reigns above; and doth not make havoc of mankind like the Royal Brute of Great Britain. Yet that we may not appear to be defective even in earthly honours, let a day be solemnly set a part for proclaiming the Charter; let it be brought forth placed on the Divine Law, the Word of God; let a crown be placed thereon, by which the world may know, that so far as we approve of monarchy, that in America THE LAW IS KING. For as in absolute governments the King is law, so in free countries the law ought to be king; and there ought to be no other. But lest any ill use should afterwards arise, let the Crown at the conclusion of the ceremony be demolished, and scattered among the people whose right it is.

A government of our own is our natural right: and when a man seriously reflects on the precariousness of human affairs, he will become convinced, that it is infinitely wiser and safer, to form a constitution of our own, in a cool deliberate manner, while we have it in our power, than to trust such an interesting event to time and chance. . . .

*   *   *

O ye that love mankind! Ye that dare oppose not only the tyranny but the tyrant, stand forth! Every spot of the old world is over-run with oppression. Freedom hath been hunted round the Globe. Asia and Africa have long expelled her. Europe regards her like a stranger, and England hath given her warning to depart. O! receive the fugitive, and prepare in time an asylum for mankind.

Of the Present Ability of America, With Some Miscellaneous Reflections.

*   *   *

'Tis not in numbers but in unity that our great strength lies: yet our present numbers are sufficient to repel the force of all the world. The Continent hath at this time the largest disciplined army of any power under Heaven: and is just arrived at that pitch of strength, in which no single Colony is able to support itself, and the whole, when united, is able to do any thing. . . .

*   *   *

The debt we may contract doth not deserve our regard if the work be but accomplished. No nation ought to be without a debt. A national debt is a national bond: and when it bears no interest is in no case a grievance. Britain is oppressed with a debt of upwards of one hundred and forty millions sterling, for which she pays upwards of four millions interest. And as a compensation for her debt, she has a large navy; America is without debt, and without a navy; but for the twentieth part of the English national debt, could have a navy as large again. . . .

No country on the globe is so happily situated, or so internally capable of raising a fleet as America. Tar, timber, iron, and cordage are her natural produce. We need go abroad for nothing. Whereas the Dutch, who make large profits by hiring out their ships of war to the Spaniards and Portuguese, are obliged to import most of the materials they use. We ought to view the building a fleet as an article of commerce, it being the natural manufactory of this country. 'Tis the best money we can lay out. A navy when finished is worth more than it cost: And is that nice point in national policy, in which commerce and protection are united. Let us build; if we want them not, we can sell; and by that means replace our paper currency with ready gold and silver.

*   *   *

In point of safety, ought we to be without a fleet? We are not the little people now, which we were sixty years ago, at that time we might have trusted our property in the streets, or fields rather, and slept securely without locks or bolts to our doors and windows. The case now is altered, and our methods of defence, ought to improve with our encrease of property. . . .

Another reason why the present time is preferable to all others is, that the fewer our numbers are, the more land there is yet unoccupied, which instead of being lavished by the king on his worthless dependants, may be hereafter applied, not only to the discharge of the present debt, but to the constant support of government. No nation under Heaven hath such an advantage as this.

The infant state of the Colonies, as it is called, so far from being against, is an argument in favour of independance. We are sufficiently numerous, and were we more so, we might be less united. 'Tis a matter worthy of observation, that the more a country is peopled, the smaller their armies are. In military numbers the ancients far exceeded the moderns: and the reason is evident, for trade being the consequence of population, men become too much absorbed thereby to attend to any thing else. Commerce diminishes the spirit both of Patriotism and military defence. And history sufficiently informs us that the bravest achievements were always accomplished in the non-age of a nation. With the encrease in commerce, England hath lost its spirit. . . .

Youth is the seed time of good habits as well in nations as in individuals. It might be difficult, if not impossible to form the Continent into one Government half a century hence. The vast variety of interests occasioned by an increase of trade and population would create confusion. Colony would be against Colony. Each being able would scorn each others assistance: and while the proud and foolish gloried in their little distinctions, the wise would lament that the union had not been formed before. Wherefore, the present time is the true time for establishing it. The intimacy which is contracted in infancy, and the friendship which is formed in misfortune, are of all others, the most lasting and unalterable. Our present union is marked with both these characters: we are young and we have been distressed; but our concord hath withstood our troubles, and fixes a memorable Æra for posterity to glory in.

The present time likewise, is that peculiar time, which never happens to a nation but once, viz. the time of forming itself into a government. Most nations have let slip the opportunity, and by that means have been compelled to receive laws from their conquerors, instead of making laws for themselves. . . .

* * *

To conclude, however strange it may appear to some, or however unwilling they may be to think so, matters not, but many strong and striking reasons may be given to shew, that nothing can settle our affairs so expeditiously as an open and determined declaration for independence. Some of which are,

First—It is the custom of Nations when any two are at war, for some other powers not engaged in the quarrel, to step in as mediators and bring about the preliminaries of a peace: But while America calls herself the subject of Great Britain, no power however well disposed she may be, can offer her mediation. Wherefore in our present state we may quarrel on for ever.

Secondly—It is unreasonable to suppose, that France or Spain will give us any kind of assistance, if we mean only to make use of that assistance, for the purpose of repairing the breach, and strengthening the connection between Britain and America; because, those powers would be sufferers by the consequences.

Thirdly—While we profess ourselves the subjects of Britain, we must in the eye of foreign nations be considered as Rebels. The precedent is some-what dangerous to their peace, for men to be in arms under the name of subjects: we on the spot can solve the paradox; but to unite resistance and subjection, requires an idea much too refined for common understanding.

Fourthly—Were a manifesto to be published and dispatched to foreign Courts, setting forth the miseries we have endured, and the peaceable methods we have ineffectually used for redress, declaring at the same time, that not being able any longer to live happily or safely, under the cruel disposition of the British Court, we had been driven to the necessity of breaking off all connections with her; at the same time, assuring all such Courts, of our peaceable disposition towards them, and of our desire of entering into trade with them: such a memorial would produce more good effects to this Continent, than if a ship were freighted with petitions to Britain.

Under our present denomination of British Subjects, we can neither be received nor heard abroad: the custom of all Courts is against us, and will be so, until by an independance we take rank with other nations.

These proceedings may at first appear strange and difficult, but like all other steps which we have already passed over, will in a little time become familiar and agreeable: and until an independance is declared, the Continent will feel itself like a man who continues putting off some unpleasant business from day to day, yet knows it must be done, hates to set about it, wishes it over, and is continually haunted with the thoughts of its necessity.

FINIS

REVIEW QUESTIONS

1. What did Paine say were some of the "material injuries" the colonies had sustained due to their dependence on Great Britain? What are the strengths and weaknesses in his argument?
2. Was Paine right to say that "Europe and not England is the parent country of America"? Why should that concept be considered a factor for separation?
3. What interests could America better pursue if independent?
4. What did Paine say would guarantee American success? Why?
5. Why did he argue for a declaration of independence and for immediate action?

THOMAS JEFFERSON

FROM *Declaration of Independence* (1776)

Thomas Jefferson (1743–1826), a Virginia planter and lawyer who emerged from the Revolution renowned as an American statesman and philosopher, levied his first major charge against the British government when he wrote A Summary View of the Rights of British America *in 1774. While arguing against Parliament's power, however, he still promoted allegiance to the king. Two years later he advocated the severance of that tie. After Richard Henry Lee, a delegate from Virginia to the Continental Congress, made the resolution that the colonies were and had the right to be independent states, the congress created a committee to draft a declaration to that effect. The committee, in turn, handed over the task to the person they believed most suited to it: Jefferson. A product of his period and place, Jefferson wrote later in 1825 that in the* Declaration of Independence *he had attempted to produce "an expression of the American Mind." Other congressional delegates had their own interpretations and agendas, however, and insisted on alterations. Jefferson recorded the changes that were made to the draft he submitted by underlining and sometimes bracketing what the delegates omitted and showing what they added in the margins.*

From Julian P. Boyd, ed., *The Papers of Thomas Jefferson*, vol. 1 (Princeton: Princeton University Press, 1950), pp. 315–19. This selection is a draft document with congressional alterations in Jefferson's "Notes of Proceedings."

A Declaration by the representatives of the United states of America, in <u>General</u> Congress assembled.

When in the course of human events it becomes necessary for one people to dissolve the political bands which have connected them with another, and to assume among the powers of the earth the separate & equal station to which the laws of nature and of nature's god entitle them, a decent respect to the opinions of mankind requires that they should declare the causes which impel them to the separation.

We hold these truths to be self evident: that all men are created equal; that they are endowed by their creator with ∧ <u>inherent and</u> inalienable rights; that among   ∧ certain these are life, liberty & the pursuit of happiness: that to secure these rights, governments are instituted among men, deriving their just powers from the conesent of the governed; that whenever any form of government becomes destructive of these ends, it is the right of the people to alter or to abolish it, & to institute new government, laying it's foundation on such principles, & organising it's powers in such form, as to them shall seem most likely to effect their safety & happiness. prudence indeed will dictate that governments long established should not be changed for light & transient causes; and accordingly all experience hath shewn that mankind are more disposed to suffer while evils are sufferable than to right them-

selves by abolishing the forms to which they are accustomed. but when a long train
of abuses & usurpations [begun at a distinguished period and] pursuing invariably the same object, evinces a design to reduce them under absolute despotism it
is their right, it is their duty to throw off such government, & to provide new
guards for their future security. such has been the patient sufferance of these
colonies; & such is now the necessity which constrains them to ∧ [expunge] their   ∧ alter
former systems of government. the history of the present king of Great Britain is
a history of ∧ [unremitting] injuries & usurpations, [among which appears no   ∧ repeated
solitary fact to contradict the uniform tenor of the rest but all have] ∧ in direct   ∧ all having
object the establishment of an absolute tyranny over these states. to prove this let
facts be submitted to a candid world [for the truth of which we pledge a faith yet
unsullied by falsehood.]

King only

he has refused his assent to laws the most wholsome & necessary for the public good.

he has forbidden his governors to pass laws of immediate & pressing importance, unless suspended in their operation till his assent should be obtained; &
when so suspended, he has utterly neglected to attend to them.

he has refused to pass other laws for the accomodation of large districts of people, unless those people would relinquish the right of representation in the legislature, a right inestimable to them, & formidable to tyrants only.

he has called together legislative bodies at places unusual, uncomfortable, and
distant from the depository of their public records, for the sole purpose of fatiguing them into compliance with his measures.

he has dissolved representative houses repeatedly [& continually] for opposing
with manly firmness his invasions on the rights of the people.

he has refused for a long time after such dissolutions to cause others to be
elected, whereby the legislative powers, incapable of annihilation, have returned
to the people at large for their exercise, the state remaining in the mean time
exposed to all the dangers of invasion from without & convulsions within.

he has endeavored to prevent the population of these states; for that purpose
obstructing the laws for naturalization of foreigners, refusing to pass others to encourage their migrations hither, & raising the conditions of new appropriations of
lands.

he has ∧ [suffered] the administration of justice [totally to cease in some of   ∧ obstructed
these states] ∧ refusing his assent to laws for establishing judiciary powers.   ∧ by

he has made [our] judges dependant on his will alone, for the tenure of their
offices, & the amount & paiment of their salaries.

he has erected a multitude of new offices [by a self assumed power] and sent
hither swarms of new officers to harrass our people and eat out their substance.

he has kept among us in times of peace standing armies [and ships of war]
without the consent of our legislatures.

he has affected to render the military independant of, & superior to the civil
power.

he has combined with others to subject us to a jurisdiction foreign to our constitutions & unacknoleged by our laws, giving his assent to their acts of pretended

King and Parliament

legislation for quartering large bodies of armed troops among us; for protecting them by a mock-trial from punishment for any murders which they should commit on the inhabitants of these states; for cutting off our trade with all parts of the world; for imposing taxes on us without our consent; for depriving us ∧ of the benefits of trial by jury; for transporting us beyond seas to be tried for pretended offences; for abolishing the free system of English laws in a neighboring province, establishing therein an arbitrary government, and enlarging it's boundaries, so as to render it at once an example and fit instrument for introducing the same absolute rule into these ∧ [states]; for taking away our charters, abolishing our most valuable laws, and altering fundamentally the forms of our governments; for suspending our own legislatures, & declaring themselves invested with power to legislate for us in all cases whatsoever.

  ∧ in many cases

  ∧ colonies

  he has abdicated government here ∧ [underline]withdrawing his governors, and declaring us out of his allegiance & protection[/underline]]

  ∧ by declaring us out of his protection & waging war against us.

  he has plundered our seas, ravaged our coasts, burnt our towns, & destroyed the lives of our people.

  he is at this time transporting large armies of foreign mercenaries to compleat the works of death, desolation & tyranny already begun with circumstances of cruelty and perfidy ∧ unworthy the head of a civilized nation.

  ∧ scarcely paralleled in the most barbarous ages, & totally

  he has constrained our fellow citizens taken captive on the high seas to bear arms against their country, to become the executioners of their friends & brethren, or to fall themselves by their hands.

  he has ∧ endeavored to bring on the inhabitants of our frontiers the merciless Indian savages, whose known rule of warfare is an undistinguished destruction of all ages, sexes, & conditions [of existence.]

  ∧ excited domestic insurrections amongst us, & has

  [he has incited treasonable insurrections of our fellow-citizens, with the allurements of forfeiture & confiscation of our property.

  he has waged cruel war against human nature itself, violating it's most sacred rights of life and liberty in the persons of a distant people who never offended him, captivating & carrying them into slavery in another hemisphere or to incur miserable death in their transportation thither. this piratical warfare, the opprobrium of *infidel* powers, is the warfare of the *Christian* king of Great Britain. determined to keep open a market where *Men* should be bought & sold, he has prostituted his negative for suppressing every legislative attempt to prohibit or to restrain this execrable commerce. and that this assemblage of horrors might want no fact of distinguished die, he is now exciting those very people to rise in arms among us, and to purchase that liberty of which he has deprived them, by murdering the people on whom he also obtruded them: thus paving off former crimes committed against the *Liberties* of one people, with crimes which he urges them to commit against the *lives* of another.]

  In every stage of these oppressions we have petitioned for redress in the most humble terms: our repeated petitions have been answered only by repeated injuries. a prince whose character is thus marked by every act which may define a tyrant is unfit to be the ruler of a ∧ people [who mean to be free. future ages will scarcely believe that the hardiness of one man adventured, within the short com-

  ∧ free

pass of twelve years only, to lay a foundation so broad & so undisguised for tyranny over a people fostered & fixed in principles of freedom.]

Nor have we been wanting in attentions to our British brethren. we have warned them from time to time of attempts by their legislature to extend ∧ [a] ju-risdiction over ∧ [these our states.] we have reminded them of the circumstances of our emigration & settlement here, [no one of which could warrant so strange a pretension: that these were effected at the expence of our own blood & treasure, unassisted by the wealth or the strength of Great Britain: that in constituting in-deed our several forms of government, we had adopted one common king, thereby laying a foundation for perpetual league & amity with them: but that submission to their parliament was no part of our constitution, nor ever in idea, if history may be credited: and,] we ∧ appealed to their native justice and magnanimity ∧ [as well as to] the ties of our common kindred to disavow these usurpations which ∧ [were likely to] interrupt our connection and correspondence. they too have been deaf to the voice of justice & of consanguinity, [and when occasions have been given them, by the regular course of their laws, of removing from their councils the dis-turbers of our harmony, they have, by their free election, re-established them in power. at this very time too they are permitting their chief magistrate to send over not only souldiers of our common blood, but Scotch & foreign mercenaries to in-vade & destroy us. these facts have given the last stab to agonizing affection, and manly spirit bids us to renounce for ever these unfeeling brethren. we must en-deavor to forget our former love for them, and to hold them as we hold the rest of mankind enemies in war, in peace friends. we might have been a free and a great people together; but a communication of grandeur & of freedom it seems is below their dignity. be it so, since they will have it. the road to happiness & to glory is open to us too. we will tread it apart from them, and] ∧ acquiesce in the necessity which denounces our [eternal] separation ∧ !

∧ an unwarrantable

∧ us

∧ have
∧ and we have conjured them by
∧ would inevitably

∧ we must therefore
∧ and hold them as we hold the rest of mankind, ene-mies in war, in peace friends.

We therefore the representatives of the United states of America in General Congress assembled do in the name, & by the authority of the good people of these [states reject & renounce all allegiance & subjection to the kings of Great Britain & all others who may hereafter claim by, through or under them: we utterly dissolve all political connection which may heretofore have subsisted between us & the people or parlia-ment of Great Britain: & finally we do assert & declare these colonies to be free & independant states,] & that as free & independant states, they

We therefore the representatives of the United states of America in Gen-eral Congress assembled, appealing to the supreme judge of the world for the rectitude of our intentions, do in the name, & by the authority of the good people of these colonies, solemnly publish & declare that these United colonies are & of right ought to be free & independant states; that they are absolved from all allegiance to the British crown, and that all political connection between them & the state of Great Britain is, & ought to be, to-tally dissolved; & that as free & inde-pendant states they have full power to have full power to levy war, conclude peace, contract alliances, establish commerce, & to do all other acts & things which independant states may of right do. and for the support of this declaration we mutually pledge to each other our lives, our fortunes & our sacred honour.

levy war, conclude peace, contract alliances, establish commerce & to do all other acts & things which independant states may of right do. and for the support of this declaration, with a firm reliance on the protection of divine providence we mutually pledge to each other our lives, our fortunes & our sacred honour.

REVIEW QUESTIONS

1. What were the charges against the king? Why were most of the condemnations addressed against him?
2. How did Jefferson's interpretation of the American mind differ from that presented by the Continental Congress via its alterations? Which version appears to be the harsher condemnation of the British government and people? Why?
3. What does this difference suggest about American perceptions and feelings towards the mother country?
4. What is distinctive about the approved concluding paragraph versus the one proposed by Jefferson? What does this difference reveal about the original author and those who altered his document?
5. How did the declaration justify independence?
6. Is this a document of construction as well as destruction? How so?
7. Does it reveal one unified nation and people or a group of states and peoples working together?

6 ✑ THE AMERICAN REVOLUTION

The American Revolution began when colonists protested English acts that infringed upon the privileges granted them as British subjects. These protests became rebellion as the issue of privileges quickly became one of rights. As James Thacher, a young physician, wrote one January day in 1775, "In no country . . . is the love of liberty more deeply rooted, or the knowledge of the rights inherent to freemen more generally diffused, or better understood, than among the British American Colonies." Although loyal British subjects both in mother country and colonies could point out the benefits of living under the British constitution, once the discontented colonists determined that a corrupt imperial government threatened their natural rights, as well as their privileges as citizens, the resistance movement exploded into both a revolution and a war for independence.

It was a thrilling, multidimensional revolution, for in the course of destroying the fetters of empire and forging new national bonds, the revolutionaries grappled with novel ideas and institutions. They did not act upon or implement everything that was proposed, nor was everything that was initiated successful, but it was an exhilarating, exasperating, and sometimes scary time of experimentation.

There were revolutionaries of all sorts active in all facets of change—political, military, and social. Political revolutionaries lambasted loyalists and lauded separatists in their struggle for the allegiance of Americans. They also bickered, dickered, and philosophized their way through the establishment of new state and national governments. Militaristic revolutionaries focused their minds and might on winning the War for American Independence. Whether serving in the Continental Army or the state regiments and militia, they battled against foreign and domestic enemies. These two groups of revolutionaries, after many setbacks, met with success, but success brought with it both questions and challenges. Many of those challenges were delivered by those who also wanted to see a societal revolution. Social revolutionaries, from those who had only begun to question *established hierarchies and conventions to those who wanted to overthrow them, presented some of the most troublesome issues of the era. While they helped initiate some changes—as soon seen in wider suffrage, an increase in private manumissions, the abolition of slavery in some states, and a greater separation between church and state—they did not meet with the same success as the other revolutionaries.*

A major issue confronting the revolutionaries was how to act upon the words that initiated and described the new world they wanted to create. They voted in new state constitutions and governments; they took up arms to ensure independence; but many stopped short—some in humorous disbelief and others in horror—when some of their associates grabbed hold of the words and applied them literally and liberally. To many revolutionaries the formation of a republic based on the notion that all free, white, adult males were legally and politically equal was quite radical enough. Indeed, they were right—it was a radical change from what was practiced in most of the world. But others argued for a new order in that new world: for all men to be equal, neither creed nor color must matter. If "men" meant humankind, then gender must be irrelevant. But in this case, at that time, such a definition was too demanding: most revolutionaries were unable or unwilling to free themselves of the social and cultural constraints by which they defined their world. Even so, the words remained, and were—and are— dynamic elements of revolution in American history.

THOMAS PAINE

FROM *The American Crisis,* Number 1 (1776)

Thomas Paine, who in January 1776 had published the pamphlet Common Sense *that rallied Americans to revolution, set his hand to rallying them to war in December. Paine had marched with the American forces as they fought the British army in New York and New Jersey late that summer and into the fall. The Americans did not do well: they were battered and bloodied in the various battles and retreats from Long Island on 27 August to Fort Lee in New Jersey on 20 November. General Washington ordered that Paine's call to arms be read to the troops as they readied themselves for action against the Hessians in Trenton.*

From Thomas Paine, *Collected Writings* (New York: Literary Classics of the United States, 1995), pp. 91–99.

December 19, 1776

These are the times that try men's souls: The summer soldier and the sunshine patriot will, in this crisis, shrink from the service of his country; but he that stands it NOW, deserves the love and thanks of man and woman. Tyranny, like hell, is not easily conquered; yet we have this consolation with us, that the harder the conflict, the more glorious the triumph. What we obtain too cheap, we esteem too lightly:—'Tis dearness only that gives every thing its value. Heaven knows how to set a proper price upon its goods; and it would be strange indeed, if so celestial an article as FREEDOM should not be highly rated. Britain, with an army to enforce her tyranny, has declared, that she has a right (*not only to* TAX) but "*to* BIND *us in* ALL CASES WHATSOEVER," and if being *bound in that manner* is not slavery, then is there not such a thing as slavery upon earth. Even the expression is impious, for so unlimited a power can belong only to GOD.

*   *   *

I have as little superstition in me as any man living, but my secret opinion has ever been, and still is, that GOD almighty will not give up a people to military destruction, or leave them unsupportedly to perish, who had so earnestly and so repeatedly sought to avoid the calamities of war, by every decent method which wisdom could invent. Neither have I so much of the infidel in me, as to suppose, that HE has relinquished the government of the world, and given us up to the care of devils; and as I do not, I cannot see on what grounds the king of Britain can look up to heaven for help against us: A common murderer, a highwayman, or a housebreaker, has as good a pretence as he.

*   *   *

I shall conclude this paper with some miscellaneous remarks on the state of our affairs; and shall begin with asking the following question, Why is it that the enemy hath left the New-England provinces, and made these middle ones the seat of war? The answer is easy: New-England is not infested with Tories, and we are. I have been tender in raising the cry against these men, and used numberless arguments to shew them their danger, but it will not do to sacrifice a world to either their folly or their baseness. The period is now arrived, in which either they or we must change our sentiments, or one or both must fall. And what is a Tory? Good GOD! what is he? I should not be afraid to go with a hundred Whigs against a thousand Tories, were they to attempt to get into arms. Every Tory is a coward, for a servile, slavish, self-interested fear is the foundation of Toryism; and a man under such influence, though he may be cruel, never can be brave.

But before the line of irrecoverable separation be drawn between us, let us reason the matter together: Your conduct is an invitation to the enemy, yet not one in a thousand of you has heart enough to join him. Howe is as much deceived by you as the American cause is injured by you. He expects you will all take up arms, and flock to his standard with muskets on your shoulders. Your opinions are of no use to him, unless you support him personally; for 'tis soldiers, and not Tories, that he wants.

I once felt all that kind of anger, which a man ought to feel, against the mean principles that are held by the Tories: A noted one, who kept a tavern at Amboy, was standing at his door, with as pretty a child in his hand, about eight or nine years old, as most I ever saw, and after speaking his mind as freely as he thought was prudent, finished with this unfatherly expression, "*Well! give me peace in my day.*" Not a man lives on the Continent but fully believes that a seperation must some time or other finally take place, and a generous parent would have said, "*If there must be trouble, let it be in my day, that my child may have peace;*" and this single reflection, well applied, is sufficient to awaken every man to duty. . . .

America did not, nor does not, want force; but she wanted a proper application of that force. Wisdom is not the purchase of a day, and it is no wonder that we should err at first sitting off. From an excess of tenderness, we were unwilling to raise an army, and trusted our cause to the temporary defence of a well meaning militia. A summer's experience has now taught us better; yet with those troops, while they were collected, we were able to set bounds to the progress of the enemy, and, thank GOD! they are again assembling. I always considered a militia as the best troops in the world for a sudden exertion, but they will not do for a long campaign. . . .

. . . I call not upon a few, but upon all; not on THIS State or THAT State, but on EVERY State; up and help us; lay your shoulders to the wheel; better have too much force than too little, when so great an object is at stake. Let it be told to the future world, that in the depth of winter, when nothing but hope and virtue could survive, that the city and the country, alarmed at one common danger, came forth to meet and to repulse it. . . .

There are cases which cannot be overdone by language, and this is one. There are persons too who see not the full extent of the evil that threatens them; they solace themselves with hopes that the enemy, if they succeed, will be merciful. It is the madness of folly to expect mercy from those who have refused to do justice; and even mercy, where conquest is the object, is only a trick of war: The cunning of the fox is as murderous as the violence of the wolfe; and we ought to guard equally against both. Howe's first object is partly by threats and partly by promises, to terrify or seduce the people to deliver up their arms, and receive mercy. The ministry recommended the same plan to Gage, and this is what the Tories call making their peace; *"a peace which passeth all understanding"* indeed! . . .

I thank GOD that I fear not. I see no real cause for fear. I know our situation well, and can see the way out of it. While our army was collected, Howe dared not risk a battle, and it is no credit to him that he decamped from the White Plains, and waited a mean opportunity to ravage the defenceless Jersies; but it is great credit to us, that, with a handful of men, we sustained an orderly retreat for near an hundred miles, brought off our ammunition, all our field-pieces, the greatest part of our stores, and had four rivers to pass. None can say that our retreat was precipitate, for we were near three weeks in performing it, that the country might have time to come in. Twice we marched back to meet the enemy and remained out till dark. The sign of fear was not seen in our camp, and had not some of the cowardly and disaffected inhabitants spread false alarms thro' the country, the Jersies had never been ravaged. Once more we are again collected and collecting; our new army at both ends of the Continent is recruiting fast, and we shall be able to open the next campaign with sixty thousand men, well armed and cloathed. This is our situation, and who will may know it. By perseverance and fortitude we have the prospect of a glorious issue; by cowardice and submission, the sad choice of a variety of evils—a ravaged country—a depopulated city—habitations without safety, and slavery without hope—our homes turned into barracks and baudy-houses for Hessians, and a future race to provide for whose fathers we shall doubt of. Look on this picture, and weep over it!—and if there yet remains one thoughtless wretch who believes it not, let him suffer it unlamented.

REVIEW QUESTIONS

1. Who were the summer soldiers and sunshine patriots?
2. How did Paine define Tories? Why did he bring them up here?
3. What reasons did Paine give Americans to convince them that they must fight? What proof did he present that they would succeed?
4. Was Paine convincing in his argument that this was a just war?

JOHN BRYAN

FROM A Revolutionary Soldier's Pension Applications (1832, 1837)

John Bryan appeared before the justices of the court of Albany, New York, on 6 September 1832 to declare that he had been a soldier for over twenty-four months during the War for American Independence. Bryan did this so as to apply for a pension under the Service-Pension Act passed by Congress in June 1832. This act did not require the applicant to prove disability or poverty as did earlier acts; it did, however, require that applicants show proof of at least two years service in the Continental Army, state troops, or militia to qualify for a full pension. Veterans who served less than two years but over six months could qualify for a partial pension. Bryan applied on the basis of his service in the state militia, during which he engaged in the bitter partisan warfare that roiled the countryside outside New York City and into Connecticut and New Jersey. The Pension Office rejected Bryan's 1832 application because he was able to establish only three months of service in the 1780 levies. Bryan gathered more evidence and witnesses and tried again in 1837 and 1845. Those who wrote reference letters for him said that he was a respectable inhabitant and good citizen.

From John Bryan, Pension Applications, R1379, *Revolutionary War Pension and Bounty-Land-Warrant Application Files*, Records of the Veterans Administration, Record Group 15, National Archives (reel 388, microfilm, David Library of the American Revolution). [Editorial insertions appear in square brackets—*Ed.*]

I was born in the City of New York, on the 4th July 1765: I lost my Father when I was about 4 years old; In the fall of 1774 I went to live with Alsop & James Hunt, brothers, Leather Dressers, then living in Queen Street (Now Pearl) in the City of New York; they were good whigs: When Genl. Washington left Long Island, they left New York, and took me with them, and went to West Farms; but the British landing on Throgs Neck, and likely to cut us off, we retired to White Plains, the enemy close on our rear, we moved to North Castle & from thence to Pound Ridge, when in 1778 the enemy followed us and burn't and destroyed every thing we had left; the brothers dissolved partnership and

James Hunt was appointed one of the Commissioners of Sequestration for the County of Westchester & entered on the duties of his office and took me with him; we were sometimes in one place and sometimes in another, till the Spring of 1780 when he took a Tory farm in a place then called A[me?] Walk, about 9 miles east of Peekskill, that one Griffin Corey had left and gone to the enemy; the winter of 1779–80 was very severe and the enemy had been locked up in New York; and as soon as the spring opened they began to make incursions into the country with Delanceys Light Horse and rob & murder every one that came in their way, the lines being unguarded the last of March or beginning of April, the Militia was ordered out to guard the lines; I was then not 15 years old till the coming 4th July: I was enrolled in Col. Samuel Drakes Regiment and took my tour of duty on the lines under the command of Lieut. Elisha Scott a very brave and useful officer, we were on the lines about 20 days during which time I suffered the greatest hardships of hunger fatigue and cold and not being more than 6 hours in one place during the whole time; being on the march, patrolling the country continually[.] Lieut. Scotts command consisted of about 20 men among whom I remember well was my friend Isaac Lawson[,] we were relieved by another detachment and returned home for a few days, but was continually on the alarm and had to watch our horses and Cattle every night, so that it may be said we were continually on duty, things continued in this way till some time in July, when it was ordered that . . . a company of 100 men raised to guard the lines the company was raised and the command given to Capt. Benjamin Stevens and Lieut. Peacock a Virginian, a very fine soldier and a gentleman[.] I was one of this company and my friend Isaac Lawson was also one of the company, and the only one of the officers or men I believe now alive, as soon as we were mustered we were marched in to the lines, we were stationed no where and every where we were continually on the Reconnoitre for nearly 4 months till the weather became so cold we could not keep the field any longer without shelter. I was on the quarter guard at Col. Jamieson's Head quarters at Doct. Flemings house a little below Bedford when Maj. Andre was taken and brought to Head quarters. Col Jamieson was not in his quarters, but I saw Capt. Hoogland receive Maj. Andre and saw his first salutation and sign of distress. During the remainder of the war I was continually on the alert under arms almost every day till the peace of 1783 since which time to the present day I have been an uniform Republican and a sincer friend to Republican men and measures. In the late war with England [War of 1812] I was one of six or seven who projected and raised at private expense a Volunteer Regiment chose the officers and had them Brevetted by Governor Topkins. Col John Mills commanded the Regiment and fell nobly fighting in his countrys cause at Sacketts Harbor. I with others contributed to the relief of the Niagara Sufferers. . . . I am an old man 67 on 4th July last, I want but little for myself and shall not want that little long[.]

*   *   *

[On 10 February 1837, Bryan appeared before a commissioner of deeds, Albany, NY, to give a supplementary statement.] In addition to the above brief sketch of my life and my military services in the Revolutionary War I can only add I was in Col. Samuel Drakes Regiment of Militia in the County of Westchester and State of New York from April 1780 to March 1783 and that I was in actual service under his command two years of that time as a private, it must be observed I was an apprentice and whatever vouchers there might have been, they were all in my masters hands as will be seen by a certified copy of an order given him in New York after peace, it was found by accident in the Comptrollers office of this State: [That certified copy read: "Sir Please to pay the Bearer Mr James Hunt or his order the amount of my wages for three months service as a soldier in the Levies raised by the authority of the state of New York under the command of Capt. Benjn. Stevenson in the year one thousand seven hundred and eighty, I having received value of him for the same and his receipt shall be a discharge from your humble servant New York May 28. 1784 John Bryan[."]] I think it very probable Mr Hunt had in his hands many papers that would fully demonstrate my services in the Revolution but he has been long dead and his papers gone or lost, so that it is impossible at this length of time to tell any thing about them as to the true periods of the War in which I served, . . . as to the nature of my services, we were what was called minute men and as we lived on the lines we were called on every few days for some services or other, we were sometimes commanded by one officer and sometimes by another, very often by the guides, as they were called, they were men under the pay of the Continental Congress in whom great confidence was placed, we were ordered on secret expeditions under their command for six, ten and fifteen days at a time and when the party returned another took its place. [I]n the year eighty two, I was detached with others to join a small detachment of continental troops to guard a depot of provisions we were under the command of a sergeant for six months before the provisions were all removed and a very important service it was to my country for had it not been for our vigilance the provisions would have all been destroyed by the Tories[.]

REVIEW QUESTIONS

1. What image does Bryan present of life in the New York City area after the British took the city?
2. What was the mission of the militia in this area? Why did it have that mission?
3. What tasks did Bryan perform?
4. Was Bryan a "free man" when he served in the militia? Did he represent the citizen-soldier?

LUDWIG VON CLOSEN

FROM The Yorktown Campaign and Siege (July–October 1781)

After battles at Freeman's Farm (19 September) and Bemis' Heights (7 October), British General John Burgoyne surrendered his army at Saratoga on 17 October 1777. The American success led to an alliance with France. Baron Ludwig von Closen served with the French troops that were sent to assist the Americans against France's old enemy. The baron was an enthusiastic observer of the American scene, leaving a detailed journal that brimmed with descriptions of the country and its citizens as well as of the armies and their exploits. Confident of himself, he was quite free in his opinions, whether they were of praise or condemnation. The major allied campaign, in which both American and French troops worked closely together, was that of Yorktown in 1781. The French troops under the Comte de Rochambeau marched with Washington's main army down to the Chesapeake Bay where they, in turn, would be supported by the French fleet under the command of Admiral comte de Grasse. Their plan was to defeat the army commanded by General Charles Cornwallis.

From Ludwig von Closen, *The Revolutionary Journal of Baron Ludwig von Closen, 1780–1783*. Trans. and ed. Evelyn M. Acomb. Published for the Institute of Early American History and Culture. Copyright © 1958 by the University of North Carolina Press. Used by permission of the publisher. [Editorial insertions that appear in square brackets are from Acomb's edition—*Ed.*]

[23 July 1781]

*   *   *

I admire the American troops tremendously! It is incredible that soldiers composed of men of every age, even of children of fifteen, of whites and blacks, almost naked, unpaid, and rather poorly fed, can march so well and withstand fire so steadfastly. The calm and calculated measures of General Washington, in whom I discover daily some new and eminent qualities, are already well known, and the entire universe accords him the homage of its highest esteem. He is certainly admirable as the leader of his army, in which everyone regards him as his friend and father.

The armies had no trouble en route, and before daybreak, they had returned to their camp.

*   *   *

[6–7 October.] On the night of the 6th–7th we opened the first parallel; it extended 3840–4480 feet and was supported on the flanks and in the center by 4 good redoubts, hastily constructed. This work was interrupted only by the batteries, whose fire had been continually directed towards the new redoubts mentioned above. Our experience was not the same on the left, where we opened on the same night an end of the parallel, with a *flying trench* to support a battery that had the dual purpose of disturbing the advanced redoubt on the besieged's right and of keeping at a distance the warships, which, being anchored close by, could have enfiladed the left of this line of attack. Since a deserter from Touraine informed the enemy of the plan for this attack, the latter turned all his attention to it and tormented it greatly with his batteries. . . .

*   *   *

[8–9] . . . As I served throughout the campaign in two capacities, that of captain of the Royal Deux-Ponts and that of aide-de-camp, I always entered the trench with the regiment and went, in addition, at least once a day to the trench, either with my general, or alone, for my instruction. It was, so-to-speak, our gallery. We worked hard on all the batteries and on finishing a branch communications trench behind the left of the parallel, so that we might have several exits. During the night, the parallel and the battery for the feint on the left were finished; it was composed of 6 mortars, of 8 inches, and of 4 pieces of twelve. Altogether, 4 men killed and 9 wounded.

*   *   *

[10] On the 10th, all our batteries were ready to fire. After repeated representations from M. de *Saint-Simon* and M. de *Boisloger* (commander of the battery on the short line of attack on the left), the general sent 2 pieces of 24 there in place of 2 of 12, so that they could fire red-hot balls on the vessels. At daybreak on the 11th, 18 barges loaded with English troops re-ascended the river, probably to disembark on the Gloucester side, but M. de Choisy's cannon prevented them from doing so. He even captured one of these ships, which had grounded, from which everyone had escaped, but he found on it one piece of 4. 3 men killed; 12 wounded.

*   *   *

[12] During the night we opened the second parallel, 1152 feet from the main fortifications, and we immediately began to construct the redoubts necessary for its security, as well as the outline of its batteries. We opened several branch communications trenches between the two parallels, that on the right running from the beginning of the large ravine in the center, and that on the left intersecting the main Hampton Road. This work, too near the besieged for him not to become acquainted with it, was very much interrupted by his batteries and flying shells. There was even a momentary volley between patrols, which encountered each other on our extreme right. The fire from our batteries on the first parallel caused those of the fortress to abate theirs enormously, and greatly favored the progress of the work. The troops in the second parallel were already almost entirely under cover by daylight. 7 men killed; 12 wounded.

*   *   *

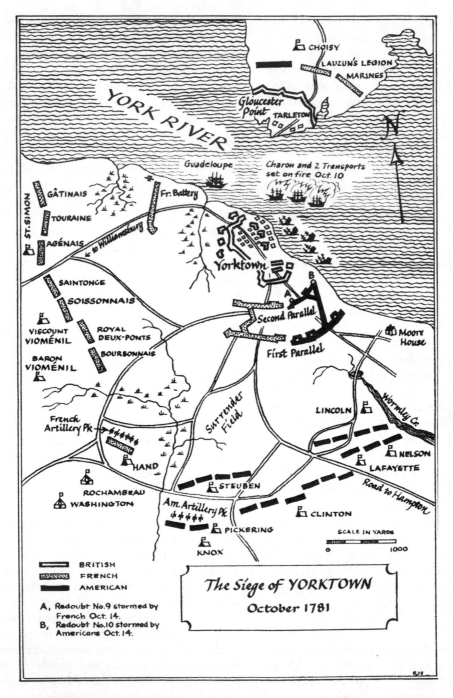

From Ludwig von Closen, *The Revolutionary Journal of Baron Ludwig von Closen,*
1780–1783, trans. and ed. Evelyn M. Acomb, p. 144.

[14–15] From the 14th to the 15th, the trench was relieved by the Gâtinais and Royal Deux-Ponts regiments, commanded by M. le Baron de Vioménil and M. le Comte de Custine. Four companies of grenadiers and chasseurs (auxiliaries) were joined to them towards evening, since it had been decided to attack the two redoubts, detached from the main fortress, with full force, at nightfall. M. le Marquis de Lafayette, at the head of the *American* light infantry, was ordered to attack the most extended redoubt, on the river bank, and M. le Baron de Vioménil, with the French, the nearest. That day I commanded 50 men in one of the redoubts, where balls and royal bombs were not scarce.

At the beginning of the night, the Touraine regiment made a feint on the left, which resulted in a rather strong fusillade, lasting 7 minutes. After this, the whole regiment retired without the loss of a single man. To deceive the enemy, M. de Choisy carried out another, nearly at the same time, at Gloucester. At 8 o'clock exactly, the four companies of grenadiers and chasseurs from Gâtinais and Royal Deux-Ponts, supported by the Gâtinais and Bourbonnais regiments, in a *column 50 feet* from them, debouched in absolute silence through the communications trench almost opposite the first of the advanced redoubts. The American column debouched at the same moment on the right wing. The arrangements of M. de Vioménil, and under him of Vicomte des Deux-Ponts and M. de l'Estrade (Lieutenant-Colonel of the Gâtinais), were so well planned that they captured the redoubt, sword in hand, and killed, wounded, and took a great number of those guarding it. M. de Lafayette did the same on his side, but he met with much less resistance. We captured in ours a major, 6 subordinate officers, and 68 men, with two small howitzers. In the little one seized by the Americans, they found only 3 small pieces. At the moment that the enemy heard our troops attacking them, they fired overhead, and this was, so-to-speak, the signal for all their garrison to fire a roulade, from the left to the right, since it believed that our attack would be general.

The sight of this fusillade and the noise made by the troops when they approached and entered the redoubts had an extraordinary effect and made an enormous impression upon me. When we heard the *Vive le Roi!* and when the fire of the captured redoubts ceased, we saw the fire of the fortress's batteries directed on the captured fortifications. It seemed as if all that side was in flames. I was very anxious to learn if we had lost many persons, and if perhaps some of my comrades had had the misfortune to be wounded. Some time afterward I was told that the Chevalier Charles de *Lameth*, one of my colleagues, and aide-de-camp, who had engaged in the fight as a volunteer (even without the general's permission), had suffered two bullet wounds, one of which had broken his knee-cap and the other had passed through his right leg; that M. de *Lutzon*, Lieutenant of the Royal Deux-Ponts, had had a light contusion of the abdomen; but that the *Vicomte des Deux-Ponts* had experienced a very severe one from grains of sand hurled in his face by a ball, and that his hearing and sight were much feared for. M. de *Sireuil* and another officer of the Gâtinais were seriously wounded.

*   *   *

[15–16] The trench was relieved from the 15th to the 16th by the Bourbonnais and Soissonnais regiments commanded by M. de Chastellux. In order to have a reserve, in case the enemy wished to recover the captured redoubts, or to attack the 2nd parallel, the Bourbonnais regiment spent the whole night of the 14th to the 15th within reach of the trench, but under cover from the fire of the fortifications. For this reason, Agénais relieved Bourbonnais at the beginning of the night. We completed the parallel and its communications and marked out a battery in front of it, between the two captured redoubts, in order to enfilade the works of the fortifications with *ricochet* fire. Two other batteries were given an order for the same kind of fire, since it is the surest way to keep the besieged from having any cover and to disconcert their batteries.

*   *   *

[16] On the 16th, at dawn, we suddenly heard some cries and a fusillade on our right, followed by something sounding like firecrackers over the Sois-

sonnais regiment, *which was prevented from firing by the prudence of its leaders.* We (the Chevalier de Haacke and I) very quickly collected our respective detachments to lead them to the trench depot, where we were to wait for new orders. In spite of the whistling of bullets around our ears, we conducted our troops there in good order and without losing a man. As soon as we put down our implements and took up our arms, we learned that the English had just spiked 4 pieces not yet mounted in a battery, that they had completely surprised one of the redoubts containing an Agénais captain and 50 men, and that they had carried him off wounded. We saw many wounded from this regiment pass by, most of them injured by bayonet thrusts. We captured 16 prisoners, who told us that the sortie had consisted of 600 men of the light infantry commanded by Lieutenant-Colonel Abercromby. Now that it was daylight, we were ordered to return to camp with our workers, and I learned from M. de Chastellux at dinner that since the Agénais pickets had immediately opposed the enemy's advance into the trench, the latter had done us very little harm, in as much as the 4 spiked pieces were in condition to fire that very evening.

Since this journal will be read only by my friends, I can add that the negligence of the Agénais regiment was the sole reason for the surprise of the redoubt and of the adjoining battery. In general, we noted that discipline and order (without speaking of bearing) were much less strictly maintained in the three regiments from the Islands. The famous *Mirabeau* (Cask), Captain of the Gâtinais, was such a drunkard that he would drink punch from one of his boots; whereas in our 6 regiments in Rochambeau's army, our leaders succeeded in enforcing a correctness, vigilance, and discipline that would do honor to Potsdam regiments (credit to whom it is due). According to the report on the 16th, at noon, we had 11 killed and 57 wounded in 24 hours.

*   *   *

[17] During the day of the 17th, the trench was relieved by the Bourbonnais and Royal Deux-Ponts regiments, commanded by M. le Vicomte de Vio-

ménil. The fire from our batteries was so formidable and their aim was so exact that at one o'clock Cornwallis sent a flag of truce to ask for a cessation of the fighting for 24 hours, in order to discuss the fate of the garrison. At first they granted him only two, but the suspension of fighting and of the work of fortification was prolonged successively on both sides until the next day, which [interrupted] the laying out of a flying trench in order to approach closer to the batteries, opposite the redoubt on the enemy's right.

[18–19] The truce was continued on the 18th in order to decide upon the capitulation, which was finally signed on the 19th. The articles were drawn up by the Vicomte de *Noailles* and the American Colonel Laurens, on the one hand, and by Colonel *Dundas* and Major *Ross*, English superior officers, on the other. As it is the custom for the troops who are in the trench when the enemy surrenders to remain there, *as at a post of honor,* until the enemy has given up the fortifications, Bourbonnais and our regiment had the honor of remaining 52 hours in the open air. Fortunately, the weather was dry, although the nights, and especially the mornings, were very cold.

[19] A detachment of the American light infantry and the Bourbonnais company of grenadiers took possession at noon on the 19th of the two redoubts of the fortifications, as provided in Article Three. At two o'clock the garrison of York marched past the combined army, which was drawn up in two lines, the French in full dress opposite the Americans. The captive army laid its arms and 22 flags on a designated spot at the end of the line, where the general staff of the army received them. The Gloucester garrison did the same before M. de Choisy.

Lord Cornwallis, under the pretext of an indisposition, excused himself from this sad ceremony, so that Brigadier-General O'Hara marched at the head of the English troops. In passing between the two armies, they showed the greatest scorn for the Americans, who, to tell the truth, were eclipsed by our army in splendor of appearance and dress, for most of these unfortunate persons were clad in small jackets of white cloth, dirty and ragged, and a number of them were almost barefoot. The English had given them the *nickname* of *Yankee-Doodle*. What does it matter! an intelligent man would say. These people are much more praiseworthy and brave to fight as they do, when they are so poorly supplied *with everything*.

The English troops seemed to be much more tired and much less heroic than the Anspach regiments, who were very handsome and very neatly dressed, better even than the Hessians. The Hessian regiment of Bose was not comparable in appearance to the two last, but it served throughout this war with the greatest distinction, and during the entire siege not a man deserted from it, whereas we received many Anspach deserters and two English nationals.

*   *   *

[20] Since M. de Rochambeau wished to keep me alert, he sent me early in the morning, on the 20th, on board the *Ville de Paris*, where I had several interesting matters to discuss on his behalf with M. de Grasse. I was so quick that I returned at 5 o'clock in the afternoon, just as they were rising from the table, so that I could accompany the general to York to see Lord Cornwallis. I will never forget how frightful and disturbing was the appearance of the city of York, from the fortifications on the crest to the strand below. One could not take three steps without running into some great holes made by bombs, some splinters, some balls, some half covered trenches, with scattered white or negro arms or legs, [and] some bits of uniforms. Most of the houses [were] riddled by cannon fire, and [there were] almost no window-panes in the houses. Most striking of all was the consternation among the few inhabitants, who feared that the little that remained to them would be pillaged by the American troops, who (they falsely said) excelled in such ventures!

We found Lord Cornwallis at his residence. His appearance gave the impression of nobility of soul, magnanimity, and strength of character; his manner seemed to say, "I have nothing with which to reproach myself, I have done my duty, and I held out as long as possible." He told us among other things in our conversation with him that he had wanted to try to force a passage towards the Gloucester side, through M. de Choisy's position, and that he had even given his orders that the Anspach troops should relieve all the posts on the night of the 16th to 17th, so that all the remainder of his army might cross the river; but that the bad weather and the lack of means to transport them all *before daylight* had checked him. After that, he had assembled a council of war, which had unanimously advised him to capitulate.

After a half-hour's talk, we left Cornwallis in order to explore part of the city and see the magazines and arsenal that the *American* quartermasters had just taken over from the English employees. The arsenal was not well stocked, but in the magazine there was clothing for three regiments: shirts, stockings, etc. There were also some merchants' shops, where the deputy quartermasters acted shamefully. It was stated in the capitulation that merchandise would be paid for, but surely half of it must have been taken *gratis*.

The day after the capture of York, General Washington expressed to the entire army his satisfaction with the good conduct, valor, and courage with which it had distinguished itself during the siege. I cannot omit saying here that I have always seen the greatest unity, much agreement on the manner of proceeding in detail, and complete accord on the means of execution prevail between General Washington and M. de Rochambeau, as well as between all the general officers and heads of the engineers and artillery of the combined army. All the reports about deserters, quarters, people to employ, the why and the wherefore, were weighed, discussed, and agreed upon in the morning [as the basis] for orders *for the next 24 hours*, and each chief was informed as to the particular instructions concerning his department. The profound knowledge of M. de Rochambeau *(who was engaged in his 15th siege)* guided *in a large measure* the successive works of the besieging army.

*   *   *

REVIEW QUESTIONS

1. Why was French assistance important to both the revolution and the war?
2. What did this account reveal about allied or combined operations? Was there much interaction, integration, or interservice rivalry?
3. Consider whether the French and Americans were comfortably applying techniques or tactics which they already knew or if they had to be innovative in this siege. Was there anything revolutionary about the troops or the warfare as described by Closen?
4. How does this siege show the effect of war on a civilian community?

SARAH OSBORN

FROM A Follower's Remembrance of Yorktown (1837)

The formation and use of the armed forces—whether militia, state troops, or the Continental Army—of the new United States illustrated both traditional and innovative aspects of military science. Most armies of the era had camp followers: men, women, and children who were attached to military members or departments for either personal or professional reasons. Despite Washington's efforts to minimize their numbers and effects, the American army had a considerable number of these people. Washington and other commanding officers therefore had to ensure that the followers would not undermine discipline and military operations but would, instead, contribute to them. As a result, these followers not only observed but participated in some of the key events of the military side of the Revolution. Sarah Osborn was in her mid-twenties when she married Aaron Osborn. She then shared the hardships and adventures of army life with him when he reenlisted in the Continental Army as a commissary sergeant with the Third New York Regiment. After the war and after her husband abandoned her for another woman, Osborn married John Benjamin, himself a veteran. In 1837 Sarah Osborn Benjamin successfully offered this account in her application for a pension: she was awarded a double pension for both her husbands' (and perhaps in recognition of her own) service.

From John C. Dann, ed., *The Revolution Remembered: Eyewitness Accounts of the War for Independence* (Chicago: University of Chicago Press, 1980), pp. 241–42, 244–46. [Editorial insertions that appear in square brackets are from Dann's edition—*Ed.*]

On this twentieth day of November, A.D. 1837, personally appeared before the Court of Common Pleas of said county of Wayne, Sarah Benjamin, a resident of Pleasant Mount in said county of Wayne and state of Pennsylvania, aged eighty-one years on the seventeenth day of the present month, who being first duly sworn according to law, doth on her oath make the following declaration in order to obtain the benefit of the provision made by the act of Congress passed July 4, 1836, and the act explanatory of said act, passed March 3, 1837.

That she was married to Aaron Osborn, who was a soldier during the Revolutionary War. . . .

That after deponent had married said Osborn, he informed her that he was returned during the war, and that he desired deponent to go with him. Deponent declined until she was informed by Captain Gregg that her husband should be put on the commissary guard, and that she should have the means of conveyance either in a wagon or on horseback. That deponent then in the same winter season in sleighs accompanied her husband and the forces under command of Captain Gregg on the east side of the Hudson river to Fishkill, then crossed the river and went down to West Point. . . .

Deponent, accompanied by her said husband and the same forces, returned during the same season to West Point. Deponent recollects no other females in company but the wife of Lieutenant Forman and of Sergeant Lamberson. . . .

Deponent further says that she and her husband remained at West Point till the departure of the army for the South, . . .

*   *   *

They . . . marched . . . for a place called Williamsburg, as she thinks, deponent alternately on horseback and on foot. There arrived, they remained two days till the army all came in by land and then marched for Yorktown, or Little York as it was then called. The York troops were posted at the right, the Connecticut troops next, and the French to the left. In about one day or less than a day, they reached the place of encampment about one mile from Yorktown. Deponent was on foot and the other females above named and her said husband still on the commissary's guard. Deponent's attention was arrested by the appearance of a large plain between them and Yorktown and an entrenchment thrown up. She also saw a number of dead Negroes lying round their encampment, whom she understood the British had driven out of the town and left to starve, or were first starved and then thrown out. Deponent took her stand just back of the American tents, say about a mile from the town, and busied herself washing, mending, and cooking for the soldiers, in which she was assisted by the other females; some men washed their own clothing. She heard the roar of the artillery for a number of days, and the last night the Americans threw up entrenchments, it was a misty, foggy night, rather wet but not rainy. Every soldier threw up for himself, as she understood, and she afterwards saw and went into the entrenchments. Deponent's said husband was there throwing up entrenchments, and deponent cooked and carried in beef, and bread, and coffee (in a gallon pot) to the soldiers in the entrenchment.

On one occasion when deponent was thus employed carrying in provisions, she met General Washington, who asked her if she "was not afraid of the cannonballs?"

She replied, "No, the bullets would not cheat the gallows," that "It would not do for the men to fight and starve too."

They dug entrenchments nearer and nearer to Yorktown every night or two till the last. While digging that, the enemy fired very heavy till about nine o'clock next morning, then stopped, and the drums from the enemy beat excessively. Deponent was a little way off in Colonel Van Schaick's or the officers' marquee and a number of officers were present, among whom was Captain Gregg, who, on account of infirmities, did not go out much to do duty.

The drums continued beating, and all at once the officers hurrahed and swung their hats, and deponent asked them, "What is the matter now?"

One of them replied, "Are not you soldier enough to know what it means?"

Deponent replied, "No."

They then replied, "The British have surrendered."

Deponent, having provisions ready, carried the same down to the entrenchments that morning, and four of the soldiers whom she was in the habit of cooking for ate their breakfasts.

Deponent stood on one side of the road and the American officers upon the other side when the British officers came out of the town and rode up to the American officers and delivered up [their swords, which the deponent] thinks were returned again, and the British officers rode right on before the army, who marched out beating and playing a melancholy tune, their drums covered with black handkerchiefs and their fifes with black ribbands tied around them, into an old field and there grounded their arms and then returned into town again to await their destiny. Deponent recollects seeing a great many American officers, some on horseback and some on foot, but cannot call them all by name. Washington, Lafayette, and Clinton were among the number. The British general at the head of the army was a large, portly man, full face, and the tears rolled down his cheeks as he passed along. She does not recollect his name, but it was not Cornwallis. She saw the latter afterwards and noticed his being a man of diminutive appearance and having cross eyes.

On going into town, she noticed two dead Negroes lying by the market house. She had the curiosity to go into a large building that stood nearby, and there she noticed the cupboards smashed to pieces and china dishes and other ware strewed around upon the floor, and among the rest a pewter cover to a hot basin that had a handle on it. She picked it up, supposing it to belong to the British, but the governor came in and claimed it as his, but said he would have the name of giving it away as it was the last one out of twelve that he could see, and accordingly presented it to deponent, and she afterwards brought it home with her to Orange County and sold it for old pewter, which she has a hundred times regretted.

*   *   *

REVIEW QUESTIONS

1. What does Osborn's account reveal about the Continental Army and about the siege of Yorktown?
2. How does her description of Yorktown support Closen's?
3. Were Osborn and others like her important to the Revolution? Why or why not?
4. Is Osborn noteworthy because she was exceptional or because she was not unique?

PENNSYLVANIA CITIZENS

Petition to the Assembly of Pennsylvania against the Slave Trade (March 1780)

African Americans, both free and enslaved, fought in the armies of both sides of the American Revolution and desired, in turn, to benefit from such service. Others had not joined in the military fight, but they also hoped that the rhetoric of the Revolution would translate into freedom and rights for blacks. "A Black Whig" wrote a sermon in 1782 glorifying American independence. As he focused on America's righteousness, he slipped in a request that Americans remember the slaves: "And now my virtuous fellow citizens, let me intreat you, that, after you have rid yourselves of the British yoke, that you will also emancipate those who have been all their life time subject to bondage."*

As Americans created new state constitutions and legislation, they grappled with the issue. Although not all acted immediately, nor provided for immediate emancipation, states from the Middle Atlantic region to New England did move to abolish slavery. Pennsylvania, for instance, passed an act for gradual emancipation in 1780 that allowed owners to retain the slaves they already had, but stipulated that children born to a slave mother after the act's passage would be servants until the age of twenty-eight and then be freed. To retain the slaves they already had, owners had to register them by November 1780; if they did not, they could lose their slaves (and a number of unregistered slaves did gain immediate freedom). Furthermore, slaves brought into the state could not be held in servitude longer than seven years unless they came in under the age of twenty-one; then they could be kept until they were twenty-eight. Finally, the act nullified laws that discriminated against blacks, stating that blacks were to be judged and punished just like other inhabitants. States south of Pennsylvania, however, did not accept general emancipation though most did relax manumission laws that allowed owners to liberate slaves individually.

"Petition to the Assembly of Pennsylvania against the Slave Trade, March 1780," Historical Society of Pennsylvania. *Sermon, On the Present Situation of the Affairs of America and Great-Britain.* Written by a Black, and printed at the Request of several Persons of distinguished Characters (Philadelphia: T. Bradford and P. Hall, 1782) Library Company of Philadelphia.

To the Representatives of the Freemen of the Commonwealth of Pennsylvania, in General Assembly met,

The Representation and Petition of the Subscribers, Citizens of Pennsylvania.

Your Petitioners have observed, with great satisfaction, the salutary effects of the Law of this State, passed on the first day of March, 1780, for the "gradual abolition of slavery."—They have also seen, with equal satisfaction, the progress which the humane and just principles of that Law have made in other States.

They, however, find themselves called upon, by the interesting nature of those principles, to suggest to the General Assembly, that vessels have been publicly equipt in this Port for the Slave Trade, and that several other practices have taken place which they conceive to be inconsistent with the spirit of the Law abovementioned; and that these, and other circumstances relating to the afflicted Africans, do, in the opinion of your Petitioners, require the further interposition of the Legislature.

Your Petitioners, therefore, earnestly request that you will again take this subject into your serious consideration, and that you will make such additions to the said Law, as shall effectually put a stop to the Slave Trade being carried on directly or indirectly in this Commonwealth, and to answer other purposes of benevolence and justice to an oppressed part of the human species.

1688 signatures

REVIEW QUESTIONS

1. Why, given that the state had just passed an act providing for gradual emancipation, did Pennsylvania citizens again petition their assembly about slavery in March 1780?
2. What was their argument?
3. Pennsylvania did not pass legislation complying with their request until 1788. Why do you think it took so long?

FROM *Massachusetts Bill of Rights* (1780)

*As the armies clashed on fields of battle, and as soldiers fought for reasons both patri-
otic and personal, American politicians and statesmen gathered in conventions, con-
gresses, and legislatures to formulate, fight over, and finally install new governments
based on principles espoused in new constitutions. The Massachusetts Bill of Rights
leads off that state's constitution of 1780. The Declaration of Rights and Frame of
Government that together formed the constitution were the result of much thought
on the nature of the Revolution and the proper relationship between a people and
their government. In 1778, when Massachusetts' provisional legislature presented its
draft of a constitution to the people for ratification, the people rejected it. They did
not like some of its provisions, its lack of a bill of rights, and, very importantly, they
did not like the government writing its own "compact." They believed that the people
should create the contract which in turn begets the government. The legislature's response in 1780 was to allow a constitutional convention to meet and decide upon the
issue, one that resulted in a constitution that embodied such Enlightenment principles
as social contract, popular sovereignty, and separation of powers.*

From Francis N. Thorpe, ed., *The Federal and State Constitutions*, vol. 3 (Washington, D.C.,
1909), pp. 1888–95.

The end of the institution, maintenance, and administration of government, is to secure the
existence of the body-politic, to protect it, and
to furnish the individuals who compose it with the
power of enjoying in safety and tranquillity their
natural rights, and the blessings of life: and whenever
these great objects are not obtained, the people have
a right to alter the government, and to take measures
necessary for their safety, prosperity, and happiness.

The body-politic is formed by a voluntary association of individuals; it is a social compact by
which the whole people covenants with each citizen and each citizen with the whole people that all
shall be governed by certain laws for the common
good. It is the duty of the people, therefore, in
framing a constitution of government, to provide
for an equitable mode of making laws, as well as
for an impartial interpretation and a faithful execution of them; that every man may, at all times,
find his security in them.

We, therefore, the people of Massachusetts, acknowledging, with grateful hearts the goodness of
the great Legislator of the universe, in affording us,
in the course of His Providence, an opportunity,
deliberately and peaceably, without fraud, violence,
or surprise, of entering into an original, explicit,
and solemn compact with each other; and of forming a new constitution of civil government, for
ourselves and posterity; and devoutly imploring
His direction in so interesting a design, do agree
upon, ordain, and establish the following Declaration of Rights, and Frame of Government, as the
Constitution of the Commonwealth of Massachusetts.

A Declaration of the Rights of the Inhabitants of the Commonwealth of Massachusetts

Article I. All men are born free and equal, and
have certain natural, essential and unalienable
rights; among which may be reckoned the right of
enjoying and defending their lives and liberties;

that of acquiring, possessing, and protecting property; in fine, that of seeking and obtaining their safety and happiness.

II. It is the right as well as the duty of all men in society, publicly, and at stated seasons, to worship the Supreme Being, the great Creator and Preserver of the universe. And no subject shall be hurt, molested, or restrained, in his person, liberty, or estate, for worshipping God in the manner and season most agreeable to the dictates of his own conscience; or for his religious profession of sentiments; provided he doth not disturb the public peace, or obstruct others in their religious worship. . . . *Freedom to worship*

As the happiness of a people and the good order and preservation of civil government essentially depend upon piety, religion, and morality, and as these cannot be generally diffused through a community but by the institution of the public worship of God and of public instructions, in piety, religion, and morality. Therefore to promote their happiness and secure the good order and preservation of their government, the people of this commonwealth have a right to invest their legislature with power to authorize and require, and the legislature shall from time to time authorize and require, the several towns. . . . and other bodies—politic or religious societies, to make suitable provision, at their own expense, for the institution of the public worship of God and the support and maintenance of public Protestant teachers of piety, religion, and morality. . . .

And the people of this commonwealth. . . . do invest their legislature with authority to enjoin upon all the subjects an attendance upon the instructions of the public teachers aforesaid. . . .

And every denomination of Christians, demeaning themselves peaceably and as good subjects of the commonwealth, shall be equally under the protection of the law; and no subordination of any one sect or denomination to another shall ever be established by law.

IV. The people of this commonwealth have the sole and exclusive right of governing themselves, as a free, sovereign, and independent State, and do, and forever hereafter shall, exercise and enjoy every

power, jurisdiction, and right, which is not, or may not hereafter be, by them expressly delegated to the United States of America, in Congress assembled.

V. All power residing originally in the people, and being derived from them, the several magistrates and officers of government, vested with authority, whether legislative, executive, or judicial, are their substitutes and agents, and are at all times accountable to them.

VI. No man, nor corporation, or association of men, have any other title to obtain advantages, or particular and exclusive privileges, distinct from those of the community, than what arises from the consideration of services rendered to the public; and this title being in nature neither hereditary, nor transmissible to children, or descendants, or relations by blood; the idea of a man born a magistrate, lawgiver, or judge, is absurd and unnatural.

VII. Government is instituted for the common good, for the protection, safety, prosperity, and happiness of the people and not for the profit, honor or private interest of any one man, family, or class of men; therefore the people alone have an incontestible unalienable, and indefeasible right to institute government; and to reform, alter, or totally change the same, when their protection, safety, prosperity, and happiness require it.

VIII. In order to prevent those who are vested with authority from becoming oppressors, the people have a right, at such periods and in such manner as they shall establish by their frame of government, to cause their public officers to return to private life; and to fill up vacant places by certain and regular elections and appointments.

IX. All elections ought to be free; and all the inhabitants of this commonwealth, having such qualifications as they shall establish by their frame of government, have an equal right to elect officers, and to be elected, for public employments.

X. Each individual of the society has a right to be protected by it in the enjoyment of his life, liberty, and property. . . . No part of the property of any individual can, with justice, be taken from him, or applied to public uses, without his own consent, or that of the representative body of the people. . . .

And whenever the public exigencies require that the property of any individual should be appropriated to public uses, he shall receive a reasonable compensation therefor.

XI. Every subject of the commonwealth ought to find a certain remedy, by having recourse to the laws, for all injuries or wrongs which he may receive in his person, property, or character. He ought to obtain right and justice freely, and without being obliged to purchase it; completely, and without any denial; promptly, and without delay, conformably to the laws.

XII. No subject shall be held to answer for any crimes or offence, until the same is fully and plainly . . . described to him; or be compelled to accuse, or furnish evidence against himself. And every subject shall have a right to produce all proofs that may be favorable to him; to meet the witnesses against him face to face, and to be fully heard in his defence by himself, or his counsel, at his election. And no subject shall be arrested, . . . or deprived of his life, liberty, or estate, but by the judgement of his peers, or the law of the land.

And the legislature shall not make any law that shall subject any person to a capital or infamous punishment, excepting for the government of the army and navy, without trial by jury. . . .

XIV. Every subject has a right to be secure from all unreasonable searches, and seizures, of his person, his houses, his papers, and all his possessions. . . . And no warrant ought to be issued but in cases, and with the formalities prescribed by the laws.

XV. In all controversies concerning property, and in all suits between two or more persons, . . . the parties have a right to a trial by jury; and this method of procedure shall be held sacred. . . .

XVI. The liberty of the press is essential to the security of freedom in a state it ought not, therefore, to be restricted in this commonwealth.

XVII. The people have a right to keep and to bear arms for the common defence. And as, in time of peace, armies are dangerous to liberty, they ought not to be maintained without the consent of the legislature; and the military power shall always be held in an exact subordination to the civil authority, and be governed by it.

XVIII. A frequent recurrence to the fundamental principles of the constitution, and a constant adherence to those of piety, justice, moderation, temperance, industry and frugality, are absolutely necessary to preserve the advantages of liberty, and to maintain a free government. The people ought, consequently, to have a particular attention to all those principles, in the choice of their officers and representatives: and they have a right to require of their lawgivers and magistrates an exact and constant observance of them, in the formation and execution of the laws necessary for the good administration of the commonwealth.

XIX. The people have a right, in an orderly and peaceable manner to assemble to consult upon the common good; give instructions to their representatives, and to request of the legislative body, by the way of addresses, petitions, or remonstrances, redress of the wrongs done them, and of the grievances they suffer.

XX. The power of suspending the laws, or the execution of the laws, ought never to be exercised but by the legislature, or by authority derived from it, to be exercised in such particular cases only as the legislature shall expressly provide for.

XXI. The freedom of deliberation, speech, and debate, in either house of the legislature, is so essential to the rights of the people, that it cannot be the foundation of any accusation or prosecution, action or complaint, in any other court or place whatsoever.

XXII. The legislature ought frequently to assemble for the redress of grievances, for correcting, strengthening, and confirming the laws, and for making new laws, as the common good may require.

XXIII. No subsidy, charge, tax, impost, or duties ought to be established, fixed, laid or levied, under any pretext whatsoever, without the consent of the people or their representatives in the legislature. *No taxation w/o consent*

XXIV. Laws made to punish for actions done before the existence of such laws, and which have not been declared crimes by preceding laws, are unjust, oppressive, and inconsistent with the fundamental principles of a free government.

XXV. No subject ought, in any case, or in any time, to be declared guilty of treason or felony by the legislature.

XXVI. No magistrate or court of law shall demand excessive bail or sureties, impose excessive fines, or inflict cruel or unusual punishments.

XXVII. In time of peace, no soldier ought to be quartered in any house without the consent of the owner; and in time of war, such quarters ought not to be made but by the civil magistrate, in a manner ordained by the legislature.

XXVIII. No person can in any case be subject to law-martial, or to any penalties or pains, by virtue of that law, except those employed in the army or navy, and except the militia in actual service, but by authority of the legislature.

XXIX. It is essential to the preservation of the rights of every individual, his life, liberty, property, and character, that there be an impartial interpretation of the laws, and administration of justice. It is the right of every citizen to be tried by judges as free, impartial, and independent as the lot of humanity will admit. It is, therefore, not only the best policy, but for the security of the rights of the people, and of every citizen, that the judges of the supreme judicial court should hold their offices as long as they behave themselves well; and that they should have honorable salaries ascertained and established by standing laws.

XXX. In the government of this commonwealth, the legislative department shall never exercise the executive and judicial powers, or either of them: the executive shall never exercise the legislative and judicial powers, or either of them: the judicial shall never exercise the legislative and executive powers, or either of them: to the end it may be a government of laws and not of men.

REVIEW QUESTIONS

1. What human rights were listed in this document? Of those, which appear to have been the most important to the people of Massachusetts? Why?
2. How did the framers balance the rights of the one—the individual—against the rights of the many—the community?
3. How did the framers ensure that political power would remain with the people; in other words, by what means was the government made answerable to the will of the people?
4. How revolutionary were the thoughts expressed in this *Bill of Rights*?

FROM *Virginia Statute of Religious Liberty* (1786)

Shortly after Virginia established a new government under its constitution of 1776, Thomas Jefferson, along with other like-minded representatives in the House of Delegates, started to propose numerous bills to reform even more fully both government and society. The Virginia Assembly quickly accepted a few of the bills, which dealt with such matters as inheritance of property, slavery, crime, education, and religion, rejected some others that seemed to require too radical a change, and then slowly worked its way through the rest, approving many of them after the war was over, when Jefferson was away representing the country in France. Jefferson's Bill for Establishing Religious Freedom was one of the latter proposals and was in response to the colony of Virginia's having sanctioned and supported the Church of England by way of law and taxes. Jefferson proposed that the state of Virginia support religious free-dom instead of any one church. The Assembly passed the bill in January 1786.

From William W. Hering, ed., *The Statutes at Large of Virginia*, 13 vols. (New York, 1819–23), 12:86.

January 16, 1786

An Act for establishing Religious Freedom

I. WHEREAS Almighty God hath created the mind free; that all attempts to influence it by temporal punishments or burthens, or by civil incapacitations, tend only to beget habits of hypocrisy and meanness, and are a departure from the plan of the Holy author of our religion, who being Lord both of body and mind, yet chose not to propagate it by coercions on either, as was in his Almighty power to do; that the impious presumption of legislators and rulers, civil as well as ecclesiastical, who being themselves but fallible and uninspired men, have assumed dominion over the faith of others, setting up their own opinions and modes of thinking as the only true and infallible, and as such endeavouring to impose them on others, hath established and maintained false religions over the greatest part of the world, and through all time; that to compel a man to furnish contributions of money for the propagation of opinions which he disbelieves, is sinful and tyrannical; that even the forcing him to support this or that teacher of his own religious persuasion, is depriving him of the comfortable liberty of giving his contributions to the particular pastor whose morals he would make his pattern, and whose powers he feels most persuasive to righteousness, and is withdrawing from the ministry those temporary rewards, which proceeding from an approbation of their personal conduct, are an additional incitement to earnest and unremitting labours for the instruction of mankind; that our civil rights have no dependence on our religious opinions, any more than our opinions in physics or geometry; that therefore the pro-

scribing any citizen as unworthy the public confidence by laying upon him an incapacity of being called to offices of trust and emolument, unless he profess or renounce this or that religious opinion, is depriving him injuriously of those privileges and advantages to which in common with his fellow-citizens he has a natural right, that it tends only to corrupt the principles of that religion it is meant to encourage, by bribing with a monopoly of worldly honours and emoluments, those who will externally profess and conform to it; that though indeed these are criminal who do not withstand such temptation, yet neither are those innocent who lay the bait in their way; that to suffer the civil magistrate to intrude his powers into the field of opinion, and to restrain the profession or propagation of principles on supposition of their ill tendency, is a dangerous fallacy, which at once destroys all religious liberty, because he being of course judge of that tendency will make his opinions the rule of judgment, and approve or condemn the sentiments of others only as they shall square with or differ from his own; that it is time enough for the rightful purposes of civil government, for its officers to interfere when principles break out into overt acts against peace and good order; and finally, that truth is great and will prevail if left to herself, that she is the proper and sufficient antagonist to error, and has nothing to fear from the conflict, unless by human interposition disarmed of her natural weapons, free argument and debate, errors ceasing to be dangerous when it is permitted freely to contradict them.

II. Be it enacted by the General Assembly, that no man shall be compelled to frequent or support any religious worship, place or ministry whatsoever, nor shall be enforced, restrained, molested, or burthened in his body or goods, nor shall otherwise suffer on account of his religious opinions or belief; but that all men shall be free to profess, and by argument to maintain, their opinion in matters of religion, and that the same shall in no wise diminish, enlarge or affect their civil capacities.

III. And though we well know that this assembly, elected by the people for the ordinary purposes of legislation only, have no power to restrain the acts of succeeding assemblies, constituted with powers equal to our own, and that therefore to declare this act to be irrevocable would be of no effect in law; yet as we are free to declare, and do declare, that the rights hereby asserted are of the natural rights of mankind and that if any act shall hereafter be passed to repeal the present, or to narrow its operation, such act will be an infringement of natural right.

REVIEW QUESTIONS

1. What was the purpose of section one?
2. Did Jefferson effectively prove his case for religious freedom? How did he answer those people with religious reservations?
3. How was freedom of religion defined in this statute?
4. Why was it deemed a natural right? And why must it be a civil liberty?

FROM *The Articles of Confederation* (Ratified 1781)

On 12 June 1776, just five days after Richard Henry Lee had moved that a resolution be adopted declaring the colonies to be free and independent states, the Second Continental Congress appointed a committee to draft a constitution for the new nation's government. Independence was declared before the committee was ready to report back, but soon thereafter, on 12 July, the committee submitted its proposal to Congress. The committee's draft, a revision of one written by John Dickinson, made Congress—as a body of national government—stronger than the states. The delegates did not approve. Reflecting Americans' fears of too strong a central government, the representatives made major changes that switched the seat of power back to the states. Writing and deciding upon these revisions was a lengthy and interrupted process, since Congress had a war to run as well, but on 17 November 1777 Congress approved The Articles of Confederation *and submitted them to the states for ratification. Although a few states signified their approval by July 1778, full ratification came neither quickly nor easily, for many thought the powers granted Congress were still too great. The major issue, however, became that of control over the western lands. Maryland refused to ratify until Virginia ceded her western land claims to the United States. When Virginia made that concession in January 1781, Maryland ratified in February, and the Articles officially went into effect on 1 March.*

From James D. Richardson, comp., *A Compilation of the Messages and Papers of the Presidents, 1789–1902*, vol. 1 (Bureau of National Literature and Art, 1904), pp. 9–18.

Agreed to by Congress November 15, 1777; Ratified and in Force, March 1, 1781

TO ALL TO WHOM these Presents shall come, we the undersigned Delegates of the States affixed to our Names send greeting. Whereas the Delegates of the United States of America in Congress assembled did on the fifteenth day of November in the Year of our Lord One Thousand Seven Hundred and Seventy seven, and the Second Year of the Independence of America agree to certain articles of Confederation and perpetual Union . . . in the Words following, viz. "Articles of Confederation and perpetual Union between the states. . . .

Art. I. The Stile of this confederacy shall be "The United States of America."

Art. II. Each state retains its sovereignty, freedom and independence, and every Power, Jurisdiction and right, which is not by this confederation expressly delegated to the United States, in Congress assembled.

Art. III. The said states hereby severally enter into a firm league of friendship with each other, for their common defence, the security of their Liberties, and their mutual and general welfare, binding themselves to assist each other, against all force offered to, or attacks made upon them, or any of them, on account of religion, sovereignty, trade, or any other pretence whatever.

Art. IV. The better to secure and perpetuate mutual friendship and intercourse among the people of the different states in this union, the free inhabitants of each of these states, paupers, vagabonds and fugitives from Justice excepted, shall be entitled to all privileges and immunities of free citizens in the several states; and the people of each state shall have free ingress and regress to and from any other state, and shall enjoy therein all the privileges of trade and commerce, subject to the same duties, impositions and restrictions as the inhabitants thereof respectively, provided that such restriction shall not extend so far as to prevent the removal of property imported into any state, to any other state of which the Owner is an inhabitant;

provided also that no imposition, duties or restriction shall be laid by any state, on the property of the united states, or either of them.

If any Person guilty of, or charged with treason, felony, or other high misdemeanor in any state, shall flee from Justice, and be found in any of the united states, he shall upon demand of the Governor or executive power, of the state from which he fled, be delivered up and removed to the state having jurisdiction of his offence.

Full faith and credit shall be given in each of these states to the records, acts and judicial proceedings of the courts and magistrates of every other state.

Art. V. For the more convenient management of the general interests of the united states, delegates shall be annually appointed in such manner as the legislature of each state shall direct, to meet in Congress on the first Monday in November, in every year, with a power reserved to each state, to recall its delegates, or any of them, at any time within the year, and to send others in their stead, for the remainder of the Year.

No state shall be represented in Congress by less than two, nor by more than seven Members; and no person shall be capable of being a delegate for more than three years in any term of six years; nor shall any person, being a delegate, be capable of holding any office under the united states, for which he, or another for his benefit receives any salary, fees or emolument of any kind.

Each state shall maintain its own delegates in a meeting of the states, and while they act as members of the committee of the states.

In determining questions in the united states, in Congress assembled, each state shall have one vote.

Freedom of speech and debate in Congress shall not be impeached or questioned in any Court, or place out of Congress, and the members of congress shall be protected in their persons from arrests and imprisonments, during the time of their going to and from, and attendance on congress, except for treason, felony, or breach of the peace.

Art. VI. No state without the Consent of the united states in congress assembled, shall send any embassy to, or receive any embassy from, or enter into any conference, agreement, or alliance or treaty with any King, prince or state; nor shall any person holding any office of profit or trust under the united states, or any of them, accept of any present, emolument, office or title of any kind whatever from any king, prince or foreign state; nor shall the united states in congress assembled, or any of them, grant any title of nobility.

No two or more states shall enter into any treaty, confederation or alliance whatever between them, without the consent of the united states in congress assembled, specifying accurately the purposes for which the same is to be entered into, and how long it shall continue.

No state shall lay any imposts or duties, which may interfere with any stipulations in treaties, entered into by the united states in congress assembled, with any king, prince or state, in pursuance of any treaties already proposed by congress, to the courts of France and Spain.

No vessels of war shall be kept up in time of peace by any state, except such number only, as shall be deemed necessary by the united states in congress assembled, for the defence of such state, or its trade; nor shall any body of forces be kept up by any state, in time of peace, except such number only as in the judgment of the united states, in congress assembled, shall be deemed requisite to garrison the forts necessary for the defence of such state; but every state shall always keep up a well regulated and disciplined militia, sufficiently armed and accoutred, and shall provide and constantly have ready for use, in public stores, a due number of field pieces and tents, and a proper quantity of arms, ammunition and camp equipage.

No state shall engage in any war without the consent of the united states in congress assembled, unless such state be actually invaded by enemies, or shall have received certain advice of a resolution being formed by some nation of Indians to invade such state, and the danger is so imminent as not to admit of a delay, till the united states in congress assembled can be consulted: nor shall any state grant commissions to any ships or vessels of war,

nor letters of marque or reprisal, except it be after a declaration of war by the united states in congress assembled, and then only against the kingdom or state and the subjects thereof, against which war has been so declared, and under such regulations as shall be established by the united states in congress assembled, unless such state be infested by pirates, in which case vessels of war may be fitted out for that occasion, and kept so long as the danger shall continue, or until the united states in congress assembled shall determine otherwise. . . .

Art. VIII. All charges of war, and all other expences that shall be incurred for the common defence or general welfare, and allowed by the united states in congress assembled, shall be defrayed out of a common treasury, which shall be supplied by the several states, . . .

Art. IX. The united states in congress assembled, shall have the sole and exclusive right and power of determining on peace and war, except in the cases mentioned in the sixth article—of sending and receiving ambassadors—entering into treaties and alliances, provided that no treaty of commerce shall be made whereby the legislative power of the respective states shall be restrained from imposing such imposts and duties on foreigners, as their own people are subjected to, or from prohibiting the exportation or importation of any species of goods or commodities whatsoever—of establishing rules for deciding in all cases, what captures on land or water shall be legal, and in what manner prizes taken by land or naval forces in the service of the united states shall be divided or appropriated.—of granting letters of marque and reprisal in times of peace—appointing courts for the trial of piracies and felonies committed on the high seas and establishing courts for receiving and determining finally appeals in all cases of captures, provided that no member of congress shall be appointed a judge of any of the said courts.

The united states in congress assembled shall also be the last resort on appeal in all disputes and differences now subsisting or that hereafter may arise between two or more states concerning boundary, jurisdiction or any other cause whatever; which authority shall always be exercised in the manner following. . . .

The united states in congress assembled shall also have the sole and exclusive right and power of regulating the alloy and value of coin struck by their own authority, or by that of the respective states—fixing the standard of weights and measures throughout the united states.—regulating the trade and managing all affairs with the Indians, not members of any of the states, provided that the legislative right of any state within its own limits be not infringed or violated—establishing and regulating post-offices from one state to another, throughout all the united states, and exacting such postage on the papers passing thro' the same as may be requisite to defray the expences of the said office—appointing all officers of the land forces, in the service of the united states, excepting regimental officers.—appointing all the officers of the naval forces, and commissioning all officers whatever in the service of the united states—making rules for the government and regulation of the said land and naval forces, and directing their operations.

The united states in congress assembled shall have authority to appoint a committee, to sit in the recess of congress, to be denominated "A Committee of the States," and to consist of one delegate from each state; and to appoint such other committees and civil officers as may be necessary for managing the general affairs of the united states under their direction—to appoint one of their number to preside, provided that no person be allowed to serve in the office of president more than one year in any term of three years; to ascertain the necessary sums of Money to be raised for the service of the united states, and to appropriate and apply the same for defraying the public expences—to borrow money, or emit bills on the credit of the united states, transmitting every half year to the respective states an account of the sums of money so borrowed or emitted,—to build and equip a navy—to agree upon the number of land forces, and to make requisitions from each state for its quota, in proportion to the number of white inhabitants in such state; which requisition shall be

binding, and thereupon the legislature of each state shall appoint the regimental officers, raise the men and cloath, arm and equip them in a soldier like manner, at the expence of the united states, and the officers and men so cloathed, armed and equipped shall march to the place appointed, and within the time agreed on by the united states in congress assembled: . . .

The united states in congress assembled shall never engage in a war, nor grant letters of marque and reprisal in time of peace, nor enter into any treaties or alliances, nor coin money, nor regulate the value thereof, nor ascertain the sums and expences necessary for the defence and welfare of the united states, or any of them, nor emit bills, nor borrow money on the credit of the united states, nor appropriate money, nor agree upon the number of vessels of war, to be built or purchased, or the number of land or sea forces to be raised, nor appoint a commander in chief of the army or navy, unless nine states assent to the same: nor shall a question on any other point, except for adjourning from day to day be determined, unless by the votes of a majority of the united states in congress assembled. . . .

Art. X. The committee of the states, or any nine of them, shall be authorised to execute, in the recess of congress, such of the powers of congress as the united states in congress assembled, by the consent of nine states, shall from time to time think expedient to vest them with; provided that no power be delegated to the said committee, for the exercise of which, by the articles of confederation, the voice of nine states in the congress of the united states assembled is requisite.

Art. XI. Canada acceding to this confederation, and joining in the measures of the united states, shall be admitted into, and entitled to all the advantages of this union: but no other colony shall be admitted into the same, unless such admission be agreed to by nine states.

Art. XII. All bills of credit emitted, monies borrowed and debts contracted by, or under the authority of congress, before the assembling of the united states, in pursuance of the present confederation, shall be deemed and considered as a charge against the united states, for payment and satisfaction whereof the said united states, and the public faith are hereby solemnly pledged.

Art. XIII. Every state shall abide by the determinations of the united states in congress assembled, on all questions which by this confederation are submitted to them. And the Articles of this confederation shall be inviolably observed by every state, and the union shall be perpetual; nor shall any alteration at any time hereafter be made in any of them; unless such alteration be agreed to in a congress of the united states, and be afterwards confirmed by the legislatures of every state.

AND WHEREAS it hath pleased the Great Governor of the World to incline the hearts of the legislatures we respectively represent in congress, to approve of, and to authorize us to ratify the said articles of confederation and perpetual union. . . . In Witness whereof we have hereunto set our

hands in Congress. Done at Philadelphia in the state of Pennsylvania the ninth Day of July in the Year of our Lord one Thousand seven Hundred and Seventy-eight, and in the third year of the independence of America.

REVIEW QUESTIONS

1. Was this a radical or conservative document?
2. What do you think were its strengths and weaknesses?
3. What were the powers assigned to Congress?
4. How did the *Articles* safeguard the states against encroachment from the central government?
5. What were the controls placed upon and the privileges granted to the representatives?

ABIGAIL AND JOHN ADAMS

FROM Family Letters on Revolutionary Matters (1776–83)

Abigail Adams recognized that the constituting of a new government was a chance to rectify gender inequities inherent in law, politics, and society. A problem for historians, however, is determining whether she was exceptional or representative of her female contemporaries. While it may be impossible to discover how many thought as she did, it is probable that those who did advocate such change tried to influence their friends and family—especially the men who participated in politics—to effect reform. Adams spent much of the war separated from her husband John, but the loving couple kept postriders busy with their constant letters on family, local, and national affairs. They also maintained a voluminous correspondence with many other people, such as their good friend Mercy Otis Warren (the learned wife of politician Joseph Warren, she would later write a history of the Revolution), and John Thaxter, Sr., the husband of Abigail Adams's aunt. While John Adams was off in Philadelphia creating a new nation or overseas in Europe representing the United States, his wife—in this act representative of so many other women—took command on the homefront. Adams and other female patriots did without their usual comforts, boycotted British goods, and took on additional burdens to maintain family farms and businesses.

From L. H. Butterfield, ed., *Adams Family Correspondence* (Cambridge, MA: Belknap Press, 1963), vol. I, pp. 362–63, 369–71, 381–83, 396–98, 401–402; vol. II, pp. 27–28, 93–94, 166–67, 306, 313–14, 390–92, 400–401; Richard Alan Ryerson, ed., *Adams Family Correspondence* (Cambridge, MA: Belknap Press, 1993), vol. V, pp. 223–24. [Editorial insertions appear in square brackets—*Ed.*]

John Adams to Abigail Adams

March 19. 1776

*   *   *

You ask, what is thought of Common sense [Paine's pamphlet]. Sensible Men think there are some Whims, some Sophisms, some artfull Addresses to superstitious Notions, some keen attempts upon the Passions, in this Pamphlet. But all agree there is a great deal of good sense, delivered in a clear, simple, concise and nervous Style.

His Sentiments of the Abilities of America, and of the Difficulty of a Reconciliation with G.B. are generally approved. But his Notions, and Plans of Continental Government are not much applauded. Indeed this Writer has a better Hand at pulling down than building.

. . . This Writer seems to have very inadequate Ideas of what is proper and necessary to be done, in order to form Constitutions for single Colonies, as well as a great Model of Union for the whole.

*   *   *

Abigail Adams to John Adams

Braintree March 31 1776

I wish you would ever write me a Letter half as long as I write you; and tell me if you may where your Fleet are gone? What sort of Defence Virginia can make against our common Enemy? Whether it is so situated as to make an able Defence? Are not the Gentery Lords and the common people vassals, are they not like the uncivilized Natives Brittain represents us to be? I hope their Riffel Men who have shewen themselves very savage and even

Blood thirsty; are not a specimen of the Generality of the people.

I am willing to allow the Colony great merrit for having produced a Washington but they have been shamefully duped by a Dunmore.

I have sometimes been ready to think that the passion for Liberty cannot be Eaquelly Strong in the Breasts of those who have been accustomed to deprive their fellow Creatures of theirs. Of this I am certain that it is not founded upon that generous and christian principal of doing to others as we would that others should do unto us.

*   *   *

I feel very differently at the approach of spring to what I did a month ago. We knew not then whether we could plant or sow with safety, whether when we had toild we could reap the fruits of our own industery, whether we could rest in our own Cottages, or whether we should not be driven from the sea coasts to seek shelter in the wilderness, but now we feel as if we might sit under our own vine and eat the good of the land.

*   *   *

Tho we felicitate ourselves, we sympathize with those who are trembling least the Lot of Boston should be theirs. But they cannot be in similar circumstances unless pusilanimity and cowardise should take possession of them. They have time and warning given them to see the Evil and shun it.—I long to hear that you have declared an independancy—and by the way in the new Code of Laws which I suppose it will be necessary for you to make I desire you would Remember the Ladies, and be more generous and favourable to them than your ancestors. Do not put such unlimited power into the hands of the Husbands. Remember all Men would be tyrants if they could. If perticuliar care and attention is not paid to the Laidies we are determined to foment a Rebelion, and will not hold ourselves bound by any Laws in which we have no voice, or Representation.

That your Sex are Naturally Tyrannical is a Truth so thoroughly established as to admit of no dispute, but such of you as wish to be happy willingly give up the harsh title of Master for the more tender and endearing one of Friend. Why then, not put it out of the power of the vicious and the Lawless to use us with cruelty and indignity with impunity. Men of Sense in all Ages abhor those customs which treat us only as the vassals of your Sex. Regard us then as Beings placed by providence under your protection and in immitation of the Supreem Being make use of that power only for our happiness.

John Adams to Abigail Adams

Ap. 14. 1776

You justly complain of my short Letters, but the critical State of Things and the Multiplicity of Avocations must plead my Excuse.—You ask where the Fleet is. The inclosed Papers will inform you. You ask what Sort of Defence Virginia can make. I believe they will make an able Defence. Their Militia and minute Men have been some time employed in training them selves, and they have Nine Battallions of regulars as they call them, maintained among them, under good Officers, at the Continental Expence. They have set up a Number of Manufactories of Fire Arms, which are busily employed. They are tolerably supplied with Powder, and are successfull and assiduous, in making Salt Petre. Their neighbouring Sister or rather Daughter Colony of North Carolina, which is a warlike Colony, and has several Battallions at the Continental Expence, as well as a pretty good Militia, are ready to assist them, and they are in very good Spirits, and seem determined to make a brave Resistance.—The Gentry are very rich, and the common People very poor. This Inequality of Property, gives an Aristocratical Turn to all their Proceedings, and occasions a strong Aversion in their Patricians, to Common Sense. But the Spirit of these Barons, is coming down, and it must submit.

It is very true, as you observe they have been duped by Dunmore. But this is a Common Case. All the Colonies are duped, more or less, at one Time and another. . . .

*   *   *

As to Declarations of Independency, be patient. Read our Privateering Laws, and our Commercial Laws. What signifies a Word.

As to your extraordinary Code of Laws, I cannot but laugh. We have been told that our Struggle has loosened the bands of Government every where. That Children and Apprentices were disobedient—that schools and Colledges were grown turbulent—that Indians slighted their Guardians and Negroes grew insolent to their Masters. But your Letter was the first Intimation that another Tribe more numerous and powerfull than all the rest were grown discontented.—This is rather too coarse a Compliment but you are so saucy, I wont blot it out.

Depend upon it, We know better than to repeal our Masculine systems. Altho they are in full Force, you know they are little more than Theory. We dare not exert our Power in its full Latitude. We are obliged to go fair, and softly, and in Practice you know We are the subjects. We have only the Name of Masters, and rather than give up this, which would compleatly subject Us to the Despotism of the Peticoat, I hope General Washington, and all our brave Heroes would fight. I am sure every good Politician would plot, as long as he would against Despotism, Empire, Monarchy, Aristocracy, Oligarchy, or Ochlocracy.—A fine Story indeed. I begin to think the Ministry as deep as they are wicked. After stirring up Tories, Landjobbers, Trimmers, Bigots, Canadians, Indians, Negroes, Hanoverians, Hessians, Russians, Irish Roman Catholicks, Scotch Renegadoes, at last they have stimulated the [————] to demand new Priviledges and threaten to rebell.

Abigail Adams to Mercy Otis Warren

Braintree April 27 1776

*   *   *

I dare say [John Adams] writes to no one unless to Portia[1] oftner than to your Friend [Warren's husband], because I know there is no one besides in whom he has an eaquel confidence. His Letters to me have been generally short, but he pleads in Excuse the critical state of affairs and the Multiplicity of avocations and says further that he has been very Busy, . . .

He is very sausy to me in return for a List of Female Grievances which I transmitted to him. I think I will get you to join me in a petition to Congress. I thought it was very probable our wise Statesmen would erect a New Government and form a new code of Laws. I ventured to speak a word in behalf of our Sex, who are rather hardly dealt with by the Laws of England which gives such unlimitted power to the Husband to use his wife Ill.

I requested that our Legislators would consider our case and as all Men of Delicacy and Sentiment are averse to Excercising the power they possess, yet as there is a natural propensity in Humane Nature to domination, I thought the most generous plan was to put it out of the power of the Arbitary and tyranick to injure us with impunity by Establishing some Laws in our favour upon just and Liberal principals.

I believe I even threatned fomenting a Rebellion in case we were not considerd, and assured him we would not hold ourselves bound by any Laws in which we had neither a voice, nor representation.

In return he tells me he cannot but Laugh at My Extrodonary Code of Laws. That he had heard their Struggle had loosned the bands of Goverment, that children and apprentices were dissabedient, that Schools and Colledges were grown turbulant, that Indians slighted their Guardians, and Negroes grew insolent to their Masters. But my

Letter was the first intimation that another Tribe more numerous and powerfull than all the rest were grown discontented. This is rather too coarse a complement, he adds, but that I am so sausy he wont blot it out.

So I have help'd the Sex abundantly, but I will tell him I have only been making trial of the Disintresstedness of his Virtue, and when weigh'd in the balance have found it wanting.

It would be bad policy to grant us greater power say they since under all the disadvantages we Labour we have the assendancy over their Hearts

And charm by accepting, by submitting sway.

I wonder Apollo and the Muses could not have indulged me with a poetical Genious. I have always been a votary to her charms but never could assend Parnassus myself.

*   *   *

Abigail Adams to John Adams

B[raintre]e May 7 1776

*   *   *

A Goverment of more Stability is much wanted in this colony, and they are ready to receive it from the Hands of the Congress, and since I have begun with Maxims of State I will add an other viz. that a people may let a king fall, yet still remain a people, but if a king let his people slip from him, he is no longer a king. And as this is most certainly our case, why not proclaim to the World in decisive terms your own importance?

Shall we not be dispiced by foreign powers for hesitateing so long at a word?

I can not say that I think you very generous to the Ladies, for whilst you are proclaiming peace and good will to Men, Emancipating all Nations, you insist upon retaining an absolute power over Wives. But you must remember that Arbitary power is like most other things which are very hard, very liable to be broken—and notwithstanding all your wise Laws and Maxims we have it in our power not only to free ourselves but to subdue

---

[1] Adams and Warren gave each other classical nicknames: Portia for Adams, Marcia for Warren.

our Masters, and without voilence throw both your natural and legal authority at our feet[.]

*   *   *

John Adams to Abigail Adams

Philadelphia July 3. 1776

*   *   *

Yesterday the greatest Question was decided, which ever was debated in America, and a greater perhaps, never was or will be decided among Men. A Resolution was passed without one dissenting Colony "that these united Colonies, are, and of right ought to be free and independent States, and as such, they have, and of Right ought to have full Power to make War, conclude Peace, establish Commerce, and to do all the other Acts and Things, which other States may rightfully do." You will see in a few days a Declaration setting forth the Causes, which have impell'd Us to this mighty Revolution, and the Reasons which will justify it, in the Sight of God and Man. A Plan of Confederation will be taken up in a few days.

When I look back to the Year 1761, and recollect the Argument concerning Writs of Assistance, in the Superiour Court, which I have hitherto considered as the Commencement of the Controversy, between Great Britain and America, and run through the whole Period from that Time to this, and recollect the series of political Events, the Chain of Causes and Effects, I am surprized at the Suddenness, as well as Greatness of this Revolution. Britain has been fill'd with Folly, and America with Wisdom, at least this is my Judgment.—Time must determine. It is the Will of Heaven, that the two Countries should be sundered forever. It may be the Will of Heaven that America shall suffer Calamities still more wasting and Distresses yet more dreadfull. If this is to be the Case, it will have this good Effect, at least: it will inspire Us with many Virtues, which We have not, and correct many Errors, Follies, and Vices, which threaten to disturb, dishonour, and destroy Us.—The Furnace of Affliction produces Refinement, in States as well as Individuals. And the new Governments we are assuming, in every Part, will require a Purification from our Vices, and an Augmentation of our Virtues or they will be no Blessings. The People will have unbounded Power. And the People are extreamly addicted to Corruption and Venality, as well as the Great.—I am not without Apprehensions from this Quarter. But I must submit all my Hopes and Fears, to an overruling Providence, in which, unfashionable as the Faith may be, I firmly believe.

Abigail Adams to John Adams

August 14 1776

*   *   *

You remark upon the deficiency of Education in your Countrymen. It never I believe was in a worse state, at least for many years. The Colledge is not in the state one could wish, the Schollars complain that their professer in Philosophy is taken of by publick Buisness to their great detriment. In this Town I never saw so great a neglect of Education. The poorer sort of children are wholly neglected, and left to range the Streets without Schools, without Buisness, given up to all Evil. The Town is not as formerly divided into Wards. There is either too much Buisness left upon the hands of a few, or too little care to do it. We daily see the Necessity of a regular Goverment. . . .

If you complain of neglect of Education in sons, What shall I say with regard to daughters, who every day experience the want of it. With regard to the Education of my own children, I find myself soon out of my debth, and destitute and deficient in every part of Education.

I most sincerely wish that some more liberal plan might be laid and executed for the Benefit of the rising Generation, and that our new constitution may be distinguished for Learning and Virtue. If we mean to have Heroes, Statesmen and Philosophers, we should have learned women. The world perhaps would laugh at me, and accuse me of vanity, But you I know have a mind too enlarged and liberal to disregard the Sentiment. If much depends as is allowed upon the early Education of youth and the first principals which are instilld take the deepest root, great benifit must arise from litirary accomplishments in women.

*   *   *

Abigail Adams to Mercy Otis Warren

August 14. 1777. Braintree
This is the memorable fourteenth of August. This day 12 years the Stamp office was distroyd. Since that time what have we endured? What have we suffer'd? Many very many memorable Events which ought to be handed down to posterity will be buried in oblivion merely for want of a proper Hand to record them, whilst upon the opposite side many venal pens will be imployd to misrepresent facts and to render all our actions odious in the Eyes of future Generations. I have always been sorry that a certain person who once put their Hand to the pen, should be discouraged, and give up so important a service. Many things would have been recorded by the penetrateing Genious of that person which thro the multiplicity of Events and the avocations of the times will wholly escape the notice of any future Historian.

The History and the Events of the present day must fill every Humane Breast with Horrour. Every week produces some Horrid Scene perpetrated by our Barbarous foes, not content with a uniform Series of cruelties practised by their own Hands, but they must let loose the infernal Savages "those dogs of War" and cry Havock to them. Cruelty, impiety and an utter oblivion of the natural Sentiments of probity and Honour with the voilation of all Laws Humane and Divine rise at one veiw and characterise a George, a How and a Burgoine.

O my dear Friend when I bring Home to my own Dwelling these tragical Scenes which are every week presented in the publick papers to us, and only in Idea realize them, my whole Soul is distress'd. Were I a man I must be in the Feild. I could not live to endure the Thought of my Habitation desolated, my children Butcherd, and I an inactive Spectator.

*   *   *

Abigail Adams to John Thaxter

Dear Sir   Braintree Febry 15 1778

*   *   *

It gives me pleasure to see so distinguished a Genious as Mrs. Macauly[2] Honourd with a Statue, yet she wanted it not to render her Name immortal. The Gentleman who erected it has sullied the glory of his deed by the narrow contracted Spirit which he discovers in the inscription, . . . Even the most Excellent monody which he wrote upon the Death of his Lady will not atone for a mind contracted enough to wish that but one woman in an age might excell, and she only for the sake of a prodigy. What must be that Genious which cannot do justice to one Lady, but at the expence of the whole Sex?

It is really mortifying Sir, when a woman possessd of a common share of understanding considers the difference of Education between the male and female Sex, even in those families where Education is attended too. Every assistance and advantage which can be procured is afforded to the sons, whilst the daughters are totally neglected in point of Literature. Writing and Arithmetick comprise all their Learning. Why should children of the same parents be thus distinguished? Why should the Females who have a part to act upon the great Theater, and a part not less important to Society, (as the care of a family and the first instruction of Children falls to their share, and if as we are told that first impressions are most durable), is it not of great importance that those who are to instill the first principals should be suiteably qualified for the Trust, Especially when we consider that families compose communities, and individuals make up the sum total. Nay why should your sex wish for such a disparity in those whom they one day intend for companions and associates. Pardon me Sir if I cannot help sometimes suspecting that this Neglect arises in some measure from an ungenerous

---

[2] Catherine Macaulay, British philosopher and author.

jealousy of rivals near the Throne—but I quit the Subject or it will run away with my pen.

*   *   *

John Thaxter to Abigail Adams

Dear Madam   York Town March 6th. 1778

Your much esteemed favor came to hand this day, in which you inform me of the departure of your "dearest Friend."[3] I sincerely wish for your sake it had been convenient and safe for you to have accompanied him: But the danger you mention must, I think, have made the voyage disagreeable and had the event taken place, doubly aggravating on his part. . . . The principle, on which you assented to his departure, was noble, and marks that zeal and attachment to the cause of our country, which has so eminently distinguished you. Honor or profit weighed not with either of you, I am certain. . . .

*   *   *

I cannot pass over that part of your agreeable favor which contain some strictures on the statue of [Mrs.] McCaulay, and the difference in point of Education between [male] and female, without an acknowledgment of the justice of the observations. They are so ingenious, and at the same time so just, that if complaisance did not suggest silence, Reason would tell me that the subterfuges of sophistication would be defyed in breaking silence and attempting to explain them away. After mentioning that our sex wish a disparity, you subjoin a suspicion that Jealousy of rivalship is the foundation of the neglect of your sex. Madam, I am positive it is too often the case. It is an "ungenerous Jealousy" as you justly term it.

*   *   *

_____

[3] John Adams left with his son, John Quincy Adams, on a diplomatic mission to Europe.

John Adams to Abigail Adams 2d

My Dear Daughter   Paris, August 13th
                              [i.e. 14th], 1783

I have received your affectionate letter of the 10th of May, with great pleasure, and another from your mother of the 28th and 29th of April, which by mistake I omitted to mention in my letter to her to-day. Your education and your welfare, my dear child, are very near my heart; and nothing in this life would contribute so much to my happiness, next to the company of your mother, as yours. I have reason to say this by the experience I have had of the society of your brother, whom I brought with me from the Hague. He is grown to be a man, and the world says they should take him for my younger brother, if they did not know him to be my son. I have great satisfaction in his behaviour, as well as in the improvements he has made in his travels, and the reputation he has left behind him wherever he has been. He is very studious and delights in nothing but books, which alarms me for his health; because, like me, he is naturally inclined to be fat. His knowledge and his judgment are so far beyond his years, as to be admired by all who have conversed with him. I lament, however, that he could not have his education at Harvard College, where his brothers shall have theirs, if Providence shall afford me the means of supporting the expense of it. . . .

You have reason to wish for a taste for history, which is as entertaining and instructive to the female as to the male sex. My advice to you would be to read the history of your own country, which although it may not afford so splendid objects as some others, before the commencement of the late war, yet since that period, it is the most interesting chapter in the history of the world, and before that period is intensely affecting to every native American. You will find among your own ancestors, by your mother's side at least, characters which deserve your attention. It is by the female world, that the greatest and best characters among men are formed. I have long been of this opinion to such a degree, that when I hear of an extraordinary man, good or bad, I naturally, or habitually inquire who was his mother? There can be nothing in life more honourable for a woman, than to contribute by her virtues, her advice, her example, or her address, to the formation of an husband, a brother, or a son, to be useful to the world.

Heaven has blessed you, my daughter, with an understanding and a consideration, that is not found every day among young women, and with a mother who is an ornament to her sex. You will take care that you preserve your own character, and that you persevere in a course of conduct, worthy of the example that is every day before you. With the most fervent wishes for your happiness, I am your affectionate father,

John Adams

REVIEW QUESTIONS

1. How conversant was Abigail Adams with the public ideas and issues of the day? Did she simply echo her husband's ideas or did she have her own opinions?
2. What did Adams think about men's attitudes and actions toward women? What did she want her husband to do about these issues? How did John Adams respond?
3. Why did Abigail Adams take up the cause of educational reform? Was that revolutionary?
4. Was her husband in agreement with her on this issue? Was her uncle, John Thaxter?
5. How did the Adams family correspondents display a regional bias even as they labored to establish a united American nation? What would have been the significance of such an attitude if held by many revolutionaries?

7 SHAPING A FEDERAL UNION

To borrow a phrase from a twentieth-century cartoon character, "We have met the enemy and he is us."[1] In the early years of the American Revolution, and on through the War for Independence, revolutionaries distanced themselves from local opponents both in word and action. Calling themselves patriots and Americans while cursing the loyalists as Tories, they tried, and often succeeded, in driving out these enemies. They also focused on and fought fiercely against the external threat: Great Britain and its armies. The necessity of dealing with these threats, as well as a shared idealistic desire to initiate a new civil millennium, tended to steer the revolutionaries through a myriad of political conflicts into consensus on what they wanted to achieve: republican states and nation. Consensus, however, although firmly founded on certain key ideas about rights and government, was in fact a rather fragile construct. Fissures and weak spots soon appeared in the philosophical and governmental systems that the revolutionaries had engineered, and the persons who discovered and exposed these were not outsiders, they were Americans. The Revolution, therefore, did not end with the ratification of the Articles of Confederation and state constitutions; nor did it end with victory in the war. It continued through the 1780s as Americans struggled with themselves over the interpretation and implementation through law and government of such ideas as life, liberty, property, and the pursuit of happiness.

At times it may seem that governing in peace is more difficult than governing in war, and so it appeared in the immediate postwar years. That transition from war to peace, from fighting for independence to living with it, proved quite difficult for Americans in the 1780s. There was so much to which they had to adjust, both in personal and political affairs. Issues that had been repressed, ignored, or temporarily compromised upon during the greater emergency now

---

[1] *Pogo* by Walt Kelly, 1970 cartoon.

demanded resolution along with the new problems that cropped up. People and events, both foreign and domestic, constantly challenged the plans and programs, including the Articles of Confederation, that leaders had drawn up during the war. While they certainly reflected revolutionary political philosophy, these schemes had also been the result of expediency and speculation as to what the nation and its people would face and want in the future. Once the future became the present, and that present became marked by problems, many—but not all— Americans clamored for amendments.

For people who tended to define pursuit of happiness in economic terms, the financial fiascoes of the postwar era proved especially disconcerting. Americans did not simply want to muddle through the adjustments that had to be made, they wanted solutions—with many demanding that they be democratic ones— that would allow them to prosper. The nation and states struggled to meet those desires as they also strove to ensure the security of the United States.

In the course of trying to cure the nation's ills, some American leaders fostered another one. They prescribed changing the federal compact and government, which raised a fever among Americans. At issue was the degree of change acceptable to the majority at that time. Some Americans wanted to slow down the changes and create a stability in which they could find the time to think things through before taking the next step. Some thought there had already been too much change. There was a fear that their dearly bought win would lead to loss. The heated debates that ensued ranged over the need for radical change versus more moderate reforms, who would lead during and after the change, and how the change would define the nation and people.

DANIEL GRAY

FROM A Proclamation of Shaysite Grievances (1786)

In the mid 1780s western Massachusetts farmers, many of whom had supported the Revolution through military service, found their pursuit of happiness challenged by the fiscal policies of the state. Anxiety and anger boiled into direct action in the summer of 1786 after the state legislature voted for more taxes but did not reform the state's monetary policy. The legislature's lack of responsiveness to the westerners' problems and requests reflected the political power of the eastern mercantile and creditor interests, but it may also have been due to an earlier lack of strong, direct participation in government by the westerners. The farmers set out to rectify that. Farmers who had already suffered through foreclosure on their lands due to their inability to pay taxes were joined by those who faced ruin because of the new taxes. Under such leaders as Daniel Shays, who had been a captain in the Continental Army, the farmers formed their own political committees (chaired by such compatriots as Daniel Gray) and armed forces. They closed courts while opening their own conventions in the counties, for they wanted to make sure that their grievances were not only heard but acted upon. Governor James Bowdoin certainly did react, but not in the way they wanted: he first suspended habeas corpus *and then called out an army.*

From George R. Minot, *The History of the Insurrection in Massachusetts in 1786 and of the Rebellion Consequent Thereon* (1788; New York: De Capo Press, 1971), pp. 82–83.

Shays's Rebellion 1786

1. An ADDRESS to the People of the several towns in the county of Hampshire, now at arms.

GENTLEMEN,

We have thought proper to inform you of some of the principal causes of the late risings of the people, and also of their present movement, viz.

1st. The present expensive mode of collecting debts, which by reason of the great scarcity of cash, will of necessity fill our gaols with unhappy debtors, and thereby a reputable body of people rendered incapable of being serviceable either to themselves or the community.

2d. The monies raised by impost and excise being appropriated to discharge the interest of governmental securities, and not the foreign debt, when these securities are not subject to taxation.

3d. A suspension of the writ of Habeas Corpus, by which those persons who have stepped forth to assert and maintain the rights of the people, are liable to be taken and conveyed even to the most distant part of the Commonwealth, and thereby subjected to an unjust punishment.

4th. The unlimited power granted to Justices of the Peace and Sheriffs, Deputy Sheriffs, and Constables, by the Riot Act, indemnifying them to the prosecution thereof; when perhaps, wholly actuated from a principle of revenge, hatred, and envy.

Furthermore, Be assured, that this body, now at arms, despise the idea of being instigated by British emissaries, which is so strenuously propagated by the enemies of our liberties: And also wish the most proper and speedy measures may be taken, to discharge both our foreign and domestick debt.

Per Order,

DANIEL GRAY,
Chairman of the Committee.

REVIEW QUESTIONS

1. How did this address serve as an assurance that the rebels were not enemies of the people or the Revolution?
2. Did they perceive their cause to be a matter of rights or economics?
3. Did the reasons they presented justify rebellion?
4. How did their grievances indicate a breakdown in the newly constituted political processes? How did they indicate an erosion in social and political deference?

GEORGE WASHINGTON

Letters about Shays's Rebellion (1786)

The eruption in Massachusetts ignited public and private outbursts within and well beyond the state. Newspaper publishers filled column upon column with reports of the insurgents' as well as the government's actions, while correspondents penned their opinions of the legality, morality, and repercussions of the rebellion. Some Americans supported the rebellion, but many others feared, deplored, and condemned it. The strong reactions showed how sensitive many Americans, including George Washington, were to both the image as well as the implementation of their republican experiment. Washington, who had resigned his commission and returned to private life as a planter after the war, was still vitally concerned about the security and interests of the new nation. To that end he encouraged attendance at the Annapolis Convention in September 1786, and then when that failed to draw enough delegates, he supported the call for a convention to take place the following year in Philadelphia. In almost constant communication with other leading revolutionaries, he continued to influence events as he offered his opinions and advice.

From John C. Fitzpatrick, *The Writings of George Washington*, vol. 29 (Washington, D.C., GPO, 1939), pp. 50–52, 121–124.

To James Madison

Mount Vernon, November 5, 1786

My dear Sir: . . . Fain would I hope, that the great, and most important of all objects, the fœderal governmt., may be considered with that calm and deliberate attention which the magnitude of it so loudly calls for at this critical moment. Let prejudices, unreasonable jealousies, and local interest yield to reason and liberality. Let us look to our National character, and to things beyond the present period. No morn ever dawned more favourably than ours did; and no day was ever more clouded than the present! Wisdom, and good examples are necessary at this time to rescue the political machine from the impending storm. Virginia has now an opportunity to set the latter, and has enough of the former, I hope, to take the lead in promoting this great and arduous work. Without some alteration in our political creed, the superstructure we have been seven years raising at the expence of so much blood and treasure, must fall. We are fast verging to anarchy and confusion!

A letter which I have just received from Genl Knox, who had just returned from Massachusetts (whither he had been sent by Congress consequent of the commotion in that State) is replete with melancholy information of the temper, and designs of a considerable part of that people. Among other things he says,

there creed is, that the property of the United States, has been protected from confiscation of Britain by the joint exertions of *all*, and therefore ought to be the *common property* of all. And he that attempts opposition to this creed is an enemy to equity and justice, and ought to be swept from off the face of the Earth.

again

They are determined to anihillate all debts public and private, and have Agrarian Laws, which are easily effected by the means of unfunded paper money which shall be a tender in all cases whatever.

He adds

The numbers of these people amount in Massachusetts to about one fifth part of several populous Counties, and to them may be collected, people of similar sentiments from the States of Rhode Island, Connecticut, and New Hampshire, so as to constitute a body of twelve or fifteen thousand desperate, and unprincipled men. They are chiefly of the young and active part of the Community.

How melancholy is the reflection, that in so short a space, we should have made such large strides towards fulfilling the prediction of our transatlantic foe! "leave them to themselves, and their government will soon dissolve." Will not the wise and good strive hard to avert this evil? Or will their supineness suffer ignorance, and the arts of self-interested designing disaffected and desperate characters, to involve this rising empire in wretchedness and contempt? What stronger evidence can be given of the want of energy in our governments than these disorders? If there exists not a power to check them, what security has a man for life, liberty, or property? To you, I am sure I need not add aught on this subject, the consequences of a lax, or inefficient government, are too obvious to be dwelt on. Thirteen Sovereignties pulling against each other, and all tugging at the f;oederal head will soon bring ruin on the whole; whereas a liberal, and energetic Constitution, well guarded and closely watched, to prevent incroachments, might restore us to that degree of respectability and consequence, to which we had a fair claim, and the brightest prospect of attaining. With sentiments of the sincerest esteem etc.

To Henry Knox

Mount Vernon, December 26, 1786

My dear Sir: . . .

Lamentable as the conduct of the Insurgents of Massachusetts is, I am exceedingly obliged to you for the advices respecting them; and pray you,

most ardently, to continue the acct. of their proceedings; because I can depend upon them from you without having my mind bewildered with those vague and contradictory reports which are handed to us in Newspapers, and which please one hour, only to make the moments of the next more bitter. I feel, my dear Genl. Knox, infinitely more than I can express to you, for the disorders which have arisen in these States. Good God! who besides a tory could have foreseen, or a Briton predicted them! were these people wiser than others, or did they judge of us from the corruption, and depravity of their own hearts? The latter I am persuaded was the case, and that notwithstanding the boasted virtue of America, we are far gone in every thing ignoble and bad.

I do assure you, that even at this moment, when I reflect on the present posture of our affairs, it seems to me to be like the vision of a dream. My mind does not know how to realize it, as a thing in actual existence, so strange, so wonderful does it appear to me! In this, as in most other matter, we are too slow. When this spirit first dawned, probably it might easily have been checked; but it is scarcely within the reach of human ken, at this moment, to say when, where, or how it will end. There are combustibles in every State, which a spark might set fire to. In this State, a perfect calm prevails at present, and a prompt disposition to support, and give energy to the f;oederal System is discovered, if the unlucky stirring of the dispute respecting the navigation of the Mississippi does not become a leaven that will ferment, and sour the mind of it.

The resolutions of the prest. Session respecting a paper emission, military certificates, &ca., have stamped justice and liberality on the proceedings of the Assembly, and By a late act, *it* seems very desirous of a General Convention to revise and amend the fœderal Constitution. Apropos, what prevented the Eastern States from attending the September meeting at Annapolis? Of all the States in the Union it should have seemed to me, that a measure of this sort (distracted as they were with internal commotions, and experiencing the want of energy in the government) would have been most pleasing to them. What are the prevailing sentiments of the one now proposed to be held at Philadelphia, in May next? and how will it be attended? . . .

*   *   *

In both your letters you intimate, that the men of reflection, principle and property in New England, feeling the inefficacy of their present government, are contemplating a change; but you are not explicit with respect to the nature of it. It has been supposed, that, the Constitution of the State of Massachusetts was amongst the most energetic in the Union; May not these disorders then be ascribed to an endulgent exercise of the powers of Administration? If your laws authorized, and your powers were adequate to the suppression of these tumults, in the first appearances of them, delay and temporizing expedients were, in my opinion improper; these are rarely well applied, and the same causes would produce similar effects in any form of government, if the powers of it are not enforced. I ask this question for information, I know nothing of the facts.

That G. B will be an unconcerned Spectator of the present insurrections (if they continue) is not to be expected. That she is at this moment sowing the Seeds of jealousy and discontent among the various tribes of Indians on our frontier admits of no doubt, in my mind. And that she will improve every opportunity to foment the spirit of turbulence within the bowels of the United States, with a view of distracting our governments, and promoting divisions, is, with me, not less certain. Her first Manœuvres will, no doubt, be covert, and may remain so till the period shall arrive when a decided line of conduct may avail her. . . . We ought not therefore to sleep nor to slumber. Vigilance in watching, and vigour in acting, is, in my opinion, become indispensably necessary. If the powers are inadequate amend or alter them, but do not let us sink into the lowest state of humiliation and contempt, and become a by-word in all the earth. I think with you that the Spring will unfold important and distressing Scenes, unless much wisdom and good management is displayed in the interim. . . .

REVIEW QUESTIONS

1. Compare Washington's summary of Henry Knox's account of the rebels' grievances to the proclamation above. Do the two support one another?
2. Does the Knox account as accepted and echoed by Washington show any interpretative biases? If so, what does it reveal about their shared attitude to the rebellion?
3. Did Washington believe the insurgents to be a small faction found only in Massachusetts? Did he believe their attitude and actions to be a threat not only to their state but others? Why or why not?
4. What did he say caused the problem? What did he believe to be the solution?
5. How did Washington use the rebellion to support his argument for governmental reform?

CONSTITUTIONAL CONVENTION

Debates on Slavery (1787)

Delegates from twelve states (Rhode Island did not appoint a representative), tasked with reforming the Articles of Confederation, *met in a Grand Convention in Philadelphia from May to September 1787. Their mission, as announced and accepted by Congress, the state governments, and the public was reform, not revolution. Yet once the delegates settled down to work, key members such as James Madison and Alexander Hamilton immediately began to push for radical change. In the debates that ensued, members argued over revolutionary social and political issues. One such issue was slavery. Many of the nation's founders desired the abolition of that institution. Just a year before, in September 1786, George Washington had written, "I never mean (unless some particular circumstance should compel me to it) to possess another slave by purchase; it being among my first wishes to see some plan adopted, by which slavery in this country may be abolished by slow, sure, and imperceptible degrees." Washington and others like him did not propose immediate emancipation, for they did not wish to upset or undermine state societies and economies, but they did want to deal with the moral and ideological dilemna that slavery posed. Their sentiments, however, did not match the resolve of the slaveholding interests.*

From *Notes of Debates in the Federal Convention of 1787 Reported by James Madison*, intro. Adrienne Koch (Athens: Ohio University Press. Intro. copyright, 1966; new, indexed ed. 1984), pp. 502–508, 530–32. [Editorial insertions that appear in square brackets are from the 1984 edition—*Ed.*]

[Tuesday, August 21]

Mr L. Martin, proposed to vary the Sect: 4. art VII. so as to allow a prohibition or tax on the importation of slaves. 1. as five slaves are to be counted as 3 free men in the apportionment of Representatives; such a clause wd. leave an encouragement to this trafic. 2. slaves weakened one part of the Union which the other parts were bound to protect: the privilege of importing them was therefore unreasonable. 3. it was inconsistent with the principles of the revolution and dishonorable to the American character to have such a feature in the Constitution.

Mr Rutlidge did not see how the importation of slaves could be encouraged by this Section. He was not apprehensive of insurrections and would readily exempt the other States from the obligation to protect the Southern against them.—Religion & humanity had nothing to do with this question. Interest alone is the governing principle with nations. The true question at present is whether the South^n States shall or shall not be parties to the Union. If the Northern States consult their interest, they will not oppose the increase of Slaves which will increase the commodities of which they will become the carriers.

Mr Elseworth was for leaving the clause as it stands. let every State import what it pleases. The morality or wisdom of slavery are considerations belonging to the States themselves. What enriches a part enriches the whole, and the States are the best judges of their particular interest. The old confederation had not meddled with this point, and he did not see any greater necessity for bringing it within the policy of the new one:

Mͬ Pinkney. South Carolina can never receive the plan if it prohibits the slave trade. In every proposed extension of the powers of the Congress, that State has expressly & watchfully excepted that of meddling with the importation of negroes. If the States be all left at liberty on this subject, S. Carolina may perhaps by degrees do of herself what is wished, as Virginia & Maryland have already done.

Adjourned

Wednesday August 22. in Convention

Art VII sect 4. resumed. Mͬ Sherman was for leaving the clause as it stands. He disapproved of the slave trade; yet as the States were now possessed of the right to import slaves, as the public good did not require it to be taken from them, & as it was expedient to have as few objections as possible to the proposed scheme of Government, he thought it best to leave the matter as we find it. He observed that the abolition of Slavery seemed to be going on in the U. S. & that the good sense of the several States would probably by degrees compleat it. He urged on the Convention the necessity of despatching its business.

Col. Mason. This infernal trafic originated in the avarice of British Merchants. The British Govͭ constantly checked the attempts of Virginia to put a stop to it. The present question concerns not the importing States alone but the whole Union. The evil of having slaves was experienced during the late war. Had slaves been treated as they might have been by the Enemy, they would have proved dangerous instruments in their hands. But their folly dealt by the slaves, as it did by the Tories. . . . Maryland & Virginia he said had already prohibited the importation of slaves expressly. N. Carolina had done the same in substance. All this would be in vain if S. Carolina & Georgia be at liberty to import. The Western people are already calling out for slaves for their new lands, and will fill that Country with slaves if they can be got thro' S. Carolina & Georgia. Slavery discourages arts & manufactures. The poor despise labor when performed by slaves. They prevent the immigration of Whites, who really enrich & strengthen a Country. They produce the most pernicious effect on manners. Every master of slaves is born a petty tyrant. They bring the judgment of heaven on a Country. As nations can not be rewarded or punished in the next world they must be in this. By an inevitable chain of causes & effects providence punishes national sins, by national calamities. He lamented that some of our Eastern brethren had from a lust of gain embarked in this nefarious traffic. As to the States being in possession of the Right to import, this was the case with many other rights, now to be properly given up. He held it essential in every point of view that the Genͤ Govͭ should have power to prevent the increase of slavery.

Mͬ Elsworth. As he had never owned a slave could not judge of the effects of slavery on character: He said however that if it was to be considered in a moral light we ought to go farther and free those already in the Country.—As slaves also multiply so fast in Virginia & & Maryland that it is cheaper to raise than import them, whilst in the sickly rice swamps foreign supplies are necessary, if we go no farther than is urged, we shall be unjust towards S. Carolina & Georgia. Let us not intermeddle. As population increases poor laborers will be so plenty as to render slaves useless. Slavery in time will not be a speck in our Country. Provision is already made in Connecticut for abolishing it. And the abolition has already taken place in Massachusetts. As to the danger of insurrections from foreign influence, that will become a motive to kind treatment of the slaves.

Mͬ Pinkney. If slavery be wrong, it is justified by the example of all the world. He cited the case of Greece Rome & other antient States; the sanction given by France England, Holland & other modern States. In all ages one half of mankind have been slaves. If the S. States were let alone they will probably of themselves stop importations. He wͩ himself as a Citizen of S. Carolina vote for it. An attempt to take away the right as proposed will produce serious objections to the Constitution which he wished to see adopted.

General PINKNEY declared it to be his firm opinion that if himself & all his colleagues were to sign the Constitution & use their personal influence, it would be of no avail towards obtaining the assent of their Constituents. S. Carolina & Georgia cannot do without slaves. As to Virginia she will gain by stopping the importations. Her slaves will rise in value, & she has more than she wants. It would be unequal to require S. C. & Georgia to confederate on such unequal terms. He said the Royal assent before the Revolution had never been refused to S. Carolina as to Virginia. He contended that the importation of slaves would be for the interest of the whole Union. The more slaves, the more produce to employ the carrying trade; The more consumption also, and the more of this, the more of revenue for the common treasury. He admitted it to be reasonable that slaves should be dutied like other imports, but should consider a rejection of the clause as an exclusion of S. Carolᵃ from the Union.

Mʳ BALDWIN had conceived national objects alone to be before the Convention, not such as like the present were of a local nature. Georgia was decided on this point. . . .

Mʳ GERRY thought we had nothing to do with the conduct of the States as to Slaves, but ought to be careful not to give any sanction to it.

Mʳ DICKENSON considered it as inadmissible on every principle of honor & safety that the importation of slaves should be authorised to the States by the Constitution. The true question was whether the national happiness would be promoted or impeded by the importation, and this question ought to be left to the National Govᵗ not to the States particularly interested. If Engᵈ & France permit slavery, slaves are at the same time excluded from both those Kingdoms. Greece and Rome were made unhappy by their slaves. He could not believe that the Southⁿ States would refuse to confederate on the account apprehended; especially as the power was not likely to be immediately exercised by the Genˡ Government.

Mʳ WILLIAMSON stated the law of N. Carolina on the subject, to wit that it did not directly prohibit the importation of slaves. It imposed a duty of £5. on each slave imported from Africa. £10 on each from elsewhere, & £50 on each from a State licensing manumission. He thought the S. States could not be members of the Union if the clause shd. be rejected, and that it was wrong to force any thing down, not absolutely necessary, and which any State must disagree to.

Mʳ KING thought the subject should be considered in a political light only. If two States will not agree to the Constitution as stated on one side, he could affirm with equal belief on the other, that great & equal opposition would be experienced from the other States. He remarked on the exemption of slaves from duty whilst every other import was subjected to it, as an inequality that could not fail to strike the commercial sagacity of the Northn. & middle States.

Mʳ LANGDON was strenuous for giving the power to the Genˡ Govt. He cᵈ not with a good conscience leave it with the States who could then go on with the traffic, without being restrained by the opinions here given that they will themselves cease to import slaves.

Genˡ PINKNEY thought himself bound to declare candidly that he did not think S. Carolina would stop her importations of slaves in any short time, but only stop them occasionally as she now does. He moved to commit the clause that slaves might be made liable to an equal tax with other imports which he he thought right & wᶜʰ wᵈ remove one difficulty that had been started.

Mʳ RUTLIDGE. If the Convention thinks that N. C. S. C. & Georgia will ever agree to the plan, unless their right to import slaves be untouched, the expectation is vain. The people of those States will never be such fools as to give up so important an interest. He was strenuous agˢᵗ striking out the Section, and seconded the motion of Genˡ Pinkney for a commitment.

*   *   *

Mʳ SHERMAN said it was better to let the S. States import slaves than to part with them, if they made that a sine qua non. He was opposed to a tax on slaves imported as making the matter worse, because it implied they were *property*. He acknowledged that if the power of prohibiting the importation should be given to the Gen! Government that it would be exercised. He thought it would be its duty to exercise the power.

*   *   *

M! RANDOLPH was for committing in order that some middle ground might, if possible, be found. He could never agree to the clause as it stands. He w^d sooner risk the constitution. He dwelt on the dilemma to which the Convention was exposed. By agreeing to the clause, it would revolt the Quakers, the Methodists, and many others in the States having no slaves. On the other hand, two States might be lost to the Union. Let us then, he said, try the chance of a commitment.

On the question for committing the remaining part of Sect. 4 & 5. of art: 7. N. H. no. Mas. abs^t Con^t ay N. J. ay P^a no. Del. no Mary^d ay. V^a ay. N. C. ay S. C. ay. Geo. ay.

*   *   *

[From Saturday August 25, 1787. In Convention.] The Report of the Committee of eleven [see friday the 24th instant] being taken up.

Gen! PINKNEY moved to strike out the words "the year eighteen hundred" as the year limiting the importation of slaves, and to insert the words "the year eighteen hundred and eight"

M! GHORUM 2^ded the motion

M! MADISON. Twenty years will produce all the mischief that can be apprehended from the liberty to import slaves. So long a term will be more dishonorable to the National character than to say nothing about it in the Constitution.

On the motion; which passed in the affirmative.

N. H. ay. Mas. ay. C^t ay. N. J. no. P^a no. Del. no. M^d ay. V^a no. N. C. ay. S. C. ay. Geo. ay.

M! Govr MORRIS was for making the clause read at once, "importation of slaves into N. Carolina, S. Carolina & Georgia shall not be prohibited &c." This he said would be most fair and would avoid the ambiguity by which, under the power with regard to naturalization, the liberty reserved to the States might be defeated. He wished it to be known also that this part of the Constitution was

a compliance with those States. If the change of language however should be objected to by the members from those States, he should not urge it.

Col: MASON was not against using the term "slaves" but ag^nt naming N. C. S. C. & Georgia, lest it should give offence to the people of those States.

M! SHERMAN liked a description better than the terms proposed, which had been declined by the old Cong^r & were not pleasing to some people. M! CLYMER concurred with M^r. Sherman

M! WILLIAMSON said that both in opinion & practice he was, against slavery; but thought it more in favor of humanity, from a view of all circumstances, to let in S. C. & Georgia on those terms, than to exclude them from the Union.

M! Govr MORRIS withdrew his motion.

M! DICKENSON wished the clause to be confined to the States which had not themselves prohibited the importation of slaves, and for that purpose moved to amend the clause so as to read "The importation of slaves into such of the States as shall permit the same shall not be prohibited by the Legislature of the U- S- until the year 1808"—which was disagreed to nem: cont:

The first part of the report was then agreed to, amended as follows.

"The migration or importation of such persons as the several States now existing shall think proper to admit, shall not be prohibited by the Legislature prior to the year 1808."

N. H. Mas. Con. M^d N. C. S. C. Geo: ay
N. J. P^a Del. Virg^a . . . . no

M! BALDWIN in order to restrain & more explicitly define "the average duty" moved to strike out of the 2^d part the words "average of the duties laid on imports" and insert "common impost on articles not enumerated" which was agreed to nem: cont:

M! SHERMAN was ag^st this 2^d part, as acknowledging men to be property, by taxing them as such under the character of slaves.

M! KING & M! LANGDON considered this as the price of the I^st part.

Gen! PINKNEY admitted that it was so.

Col: MASON. Not to tax, will be equivalent to a bounty on the importation of slaves.

Mr GHORUM thought that Mr Sherman should consider the duty, not as implying that slaves are property, but as a discouragement to the importation of them.

Mr Govr MORRIS remarked that as the clause now stands it implies that the Legislature may tax freemen imported.

Mr SHERMAN in answer to Mr Ghorum observed that the smallness of the duty shewed revenue to be the object, not the discouragement of the importation.

Mr MADISON thought it wrong to admit in the Constitution the idea that there could be property in men. The reason of duties did not hold, as slaves are not like merchandize, consumed, &c

Col. MASON (in answ.^r to Govr Morris) the provision as it stands was necessary for the case of Convicts in order to prevent the introduction of them.

It was finally agreed nem: contrad: to make the clause read "but a tax or duty may be imposed on such importation not exceeding ten dollars for each person," and then the 2d. part as amended was agreed to.

*   *   *

REVIEW QUESTIONS

1. During the debates, what were the arguments for and against the importation of slaves—and by extension, for and against the entire institution of slavery?
2. How and why did the delegates finally arrive at a compromise if not a consensus on this issue?
3. How did these debates affect the representation and regulation of slavery (in particular, see Art. I, Sections 2 & 9; Art. IV, Section 2) in the Constitution?
4. Given that the Constitution did not abolish slavery, do the arguments presented here indicate that the Revolution initiated change with respect to that institution both in attitude and practice?

Constitution of the United States (1787)

Hot as it was outside the Pennsylvania State House (now called Independence Hall), it was even hotter within as the delegates to the Constitutional Convention debated behind closed doors and windows. While some representatives hoped that reforms would include moral and ideological imperatives, most saw the creation of a federal government that would work more effectively and protect the nation's interests as the first priority. After many debates, committee meetings, and compromises over the proper form and function of their national government, the twelve state delegations (minus some delegates who had left earlier and three who refused to sign) approved the final draft of the Constitution on 17 September. They then sent it on to Congress.

From James D. Richardson, comp., *A Compilation of the Messages and Papers of the Presidents, 1789–1902*, vol. I (Bureau of National Literature and Art, 1904), pp. 21–38.

We the people of the United States, in order to form a more perfect Union, establish Justice, insure domestic Tranquility, provide for the common defence, promote the general Welfare, and secure the Blessings of Liberty to ourselves and our Posterity, do ordain and establish this Constitution for the United States of America.

ARTICLE. I

Section. 1. All legislative Powers herein granted shall be vested in a Congress of the United States, which shall consist of a Senate and House of Representatives.

Section. 2. The House of Representatives shall be composed of Members chosen every second Year by the People of the several States, and the Electors in each State shall have the Qualifications requisite for Electors of the most numerous Branch of the State Legislature.

No Person shall be a Representative who shall not have attained to the Age of twenty five Years, and been seven Years a Citizen of the United States, and who shall not, when elected, be an Inhabitant of that State in which he shall be chosen.

Representatives and direct Taxes shall be apportioned among the several States which may be included within this Union, according to their respective Numbers, which shall be determined by adding to the whole Number of free Persons, including those bound to Service for a Term of Years, and excluding Indians not taxed, three fifths of all other Persons. The actual Enumeration shall be made within three Years after the first Meeting of the Congress of the United States, and within every subsequent Term of ten Years, in such Manner as they shall by Law direct. The Number of Representatives shall not exceed one for every thirty Thousand, but each State shall have at Least one Representative; and until such enumeration shall be made, the State of New Hampshire shall be entitled to chuse three, Massachusetts eight, Rhode-Island and Providence Plantations one, Connecticut five, New-York six, New Jersey four,

Pennsylvania eight, Delaware one, Maryland six, Virginia ten, North Carolina five, South Carolina five, and Georgia three.

When vacancies happen in the Representation from any state, the Executive Authority thereof shall issue Writs of Election to fill such Vacancies.

The House of Representatives shall chuse their Speaker and other Officers; and shall have the sole Power of Impeachment.

Section. 3. The Senate of the United States shall be composed of two Senators from each State, chosen by the legislature thereof, for six Years; and each Senator shall have one Vote.

Immediately after they shall be assembled in Consequence of the first Election, they shall be divided as equally as may be into three Classes. The Seats of the Senators of the first Class shall be vacated at the Expiration of the second Year, of the second Class at the Expiration of the fourth Year, and of the third Class at the Expiration of the sixth Year, so that one third maybe chosen every second Year; and if Vacancies happen by Resignation, or otherwise, during the Recess of the Legislature of any State, the Executive thereof may make temporary Appointments until the next Meeting of the Legislature, which shall then fill such Vacancies.

No Person shall be a Senator who shall not have attained to the Age of thirty Years, and been nine Years a Citizen of the United States, and who shall not, when elected, be an Inhabitant of that State for which he shall be chosen.

The Vice President of the United States shall be President of the Senate, but shall have no Vote, unless they be equally divided.

The Senate shall chuse their other Officers, and also a President pro tempore, in the Absence of the Vice President, or when he shall exercise the Office of President of the United States.

The Senate shall have the sole Power to try all Impeachments. When sitting for that Purpose, they shall be on Oath or Affirmation. When the President of the United States is tried, the Chief Justice shall preside: And no Person shall be convicted without the Concurrence of two thirds of the Members present.

Judgment in Cases of Impeachment shall not extend further than to removal from Office, and disqualification to hold and enjoy any Office of honor, Trust or Profit under the United States: but the Party convicted shall nevertheless be liable and subject to Indictment, Trial, Judgment and Punishment, according to Law.

Section. 4. The Times, Places and Manner of holding Elections for Senators and Representatives, shall be prescribed in each State by the Legislature thereof, but the Congress may at any time by Law make or alter such Regulations, except as to the Places of chusing Senators.

The Congress shall assemble at least once in every Year, and such Meeting shall be on the first Monday in December, unless they shall by Law appoint a different Day.

Section. 5. Each House shall be the Judge of the Elections, Returns and Qualifications of its own Members, and a Majority of each shall constitute a Quorum to do Business; but a smaller Number may adjourn from day to day, and may be authorized to compel the Attendance of absent Members, in such Manner, and under such Penalties as each House may provide.

Each House may determine the Rules of its Proceedings, punish its Members for disorderly Behaviour, and, with the Concurrence of two thirds, expel a Member.

Each House shall keep a Journal of its Proceedings, and from time to time publish the same, excepting such Parts as may in their Judgment require Secrecy; and the Yeas and Nays of the Members of either House on any question shall, at the Desire of one fifth of those Present, be entered on the Journal.

Neither House, during the Session of Congress, shall, without the Consent of the other, adjourn for more than three days, nor to any other Place than that in which the two Houses shall be sitting.

Section. 6. The Senators and Representatives shall receive a Compensation for their Services, to be ascertained by Law, and paid out of the Treasury of the United States. They shall in all Cases, except Treason, Felony and Breach of the Peace, be privileged from Arrest during their Attendance at the Session of their respective Houses, and in going to and returning from the same; and for any Speech or Debate in either House, they shall not be questioned in any other Place.

No Senator or Representative shall, during the Time for which he was elected, be appointed to any civil Office under the Authority of the United States, which shall have been created, or the Emoluments whereof shall have been encreased during such time; and no Person holding any Office under the United States, shall be a Member of either House during his Continuance in Office.

Section. 7. All Bills for raising Revenue shall originate in the House of Representatives; but the Senate may propose or concur with Amendments as on other Bills.

Every Bill which shall have passed the House of Representatives and the Senate shall, before it become a Law, be presented to the President of the United States; If he approve he shall sign it, but if not he shall return it, with his Objections to that House in which it shall have originated, who shall enter the Objections at large on their Journal, and proceed to reconsider it. If after such Reconsideration two thirds of that House shall agree to pass the Bill, it shall be sent, together with the Objections, to the other House, by which it shall likewise be reconsidered, and if approved by two thirds of that House, it shall become a Law. But in all such Cases the Votes of both Houses shall be determined by yeas and Nays, and the Names of the Persons voting for and against the Bill shall be entered on the Journal of each House respectively. If any Bill shall not be returned by the President within ten Days (Sundays excepted) after it shall have been presented to him, the Same shall be a Law, in like Manner as if he had signed it, unless the Congress by their Adjournment prevent its Return, in which Case it shall not be a Law.

Every Order, Resolution, or Vote to which the Concurrence of the Senate and House of Representatives may be necessary (except on a question of Adjournment) shall be presented to the President of the United States; and before the Same shall take Effect, shall be approved by him, or being disapproved by him, shall be repassed by two thirds of the Senate and House of Representatives, according to the Rules and Limitations prescribed in the Case of a Bill.

Section. 8. The congress shall have Power To lay and collect Taxes, Duties, Imposts and Excises, to pay the Debts and provide for the common Defence and general Welfare of the United States; but all Duties, Imposts and Excises shall be uniform throughout the United States.

To borrow Money on the credit of the United States;

To regulate Commerce with foreign Nations, and among the several States, and with the Indian Tribes;

To establish an uniform Rule of Naturalization, and uniform Laws on the subject of Bankruptcies throughout the United States;

To coin Money, regulate the Value thereof, and of foreign Coin, and fix the Standard of Weights and Measures;

To provide for the Punishment of counterfeiting the Securities and current Coin of the United States;

To establish Post Offices and Post Roads;

To promote the Progress of Science and useful Arts, by securing for limited Times to Authors and Inventors the exclusive Right to their respective Writings and Discoveries;

To constitute Tribunals inferior to the supreme Court;

To define and punish Piracies and Felonies committed on the high Seas, and Offences against the Law of Nations;

To declare War, grant Letters of Marque and Reprisal, and make Rules concerning Captures on land and Water;

To raise and support Armies, but no Appropriation of Money to that Use shall be for a longer Term than two Years;

To provide and maintain a Navy;

To make Rules for the Government and Regulation of the land and naval Forces;

To provide for calling forth the Militia to execute the Laws of the Union, suppress Insurrections and repel Invasions;

To provide for organizing, arming, and disciplining, the Militia, and for governing such Part of them as may be employed in the Service of the United States, reserving to the States respectively, the Appointment of the Officers, and the Authority of training the Militia according to the discipline prescribed by Congress;

To exercise exclusive Legislation in all Cases whatsoever, over such District (not exceeding ten Miles square) as may, by Cession of particular States, and the Acceptance of Congress, become the Seat of the Government of the United States, and to exercise like Authority over all Places purchased by the Consent of the Legislature of the State in which the Same shall be, for the Erection of Forts, Magazines, Arsenals, dock-Yards, and other needful Buildings;—And

To make all Laws which shall be necessary and proper for carrying into Execution the foregoing Powers, and all other Powers vested by this Constitution in the Government of the United States, or in any Department or Officer thereof.

Section. 9. The Migration or Importation of such Persons as any of the States now existing shall think proper to admit, shall not be prohibited by the Congress prior to the Year one thousand eight hundred and eight, but a Tax or duty may be imposed on such Importation, not exceeding ten dollars for each Person.

The Privilege of the Writ of Habeas Corpus shall not be suspended, unless when in Cases of Rebellion or Invasion the public Safety may require it.

No Bill of Attainder or ex post facto Law shall be passed.

No Capitation, or other direct, Tax shall be laid, unless in Proportion to the Census or Enumeration herein before directed to be taken.

No Tax or Duty shall be laid on Articles exported from any State.

No Preference shall be given by any Regulation of Commerce or Revenue to the Ports of one State over those of another: nor shall Vessels bound to, or from, one State, be obliged to enter, clear, or pay Duties in another.

No Money shall be drawn from the Treasury, but in Consequence of Appropriations made by Law, and a regular Statement and Account of the Receipts and Expenditures of all public Money shall be published from time to time.

No Title of Nobility shall be granted by the United States: And no Person holding any Office of Profit or trust under them, shall, without the Consent of the Congress, accept of any present, Emolument, Office, or Title, of any kind whatever, from any King, prince, or foreign State.

Section. 10. No State shall enter into any Treaty, Alliance, or Confederation; grant Letters of Marque and Reprisal; coin Money; emit Bills of Credit; make any Thing but gold and silver Coin a Tender in Payment of Debts; pass any Bill of Attainder, ex post facto Law, or Law impairing the Obligation of Contracts, or grant any Title of Nobility.

No State shall, without the Consent of the Congress, lay any Imposts or Duties on Imports or Exports, except what may be absolutely necessary for executing it's inspection Laws: and the net Produce of all Duties and Imposts, laid by any State on Imports or Exports, shall be for the Use of the Treasury of the United States; and all such Laws shall be subject to the Revision and Controul of the Congress.

No State shall, without the Consent of Congress, lay any Duty of Tonnage, keep Troops, or Ships of War in time of Peace, enter into any Agreement or Compact with another State, or with a foreign Power, or engage in War, unless actually invaded, or in such imminent Danger as will not admit of delay.

Article. II

Section. 1. The executive Power shall be vested in a President of the United States of America. He shall hold his Office during the term of four Years, and, together with the Vice President, chosen for the same Term, be elected, as follows.

Each State shall appoint, in such Manner as the Legislature thereof may direct, a Number of Electors, equal to the whole Number of Senators and Representatives to which the State may be entitled in the Congress: but no Senator or Representative, or Person holding an Office of Trust or Profit under the United States, shall be appointed an Elector.

The Electors shall meet in their respective States, and vote by Ballot for two Persons, of whom one at least shall not be an Inhabitant of the same State with themselves. And they shall make a List of all the Persons voted for, and of the Number of Votes for each; which List they shall sign and certify, and transmit sealed to the Seat of the Government of the United States, directed to the President of the Senate. The President of the Senate shall, in the Presence of the Senate and House of Representatives, open all the Certificates, and the Votes shall then be counted. The Person having the greatest Number of Votes shall be the President, if such Number be a Majority of the whole Number of Electors appointed; and if there be more than one who have such Majority, and have an equal Number of Votes, then the House of Representatives shall immediately chuse by Ballot one of them for President; and if no Person have a Majority, then from the five highest on the List the said House shall in like Manner chuse the President. But in chusing the President, the Votes shall be taken by States, the Representation from each State having one Vote; A quorum for this Purpose shall consist of a Member or Members from two thirds of the States, and a Majority of all the States shall be necessary to a Choice. In every Case, after the Choice of the President, the Person having the greatest Number of Votes of the Electors shall be the Vice President. But if there should remain two or more who have equal Votes, the Senate shall chuse from them by Ballot the Vice President.

The Congress may determine the Time of chusing the Electors, and the Day on which they shall give their Votes; which Day shall be the same throughout the United States.

No Person except a natural born Citizen, or a Citizen of the United States, at the time of the Adoption of this Constitution, shall be eligible to the Office of President, neither shall any Person be eligible to that Office who shall not have attained to the Age of thirty five Years, and been fourteen Years a Resident within the United States.

In Case of the Removal of the President from office, or of his Death, Resignation, or Inability to discharge the Powers and Duties of the said Office, the Same shall devolve on the Vice President, and the Congress may by Law provide for the Case of Removal, Death, Resignation or Inability, both of the President and Vice President, declaring what Officer shall then act as President, and such Officer shall act accordingly, until the Disability be removed, or a President shall be elected.

The President shall, at stated Times, receive for his Services, a Compensation, which shall neither be encreased or diminished during the Period for which he shall have been elected, and he shall not receive within that Period any other Emolument from the United States, or any of them.

Before he enters on the Execution of his Office, he shall take the following Oath or Affirmation:— "I do solemnly swear (or affirm) that I will faithfully execute the Office of President of the United States, and will to the best of my Ability, preserve, protect and defend the Constitution of the United States."

Section. 2. The President shall be Commander in Chief of the Army and Navy of the United States, and of the Militia of the several States, when called into the actual Service of the United States; he may require the Opinion, in writing, of the principal Officer in each of the executive Departments, upon any Subject relating to the Duties of their respective Offices, and he shall have Power to grant Reprieves and Pardons for Offences against the United States, except in Cases of Impeachment.

He shall have Power, by and with the Advice and Consent of the Senate, to make Treaties, provided two thirds of the Senators present concur; and he shall nominate, and by and with the Advice and Consent of the Senate, shall appoint Ambas-

sadors, other public Ministers and Consuls, Judges of the supreme Court, and all other Officers of the United States, whose Appointments are not herein otherwise provided for, and which shall be established by Law; but the Congress may by Law vest the Appointment of such inferior Officers, as they think proper, in the President alone, in the Courts of Law, or in the Heads of Departments.

The President shall have Power to fill up all Vacancies that may happen during the Recess of the Senate, by granting Commissions which shall expire at the End of their next Session.

Section. 3. He shall from time to time give to the Congress Information of the State of the Union, and recommend to their Consideration such Measures as he shall judge necessary and expedient; he may, on extraordinary Occasions, convene both Houses, or either of them, and in Case of Disagreement between them, with Respect to the Time of Adjournment, he may adjourn them to such Time as he shall think proper; he shall receive Ambassadors and other public Ministers; he shall take Care that the Laws be faithfully executed, and shall Commission all the Officers of the United States.

Section. 4. The President, Vice President and all civil Officers of the United States, shall be removed from Office on Impeachment for, and Conviction of, Treason, Bribery, or other high Crimes and Misdemeanors.

ARTICLE. III

Section. 1. The judicial Power of the United States, shall be vested in one supreme Court, and in such inferior Courts as the Congress may from time to time ordain and establish. The Judges, both of the supreme and inferior Courts, shall hold their Offices during good Behavior, and shall, at stated Times, receive for their Services, a Compensation, which shall not be diminished during their Continuance in Office.

Section. 2. The judicial Power shall extend to all Cases, in Law and Equity, arising under this Constitution, the Laws of the United States, and Treaties made, or which shall be made, under their Authority;—to all Cases affecting Ambassadors, other public Ministers and Consuls;—to all Cases of admiralty and maritime Jurisdiction;—to Controversies to which the United States shall be a Party;—to Controversies between two or more States;—between a State and Citizens of another State;—between Citizens of different States;—between Citizens of the same State claiming Lands under Grants of different States, and between a State, or the Citizens thereof, and foreign States, Citizens or Subjects.

In all cases affecting Ambassadors, other public Ministers and Consuls, and those in which a State shall be Party, the supreme Court shall have original Jurisdiction. In all the other Cases before mentioned, the supreme Court shall have appellate Jurisdiction, both as to Law and Fact, with such Exceptions, and under such Regulations as the Congress shall make.

The Trial of all Crimes, except in Cases of Impeachment, shall be by Jury; and such Trial shall be held in the State where the said Crimes shall have been committed; but when not committed within any State, the Trial shall be at such Place or Places as the Congress may by Law have directed.

Section. 3. Treason against the United States, shall consist only in levying War against them, or in adhering to their Enemies, giving them Aid and Comfort. No Person shall be convicted of Treason unless on the Testimony of two Witnesses to the same overt Act, or on Confession in open Court.

The Congress shall have Power to declare the Punishment of Treason, but no Attainder of Treason shall work Corruption of Blood, or Forfeiture except during the Life of the Person attainted.

Article. IV

Section. 1. Full Faith and Credit shall be given in each State to the public Acts, Records, and judicial Proceedings of every other State. And the Congress may by general Laws prescribe the Manner in which such Acts, Records and Proceedings shall be proved, and the Effect thereof.

Section. 2. The Citizens of each State shall be entitled to all Privileges and Immunities of Citizens in the several States.

A Person charged in any State with Treason, Felony, or other Crime, who shall flee from Justice, and be found in another State, shall on Demand of the executive Authority of the State from which he fled, be delivered up, to be removed to the State having Jurisdiction of the Crime.

No Person held to Service or Labour in one State, under the Laws thereof, escaping into another, shall, in Consequence of any Law or Regulation therein, be discharged from such Service or Labour, but shall be delivered up on Claim of the Party to whom such Service or Labour may be due.

Section. 3. New States may be admitted by the Congress into this Union; but no new State shall be formed or erected within the Jurisdiction of any other State; nor any State be formed by the Junction of two or more States, or Parts of States, without the consent of the Legislatures of the States concerned as well as of the Congress.

The Congress shall have Power to dispose of and make all needful Rules and Regulations respecting the Territory or other Property belonging to the United States; and nothing in this Constitution shall be so construed as to Prejudice any Claims of the United States, or of any particular States.

Section. 4. The United States shall guarantee to every State in this Union a Republican Form of Government, and shall protect each of them against Invasion; and on Application of the Legislature, or of the Executive (when the Legislature cannot be convened) against domestic Violence.

Article. V

The Congress, whenever two thirds of both Houses shall deem it necessary, shall propose

Amendments to this Constitution, or, on the Application of the Legislatures of two thirds of the several States shall call a Convention for proposing Amendments, which, in either Case, shall be valid to all Intents and Purposes, as Part of this Constitution, when ratified by the Legislatures of three fourths of the several States, or by Conventions in three fourths thereof, as the one or the other Mode of Ratification may be proposed by the Congress; Provided that no Amendment which may be made prior to the Year One thousand eight hundred and eight shall in any Manner affect the first and fourth Clauses in the Ninth Section of the first Article; and that no State, without its Consent, shall be deprived of its equal Suffrage in the Senate.

Article. VI

All Debts contracted and Engagements entered into, before the Adoption of this Constitution, shall be as valid against the United States under this Constitution, as under the Confederation.

This Constitution, and the Laws of the United States which shall be made in Pursuance thereof; and all Treaties made, or which shall be made, under the Authority of the United States, shall be the supreme Law of the Land; and the Judges in every State shall be bound thereby, any Thing in the Constitution or Laws of any State to the Contrary notwithstanding.

The Senators and Representatives before mentioned, and the Members of the several State Legislatures, and all executive and judicial Officers, both of the United States and of the several States, shall be bound by Oath or Affirmation, to support this Constitution; but no religious Test shall ever be required as a Qualification to any Office or public Trust under the United States.

Article. VII

The Ratification of the Conventions of nine States, shall be sufficient for the Establishment of this Constitution between the States so ratifying the Same.

Done in Convention by the Unanimous Consent of the States present the Seventeenth Day of September in the Year of our Lord one thousand seven hundred and Eighty seven and of the Independence of the United States of America the Twelfth. In witness thereof We have hereunto subscribed our Names,

G°: WASHINGTON—Presid.
and deputy from Virginia

New Hampshire { John Langdon
Nicholas Gilman

Massachusetts { Nathaniel Gorham
Rufus King

Connecticut { Wm Saml Johnson
Roger Sherman

New York   Alexander Hamilton

New Jersey { Wil: Livingston
David A. Brearley.
Wm Paterson.
Jona: Dayton

Pennsylvania { B. Franklin
Thomas Mifflin
Robt Morris
Geo. Clymer
Thos. FitzSimons
Jared Ingersoll
James Wilson
Gouv Morris

Delaware { Geo: Read
Gunning Bedford jun
John Dickinson
Richard Bassett
Jaco: Broom

Maryland { James McHenry
Dan of St Thos Jenifer
Danl Carroll

Virginia { John Blair—
James Madison Jr.

North Carolina { Wm. Blount
Richd Dobbs Spaight.
Hu Williamson

South Carolina { J. Rutledge
Charles Cotesworth Pinckney
Charles Pinckney
Pierce Butler.

Georgia { William Few
Abr Baldwin

Review Questions

1. What major political principles were not only articulated but activated by the Constitution?
2. How does the Constitution reveal not only the intellectual background of the Founders but their practical experiences as well?
3. Can you tell which provisions were the result of consensus and which were due to compromise? What does such a comparison reveal about the founders and the foundation of the government?
4. What provisions appear to be most open to differing interpretations? Why are the different possibilities for interpretation significant?

JAMES WILSON

FROM Wilson's Defense of the Constitution at the Pennsylvania Convention (1787)

As the Constitution—and the government it would create—could only be ratified by the people, the Confederation Congress submitted the document to the states where the issue would be decided by special ratifying conventions. That was a noble nod to government by the people, but the convention delegates also bowed to political neces-sity in Article VII of the Constitution: only nine of the state conventions had to vote aye for the Constitution to be ratified. But to found the new government upon the ac-ceptance of only nine states would not have boded well for the strength and unity of the new nation, so the Constitution's supporters set out to make ratification a unani-mous mandate for change. It was not quite the mandate they sought, for while all of the states did eventually ratify the Constitution, North Carolina and Rhode Island waiting until after the new government had commenced operations, unanimity came only after vigorous debate with and concessionary promises to those against the pro-posed change.

Within days of Delaware's (the first state to ratify) vote, Pennsylvania ratified the Constitution on 12 December 1787. As in many of the states, the Federalists, those who supported a strong, national government, had taken the lead and established the agenda. This group benefited from some exceptional leaders who knew how to articu-late clearly the reasons for a general government and champion its adoption. Among those leaders was James Wilson. Born in Scotland and educated at Edinburgh and Saint Andrews Universities there, Wilson was a profound legal scholar and revolu-tionary. He was a signer of the Declaration of Independence as well as the Constitu-tion and would eventually serve on the Supreme Court.

From Jonathan Elliot, ed., *The Debates in the Several State Conventions on the Adoption of the Federal Constitution*, vol. 2 (1836; New York: Burt Franklin Reprints, 1974), pp. 418–19, 435–37, 443–44, 455–58, 462–63.

The system proposed, by the late Convention, for the government of the United States, is now before you. Of that Convention I had the honor to be a member. As I am the only mem-ber of that body who has the honor to be also a member of this, it may be expected that I should prepare the way for the deliberations of this assembly, by unfolding the difficulties which the late Convention were obliged to encounter; by pointing out the end which they proposed to ac-complish; and by tracing the general principles which they have adopted for the accomplishment of that end.

To form a good system of government for a single city or state, however limited as to territory, or inconsiderable as to numbers, has been thought to require the strongest efforts of human genius. With what conscious diffidence, then, must the members of the Convention have revolved in their minds the immense undertaking which was before them. Their views could not be confined to a small or a single community, but were expanded to a great number of states; several of which contain an extent of territory, and resources of population, equal to those of some of the most respectable kingdoms on the other side of the Atlantic. Nor were even these the only objects to be comprehended within their deliberations. Numerous states yet unformed, myriads of the human race, who will inhabit regions hitherto uncultivated, were to be affected by the result of their proceedings. It was necessary, therefore, to form their calculations on a scale commensurate to a large portion of the globe.

*   *   *

The difficulty of the business was equal to its magnitude. No small share of wisdom and address is requisite to combine and reconcile the jarring interests that prevail, or seem to prevail, in a single community. The United States contain already thirteen governments mutually independent. Those governments present to the Atlantic a front of fifteen hundred miles in extent. Their soil, their climates, their productions, their dimensions, their numbers, are different. In many instances, a difference, and even an opposition, subsists among their interests; and a difference, and even an opposition, is imagined to subsist in many more. An apparent interest produces the same attachment as a real one, and is often pursued with no less perseverance and vigor. When all these circumstances are seen, and attentively considered, will any member of this honorable body be surprised that such a diversity of things produced a proportionate diversity of sentiment? Will he be surprised that such a diversity of sentiment rendered a spirit of mutual forbearance and conciliation indispensably necessary to the success of the great work? . . .

*   *   *

I am called upon to give a reason why the Convention omitted to add a bill of rights to the work before you. I confess, sir, I did think that, in point of propriety, the honorable gentleman ought first to have furnished some reasons to show such an addition to be necessary; it is natural to prove the affirmative of a proposition; and, if he had established the propriety of this addition, he might then have asked why it was not made.

I cannot say, Mr. President, what were the reasons of every member of that Convention for not adding a bill of rights. I believe the truth is, that such an idea never entered the mind of many of them. I do not recollect to have heard the subject mentioned till within about three days of the time of our rising; and even then, there was no direct motion offered for any thing of the kind. I may be mistaken in this; but as far as my memory serves me, I believe it was the case. A proposition to adopt a measure that would have supposed that we were throwing into the general government every power not expressly reserved by the people, would have been spurned at, in that house, with the greatest indignation. Even in a single government, if the powers of the people rest on the same establishment as is expressed in this Constitution, a bill of rights is by no means a necessary measure. In a government possessed of enumerated powers, such a measure would be not only unnecessary, but preposterous and dangerous. Whence comes this notion, that in the United States there is no security without a bill of rights? Have the citizens of South Carolina no security for their liberties? They have no bill of rights. Are the citizens on the eastern side of the Delaware less free, or less secured in their liberties, than those on the western side? The state of New Jersey has no bill of rights. The state of New York has no bill of rights. The states of Connecticut and Rhode Island have no bill of rights. I know not whether I have exactly enumerated the states who have not thought it necessary to add *a bill of rights* to their constitutions; but this enumeration, sir, will serve to show by experience, as well as principle, that, even in single governments, a bill of rights is not an essential or necessary measure. But in a government consisting of enumerated powers, such as is proposed for the United States, a bill of rights would not only be unnecessary, but, in my humble judgment, highly imprudent. In all societies, there are many powers and rights which cannot be particularly enumerated. A bill of rights annexed to a constitution is *an enumeration of the powers* reserved. If we attempt an enumeration, every thing that is not enumerated is presumed to be given. The consequence is, that an imperfect enumeration would throw all implied power into the scale of the government, and the rights of the people would be rendered incomplete. On the other hand, an imperfect enumeration of the powers of government reserves all implied power to the people; and by that means the constitution becomes incomplete. But of the two, it is much safer to run the risk on the side of the constitution; for an omission in the enumeration of the powers of government is neither so dangerous nor important as an omission in the enumeration of the rights of the people.

* * *

To every suggestion concerning a bill of rights, the citizens of the United States may always say, We reserve the right to do what we please.

* * *

. . . Upon what principle is it contended that the sovereign power resides in the state governments? The honorable gentleman has said truly, that there can be no subordinate sovereignty. Now, if there cannot, my position is, that the sovereignty resides in the people; they have not parted with it; they have only dispensed such portions of power as were conceived necessary for the public welfare. This Constitution stands upon this broad principle. I know very well, sir, that the people have hitherto been shut out of the federal government; but it is not meant that they should any longer be dispossessed of their rights. In order to recognize this leading principle, the proposed system sets out with a declaration that its existence depends upon the supreme authority of the people alone. We have heard much about a consolidated government. I wish the honorable gentleman would condescend to give us a definition of what he meant by it. I think this the more necessary, because I apprehend that the term, in the numerous times it has been

used, has not always been used in the same sense. It may be said, and I believe it has been said, that a consolidated government is such as will absorb and destroy the governments of the several states. If it is taken in this view, the plan before us is not a consolidated government, as I showed on a former day, and may, if necessary, show further on some future occasion. On the other hand, if it is meant that the general government will take from the state governments their power in some particulars, it is confessed, and evident, that this will be its operation and effect.

When the principle is once settled that *the people* are the source of authority, the consequence is, that they may take from the subordinate governments powers with which they have hitherto trusted them, and place those powers in the general government, if it is thought that there they will be productive of more good. They can distribute one portion of power to the more contracted circle, called *state governments*; they can also furnish another proportion to the government of the United States. . . .

* * *

I consider the people of the United States as forming one great community; and I consider the people of the different states as forming communities, again, on a lesser scale. From this great division of the people into distinct communities, it will be found necessary that different proportions of legislative powers should be given to the governments, according to the nature, number, and magnitude of their objects.

Unless the people are considered in these two views, we shall never be able to understand the principle on which this system was constructed. I view the states as made *for* the people, as well as by them, and not the people as made for the states; the people, therefore, have a right, whilst enjoying the undeniable powers of society, to form either a general government, or state governments, in what manner they please, or to accommodate them to one another, and by this means preserve them all. This, I say, is the inherent and unalienable right of the people; . . .

*   *   *

. . . My position is, sir, that, in this country, the supreme, absolute, and uncontrollable power resides in the people at large; that they have vested certain proportions of this power in the state governments; but that the fee-simple continues, resides, and remains, with the body of the people. Under the practical influence of this great truth, we are now sitting and deliberating, and under its operation, we can sit as calmly and deliberate as coolly, in order to change a constitution, as a legislature can sit and deliberate under the power of a constitution, in order to alter or amend a law. It is true, the exercise of this power will not probably be so frequent, nor resorted to on so many occasions, in one case as in the other; but the recognition of the principle cannot fail to establish it more firmly. But, because this recognition is made in the proposed Constitution, an exception is taken to the whole of it; for we are told it is a violation of the present Confederation—*a Confederation of sovereign states.* I shall not enter into an investigation of the present Confederation, but shall just remark that its principle is not the principle of free governments. The people of the United States are not, as such, represented in the present Congress; and, considered even as the component parts of the several states, they are not represented in proportion to their numbers and importance.

*   *   *

REVIEW QUESTIONS

1. How did Wilson justify his assumption of a commanding role in the Pennsylvania convention? Did this tactic benefit the Federalists and weaken their opponents?
2. One reason the Antifederalists attacked the proposed Constitution was that it lacked a Bill of Rights. How did Wilson counter this criticism?
3. What is the relationship between sovereignty and political power? In delegating the latter, do the people lose the former?
4. How did Wilson illustrate or define the federal system as it would operate under the Constitution?

PATRICK HENRY AND GEORGE MASON

FROM Arguments against Ratification at the Virginia Convention (1788)

When the delegates to the Virginia convention debated the Constitution in June 1788, they did so under the assumption that an aye vote there would provide the vital, deciding ninth affirmative needed for ratification. As it turned out, New Hampshire provided that necessary vote; but acting without that knowledge and aware that other states deemed Virginia's acceptance critical to the success of a new government, these delegates were especially primed to do battle. Adding to the dynamism of this particular convention was the caliber of the participants: there were exceptional men among both the proponents of and opponents to the Constitution. Among its champions were

Edmund Pendleton, James Madison, George Nicholas, and John Marshall. Opposing them was a formidable team that included, to name just a few, George Mason, Richard Henry Lee, James Monroe, and its leader Patrick Henry. Henry had served as a wartime governor of the state but had made his reputation through his inflammatory rhetoric as a young revolutionary. In the following selection he once again uses his oratory talents as well as legal skills to try to guide public affairs as he presents impassioned, imaginative, and negative arguments.

From Jonathan Elliot, ed., *The Debates in the Several State Conventions on the Adoption of the Federal Constitution*, vol. 3 (1836; New York: Burt Franklin Reprints, 1974), pp. 6, 21–23, 29–34, 44–59, 445–48, 589–91.

Wednesday, 4 June 1788

The Convention, according to the order of the day, resolved itself into a committee of the whole Convention, to take into consideration the proposed plan of government, Mr. Wythe in the chair.

Mr. HENRY moved,—

That the act of Assembly appointing deputies to meet at Annapolis to consult with those from some other states, on the situation of the commerce of the United States—the act of Assembly appointing deputies to meet at Philadelphia, to revise the Articles of Confederation—and other public papers relative thereto—should be read.

Mr. PENDLETON then spoke to the following effect: Mr. Chairman, we are not to consider whether the federal Convention exceeded their powers. It strikes my mind that this ought not to influence our deliberations. This Constitution was transmitted to Congress by that Convention; by the Congress transmitted to our legislature; by them recommended to the people; the people have sent us hither to determine whether this government be a proper one or not. I did not expect these papers would have been brought forth. Although those gentlemen were only directed to consider the defects of the old system, and not devise a new one, if they found it so thoroughly defective as not to admit a revising, and submitted a new system to our consideration, which the people have deputed us to investigate, I cannot find any degree of propriety in reading those papers.

Mr. HENRY then withdrew his motion.

The clerk proceeded to read the preamble, and the two first sections of the first article.

*   *   *

Mr. HENRY. Mr. Chairman, the public mind, as well as my own, is extremely uneasy at the proposed change of government. Give me leave to form one of the number of those who wish to be thoroughly acquainted with the reasons of this perilous and uneasy situation, and why we are brought hither to decide on this great national question. I consider myself as the servant of the people of this commonwealth, as a sentinel over their rights, liberty, and happiness. I represent their feelings when I say that they are exceedingly uneasy at being brought from that state of full security, which they enjoyed, to the present delusive appearance of things. A year ago, the minds of our citizens were at perfect repose. Before the meeting of the late federal Convention at Philadelphia, a general peace and a universal tranquillity prevailed in this country; but, since that period, they are exceedingly uneasy and disquieted. When I wished for an appointment to this Convention, my mind was extremely agitated for the situation of public affairs. I conceived the republic to be in extreme danger. If our situation be thus uneasy, whence has arisen this fearful jeopardy? It arises from this fatal system; it arises from a proposal to change our government—a proposal that goes to the utter annihilation of the most solemn engagements of the states—a proposal of establishing nine states into a confederacy, to the eventual exclusion of four states. It goes to the annihilation of those solemn treaties we have formed with foreign nations.

The present circumstances of France—the good offices rendered us by that kingdom—require our most faithful and most punctual adherence to our treaty with her. We are in alliance with the Spaniards, the Dutch, the Prussians; those treaties bound us as thirteen states confederated together. Yet here is a proposal to sever that confederacy. Is it possible that we shall abandon all our treaties and national engagements?—and for what? I expected to hear the reasons for an event so unexpected to my mind and many others. Was our civil polity, or public justice, endangered or sapped? Was the real existence of the country threatened, or was this preceded by a mournful progression of events? This proposal of altering our federal government is of a most alarming nature! Make the best of this new government—say it is composed by any thing but inspiration—you ought to be extremely cautious, watchful, jealous of your liberty; for, instead of securing your rights, you may lose them forever. . . . It will be necessary for this Convention to have a faithful historical detail of the facts that preceded the session of the federal Convention, and the reasons that actuated its members in proposing an entire alteration of government, and to demonstrate the dangers that awaited us. If they were of such awful magnitude as to warrant a proposal so extremely perilous as this, I must assert, that this Convention has an absolute right to a thorough discovery of every circumstance relative to this great event. And here I would make this inquiry of those worthy characters who composed a part of the late federal Convention. I am sure they were fully impressed with the necessity of forming a great consolidated government, instead of a confederation. That this is a consolidated government is demonstrably clear; and the danger of such a government is, to my mind, very striking I have the highest veneration for those gentlemen; but, sir, give me leave to demand, What right had they to say, *We, the people*? My political curiosity, exclusive of my anxious solicitude for the public welfare, leads me to ask, Who authorized them to speak the language of, *We, the people*, instead of,

We, the states? States are the characteristics and the soul of a confederation. If the states be not the agents of this compact, it must be one great, consolidated, national government, of the people of all the states. . . . It is not mere curiosity that actuates me: I wish to hear the real, actual, existing danger, which should lead us to take those steps, so dangerous in my conception. Disorders have arisen in other parts of America; but here, sir, no dangers, no insurrection or tumult have happened; every thing has been calm and tranquil. But, notwithstanding this, we are wandering on the great ocean of human affairs. . . . The federal Convention ought to have amended the old system; for this purpose they were solely delegated; the object of their mission extended to no other consideration. You must, therefore, forgive the solicitation of one unworthy member to know what danger could have arisen under the present Confederation, and what are the causes of this proposal to change our government.

*   *   *

Mr. GEORGE MASON. Mr. Chairman, whether the Constitution be good or bad, the present clause clearly discovers that it is a national government, and no longer a Confederation. I mean that clause which gives the first hint of the general government laying direct taxes. The assumption of this power of laying direct taxes does, of itself, entirely change the confederation of the states into one consolidated government. This power, being at discretion, unconfined, and without any kind of control, must carry every thing before it. The very idea of converting what was formerly a confederation to a consolidated government, is totally subversive of every principle which has hitherto governed us. This power is calculated to annihilate totally the state governments. Will the people of this great community submit to be individually taxed by two different and distinct powers? Will they suffer themselves to be doubly harassed? These two concurrent powers cannot exist long together; the one will destroy the other: the general government being paramount to, and in every respect more powerful than the state governments, the latter must give way to the former. Is it to be supposed that one national government will suit so extensive a country, embracing so many climates, and containing inhabitants so very different in manners, habits, and customs? It is ascertained, by history, that there never was a government over a very extensive country without destroying the liberties of the people: history also, supported by the opinions of the best writers, shows us that monarchy may suit a large territory, and despotic governments ever so extensive a country, but that popular governments can only exist in small territories. . . . It would be impossible to have a full and adequate representation in the general government; it would be too expensive and too unwieldy. We are, then, under the necessity of having this a very inadequate representation. Is this general representation to be compared with the real, actual, substantial representation of the state legislatures? It cannot bear a comparison. To make representation real and actual, the number of representatives ought to be adequate; they ought to mix with the people, think as they think, feel as they feel,—ought to be perfectly amenable to them, and thoroughly acquainted with their interest and condition. Now, these great ingredients are either not at all, or in a small degree, to be found in our federal representatives; so that we have no real, actual, substantial representation: but I acknowledge it results from the nature of the government. The necessity of this inconvenience may appear a sufficient reason not to argue against it; but, sir, it clearly shows that we ought to give power with a sparing hand to a government thus imperfectly constructed. To a government which, in the nature of things, cannot but be defective, no powers ought to be given but such as are absolutely necessary. There is one thing in it which I conceive to be extremely dangerous. Gentlemen may talk of public virtue and confidence; we shall be told that the House of Representatives will consist of the most virtuous men on the continent, and that in their hands we may trust our dearest rights. This, like all other assemblies, will be composed of some bad and some good men; and, considering the natural lust of power so inherent in man, I fear the thirst of power will prevail to oppress the people. . . . But my principal objection is,

that the Confederation is converted to one general consolidated government, which, from my best judgment of it, (and which perhaps will be shown, in the course of this discussion, to be really well founded,) is one of the worst curses that can possibly befall a nation. Does any man suppose that one general national government can exist in so extensive a country as this? I hope that a government may be framed which may suit us, by drawing a line between the general and state governments, and prevent that dangerous clashing of interest and power, which must, as it now stands, terminate in the destruction of one or the other. When we come to the judiciary, we shall be more convinced that this government will terminate in the annihilation of the state governments: the question then will be, whether a consolidated government can preserve the freedom and secure the rights of the people.

If such amendments be introduced as shall exclude danger, I shall most gladly put my hand to it. When such amendments as shall, from the best information, secure the great essential rights of the people, shall be agreed to by gentlemen, I shall most heartily make the greatest concessions, and concur in any reasonable measure to obtain the desirable end of conciliation and unanimity. . . .

*   *   *

Thursday, 5 June 1788

Mr. HENRY. . . .

I rose yesterday to ask a question which arose in my own mind. When I asked that question, I thought the meaning of my interrogation was obvious. The fate of this question and of America may depend on this. Have they said, We, the states? Have they made a proposal of a compact between states? If they had, this would be a confederation. It is otherwise most clearly a consolidated government. The question turns, sir, on that poor little thing—the expression, We, the *people*, instead of the *states*, of America. I need not take much pains to show that the principles of this system are extremely pernicious, impolitic, and dangerous. Is this a monarchy, like England—a compact between prince and people, with checks on the former to secure the liberty of the latter? Is this a confederacy, like Holland—an association of a number of independent states, each of which retains its individual sovereignty? It is not a democracy, wherein the people retain all their rights securely. Had these principles been adhered to, we should not have been brought to this alarming transition, from a confederacy to a consolidated government. . . . Here is a resolution as radical as that which separated us from Great Britain. It is radical in this transition; our rights and privileges are endangered, and the sovereignty of the states will be relinquished: and cannot we plainly see that this is actually the case? The rights of conscience, trial by jury, liberty of the press, all your immunities and franchises, all pretensions to human rights and privileges, are rendered insecure, if not lost, by this change, so loudly talked of by some, and inconsiderately by others. Is this tame relinquishment of rights worthy of freemen? Is it worthy of that manly fortitude that ought to characterize republicans? . . . You are not to inquire how your trade may be increased, nor how you are to become a great and powerful people, but how your liberties can be secured; for liberty ought to be the direct end of your government.

*   *   *

What, sir, is the genius of democracy? Let me read that clause of the bill of rights of Virginia which relates to this: 3d clause:—that government is, or ought to be, instituted for the common benefit, protection, and security of the people, nation, or community. Of all the various modes and forms of government, that is best, which is capable of producing the greatest degree of happiness and safety, and is most effectually secured against the danger of mal-administration; and that whenever any government shall be found inadequate, or contrary to those purposes, a majority of the community hath an indubitable, unalienable, and indefeasible right to reform, alter, or abolish it, in such manner as shall be judged most conducive to the public weal.

This, sir, is the language of democracy—that a majority of the community have a right to alter government when found to be oppressive. But how

different is the genius of your new Constitution from this! How different from the sentiments of freemen, that a contemptible minority can prevent the good of the majority! If, then, gentlemen, standing on this ground, are come to that point, that they are willing to bind themselves and their posterity to be oppressed, I am amazed and inexpressibly astonished. . . .

A standing army we shall have, also, to execute the execrable commands of tyranny; and how are you to punish them? Will you order them to be punished? Who shall obey these orders? Will your mace-bearer be a match for a disciplined regiment? In what situation are we to be? The clause before you gives a power of direct taxation, unbounded and unlimited, exclusive power of legislation, in all cases whatsoever, for ten miles square, and over all places purchased for the erection of forts, magazines, arsenals, dockyards, &c. What resistance could be made? The attempt would be madness. You will find all the strength of this country in the hands of your enemies; their garrisons will naturally be the strongest places in the country. Your militia is given up to Congress, also, in another part of this plan: they will therefore act as they think proper: all power will be in their own possession. . . .

*   *   *

. . . An opinion has gone forth, we find, that we are contemptible people: the time has been when we were thought otherwise. Under the same despised government, we commanded the respect of all Europe: wherefore are we now reckoned otherwise? The American spirit has fled from hence: it has gone to regions where it has never been expected; it has gone to the people of France, in search of a splendid government—a strong, energetic government. Shall we imitate the example of those nations who have gone from a simple to a splendid government? Are those nations more worthy of our imitation? What can make an adequate satisfaction to them for the loss they have suffered in attaining such a government—for the loss of their liberty? If we admit this consolidated government, it will be because we like a great, splendid one.

Some way or other we must be a great and mighty empire; we must have an army, and a navy, and a number of things. When the American spirit was in its youth, the language of America was different: liberty, sir, was then the primary object. We are descended from a people whose government was founded on liberty: our glorious forefathers of Great Britain made liberty the foundation of every thing. That country is become a great, mighty, and splendid nation; not because their government is strong and energetic, but, sir, because liberty is its direct end and foundation. We drew the spirit of liberty from our British ancestors: by that spirit we have triumphed over every difficulty. But now, sir, the American spirit, assisted by the ropes and chains of consolidation, is about to convert this country into a powerful and mighty empire. If you make the citizens of this country agree to become the subjects of one great consolidated empire of America, your government will not have sufficient energy to keep them together. Such a government is incompatible with the genius of republicanism. There will be no checks, no real balances, in this government. What can avail your specious, imaginary balances, your rope-dancing, chain-rattling, ridiculous ideal checks and contrivances? But, sir, we are not feared by foreigners; we do not make nations tremble. Would this constitute happiness, or secure liberty? I trust, sir, our political hemisphere will ever direct their operations to the security of those objects.

Consider our situation, sir: go to the poor man, and ask him what he does. He will inform you that he enjoys the fruits of his labor, under his own fig-tree, with his wife and children around him, in peace and security. Go to every other member of society,—you will find the same tranquil ease and content; you will find no alarms or disturbances. Why, then, tell us of danger, to terrify us into an adoption of this new form of government? And yet who knows the dangers that this new system may produce? They are out of the sight of the common people: they cannot foresee latent consequences. I dread the operation of it on the middling and lower classes of people: it is for them I fear the adoption of this system. . . .

*   *   *

Monday, 14 June 1788

Mr. HENRY. Mr. Chairman, the necessity of a bill of rights appears to me to be greater in this government than ever it was in any government before. I have observed already, that the sense of the European nations, and particularly Great Britain, is against the construction of rights being retained which are not expressly relinquished. I repeat, that all nations have adopted this construction—that all rights not expressly and unequivocally reserved to the people are impliedly and incidentally relinquished to rulers, as necessarily inseparable from the delegated powers. It is so in Great Britain; for every possible right, which is not reserved to the people by some express provision or compact, is within the king's prerogative. It is so in that country which is said to be in such full possession of freedom. . . .

*   *   *

If you intend to reserve your unalienable rights, you must have the most express stipulation; for, if implication be allowed, you are ousted of those rights. If the people do not think it necessary to reserve them, they will be supposed to be given up. How were the congressional rights defined when the people of America united by a confederacy to defend their liberties and rights against the tyrannical attempts of Great Britain? The states were not then contented with implied reservation. No, Mr. Chairman. It was expressly declared in our Confederation that every right was retained by the states, respectively, which was not given up to the government of the United States. But there is no such thing here. You, therefore, by a natural and unavoidable implication, give up your rights to the general government.

*   *   *

. . . A bill of rights is a favorite thing with the Virginians and the people of the other states likewise. It may be their prejudice, but the government ought to suit their geniuses; otherwise, its operation will be unhappy. A bill of rights, even if its necessity be doubtful, will exclude the possibility of dispute; and, with great submission, I think the best way is to have no dispute. In the present Constitution, they are restrained from issuing general warrants to search suspected places, or seize persons not named, without evidence of the commission of a fact, &c. There was certainly some celestial influence governing those who deliberated on that Constitution; for they have, with the most cautious and enlightened circumspection, guarded those indefeasible rights which ought ever to be held sacred! . . .

*   *   *

Tuesday, 24 June 1788 [Mr. Henry]

*   *   *

With respect to that part of the proposal which says that every power not granted remains with the people, it must be previous to adoption, or it will involve this country in inevitable destruction. To talk of it as a thing subsequent, not as one of your unalienable rights, is leaving it to the casual opinion of the Congress who shall take up the consideration of that matter. They will not reason with you about the effect of this Constitution. They will not take the opinion of this committee concerning its operation. They will construe it as they please. If you place it subsequently, let me ask the consequences. Among ten thousand *implied powers* which they may assume, they may, if we be engaged in war, liberate every one of your slaves if they please. And this must and will be done by men, a majority of whom have not a common interest with you. They will, therefore, have no feeling of your interests. It has been repeatedly said here, that the great object of a national government was national defence. That power which is said to be intended for security and safety may be rendered detestable and oppressive. If they give power to the general government to provide for the *general defence*, the means must be commensurate to the end. All the means in the possession of the people must be given to the government which is intrusted with the public defence. In this state there are two hundred and thirty-six thousand blacks,

and there are many in several other states. But there are few or none in the Northern States; and yet, if the Northern States shall be of opinion that our slaves are numberless, they may call forth every national resource. May Congress not say, *that every black man must fight?* Did we not see a little of this last war? We were not so hard pushed as to make emancipation general; but acts of Assembly passed that every slave who would go to the army should be free. Another thing will contribute to bring this event about. Slavery is detested. We feel its fatal effects—we deplore it with all the pity of humanity. Let all these considerations, at some future period, press with full force on the minds of Congress. Let that urbanity, which I trust will distinguish America, and the necessity of national defence,—let all these things operate on their minds; they will search that paper, and see if they have power of manumission. And have they not, sir? Have they not power to provide for the general defence and welfare? May they not think that these call for the abolition of slavery? May they not pronounce all slaves free, and will they not be warranted by that power? This is no ambiguous implication or logical deduction. The paper speaks to the point: they have the power in clear, unequivocal terms, and will clearly and certainly exercise it. As much as I deplore slavery, I see that prudence forbids its abolition. I deny that the general government ought to set them free, because a decided majority of the states have not the ties of sympathy and fellow-feeling for those whose interest would be affected by their emancipation. The majority of Congress is to the north, and the slaves are to the south.

In this situation, I see a great deal of the property of the people of Virginia in jeopardy, and their peace and tranquillity gone. I repeat it again, that it would rejoice my very soul that every one of my fellow-beings was emancipated. As we ought with gratitude to admire that decree of Heaven which has numbered us among the free, we ought to lament and deplore the necessity of holding our fellowmen in bondage. But is it practicable, by any human means, to liberate them without producing the most dreadful and ruinous consequences? We ought to possess them in the manner we inherited them from our ancestors, as their manumission is incompatible with the felicity of our country. But we ought to soften, as much as possible, the rigor of their unhappy fate. I know that, in a variety of particular instances, the legislature, listening to complaints, have admitted their emancipation. Let me not dwell on this subject. I will only add that this, as well as every other property of the people of Virginia, is in jeopardy, and put in the hands of those who have no similarity of situation with us. This is a local matter, and I can see no propriety in subjecting it to Congress.

With respect to subsequent amendments, proposed by the worthy member, I am distressed when I hear the expression. It is a new one altogether, and such a one as stands against every idea of fortitude and manliness in the states, or any one else. Evils admitted in order to be removed subsequently, and tyranny submitted to in order to be excluded by a subsequent alteration, are things totally new to me. . . . I ask, does experience warrant such a thing from the beginning of the world to this day? Do you enter into a compact first, and afterwards settle the terms of the governent? . . .

*   *   *

REVIEW QUESTIONS

1. How did Patrick Henry define the difference between a confederation and a consolidated, national government? Why did he see the latter as so dangerous?
2. How did Henry address local, material concerns? How did he present ideological, political ones?
3. Did he appear to be more worried about states' rights or people's rights?
4. What were George Mason's particular worries? How did his argument supplement Henry's?
5. Were Patrick Henry and George Mason reactionaries in their distrust of constitutional innovation or were they still revolutionaries?

JAMES MADISON

The Federalist Papers, No. 45 (1788)

James Madison, a principal framer of the Constitution at the Federal (later called Constitutional) Convention, defended this conception of a new, stronger, central government at the Virginia ratifying convention. His powerful rebuttals and counterarguments were the products of his extensive study of governments, his participation in the Constitutional Convention's debates, and his writing a great many of the essays published under the title of The Federalist.

Alexander Hamilton devised The Federalist Papers *to overwhelm the strong opposition to the Constitution's ratification in New York. He planned the series of letters to illuminate both the pros of a new government under the Constitution as well as the cons of a government under the Articles of Confederation. To help him in the intensive writing campaign (that resulted in eighty-five essays between October 1787 and May 1788), he recruited Madison and John Jay. All three wrote under the pseudonym "Publius." The letters originally appeared in New York newspapers and were then collected into a two-volume book, which Hamilton hoped would influence the delegates at the New York ratification convention while Madison wished for the same in Virginia. In each case, the essays were not as persuasive as their authors had desired; but* The Federalist Papers *did help people interpret the Constitution once it was adopted.*

From Alexander Hamilton, James Madison, and John Jay, *The Federalist Papers.* Edited by Garry Wills (New York: Bantam Books, 1982), pp. 232–37.

The Federalist No. 45

January 26, 1788

To the People of the State of New York.

Having shewn that no one of the powers transferred to the federal Government is unnecessary or improper, the next question to be considered is whether the whole mass of them will be dangerous to the portion of authority left in the several States.

The adversaries to the plan of the Convention instead of considering in the first place what degree of power was absolutely necessary for the purposes of the federal Government, have exhausted themselves in a secondary enquiry into the possible consequences of the proposed degree of power, to the Governments of the particular States. But if the Union, as has been shewn, be essential, to the security of the people of America against foreign danger; if it be essential to their security against contentions and wars among the different States; if it be essential to guard them against those violent and oppressive factions which embitter the blessings of liberty, and against those military establishments which must gradually poison its very fountain; if, in a word the Union be essential to the happiness of the people of America, is it not preposterous, to urge as an objection to a government without which the objects of the Union cannot be attained, that such a Government may derogate from the importance of the Governments of the individual States? Was then the American revolution effected, was the American confederacy formed, was the precious blood of thousands spilt, and the hard earned substance of millions lavished,

not that the people of America should enjoy peace, liberty and safety; but that the Governments of the individual States, that particular municipal establishments, might enjoy a certain extent of power, and be arrayed with certain dignities and attributes of sovereignty? We have heard of the impious doctrine in the old world that the people were made for kings, not kings for the people. Is the same doctrine to be revived in the new, in another shape, that the solid happiness of the people is to be sacrificed to the views of political institutions of a different form? It is too early for politicians to presume on our forgetting that the public good, the real welfare of the great body of the people is the supreme object to be pursued; and that no form of Government whatever, has any other value, than as it may be fitted for the attainment of this object. Were the plan of the Convention adverse to the public happiness, my voice would be, reject the plan. Were the Union itself inconsistent with the public happiness, it would be, abolish the Union. In like manner as far as the sovereignty of the States cannot be reconciled to the happiness of the people, the voice of every good citizen must be, let the former be sacrificed to the latter. How far the sacrifice is necessary, has been shewn. How far the unsacrificed residue will be endangered, is the question before us.

Several important considerations have been touched in the course of these papers, which discountenance the supposition that the operation of the federal Government will by degrees prove fatal to the State Governments. The more I revolve the subject the more fully I am persuaded that the balance is much more likely to be disturbed by the preponderancy of the last than of the first scale.

We have seen in all the examples of antient and modern confederacies, the strongest tendency continually betraying itself in the members to despoil the general Government of its authorities, with a very ineffectual capacity in the latter to defend itself against the encroachments. Although in most of these examples, the system has been so dissimilar from that under consideration, as greatly to weaken any inference concerning the latter from the fate of the former; yet as the States will retain under the proposed Constitution a very extensive portion of active sovereignty, the inference ought not to be wholly disregarded. In the Achæan league, it is probable that the federal head had a degree and species of power, which gave it a considerable likeness to the government framed by the Convention. The Lycian confederacy, as far as its principles and form are transmitted, must have borne a still greater analogy to it. Yet history does not inform us that either of them ever degenerated or tended to degenerate into one consolidated government. On the contrary, we know that the ruin of one of them proceeded from the incapacity of the federal authority to prevent the dissentions, and finally the disunion of the subordinate authorities. These cases are the more worthy of our attention, as the external causes by which the component parts were pressed together, were much more numerous and powerful than in our case; and consequently, less powerful ligaments within, would be sufficient to bind the members to the head, and to each other.

*   *   *

The State Governments will have the advantage of the federal Government, whether we compare them in respect to the immediate dependence of the one or the other; to the weight of personal influence which each side will possess; to the powers respectively vested in them; to the predilection and probable support of the people; to the disposition and faculty of resisting and frustrating the measures of each other.

The State Governments may be regarded as constituent and essential parts of the federal Government; whilst the latter is nowise essential to the operation or organisation of the former. Without the intervention of the State Legislatures, the President of the United States cannot be elected at all. They must in all cases have a great share in his appointment, and will perhaps in most cases of themselves determine it. The Senate will be elected absolutely and exclusively by the State Legislatures. Even the House of Representatives, though drawn immediately from the people, will be chosen very much under the influence of that class of men, whose influence over the people obtains for themselves an election into the State Legislatures. Thus each of the principal branches of the federal Government will owe its existence more or less to the favor of the State Governments, and must consequently feel a dependence, which is much more likely to beget a disposition too obsequious, than too overbearing towards them. On the other side, the component parts of the State Governments will in no instance be indebted for their appointment to the direct agency of the federal government, and very little if at all, to the local influence of its members.

The number of individuals employed under the Constitution of the United States, will be much smaller, than the number employed under the particular States. There will consequently be less of personal influence on the side of the former, than of the latter. The members of the legislative, executive and judiciary departments of thirteen and more States; the justices of peace, officers of militia, ministerial officers of justice, with all the county corporation and town-officers, for three millions and more of people, intermixed and having particular acquaintance with every class and circle of people, must exceed beyond all proportion, both in number and influence, those of every description who will be employed in the administration of the federal system. Compare the members of the three great departments, of the thirteen States, excluding from the judiciary department the justices of peace, with the members of the corresponding departments of the single Government of the Union; compare the militia officers of three millions of people, with the military and marine officers of any establishment which is within the compass of probability, or I may add, of possibility, and in this view alone, we may pronounce the advantage of the States to be decisive. If the federal Government is to have collectors of revenue, the State Governments will have theirs also. And as those of the former will be principally on the seacoast, and not very numerous; whilst those of the latter will be spread over the face of the country, and will be very numerous, the advantage in this view also lies on the same side. It is true that the confederacy is to possess, and may exercise, the power of collecting internal as well as external taxes throughout the States: But it is probable that this power will not be resorted to, except for supplemental purposes of revenue; that an option will then be given to the States to supply their quotas by previous collections of their own; and that the eventual collection under the immediate authority of the Union, will generally be made by the officers, and according to the rules, appointed by the several States. Indeed it is extremely probable that in other instances, particularly in the organisation of the judicial power, the officers of the States will be cloathed with the correspondent authority of the Union. Should it happen however that separate collectors of internal revenue should be appointed under the federal Government, the influence of the whole number would not be a comparison with that of the multitude of State officers in the opposite scale. . . .

The powers delegated by the proposed Constitution to the Federal Government, are few and defined. Those which are to remain in the State Governments are numerous and indefinite. The former will be exercised principally on external objects, as war, peace, negociation, and foreign commerce; with which last the power of taxation will for the most part be connected. The powers reserved to the several States will extend to all the objects, which, in the ordinary course of affairs, concern the lives, liberties and properties of the people; and the internal order, improvement, and prosperity of the State.

The operations of the Federal Government will be most extensive and important in times of war and danger; those of the State Governments, in times of peace and security. As the former periods will probably bear a small proportion to the latter, the State Governments will here enjoy another advantage over the Federal Government. The more adequate indeed the federal powers may be rendered to the national defence, the less frequent will be those scenes of danger which might favour their ascendency over the governments of the particular States.

If the new Constitution be examined with accuracy and candour, it will be found that the change which it proposes, consists much less in the addition of NEW POWERS to the Union, than in the invigoration of its ORIGINAL POWERS. The regulation of commerce, it is true, is a new power; but that seems to be an addition which few oppose, and from which no apprehensions are entertained. The powers relating to war and peace, armies and fleets, treaties and finance, with the other more considerable powers, are all vested in the existing Congress by the articles of Confederation. The proposed change does not enlarge these powers; it only substitutes a more effectual mode of administering them. The change relating to taxation, may be regarded as the most important. And yet the present Congress have as compleat authority to REQUIRE of the States indefinite supplies of money for the common defence and general welfare, as the future Congress will have to require them of individual citizens; and the latter will be no more bound than the States themselves have been, to pay the quotas respectively taxed on them. Had the States complied punctually with the articles of confederation, or could their compliance have been enforced by as peaceable means as may be used with success towards single persons, our past experience is very far from countenancing an opinion that the State Governments would have lost their constitutional powers, and have gradually undergone an entire consolidation. To maintain that such an event would have ensued, would be to say at once, that the existence of the State Governments is incompatible with any system whatever that accomplishes the essential purposes of the Union.

PUBLIUS.

REVIEW QUESTIONS

1. What anti-federalist arguments did Madison counter in this essay?
2. Why did he begin his essay with questions about the ends or goals of a federal government? What did he say was the ultimate goal of government?
3. How did Madison try to neutralize fears of stronger federal authority? Did he provide speculations or certainties?
4. How did he compare federal and state powers? Why did he say the latter would generally still have the advantage?

8 ∽ THE FEDERALIST ERA

The citizens of the new nation may have ratified their Constitution, but they still had to translate the words into actions. They proceeded by inaugurating a new government in 1789. Yet again, that was not enough, for they had to figure out what that government truly could and could not do. With that in mind, the American people debated the initiation, amendment, and interpretation of the rules by which they wanted to live. The revolutionaries had taken historical and transatlantic intellectual and political concepts, translated them into a language and form—an idiom—readily understood by Americans, and applied them to the American situation. The founders then had to make those words serve the new government—which involved some reinterpretation. As they labored to create a government and govern at the same time, the founders debated fiercely over whether they were undermining some of their revolutionary and constitutional concepts in the process. In the midst of these debates, having already established the Constitution as the organic law of the United States, the founders proceeded to build upon it with both administrative and statutory constructions. In doing so, they set precedents by which later generations would govern and judge themselves.

Federalists gained power first and set out to create not only a government in their image but also a nation to fit their vision. In many ways they succeeded, but not without encountering opposition, a resistance that had first been mounted against the ratification of the Constitution. In what was both a concession to the merit of their opponents' arguments as well as an expediency to gain ratification, the Federalists compromised over incorporating a Bill of Rights into the Constitution. Their subsequent policies and programs, whether on domestic or foreign issues, were also challenged—and sometimes changed—by the opponents who came to be known as the Democratic Republicans.

Although most Americans said they deplored the rise of factionalism that undermined consensus, they continued to fight over how the Constitution was to be interpreted and implemented, thus contributing to the rise of a new institution— the political party—during the administrations of George Washington and John Adams. Both parties wanted to make the United States a viable nation: one with a financially sound foundation. Both Federalists and Republicans were concerned about national honor, interests, and security. These issues were top priorities in the 1790s as the nation tried to counter foreign intrigues directed against it at home as well as the foreign conflicts that encroached on its endeavors abroad, The Federalists and Republicans wanted a stable government that was respected nationally and internationally; and both wanted to ensure citizen rights. But they could not always agree on how to define or ensure these ends. For instance, the Federalists and Republicans differed on what was economically—a manufacturing or agricultural orientation—or diplomatically—fostering British or French connections—best for the nation. Therefore debates over programs that addressed immediate material concerns often became battles over differing visions for America's future and over what would have even more lasting repercussions: constitutional interpretation.

These conflicts revealed that consensus was an ideal that was often surrendered to more pragmatic compromise. Union, at times, seemed more important than unity. While some may have deplored compromise as the lesser sibling to consensus, others accepted it as another check within the new system they had created. The factions or parties checked one another as they dealt with sectionalism, economic interests, and competing images of America's future.

ALEXANDER HAMILTON

FROM The First Report on Public Credit (1790)

Alexander Hamilton (1755–1804) plunged into revolutionary action soon after his arrival in New York from the West Indies in 1773. He served in the Continental Army and then in the Confederation Congress. Never happy with the Articles of Confederation, he was an early proponent of constitutional reform. A firm advocate of a strong, even aristocratic, centralized government, he participated in the Constitutional Convention, wrote many of The Federalist *essays that promoted the new constitution, and helped push through ratification in New York. Washington rewarded his intelligent, energetic ex-aide-de-camp by appointing him the first Secretary of the United States Treasury. Hamilton embraced the challenge and opportunity to create a financial and economic program for the young nation. Most of his proposals were not innovations unique to the United States; he borrowed readily from European and especially English precedents on such revenue methods as tariffs and excise taxes.*

Hamilton was, however, innovative in how he pieced together his policy and how he planned to implement it. The secretary submitted a series of reports to Congress that outlined what has been called the Hamiltonian program: the First Report on the Public Credit, January 1790; the Second Report on Public Credit and the Report on a National Bank in December 1790; the Report on the Establishment of a Mint in January 1791; and the Report on Manufactures in December 1791. After debate and some amendment, all but the last one were adopted.

From *The Papers of Alexander Hamilton*, vol. 6, edited by Harold C. Syrett. Copyright © 1962 by Columbia University Press. Reprinted with permission of the publisher. [Editorial insertions that appear in square brackets are from Syrett's edition—*Ed.*]

Treasury Department, January 9, 1790.
[Communicated on January 14, 1790]
[To the Speaker of the House of Representatives]

The Secretary of the Treasury, in obedience to the resolution of the House of Representatives, of the twenty-first day of September last, has, during the recess of Congress, applied himself to the consideration of a proper plan for the support of the Public Credit, with all the attention which was due to the authority of the House, and to the magnitude of the object.

In the discharge of this duty, he has felt, in no small degree, the anxieties which naturally flow from a just estimate of the difficulty of the task, from a well-founded diffidence of his own qualifications for executing it with success, and from a deep and solemn conviction of the momentous nature of the truth contained in the resolution under which his investigations have been conducted, "That an *adequate* provision for the support of the Public Credit, is a matter of high importance to the honor and prosperity of the United States."

*   *   *

In the opinion of the Secretary, the wisdom of the House, in giving their explicit sanction to the proposition which has been stated, cannot but be applauded by all, who will seriously consider, and trace through their obvious consequences, these plain and undeniable truths.

That exigencies are to be expected to occur, in the affairs of nations, in which there will be a necessity for borrowing.

That loans in times of public danger, especially from foreign war, are found an indispensable resource, even to the wealthiest of them.

And that in a country, which, like this, is possessed of little active wealth, or in other words, little monied capital, the necessity for that resource, must, in such emergencies, be proportionably urgent.

And as on the one hand, the necessity for borrowing in particular emergencies cannot be doubted, so on the other, it is equally evident, that to be able to borrow upon *good terms*, it is essential that the credit of a nation should be well established.

For when the credit of a country is in any degree questionable, it never fails to give an extravagant premium, in one shape or another, upon all the loans it has occasion to make. Nor does the evil end here; the same disadvantage must be sustained upon whatever is to be bought on terms of future payment.

From this constant necessity of *borrowing* and *buying dear*, it is easy to conceive how immensely the expenses of a nation, in a course of time, will be augmented by an unsound state of the public credit.

To attempt to enumerate the complicated variety of mischiefs in the whole system of the social œconomy, which proceed from a neglect of the maxims that uphold public credit, and justify the solicitude manifested by the House on this point, would be an improper intrusion on their time and patience.

In so strong a light nevertheless do they appear to the Secretary, that on their due observance at the present critical juncture, materially depends, in his judgment, the individual and aggregate prosperity of the citizens of the United States; their relief from the embarrassments they now experience; their character as a People; the cause of good government.

If the maintenance of public credit, then, be truly so important, the next enquiry which suggests itself is, by what means it is to be effected? The ready answer to which question is, by good faith, by a punctual performance of contracts. States, like individuals, who observe their engagements, are respected and trusted: while the reverse is the fate of those, who pursue an opposite conduct.

*   *   *

While the observance of that good faith, which is the basis of public credit, is recommended by the strongest inducements of political expediency, it is enforced by considerations of still greater authority. There are arguments for it, which rest on the immutable principles of moral obligation. And in proportion as the mind is disposed to contemplate, in the order of Providence, an intimate connection between public virtue and public happiness, will be its repugnancy to a violation of those principles.

This reflection derives additional strength from the nature of the debt of the United States. It was the price of liberty. The faith of America has been repeatedly pledged for it, and with solemnities, that give peculiar force to the obligation. There is indeed reason to regret that it has not hitherto been kept; that the necessities of the war, conspiring with inexperience in the subjects of finance, produced direct infractions: and that the subsequent period has been a continued scene of negative violation, or non-compliance. But a diminution of this regret arises from the reflection, that the last seven years have exhibited an earnest and uniform effort, on the part of the government of the union, to retrieve the national credit, by doing justice to the creditors of the nation; and that the embarrassments of a defective constitution, which defeated this laudable effort, have ceased.

*   *   *

It cannot but merit particular attention, that among ourselves the most enlightened friends of good government are those, whose expectations are the highest.

To justify and preserve their confidence; to promote the encreasing respectability of the American name; to answer the calls of justice; to restore landed property to its due value; to furnish new resources both to agriculture and commerce; to cement more closely the union of the states; to add to their security against foreign attack; to establish public order on the basis of an upright and liberal policy. These are the great and invaluable ends to be secured, by a proper and adequate provision, at the present period, for the support of public credit.

To this provision we are invited, not only by the general considerations, which have been noticed, but by others of a more particular nature. It will procure to every class of the community some important advantages, and remove some no less important disadvantages.

The advantage to the public creditors from the increased value of that part of their property which constitutes the public debt, needs no explanation.

But there is a consequence of this, less obvious, though not less true, in which every other citizen is interested. It is a well known fact, that in countries in which the national debt is properly funded, and an object of established confidence, it answers most of the purposes of money. Transfers of stock or public debt are there equivalent to payments in specie; or in other words, stock, in the principal transactions of business, passes current as specie. The same thing would, in all probability happen here, under the like circumstances.

The benefits of this are various and obvious.

First. Trade is extended by it; because there is a larger capital to carry it on, and the merchant can at the same time, afford to trade for smaller profits; as his stock, which, when unemployed, brings him in an interest from the government, serves him also as money, when he has a call for it in his commercial operations.

Secondly. Agriculture and manufactures are also promoted by it: For the like reason, that more capital can be commanded to be employed in both; and because the merchant, whose enterprize in foreign trade, gives to them activity and extension, has greater means for enterprize.

Thirdly. The interest of money will be lowered by it; for this is always in a ratio, to the quantity of money, and to the quickness of circulation. This circumstance will enable both the public and individuals to borrow on easier and cheaper terms.

And from the combination of these effects, additional aids will be furnished to labour, to industry, and to arts of every kind.

*   *   *

It is agreed on all hands, that that part of the debt which has been contracted abroad, and is denominated the foreign debt, ought to be provided for, according to the precise terms of the contracts relating to it. The discussions, which can arise, therefore, will have reference essentially to the domestic part of it, or to that which has been contracted at home. It is to be regretted, that there is not the same unanimity of sentiment on this part, as on the other.

The Secretary has too much deference for the opinions of every part of the community, not to have observed one, which has, more than once, made its appearance in the public prints, and which is occasionally to be met with in conversation. It involves this question, whether a discrimination ought not to be made between original holders of the public securities, and present possessors, by purchase. Those who advocate a discrimination are for making a full provision for the securities of the former, at their nominal value; but contend, that the latter ought to receive no more than the cost to them, and the interest: And the idea is sometimes suggested of making good the difference to the primitive possessor.

In favor of this scheme, it is alledged, that it would be unreasonable to pay twenty shillings in the pound, to one who had not given more for it than three or four. And it is added, that it would be hard to aggravate the misfortune of the first owner, who, probably through necessity, parted with his property at so great a loss, by obliging him to contribute to the profit of the person, who had speculated on his distresses.

The Secretary, after the most mature reflection on the force of this argument, is induced to reject the doctrine it contains, as equally unjust and impolitic, as highly injurious, even to the original holders of public securities; as ruinous to public credit.

It is inconsistent with justice, because in the first place, it is a breach of contract; in violation of the rights of a fair purchaser.

The nature of the contract in its origin, is, that the public will pay the sum expressed in the security, to the first holder, or his *assignee*. The *intent*, in making the security assignable, is, that the proprietor may be able to make use of his property, by selling it for as much as it *may be worth in the market*, and that the buyer may be *safe* in the purchase.

*   *   *

The impolicy of a discrimination results from two considerations; one, that it proceeds upon a principle destructive of that *quality* of the public debt, or the stock of the nation, which is essential to its capacity for answering the purposes of money—that is the *security* of *transfer*; the other, that as well on this account, as because it includes a breach of faith, it renders property in the funds less valuable; consequently induces lenders to demand a higher premium for what they lend, and produces every other inconvenience of a bad state of public credit.

It will be perceived at first sight, that the transferable quality of stock is essential to its operation as money, and that this depends on the idea of complete security to the transferree, and a firm persuasion, that no distinction can in any circumstances be made between him and the original proprietor.

*   *   *

But there is still a point in view in which it will appear perhaps even more exceptionable, than in either of the former. It would be repugnant to an express provision of the Constitution of the United

States. This provision is, that "all debts contracted and engagements entered into before the adoption of that Constitution shall be as valid against the United States under it, as under the confederation." which amounts to a constitutional ratification of the contracts respecting the debt, in the state in which they existed under the confederation. And resorting to that standard, there can be no doubt, that the rights of assignees and original holders, must be considered as equal.

*　　*　　*

The Secretary concluding, that a discrimination, between the different classes of creditors of the United States, cannot with propriety be *made*, proceeds to examine whether a difference ought to be permitted to *remain* between them, and another description of public creditors—Those of the states individually.

The Secretary, after mature reflection on this point, entertains a full conviction, that an assumption of the debts of the particular states by the union, and a like provision for them, as for those of the union, will be a measure of sound policy and substantial justice.

It would, in the opinion of the Secretary, contribute, in an eminent degree, to an orderly, stable and satisfactory arrangement of the national finances.

Admitting, as ought to be the case, that a provision must be made in some way or other, for the entire debt; it will follow, that no greater revenues will be required, whether that provision be made wholly by the United States, or partly by them, and partly by the states separately.

The principal question then must be, whether such a provision cannot be more conveniently and effectually made, by one general plan issuing from one authority, than by different plans originating in different authorities.

*　　*　　*

The Secretary now proceeds to a consideration of the necessary funds.

It has been stated that the debt of the United States consists of

	Dollars.	Cents.
The foreign debt, amounting, with arrears of interest, to	11,710,378	62
And the domestic debt amounting, with like arrears, computed to the end of the year 1790, to	42,414,085	94
Making together, Dollars	54,124,464	56

The interest on the domestic debt is computed to the end of this year, because the details of carrying any plan into execution, will exhaust the year.

	Dollars.	Cents.
The annual interest of the foreign debt has been stated at	542,599	66
And the interest on the domestic debt at four per cent. would amount to	1,696,563	43
Making together, Dollars	2,239,163	09

Thus to pay the interest of the foreign debt, and to pay four per cent on the whole of the domestic debt, principal and interest, forming a new capital, will require a yearly

income of 2,239,163 dollars, 9 cents.

The sum which, in the opinion of the Secretary, ought now to be provided in addition to what the current service will require.

*　　*　　*

With regard to the instalments of the foreign debt, these, in the opinion of the Secretary, ought to be paid by new loans abroad. Could funds be conveniently spared, from other exigencies, for paying them, the United States could ill bear the drain of cash, at the present juncture, which the measure would be likely to occasion.

But to the sum which has been stated for payment of the interest, must be added a provision for the current service. This the Secretary estimates at six hundred thousand dollars; making, with the amount of the interest, two millions, eight hundred and thirty-nine thousand, one hundred and sixty-three dollars, and nine cents.

This sum may, in the opinion of the Secretary, be obtained from the present duties on imports and tonnage, with the additions, which, without any possible disadvantage either to trade, or agriculture, may be made on wines, spirits, including those distilled within the United States, teas and coffee.

The Secretary conceives, that it will be sound policy, to carry the duties upon articles of this kind, as high as will be consistent with the practicability of a safe collection. This will lessen the necessity, both of having recourse to direct taxation, and of accumulating duties where they would be more inconvenient to trade, and upon objects, which are more to be regarded as necessaries of life.

That the articles which have been enumerated, will, better than most others, bear high duties, can hardly be a question. They are all of them, in reality—luxuries—the greatest part of them foreign luxuries; some of them, in the excess in which they are used, pernicious luxuries. And there is, perhaps, none of them, which is not consumed in so great abundance, as may, justly, denominate it, a source of national extravagance and impoverishment. The consumption of ardent spirits particularly, no doubt very much on account of their cheapness, is carried to an extreme, which is truly to be regretted, as well in regard to the health and the morals, as to the œconomy of the community.

Should the increase of duties tend to a decrease of the consumption of those articles, the effect would be, in every respect desirable. The saving which it would occasion, would leave individuals more at their ease, and promote a more favourable balance of trade. As far as this decrease might be applicable to distilled spirits, it would encourage the substitution of cyder and malt liquors, benefit agriculture, and open a new and productive source of revenue.

It is not however, probable, that this decrease would be in a degree, which would frustrate the expected benefit to the revenue from raising the duties. Experience has shewn, that luxuries of every kind, lay the strongest hold on the attachments of mankind, which, especially when confirmed by habit, are not easily alienated from them.

The same fact affords a security to the merchant, that he is not likely to be prejudiced by considerable duties on such articles. They will usually command a proportional price. The chief things in this view to be attended to, are, that the terms of payment be so regulated, as not to require inconvenient advances, and that the mode of collection be secure.

*   *   *

Persuaded as the Secretary is, that the proper funding of the present debt, will render it a national blessing: Yet he is so far from acceding to the position, in the latitude in which it is sometimes laid down, that "public debts are public benefits," a position inviting to prodigality, and liable to dangerous abuse,—that he ardently wishes to see it incorporated, as a fundamental maxim, in the system of public credit of the United States, that the creation of debt should always be accompanied with the means of extinguishment. This he regards as the true secret for rendering public credit immortal. And he presumes, that it is difficult to conceive a situation, in which there may not be an adherence to the maxim. At least he feels an unfeigned solicitude, that this may be attempted by the United States, and that they may commence their measures for the establishment of credit, with the observance of it.

*   *   *

REVIEW QUESTIONS

1. Did Hamilton's program expand the power of the central government?
2. Why was it so important to establish the credit of the United States?
3. If, as Hamilton pointed out, the ratification of the Constitution had already put the public credit on a firmer foundation, why was there need of a formal economic program?

4. How did he propose to redeem the nation's debt at the individual and state levels? Did he acknowledge controversies or answer objections via his proposals?

5. Why did Hamilton argue that increasing the duties on certain products would have more than economic benefits?

THOMAS JEFFERSON

FROM *Notes on the State of Virginia* (1785)

Hamilton wanted to manage the country's economy as well as its finances, for he believed that the United States should promote an economic system that was as exceptional as its political one. While most other Americans, Secretary of State Thomas Jefferson included, agreed with that idea in principle, they disagreed on the particulars. Jefferson articulated the prevailing agrarian vision when he eloquently described his dream for America in his Notes on the State of Virginia. *Besides extolling the virtues of an agriculturally based economy, Jefferson also commented on American flora and fauna, Native American issues, the problem of slavery, the promise of education, and the organization of government. Jefferson began the work as a series of essay answers to a questionnaire sent out by an official, François Barbé-Marbois, with the French legation at Philadelphia in 1780, sending him his original answers in December 1781. Jefferson continued to revise and add new material to the work until it was published as a book, first in Paris in 1785, and then in London.*

From Thomas Jefferson, *Notes on the State of Virginia*, intro. Thomas Perkins Abernathy (New York: Harper Torch Books, 1964), pp. 156–58.

Query XIX

The present state of manufactures, commerce, interior and exterior trade?

We never had an interior trade of any importance. Our exterior commerce has suffered very much from the beginning of the present contest. During this time we have manufactured within our families the most necessary articles of clothing. Those of cotton will bear some comparison with the same kinds of manufacture in Europe; but those of wool, flax and hemp are very coarse, unsightly, and unpleasant; and such is our attachment to agriculture, and such our preference for foreign manufactures, that be it wise or unwise, our people will certainly return as soon as they can, to the raising raw materials, and exchanging them for finer manufactures than they are able to execute themselves.

The political economists of Europe have established it as a principle, that every State should endeavor to manufacture for itself; and this principle, like many others, we transfer to America, without calculating the difference of circumstance which should often produce a difference of result. In Europe the lands are either cultivated, or locked up against the cultivator. Manufacture must therefore be resorted to of necessity not of choice, to support the surplus of their people. But we have an immensity of land courting the industry of the husbandman. Is it best then that all our citizens should be employed in its improvement, or that one half should be called off from that to exercise manufactures and handicraft arts for the other? Those who labor in the earth are the chosen people of God, if ever He had a chosen people, whose breasts He has made His peculiar deposit for substantial and genuine virtue. It is the focus in which he keeps alive that sacred fire, which otherwise might escape from the face of the earth. Corruption of morals in the mass of cultivators is a phenomenon of which no age nor nation has furnished an example. It is the mark set on those, who, not looking up to heaven, to their own soil and industry, as does the husbandman, for their subsistence, depend for it on casualties and caprice of customers. Dependence begets subservience and venality, suffocates the germ of virtue, and prepares fit tools for the designs of ambition. This, the natural progress and consequence of the arts, has sometimes perhaps been retarded by accidental circumstances; but, generally speaking, the proportion which the aggregate of the other classes of citizens bears in any State to that of its husbandmen, is the proportion of its unsound to its healthy parts, and is a good enough barometer whereby to measure its degree of corruption. While we have land to labor then, let us never wish to see our citizens occupied at a workbench, or twirling a distaff. Carpenters, masons, smiths, are wanting in husbandry; but, for the general operations of manufacture, let our workshops remain in Europe. It is better to carry provisions and materials to workmen there, than bring them to the provisions and materials, and with them their manners and principles. The loss by the transportation of commodities across the Atlantic will be made up in happiness and permanence of government. The mobs of great cities add just so much to the support of pure government, as sores do to the strength of the human body. It is the manners and spirit of a people which preserve a republic in vigor. A degeneracy in these is a canker which soon eats to the heart of its laws and constitution.

REVIEW QUESTIONS

1. Why did Jefferson dismiss European political-economic theory as being irrelevant to or improper for the American situation?
2. What did Jefferson say differentiated America from Europe?
3. Why did he believe an agrarian economy begat a better society?
4. Were Jefferson's comments those of an economist or a revolutionary?

TENCH COXE

FROM *A View of the United States of America* (1794)

When the War for American Independence began, Tench Coxe (1755–1824) was a Philadelphia merchant who chose to remain loyal to the crown. While that allegiance placed him in good stead when the British army occupied the city between September 1777 and June 1778, it did quite the reverse once the British left: the revolutionaries charged him with treason. He escaped conviction due to family connections and his own acts of repentence, including taking the patriot oath of allegiance. Politically am-

bitious, Coxe then set out to cultivate the appropriate connections and influence the development of the new nation. He promoted the ratification of the Constitution and then, once the new government was formed, he acted as an unofficial advisor to his friends in Congress. This, along with the fact that Coxe had already been making a reputation for himself as a political economist through his writings, put him in the right position to apply to Hamilton when the position of assistant secretary of the Treasury became available in the spring of 1790. Within this department, the largest of the executive offices, Coxe advised and assisted in the implementation of Hamilton's economic strategies. While they were in agreement on many issues of public policy, Coxe, at least partly due to envy and frustration at his lack of advancement, eventually transferred his allegiance from Hamilton and the Federalists to Jefferson and the Democratic Republicans. Although his political allegiances changed, Coxe remained consistent in his advocacy of a diversified national economy. He championed agriculture even as he continued to echo Hamilton in promoting industry and internal improvements so as to build a more powerful a well as self-sufficient nation. He promoted this economic program in his book, A View of the United States of America, *which was actually a collection of articles that he had previously published. Although focused on reform, the book also presented an idyllic vision of the United States.*

From Tench Coxe, *A View of the United States of America* (1794; New York: Reprints of Economic Classics, Augustus M. Kelley, Bookseller, 1965), pp. 84–105.

A Concise General View of the United States, for the Information of Migrators from Foreign Countries.

*   *   *

THE United States of America are situated in the northern division of that extensive portion of the globe, between the thirty-first and forty-sixth degrees of northern latitude. . . .

In so very extended a scene, it will be naturally expected, that the fruits of the earth are many and various: and accordingly we find, in the present half-tried state of the capacities of our soil and climate, a list of invaluable productions present themselves, some found by the first discoverers of the country—others introduced by mere accident—and others transported from Europe, during the simple state of agriculture in the last century. In our southern latitudes, in-

cluding the states of Georgia, South Carolina and North Carolina, rice, much superior to that of Italy or the Levant, is raised in very great quantities. . . .

Tobacco is a staple article of all the states, from Georgia as far north as Maryland, including both. Virginia, alone, generally exported before the revolution, 55,000 hogsheads, weighing fifty-five millions of pounds—Maryland 30,000 hogsheads. The Carolinas and Georgia, which raised but little of this article before the revolution, have, of late years, produced very large quantities: and as Virginia and Maryland are turning more of their attention to the cultivation of wheat, Indian corn, flax, and hemp, the Carolinas and Georgia will probably extend the cultivation of this plant, to which their soil and climate are well suited.

Indigo is produced by North Carolina, South Carolina, and Georgia: but this, and the other two articles before mentioned, are raised in much less proportions in North Carolina, than in South Carolina and Georgia. . . .

Cotton has been lately adopted as an article of culture in the southern states: and if the prices of rice, tobacco, and indigo decline, it must be very beneficial to the owners and purchasers of lands in that part of our union. . . . As our people will increase very rapidly by emigration, and the course of nature, it is certain we cannot procure wool from our own internal resources in sufficient quantities. The owners of cotton plantations may therefore expect a constant and great demand for this article, as a substitute for wool, besides its ordinary uses for light goods.

Tar, pitch, and turpentine are produced in immense quantities in North Carolina, which state ships more of these articles, particularly the last, than all the rest of our union. Tar and pitch are also produced in the southern parts of Jersey, and more or less in all the states southward of that.

Besides these, myrtle wax, and those two invaluable timbers, the live oak and red cedar, are abundant in the Carolinas and Georgia: and they have Indian corn, hemp, flax, boards, staves, shingles, leather, beef, pork, butter, minerals, fossils, and many other articles in common with the middle, or eastern states; also skins, furs and ginseng from their Indian country.

The wheat country of the United States lies in Virginia, Maryland, Delaware, Pennsylvania, New-Jersey and New-York, and the westernmost parts of Connecticut, as also the western parts of the two Carolinas, and probably of Georgia, for their own use. The character of the American flour is so well known, that it is unnecessary to say any thing in commendation of it here. Virginia exported before the war 800,000 bushels of wheat—Maryland above half that quantity. The export of flour from Pennsylvania (with the wheat) was equivalent to 1,200,000 bushels in 1788, and about 2,000,000 of bushels in 1789, which, however, was a very favourable year. New-York exports in flour and wheat equivalent to 1,000,000 of bushels. In the wheat states are also produced great quantities of Indian corn, or maize. Virginia formerly exported half a million of bushels. Maryland ships a great deal of this article, and considerable quantities, raised in Virginia, Delaware, Pennsylvania, New-Jersey, New-York, and Connecticut, are exported—as are the wheat and flour of the last five states, from Philadelphia and New-York, there being little foreign trade from Delaware or Jersey[—and the western parts of Connecticut shipping with less expense from the ports on Hudson's river than those of their own state.

Hemp and flax are raised in very large quantities throughout the United States: . . . Large portions of the new lands of all the states are well suited to hemp and flax.

Though sheep are bred in all parts of America, yet the most populous scenes in the middle states, and the eastern states which have been long settled, and particularly the latter, are the places where they thrive best. In the eastern or New-England states, they form one of the greatest objects of the farmer's attention, and one of his surest sources of profit. The demand for wool, which has of late increased exceedingly with the rapid growth of our manufactures, will add considerably to the former great profits of sheep: and the consumption of their meat by the manufacturers, will render them still more beneficial.

Horned or neat cattle are also bred in every part of the United States. In the western counties of Virginia, the Carolinas, Georgia, and Kentucky, where they have extensive ranges, and mild winters, without snows of any duration, they run at large, and multiply very fast. In the middle states, cattle require more of the care and attention they usually receive in Europe, and they are generally good; often very large. But in the eastern states, whose principal objects on the land, have until lately been pasturage and grazing, cattle are very numerous indeed, and generally large. Cheese is, of course, most abundant in those states. No European country can exceed the United States in the valuable article of salt provisions. Our exports of this kind are every day increasing; as the raising of cattle is peculiarly profitable to farmers, the greater part of whom have no more land, than they can cultivate even with the plough. Barley and oats are the productions of every state, though least cultivated to the southward. Virginia however is turning her attention to barley, as also Maryland, and can raise great quantities.

Masts, spars, staves, heading, boards, plank, scantling, and square timber, are shipped from almost all the states: New-Hampshire, and the adjoining province of Maine, which is connected with Massachusetts, are among the most plentiful scenes. In New-York they abound: and in North Carolina and Georgia, the pitch-pine plank, and scantling, and white oak staves, are excellent, and abundant, especially in the former. The stock of these articles on the Chesapeak and Delaware bays is more exhausted: but yet there is a great deal on the rivers of both for exportation, besides abundance for home consumption. Considerable quantities are also brought to the Charleston market, but a large part of them is from the adjacent states of Georgia and North Carolina. When their internal navigation shall be improved, South-Carolina will open new sources of these articles.

*   *   *

A grand dependence of the eastern states is on their valuable fisheries. A detail of these is unnecessary. It is sufficient to say, that, with a small exception in favour of New-York, *the whole great sea fishery* of the United States, is carried on by New-England: and it is in a variety of ways highly beneficial to our landed and manufacturing interests. Massachusetts very far exceeds all the other states, in the fishing business.

Iron is abundant throughout the union, except in the Delaware state; which can draw it as conveniently from the other states on the Delaware river, as if it were in her own bowels. Virginia is supposed to be the state most pregnant with minerals and fossils of any in our union.

Deer-skins, and a variety of furs, are obtained by all the states from the Indian country; either directly, or through the medium of their neighbours. Hitherto they have been exported in large quantities.: but from the rapid progress of our manufactures, that exportation must diminish.

The article of pork, so important in war, navigation and trade, merits particular notice. The plenty of mast or nuts of the oak and beech, in some places, and Indian corn every where, occasion ours to be very fine, and abundant. . . .

Cider can be produced with ease in considerable quantities, from Virginia inclusive to the most northern states, as also in the western country of the Carolinas and Georgia: but New-Jersey and New-England have hitherto paid most attention to this drink. An exquisite brandy is distilled from the extensive peach-orchards, which grow upon the numerous rivers of the Chesapeak, in North Carolina, in Georgia, and in Pennsylvania, and may be made in the greater part of our country.

*   *   *

Rye is produced generally through all the states north of the Carolinas, and in the western parts of the three southern states. But the detail of American productions, and the parts in which they most abound, would be very lengthy. It will therefore be sufficient to say, that, in addition to the above capital articles, the United States produce or contain flaxseed, spelts, lime-stone, allum, saltpetre, lead, copper, coal, free-stone, marble, stone for wares, potters' clay, brick clay, a variety of ship-timber, shingles, holly, beech, poplar, curled maple, black walnut, wild cherry, and other woods suitable for cabinet makers, shingles of cedar and cypress, myrtle-wax, bees-wax, butter, tallow, hides, leather, tanners' bark, maple sugar, hops, mustard-seed, potatoes, and all the other principal vegetables; apples, and all the other principal fruits; clover, and all the other principal grasses. On the subject of our productions, it is only necessary to add, that they must be numerous, diversified, and extremely valuable, as the various parts of our country, lie in the same latitudes as Spain, Portugal, the middle and southern provinces of France, the fertile island of Sicily, and the greater part of Italy, European and Asiatic Turkey, and the kingdom of China, which maintains by its own agriculture more people than any country in the world.

The lands of the United States, though capable of producing so great a variety of necessary and useful articles, are much cheaper than in Europe. Farms which lie in such of our states as have been longest settled and improved, can be purchased for less money than the medium value of farming lands in any civilized part of the world: and our new lands, as well within the particular bounds of the several states, as those in the western territory of our confederated republic, are to be procured at very low prices, . . .

Labouring people in the farming, manufacturing, and mechanical trades, can have constant employment, and better wages, than in the dearest countries of Europe; because we have so much land, so many new dwelling-houses, work-shops, barns, and other buildings to erect, and so many new trades and manufactories to establish. And though the wages of the industrious poor are very good, yet the necessaries of life are cheaper than in Europe, and the articles used are more comfortable and pleasing. The medium price of meat and fish in many parts of America, is lower than the price of flour in Europe, especially if bought by the carcase. . . . Add to this, many principal necessaries and conveniencies of life are entirely free from excise or duty, at this time; and will be lightly charged for a long while to come—such as home-made malt liquors and cider, coal and firewood, candles, oil, soap, tobacco, and leather, none of which pay excise, and even foreign salt pays only about sixpence sterling duty on importation, and no excise whatever. Nor have we any window-tax or hearth-money, nor several other taxes, by which large sums are raised in Europe.

Many things are daily presenting themselves, by which the profits of land will be greatly enhanced in this country. We have hitherto imported a great part of our drink from abroad, viz. rum, brandy, gin, &c. but we find, if we extend our breweries so far as to render these spirituous liquors unnecessary, that we shall want above two millions of bushels of barley for the purpose, and large quantities of hops, besides having use for a further part of the immense quantities of firewood and coal with which our country abounds. We have also obtained the European cotton mill, by means of which, and a few of our innumerable mill seats, the owners of lands, in the six southern states, will be called upon to supply great quantities of cotton. The movements of a mill for spinning flax, hemp, and combed wool, have also been constructed here, by which our farmers, throughout the union, will

be called upon to supply further quantities of flax and hemp, and to increase their sheep. The rolling mill for iron and other metals—and the tilt-hammer for all large iron work—have been brought into extensive use, and will no doubt be erected in all the states. . . .

There is a striking invaluable difference between the navigable waters of the United States and those of any country in the old world. The Elbe is the only river in Europe, which will permit a sea vessel to sail up it for so great a length as seventy miles. The Hudson's, or North-River, between the states of New-York and New-Jersey, is navigated by sea vessels one hundred and eighty miles from the ocean; the Delaware, between Pennsylvania, New-Jersey and the Delaware state, one hundred and sixty miles; the Patowmac, between Virginia and Maryland, three hundred miles: and there are several other rivers, bays, and sounds, of extensive navigation, far exceeding the great river Elbe. The inland boatable waters and lakes are equally numerous and great.

In a country thus circumstanced, producing the great raw materials for manufactures, and possessing unlimited powers by water and resources of fuel, subject also to considerable charges upon the importation of foreign fabrics, *to neglect manufactures would have been highly criminal.* These important ideas have taken full possession of the American mind. The theory is now every where approved: and in New England, Pennsylvania, and several other states, the practice has been taken up with considerable spirit and very extensively. Master workmen in every manufacturing and mechanical art (except those of superfluous or luxurious kinds) with their journeymen and labourers, must succeed here. The freight, insurance, and other charges of a long voyage, of more than three thousand miles and the duties laid here, operate greatly in favour of American fabrics. Manufactures by fire, water, and emigrating workmen, must succeed even in the most agricultural of our states, and will meet every encouragement in the New England states, and others whose lands are nearly full. A regard for the republican manners of our country, renders it a duty to warn the manufacturers of very fine, superflous, and luxurious articles, not to emigrate to these states. Gold and silver and other laces, embroidery, jewellery, rich silks and silk velvets, fine cambrics, fine lawns, fine muslins, and articles of that expensive nature, have yet few wearers here.

Ship-building is an art for which the United States are peculiarly qualified by their skill in the construction, and by the materials, with which this country abounds: and they are strongly tempted to pursue it by their commercial spirit, by the capital fisheries in their bays and on their coasts, and by the productions of a great and rapidly increasing agriculture. They build their oak vessels on lower terms than the cheapest European vessels of fir, pine, and larch. . . . In such a country, the fisheries and commerce, with due care and attention on the part of government, must be profitable.

*   *   *

The people of the principal European nations will find themselves more *at home* in America than in any foreign country, to which they can emigrate. The English, German, and Dutch languages are fluently spoken by large bodies of our citizens, who have emigrated from those countries, or who are the descendants of emigrants. The French language is also spoken by many in our towns. There are many emigrants from other nations, and the descendants of such emigrants. Our population has been derived from England, Scotland, Wales, Ireland, Germany, the United Netherlands, Sweden, and France, and a few from several other countries. It is computed to be above three millions at this time:[1] and the population of no country can increase so rapidly: because living is no where so cheap, and we are constantly gaining people from the nations of the old world.

The state of literature in the United States is respectable, and is rapidly advancing and extending. Seminaries of learning are spread from north to south. There are five universities, no one of which, however is on a very extensive scale—fourteen colleges, and forty eight public academies, besides very many establishments of schools, in the townships or hundreds, and under the care of religious corporations and societies. There is scarcely an instance of a state constitution, which does not recognize the utility of public schools, and the necessity of supporting and increasing them. Liberal grants of land and other real estates, and of monies, for these salutary purposes, have been and are continually made.

The situation of civil liberty in America is so universally known that it is scarcely necessary to add any thing upon that head. Yet it may not be amiss briefly to mention, that no man can be convicted of any crime in the United States, without the unanimous verdict of twelve jurymen—that he cannot be deprived of any money, lands, or other property, nor punished in his person, but by some known law, made and published before the circumstance or act in question took place—that all foreigners may freely exercise their trades and employments, on landing in our country, upon equal terms with our own natural born citizens— that they may return at any time, to their native country, without hindrance or molestation, and may take with them the property they brought hither, or what they may have afterwards acquired here—that if they choose to remain among us, they will become completely naturalized free citizens by only two years residence; but may purchase and hold lands on the day of their arrival, and that a free citizen of the United States has a right, directly or indirectly, to elect every officer of the state in which he lives, and every officer of the United States.

The situation of religious rights in the American states, though also well known, is too important, too precious a circumstance, to be omitted. Almost every sect and form of christianity is known here—as also the Hebrew church. None are merely tolerated. All are admitted, aided by mutual charity and concord, and equally supported and cherished by the laws. . . .

---

[1] It was a matter of agreeable surprise, that our population in 1791, proved to be about 4,000,000. [Footnote from Coxe's edition—*Ed.*]

At the time of the foregoing publication, the the exports of the United States amounted to above 18,000,000 of dollars. The progress of industry had advanced them in 1792, to the sum of 21,000,000 of dollars. A very large proportion of this increase, consists in articles for the sustenance of man—the food of our increasing manufacturers, or the prime necessaries of other countries. The useful art of ship-building has kept more than equal pace with our agriculture, because it has felt the impulse of the revival of the fisheries, and of foreign demand. The price of iron, which is a good general index of industry and arts, has been greatly advanced by the progress of public and private improvements, and useful manufactures: and eleven great and important canals have been actually commenced in a country, which before the late revolution did not exhibit a single instance of those invaluable improvements.

REVIEW QUESTIONS

1. How could this essay be interpreted as a cultural as well as an economic commentary?
2. Why and how did Coxe present some of the results of the Revolution to his readers?
3. Does this essay provide evidence of a burgeoning nationalism?
4. Did Coxe present solely the facts or did he engage in some conjecture or wishful thinking? Did his merchant background flavor his presentation?

FROM The Conference Concerning the Insurrection in Western Pennsylvania (1794)

In support of Hamilton's economic program, Congress passed legislation in 1791 and 1792 establishing excise taxes on distilled spirits (including whiskey, which may be distilled from fermented rye, wheat, corn, or barley). Many western Pennsylvanians vehemently protested these duties, for they amounted to a tax on the grains they grew and thus affected their livelihood. They conducted meetings, called for the creation of a committee to prepare a case to send to Congress, as well as committees of correspondence in the affected counties to coordinate actions, and passed resolutions to interfere with or obstruct those collecting the duties. Hamilton later scoffed at the idea that the latter had been legal: "Legal measures may be pursued to procure the repeal of a law, but to obstruct *its operation presents a contradiction in terms."* Despite a congressional attempt to placate protestors through new legislation revising the excise in June 1794, vehemence escalated into violence. By July western Pennsylvania was the scene of insurrection. Protestors intimidated those collecting and paying the excise by abusing persons and destroying property. They stole the mail of officials involved in the crisis and threatened government in Pittsburgh. The Whiskey Rebellion set off a debate within the administration and between some federal and state officials over the proper course of action.*

From Alexander Hamilton, *The Papers of Alexander Hamilton*, vol. 17, ed. Harold C. Syrett (New York: Columbia University Press, 1972), pp. 9–13. [Editorial insertions appear in square brackets—*Ed.*] *Hamilton to Washington, Treasury Department [5 August 1794], p. 40.

"Conference Concerning the Insurrection in Western Pennsylvania" [Philadelphia, 2 August 1794. Attendees from the federal government were President George Washington, Secretary of State Edmund Randolph, Secretary of Treasury Alexander Hamilton, Secretary of War Henry Knox, and Attorney General William Bradford; and those from Pennsylvania were Governor Thomas Mifflin, Chief Justice Thomas McKean, Attorney General Jared Ingersoll, and Alexander J. Dallas, secretary of the Commonwealth.]

The President opened the business by stating that it was hardly necessary to prepare the subject of the conference, as it was generally understood, and the circumstances which accompanied it were such as to strike at the root of all law & order; that he was clearly of opinion that the most spirited & firm measures were necessary to rescue the State as well as the general government from the impending danger, for if such proceedings were tolerated there was an end to our Constitutions & laws. He then observed that there were some papers besides those already communicated to the Gov'r which would throw additional light on the subject, and he presented them to the Secretary of State who read them aloud.

*   *   *

The President declared his determination to go every length that the Constitution and Laws would permit, but no further; he expressed a wish for the co-operation of the State Government, and he enquired whether the Governor could not adopt some preliminary measures under the State Laws, as the measures of the Gen'l Gov't would be slow, and depended on the certificate of Judge Wilson, to whom the documents had been delivered for his consideration. [At an earlier meeting, Washington's cabinet decided that the information should be brought before an associate justice to be evaluated under the 2 May 1792 "Act to provide for calling forth the Militia to execute the laws of the Union, suppress insurrections, and repel invasion." Justice James Wilson of the Supreme Court evaluated the

evidence and on 4 August informed the President that in Washington and Allegheny counties execution of the laws of the United States was being obstructed "by Combinations too powerful to be suppressed by the ordinary Course of judicial Proceedings, or by the Powers vested in the Marshal of that District."]

The Secretary of State read the act of Congress under which the Gen'l Gov't were proceeding and repeated the enquiries, whether some more expeditious, preliminary course, could not be pursued, referring to a particular act of the state.

The officers of the State Government remaining silent for some time, the Att'y Gen'l of the U.S. turned to the act of 22d Sept., '83 [referring to state legislation: "An Additional Supplement to an Act, Entitled 'An Act for the Regulation of the Militia of the Commonwealth of Pennsylvania' "], authorizing calls of the Militia on sudden emergencies, but the Secretary of the Comm'th referred him to a note in the index, subjoined to title militia, and suggested his opinion that the law referred to was repealed, whereupon the Att'y Gen'l of the U.S. asked the Sec'y of the Com'th, what was his opinion respecting the power of the Governor to call out the Militia on such occasions, to which the secretary replied, that as an individual he had no objection to give a private opinion—that independent of the law referred to, or any other special law, the executive Magistrate was charged with the care of seeing the laws faithfully executed, and that upon the requisition of the civil authority declaring it incompetent to the task, the very nature of the Executive Magistrate's duty and obligations, required that he should aid the civil authority by an exertion of the military force of the Government.

The intention of proceeding against the Rioters in Allegheny co., being declared by the President, the Chief Justice expressed it as his positive opinion, that the judiciary power was equal to the task of quelling and punishing the riots, and that the employment of a military force, at this period, would be as bad as anything that the Rioters had done—equally unconstitutional and illegal.

The opinion of the Secretary of the Treasury was introduced by argument upon the general necessity of maintaining the Government in its regular authority. He referred to the various co-operating sources of opposition to the Constitution and laws of the U.S., (The Judiciary, excise, Mississippi navigation, erecting a new State, &c., &c.,) and insisted upon the propriety of an immediate resort to Military force. He said that it would not be sufficient to quell the existing riot to restore us to the state in which we were a few weeks back; for, before the present outrages, there was equal opposition to the laws of the U.S. [as above, Hamilton was referring to various cases and events that dealt with the exercise of federal authority], though not expressed in the same manner; but that now the crisis was arrived when it must be determined whether the Government can maintain itself, and that the exertion must be made, not only to quell the rioters, but to protect the officers of the Union in executing their offices, and in compelling obedience to the laws.

The Secretary of the Com'th stated, as information, that in a conversation with Judge Addison [Alexander Addison, presiding judge of the County Court of the western district of Pennsylvania], the Judge had declared it as his opinion that if the business was left to the courts, the rioters might be prosecuted and punished, and the matter peaceably terminated; but that a resort to military force, would unite in the resistance, the peaceable as well as riotous opponents of the excise, upon the Idea that the military was intended to dragoon them equally into submission. He also stated that similar riots against the excise had been punished in the State courts.

The secretary of the Treasury observed, that the Judge alluded was among those who had most promoted the opposition in an insidious manner, that perhaps it would lead to a disagreeable animadversion to point out the particulars of the Judge's conduct; but that they were stated at large in a report to the President, which the President said was the case. [Conference minutes ended there.]

REVIEW QUESTIONS

1. Why did Washington want the federal government to intervene in this Pennsylvania insurrection? What kind of intervention was he suggesting? Did he propose unilateral federal action?
2. Why did Hamilton push for military action?
3. How did the state officials respond to the proposals of the federal authorities?
4. What does this episode reveal about the exercise of government in the early 1790s?

GEORGE WASHINGTON

FROM Farewell Address (1796)

The founding financiers wanted to make the United States independent in an economic as well as political sense; and yet, in their promotion of a diversified economy, they also advocated the expansion of foreign trade. They wanted to create more markets abroad to offset the use of this country as a market for other nations. Such a plan generally meant establishing ties to other nations, but American leaders tried to avoid such connections by supporting a concept of free trade. Most Americans wanted to be free of entangling alliances as they pursued their interests abroad as well as at home. Unfortunately for them, European nations, especially Britain and France, were not willing to grant the Americans such autonomy in international relations. Struggling to maintain their power and contain adversaries in an era of revolution and war, these countries challenged and intervened in the domestic and foreign affairs of the United States. President Washington strove to counter these attacks on the nation's honor and interests as he labored to ensure the nation's security. He addressed these issues in the valedictory statement that he had published in the American Daily Advertiser *on 19 September 1796. After informing the American people that he was retiring from office, he offered them some advice. His recommendations as they pertained to foreign relations influenced the creation and implementation of American foreign policy into the twentieth century.*

From George Washington, *The Writings of George Washington from the Original Manuscript Sources, 1745–1799*, vol. 35, ed. John C. Fitzpatrick, (Washington, D.C.: GPO, 1940), pp. 214–36. [Editorial insertions appear in square brackets—*Ed.*]

United States, September 19, 1796

*   *   *

. . . [A] solicitude for your welfare, which cannot end but with my life, and the apprehension of danger, natural to that solicitude, urge me on an occasion like the present, to offer to your solemn contemplation, and to recommend to your frequent review, some sentiments; which are the result of much reflection, of no inconsiderable observation, and which appear to me all important to the permanency of your felicity as a People. . . .

*   *   *

The Unity of Government which constitutes you one people is also now dear to you. It is justly so; for it is a main Pillar in the Edifice of your real independence, the support of your tranquility at home; your peace abroad; of your safety; of your prosperity; of that very Liberty which you so highly prize. But as it is easy to foresee, that from different causes and from different quarters, much pains will be taken, many artifices employed, to weaken in your minds the conviction of this truth; as this is the point in your political fortress against which the batteries of internal and external enemies will be most constantly and actively (though often covertly and insidiously) directed, it is of infinite moment, that you should properly estimate the immense value of your national Union to your collective and individual happiness; that you should cherish a cordial, habitual and immoveable attachment to it; accustoming yourselves to think and speak of it as of the Palladium of your political safety and prosperity; watching for its preservation with jealous anxiety; discountenancing whatever may suggest even a suspicion that it can in any event be abandoned, and indignantly frowning upon the first dawning of every attempt to alienate any portion of our Country from the rest, or to enfeeble the sacred ties which now link together the various parts.

For this you have every inducement of sympathy and interest. Citizens by birth or choice, of a common country, that country has a right to concentrate your affections. The name of AMERICAN, which belongs to you, in your national capacity, must always exalt the just pride of Patriotism, more than any appellation derived from local discriminations. With slight shades of difference, you have the same Religeon, Manners, Habits and political Principles. You have in a common cause fought and triumphed together. The independence and liberty you possess are the work of joint councils, and joint efforts; of common dangers, sufferings and successes.

But these considerations, however powerfully they address themselves to your sensibility are greatly outweighed by those which apply more immediately to your Interest. Here every portion of our country finds the most commanding motives for carefully guarding and preserving the Union of the whole.

The *North*, in an unrestrained intercourse with the *South*, protected by the equal Laws of a common government, finds in the productions of the latter, great additional resources of Maratime and commercial enterprise and precious materials of manufacturing industry. The *South* in the same Intercourse, benefitting by the Agency of the *North*, sees its agriculture grow and its commerce expand. Turning partly into its own channels the seamen of the *North*, it finds its particular navigation envigorated; and while it contributes, in different ways, to nourish and increase the general mass of the National navigation, it looks forward to the protection of a Maratime strength, to which itself is unequally adapted. The *East*, in a like intercourse with the *West*, already finds, and in the progressive improvement of interior communications, by land and water, will more and more find a valuable vent for the commodities which it brings from abroad, or manufactures at home. The *West* derives from the *East* supplies requisite to its growth and comfort, and what is perhaps of still greater consequence, it must of necessity owe the *secure* enjoyment of indispensable *outlets* for its own productions to the weight, influence, and the future Maritime strength of the Atlantic side of the Union, directed by an indissoluble community of Interest as *one Nation*. Any other tenure by which the *West* can hold this essential advantage, whether derived from its own seperate strength, or from an apostate and unnatural connection with any foreign Power, must be intrinsically precarious.

While then every part of our country thus feels an immediate and particular Interest in Union, all the parts combined cannot fail to find in the united mass of means and efforts greater strength, greater resource, proportionably greater security from external danger, a less frequent interruption of their Peace by foreign Nations; and, what is of inestimable value! they must derive from Union an exemption from those broils and Wars between themselves, which so frequently afflict neighbouring countries, not tied together by the same gov-

ernment; . . . Hence likewise they will avoid the necessity of those overgrown Military establishments, which under any form of Government are inauspicious to liberty, and which are to be regarded as particularly hostile to Republican Liberty: In this sense it is, that your Union ought to be considered as a main prop of your liberty, and that the love of the one ought to endear to you the preservation of the other.

*   *   *

In contemplating the causes wch. may disturb our Union, it occurs as matter of serious concern, that any ground should have been furnished for characterizing parties by *Geographical* discriminations: *Northern* and *Southern*; *Atlantic* and *Western*; whence designing men may endeavour to excite a belief that there is a real difference of local interests and views. One of the expedients of Party to acquire influence, within particular districts, is to misrepresent the opinions and aims of other Districts. You cannot shield yourselves too much against the jealousies and heart burnings which spring from these misrepresentations. They tend to render Alien to each other those who ought to be bound together by fraternal affection. . . .

To the efficacy and permanency of Your Union, a Government for the whole is indispensable. No Alliances however strict between the parts can be an adequate substitute. They must inevitably experience the infractions and interruptions which all Alliances in all times have experienced. Sensible of this momentous truth, you have improved upon your first essay, by the adoption of a Constitution of Government, better calculated than your former for an intimate Union, and for the efficacious management of your common concerns. This government, . . . has a just claim to your confidence and your support. Respect for its authority, compliance with its Laws, acquiescence in its measures, are duties enjoined by the fundamental maxims of true Liberty. The basis of our political systems is the right of the people to make and to alter their Constitutions of Government. But the Constitution which at any time exists, 'till changed by an explicit and authentic act of the whole People, is sacredly obligatory upon all. The very idea of the power and the right of the People to establish Government presupposes the duty of every Individual to obey the established Government.

All obstructions to the execution of the Laws, all combinations and Associations, under whatever plausible character, with the real design to direct, controul counteract, or awe the regular deliberation and action of the Constituted authorities are distructive of this fundamental principle and of fatal tendency. They serve to organize faction, to give it an artificial and extraordinary force; to put in the place of the delegated will of the Nation, the will of a party; often a small but artful and enterprizing minority of the Community; and, according to the alternate triumphs of different parties, to make the public administration the Mirror of the ill concerted and incongruous projects of faction, rather than the organ of consistent and wholesome plans digested by common councils and modefied by mutual interests. . . .

*   *   *

[The Spirit of Party] serves always to distract the Public Councils and enfeeble the Public administration. It agitates the Community with ill founded jealousies and false alarms, kindles the animosity of one part against another, foments occasionally riot and insurrection. It opens the door to foreign influence and corruption, which find a facilitated access to the government itself through the channels of party passions. Thus the policy and and [*sic*][1] the will of one country, are subjected to the policy and will of another.

There is an opinion that parties in free countries are useful checks upon the Administration of the Government and serve to keep alive the spirit of Liberty. This within certain limits is probably true, and in Governments of a Monarchical cast Patriotism may look with endulgence, if not with favour, upon the spirit of party. But in those of the popular character, in Governments purely elective, it is a spirit not to be encouraged. From their natural tendency, it is certain there will always be

enough of that spirit for every salutary purpose. And there being constant danger of excess, the effort ought to be, by force of public opinion, to mitigate and assuage it. . . .

It is important, likewise, that the habits of thinking in a free Country should inspire caution in those entrusted with its administration, to confine themselves within their respective Constitutional spheres; avoiding in the exercise of the Powers of one department to encroach upon another. The spirit of encroachment tends to consolidate the powers of all the departments in one, and thus to create whatever the form of government, a real despotism. . . .

*   *   *

'Tis substantially true, that virtue or morality is a necessary spring of popular government. The rule indeed extends with more or less force to every species of free Government. Who that is a sincere friend to it, can look with indifference upon attempts to shake the foundation of the fabric

Promote then as an object of primary importance, Institutions for the general diffusion of knowledge. In proportion as the structure of a government gives force to public opinion, it is essential that public opinion should be enlightened

As a very important source of strength and security, cherish public credit. One method of preserving it is to use it as sparingly as possible: avoiding occasions of expence by cultivating peace, but remembering also that timely disbursements to prepare for danger frequently prevent much greater disbursements to repel it; avoiding likewise the accumulation of debt, not only by shunning occasions of expence, but by vigorous exertions in time of Peace to discharge the Debts which unavoidable wars may have occasioned, not ungenerously throwing upon posterity the burthen which we ourselves ought to bear. The execution of these maxims belongs to your Representatives, but it is necessary that public opinion should cooperate. To facilitate to them the performance of their duty, it is essential that you should practically bear in mind, that towards the payment of debts there must be Revenue; that to have Revenue there must

---

[1]Editorial insertion from Fitzpatrick's edition.

be taxes; that no taxes can be devised which are not more or less inconvenient and unpleasant; . . .

Observe good faith and justice towds. all Nations. Cultivate peace and harmony with all. Religion and morality enjoin this conduct; and can it be that good policy does not equally enjoin it? It will be worthy of a free, enlightened, and, at no distant period, a great Nation, to give to mankind the magnanimous and too novel example of a People always guided by an exalted justice and benevolence. . . .

In the execution of such a plan nothing is more essential than that permanent, inveterate antipathies against particular Nations and passionate attachments for others should be excluded; and that in place of them just and amicable feelings towards all should be cultivated. The Nation, which indulges towards another an habitual hatred, or an habitual fondness, is in some degree a slave. It is a slave to its animosity or to its affection, either of which is sufficient to lead it astray from its duty and its interest. . . .

*   *   *

Against the insidious wiles of foreign influence, (I conjure you to believe me fellow citizens) the jealousy of a free people ought to be *constantly* awake; since history and experience prove that foreign influence is one of the most baneful foes of Republican Government. But that jealousy to be useful must be impartial; else it becomes the instrument of the very influence to be avoided, instead of a defence against it. . . .

The Great rule of conduct for us, in regard to foreign Nations is in extending our commercial relations to have with them as little *political* connection as possible. So far as we have already formed engagements let them be fulfilled, with perfect good faith. Here let us stop.

Europe has a set of primary interests, which to us have none, or a very remote relation. Hence she must be engaged in frequent controversies, the causes of which are essentially foreign to our concerns. Hence therefore it must be unwise in us to implicate ourselves, by artificial ties, in the ordinary vicissitudes of her politics, or the ordinary combinations and collisions of her friendships, or enmities:

Our detached and distant situation invites and enables us to pursue a different course. If we remain one People, under an efficient government, the period is not far off, when we may defy material injury from external annoyance; when we may take such an attitude as will cause the neutrality we may at any time resolve upon to be scrupulously respected; when belligerent nations, under the impossibility of making acquisitions upon us, will not lightly hazard the giving us provocation; when we may choose peace or war, as our interest guided by our justice shall Counsel.

Why forego the advantages of so peculiar a situation? Why quit our own to stand upon foreign ground? Why, by interweaving our destiny with that of any part of Europe, entangle our peace and prosperity in the toils of European Ambition, Rivalship, Interest, Humour or Caprice?

'Tis our true policy to steer clear of permanent Alliances, with any portion of the foreign world. So far, I mean, as we are now at liberty to do it, for let me not be understood as capable of patronising infidility to existing engagements (I hold the maxim no less applicable to public than to private affairs, that honesty is always the best policy). I repeat it therefore, let those engagements be observed in their genuine sense. But in my opinion, it is unnecessary and would be unwise to extend them.

Taking care always to keep ourselves, by suitable establishments, on a respectably defensive posture, we may safely trust to temporary alliances for extraordinary emergencies.

Harmony, liberal intercourse with all Nations, are recommended by policy, humanity and interest. But even our Commercial policy should hold an equal and impartial hand: neither seeking nor granting exclusive favours or preferences; consulting the natural course of things; diffusing and deversifying by gentle means the streams of Commerce, but forcing nothing; establishing with Powers so disposed; in order to give to trade a stable course, to define the rights of our Merchants, and to enable the Government to support them; conventional rules of intercourse, the best that present circumstances and mutual opinion will permit, but temporary, and liable to be from time to time abandoned or varied, as experience and circumstances shall dictate; constantly keeping in view, that 'tis folly in one Nation to look for disinterested favors from another; that it must pay with a portion of its Independence for whatever it may accept under that character; that by such acceptance, it may place itself in the condition of having given equivalents for nominal favours and yet of being reproached with ingratitude for not giving more. There can be no greater error than to expect, or calculate upon real favours from Nation to Nation. 'Tis an illusion which experience must cure, which a just pride ought to discard.

In offering to you, my Countrymen these counsels of an old and affectionate friend, I dare not hope they will make the strong and lasting impression, I could wish; that they will controul the usual current of the passions, or prevent our Nation from running the course which has hitherto marked the Destiny of Nations: But if I may even flatter myself, that they may be productive of some partial benefit, some occasional good; that they may now and then recur to moderate the fury of party spirit, to warn against the mischiefs of foreign Intriegue, to guard against the Impostures of pretended patriotism; this hope will be a full recompence for the solicitude for your welfare, by which they have been dictated.

*   *   *

REVIEW QUESTIONS

1. In voicing some concerns and offering advice, Washington revealed some of the problems and conflicts undermining the republic's stability and success. What were they?
2. What did he believe were the nation's particular strengths?
3. What did Washington recommend to preserve the nation's union and liberty?
4. Were his recommendations idealistic or practical? Why?

FROM Alien and Sedition Acts (1798)

Washington, his successor John Adams, and the Federalist Congress came under increasing attack by the public and in the press in the 1790s. It was difficult to determine whether the press was simply reporting public sentiment or feeding it, but the leaders being criticized tended to believe the latter. They deplored what was happening for personal reasons, but they also worried about the power of the press in fostering dissent and division.

Foreign affairs highlighted and contributed to domestic schisms. Washington had warned against hostile foreign influences in his Farewell Address, but the Federalist-dominated Congress, with President Adams's concurrence, moved beyond mere warnings to legislate for the containment of dissent—whether it was foreign or domestically generated. In 1798, a year already fraught with international problems, namely the growing conflict with France, Congress escalated the domestic political crisis by passing acts that could be interpreted as demanding deferential behavior and orderly, even unquestioning, compliance with national policies.

From Richard Peters, ed., *The Public Statutes at Large of the United States of America from the organization of the government in 1789, to March, 1845*, vol. I (Boston: Little, Brown, and Company, 1853), pp. 566–69, 570–72, 577–78, 596–97.

The Naturalization Act (18 June 1798; repealed 1802)

CHAP. LIV.—*An Act supplementary to and to amend the act, intituled "An act to establish an uniform rule of naturalization; and to repeal the act heretofore passed on that subject."*

SECTION 1. *Be it enacted by the Senate and House of Representatives of the United States of America in Congress assembled,* That no alien shall be admitted to become a citizen of the United States, or of any state, unless in the manner prescribed by the act, intituled "An act to establish an uniform rule of naturalization; and to repeal the act heretofore passed on that subject," he shall have declared his intention to become a citizen of the United States, five years, at least, before his admission, and shall, at the time of his application to be admitted, declare and prove, to the satisfaction of the court having jurisdiction in the case, that he has resided within the United States fourteen years, at least, and within the state or territory where, or for which such court is at the time held, five years, at least, besides conforming to the other declarations, renunciations and proofs, by the said act required, any thing therein to the contrary hereof notwithstanding: *Provided,* that any alien, who was residing within the limits, and under the jurisdiction of the United States, before the twenty-ninth day of January, one thousand seven hundred and ninety-five, may, within one year after the passing of this act—and any alien who shall have made the declaration of his intention to become a citizen of the United States, in conformity to the provisions of the act, intituled "An act to establish an uniform

rule of naturalization, and to repeal the act heretofore passed on that subject," may, within four years after having made the declaration aforesaid, be admitted to become a citizen, in the manner prescribed by the said act, upon his making proof that he has resided five years, at least, within the limits, and under the jurisdiction of the United States: *And provided also,* that no alien, who shall be a native, citizen, denizen or subject of any nation or state with whom the United States shall be at war, at the time of his application, shall be then admitted to become a citizen of the United States.

*   *   *

SEC. 4. *And be it further enacted,* That all white persons, aliens, (accredited foreign ministers, consuls, or agents, their families and domestics, excepted) who, after the passing of this act, shall continue to reside, or who shall arrive, or come to reside in any port or place within the territory of the United States, shall be reported, if free, and of the age of twenty-one years, by themselves, or being under the age of twenty-one years, or holden in service, by their parent, guardian, master or mistress in whose care they shall be, to the clerk of the district court of the district, if living within ten miles of the port or place, in which their residence or arrival shall be, and otherwise, to the collector of such port or place, or some officer or other person there, or nearest thereto, who shall be authorized by the President of the United States, to register aliens: And report, as aforesaid, shall be made in all cases of residence, within six months from and after the passing of this act, and in all after cases, within forty-eight hours after the first arrival or coming into the territory of the United States, and shall ascertain the sex, place of birth, age, nation, place of allegiance or citizenship, condition or occupation, and place of actual or intended residence within the United States, of the alien or aliens reported, and by whom the report is made. And it shall be the duty of the clerk, or other officer, or person authorized, who shall receive such report, to record the same in a book to be kept for that purpose, and to grant to the person making the report, and to each individual concerned therein, whenever required, a certificate of such report and registry; . . .

SEC. 5. *And be it further enacted,* That every alien who shall continue to reside, or who shall arrive, as aforesaid, of whom a report is required as aforesaid, who shall refuse or neglect to make such report, and to receive a certificate thereof, shall forfeit and pay the sum of two dollars; and any justice of the peace, or other civil magistrate, who has authority to require surety of the peace, shall and may, on complaint to him made thereof, cause such alien to be brought before him, there to give surety of the peace and good behaviour during his residence within the United States, or for such term as the justice or other magistrate shall deem reasonable, and until a report and registry of such alien shall be made, and a certificate thereof, received as aforesaid; and in failure of such surety, such alien shall and may be committed to the common gaol, and shall be there held, until the order which the justice or magistrate shall and may reasonably make, in the premises, shall be performed. And every person, whether alien, or other, having the care of any alien or aliens, under the age of twenty-one years, or of any white alien holden in service, who shall refuse and neglect to make report thereof, as aforesaid, shall forfeit the sum of two dollars, for each and every such minor or servant, monthly, and every month, until a report and registry, and a certificate thereof, shall be had, as aforesaid.

*   *   *

The Alien Act
(25 June 1798; expired)

CHAP. LVIII.—*An Act concerning Aliens. (u)*

SECTION 1. *Be it enacted by the Senate and House of Representatives of the United States of America in Congress assembled,* That it shall be lawful for the President of the United States at any time during the continuance of this act, to *order* all such *aliens* as he shall judge dangerous to the peace and safety of the United States, or shall have reasonable grounds to suspect are concerned in any reasonable or secret machinations against the government thereof, to depart out of the territory of the United States, within such time as shall be expressed in such order, which order shall be served on such alien by delivering him a copy thereof, or leaving the same at his usual abode, and returned to the office of the Secretary of State, by the marshal or other person to whom the same shall be directed. And in case any alien, so ordered to depart, shall be found at large within the United States after the time limited in such order for his departure, and not having obtained a *license* from the President to reside therein, or having obtained such *license* shall not have conformed thereto, every such alien shall, on conviction thereof, be imprisoned for a term not exceeding three years, and shall never after be admitted to become a citizen of the United States. *Provided always, and be it further enacted,* that if any alien so ordered to depart shall prove to the satisfaction of the President, by evidence to be taken before such person or persons as the President shall direct, who are for that purpose hereby authorized to administer oaths, that no injury or danger to the United States will arise from suffering such alien to reside therein, the President may grant a *license* to such alien to remain within the United States for such time as he shall judge proper, and at such place as he may designate. And the President may also require of such alien to enter into a bond to the United States, in such penal sum as he may direct, with one or more sufficient sureties to the satisfaction of the person authorized by the President to take the same, conditioned for the good behavior of such alien during his residence in the United States, and not violating his license, which license the President may revoke, whenever he shall think proper.

SEC. 2. *And be it further enacted,* That it shall be lawful for the President of the United States, whenever he may deem it necessary for the public safety, to order to be removed out of the territory thereof, any alien who may or shall be in prison in pursuance of this act; and to cause to be arrested and sent out of the United States such of those aliens as shall have been ordered to depart therefrom and shall not have obtained a license as aforesaid, in all cases where, in the opinion of the President, the public safety requires a speedy removal. And if any alien so removed or sent out of the United States by the President shall voluntarily return thereto, unless by permission of the President of the United States, such alien on conviction thereof, shall be imprisoned so long as, in the opinion of the President, the public safety may require.

*   *   *

The Alien Enemy Act (6 July 1798; expired)

CHAP. LXVI.—*An Act respecting Alien Enemies. (a)*

SECTION 1. *Be it enacted by the Senate and House of Representatives of the United States of America in Congress assembled,* That whenever there shall be a declared war between the United States and any foreign nation or government, or any invasion or predatory incursion shall be perpetrated, attempted, or threatened against the territory of the United States, by any foreign nation or government, and the President of the United States shall make public proclamation of the event, all natives, citizens, denizens, or subjects of the hostile nation or government, being males of the age of fourteen years and upwards, who shall be within the United States, and not actually naturalized, shall be liable to be apprehended, restrained, secured and removed as alien enemies. And the President of the United States . . . is hereby authorized, . . . to direct the conduct to be observed, on the part of the United States, towards the aliens who shall become liable, as aforesaid; the manner and degree of the restraint to which they shall be subject, and in what cases, and upon what security their residence shall be permitted, and to provide for the removal of those, who, not being permitted to reside within the United States, shall refuse or neglect to depart therefrom; and to establish any other regulations which shall be found necessary in the premises and for the public safety: Provided, that aliens resident within the United States, who shall become liable as enemies, in the manner aforesaid, and who shall not be chargeable with actual hostility, or other crime against the public safety, shall be allowed, for the recovery, disposal, and removal of their goods and effects, and for their departure, the full time which is, or shall be stipulated by any treaty, where any shall have been between the United States, and the hostile nation or government, of which they shall be natives, citizens, denizens or subjects: and where no such treaty shall have existed, the President of the United States may ascertain and declare such reasonable time as may be consistent with the public safety, and according to the dictates of humanity and national hospitality.

SEC. 2. *And be it further enacted,* That after any proclamation shall be made as aforesaid, it shall be the duty of the several courts of the United States, and of each state, having criminal jurisdiction, and of the several judges and justices of the courts of the United States, . . . upon complaint, against any alien or alien enemies, as aforesaid, . . . to cause such alien or aliens to be duly apprehended and convened before such court, judge or justice; and after a full examination and hearing on such complaint, and sufficient cause therefor appearing, shall and may order such alien or aliens to be removed out of the territory of the United States, or to give sureties of their good behaviour, or to be otherwise restrained, . . .

*   *   *

The Sedition Act
(14 July 1798; expired)

CHAP. LXXIV.—*An Act in addition to the act, entitled "An act for the punishment of certain crimes against the United States."*

SECTION 1. *Be it enacted by the Senate and House of Representatives of the United States of America, in Congress assembled*, That if any persons shall unlawfully combine or conspire together, with intent to oppose any measure or measures of the government of the United States, which are or shall be directed by proper authority, or to impede the operation of any law of the United States, or to intimidate or prevent any person holding a place or office in or under the government of the United States, from undertaking, performing or executing his trust or duty; and if any person or persons, with intent as aforesaid, shall counsel, advise or attempt to procure any insurrection, riot, unlawful assembly, or combination, whether such conspiracy, threatening, counsel, advice, or attempt shall have the proposed effect or not, he or they shall be deemed guilty of a high misdemeanor, and on conviction, before any court of the United States having jurisdiction thereof, shall be punished by a fine not exceeding five thousand dollars, and by imprisonment during a term not less than six months nor exceeding five years; and further, at the discretion of the court may be holden to find sureties for his good behaviour in such sum, and for such time, as the said court may direct.

SEC. 2. *And be it further enacted*, That if any person shall write, print, utter or publish, or shall cause or procure to be written, printed, uttered or published, or shall knowingly and willingly assist or aid in writing, printing, uttering or publishing any false, scandalous and malicious writing or writings against the government of the United States, or either house of the Congress of the United States, or the President of the United States, with intent to defame the said government, or either house of the said Congress, or the said President, or to bring them, or either of them, into contempt or disrepute; or to excite against them, or either or any of them, the hatred of the good people of the United States, or to stir up sedition within the United States, or to excite any unlawful combinations therein, for opposing or resisting any law of the United States, or any act of the President of the United States, done in pursuance of any such law, or of the powers in him vested by the constitution of the United States, or to resist, oppose, or defeat any such law or act, or to aid, encourage or abet any hostile designs of any foreign nation against the United States, their people or government, then such person, being thereof convicted before any court of the United States having jurisdiction thereof, shall be punished by a fine not exceeding two thousand dollars, and by imprisonment not exceeding two years.

SEC. 3. *And be it further enacted and declared*, That if any person shall be prosecuted under this act, for the writing or publishing any libel aforesaid, it shall be lawful for the defendant, upon the trial of the cause, to give in evidence in his defence, the truth of the matter contained in the publication charged as a libel. And the jury who shall try the cause, shall have a right to determine the law and the fact, under the direction of the court, as in other cases.

*   *   *

REVIEW QUESTIONS

1. By passing the Alien and Sedition Acts, were the Federalist legislators reacting to a national or a political threat?
2. What do these acts suggest about their conception of loyalty and citizenship?

3. How did the Alien Act pick up from and strengthen provisions in the Naturalization Act? Was the Alien Act anti-immigrant or pro-security?

4. Did the later two alien acts expand presidential power?

5. Was the Sedition Act a defense of order or an offense against citizens' rights? Did the act, in effect, define dissent as treachery?

6. How could a person charged under the provisions of this act defend her or himself?

FROM Kentucky and Virginia Resolutions (1798 and 1799)

Federalists received neither the respect nor domestic peace they wanted with the above legislation; instead, the acts provoked more challenges by their opponents. Republicans denounced the Alien and Sedition Acts as unconstitutional. In their outrage and through their endeavors to have the acts immediately repealed, some Republicans advanced new or revised theories on how to check the powers of the national government. Their ideas on state interposition and nullification of national legislation would be revised by later theorists and used in even more divisive political wrangles. Thomas Jefferson and James Madison presented these ideas in the Kentucky and Virginia Resolutions respectively (Jefferson drafted Kentucky's argument; John Breckinridge actually presented them to that state's legislature). Their proposals were controversial, so much so that, despite their attempts to persuade other states to pass supporting legislation, many states passed statements—though none so short and scathing perhaps as Delaware's—denouncing the resolutions. Despite such denunciations, however, many Americans agreed that the Federalists had overstepped their authority and infringed on the peoples' rights, and thus, although they lost this political battle, the Republicans won the "war" in the election of 1800.

From Jonathan Elliot, ed., *The Debates in the Several State Conventions on the Adoption of the Federal Constitution*, vol. 4 (1836; New York: Burt Franklin Reprints, 1974), pp. 528–29, 532, 540–45.

Kentucky Resolutions of 1798 and 1799.

[HOUSE OF REPRESENTATIVES, *November* 10, 1798]

1. *Resolved*, That the several states composing the United States of America are not united on the principle of unlimited submission to their general government; but that, by compact, under the style and title of a Constitution for the United States, and of amendments thereto, they constituted a general government for special purposes, delegated to that government certain definite powers, reserving, each state to itself, the residuary mass of right to their own self-government; and that whensoever the general government assumes undelegated powers, its acts are unauthoritative, void, and of no

force; that to this compact each state acceded as a state, and is an integral party; that this government, created by this compact, was not made the exclusive or final judge of the extent of the powers delegated to itself, since that would have made its discretion, and not the Constitution, the measure of its powers; but that, as in all other cases of compact among parties having no common judge, *each party has an equal right to judge for itself, as well of infractions as of the mode and measure of redress.*

2. *Resolved,* That the Constitution of the United States having delegated to Congress a power to punish treason, counterfeiting the securities and current coin of the United States, piracies and felonies committed on the high seas, and offences against the laws of nations, and no other crimes whatever; and it being true, as a general principle, and one of the amendments to the Constitution having also declared "that the powers not delegated to the United States by the Constitution, nor prohibited by it to the states, are reserved to the states respectively, or to the people,"—therefore, also, the same act of Congress, passed on the 14th day of July, 1798, and entitled "An Act in Addition to the Act entitled `An Act for the Punishment of certain Crimes against the United States;'" as also the act passed by them on the 27th day of June, 1798, entitled "An Act to punish Frauds committed on the Bank of the United States," (and all other their acts which assume to create, define, or punish crimes other than those enumerated in the Constitution,) are altogether void, and of no force; and that the power to create, define, and punish, such other crimes is reserved, and of right appertains, solely and exclusively, to the respective states, each within its own territory.

3. *Resolved,* That it is true, as a general principle, and is also expressly declared by one of the amendments to the Constitution, that "the powers not delegated to the United States by the Constitution, nor prohibited by it to the states, are reserved to the states respectively, or to the people;" and that, no power over the freedom of religion, freedom of speech, or freedom of the press, being delegated to the United States by the Constitution,

nor prohibited by it to the states, all lawful powers respecting the same did of right remain, and were reserved to the states, or to the people; that thus was manifested their determination to retain to themselves the right of judging how far the licentiousness of speech, and of the press, may be abridged without lessening their useful freedom, and how far those abuses which cannot be separated from their use, should be tolerated rather than the use be destroyed; and thus also they guarded against all abridgment, by the United States, of the freedom of religious principles and exercises, and retained to themselves the right of protecting the same, as this, stated by a law passed on the general demand of its citizens, had already protected them from all human restraint or interference; and that, in addition to this general principle and express declaration, another and more special provision has been made by one of the amendments to the Constitution, which expressly declares, that "Congress shall make no laws respecting an establishment of religion, or prohibiting the free exercise thereof, or abridging the freedom of speech, or of the press," thereby guarding, in the same sentence, and under the same words, the freedom of religion, of speech, and of the press, insomuch that whatever violates either throws down the sanctuary which covers the others,—and that libels, falsehood, and defamation, equally with heresy and false religion, are withheld from the cognizance of federal tribunals. That therefore the act of the Congress of the United States, passed on the 14th of July, 1798, entitled "An Act in Addition to the Act entitled `An Act for the Punishment of certain Crimes against the United States,'" which does abridge the freedom of the press, is not law, but is altogether void, and of no force.

4. *Resolved,* That alien friends are under the jurisdiction and protection of the laws of the state wherein they are; that no power over them has been delegated to the United States, nor prohibited to the individual states, . . . [thus] the act of the Congress of the United States, passed the 22d day of June, 1798, entitled "An Act concerning Aliens," which assumes power over alien friends not dele-

gated by the Constitution, is not law, but is altogether void and of no force.

5. *Resolved*, That, in addition to the general principle, as well as the express declaration, that powers not delegated are reserved, another and more special provision inserted in the Constitution from abundant caution, has declared, "that the migration or importation of such persons as any of the states now existing shall think proper to admit, shall not be prohibited by the Congress prior to the year 1808." That this commonwealth does admit the migration of alien friends described as the subject of the said act concerning aliens; . . .

6. *Resolved*, That the imprisonment of a person under the protection of the laws of this commonwealth, on his failure to obey the simple order of the President to depart out of the United States, as is undertaken by the said act, entitled, "An Act concerning Aliens," is contrary to the Constitution, one amendment in which has provided, that "no person shall be deprived of liberty without due process of law;" and that another having provided, "that, in all criminal prosecutions, the accused shall enjoy the right of a public trial by an impartial jury, to be informed as to the nature and cause of the accusation, to be confronted with the witnesses against him, to have compulsory process for obtaining witnesses in his favor, and to have assistance of counsel for his defence," the same act undertaking to authorize the President to remove a person out of the United States who is under the protection of the law, on his own suspicion, without jury, without public trial, without confrontation of the witnesses against him, without having witnesses in his favor, without defence, without counsel—contrary to these provisions also of the Constitution—is therefore not law, but utterly void, and of no force.

*   *   *

7. *Resolved*, That the construction applied by the general government (as is evident by sundry of their proceedings) to those parts of the Constitution of the United States which delegate to Congress power to lay and collect taxes, duties, imposts, excises; to pay the debts, and provide for the common defence and general welfare, of the United States, and to make all laws which shall be necessary and proper for carrying into execution the powers vested by the Constitution in the government of the United States, or any department thereof, goes to the destruction of all the limits prescribed to their power by the Constitution; that words meant by that instrument to be subsidiary only to the execution of the limited powers, ought not to be so construed as themselves to give unlimited powers, nor a part so to be taken as to destroy the whole residue of the instrument; that the proceedings of the general government, under color of those articles, will be a fit and necessary subject for revisal and correction at a time of greater tranquillity, while those specified in the preceding resolutions call for immediate redress.

*   *   *

9. *Resolved*, lastly, That the governor of this commonwealth be, and is, authorized and requested to communicate the preceding resolutions to the legislatures of the several states, to assure them that this commonwealth considers union for special national purposes, and particularly for those specified in their late federal compact, to be friendly to the peace, happiness, and prosperity, of all the states: that, faithful to that compact, according to the plain intent and meaning in which it was understood and acceded to by the several parties, it is sincerely anxious for its preservation; that it does also believe, that, to take from the states all the powers of self-government, and transfer them to a general and consolidated government, without regard to the special government, and reservations solemnly agreed to in that compact, is not for the peace, happiness, or prosperity of these states; . . . that the friendless alien has been selected as the safest subject of a first experiment; but the citizen will soon follow, or rather has already followed; for already has a Sedition Act marked him as a prey: That these and successive acts of the same character, unless arrested on the threshold, may tend to drive these states into revolution and blood, and will furnish new calumnies against republican governments, and new pretexts for those who wish it

to be believed that man cannot be governed but by a rod of iron; . . .

In questions of power, then, let no more be said of confidence in man, but bind him down from mischief by the chains of the Constitution. That this commonwealth does therefore call on its co-states for an expression of their sentiments on the acts concerning aliens, and for the punishment of certain crimes herein before specified, plainly declaring whether these acts are or are not authorized by the federal compact. . . . That they will view this as seizing the rights of the states, and consolidating them in the hands of the general government, with a power assumed to bind the states, not merely in cases made federal, but in all cases whatsoever, by laws made, not with their consent, but by others against their consent, that this would be to surrender the form of government we have chosen, and live under one deriving its powers from its own will, and not from our authority; and that the co-states, recurring to their natural rights not made federal, will concur in declaring these void and of no force, and will each unite with this commonwealth in requesting their repeal at the next session of Congress.

HOUSE OF REPRESENTATIVES,
Thursday, Nov. 14, 1799.

*   *   *

The representatives of the good people of this commonwealth, in General Assembly convened, having maturely considered the answers of sundry states in the Union to their resolutions, passed the last session, respecting certain unconstitutional laws of Congress, commonly called the Alien and Sedition Laws, would be faithless, indeed, to themselves, and to those they represent, were they silently to acquiesce in the principles and doctrines attempted to be maintained in all those answers, that of Virginia only excepted. To again enter the field of argument, and attempt more fully or forcibly to expose the unconstitutionality of those obnoxious laws, would, it is apprehended, be as unnecessary as unavailing. We cannot, however, but lament that, in the discussion of those interesting

subjects by sundry of the legislatures of our sister states, unfounded suggestions and uncandid insinuations, derogatory to the true character and principles of this commonwealth, have been substituted in place of fair reasoning and sound argument. . . . Lest, however, the silence of this commonwealth should be construed into an acquiescence in the doctrines and principles advanced, and attempted to be maintained, by the said answers; or at least those of our fellow-citizens, throughout the Union, who so widely differ from us on those important subjects, should be deluded by the expectation that we shall be deterred from what we conceive our duty, or shrink from the principles contained in those resolutions,—therefore,

Resolved, That this commonwealth considers the federal Union, upon the terms and for the purposes specified in the late compact, conducive to the liberty and happiness of the several states: That it does now unequivocally declare its attachment to the Union, and to that compact, agreeably to its obvious and real intention, and will be among the last to seek its dissolution: That, if those who administer the general government be permitted to transgress the limits fixed by that compact, by a total disregard to the special delegations of power therein contained, an annihilation of the state governments, and the creation, upon their ruins, of a general consolidated government, will be the inevitable consequence: That the principle and construction, contended for by sundry of the state legislatures, that the general government is the exclusive judge of the extent of the powers delegated to it, stop not short of *despotism*—since the discretion of those who administer the government, and not the *Constitution*, would be the measure of their powers: That the several states who formed that instrument, being sovereign and independent, have the unquestionable right to judge of the infraction: and, *That a nullification, by those sovereignties, of all unauthorized acts done under color of that instrument, is the rightful remedy:* That this commonwealth does, under the most deliberate reconsideration, declare, that the said Alien and Sedition Laws are, in their opinion, palpable violations of the said Constitution; and, however cheerfully it may be disposed to surrender its opinion to a majority of its sister states, in matters of ordinary or doubtful policy, yet, in momentous regulations like the present, which so vitally wound the best rights of the citizen, it would consider a silent acquiescence as highly criminal: That, although this commonwealth, as a party to the federal compact, will bow to the laws of the Union, yet it does, at the same time, declare, that it will not now, or ever hereafter, cease to oppose, in a constitutional manner, every attempt, at what quarter soever offered, to violate that compact: And finally, in order that no pretext or arguments may be drawn from a supposed acquiescence, on the part of this commonwealth, in the constitutionality of those laws, and be thereby used as precedents for similar future violations of the federal compact, this commonwealth does now enter against them its solemn PROTEST.

*   *   *

Virginia Resolutions of 1798,

PRONOUNCING THE ALIEN AND SEDITION LAWS TO BE UNCONSTITUTIONAL, AND DEFINING THE RIGHTS OF THE STATES.

DRAWN BY MR. MADISON.

In the Virginia House of Delegates, Friday, *December* 21, 1798.

Resolved, That the General Assembly of Virginia doth unequivocally express a firm resolution to maintain and defend the Constitution of the United States, and the Constitution of this state, against every aggression, either foreign or domestic; and that they will support the government of the United States in all measures warranted by the former.

That this Assembly most solemnly declares a warm attachment to the union of the states, to maintain which it pledges its powers; and that, for this end, it is their duty to watch over and oppose every infraction of those principles which constitute the only basis of that union, because a faithful observance of them can alone secure its existence and the public happiness.

That this Assembly doth explicitly and peremptorily declare, that it views the powers of the federal government as resulting from the compact to which the states are parties, as limited by the plain sense and intention of the instrument constituting that compact, as no further valid than they are authorized by the grants enumerated in that compact; and that, in case of a deliberate, palpable, and dangerous exercise of other powers, not granted by the said compact, the states, who are parties thereto, have the right, and are in duty bound, to interpose, for arresting the progress of the evil, and for maintaining, within their respective limits, the authorities, rights, and liberties, appertaining to them.

That the General Assembly doth also express its deep regret, that a spirit has, in sundry instances, been manifested by the federal government to enlarge its powers by forced constructions of the constitutional charter which defines them; and that indications have appeared of a design to expound certain general phrases (which, having been copied from the very limited grant of powers in the former Articles of Confederation, were the less liable to be misconstrued) so as to destroy the meaning and effect of the particular enumeration which necessarily explains and limits the general phrases, and so as to consolidate the states, by degrees, into one sovereignty, the obvious tendency and inevitable result of which would be, to transform the present republican system of the United States into an absolute, or, at best, a mixed monarchy.

That the General Assembly doth particularly PROTEST against the palpable and alarming infractions of the Constitution, in the two late cases of the "Alien and Sedition Acts," passed at the last session of Congress; the first of which exercises a power nowhere delegated to the federal government, and which, by uniting legislative and judicial powers to those of executive, subverts the general principles of free government, as well as the particular organiza-

tion and positive provisions of the Federal Constitution; and the other of which acts exercises, in like manner, a power not delegated by the Constitution, but, on the contrary, expressly and positively forbidden by one of the amendments thereto—a power which, more than any other, ought to produce universal alarm, because it is levelled against the right of freely examining public characters and measures, and of free communication among the people thereon, which has ever been justly deemed the only effectual guardian of every other right.

That this state having, by its Convention, which ratified the Federal Constitution, expressly declared that, among other essential rights, "the liberty of conscience and the press cannot be cancelled, abridged, restrained, or modified, by any authority of the United States," and from its extreme anxiety to guard these rights from every possible attack of sophistry and ambition, having, with other states, recommended an amendment for that purpose, which amendment was, in due time, annexed to the Constitution,—it would mark a reproachful inconsistency, and criminal degeneracy, if an indifference were now shown to the most palpable violation of one of the rights thus declared and secured, and to the establishment of a precedent which may be fatal to the other.

That the good people of this commonwealth, having ever felt, and continuing to feel, the most sincere affection for their brethren of the other states; the truest anxiety for establishing and perpetuating the union of all; and the most scrupulous fidelity to that Constitution, which is the pledge of mutual friendship, and the instrument of mutual happiness,—the General Assembly doth solemnly appeal to the like dispositions in the other states, in confidence that they will concur with this commonwealth in declaring, as it does hereby declare, that the acts aforesaid are unconstitutional; and that the necessary and proper measures will be taken *by each* for coöperating with this state, in maintaining unimpaired the authorities, rights, and liberties, reserved to the states respectively, or to the people.

*   *   *

State of Delaware.

IN THE HOUSE OF REPRESENTATIVES,
February 1, 1799.

Resolved, By the Senate and House of Representatives of the state of Delaware, in General Assembly met, that they consider the resolutions from the state of Virginia as a very unjustifiable interference with the general government and constituted authorities of the United States, and of dangerous tendency, and therefore not fit sub-ject for the further consideration of the General Assembly.

*   *   *

REVIEW QUESTIONS

1. What body, or bodies, did Jefferson argue had the right to determine the constitutionality of congressional acts? If an act was determined to be unconstitutional could it be declared null and void?

2. Jefferson not only argued that the creation of such legislation by the national government but its contents were unconstitutional. Was this second argument a defense of civil rights?

3. How did Jefferson's interpretation of the *Constitution* form the basis of his arguments? Was his a strict (literal) or broad (flexible) interpretation?

4. In the Virginia Resolutions, did Madison's assertion that the states were duty bound to interpose to arrest the progress of evil and maintain rights supplement or modify Jefferson's challenge? Did Madison's argument include an admonition against a broad or loose interpretation of the *Constitution*?

5. Why would Delaware's legislature have considered Virginia's (and, by inference, Kentucky's) resolutions to have been dangerous?

9 ∾ THE EARLY REPUBLIC

Americans inaugurated a new president and a new century in 1801. Revolutionary as it was for a nation's people to transfer power peacefully from a current head of state to a new one, and in the process from one interest group or political party to another, this was not another revolutionary era. While some citizens celebrated by talking of radical change or engaging in millenialist rhetoric, most sought assurance that the establishment created in the old century would continue in the new. As most of the nation's leaders had earned their original laurels in the Revolution, Americans could be assured that its principles and institutions would continue to be the foundation of government. But in moving into the future with a new president—one they had elected because he espoused a strict interpretation of the Constitution and a limited federal government—American citizens did indicate a desire for some course corrections on the nation's journey to security and prosperity.

The new chief executive of the nation, Thomas Jefferson, and the new chief justice, John Marshall, jousted again and again over what should be the proper interpretation and implementation of the Constitution. The Federalists, voted out of the executive branch and relegated to minority status in the legislative branch, made the judiciary their bulwark. As the champions for each side battled in Congress, courts, and finally in the Supreme Court itself, Marshall, Jefferson, and James Madison (first as Jefferson's secretary of state and then as president), further defined the powers of their own respective branches as well as the limits of the others. In the course of their political and legal contests, these leaders, like Washington and Hamilton before them, set precedents upon which later officials would base their decisions and actions.

Jefferson presided over a growing nation—both in population and territory —which presented particular challenges to its government. Upon taking office, Jefferson faced a major foreign threat to the nation's interests and security: Napoleon Bonaparte. In November 1799 General Bonaparte made himself first consul of France (he declared himself emperor in 1804). Napoleon wanted not only to extend France's domain in Europe but to reestablish its empire in North America. Jefferson learned of his plans and immediately took steps to counter them, engaging both explorers and diplomats to secure his country's claims. Due to that American initiative and persistance, and because of various problems both in Europe and in the Caribbean, Napoleon sold the vast territory west of the Mississippi River to the United States in 1803.

While the United States thus resolved one impediment to its national interests, it was left with what many citizens deemed an even greater one: Native American resistance. Jefferson was willing to protect Indian interests on what lands the tribes still held, but he was primarily interested in supporting white settlement of the West. Jefferson and his successors not only bought Indian lands via treaties, they promoted land exchanges in which Native Americans traded their lands east of the Mississippi for lands to the west of it. As most Indians were not willing to do this, successive presidential administrations grappled again and again with the problem of how to foster peaceful coexistance with and assimilation of Native Americans. When economic and cultural coercion did not work, they adopted policies of force.

As the nation struggled with this western challenge, it also tried to counter trans-Atlantic threats to its interests. Problems had arisen due to European conflicts, primarily British-French warfare, and the continuing growth and strength of the British empire. British dominance on the high seas led to disagreements over maritime rights. Americans, insecure because of the British presence in Canada, also accused the British of inciting Indians against them. As such American weaknesses were revealed, militants in both parties, but especially Republicans, called for a war to defend the nation's honor, rights, and institutions. The result was what some citizens called the "second war of American independence." The title was perhaps apt, for whereas the first had been a war for independence, this was a war coming out of American insistence that its independence and autonomy be not only acknowledged but respected. Yet, even given such a noblesounding aim, the War of 1812 was not a popular one, nor one well waged: it was a war that both united and divided Americans.

THOMAS JEFFERSON

FROM First Inaugural Address (1801)

The election of 1800 was not a polite political duel. There was much verbal mudsling-ing as well as intra- and interparty blows and backstabbing. Alexander Hamilton's disputes with John Adams weakened the Federalist Party from within, while reactions to the administration's policies battered it from without. As a result of those conflicts and the Republican Party's attractive promises, Americans elected Thomas Jefferson to be the third president of the United States. The inauguration was conducted on 4 March in the new capital of the country, Washington, DC, and, with the president figuratively honoring the people and states by whose power he served, at the new home of the Congress, the Capitol.

From James D. Richardson, ed., *A Compilation of the Messages and Papers of the Presidents, 1789–1902*, vol. I (Bureau of National Literature and Art, 1904), pp. 321–24. [Editorial inser-tions appear in square brackets—*Ed.*]

Friends and Fellow-Citizens.

Called upon to undertake the duties of the first executive office of our country, I avail myself of the presence of that portion of my fellow-citizens which is here assembled to express my grateful thanks for the favor with which they have been pleased to look toward me, to declare a sincere consciousness that the task is above my talents, and that I approach it with those anxious and awful presentiments which the greatness of the charge and the weakness of my powers so justly inspire. A rising nation, spread over a wide and fruitful land, traversing all the seas with the rich productions of their industry, engaged in commerce with nations who feel power and forget right, advancing rapidly to destinies beyond the reach of mortal eye—when I contemplate these transcendent objects, and see the honor, the happiness, and the hopes of this beloved country committed to the issue and the auspices of this day, I shrink from the contempla-tion, and humble myself before the magnitude of the undertaking. Utterly, indeed, should I despair did not the presence of many whom I here see re-mind me that in the other high authorities pro-vided by our Constitution I shall find resources of

wisdom, of virtue, and of zeal on which to rely un-der all difficulties. To you, then, gentlemen, who are charged with the sovereign functions of legisla-tion, and to those associated with you, I look with encouragement for that guidance and support which may enable us to steer with safety the vessel in which we are all embarked amidst the conflict-ing elements of a troubled world.

During the contest of opinion through which we have passed the animation of discussions and of exertions has sometimes worn an aspect which might impose on strangers unused to think freely and to speak and to write what they think; but this being now decided by the voice of the nation, an-nounced according to the rules of the Constitu-tion, all will, of course, arrange themselves under the will of the law, and unite in common efforts for the common good. All, too, will bear in mind this sacred principle, that though the will of the major-ity is in all cases to prevail, that will to be rightful must be reasonable; that the minority possess their equal rights, which equal law must protect, and to violate would be oppression. Let us, then, fellow-citizens, unite with one heart and one mind. Let us restore to social intercourse that harmony and affection without which liberty and even life itself are but dreary things. And let us reflect that, having banished from our land that religious intolerance under which mankind so long bled and suffered, we have yet gained little if we countenance a political intolerance as despotic, as wicked, and capable of as bitter and bloody persecutions. . . . [E]very difference of opinion is not a difference of principle. We have called by different names brethren of the same principle. We are all Republicans, we are all Federalists. If there be any among us who would wish to dissolve this Union or to change its republican form, let them stand undisturbed as monuments of the safety with which error of opinion may be tolerated where reason is left free to combat it. I know, indeed, that some honest men fear that a republican government can not be strong, that this Government is not strong enough; but would the honest patriot, in the full tide of successful experiment, abandon a government which has so far kept us free and firm on the theoretic and visionary fear that this Government, the world's best hope, may by possibility want energy to preserve itself? I trust not. I believe this, on the contrary, the strongest Government on earth. I believe it the only one where every man, at the call of the law, would fly to the standard of the law, and would meet invasions of the public order as his own personal concern. Sometimes it is said that man can not be trusted with the government of himself. Can he, then, be trusted with the government of others? Or have we found angels in the forms of kings to govern him? Let history answer this question.

Let us, then, with courage and confidence pursue our own Federal and Republican principles, our attachment to union and representative government. Kindly separated by nature and a wide ocean from the exterminating havoc of one quarter of the globe; too high-minded to endure the degradations of the others; possessing a chosen country, with room enough for our descendants to the thousandth and thousandth generation; entertaining a due sense of our equal right to the use of our own faculties, to the acquisitions of our own industry, to honor and confidence from our fellow-citizens, resulting not from birth, but from our actions and their sense of them; enlightened by a benign religion, professed, indeed, and practiced in various forms, yet all of them inculcating honesty, truth, temperance, gratitude, and the love of man; acknowledging and adoring an overruling Providence, which by all its dispensations proves that it delights in the happiness of man here and his greater happiness hereafter—with all these blessings, what more is necessary to make us a happy and a prosperous people? Still one thing more, fellow-citizens—a wise and frugal Government, which shall restrain men from injuring one another, shall leave them otherwise free to regulate their own pursuits of industry and improvement, and shall not take from the mouth of labor the bread it has earned. This is the sum of good government, and this is necessary to close the circle of our felicities.

About to enter, fellow-citizens, on the exercise of duties which comprehend everything dear and valuable to you, it is proper you should understand what I deem the essential principles of our Government, and consequently those which ought to shape its Administration. I will compress them within the narrowest compass they will bear, stating the general principle, but not all its limitations. Equal and exact justice to all men, of whatever state or persuasion, religious or political; peace, commerce, and honest friendship with all nations, entangling alliances with none; the support of the State governments in all their rights, as the most competent administrations for our domestic concerns and the surest bulwarks against antirepublican tendencies; the preservation of the General Government in its whole constitutional vigor, as the sheet anchor of our peace at home and safety abroad; a jealous care of the right of election by the people—a mild and safe corrective of abuses which are lopped by the sword of revolution where peaceable remedies are unprovided; absolute acquiescence in the decisions of the majority, the vital principle of republics, from which is no appeal but to force, the vital principle and immediate parent of despotism; a well-disciplined militia, our best reliance in peace and for the first moments of war, till regulars may relieve them; the supremacy of the civil over the military authority; economy in the public expense, that labor may be lightly burthened; the honest payment of our debts and sacred preservation of the public faith; encouragement of agriculture, and of commerce as its handmaid; the diffusion of information and arraignment of all abuses at the bar of the public reason; freedom of religion; freedom of the press, and freedom of person under the protection of the habeas corpus, and trial by juries impartially selected. These principles form the bright constellation which has gone before us and guided our steps through an age of revolution and reformation. The wisdom of our sages and blood of our heroes have been devoted to their attainment. They should be the creed of our political faith, the text of civic instruction, the touchstone by which to try the services of those we trust; and should we wander from them in moments of error or of alarm, let us hasten to retrace our steps and to regain the road which alone leads to peace, liberty, and safety.

. . . I have learnt to expect that it will rarely fall to the lot of imperfect man to retire from this station with the reputation and the favor which bring him into it. Without pretensions to that high confidence you reposed in our first and greatest revolutionary character, . . . I ask so much confidence only as may give firmness and effect to the legal administration of your affairs. I shall often go wrong through defect of judgment. When right, I shall often be thought wrong by those whose positions will not command a view of the whole ground. I ask your indulgence for my own errors, which will never be intentional, and your support against the errors of others, who may condemn what they would not if seen in all its parts. The approbation implied by your suffrage is a great consolation to me for the past, and my future solicitude will be to retain the good opinion of those who have bestowed it in advance, to conciliate that of others by doing them all the good in my power, and to be instrumental to the happiness and freedom of all.

*   *   *

REVIEW QUESTIONS

1. Did Jefferson speak of continuity or change?
2. How did he define the president's powers and relationship with the legislative branch?
3. How did he define the federal government's power and responsibilities?
4. Did he speak of or imply a belief in American exceptionalism?
5. Were the sentiments expressed in this address in agreement with his earlier opinions (see Chapters 7 and 8)?

FROM *Marbury v. Madison* (1801)

The Federalists lost Congress as well as the presidency in the elections of 1800, but before they handed over their seats and votes to the Jeffersonian Republicans, the Sixth Congress passed the Judiciary Act of 1801. Besides providing for a reduction in the number of Supreme Court justices, it also created sixteen circuit courts with a judge for each, and increased the number of attorneys, clerks, and marshals associated with the judicial branch. Before leaving office, President Adams named John Marshall as chief justice and appointed a significant number of Federalists to the newly established positions. These last-minute commissions became known as the "midnight appointments." Unfortunately for some of those selected for the new offices, their commissions were not delivered before Jefferson took office. Jefferson, resisting the Federalist power play and trying to contain Federalist entrenchment in the judiciary made a power play of his own by directing his secretary of state, James Madison, not to deliver the remaining commissions. When William Marbury did not receive his letter of appointment to a justice of the peace position in the District of Columbia, he sued for a writ of mandamus (an order issued by a higher court to a lower one or to other government agencies and officials) to force its delivery. The Supreme Court, led by Marshall, in ruling on the case, not only exercised its own power but expanded it.

From William Cranch, ed., *Reports of Cases Argued and Adjudged in the Supreme Court of the United States, in August and December Terms, 1801, and February Term, 1803*, 3rd ed., vol. I (Philadelphia: Carey & Lea, 1830), pp. 49–72. [Editorial insertion appear in square brackets—*Ed.*]

*   *   *

Mr. Chief Justice MARSHALL delivered the opinion of the court.

At the last term, on the affidavits then read and filed with the clerk, a rule was granted in this case, requiring the secretary of state to show cause why a mandamus should not issue, directing him to deliver to William Marbury his commission as a justice of the peace for the county of Washington, in the district of Columbia.

No cause has been shown, and the present motion is for a mandamus. The peculiar delicacy of this case, the novelty of some of its circumstances, and the real difficulty attending the points which occur in it, require a complete exposition of the principles on which the opinion to be given by the court is founded.

*   *   *

The first object of inquiry is,

1. Has the applicant a right to the commission he demands?

His right originates in an act of congress passed in February 1801, concerning the district of Columbia.

*   *   *

It appears from the affidavits, that in compliance with this law, a commission for William Marbury as a justice of peace for the county of Washington was signed by John Adams, then president of the United States; after which the seal of the United States was affixed to it; but the commission has never reached the person for whom it was made out.

In order to determine whether he is entitled to this commission, it becomes necessary to inquire whether he has been appointed to the office. For if he has been appointed, the law continues him in office for five years, and he is entitled to the possession of those evidences of office, which, being completed, became his property.

The second section of the second article of the constitution declares, "the president shall nominate, and, by and with the advice and consent of the senate, shall appoint ambassadors, other public ministers and consuls, and all other officers of the United States, whose appointments are not otherwise provided for."

The third section declares, that "he shall commission all the officers of the United States."

An act of congress directs the secretary of state to keep the seal of the United States, "to make out and record, and affix the said seal to all civil commissions to officers of the United States to be appointed by the president, by and with the consent of the senate, or by the president alone; provided that the said seal shall not be affixed to any commission before the same shall have been signed by the president of the United States."

*   *   *

The acts of appointing to office, and commissioning the person appointed, can scarcely be considered as one and the same; since the power to perform them is given in two separate and distinct sections of the constitution.

*   *   *

It follows too, from the existence of this distinction, that, if an appointment was to be evidenced by any public act other than the commission, the performance of such public act would create the officer; and if he was not removable at the will of the president, would either give him a right to his commission, or enable him to perform the duties without it.

*   *   *

This is an appointment made by the president, by and with the advice and consent of the senate, and is evidenced by no act but the commission itself. In such a case therefore the commission and the appointment seem inseparable; it being almost impossible to show an appointment otherwise than by proving the existence of a commission: still the commission is not necessarily the appointment; though conclusive evidence of it.

*   *   *

The commission being signed, the subsequent duty of the secretary of state is prescribed by law, and not to be guided by the will of the president. He is to affix the seal of the United States to the commission, and is to record it.

This is not a proceeding which may be varied, if the judgment of the executive shall suggest one more eligible, but is a precise course accurately marked out by law, and is to be strictly pursued. It is the duty of the secretary of state to conform to the law, and in this he is an officer of the United States, bound to obey the laws. He acts, in this respect, as has been very properly stated at the bar, under the authority of law, and not by the instructions of the president. . . .

*   *   *

It is therefore decidedly the opinion of the court, that when a commission has been signed by the president, the appointment is made; and that the commission is complete when the seal of the United States has been affixed to it by the secretary of state.

Where an officer is removable at the will of the executive, the circumstance which completes his appointment is of no concern; because the act is at any time revocable; and the commission may be arrested, if still in the office. But when the officer is not removable at the will of the executive, the appointment is not revocable and cannot be annulled. It has conferred legal rights which cannot be resumed.

The discretion of the executive is to be exercised until the appointment has been made. But having once made the appointment, his power over the office is terminated in all cases, where by law the officer is not removable by him. The right to the office is *then* in the person appointed, and he has the absolute, unconditional power of accepting or rejecting it.

Mr. Marbury, then, since his commission was signed by the president and sealed by the secretary of state, was appointed; and as the law creating the office gave the officer a right to hold for five years independent of the executive, the appointment was not revocable; but vested in the officer legal rights which are protected by the laws of his country.

To withhold the commission, therefore, is an act deemed by the court not warranted by law, but violative of a vested legal right.

This brings us to the second inquiry; which is,

2. If he has a right, and that right has been violated, do the laws of his country afford him a remedy?

The very essence of civil liberty certainly consists in the right of every individual to claim the protection of the laws, whenever he receives an injury. One of the first duties of government is to afford that protection. . . .

*   *   *

The government of the United States has been emphatically termed a government of laws, and not of men. It will certainly cease to deserve this high appellation, if the laws furnish no remedy for the violation of a vested legal right.

If this obloquy is to be cast on the jurisprudence of our country, it must arise from the peculiar character of the case.

It behoves us then to inquire whether there be in its composition any ingredient which shall exempt from legal investigation, or exclude the injured party from legal redress. . . .

*   *   *

It follows then that the question, whether the legality of an act of the head of a department be examinable in a court of justice or not, must always depend on the nature of that act.

If some acts be examinable, and others not, there must be some rule of law to guide the court in the exercise of its jurisdiction.

In some instances there may be difficulty in applying the rule to particular cases; but there cannot, it is believed, be much difficulty in laying down the rule.

*   *   *

. . . [W]here the heads of departments are the political or confidential agents of the executive, merely to execute the will of the president, or rather to act in cases in which the executive possesses a constitutional or legal discretion, nothing can be more perfectly clear than that their acts are only politically examinable. But where a specific duty is assigned by law, and individual rights depend upon the performance of that duty, it seems equally clear that the individual who considers himself injured has a right to resort to the laws of his country for a remedy.

If this be the rule, let us inquire how it applies to the case under the consideration of the court.

The power of nominating to the senate, and the power of appointing the person nominated, are political powers, to be exercised by the president according to his own discretion. When he has

made an appointment, he has exercised his whole power, and his discretion has been completely applied to the case. If, by law, the officer be removable at the will of the president, then a new appointment may be immediately made, and the rights of the officer are terminated. But . . . if the officer is by law not removable at the will of the president, the rights he has acquired are protected by the law, and are not resumable by the president. . . .

*   *   *

It is then the opinion of the court,

1. That by signing the commission of Mr. Marbury, the president of the United States appointed him a justice of peace for the county of Washington in the district of Columbia; and that the seal of the United States, affixed thereto by the secretary of state, is conclusive testimony of the verity of the signature, and of the completion of the appointment; and that the appointment conferred on him a legal right to the office for the space of five years.
2. That, having this legal title to the office, he has a consequent right to the commission; a refusal to deliver which is a plain violation of that right, for which the laws of his country afford him a remedy.

It remains to be inquired whether,

3. He is entitled to the remedy for which he applies. This depends on,
   1. The nature of the writ applied for. And,
   2. The power of this court.
   3. The nature of the writ.

*   *   *

This writ, if awarded, would be directed to an officer of government, and its mandate to him would be, to use the words of Blackstone,[1] "to do a

---

[1] Sir William Blackstone (d. 1780): lawyer, historian, judge, and author of *Commentaries on the Laws of England—Ed.*

particular thing therein specified, which appertains to his office and duty, and which the court has previously determined or at least supposes to be consonant to right and justice." Or, in the words of Lord Mansfield,[2] the applicant, in this case, has a right to execute an office of public concern, and is kept out of possession of that right.

These circumstances certainly concur in this case.

Still, to render the mandamus a proper remedy, the officer to whom it is to be directed, must be one to whom, on legal principles, such writ may be directed: and the person applying for it must be without any other specific and legal remedy.

1. With respect to the officer to whom it would be directed. The intimate political relation, subsisting between the president of the United States and the heads of departments, necessarily renders any legal investigation of the acts of one of those high officers peculiarly irksome, as well as delicate: . . . [I]t is not wonderful that in such a case as this, the assertion, by an individual, of his legal claims in a court of justice, to which claims it is the duty of that court to attend, should at first view be considered by some, as an attempt to intrude into the cabinet, and to intermeddle with the prerogatives of the executive.

It is scarcely necessary for the court to disclaim all pretensions to such a jurisdiction. . . . The province of the court is, solely, to decide on the rights of individuals, not to inquire how the executive, or executive officers, perform duties in which they have a discretion. Questions, in their nature political, or which are, by the constitution and laws, submitted to the executive, can never be made in this court.

But, if this be not such a question; if so far from being an intrusion into the secrets of the cabinet, it respects a paper, which, according to law, is upon record, . . . if it be no intermeddling with a subject, over which the executive can be considered as having exercised any control; what is there in the exalted station of the officer, which shall bar a cit-

izen from asserting, in a court of justice, his legal rights, or shall forbid a court to listen to the claim; or to issue a mandamus, directing the performance of a duty, not depending on executive discretion, but on particular acts of congress and the general principles of law?

*   *   *

This, then, is a plain case of a mandamus, either to deliver the commission, or a copy of it from the record; and it only remains to be inquired,

Whether it can issue from this court.

The act [Judiciary Act of 1789] to establish the judicial courts of the United States authorizes [via Section 13] the supreme court "to issue writs of mandamus, in cases warranted by the principles and usages of law, to any courts appointed, or persons holding office, under the authority of the United States."

The secretary of state, being a person, holding an office under the authority of the United States, is precisely within the letter of the description; and if this court is not authorized to issue a writ of mandamus to such an officer, it must be because the law is unconstitutional, and therefore absolutely incapable of conferring the authority, and assigning the duties which its words purport to confer and assign.

The constitution [Article III] vests the whole judicial power of the United States in one supreme court, and such inferior courts as congress shall, from time to time, ordain and establish. This power is expressly extended to all cases arising under the laws of the United States; and consequently, in some form, may be exercised over the present case because the right claimed is given by a law of the United States.

In the distribution of this power it is declared that "the supreme court shall have original jurisdiction in all cases affecting ambassadors, other public ministers and consuls, and those in which a state shall be a party. In all other cases, the supreme court shall have appellate jurisdiction."

It has been insisted at the bar, that as the original grant of jurisdiction to the supreme and inferior courts is general, and the clause [Section 2]

---

[2] William Murray, first Earl of Mansfield (d. 1793): Lord Chief Justice of the King's Bench, 1756–1788—*Ed.*

assigning original jurisdiction to the supreme court, contains no negative or restrictive words; the power remains to the legislature to assign original jurisdiction to that court in other cases than those specified in the article which has been recited; provided those cases belong to the judicial power of the United States.

If it had been intended to leave it in the discretion of the legislature to apportion the judicial power between the supreme and inferior courts according to the will of that body, it would certainly have been useless to have proceeded further than to have defined the judicial power, and the tribunals in which it should be vested. The subsequent part of the section is mere surplusage, is entirely without meaning, if such is to be the construction. If congress remains at liberty to give this court appellate jurisdiction, where the constitution has declared their jurisdiction shall be original; and original jurisdiction where the constitution has declared it shall be appellate; the distribution of jurisdiction made in the constitution, is form without substance.

Affirmative words are often, in their operation, negative of other objects than those affirmed; and in this case, a negative or exclusive sense must be given to them or they have no operation at all.

*   *   *

When an instrument organizing fundamentally a judicial system, divides it into one supreme, and so many inferior courts as the legislature may ordain and establish; then enumerates its powers, and proceeds so far to distribute them, as to define the jurisdiction of the supreme court by declaring the cases in which it shall take original jurisdiction, and that in others it shall take appellate jurisdiction, the plain import of the words seems to be, that in one class of cases its jurisdiction is original, and not appellate: in the other it is appellate, and not original. If any other construction would render the clause inoperative, that is an additional reason for rejecting such other construction, and for adhering to the obvious meaning.

To enable this court then to issue a mandamus, it must be shown to be an exercise of appellate jurisdiction, or to be necessary to enable them to exercise appellate jurisdiction.

It has been stated at the bar that the appellate jurisdiction may be exercised in a variety of forms, and that if it be the will of the legislature that a mandamus should be used for that purpose, that will must be obeyed. This is true; yet the jurisdiction must be appellate, not original.

It is the essential criterion of appellate jurisdiction, that it revises and corrects the proceedings in a cause already instituted, and does not create that case. Although, therefore, a mandamus may be directed to courts, yet to issue such a writ to an officer for the delivery of a paper, is in effect the same as to sustain an original action for that paper, and therefore seems not to belong to appellate, but to original jurisdiction. Neither is it necessary in such a case as this, to enable the court to exercise its appellate jurisdiction.

The authority, therefore, given to the supreme court, by the act establishing the judicial courts of the United States, to issue writs of mandamus to public officers, appears not to be warranted by the constitution; and it becomes necessary to inquire whether a jurisdiction, so conferred, can be exercised.

The question, whether an act, repugnant to the constitution, can become the law of the land, is a question deeply interesting to the United States; but, happily, not of an intricacy proportioned to its interest. . . .

That the people have an original right to establish, for their future government, such principles as, in their opinion, shall most conduce to their own happiness, is the basis on which the whole American fabric has been erected. The exercise of this original right is a very great exertion; nor can it nor ought it to be frequently repeated. The principles, therefore, so established are deemed fundamental. And as the authority, from which they proceed, is supreme, and can seldom act, they are designed to be permanent.

This original and supreme will organizes the government, and assigns to different departments their respective powers. It may either stop here; or establish certain limits not to be transcended by those departments.

The government of the United States is of the latter description. The powers of the legislature are defined and limited; and that those limits may not be mistaken or forgotten, the constitution is written. . . . The constitution is either a superior, paramount law, unchangeable by ordinary means, or it is on a level with ordinary legislative acts, and like other acts, is alterable when the legislature shall please to alter it.

If the former part of the alternative be true, then a legislative act contrary to the constitution is not law: if the latter part be true, then written constitutions are absurd attempts, on the part of the people, to limimit [*sic*] a power in its own nature illimitable.

Certainly all those who have framed written constitutions contemplate them as forming the fundamental and paramount law of the nation, and consequently the theory of every such government must be, that an act of the legislature repugnant to the constitution is void.

*   *   *

If an act of the legislature, repugnant to the constitution, is void, does it, notwithstanding its invalidity, bind the courts and oblige them to give it effect? Or, in other words, though it be not law, does it constitute a rule as operative as if it was a law? This would be to overthrow in fact what was established in theory; and would seem, at first view, an absurdity too gross to be insisted on. It shall, however, receive a more attentive consideration.

It is emphatically the province and duty of the judicial department to say what the law is. Those who apply the rule to particular cases, must of necessity expound and interpret that rule. If two laws conflict with each other, the courts must decide on the operation of each.

So if a law be in opposition to the constitution: if both the law and the constitution apply to a particular case, so that the court must either decide that case conformably to the law, disregarding the constitution; or conformably to the constitution, disregarding the law: the court must determine which of these conflicting rules governs the case. This is of the very essence of judicial duty.

If then the courts are to regard the constitution; and the constitution is superior to any ordinary act of the legislature; the constitution, and not such ordinary act, must govern the case to which they both apply.

*   *   *

The judicial power of the United States is extended to all cases arising under the constitution.

Could it be the intention of those who gave this power, to say that, in using it, the constitution should not be looked into? That a case arising under the constitution should be decided without examining the instrument under which it arises?

This is too extravagant to be maintained.

In some cases then, the constitution must be looked into by the judges. And if they can open it at all, what part of it are they forbidden to read, or to obey?

There are many other parts of the constitution which serve to illustrate this subject.

It is declared that "no tax or duty shall be laid on articles exported from any state." Suppose a duty on the export of cotton, of tobacco, or of flour; and a suit instituted to recover it. Ought judgment to be rendered in such a case? ought the judges to close their eyes on the constitution, and only see the law.

*   *   *

"No person," says the constitution, "shall be convicted of treason unless on the testimony of two witnesses to the same overt act, or on confession in open court."

Here the language of the constitution is addressed especially to the courts. It prescribes, directly for them, a rule of evidence not to be departed from. If the legislature should change that rule, and declare *one* witness, or a confession *out* of court, sufficient for conviction, must the constitutional principle yield to the legislative act?

From these and many other selections which might be made, it is apparent, that the framers of the constitution contemplated that instrument as a rule for the government of *courts*, as well as of the legislature.

Why otherwise does it direct the judges to take an oath to support it? This oath certainly applies, in an especial manner, to their conduct in their official character. How immoral to impose it on them, if they were to be used as the instruments, and the knowing instruments, for violating what they swear to support!

* * *

Why does a judge swear to discharge his duties agreeably to the constitution of the United States, if that constitution forms no rule for his government? if it is closed upon him and cannot be inspected by him.

* * *

It is also not entirely unworthy of observation, that in declaring what shall be the supreme law of the land, the constitution itself is first mentioned; and not the laws of the United States generally, but those only which shall be made in pursuance of the constitution, have that rank.

Thus, the particular phraseology of the constitution of the United States confirms and strengthens the principle, supposed to be essential to all written constitutions, that a law repugnant to the constitution is void, and that courts, as well as other departments, are bound by that instrument.

The rule must be discharged.

REVIEW QUESTIONS

1. What were the specific inquiries or issues brought before the court? How did Marshall justify or explain the opinion of the court on each of these issues?
2. Did the court illuminate an important duality in the duties of cabinet officers? How did it differentiate between political and legal responsibilities?
3. Why was there a question about the proper jurisdiction or procedure for this case? If the Judiciary Act of 1789 gave the Supreme Court the power to originate a writ of mandamus, why did the court dispute it?
4. Was the Supreme Court defining or checking the powers of the executive and judicial branches in this case? If so, how?

MERIWETHER LEWIS AND WILLIAM CLARK

Journals of Exploration (1804–05)

President Jefferson in his inaugural address spoke of Americans "possessing a chosen country, with room enough for our descendants to the thousandth and thousandth generation." Such a conclusion, or rather, such hyperbole, was due to the expansiveness of the land then claimed by the United States as well as of Jefferson's vision. In this Jefferson echoed the American people, for many still believed that it would take generations to settle the territory out to the Mississippi and some had already come to contemplate expansion to the Pacific Ocean. Given the development of such a mental map—as well as the threat to national interests and security should France occupy the interior of the continent—Jefferson's decision to acquire the Louisiana Territory was a reasonable one. Even before the purchase was complete, Jefferson authorized an expedition to explore the northwestern frontier. This was due to simple curiosity—a desire to know who and what was out there—as well as a need to know what the United States was acquiring. He appointed Meriwether Lewis, a captain in the regular army who had extensive frontier experience as well as an avid interest in nature, and William Clark, a former lieutenant in the army who also was fascinated with nature and was now recommissioned, as commanders of the "Corps of Discovery." Jefferson gave them a multifaceted mission: they were to inform the natives of the government's acquisition, establish friendly relations with them, and record their languages and ways; they were to make topographical and horticultural studies; and, if possible, they were to find a viable trade route through the new territory. The expedition of forty to fifty men (of which only some were to go out to the Pacific) set out from the St. Louis area in May 1804. They traveled up the Missouri to Mandan territory in what is now North Dakota with the intention of wintering there before the permanent party continued west in the spring.

From John Bakeless, ed., *The Journals of Lewis and Clark*, (New York: Mentor Books, 1964), pp. 98–127. This is a heavily edited, including modern spelling and grammar, version of the Reuben G. Thwaites edition. [Editorial insertions that appear in square brackets are from the Bakeless edition—*Ed.*]

*   *   *

31st of October, 1804

A fine morning. The chief of the Mandans sent a second chief to invite us to his lodge to receive some corn and hear what he had to say. I walked down and, with great ceremony, was seated on a robe by the side of the chief. He threw a handsome robe over me, and after smoking the pipe with several old men around, the chief spoke:

Said he believed what we had told them, and that peace would be general, which not only gave him satisfaction but all his people: they could now hunt without fear, and their women could work in the fields without looking every moment for the enemy; and put off their moccasins at night. [Sign of peace: undress.] As to the Arikaras, we will show you that we wish peace with all, and do not make war on any without cause. That chief—pointing to the second—and some brave men will accompany the Arikara chief now with you to his village and nation, to smoke with that people. When you came up, the Indians in the neighboring villages, as well as those out hunting, when they heard of you, had

great expectations of receiving presents. Those hunting, immediately on hearing, returned to the village; and all were disappointed, and some dissatisfied. As to himself, he was not much so; but his village was. He would go and see his Great Father, &c.

He had put before me two of the steel traps which were robbed from the French a short time ago, and about twelve bushels of corn, which were brought and put before me by the women of the village. After the chief finished and smoked in great ceremony, I answered the speech, which satisfied them very much, and returned to the boat. Met the principal chief of the third village, and the Little Crow, both of whom I invited into the cabin, and smoked and talked with for about one hour.

Soon after those chiefs left us, the grand chief of the Mandans came, dressed in the clothes we had given, with his two small sons, and requested to see the men dance, which they very readily gratified him in. . . .

1st of November, 1804

The wind hard from the N.W. Mr. McCracken, a trader, set out at 7 o'clock, to the fort on the Assiniboine. By him sent a letter (enclosing a copy of the British Minister's protection) to the principal agent of the Company.

At about 10 o'clock, the chiefs of the lower village came, and after a short time informed us they wished we would call at their village and take some corn; that they would make peace with the Arikaras; they never made war against them but after the Arikaras killed their chiefs. They killed them like birds, and were tired of killing them, and would send a chief and some brave men to the Arikaras to smoke with that people.

*   *   *

2nd November, 1804

This morning at daylight, I went down the river with my men, to look for a proper place to winter. Proceeded down the river three miles, and found a place well supplied with wood, and returned. Captain Lewis went to the village to hear what they had to say, and I fell down, and formed a camp, near where a small camp of Indians were hunting. Cut down the trees around our camp. In the evening, Captain Lewis returned with a present of 11 bushels of corn. Our Arikara chief set out, accompanied by one chief of Mandans and several brave men of Minnetarees and Mandans. He called for some small article which we had promised, but as I could not understand him, he could not get it. [Afterward he did get it.] The wind from the S.E. A fine day. Many Indians to view us today.

4th November, 1804

A fine morning. We continued to cut down trees and raise our houses. A Mr. Charbonneau[1] interpreter for the Gros Ventre nation, came to see us, and informed that he came down with several Indians from a hunting expedition up the river, to hear what we had told the Indians in council. This man wished to hire as an interpreter. The wind rose this evening from the east, and clouded up. Great numbers of Indians pass, hunting, and some on the return.

---

[1] "Mr. Charbonneau" was Toussaint Charbonneau, husband of Sacagawea, and of another Shoshone girl as well. [Footnote from Bakeless edition—*Ed.*]

*   *   *

12th November, 1804

A very cold night. Early this morning, The Big White, principal chief of the lower village of the Mandans, came down. He packed about 100 pounds of fine meat on his squaw for us. We made some small presents to the squaw and child, gave a small ax with which she was much pleased. Three men sick with the [blank in MS.]. Several. Wind changeable. Very cold evening. Freezing all day. Some ice on the edges of the river.

Swans passing to the south. The hunters we sent down the river to hunt have not returned.

The Mandans speak a language peculiar to themselves, very much [blank in MS.]. They can raise about 350 men; the Wetersoons or Mahas, 80; and the Big Bellies, or Minnetarees, about 600 or 650 men. The Mandans and Sioux have the same word for water. The Big Bellies or Minnetarees and Raven [Wetersoon, as also the Crow or Raven] Indians speak nearly the same language, and the presumption is they were originally the same nation. The Raven Indians have 400 lodges and about 1,200 men, and follow the buffalo, or hunt for their subsistence in the plains, and on the Côte Noire and Rocky Mountains, and are at war with the Sioux and Snake Indians.

The Big Bellies and Wetersoons are at war with the Snake Indians and Sioux, and were at war with the Arikaras until we made peace a few days past. The Mandans are at war with all who make war [on them—at present with the Sioux] only, and wish to be at peace with all nations. Seldom the aggressors.

*   *   *

22nd of November, 1804

A fine morning. Dispatched a pirogue and 5 men under the direction of Sergeant Pryor, to the second village, for 100 bushels of corn in ears, which Mr. Jussome let us have. [Did not get more than 30 bushels.] I was alarmed about 10 o'clock by the sentinel, who informed that an Indian was about to kill his wife, in the interpreter's fire [*i.e., lodge*] about 60 yards below the works. I went down and spoke to the fellow about the rash act he was likely to commit, and forbade any act of the kind near the Fort.

Some misunderstanding took place between this man and his wife, about 8 days ago, and she came to this place, and continued with the squaws of the interpreters. [He might lawfully have killed her for running away.] Two days ago, he returned to the village. In the evening of the same day, she came to the interpreter's fire, apparently much beaten and stabbed in 3 places. We directed that no man of this party have any intercourse with this woman under the penalty of punishment. He, the husband, observed that one of our sergeants slept with his wife, and if he wanted her he would give her to him.

We directed the sergeant (Ordway) to give the man some articles, at which time I told the Indian that I believed not one man of the party had touched his wife except the one he had given the use of her for a night, in his own bed;[2] no man of the party should touch his squaw, or the wife of any Indian, nor did I believe they touched a woman if they knew her to be the wife of another man, and advised him to take his squaw home and live happily together in future. At this time the grand chief of the nation arrived, and lectured him, and they both went off, apparently dissatisfied.

*   *   *

30th of November, 1804

This morning at 8 o'clock, an Indian called from the other side, and informed that he had something of consequence to communicate. We sent a pirogue for him, and he informed us as follows: "Five men of the Mandan nation, out hunting in a S.W. direction about eight leagues, were surprised by a large party of Sioux and Pawnees. One man was killed and two wounded with arrows, and 9 horses taken; 4 of the Wetersoon nation were missing, and they expected to be attacked by the Sioux, &c." We thought it well to show a disposition to aid and assist them against their enemies, particularly those who came in opposition to our councils. And I determined to go to the town with some men and, if the Sioux were coming to attack the nation, to collect the warriors from each village and meet them. Those ideas were also those of Captain Lewis.

I crossed the river in about an hour after the arrival of the Indian express with 23 men including the interpreters, and flanked the town and came up on the back part. The Indians, not expecting to receive such strong aid in so short a time, were much surprised, and a little alarmed at the formidable appearance of my party. The principal chiefs met me some distance from the town (say 200 yards) and invited me in to town. I ordered my party into different lodges, &c. I explained to the nation the cause of my coming in this formidable manner to their town was to assist and chastise the enemies of our dutiful children. I requested the grand chief to repeat the circumstances as they happened, which he did, as was mentioned by the express in the morning.

I then informed them that if they would assemble their warriors and those of the different towns, I would go to meet the army of Sioux, &c., and chastise them for taking the blood of our dutiful children, &c. After a conversation of a few minutes among themselves, one chief—The Big Man, a Cheyenne—said they now saw that what we had told them was the truth: that when we expected the enemies of their nation were coming to attack them, or had spilled their blood, we were ready to protect them, and kill those who would not listen to our good talk. His people had listened to what we had told them, and fearlessly went out to hunt in small parties believing themselves to be safe from the other nations, and were killed by the Pawnees and Sioux.

"I knew," said he, "that the Pawnees were liars, and told the old chief who came with you (to confirm a peace with us) that his people were liars and bad men, and that we killed them like the

---

[2] Among these Indians, a husband had the right to give (or sell) his wife's favors to anyone he pleased. Surreptitious adultery was an offense, which the husband might punish, practically as he pleased. But a woman who yielded to another at her husband's order was merely doing her duty as a wife. [Footnote from Bakeless edition—*Ed.*]

buffalo—when we pleased. We had made peace several times and your nation has always commenced the war. We do not want to kill you, and will not suffer you to kill us or steal our horses. We will make peace with you as our two fathers have directed, and they shall see that we will not be the aggressors. But we fear the Arikaras will not be at peace long. My father, those are the words I spoke to the Arikaras in your presence. You see they have not opened their ears to your good counsels, but have spilled our blood.

"Two Arikaras, whom we sent home this day, for fear of our people's killing them in their grief, informed us when they came here several days ago, that two towns of the Arikaras were making their moccasins, and that we had best take care of our horses, &c. Numbers of Sioux were in their towns and, they believed, not well disposed toward us. Four of the Wetersoons are now absent. They were to have been back in 16 days; they have been out 24. We fear they have fallen. My father, the snow is deep and it is cold. Our horses cannot travel through the plains. Those people who have spilt our blood have gone back. If you will go with us in the spring after the snow goes off, we will raise the warriors of all the towns and nations around about us, and go with you."

I told this nation that we should be always willing and ready to defend them from the insults of any nation who would dare to come to do them injury, during the time we remained in their neighborhood, and requested that they would inform us of any party who might at any time be discovered by their patrols or scouts. I was sorry that the snow in the plains had fallen so deep since the murder of the young chief by the Sioux as prevented their horses from traveling. I wished to meet those Sioux and all others who will not open their ears, but make war on our dutiful children, and let you see that the warriors of your Great Father will chastise the enemies of his dutiful children the Mandans, Wetersoons, and Minnetarees, who have opened their ears to his advice. You say that the Pawnees or Arikaras were with the Sioux. Some bad men may have been with the Sioux. You know there are bad men in all nations. Do not get mad with the

Arikaras until we know if those bad men are countenanced by their nation, and we are convinced those people do not intend to follow our counsels. You know that the Sioux have great influence over the Arikaras, and perhaps have led some of them astray. You know that the Arikaras are dependent on the Sioux for their guns, powder, and ball; and it was policy in them to keep on as good terms as possible with the Sioux until they had some other means of getting those articles, &c. You know yourselves that you are compelled to put up with little insults from the Crees and Assiniboines (or Stone Indians) because if you go to war with those people, they will prevent the traders in the north from bringing you guns, powder, and ball, and by that means distress you very much. But when you will have certain supplies from your Great American Father of all those articles, you will not suffer any nation to insult you, &c.

After about two hours' conversation on various subjects, all of which tended toward their situation, &c., I informed them I should return to the Fort. The chief said they all thanked me very much for the fatherly protection which I showed toward them; that the village had been crying all the night and day for the death of the brave young man who fell, but now they would wipe away their tears and rejoice in their father's protection, and cry no more.

I then paraded and crossed the river on the ice, and came down on the north side. The snow so deep, it was very fatiguing. Arrived at the Fort after night, gave a little taffee[3] [dram] to my party. A cold night. The river rose to its former height. The chief frequently thanked me for coming to protect them; and the whole village appeared thankful for that measure.

1st of December, 1804

Wind from the N.W. All hands engaged in getting pickets, &c. At 10 o'clock, the half-brother of the man who was killed came and informed us that, after my departure last night, six Chiens [Cheyennes]—so called by the French—or Sharha Indians, had arrived with a pipe, and said that their

---

[3] A local rum. [Footnote from Bakeless edition—*Ed.*]

nation was at one day's march and intended to come and trade, &c. Three Pawnees had also arrived from the nation. Their nation was then within 3 days' march, and were coming on to trade with us. Three Pawnees accompanied these Cheyennes. The Mandans call all Arikaras Pawnees; they don't use the name of Arikaras, but the Arikaras call themselves Arikaras. The Mandans apprehended danger from the Sharhas, as they were at peace with the Sioux; and wished to kill them and the Arikaras (or Pawnees), but the chiefs informed the nation it was our wish that they should not be hurt and forbid their being killed, &c. We gave a little tobacco, &c., and this man departed, well satisfied with our counsels and advice to him.

In the evening a Mr. G. Henderson arrived, in the employ of the Hudson's Bay Company, sent to trade with the Gros Ventres, or Big Bellies, so called by the French traders.

*   *   *

7th of December, 1804

A very cold day. Wind from the N.W. The Big White, grand chief of the first village, came and informed us that a large drove of buffalo was near, and his people were waiting for us to join them in a chase. Captain Lewis took 15 men and went out and joined the Indians who were, at the time he got up, killing the buffalo, on horseback with arrows, clothed. This man was not in the least injured. Customs, and the habits of those people, have inured them to bear more cold than I thought it possible for man to endure. Sent out 3 men to hunt elk, below, about 7 miles.

13th of January, 1805

A cold, clear day. Great numbers of Indians move down the river to hunt. Those people kill a number of buffalo near their villages and save a great proportion of the meat. Their custom of making [sharing] this article of life general leaves them more than half of their time without meat. Their corn and beans, &c., they keep for the summer, and as a reserve in case of an attack from the Sioux, of which they are always in dread, and seldom go far to hunt except in large parties. About

½ the Mandan nation passed today, to hunt on the river below. They will stay out some days. Mr. Charbonneau, our interpreter, and one man who accompanied him to some lodges of the Minnetarees near the Turtle Hill, returned, both frozen in their faces. Charbonneau informs me that the clerk of the Hudson's Bay Company, with the Minnetarees, has been speaking some few expressions unfavorable toward us, and that it is said the N.W. Company intends building a fort at the Minnetarees. He saw the Grand Chief of the Big Bellies, who spoke slightingly of the Americans, saying if we would give our great flag to him he would come to see us.

*   *   *

Fort Mandan, April 7th, 1805

Having on this day at 4 P.M. completed every arrangement necessary for our departure, we dismissed the barge and crew, with orders to return without loss of time to St. Louis. A small canoe with two French hunters accompanied the barge. These men had ascended the Missouri with us the last year as *engagés*. The barge crew consisted of six soldiers and two [blank space in MS.] Frenchmen. Two Frenchmen and an Arikara Indian also take their passage in her as far as the Arikara villages, at which place we expect Mr. Tabeau to embark, with his peltry, who, in that case, will make an addition of two, perhaps four, men to the crew of the barge.

We gave Richard Warfington, a discharged corporal, the charge of the barge and crew, and confided to this care likewise our dispatches to the government, letters to our private friends, and a number of articles to the President of the United States. One of the Frenchmen, by the name of Joseph Gravelines, an honest, discreet man, and an excellent boatman, is employed to conduct the barge as a pilot. We have therefore every hope that the barge and, with her, our dispatches will arrive safe at St. Louis. Mr. Gravelines, who speaks the Arikara language extremely well, has been employed to conduct a few of the Arikara chiefs to the seat of government, who have promised us to descend in the barge to St. Louis with that view.

At the same moment that the barge departed from Fort Mandan, Captain Clark embarked with our party and proceeded up the river. As I had used no exercise for several weeks, I determined to walk on shore as far as our encampment of this evening. Accordingly I continued my walk on the north side of the river about six miles, to the upper village of the Mandans, and called on The Black Cat, or Posecopsehá, the Great Chief of the Mandans. He was not at home. I rested myself a few minutes and, finding that the party had not arrived, I returned about two miles and joined them at their encampment on the N. side of the river opposite the lower Mandan village.

*   *   *

Our party now consisted of the following individuals:

Sergeants:

John Ordway
Nathaniel Pryor
Patrick Gass

Privates:

William Bratton
John Colter
Reuben Fields
Joseph Fields
John Shields
George Gibson
George Shannon
John Potts
John Collins
Joseph Whitehouse
Richard Windsor
Alexander Willard
Hugh Hall
Silas Goodrich
Robert Frazer
Peter Cruzat
John Baptiste Lepage
Francis Labiche
Hugh McNeil
William Warner
Thomas P. Howard
Peter Wiser
John B. Thompson

Interpreters: George Drouilliard and Toussaint Charbonneau; also a black man by the name of York, servant to Captain Clark; an Indian woman, wife to Charbonneau, with a young child; and a Mandan man who had promised us to accompany us as far as the Snake Indians, with a view to bring about a good understanding and friendly intercourse between that nation and his own, the Minnetarees and Amahamis.

Our vessels consisted of six small canoes and two large pirogues. This little fleet, although not quite so respectable as that of Columbus or Captain Cook, was still viewed by us with as much pleasure as those deservedly famed adventurers ever beheld theirs, and, I daresay, with quite as much anxiety for their safety and preservation. We were now about to penetrate a country at least two thousand miles in width, on which the foot of civilized man had never trod. The good or evil it had in store for us was for experiment yet to determine, and these little vessels contained every article by which we were to expect to subsist or defend ourselves. However, as the state of mind in which we are, generally gives the coloring to events, when the imagination is suffered to wander into futurity, the picture which now presented itself to me was a most pleasing one.

Entertaining as I do the most confident hope of succeeding on a voyage which had formed a darling project of mine for the last ten years, I could but esteem this moment of my departure as among the most happy of my life. The party are in excellent health and spirits, zealously attached to the enterprise, and anxious to proceed. Not a whisper or murmur of discontent to be heard among them, but all act in unison and with the most perfect harmony.

*   *   *

REVIEW QUESTIONS

1. Lewis and Clark wanted recognition, good relations, and assistance from the Mandan and the other local Native American tribes. What did these tribes want from the explorers in return?

2. What customs—social, political, and/or military—did the explorers find to be noteworthy?

3. What do these notes reveal about both the subjects and the writers?

4. What do the entries reveal about intertribal relations in the area?

5. Why do you think such relations and conflicts were important to the explorers and their government?

THE *PENNSYLVANIA GAZETTE*

FROM The Indian Prophet and His Doctrine (1812)

As the United States government, through such representatives as Lewis and Clark, attempted to establish cordial relations with Native American tribes in the far northwest territories, it faced increasing hostility from tribes resisting the encroachment of settlers from the Ohio country to the Mississippi territory. Through various treaties the federal government had acquired millions of acres of land for its citizens, yet many settlers invaded lands that their government acknowledged as still belonging to the Indians. Native Americans responded angrily and sometimes violently to these incursions.

Many Indians also became concerned that continued contact and conflict with the Euro-Americans was undermining not only their autonomy but their cultures. Particularly worrisome was the illegal trade in alcohol: as frustrated tribesmen tried to drown their sorrows, they created more problems for their people. This situation created chaos in many villages, especially those of the Shawnee. Although many Shawnees blamed outside sources for their troubles, others believed that in neglecting their own traditions they had brought these evils upon themselves. During these difficult times, a pair of Native American brothers, Lalawethika and Tecumseh, each with a different world vision, assumed leadership roles within the tribe, and ultimately came to influence other tribes as well. Lalawethika, an alcoholic who had been unsuccessful much of his life, renounced his former ways upon experiencing visions in 1805, renamed himself Tenskwatawa (meaning "The Open Door": he came to be called the Prophet), and set out to reclaim his people from evil and revitalize their culture. Over the next few years the people of many tribes participated in this religious and cultural revival. The Ottawa warrior Le Maigouis, for example, as revealed in the document below, passed on the Prophet's message to his people as he traveled among their villages in Michigan. Although the Prophet said he wanted to maintain peace, some of his followers started to attack white settlers. As relations deteriorated, William Henry Harrison, governor of the Indiana territory, completed the negotiations for the Treaty of Fort Wayne in 1809, which led to a rupture of relations. Riding the wave of hostil-

ity, Tecumseh began to exert more influence than his brother as he called for political and military solutions to the Indians' problems.

From "The Indian Prophet and His Doctrine," The *Pennsylvania Gazette*, 11 March 1812. [Editorial insertion that appear in square brackets are from the original printing—*Ed.*]

As this man has been for some years making a figure among the Savages to the Westward, and seems to be attempting something like becoming another MAHOMET, it may not be uninteresting to our readers, to peruse the following *substance* of a GREAT TALK, which he circulated among the different tribes of Western Indians, when he first gave himself out for a Prophet; or, ADAM *come again on the earth*. It gives a strong clue to his character, his policy and his views. It shews, that his object is to unite the different tribes, and to render the savages more truly *savage* and Independent, by *prohibiting commerce* and by establishing a perfect system of *Non-Intercourse* with the Whites; in short, by enabling the Aborigines to depend more on their own internal resources, and to restore the savage character to its native vigour and perfection. This *Talk* was communicated, a few days after its delivery, to the Editor of the Washingtonian, while at Fort Michilimakinak, by a trader of unquestionable veracity, who had intermarried with them, and had long resided in the Indian Country. It was procured from his *Squaw* and several intelligent Indians present, who confided it to him, as an adopted member of their family.—EDITOR.]

Substance of a TALK, held at Le Maionitinong, entrance of Lake Michigan, by the Indian Chief, LEMAIGOUIS, May 4, 1807, . . . addressed to the different tribes of Indians.

*   *   *

"*My Children!*

*   *   *

The Great Spirit bids me say to you thus. *My Children!* Have very little to do [with the Americans]. They proceeded from the froth of the *Great Lake*, [the sea] when it was troubled, and were driven on shore by a strong east wind.—They are very numerous. But I HATE THEM—BECAUSE THEY TAKE AWAY YOUR LANDS, which were not made for them—the Whites I placed on the other side of the Great Water, to be another people, separate from you. To them I gave different manners, customs, animals, and vegetables. You may salute them; but must not shake hands.

My Children! You must not get drunk. It displeases the Great Spirit. And on no account drink WHISKEY. It was made by the *Big Knives*, without my permission. It makes you sick, and burns your insides; It destroys you. . . .

*   *   *

My Children! To you I have given Deer, Bears, and all wild animals; wild fowls and fish, corn and squashes; for yourselves only, and not for white men. To them I have given Oxen, Cows, Sheep, and all other domestic animals, for themselves only; therefore, you are not to keep any of their animals, nor any living thing made for them. You are not to plant more corn, than you want for your own use; you must not sell it to them unless they are starving, and then only *by measure*, lest they cheat you. When you plant, you must help each other, and then the Great Spirit will give you good crops.

My Children! I made all the trees of the woods. The maple tree I made, that you might have sugar for your children. I love the maple tree, which you spoil and give pain to (for it has feeling like yourselves) by cutting it too much, to make sugar for the Whites. They have another sugar, which I made for them. If you make more sugar than you want for yourselves, you shall die, and the maple tree shall yield no more water. If a white man needs a little sugar, you may sell him very little; but always by weight.—But even this I dislike, because it burns your kettles, which you must not destroy.

My Children! You must pay the Whites only half their credits; *because they cheat you.* You may sell them only peltries, canoes, gums, &c. but no wild meat. . . . You may give them a little dried meat, without any bone; because they burn the bones, so that the animals cannot come again on the earth. This is the reason why they are so few and so lean. You complain that the animals are few on the earth. How can it be otherwise, when you destroy them yourselves. You take only their skin, and leave their bodies to rot. When I pass by and see them thus, I take them back that they come no more to you again.

My Children! You must not dress like the Whites; but pluck out your hair, as in former times; and wear the feather of the eagle on your head. And when it is not too cold you must go naked, (excepting your breech-cloth) with your bodies painted, &c. When I see you thus, I am well pleased.

COURTSHIP, MARRIAGE, &c.

[Here the Prophet goes on to prescribe rules to be observed in courtship and matrimony. He forbids their women to live with a white man, unless they are lawfully married. "But" adds he "this I dislike. Let the whites marry only whites, and the Indians marry Indians. Because I *made you to be two distinct people.*" When they marry, they must be of mature years, and of nearly equal ages.]

*   *   *

"*My Children!* When you dance you are not to dance the *Ouabanna,* nor the *Poigan* or *pipe dance* [social dances.] I did not place you on the earth to dance these dances. When you dance you are to be naked, and painted, with your feather on your head, and dance among yourselves, holding the *Poigamaugan,* [war club] or some other club, in your hands; and then I shall look on with pleasure.

My Children! You are to make for yourselves PAKATOUANACS (or *Crosses,*) which you are always to carry with you; as it pleases me to see you play at that game. Your women must have handsome *Pasaquanacs,* that they may play also; for I made you to amuse yourselves. You are not to beat your wives. If you strike them with your fist, or kick

them, the part which touches them will be wanting to you when you are gone from this life. If you punish them, use a small switch, and have pity.

[He directs them to keep but one dog each, because by keeping too many they starve them. At their *feasts and councils* they must not use fire procured from *flint and steel*; but *as they formerly did*—(probably by *friction.*) And they are strictly forbidden to fight and kill each other; but enjoined to cultivate friendship and union among their several tribes, and, on no occasion, to smoke pure tobacco.]

*   *   *

Now *My Children,* I charge you not to speak of this talk to the whites; and every Indian village must send me two deputies, to be instructed, lest they be cut off from the face of the earth. The world is not as it was at first, but it is broken, and *leans down*; and those that are on the slope, from the *Chippewas,* and further, will all die, if the earth should fall; therefore, if they would live, let them send to me two persons from each village, that they may be instructed, so as to prevent it."

NOTES.

The prophet says the *Great Spirit* opened to him a door, and shewed him all wild animals, *very large and fat*—and said "Look!—these are the animals I made, when I created you."—He then opened another door, and shewed me all wild animals *very small and lean.* "Look! said he again—These are the animals you now have on earth."

Men with hats.—The French were the first Whites seen by the Western Indians, and were called by them the *men with hats.* They are, in general, more partial to the French than to any other nation. It is a remark, I have heard more than once by traders, that these western savages "*love* the French, *respect* the English, and *hate* the Americans." But they certainly *fear* us more than both the others; and this alone has kept them quiet so long.

*   *   *

PAKATOUANACS, Heavy batts—for playing a kind of wicket ball, an athletic game common among the

Savages, and well calculated to give them strength and agility.

PASSAQUANACS—These also are *Ball-Sticks* for the use of their women; two balls are tied together by a thong about six inches in length, and by these sticks they are thrown at a certain goal; and sometimes at each other, when they are used for defence and to catch the balls. This game has the same object as the other; to render them more hardy, active and athletic.

On receiving the above Talk, it was communicated to his Excellency Governor HULL, with a letter, of which the following is an extract.—It may serve to shew what views were then entertained of this impostor, and his designs.

[WASHINGTONIAN.]

"Extract of a letter from the Commanding Officer, at Fort Michilimakinak, to his Excellency Gov. Hull, dated May 20, 1807."

SIR,

I have thought it my duty to state to your excellency, that there appears to be an extensive movement among the SAVAGES of this quarter, which seems to carry with it much of the *dark* and *mysterious*. Belts of *wampum* are rapidly circulating, from one tribe to another; and a spirit is prevailing, by no means pacific. What I have been able to learn, through sources to be relied on, leaves little room for conjecture, as to the object of their hostile dispositions; and the enclosed *Talk*, which has been industriously circulated, and which seems to have had considerable effect on their minds, needs no comment.

It ought to be observed, that this *Talk* is freely communicated in open council, where old and young, of both sexes, are allowed to assemble. There is, however, *another Talk*, known only in the private counsel of the chiefs and warriors. From the letter and spirit of the former, we may infer the complexion and views of the latter. *There is certainly mischief at the bottom:*—And there can be no doubt in my mind, but that the object and intention of this MANITOU, or *second* ADAM, under the pretense of restoring to the Aborigines their former independence, and to the savage character its ancient energy, is, in reality, to induce a general effort to *rally*—and sooner or later to strike, somewhere, a desperate blow. I cannot say, that I apprehend an immediate attack. Perhaps my character as a soldier, might be called in question, were I to admit the *possibility* of a thing, which to me would deem so *improbable*; but, aware, as I am, of the insidiousness and treachery of these people, I have thought it no more than prudence to *watch their motions*—and to be in constant readiness to receive them, either with the *olive-branch*, or the *bayonet*, as circumstances might require.

Many fabulous and foolish stories are circulated, to impress the idea of their GREAT PROGENITOR'S *Divinity and Mission:*—But whether he is, really, the *Envoy of Heaven*, or only an EMISSARY *from the Cabinet of* ST. CLOUD—I would not presume to decide.

He is represented, as being seen only on an elevated scaffold, sitting or kneeling *on a cross*, and in a constant attitude of devotion. It is even said he can *fly*—and that the multitude of his disciples, who visit him, are miraculously fed by a profusion of wild animals, which are thronging about him for that purpose.—All this is eagerly swallowed—and the severe denunciations of his penal code terrify them at once into an adoption of his Creed. This new system is so artfully interwoven with their ancient superstitions and their modern prejudices, that they receive the whole with a religious enthusiasm.

The *Herald*, or *Preacher*, of this new religion here (LEMAIGOUIS) is brother to the principal chief in this quarter. He has gone to *Lake Superior* to initiate the savages there into its mysteries, and is expected to return to *L'Arbre Croche* immediately, when, it is said, *he is to be met by all the War Chiefs, to whom he is to communicate something further.* . . .

I have not a doubt but securing him, and immediately calling together the CHIEFS, in order to open their eyes to the real views of this *impostor*, will be the means of preventing at least the Chippewas and Attawas of this part of the country from entering into the combination, that is either formed or forming, *as I believe*, against our people and government."

REVIEW QUESTIONS

1. As Le Maigouis noted in his talk, Tenskwatawa addressed both the problems facing the Native Americans and solutions. What were they?
2. How did the Prophet intend to preserve Native Americans from Euro-Americans?
3. How did the commanding officer of Fort Michilimakinak interpret the attitudes and actions of Native Americans who adhered to the Prophet's doctrine?
4. Was the commander an objective commentator?

JAMES MADISON

FROM Presidential Message to Congress (1 June 1812)

The United States, a nation building its economy through foreign trade as well as domestic agriculture, first found opportunity but then obstruction in the European warfare that resumed in 1803. The government established a policy of neutral trade, a policy its ministers tried to ensure an acceptance of abroad, but both Britain and France ignored it as they tried to restrict trade with the enemy. Jefferson, the former revolutionary that he was, resorted to a favorite American tactic: embargo. This ill-fated attempt at economic coercion did not work for him, nor for his successor James Madison. In June 1812 the British government reconsidered its position and revoked the orders that had provoked the Americans, but it was too late. Madison sent a secret message to Congress indicting British actions on 1 June. After reading it and reflecting on all the issues, the House of Representatives and then the Senate debated a war bill. The Senate finally passed the bill on 17 June with a 19–13 vote. Madison signed it on the 18th and thus the War of 1812 began.

From James D. Richardson, comp., *A Compilation of the Messages and Papers of the Presidents, 1789–1902*, vol. 1 (Bureau of National Literature and Art, 1904), pp. 499–505.

WASHINGTON, *June 1, 1812.*
To the Senate and House of Representatives of the United States:

*   *   *

Without going back beyond the renewal in 1803 of the war in which Great Britain is engaged, and

omitting unrepaired wrongs of inferior magnitude, the conduct of her Government presents a series of acts hostile to the United States as an independent and neutral nation.

British cruisers have been in the continued practice of violating the American flag on the great highway of nations, and of seizing and carrying off persons sailing under it, not in the exercise of a belligerent right founded on the law of nations against an enemy, but of a municipal prerogative over British subjects. British jurisdiction is thus extended to neutral vessels in a situation where no laws can operate but the law of nations and the laws of the country to which the vessels belong, . . . Could the seizure of British subjects in such cases be regarded as within the exercise of a belligerent right, the acknowledged laws of war, which forbid an article of captured property to be adjudged without a regular investigation before a competent tribunal, would imperiously demand the fairest trial where the sacred rights of persons were at issue. In place of such a trial these rights are subjected to the will of every petty commander.

The practice, hence, is so far from affecting British subjects alone that, under the pretext of searching for these, thousands of American citizens, under the safeguard of public law and of their national flag, have been torn from their country and from everything dear to them; have been dragged on board ships of war of a foreign nation and exposed, under the severities of their discipline, to be exiled to the most distant and deadly climes, to risk their lives in the battles of their oppressors, and to be the melancholy instruments of taking away those of their own brethren.

Against this crying enormity, which Great Britain would be so prompt to avenge if committed against herself, the United States have in vain exhausted remonstrances and expostulations, . . .

British cruisers have been in the practice also of violating the rights and the peace of our coasts. They hover over and harass our entering and departing commerce. To the most insulting pretensions they have added the most lawless proceedings in our very harbors, and have wantonly spilt American blood within the sanctuary of our territorial jurisdiction. . . .

Under pretended blockades, without the presence of an adequate force and sometimes without the practicability of applying one, our commerce has been plundered in every sea, the great staples of our country have been cut off from their legitimate markets, and a destructive blow aimed at our agricultural and maritime interests. . . .

Not content with these occasional expedients for laying waste our neutral trade, the cabinet of Britain resorted at length to the sweeping system of blockades, under the name of orders in council, which has been molded and managed as might best suit its political views, its commercial jealousies, or the avidity of British cruisers.

To our remonstrances against the complicated and transcendent injustice of this innovation the first reply was that the orders were reluctantly adopted by Great Britain as a necessary retaliation on decrees of her enemy proclaiming a general blockade of the British Isles at a time when the naval force of that enemy dared not issue from his own ports. She was reminded without effect that her own prior blockades, unsupported by an adequate naval force actually applied and continued, were a bar to this plea; that executed edicts against millions of our property could not be retaliation on edicts confessedly impossible to be executed; that retaliation, to be just, should fall on the party setting the guilty example, not on an innocent party which was not even chargeable with an acquiescence in it.

*   *   *

It has become, indeed, sufficiently certain that the commerce of the United States is to be sacrificed, not as interfering with the belligerent rights of Great Britain; not as supplying the wants of her enemies, which she herself supplies; but as interfering with the monopoly which she covets for her own commerce and navigation. . . .

Anxious to make every experiment short of the last resort of injured nations, the United States have withheld from Great Britain, under successive modifications, the benefits of a free intercourse with their market, the loss of which could not but outweigh the profits accruing from her restrictions of our commerce with other nations. And to entitle these experiments to the more favorable consideration they were so framed as to enable her place her adversary under the exclusive oper of them. To these appeals her Government has been equally inflexible, as if willing to make sacrifices of every sort rather than yield to the claims of justice or renounce the errors of a false pride. Nay, so far were the attempts carried to overcome the attachment of the British cabinet to its unjust edicts that it received every encouragement within the competency of the executive branch of our Government to expect that a repeal of them would be followed by a war between the United States and France, unless the French edicts should also be repealed. Even this communication, although silencing forever the plea of a disposition in the United States to acquiesce in those edicts originally the sole plea for them, received no attention.

*　*　*

There was a period when a favorable change in the policy of the British cabinet was justly considered as established. The minister plenipotentiary of His Britannic Majesty here proposed an adjustment of the differences more immediately endangering the harmony of the two countries. The proposition was accepted with the promptitude and cordiality corresponding with the invariable professions of this Government. A foundation appeared to be laid for a sincere and lasting reconciliation. The prospect, however, quickly vanished. The whole proceeding was disavowed by the British Government without any explanations which could at that time repress the belief that the disavowal proceeded from a spirit of hostility to the commercial rights and prosperity of the United States; and it has since come into proof that at the very moment when the public minister was holding the language of friendship and inspiring confidence in the sincerity of the negotiation with which he was charged a secret agent of his Government was employed in intrigues having for their object a subversion of our Government and a dismemberment of our happy union.

In reviewing the conduct of Great Britain toward the United States our attention is necessarily drawn to the warfare just renewed by the savages on one of our extensive frontiers—a warfare which is known to spare neither age nor sex and to be distinguished by features peculiarly shocking to humanity. It is difficult to account for the activity and combinations which have for some time been developing themselves among tribes in constant intercourse with British traders and garrisons without connecting their hostility with that influence and without recollecting the authenticated examples of such interpositions heretofore furnished by the officers and agents of that Government.

Such is the spectacle of injuries and indignities which have been heaped on our country, and such the crisis which its unexampled forbearance and conciliatory efforts have not been able to avert. It might at least have been expected that an enlightened nation, if less urged by moral obligations or invited by friendly dispositions on the part of the United States, would have found in its true interest alone a sufficient motive to respect their rights and their tranquillity on the high seas; that an enlarged policy would have favored that free and general circulation of commerce in which the British nation is at all times interested, and which in times of war is the best alleviation of its calamities to herself as well as to other belligerents; and more especially that the British cabinet would not, for the sake of a precarious and surreptitious intercourse with hostile markets, have persevered in a course of measures which necessarily put at hazard the invaluable market of a great and growing country, disposed to cultivate the mutual advantages of an active commerce.

Other counsels have prevailed. Our moderation and conciliation have had no other effect than to encourage perseverance and to enlarge pretensions. We behold our seafaring citizens still the daily victims of lawless violence, committed on the great common and highway of nations, even within sight of the country which owes them protection. We behold our vessels, freighted with the products of our soil and industry, or returning with the honest proceeds of them, wrested from their lawful destinations, confiscated by prize courts no longer the organs of public law but the instruments of arbitrary edicts, and their unfortunate crews dispersed and lost, or forced or inveigled in British ports into British fleets, whilst arguments are employed in support of these aggressions which have no foundation but in a principle equally supporting a claim to regulate our external commerce in all cases whatsoever.

We behold, in fine, on the side of Great Britain a state of war against the United States, and on the side of the United States a state of peace toward Great Britain.

Whether the United States shall continue passive under these progressive usurpations and these accumulating wrongs, or, opposing force to force in defense of their national rights, shall commit a just cause into the hands of the Almighty Disposer of Events, avoiding all connections which might entangle it in the contest or views of other powers, and preserving a constant readiness to concur in an honorable reestablishment of peace and friendship, is a solemn question which the Constitution wisely confides to the legislative department of the Government. In recommending it to their early delib-

erations I am happy in the assurance that the decision will be worthy the enlightened and patriotic councils of a virtuous, a free, and a powerful nation.

*   *   *

JAMES MADISON.

REVIEW QUESTIONS

1. What were Madison's indictments against Great Britain?
2. What appear to have been the most grievous injuries to the United States? Why?
3. Was there any echo of the Revolution's rhetoric or ideology in this message?
4. Was Madison asking for war?

ABIGAIL ADAMS

FROM Letter to Mercy Otis Warren (December 1812)

Americans were by no means united over the need for war, much less its prosecution. Many believed that a militant segment in Congress, the War Hawks, had pushed the nation into this conflict. While most Republicans voted for the declaration of war, the Federalists in Congress voted against it. Yet there were a few Federalists who eventually supported the nation's war efforts. Furthermore, Americans tended to be divided along regional lines over this conflict. New Englanders were generally against the war while southerners and westerners showed more support. Abigail Adams was an exception to this generalization. This New England woman could not participate publicly in the political process, but she was an avid observer and commentator on the political scene. Although she was essentially a Federalist in her beliefs, once the war began she put nation before party.

From Charles F. Adams, ed., *Correspondence Between John Adams and Mercy Otis Warren,* (New York: Arno Press, 1972), pp. 501–502.

Mrs. Abigail Adams to Mrs. Mercy Warren

QUINCY, Dec. 30, 1812

MY DEAR MADAM,—

*   *   *

So long as we are inhabitants of this earth, and possess any of our faculties, we cannot be indifferent to the state of our country, our posterity, and our friends. Personally, we have arrived so near the close of the drama that we can experience but few of the evils which await the rising generation. We have passed through one revolution, and happily arrived at the goal; but the ambition, injustice, and plunder of foreign powers have again involved us in war, the termination of which is not given us to see.

If we have not the "gorgeous palaces or the cloud-capped towers" of Moscow to be levelled with the dust, nor a million of victims to sacrifice upon the altar of ambition, we have our firesides, our comfortable habitations, our cities, our churches, and our country to defend, our rights, privileges, and independence to preserve.

And for these are we not justly contending? Thus it appears to me. Yet I hear from our pulpits, and read from our presses, that it is an unjust, a wicked, a ruinous, and unnecessary war.

If I give an opinion with respect to the conduct of our native State, I cannot do it with approbation. She has had much to complain of, as it respected a refusal of naval protection; yet that cannot justify her in paralyzing the arm of Government, when raised for her defence and that of the nation. A house divided against itself,—and upon that foundation do our enemies build their hopes of subduing us. May it prove a sandy one to them!

You once asked, What does Mr. Adams think of Napoleon? The reply was, I think that, after having been the scourge of nations, he should himself be destroyed. We have seen him run an astonishing career. Is not his measure full? Like Charles XII. of Sweden he may find in Alexander another Peter.

Much, my friend, might we moralize upon these great events; but we know but in part, and we see but in part. The longer I live, the more wrapt in clouds and darkness does the future appear to me.

"Who sees with equal eye, as God of all,
A hero perish or a sparrow fall:
Atoms to atoms into ruin hurled,
And now a bubble burst, and now a world."

*   *   *

Your affectionate   ABIGAIL ADAMS

REVIEW QUESTIONS

1. Why did Adams believe the war to be a just one?
2. Would she have qualified as a War Hawk?
3. What did she think about the actions of Massachusetts?
4. What does this letter reveal about nationalism versus sectionalism in the country?

FROM *Report and Resolutions of the Hartford Convention* (1815)

The Federalist Party dominated New England politics and, because its adherents held the majority of offices, it controlled state and local governments. It used that power to challenge the authority of national officers and test the bonds of union. Taking the

Revolution as a guide, Massachusetts Federalists called for a convention in which to discuss the defense of their region and its relationship to the national government. Their legislature responded in the fall of 1814 by contacting the other New England states and by choosing delegates to represent Massachusetts in the convention. Connecticut and Rhode Island responded positively and sent delegates. Federalist leaders in Vermont and New Hampshire objected to the convention, but a couple of counties from those states did send delegates. While critics had feared that only extremists would be sent, most of the representatives were in fact moderates. The twenty-six delegates met at Hartford, Connecticut, from 15 December 1814 to 5 January 1815.

From Theodore Dwight, *History of the Hartford Convention* (New York: N. J. White, 1833), pp. 358ff.

January 4, 1815

. . . Nothing more can be attempted in this report than a general allusion to the principal outlines of the policy which has produced this vicissitude. Among these may be enumerated—

First.—A deliberate and extensive system for effecting a combination among certain states, by exciting local jealousies and ambition, so as to secure to popular leaders in one section of the Union, the control of public affairs in perpetual succession. To which primary object most other characteristics of the system may be reconciled.

Secondly.—The political intolerance displayed and avowed in excluding from office men of unexceptionable merit, for want of adherence to the executive creed.

Thirdly.—The infraction of the judiciary authority and rights, by depriving judges of their offices in violation of the constitution.

Fourthly.—The abolition of existing taxes, requisite to prepare the country for those changes to which nations are always exposed, with a view to the acquisition of popular favor.

Fifthly.—The influence of patronage in the distribution of offices, which in these states has been almost invariably made among men the least entitled to such distinction, and who have sold themselves as ready instruments for distracting public opinion, and encouraging administration to hold in contempt the wishes and remonstrances of a people thus apparently divided.

Sixthly.—The admission of new states into the Union formed at pleasure in the western region, has destroyed the balance of power which existed among the original States, and deeply affected their interest.

Seventhly.—The easy admission of naturalized foreigners, to places of trusts, honor or profit, operating as an inducement to the malcontent subjects of the old world to come to these States, in quest of executive patronage, and to repay it by an abject devotion to executive measures.

Eighthly.—Hostility to Great Britain and partiality to the late government of France, adopted as coincident with popular prejudice, and subservient to the main object, party power. Connected with these must be ranked erroneous and distorted estimates of the power and resources of those nations, of the probable results of their controversies, and of our political relations to them respectively.

Lastly and principally.—A visionary and superficial theory in regard to commerce, accompanied by a real hatred but a feigned regard to its interests, and a ruinous perseverance in efforts to render it an instrument of coercion and war.

But it is not conceivable that the obliquity of any administration could, in so short a period, have so nearly consummated the work of national ruin, unless favoured by defects in the constitution.

To enumerate all the improvements of which that instrument is susceptible, and to propose such amendments as might render it in all respects perfect, would be a task which this convention has not thought proper to assume. They have confined their attention to such as experience has demonstrated to be essential, and even among these, some are considered entitled to a more serious attention than others. They are suggested without any intentional disrespect to other states, and are meant to be such as all shall find an interest in promoting. Their object is to strengthen, and if possible to perpetuate, the union of the states, by removing the grounds of existing jealousies, and providing for a fair and equal representation, and a limitation of powers, which have been misused. . . .

THEREFORE RESOLVED,

That it be and hereby is recommended to the legislatures of the several states represented in this Convention, to adopt all such measures as may be necessary effectually to protect the citizens of said states from the operation and effects of all acts which have been or may be passed by the Congress of the United States, which shall contain provisions, subjecting the militia or other citizens to forcible drafts, conscriptions, or impressments, not authorised by the constitution of the United States.

Resolved, That it be and hereby is recommended to the said Legislatures, to authorize an immediate and earnest application to be made to the government of the United States, requesting their consent to some arrangement, whereby the said states may, separately or in concert, be empowered to assume upon themselves the defence of their territory against the enemy; and a reasonable portion of the taxes, collected within said States, may be paid into the respective treasuries thereof, and appropriated to the payment of the balance due said states, and to the future defence of the same. The amount so paid into the said treasuries to be credited, and the disbursements made as aforesaid to be charged to the United States.

Resolved, That it be, and hereby is, recommended to the legislatures of the aforesaid states, to pass laws (where it has not already been done) authorizing the governors or commanders-in-chief of their militia to make detachments from the same, or to form voluntary corps, as shall be most convenient and conformable to their constitutions, and to cause the same to be well armed, equipped,

and disciplined, and held in readiness for service; and upon the request of the governor of either of the other states to employ the whole of such detachment or corps, as well as the regular forces of the state, or such part thereof as may be required and can be spared consistently with the safety of the state, in assisting the state, making such request to repel any invasion thereof which shall be made or attempted by the public enemy.

Resolved, That the following amendments of the constitution of the United States be recommended to the states represented as aforesaid, to be proposed by them for adoption by the state legislatures, and in such cases as may be deemed expedient by a convention chosen by the people of each state.

And it is further recommended, that the said states shall persevere in their efforts to obtain such amendments, until the same shall be effected.

First. Representatives and direct taxes shall be apportioned among the several states which may be included within this Union, according to their respective numbers of free persons, including those bound to serve for a term of years, and excluding Indians not taxed, and all other persons.

Second. No new state shall be admitted into the Union by Congress, in virtue of the power granted by the constitution, without the concurrence of two thirds of both houses.

Third. Congress shall not have power to lay any embargo on the ships or vessels of the citizens of the United States, in the ports or harbours thereof, for more than sixty days.

Fourth. Congress shall not have power, without the concurrence of two thirds of both houses, to interdict the commercial intercourse between the United States and any foreign nation, or the dependencies thereof.

Fifth. Congress shall not make or declare war, or authorize acts of hostility against any foreign nation, without the concurrence of two thirds of both houses, except such acts of hostility be in defence of the territories of the United States when actually invaded.

Sixth. No person who shall hereafter be naturalized, shall be eligible as a member of the senate or house of representatives of the United States, nor capable of holding any civil office under the authority of the United States.

Seventh. The same person shall not be elected president of the United States a second time; nor shall the president be elected from the same state two terms in succession.

Resolved, That if the application of these states to the government of the United States, recommended in a foregoing resolution, should be unsuccessful and peace should not be concluded, and the defence of these states should be neglected, as it has since the commencement of the war, it will, in the opinion of this convention, be expedient for the legislatures of the several states to appoint delegates to another convention, to meet at Boston

. . . with such powers and instructions as the exigency of a crisis so momentous may require.

REVIEW QUESTIONS

1. Why do you suppose both moderate and extremist Federalists praised this report?
2. What were the delegates' grievances?
3. How did these complaints illuminate the shifting dynamics of the nation?
4. What were the proposed solutions? Did these include radical amendment of the *Constitution*?
5. Did any of the solutions suggest the empowerment of state government against the national government?

THE *PENNSYLVANIA GAZETTE*

FROM Newspaper Accounts of the War of 1812 (August–September 1814)

In March 1814 British forces and their allies marched into the French capital; in August the British marched into the American capital. With Europe once more at peace that spring, the British government was able to concentrate its attention on the war across the Atlantic. As it sent over more ships and soldiers, and as the American government increased its enlistment inducements so as to strengthen its forces, the conflict escalated. There was much action on the Great Lakes and along the Canadian-American border, but neither side could break through there. Elsewhere the story differed: while the United States was able to maintain its strength and control in the West, it proved vulnerable in the East. With the support of their navy, British forces were able to occupy eastern Maine by September. Embarrassing as that was for the Americans, the ultimate insult had been the invasion of the Chesapeake and the burning of Washington in August. Admirals Alexander Cochrane and George Cockburn conducted the invasion, along with General Robert Ross who commanded the British troops, numbering over 4,000, that actually took the city. General William Winder, charged by President Madison with the defense of the capital, had a mixed force of regulars and militia, as well as sailors and marines numbering approximately 7,000 with which to block the British.

From the *Pennsylvania Gazette*, 24 and 31 August, 7 September 1814.

British Fleet in the Chesapeake

*   *   *

From the Norfolk Ledger, August 17

Yesterday morning, at half past eight, a fleet of the enemy's ships entered our capes, consisting of five ships of the line, six frigates, one sloop of war, a tender, and ten transports. They came in with a fair wind and tide, and continued up the bay until our informant lost sight of them.—The wind having blown fresh to the southward all night, and still continuing, if this fleet is bound as high as Baltimore, it will be there by this evening.

It is presumed these ships are from Bermuda.

We have no information or knowledge of any circumstances to warrant us in asserting that admiral Cochrane has arrived.

It would be difficult from the detached manner in which the enemy's ships have entered our bay, to form any conjecture of his force, naval or military. Taking a view of the conjectural arrivals, and those we know, we should imagine that the enemy can land about 7000 soldiers and marines, and about 2000 to 3000 seamen.

POSTSCRIPT

It was reported this morning, and generally believed, that eight sail more of the enemy's ships came into the capes last evening. We can say, upon good authority, that no such account has been received at head quarters, by the express which left the bay shore this morning, and we have conversed with an intelligent gentleman, who left the sea beach, about ten miles to the southward of Cape Henry, at 4 o'clock yesterday afternoon; he reports that there was not any vessel in sight at that time.

From the Baltimore Fed. Gazette, Aug. 19.

The Enemy Approaching

The British fleet in the Chesapeake having received a large reinforcement, are again moving up the bay. They are yet too distant to ascertain the intended object of attack, but the prompt and vigorous preparations on the part of the officers in command here, will prevent any confusion or unnecessary alarm. It is the enemy of the nation invading our country. In opposing him we will know no distinction of party or opinion; in this cause Americans will always be united.

A gentleman just arrived from Annapolis, states, that yesterday afternoon four vessels were off Holland's Island, viz. a frigate, a schr. a sloop and a small bay craft, and one frigate in sight of Annapolis.

From the Merchant's Coffee House Books

An express arrived in town last night from Washington with accounts that six 74's, eight frigates and a number of transports, to the number of *FORTY-SIX* sail in all, came into the Bay on the 16th and 17th, and proceeded up. It is said three sail were in sight of Annapolis yesterday.

An express to gen. Smith from the President, requesting him to hold half of his brigade in readiness to march in fifteen minutes upon the order of brigadier-general Winder.

☞ In addition to the above, we have received the following from our correspondent at Baltimore.

SATURDAY, AUG. 20

Information has been received this morning, that a part of the enemy's force is proceeding up the Potomac, and the residue up the Patuxent; and it is presumed their object is to land and march from the respective rivers to the city of Washington. The preparations here for resistance and defence will not be relaxed in consequence of this movement, and our citizens of all classes evince the greatest alacrity in obeying the orders of their respective officers.

Orders have been received from brig. general Winder for a part of the troops here to march tomorrow towards Washington, to watch the motions of the enemy. We have understood that the 5th regiment of infantry, two companies of artillery, the rifle corps, and the whole of the force under brig. gen. Stansbury, near this city, will march, in obedience to those orders.

From the Baltimore Patriot, of August 27

*   *   *

Authentic Account of the Capture of Washington

[The following is a correct, and very interesting account of the loss of Washington, from unquestionable authority.—The concluding suggestions are such as ought to receive the most serious attention from all officers, who are entrusted with the defence of the country.]

To the Editors of the Baltimore Patriot
               Friday evening, Aug. 26th, 1814
GENTLEMEN,—Having witnessed the late unhappy occurrences at Washington, I will, agreeably to your request, put them on paper; that if necessary, they may be used to correct some of the many erroneous reports which are circulating.

I arrived at Washington on Sunday the 21st inst. At that time the officers of government and the citizens were very apprehensive of an attack from the British, who had landed a force on the Patuxent. Their number had not been ascertained, but reports were various, stating them from 4000 to 10,000. Gen. Winder was stationed near the Wood Yard, with about 2000 men, hourly expecting large reinforcements from every quarter, particularly from Baltimore, 3000 men having been ordered to march immediately from that place. On Sunday, the public offices were all engaged in packing and sending off their books and the citizens their furniture. On Monday, this business was continued with great industry, and many families left the city. The specie was removed from all the Banks in the District. Reports were very current, that Winder had received large reinforcements; so that it was believed by many well informed persons, that he would have 10,000 men embodied in the course of the week. In the expectation that there was a very considerable force collected, the President, accompanied by the Secretaries of War and of the Navy, left the city for the camp.—

They arrived there late that night; and the next morning finding but 8000 men, and learning that the Baltimore troops were encamped at Bladensburg, they return-to the city on Tuesday to make further arrangements—All the books and papers were sent off, and the citizens generally left the place.

In the course of that day, a scouting party from General Winder's army had a skirmish with the British advance guard, and returned to camp with such tidings as induced Gen. Winder to retire to the city with his army, which he accomplished by nine o'clock in the evening, burnt the old bridge which crossed the Potomac, and encamped on the hill directly above the other bridge, about one mile and an half from the Navy-yard, and prepared to defend that passage. In the event of the British being too strong, the bridge was to be blown up, for which he had every thing prepared. At this post he remained all night, expecting the enemy's forces. On Wednesday morning I walked through the army, and remained at the bridge until 10 o'clock, when advice was received, that the enemy had taken the Bladensburg road. The troops were immediately put in motion, and by 12 o'clock the whole were on their march, in the hope of forming a junction with the Baltimore troops, before the enemy reached Bladensburg. This was only partially accomplished when the battle commenced, and was contested by the Baltimore troops, and by the men from the flotilla, with great spirit and gallantry, till it appeared useless for so small a force, very badly supported, to stand against 6000 regulars, all picked men, and well supplied. A retreat was ordered, when the President, who had been on horseback, with the army, the whole day, retired from the mortifying scene, and left the city on horseback, accompanied by General Mason and Mr. Carroll. At Georgetown the President met his Lady, she having left the city only half an hour before him, having remained, with great firmness and composure, at the President's house, until a messenger brought her the tidings, that the British were within a few miles of the city, and that our army were retreating, without any chance of being rallied so as to check their march.

The President and Sec'ry of State went to Virginia, with their families; the other officers of government went to Fredericktown, where the government is said to be formed, and where the President intends to meet his secretaries next week. I remained at the President's house until all our army had passed, and 99 hundredths of the citizens gone, leaving nothing but bare walls. I fell into the trail of the army, and marched about four miles on the Frederick road. Being much fatigued, I turned off into a wood, and found good quarters in a farm-house, on the hill back of Pearce's. Soon after reaching there, at nine o'clock on Wednesday evening, a signal gun was discharged, and the President's house, the capitol, and many other public buildings, were at the same moment in a blaze, which continued nearly all night.

On Thursday morning I proceeded on with the army to Montgomery Courthouse, where Gen. Winder's head-quarters were established. I had some conversation with him. He appeared to regret very much, that he had not been enabled to have made a greater resistance, altho' he was perfectly satisfied that a successful resistance could not have been made, with the force in the neighbourhood of Washington; since, if all had been brought together before the action, it would not have been so large as that opposed to him, and our force was principally militia, and that of the enemy all regulars, and picked men.

The uncertanty on which road the enemy intended to attack the city compelled him to keep his forces divided, and their being divided occasioned frequent marches and counter marches, which at this hot season was quite too much for our militia, particularly as the quarter master's department was either shamefully neglected, or the officers unable to procure supplies. For it is a fact that our men suffered severely, not only for accommodations, but for bread and meat; and after retreating to the courthouse at Montgomery, they could not get quarters or provisions, not even a tent to cover them from the rain.

It is to be hoped, that the officers of the army, in every part of the U.S. will take warning from this sad lesson, and provide an abundance of provisions and tents, for it is impossible for men to fight, if they are not well fed; and if they are not sheltered from the rains and the fogs when they sleep. Our army may with truth be said to have been beaten by fatigue, before they saw the enemy.

From the National Intelligencer
WASHINGTON CITY, Aug. 30

*   *   *

The Fate of War

Has befallen the city of Washington. It was taken by the enemy on Wednesday, the 24th inst. and evacuated by them in the course of Thursday night, after destroying the interior and combustible part of the Capitol, of the President's house, and of the public offices. The Navy-Yard was burnt by order of our officers, on learning that the enemy was in possession of the City. . . .

*   *   *

REVIEW QUESTIONS

1. Was there any partisanship apparent in the reporting of these events?
2. How did government officials and civilian residents of Washington prepare for the attack?
3. What reasons were given to explain why American forces could not hold the nation's capital

against the British? Which do you believe to have been most significant? Why?

4. How long did it take for the British to occupy the city, and what did they do in the process?

FROM The Treaty of Ghent (December 1814)

Within days of the war's beginning, Madison sought a diplomatic end to the war and to the causes that had started it. It took over a year, but the British finally agreed to negotiate. It took another six months before the commissioners assembled at Ghent, Belgium, and began to conduct negotiations that lasted from 8 August to 24 December 1814. Great Britain sent three envoys to Ghent; they were not its top diplomats for those were involved in more critical European affairs. The United States, on the other hand, produced a particularly strong team to defend its interests; although, as it turned out, the government was willing to drop some of its demands in order to end the war. Britain, which had initially wanted lands set aside for the western Indians (a matter of caring for their allies and creating a buffer zone between the United States and Canada in the Northwest) and had asked for part of Maine, American demilitarization of the Great Lakes, and limits on American fishing in Canadian waters, also proved flexible about its demands, especially when the alternative was another costly and unpopular year of war.

From Treaties, Conventions, International Acts, Protocols and Agreements between the United States of America and Other Powers, 1776–1909, *vol. I (Washington, D.C.: Government Printing Office, 1910), pp. 612–19.*

1814.
TREATY OF PEACE AND AMITY.
(TREATY OF GHENT.)

Concluded at Ghent December 24, 1814; ratification advised by the Senate February 16, 1815; ratified by the President February 17, 1815; ratifications exchanged February 17, 1815; proclaimed February 18, 1815.

*   *   *

His Britannic Majesty and the United States of America, desirous of terminating the war which has unhappily subsisted between the two countries, and of restoring, upon principles of perfect reciprocity, peace, friendship and good understanding between them, have, for that purpose, appointed their respective Plenipotentiaries, that is to say:

His Britannic Majesty, on his part, has appointed the Right Honourable James Lord Gambier, late Admiral of the White, now Admiral of the Red Squadron of His Majesty's fleet, Henry Goulburn, Esquire, a member of the Imperial Parliament, and Under Secretary of State, and William Adams, Esquire, Doctor of Civil Laws; and the President of the United States, by and with the advice and consent of the Senate thereof, has appointed John Quincy Adams, James A. Bayard, Henry Clay, Jonathan Russell, and Albert Gallatin, citizens of the United States;

Who, after a reciprocal communication of their respective full powers, have agreed upon the following articles:

ARTICLE I.

There shall be a firm and universal peace between His Britannic Majesty and the United States, and between their respective countries, territories, cities, towns and people, of every degree, without exception of places or persons. All hostilities, both by sea and land, shall cease as soon as this treaty shall have been ratified by both parties, as hereinafter mentioned. All territory, places and possessions whatsoever, taken by either party from the other during the war, or which may be taken after the signing of this treaty, excepting only the islands hereinafter mentioned, shall be restored without delay. . . .

ARTICLE II.

Immediately after the ratifications of this treaty by both parties, as hereinafter mentioned, orders shall be sent to the armies, squadrons, officers, subjects and citizens of the two Powers to cease from all hostilities. . . .

ARTICLE III.

All prisoners of war taken on either side, as well by land as by sea, shall be restored as soon as practicable after the ratifications of this treaty, as hereinafter mentioned, on their paying the debts which they have contracted during their captivity. The two contracting parties respectively engage to discharge, in specie, the advances which may have been made by the other for the sustenance and maintenance of such prisoners.

ARTICLE IV.

Whereas it was stipulated by the second article in the treaty of peace of one thousand seven hundred and eighty-three, between His Britannic Majesty and the United States of America, that the boundary of the United States should comprehend all islands within twenty leagues of any part of the shores of the United States, and lying between lines to be drawn due east from the points where the aforesaid boundaries, between Nova Scotia on the one part, and East Florida on the other, shall respectively touch the Bay of Fundy and the Atlantic Ocean, excepting such islands as now are, or heretofore have been, within the limits of Nova Scotia; and whereas the several islands in the Bay of Passamaquoddy, which is part of the Bay of Fundy, and the Island of Grand Menan, in the said Bay of Fundy, are claimed by the United States as being comprehended within their aforesaid boundaries, which said islands are claimed as belonging to His Britannic Majesty, as having been, at the time of and previous to the aforesaid treaty of one thousand seven hundred and eighty-three, within the limits of the Province of Nova Scotia; In order, therefore, finally to decide upon these claims, it is agreed that they shall be referred to two Commissioners to be appointed in the following manner, viz: One Commissioner shall be appointed by His Britannic Majesty, and one by the President of the United States, by and with the advice and consent of the Senate thereof; and the said two Commissioners so appointed shall be sworn impartially to examine and decide upon the said claims according to such evidence as shall be laid before them on the part of His Britannic Majesty and of the United States respectively. . . . The said Commissioners shall, by a declaration or report under their hands and seals, decide to which of the two contracting parties the several islands aforesaid do respectively belong, in conformity with the true intent of the said treaty of peace of one thousand seven hundred and eighty-three. . . .

ARTICLE V.

Whereas neither that point of the highlands lying due north from the source of the river St. Croix, and designated in the former treaty of peace between the two Powers as the northwest angle of Nova Scotia, nor the northwesternmost head of Connecticut River, has yet been ascertained: and whereas that part of the boundary line between the dominions of the two Powers which extends from the source of the river St. Croix directly north to the abovementioned northwest angle of Nova Scotia, thence along the said highlands which divide those rivers that empty themselves into the river St. Lawrence from those which fall into the Atlantic Ocean to the northwesternmost head of Connecticut River, thence down along the middle of that river to the forty-fifth degree of north latitude; thence by a line due west on said latitude until it strikes the river Iroquois or Cataraquy, has not yet been surveyed: it is agreed that for these several purposes two Commissioners shall be appointed, sworn and authorized to act exactly in the manner directed with respect to those mentioned in the next preceding article, unless otherwise specified in the present article. . . . The said Commissioners shall have power to ascertain and determine the points above mentioned, in conformity with the provisions of the said treaty of peace of one thousand seven hundred and eighty-three, and shall cause the boundary aforesaid, from the source of the river St. Croix to the river Iroquois or Cataraquy, to be surveyed and marked according to the said provisions. . . .

ARTICLE VI.

Whereas by the former treaty of peace that portion of the boundary of the United States from the point where the forty-fifth degree of north latitude strikes the river Iroquois or Cataraquy to the Lake Superior, was declared to be "along the middle of said river into Lake Ontario, through the middle of said lake, until it strikes the communication by water between that lake and Lake Erie, thence along the middle of said communication into Lake Erie, through the middle of said lake until it arrives at the water communication into the Lake Huron, thence through the middle of said lake to the water communication between that lake and Lake Superior;" and whereas doubts have arisen what was the middle of the said river, lakes and water communications, and whether certain islands lying in the same were within the dominions of His Britannic Majesty or of the United States: In order, therefore, finally to decide these doubts, they shall be referred to two Commissioners, to be appointed, sworn and authorized to act exactly in the manner directed with respect to those mentioned in the next preceding article, unless otherwise specified in this present article. . . .

ARTICLE VII.

It is further agreed that the said two last-mentioned Commissioners, after they shall have executed the duties assigned to them in the preceding article, shall be, and they are hereby, authorized upon their oaths impartially to fix and determine, according to the true intent of the said treaty of peace of one thousand seven hundred and eighty-three, that part of the boundary between the dominions of the two Powers which extends from the water communication between Lake Huron and Lake Superior, to the most northwestern point of the Lake of the Woods, to decide to which of the two parties the several islands lying in the lakes, water communications and rivers, forming the said boundary, do respectively belong, in conformity with the true intent of the said treaty of peace of one thousand seven hundred and eighty-three; and to cause such parts of the said boundary as require it to be surveyed and marked. . . .

*   *   *

ARTICLE VIII.

The several boards of two Commissioners mentioned in the four preceding articles shall respectively have power to appoint a Secretary, and to employ such surveyors or other persons as they shall judge necessary. Duplicates of all their respective reports, declarations, statements and decisions and of their accounts, and of the journal of their proceedings, shall be delivered by them to the agents of His Britannic Majesty and to the agents of the United States, who may be respectively appointed and authorized to manage the business on behalf of their respective Governments. . . .

ARTICLE IX.

The United States of America engage to put an end, immediately after the ratification of the present treaty, to hostilities with all the tribes or nations of Indians with whom they may be at war at the time of such ratification; and forthwith to restore to such tribes or nations, respectively, all the possessions, rights and privileges which they may have enjoyed or been entitled to in one thousand eight hundred and eleven, previous to such hostilities: Provided always that such tribes or nations shall agree to desist from all hostilities against the United States of America, their citizens and subjects, upon the ratification of the present treaty being notified to such tribes or nations, and shall so desist accordingly. And His Britannic Majesty engages, on his part, to put an end immediately after the ratification of the present treaty, to hostilities with all the tribes or nations of Indians with whom he may be at war at the time of such ratification, and forthwith to restore to such tribes or nations respectively all the possessions, rights and privileges which they may have enjoyed or been entitled to in one thousand eight hundred and eleven, previous to such hostilities: Provided always that such tribes or nations shall agree to desist from all hostilities against His Britannic Majesty, and his subjects, upon the ratification of the present treaty being notified to such tribes or nations, and shall so desist accordingly.

ARTICLE X.

Whereas the traffic in slaves is irreconcilable with the principles of humanity and justice, and whereas both His Majesty and the United States are desirous of continuing their efforts to promote its entire abolition, it is hereby agreed that both the contracting parties shall use their best endeavors to accomplish so desirable an object.

ARTICLE XI.

This treaty, when the same shall have been ratified on both sides, without alteration by either of the contracting parties, and the ratifications mutually exchanged, shall be binding on both parties, and the ratifications shall be exchanged at Washington, in the space of four months from this day, or sooner if practicable.

*   *   *

REVIEW QUESTIONS

1. Was there anything in this treaty to suggest that "Mr. Madison's War" had been a "second war of independence"?
2. Were the issues that started the war (see Madison's war message) resolved in the Treaty of Ghent?
3. What did the treaty do?
4. Did the treaty change the relationship between the United States and Britain?
5. Was this a successful treaty ending a successful war?

10 ⟡ NATIONALISM AND SECTIONALISM

Over the dozen years, from 1816 to 1828, that began with the election of James Monroe and ended with that of Andrew Jackson to the presidency, the American people reflected and acted upon such issues as national history, honor, and improvement. The revolutionary generation was dying off and a new cast of characters began to tread upon the nation's stage. As those who had played their parts bowed off into the wings, they tried to make sure that they would not be forgotten. Their endeavors were aided by transitional figures, such as Monroe and John Quincy Adams, who had entered adulthood during the Revolution and used the lessons of their youth first to support the leaders of the early Republic and then continue their work. Those arriving upon the stage applauded their predecessors even as they set about changing the setting, tempo, and temper of the play.

The transition was both gross and subtle, marked by significant changes in characters and quieter modifications of costume—Monroe wore suits "of somewhat antiquated fashion, with shoe-and-knee buckles" (as Adams recorded in 1821) at both of his inaugurations whereas most American men had begun to wear trousers, rather than buckled knee britches, even for formal events. Between 1816 and 1828 most of the remaining revolutionary leaders died: both Thomas Jefferson and John Adams died on 4 July 1826. Many of their compatriots also passed from the scene, but many others were still around, some in dire financial straits, to prick the nation's memory. Congress responded by passing legislation to provide pensions for the soldiers of the Revolution. The young nation also commemorated its past by feting General Marie Joseph Lafayette on his visit to the states during 1824 and 1825 even as it celebrated its present by showing him how much the country had grown.

The developing nation had indeed altered much, in form if not in substance. Americans had extended their country's borders and continued to stretch them. Within those borders, they argued over and then implemented internal improvements, such as roads and the development of waterways, to foster prosperity and

285

power. While most, if not all, Americans looked at these transportation networks primarily as commercial necessities, a few leaders also saw them as contributing to the nation's security—they could thus move the military more efficiently to meet threats posed by Indian tribes and foreign nations. As Native American resistance grew, so too did the response of the United States: the Seminoles and Andrew Jackson illustrated the dynamics of this aggression. The nation was also intent on containing British imperial possessions to the north in Canada and pushing Spain off the continent altogether.

Territorial and economic growth stimulated the growth of American nationalism. As the Federalist Party disappeared and Republicans adopted and adapted some of its ideas and projects—including a national bank—as their own, some Americans could hope that political partisanship was a thing of the past. That quickly proved to be wishful thinking, for one party could not accommodate all beliefs or all political players. Schisms developed within the party as its leaders jockeyed for power and the intense rivalry and deal-making that marked the election of Adams to the presidency in 1824 split the party. Andrew Jackson stormed out of its ranks and helped create the new Democratic Party, and then went on to win the election of 1828.

Schisms also developed between sections of the country. There arose new North/South issues that were related to or exacerbated by the rise of the West. The question of Missouri statehood awakened people to the fact that the states had not surmounted all the domestic dangers to their union. The result was that even as citizens celebrated the nation's power, they started to worry about national dissolution.

Sectional sentiments challenged nationalism, but the latter remained strong among the American people. Nationalism also prevailed due to the ideologies and actions of the country's leaders in the executive and judicial branches. Adams and Monroe secured the United States as a continental power and endeavored to extend it as a hemispheric one. Although the United States was not a leading world power, Adams and Monroe were determined to maintain its national honor and autonomy. John Marshall, the Chief Justice of the Supreme Court, was just as determined to preserve the power of the national government against encroachments from the states.

JAMES MONROE

FROM President Monroe's First Annual Address to Congress (December 1817)

In 1816 the old Federalist Party, with its last gasps, nominated Rufus King to run for the presidency against the Democratic-Republican Party's candidate, James Monroe. It was no contest. Monroe represented continuity to Americans who were grappling with escalating changes. Many, if not most, embraced change, but perhaps in an attempt to control it, they—or more precisely, their electors—seemed to desire stability in the White House. Monroe was another Virginian, following Madison, Jefferson, and Washington, and he had been engaged in public service since the Revolution—as first soldier, then statesman. Monroe, reflecting both his personal as well as his country's history, wanted to ensure national autonomy and power against international pressures even as he acted to restrict the application of that power upon the states. Monroe served for two terms; in the first he reaped the benefits of postwar peace, prosperity, and pride. It was the so-called "Era of Good Feelings."

From Stanislaus Murray Hamilton, ed., *The Writings of James Monroe*, vol. VI (1902; New York: AMS Press, 1969), pp. 33–44.

WASHINGTON, December 2, 1817.

*Fellow Citizens of the Senate and
of the House of Representatives:*

At no period of our political existence had we so much cause to felicitate ourselves at the prosperous and happy condition of our country. The abundant fruits of the earth have filled it with plenty. An extensive and profitable commerce has greatly augmented our revenue. The public credit has attained an extraordinary elevation. Our preparations for defense in case of future wars, from which, by the experience of all nations, we ought not to expect to be exempted, are advancing under a well digested system with all the despatch which so important a work will admit. Our free government founded on the interest and affections of the people, has gained and is daily gaining strength. Local jealousies are rapidly yielding to more generous, enlarged and enlightened views of national policy. For advantages so numerous and highly important it is our duty to unite in grateful acknowledgments to that Omnipotent Being from whom they are derived and in unceasing prayer that he will endow us with virtue and strength to maintain and hand them down in their utmost purity to our latest posterity.

*   *   *

The negotiations with Spain for spoliations on our commerce and the settlements of boundaries remains essentially in the state it held by the communications that were made to Congress by my predecessor. . . .

It was anticipated at an early stage that the contest between Spain and the Colonies would become highly interesting to the United States. It was natural that our citizens should sympathize in events which affected their neighbors. It seemed probable also that the prosecution of the conflict along our coast and in contiguous countries would occasionally interrupt our commerce and otherwise affect the persons and the property of our citizens. These anticipations have been realized. Such injuries have been received from persons acting under authority of both the parties, and for which redress has in most instances been withheld. Through every stage of the conflict the United States have maintained an impartial neutrality, giving aid to neither of the parties in men, money, ships or munitions of war. They have regarded the contest not in the light of an ordinary insurrection or rebellion, but as a civil war between parties nearly equal, having as to neutral powers equal rights. Our ports have been open to both, and every article, the fruit of our soil or of the industry of our citizens which either was permitted to take has been equally free to the other. Should the Colonies establish their independence, it is proper now to state that this Government neither seeks, nor would accept from them any advantage in commerce or otherwise which will not be equally open to all other nations. The Colonies will, in that event, become independent States, free from any obligation to or connection with us, which it may not then be their interest to form on the basis of a fair reciprocity.

In the summer of the present year an expedition was set on foot against East Florida by persons claiming to act under the authority of some of the Colonies, who took possession of Amelia Island at the mouth of the St. Marys River, near the boundary of the State of Georgia. As this Province lies Eastward of the Mississippi, and is bounded by the United States and the ocean on every side and has been the subject of negotiation with the Government of Spain as an indemnity for losses by spoliation or in exchange for territory of equal value westward of the Mississippi—a fact well known to the world—it excited surprise that any countenance should be given to this measure by any of the colonies. As it would be difficult to reconcile it with the friendly relations existing between the United States and the colonies, a doubt was entertained whether it had been authorized by them or any of them. This doubt has gained strength by the circumstances which have unfolded themselves in the prosecution of the enterprise, which have marked it as a mere private unauthorized adventure. Projected and commenced with an incompetent force, reliance seems to have been placed on what might be drawn, in defiance of our laws, from within our limits; and of late, as their resources have failed, it has assumed a more marked character of unfriendliness to us, the island being made a channel for the illicit introduction of slaves from Africa into the United States, an asylum for fugitive slaves from the neighboring States, and a port for smuggling of every kind.

A similar establishment was made at an earlier period by persons of the same description in the Gulf of Mexico at a place called Galvezton within the limits of the United States, as we contend, under the cession of Louisiana. This enterprize has been marked in a more signal manner by all the objectionable circumstances which characterized the other and more particularly by the equipment of privateers which have annoyed our commerce and by smuggling. These establishments, if ever sanctioned by any authority whatever, which is not believed, have abused their trust and forfeited all claim to consideration. A just regard for the rights and interests of the United States required that they should be suppressed, and orders have been accordingly issued to that effect. . . .

*   *   *

From several of the Indian tribes inhabiting the country bordering on Lake Erie purchases have been made of lands on conditions very favorable to the United States, and, as it is presumed, not less so to the tribes themselves.

By these purchases the Indian title, with moderate reservations, has been extinguished to the whole of the land within the limits of the State of Ohio, and to a part of that in the Michigan Territory and of the State of Indiana. From the Cherokee tribe a tract has been purchased in the State of Georgia and an arrangement made by which in exchange for lands beyond the Mississippi, a great part, if not the whole of the land belonging to that tribe eastward of that river in the States of North Carolina, Georgia and Tennessee and in the Alabama Territory will soon be acquired. By these acquisitions and others that may reasonably be expected soon to follow, we shall be enabled to extend our settlements from the inhabited parts of the State of Ohio along Lake Erie into the Michigan Territory, and to connect our settlements by degrees through the State of Indiana and the Illinois Territory to that of Missouri. A similar and equally advantageous effect will soon be produced to the South, through the whole extent of the States and Territory which border on the waters emptying into the Mississippi and the Mobile. In this progress, which the rights of nature demand, and nothing can prevent, marking a growth rapid and gigantic, it is our duty to make new efforts for the preservation, improvement, and civilization of the native inhabitants. The hunter state can exist only in the vast uncultivated desert. It yields to the more dense and compact form and greater force of civilized population; and of right it ought to yield, for the earth was given to mankind to support the greatest number of which it is capable, and no tribe or people have a right to withhold from the wants of others more than is necessary for their own support and comfort. It is gratifying to know that the reservations of land made by the treaties with the tribes on Lake Erie were made with a view to individual ownership among them and to the cultivation of the soil by all, and that an annual stipend has been pledged to supply their other wants. It will merit the consideration of Congress whether other provision, not stipulated by treaty ought to be made for these tribes and for the advancement of the liberal and humane policy of the United States toward all the tribes within our limit, and more particularly for their improvement in the arts of civilized life.

Among the advantages incident to these purchases and to those which have preceded, the security which thereby may be afforded to our inland frontiers is peculiarly important. With a strong barrier, consisting of our own people, thus planted on the Lakes, the Mississippi, and the Mobile, with the protection to be derived from the regular force, Indian hostilities, if they do not altogether cease, will henceforth lose their terror. Fortifications in those quarters to any extent will not be necessary, and the expense attending them may be saved. A people accustomed to the use of firearms only, as the Indian tribes are, will shun even moderate works which are defended by cannon. Great fortifications will therefore be requisite in future only along the coast and at some points in the interior connected with it. On these will the safety of our towns and the commerce of our great rivers, from the Bay of Fundy to the Mississippi, depend. On these, therefore, should the utmost attention, skill and labor be bestowed. A considerable and rapid augmentation in the value of all the public lands, proceeding from these and other obvious causes, may henceforward be expected. The difficulties attending early emigrations will be dissipated even in the most remote parts. Several new States have been admitted into our Union to the west and South and Territorial governments, happily organized, established over every other portion in which there is vacant land for sale. In terminating Indian hostilities, as must soon be done, in a formidable shape at least, the emigration which has heretofore been great, will probably increase and the augmentation in its value be in like proportion. The great increase of our population throughout the Union will alone produce an important effect, and in no quarter will it be so sensibly felt as in those in contemplation. The public lands are a public stock which ought to be disposed of to the best advantage for the nation. The nation should therefore derive the profit proceeding from the continual rise in their value. Every encouragement should be given to the emigrants consistent with a fair competition between them, but that competition should operate in the first sale to the advantage of the nation rather than of individuals. . . .

When we consider the vast extent of territory within the United States, the great amount and value of its productions, the connection of its parts, and other circumstances on which their prosperity and happiness depend, we cannot fail to entertain a high sense of the advantage to be derived from the facility which may be afforded in the intercourse between them by means of good roads and canals. Never did a country of such vast extent offer equal inducements to an improvement of this kind, nor ever were consequences of such magnitude involved in them. As this subject was acted on by Congress at the last session, and there may be a disposition to revive it at the present, I have brought it into view for the purpose of communicating my sentiments on a very important circumstance connected with it with that freedom and candor which a regard for the public interest and a proper respect for Congress require. A difference of opinion has existed from the first formation of our Constitution to the present time among our most enlightened and virtuous citizens respecting the right of Congress to establish such a system of improvement. Taking into view the trust with which I am now honored, it would be improper after what has passed that this discussion should be revived with an uncertainty of my opinion respecting the right. Disregarding early impressions, I have bestowed on the subject all the deliberation which its great importance and a just sense of my duty required, and the result is a settled conviction in my mind that Congress do not possess the right. It is not contained in any of the specified powers granted to Congress, nor can I consider it incidental to or a necessary means, viewed on the most liberal scale, for carrying into effect any of the powers which are specifically granted. In communicating this result, I cannot resist the obligation which I feel to suggest to Congress the propriety of recommending to the States, the adoption of an Amendment to the Constitution which shall give to Congress the right in question. . . .

*   *   *

In contemplating the happy situation of the United States, our attention is drawn with peculiar interest to the surviving officers and soldiers of our Revolutionary Army, who so eminently contributed by their services to lay its foundation. Most of those very meritorious citizens have paid the debt of nature and gone to repose. It is believed that among the survivors there are some not provided for by existing laws, who are reduced to indigence and even to real distress. These men have a claim on the gratitude of their country, and it will do honor to their country to provide for them. . . .

*   *   *

REVIEW QUESTIONS

1. Did Monroe see nationalism or sectionalism as the predominant force in American politics? Why?
2. How did the insurrections in Spain's colonies affect American foreign policy?
3. Was security the dominant theme of this address? Explain.
4. How did Monroe describe American civilization and its destiny?

JOHN QUINCY ADAMS

Observations on Jackson and the Spanish Florida Situation (1818–19)

President Monroe made John Quincy Adams his secretary of state. It was a provident appointment, for Adams had long been engaged in diplomacy to good effect for his country: he had been part of the commission that negotiated the Treaty of Ghent which ended the War of 1812, and he had represented the United States in the Netherlands, Prussia, Russia, and Great Britain. Adams had also served in the Senate, the legislative branch with the duty to advise the president on treaties and ambassadors. His heritage, education, and experience molded his perceptions and policies to the point that he generally—the issue of slavery would later test him on this—put nation before section or state. He believed that the United States should have dominion over the North American continent and labored to that end. As secretary of state he negotiated the Convention of 1818 with the British, establishing, among other things, boundary and fishing rights, as well as the Transcontinental Treaty of 1819 with Spain (also called the Adams-Onis Treaty). Adams was also a major influence in the creation of what has become known as the Monroe Doctrine. He could so expand American property and power because of a growing American population, economy, and militarism. The latter was seen in the actions of, and popular reactions to (especially in the South and West), General Andrew Jackson's campaign against the Seminole Indians in 1817–18.

From Allan Nevins, ed., *The Diary of John Quincy Adams, 1794–1845* (1928; New York: Charles Scribner's Sons, 1951), pp. 196–201. [Editorial insertions appear in square brackets—Ed.]

*   *   *

May. 4. [1818]—The President sent me word this morning that he had returned from his short tour to Virginia. When I called at his house, I found there Mr. Calhoun and Mr. Crowninshield: Mr. Crawford came in shortly afterwards. The dispatches from General Jackson were just received, containing the account of his progress in the war against the Seminole Indians, and his having taken the Spanish fort of St. Mark's, in Florida, where they had taken refuge. They hung some of the Indian prisoners, as it appears, without due regard to humanity. A Scotchman by the name of Arbuthnot was found among them, and Jackson appears half inclined to take his life. Crawford some time ago proposed to send Jackson an order to give no quarter to any white man found with the Indians. I objected to it then, and this day avowed that I was not prepared for such a mode of warfare.

*   *   *

June 9.—We spent the evening at the French Minister Hyde de Neuville's, a small musical party. Mr. Bagot spoke to me of certain publications in the newspapers, mentioning the execution by sentences of court-martial, under the orders of General Jackson, of two Englishmen, named Arbuthnot and Ambrister, taken with the Seminole Indians in this war. These publications say that the evidence against them proved the greatest perfidy on the part of the British Government. Mr. Bagot was very much hurt by this charge of perfidy, for which he said there was not the slightest foundation.

June 18.—The President spoke of the taking of Pensacola by General Jackson, contrary to his orders, and, as it is now reported, by storm. This, and other events in this Indian war, makes many difficulties for the Administration.

*   *   *

July 10.—Had an interview at the office with Hyde de Neuville, the French Minister—all upon our affairs with Spain. He says that Spain will cede the Floridas to the United States, and let the lands go for the indemnities due to our citizens, and he urged that we should take the Sabine for the western boundary, which I told him was impossible. He urged this subject very strenuously for more than an hour. As to Onis's note of invective against General Jackson, which I told him as a good friend to Onis he should advise him to take back, he said I need not answer it for a month or two, perhaps not at all, if in the meantime we could come to an arrangement of the other differences.

July 15.—Attended the Cabinet meeting at the President's, from noon till five o'clock. The subject of deliberation was General Jackson's late transactions in Florida, particularly the taking of Pensacola. The President and all the members of the Cabinet, except myself, are of opinion that Jackson acted not only without, but against, his instructions: that he has committed war upon Spain, which cannot be justified, and in which, if not disavowed by the Administration, they will be abandoned by the country. My opinion is that there was no real, though an apparent, violation of his instructions: that his proceedings were justified by the necessity of the case, and by the misconduct of the Spanish commanding officers in Florida. The

question is embarrassing and complicated, not only as involving that of an actual war with Spain, but that of the Executive power to authorize hostilities without a declaration of war by Congress. There is no doubt that defensive acts of hostility may be authorized by the Executive; but Jackson was authorized to cross the Spanish line in pursuit of the Indian enemy . . . [.]

Calhoun, the Secretary at War, generally of sound, judicious, and comprehensive mind, seems in this case to be personally offended with the idea that Jackson has set at nought the instructions of the Department. The President supposes there might be cases which would have justified Jackson's measures, but that he has not made out his case.

July 16.—Second cabinet meeting at the President's, and the question of the course to be pursued with relation to General Jackson's proceedings in Florida recurred. As the opinion is unanimously against Jackson excepting mine, my range of argument now is only upon the degree to which his acts are to be disavowed. It was urged that the public dissatisfaction at the taking of Pensacola is so great that the Administration must immediately and publicly disclaim having given any authority for it, and publish all the instructions given to him to throw the blame entirely upon him.

July 17.—Cabinet meeting at the President's—the discussion continued upon the answer to be given to Onis, and the restoration of Florida to Spain. The weakness and palsy of my right hand make it impossible for me to report this discussion, in which I continue to oppose the unanimous opinions of the President, the Secretary of the Treasury Crawford, the Secretary of War Calhoun, and the Attorney-General Wirt. I have thought that the whole conduct of General Jackson was justifiable under his orders, although he certainly had none to take any Spanish fort. My principle is that everything he did was defensive; that as such it was neither war against Spain nor violation of the Constitution.

July 21.—A Cabinet meeting, at which the second draft of my letter to Mr. Onis was read and finally fixed. Mr. Wirt read what he called a second edition of his article for the *National Intelligencer*. I strenuously re-urged my objections, especially to a paragraph declaring that the President thought he had no constitutional power to have authorized General Jackson to take Pensacola . . . [.] I finally gave up the debate, acquiescing in the determination which had been taken. The Administration were placed in a dilemma from which it is impossible for them to escape censure by some, and factious crimination by many. If they avow and approve Jackson's conduct, they incur the double responsibility of having commenced a war against Spain, and of warring in violation of the Constitution without the authority of Congress. If they disavow him, they must give offence to all his friends, encounter the shock of his popularity, and have the appearance of truckling to Spain. For all this I should be prepared. But the mischief of this determination lies deeper; 1. It is weakness, and confession of weakness. 2. The disclaimer of power in the Executive is of dangerous example and of evil consequences. 3. There is injustice to the officer in disavowing him, when in principle he is strictly justifiable . . . [.]

Calhoun says he has heard that the court-martial at first acquitted the two Englishmen, but that Jackson sent the case back to them. He says, also, that last winter there was a company formed in Tennessee, who sent Jackson's nephew to Pensacola and purchased Florida lands, and that Jackson himself is reported to be interested in the speculation. I hope not.

*   *   *

January 23. [1819]—As I was going to the President's, General Jackson and his suite were going out. The President called him and Colonel Butler back, and introduced them to me. The General arrived this morning from his residence at Nashville, Tennessee, and had already called at my office. Among the rumors which have been circulated by the cabal now intriguing in Congress against Jackson, it has been very industriously whispered that Mr. Jefferson and Mr. Madison had declared themselves in very strong terms against him. I had mentioned this report a few days since to the

President, who told me that he was convinced there was no foundation for it. This morning he showed me in confidence a letter he had just received from Mr. Jefferson. It not only expresses full satisfaction with the course pursued by the Administration, but mentions my letters of 12th March last to Onis, and of 28th November to Erving, in terms which it would not become me to repeat. He advises that they, with others of my letters to Onis, should be translated into French and communicated to every Government in Europe, as a thorough vindication of the conduct and policy of this Government.

*   *   *

February 3.—General Jackson came to my house this morning, and I showed him the boundary line which has been offered to the Spanish Minister, and that which we proposed to offer upon Melish's map. He said there were many individuals who would take exception to our receding so far from the boundary of the Rio del Norte, which we claim, as the Sabine, and the enemies of the Administration would certainly make a handle of it to assail them: but the possession of the Floridas was of so great importance to the southern frontier of the United States, and so essential even to their safety, that the vast majority of the nation would be satisfied with the western boundary as we propose, if we obtain the Floridas. He showed me on the map the operations of the British force during the late war, and remarked that while the mouths of the Florida rivers should be accessible to a foreign naval force there would be no security for the United States.

He also entered into conversation upon the subject of discussion now pending in the House of Representatives on his proceedings in the late Seminole War, upon that which is preparing in the Senate under the auspices of Mr. Forsyth, of Georgia, and upon the general order given by Jackson in 1817, which was considered as setting at defiance the War Department. He imputed the whole to Mr. Crawford's resentments against him on account of his having at the last Presidential election supported Mr. Monroe against him; said there was not a single officer in the army known to have been at that time in favor of Monroe whom Crawford had not since insulted: that Mr. Monroe was of an open, fair, unsuspecting character, amiable in the highest degree, and would not believe human nature capable of the baseness which Crawford, while holding a confidential office under him, was practising against him.

I told Jackson that Mr. Crawford had never in any of the discussions on the Seminole War said a word which led me to suppose he had any hostile feeling against him. He replied that, however that might be, Crawford was now setting the whole delegation of Georgia against him, and by intentional insult and the grossest violation of all military principle had compelled him to issue the order of 1817. Crawford, he said, was a man restrained by no principle, and capable of any baseness . . . [.] Crawford was now canvassing for the next Presidential election, and actually wrote a letter to Clay proposing a coalition with him to overthrow Mr. Monroe's Administration.

That Crawford has written such a letter to Clay as Jackson has informed, is to the last degree improbable. He has too much discretion to have put himself so much in Clay's power. But that all his conduct is governed by his views to the Presidency, as the immediate successor to Mr. Monroe, and that his hopes depend upon a result unfavorable to the success, or at least to the popularity of the Administration, is perfectly clear. The important and critical interests of the country are those the management of which belongs to the Department of State. Those incidental to the Treasury are in a state which would give an able financier an opportunity to display his talents: but Crawford has no talents as a financier. He is just, and barely, equal to the current routine of the business of his office. His talent is intrigue. And as it is in the foreign affairs that the success or failure of the Administration will be most conspicuous, and as their success would promote the reputation and influence, and their failure would lead to the disgrace, of the Secretary of State, Crawford's personal views centre in the ill success of the Administration in its foreign relations; and, perhaps unconscious of his own

motives, he will always be impelled to throw obstacles in its way, and to bring upon the Department of State especially any feeling of public dissatisfaction that he can.

*　　*　　*

Feb. 22.—Mr. Onis came at eleven, with Mr. Stoughton, one of the persons attached to his Legation. The two copies of the treaty made out at his house were ready: none of ours were entirely finished. We exchanged the original full powers on both sides, which I believe to be the correct course on the conclusion of treaties, though at Ghent, and on the conclusion of the Convention of 3d July, 1815, the originals were only exhibited and copies exchanged. I had one of the copies of the treaty, and Mr. Onis the other. I read the English side, which he collated, and he the Spanish side, which I collated. We then signed and sealed both copies on both sides—I first on the English and he first on the Spanish side . . . [.]

The acquisition of the Floridas has long been an object of earnest desire to this country. The acknowledgment of a definite line of boundary to the South Sea forms a great epoch in our history. The first proposal of it in this negotiation was my own, and I trust it is now secured beyond the reach of revocation. It was not even among our claims by the Treaty of Independence with Great Britain. It was not among our pretensions under the purchase of Louisiana—for that gave us only the range of the Mississippi and its waters. I first introduced it in the written proposal of 31st October last, after having discussed it verbally both with Onis and De Neuville. It is the only peculiar and appropriate right acquired by this treaty in the event of its ratification.

*　　*　　*

REVIEW QUESTIONS

1. What did Jackson do that so disturbed the Spanish minister, Luís de Onís y Gonzales, and the British minister, Sir Charles Bagot?

2. Why did Jackson's actions create difficulties for Monroe's administration?

3. Did Adams approve or disapprove of Jackson's actions? Why?

4. Does it appear that Jackson's actions helped or hindered Adams in his negotiations with Spain?

5. Did Adams have to worry about domestic politics when implementing his foreign policy?

JOHN QUINCY ADAMS

Reflections on the Missouri Question (1820)

The nation wrestled not only with matters of state but with matters within the states as well. The question of Missouri's admittance to the union had "excited feelings & raised difficulties, of an internal nature, which did not exist before." Actually the difficulties—those concerning the extension of slavery, the corresponding expansion of slaveholder power, and the respective rights of the people, states, and Congress—were not totally new, but while they had been subdued in the "Era of Good Feelings," they now burst forth in greater vigor and viciousness. The debate began in early 1819 when there were enough people in the territory around and including the town of St. Louis to constitute a new state. Considering how the nation had celebrated the admittance of each new state up to this time as a confirmation of America's power and prosperity, there should not have been a problem. One developed, however, when Representative James Tallmadge, Jr., of New York proposed that Congress make a prohibition on the future importation of slaves into the area and introduce a system of gradual manumission as a condition of admission. Slaveowners in Missouri and elsewhere countered by arguing that Congress did not have the right to so restrict a state's power and an individual's right to control his property. John Quincy Adams, because of personal inclination as well as his professional responsibility to advise the president, observed and commented on the "Missouri question" as Congress and country debated the issue for over a year.

From Allan Nevins, ed., *The Diary of John Quincy Adams, 1794–1845* (1928. New York: Charles Scribner's Sons, 1951), pp. 225–32. [Editorial insertions appear in square brackets —*Ed.*]

*   *   *

Jan. 24.—I walked with R. M. Johnson to the Senate chamber and heard Mr. Pinkney close his Missouri speech. There was a great crowd of auditors. Many ladies, among whom several seated on the floor of the Senate. His eloquence was said to be less overpowering than it had been last Friday. His language is good, his fluency without interruption or hesitation, his manner impressive, but his argument weak, from the inherent weakness of his cause.

Feb. 11.—I went up to the Capitol and heard Mr. King in the Senate, upon what is called the Missouri question. He had been speaking perhaps an hour before I went in, and I heard him about an hour. His manner is dignified, grave, earnest, but not rapid or vehement. There was nothing new in his argument, but he unravelled with ingenious and subtle analysis many of the sophistical tissues of the slave-holders. He laid down the position of the natural liberty of man, and its incompatibility with slavery in any shape. He also questioned the Constitutional right of the President and Senate to make the Louisiana Treaty; but he did not dwell upon those points, nor draw the consequences from them which I should think important in speaking to that subject. He spoke, however, with great power, and the great slaveholders in the House gnawed their lips and clenched their fists as they heard him . . . We attended an evening party at Mr. Calhoun's, and heard of nothing but the Missouri question and Mr. King's speeches. The slave-holders cannot hear of them without being seized with cramps. They call them seditious and inflammatory, when their greatest real defect is their timidity. Never since human sentiments and human conduct were influenced by human speech was there a theme for eloquence like the free side of this question now before Congress of this Union. By what fatality does it happen that all the most eloquent orators of the body are on its slavish side? There is a great mass of cool judgment and plain sense on the side of freedom and humanity, but the ardent spirits and passions are on the side of oppression. Oh, if but one man could arise with a genius capable of comprehending, a heart capable of supporting, and an utterance capable of communicating those eternal truths that belong to this question, to lay bare in all its nakedness that outrage upon the goodness of God, human slavery, now is the time, and this is the occasion, upon which such a man would perform the duties of an angel upon earth!

Feb. 13.—Attended the divine service at the Capitol, and heard Mr. Edward Everett, the Professor of the Greek language at Harvard University, a young man of shining talents and of illustrious promise. His text was from I Cor. vii. 29: "Brethren, the time is short," and it was without comparison the most splendid composition as a sermon that I ever heard delivered. . . . Mr. Clay, with whom I walked, after the service, to call upon Chief-Justice Marshall, told me that although Everett had a fine fancy and a chaste style of composition, his manner was too theatrical, and he liked Mr. Holley's manner better.

Clay started, however, immediately to the Missouri question, yet in debate before both Houses of Congress, and, alluding to a strange scene at Richmond, Virginia, last Wednesday evening, said it was a shocking thing to think of, but he had not a doubt that within five years from this time the Union would be divided into three distinct confederacies. I did not incline to discuss the subject with him. We found Judges Livingston and Story with the Chief Justice.

*   *   *

February 23.—A. Livermore and W. Plumer, Junr, members of the House of Representatives from New Hampshire, called upon me, and, conversing on the Missouri slave question, which at this time agitates Congress and the Nation, asked my opinion of the propriety of agreeing to a compromise. The division in Congress and the nation is nearly equal on both sides. The argument on the free side is, the moral and political duty of preventing the extension of slavery in the immense country from the Mississippi River to the South Sea. The argument on the slave side is, that Congress have no power by the Constitution to prohibit slavery in any State, and, the zealots say, not in any Territory. The proposed compromise is to admit Missouri, and hereafter Arkansas, as States, without any restriction upon them regarding slavery, but to prohibit the future introduction of slaves in all Territories of the United States north of 36° 30' latitude. I told these gentlemen that my opinion was, the question could be settled no otherwise than by a compromise.

Feb. 24.—I had some conversation with Calhoun on the slave question pending in Congress. He said he did not think it would produce a dissolution of the Union, but, if it should, the South would be from necessity compelled to form an alliance, offensive and defensive, with Great Britain.

I said that would be returning to the colonial state.

He said, yes, pretty much, but it would be forced upon them. I asked him whether he thought, if by the effect of this alliance, offensive and defensive, the population of the North should be cut off from its natural outlet upon the ocean, it would fall back upon its rocks bound hand and foot, to starve, or whether it would not retain its powers of locomotion to move southward by land. Then, he said, they would find it necessary to make their communities all military. I pressed the conversation no further: but if the dissolution of the Union should result from the slave question, it is as obvious as anything that can be foreseen of futurity, that it must shortly afterwards be followed by the universal emancipation of the slaves. A more remote but perhaps not less certain consequence would be the extirpation of the African race on this continent, by the gradually bleaching process of intermixture, where the white portion is already so predominant, and by the destructive progress of emancipation, which, like all great religious and political reformations, is terrible in its means though happy and glorious in its end. Slavery is the great and foul stain upon the North American Union, and it is a contemplation worthy of the most exalted soul whether its total abolition is or is not practicable: if practicable, by what it may be effected, and if a choice of means be within the scope of the object, what means would accomplish it at the smallest cost of human suffering. A dissolution, at least temporary, of the Union, as now constituted, would be certainly necessary . . . [.] The Union might then be reorganized on the fundamental principle of emancipation. This object is vast in its compass, awful in its prospects, sublime and beautiful in its issue.

*   *   *

Washington, March 2, 1820.—The compromise of the slave question was this day completed in Congress. The Senate have carried their whole point, barely consenting to the formality of separating the bill for the admission of the State of Maine into the Union from that for authorizing the people of the Territory of Missouri to form a State Government. The condition that slavery should be prohibited by their Constitution, which the House of Representatives had inserted, they have abandoned. Missouri and Arkansas will be slave States, but to the Missouri bill a section is annexed, prohibiting slavery in the remaining part of the Louisiana cession north of latitude 36° 30'. This compromise, as it is called, was finally carried this evening by a vote of ninety to eighty-seven in the House of Representatives, after successive days and almost nights of stormy debate.

March 3.—When I came this day to my office, I found there a note requesting me to call at one o'clock at the President's house. It was then one, and I immediately went over. He expected that the two bills, for the admission of Maine, and to enable Missouri to make a Constitution, would have been brought to him for his signature, and he had summoned all the members of the Administration to ask their opinions in writing, to be deposited in the Department of State, upon two questions: 1, Whether Congress had a Constitutional right to prohibit slavery in a Territory: and 2, Whether the eighth section of the Missouri bill (which interdicts slavery forever in the Territory north of thirty-six and a half latitude) was applicable only to the Territorial State, or could extend to it after it should become a State.

As to the first question, it was unanimously agreed that Congress have the power to prohibit slavery in the Territories . . . [.] I had no doubt of the right of Congress to interdict slavery in the Territories, and urged that the power contained in the term "dispose of" included the authority to do everything that could be done with it as mere property, and that the additional words, authorizing needful rules and regulations respecting it, must have reference to persons connected with it, or could have no meaning at all. As to the force of the term needful, I observed, it was relative, and must always be supposed to have reference to some end. Needful to what end? Needful in the Constitution of the United States to any of the ends for which that compact was formed. Those ends are declared in its preamble: to establish justice, for example. What can be more needful for the establishment of justice than the interdiction of slavery where it does not exist? . . [.]

After this meeting, I walked home with Calhoun, who said that the principles which I had avowed were just and noble: but that in the Southern country, whenever they were mentioned, they were always understood as applying only to white men. Domestic labor was confined to the blacks, and such was the prejudice, that if he, who was the most popular man in his district, were to keep a white servant in his house, his character and reputation would be irretrievably ruined.

I said that this confounding of the ideas of servitude and labor was one of the bad effects of slavery: but he thought it attended with many excellent consequences. It did not apply to all kinds of labor—not, for example, to farming. He himself had often held the plough: so had his father. Manufacturing and mechanical labor was not degrading. It was only manual labor—the proper work of slaves. No white person could descend to that. And it was the best guarantee to equality among the whites. It produced an unvarying level among them. It not only did not excite, but did not even admit of inequalities, by which one white man could domineer over another.

I told Calhoun I could not see things in the same light. It is, in truth, all perverted sentiment—mistaking labor for slavery and dominion for freedom. The discussion of this Missouri question has betrayed the secret of their souls. In the abstract they admit that slavery is an evil, they disclaim all participation in the introduction of it, and cast it all upon the shoulders of our old Grandam Britain. But when probed to the quick upon it, they show at the bottom of their souls pride and vainglory in their condition of masterdom. They fancy themselves more generous and noble-hearted than the plain freemen who labor for subsistence. They look down upon the simplicity of a Yankee's manners, because he has no habits of overbearing like theirs and cannot treat negroes like dogs. It is among the evils of slavery that it taints the very sources of moral principle. It establishes false estimates of virtue and vice: for what can be more false and heartless than this doctrine which makes the first and holiest rights of humanity to depend upon the color of the skin? . . [.]

I have favored this Missouri compromise, believing it to be all that could be effected under the present Constitution, and from extreme unwillingness to put the Union at hazard. But perhaps it would have been a wiser as well as a bolder course to have persisted in the restriction upon Missouri, till it should have terminated in a convention of the States to revise and amend the Constitution. This would have produced a new Union of thirteen or fourteen States unpolluted with slavery, with a great and glorious object to effect, namely, that of rallying to their standard the other States by the universal emancipation of their slaves. If the Union must be dissolved, slavery is precisely the question upon which it ought to break. For the present, however, this contest it laid asleep.

*   *   *

REVIEW QUESTIONS

1. Why did the question of Missouri statehood provoke such a crisis? What were the moral and constitutional issues involved?
2. What appeared to have the most weight with the politicians? Does this issue appear to have affected the nature of the compromise?
3. What was Adams's position on the problem and the compromise?
4. Do these entries reveal Adams to be a believer in strict or loose construction of the Constitution? What do they reveal about Monroe?

FROM *McCulloch v. Maryland* (1819)

Maryland's legislature passed an act that permitted the state to tax the operations of the Second Bank of the United States as it operated within its borders. An officer of the Baltimore branch, James McCulloch, then went to court to refute and stop such taxation. When the Baltimore County Court decided against him, he appealed to the Court of Appeals of the State of Maryland, and when that court upheld the lower court, he appealed to the Supreme Court. John Marshall, the Chief Justice, delivered the unanimous ruling of the Court and provided an extensive justification. That the Court ruled for the bank was not surprising: by 1816, when the Second Bank was chartered, most Americans, Jeffersonian Republicans included, had come to accept that incorporation of the bank was constitutional. By 1819, however, the bank was coming under increasing attack as the people and states struggled with an economic depression. In the midst of this backlash, the question before the Court was that of the constitutionality of a state tax on a properly incorporated national institution. But Marshall did not focus on that alone; he went back to the whole issue of how to determine constitutionality. In effect, the decision itself was not as important—in terms of historical legal precedents—as how the decision was reached. McCulloch v. Maryland thus became much more than the case about the bank; it became a, if not the, fundamental, nationalistic defense of a broad construction of the Constitution.

From Gerald Gunther, ed., *John Marshall's Defense of McCulloch* v. *Maryland* (Stanford: Stanford University Press, 1969), pp. 23–51. [Editorial insertions appear in square brackets—*Ed.*]

Mr. Chief Justice MARSHALL delivered the opinion of the Court.

*   *   *

The first question made in the cause is, has Congress power to incorporate a bank?

It has been truly said, that this can scarcely be considered as an open question, entirely unprejudiced by the former proceedings of the nation respecting it. The principle now contested was introduced at a very early period of our history, has been recognized by many successive legislatures, and has been acted upon by the judicial department, in cases of peculiar delicacy, as a law of undoubted obligation.

*   *   *

The power now contested was exercised by the first Congress elected under the present constitution. The bill for incorporating the bank of the United States did not steal upon an unsuspecting legislature, and pass unobserved. Its principle was completely understood, and was opposed with equal zeal and ability. After being resisted, first in the fair and open field of debate, and afterwards in the executive cabinet, with as much persevering talent as any measure has ever experienced, and being supported by arguments which convinced minds as pure and as intelligent as this country can boast, it became a law. The original act was permitted to expire; but a short experience of the embarrassments to which the refusal to revive it exposed the government, convinced those who were most prejudiced against the measure of its necessity, and

induced the passage of the present law. It would require no ordinary share of intrepidity to assert that
a measure adopted under these circumstances was
a bold and plain usurpation, to which the constitution gave no countenance.

*   *   *

In discussing this question, the counsel for the
State of Maryland have deemed it of some importance, in the construction of the constitution, to
consider that instrument not as emanating from
the people, but as the act of sovereign and independent States. The powers of the general government, it has been said, are delegated by the States,
who alone are truly sovereign; and must be exercised in subordination to the States, who alone
possess supreme dominion.

It would be difficult to sustain this proposition.
The Convention which framed the constitution
was indeed elected by the State legislatures. But the
instrument, when it came from their hands, was a
mere proposal, without obligation, or pretensions
to it. It was reported to the then existing Congress
of the United States, with a request that it might
"be submitted to a Convention of Delegates, chosen in each State by the people thereof, under the
recommendation of its Legislature, for their assent
and ratification." This mode of proceeding was
adopted; and by the Convention, by Congress, and
by the State Legislatures, the instrument was submitted to the people. They acted upon it in the
only manner in which they can act safely, effectively, and wisely, on such a subject, by assembling
in Convention. . . .

From these Conventions the constitution derives its whole authority. The government proceeds
directly from the people; . . . It required not the
affirmance, and could not be negatived, by the
State governments. The constitution, when thus
adopted, was of complete obligation, and bound
the State sovereignties.

*   *   *

This government is acknowledged by all to be one
of enumerated powers. The principle, that it can
exercise only the powers granted to it, would seem

too apparent to have required to be enforced by all
those arguments which its enlightened friends,
while it was depending before the people, found it
necessary to urge. That principle is now universally
admitted. But the question respecting the extent of
the powers actually granted, is perpetually arising,
and will probably continue to arise, as long as our
system shall exist.

In discussing these questions, the conflicting
powers of the general and State governments must
be brought into view, and the supremacy of their
respective laws, when they are in opposition, must
be settled.

If any one proposition could command the
universal assent of mankind, we might expect it
would be this—that the government of the Union,
though limited in its powers, is supreme within its
sphere of action. This would seem to result necessarily from its nature. It is the government of all;
its powers are delegated by all; it represents all, and
acts for all. . . . But this question is not left to mere
reason: the people have, in express terms, decided
it, by saying, "this constitution, and the laws of the
United States, which shall be made in pursuance
thereof," "shall be the supreme law of the land," and
by requiring that the members of the State legislatures, and the officers of the executive and judicial
departments of the States, shall take the oath of fidelity to it.

The government of the United States, then,
though limited in its powers, is supreme; and its
laws, when made in pursuance of the constitution,
form the supreme law of the land, "any thing in the
constitution or laws of any State to the contrary
notwithstanding."

Among the enumerated powers, we do not find
that of establishing a bank or creating a corporation. But there is no phrase in the instrument
which, like the articles of confederation, excludes
incidental or implied powers; and which requires
that every thing granted shall be expressly and
minutely described. . . . [A constitution's] nature,
therefore, requires, that only its great outlines
should be marked, its important objects designated, and the minor ingredients which compose
those objects be deduced from the nature of the

objects themselves. That this idea was entertained by the framers of the American constitution, is not only to be inferred from the nature of the instrument, but from the language. Why else were some of the limitations, found in the ninth section of the 1st article, introduced? It is also, in some degree, warranted by their having omitted to use any restrictive term which might prevent its receiving a fair and just interpretation. In considering this question, then, we must never forget, that it is *a constitution* we are expounding.

Although, among the enumerated powers of government, we do not find the word "bank" or "incorporation," we find the great powers to lay and collect taxes; to borrow money; to regulate commerce; to declare and conduct a war; and to raise and support armies and navies. The sword and the purse, all the external relations, and no inconsiderable portion of the industry of the nation, are entrusted to its government. . . . [A] government, entrusted with such ample powers, on the due execution of which the happiness and prosperity of the nation so vitally depends, must also be entrusted with ample means for their execution. . . . Can we adopt that construction (unless the words imperiously require it), which would impute to the framers of that instrument, when granting these powers for the public good, the intention of impeding their exercise by withholding a choice of means? If, indeed, such be the mandate of the constitution, we have only to obey; but that instrument does not profess to enumerate the means by which the powers it confers may be executed; nor does it prohibit the creation of a corporation, if the existence of such a being be essential to the beneficial exercise of those powers. It is, then, the subject of fair inquiry, how far such means may be employed.

*   *   *

The government which has a right to do an act, and has imposed on it the duty of performing that act, must, according to the dictates of reason, be allowed to select the means; and those who contend that it may not select any appropriate means, that one particular mode of effecting the object is ex-

cepted, take upon themselves the burden of establishing that exception.

The creation of a corporation, it is said, appertains to sovereignty. This is admitted. But to what portion of sovereignty does it appertain? Does it belong to one more than to another? In America, the powers of sovereignty are divided between the government of the Union, and those of the States. They are each sovereign, with respect to the objects committed to it, and neither sovereign with respect to the objects committed to the other. We cannot comprehend that train of reasoning which would maintain, that the extent of power granted by the people is to be ascertained, not by the nature and terms of the grant, but by its date. Some State constitutions were formed *before*, some *since* that of the United States. We cannot believe that their relation to each other is in any degree dependent upon this circumstance. . . . The power of creating a corporation, though appertaining to sovereignty, is not, like the power of making war, or levying taxes, or of regulating commerce, a great substantive and independent power, which cannot be implied as incidental to other powers, or used as a means of executing them. It is never the end for which other powers are exercised, but a means by which other objects are accomplished. . . . No city was ever built with the sole object of being incorporated, but is incorporated as affording the best means of being well governed. The power of creating a corporation is never used for its own sake, but for the purpose of effecting something else. No sufficient reason is, therefore, perceived, why it may not pass as incidental to those powers which are expressly given, if it be a direct mode of executing them.

But the constitution of the United States has not left the right of Congress to employ the necessary means, for the execution of the powers conferred on the government, to general reasoning. To its enumeration of powers is added that of making "all laws which shall be necessary and proper, for carrying into execution the foregoing powers, and all other powers vested by this constitution, in the government of the United States, or in any department thereof."

The counsel for the State of Maryland have urged various arguments, to prove that this clause, though in terms a grant of power, is not so in effect; but is really restrictive of the general right, which might otherwise be implied, of selecting means for executing the enumerated powers.

*　　*　　*

But the argument on which most reliance is placed, is drawn from the peculiar language of this clause. Congress is not empowered by it to make all laws, which may have relation to the powers conferred on the government, but such only as may be "*necessary and proper*" for carrying them into execution. The word "*necessary*," is considered as controlling the whole sentence, and as limiting the right to pass laws for the execution of the granted powers, to such as are indispensable, and without which the power would be nugatory. That it excludes the choice of means, and leaves to Congress, in each case, that only which is most direct and simple.

Is it true, that this is the sense in which the word "necessary" is always used? Does it always import an absolute physical necessity, so strong, that one thing, to which another may be termed necessary, cannot exist without that other? We think it does not. If reference be had to its use, in the common affairs of the world, or in approved authors, we find that it frequently imports no more than that one thing is convenient, or useful, or essential to another. To employ the means necessary to an end, is generally understood as employing any means calculated to produce the end, and not as being confined to those single means, without which the end would be entirely unattainable. Such is the character of human language, that no word conveys to the mind, in all situations, one single definite idea; and nothing is more common than to use words in a figurative sense. Almost all compositions contain words, which, taken in their rigorous sense, would convey a meaning different from that which is obviously intended. It is essential to just construction, that many words which import something excessive, should be understood in a more mitigated sense—in that sense which common usage justifies. The word "necessary" is of this description. It has not a fixed character peculiar to itself. It admits of all degrees of comparison; and is often connected with other words, which increase or diminish the impression the mind receives of the urgency it imports. A thing may be necessary, very necessary, absolutely or indispensably necessary. To no mind would the same idea be conveyed, by these several phrases. . . . This word, then, like others, is used in various senses; and, in its construction, the subject, the context, the intention of the person using them, are all to be taken into view.

Let this be done in the case under consideration. The subject is the execution of those great powers on which the welfare of a nation essentially depends. It must have been the intention of those who gave these powers, to insure, as far as human prudence could insure, their beneficial execution. This could not be done by confining the choice of means to such narrow limits as not to leave it in the power of Congress to adopt any which might be appropriate, and which were conducive to the end. This provision is made in a constitution intended to endure for ages to come, and, consequently, to be adapted to the various *crises* of human affairs. To have prescribed the means by which government should, in all future time, execute its powers, would have been to change, entirely, the character of the instrument, . . .

*　　*　　*

But the argument which most conclusively demonstrates the error of the construction contended for by the counsel for the State of Maryland, is founded on the intention of the Convention, as manifested in the whole clause. . . . This clause, as construed by the State of Maryland, would abridge, and almost annihilate this useful and necessary right of the legislature to select its means. That this could not be intended, is, we should think, had it not been already controverted, too apparent for controversy. . . .

*　　*　　*

The result of the most careful and attentive consideration bestowed upon this clause is, that if it does not enlarge, it cannot be construed to restrain the powers of Congress, or to impair the right of the legislature to exercise its best judgment in the selection of measures to carry into execution the constitutional powers of the government. . . .

We admit, as all must admit, that the powers of the government are limited, and that its limits are not to be transcended. But we think the sound construction of the constitution must allow to the national legislature that discretion, with respect to the means by which the powers it confers are to be carried into execution, which will enable that body to perform the high duties assigned to it, in the manner most beneficial to the people. Let the end be legitimate, let it be within the scope of the constitution, and all means which are appropriate, which are plainly adapted to that end, which are not prohibited, but consist with the letter and spirit of the constitution, are constitutional.

*   *   *

If a corporation may be employed indiscriminately with other means to carry into execution the powers of the government, no particular reason can be assigned for excluding the use of a bank, if required for its fiscal operations. To use one, must be within the discretion of Congress, if it be an appropriate mode of executing the powers of government. That it is a convenient, a useful, and essential instrument in the prosecution of its fiscal operations, is not now a subject of controversy. . . .

But, were its necessity less apparent, none can deny its being an appropriate measure; and if it is, the degree of its necessity, as has been very justly observed, is to be discussed in another place. Should Congress, in the execution of its powers, adopt measures which are prohibited by the constitution; or should Congress, under the pretext of executing its powers, pass laws for the accomplishment of objects not entrusted to the government; it would become the painful duty of this tribunal, should a case requiring such a decision come before it, to say that such an act was not the law of the land. But where the law is not prohibited, and is really calculated to effect any of the objects entrusted to the government, to undertake here to

inquire into the degree of its necessity, would be to pass the line which circumscribes the judicial department, and to tread on legislative ground. This court disclaims all pretensions to such a power.

*   *   *

After the most deliberate consideration, it is the unanimous and decided opinion of this Court, that the act to incorporate the Bank of the United States is a law made in pursuance of the constitution, and is a part of the supreme law of the land.

*   *   *

It being the opinion of the Court, that the act incorporating the bank is constitutional; and that the power of establishing a branch in the State of Maryland might be properly exercised by the bank itself, we proceed to inquire—

. . . Whether the State of Maryland may, without violating the constitution, tax that branch?

That the power of taxation is one of vital importance; that it is retained by the States; that it is not abridged by the grant of a similar power to the government of the Union; that it is to be concurrently exercised by the two governments: are truths which have never been denied. But, such is the paramount character of the constitution, that its capacity to withdraw any subject from the action of even this power, is admitted. The States are expressly forbidden to lay any duties on imports or exports, except what may be absolutely necessary for executing their inspection laws. If the obligation of this prohibition must be conceded—if it may restrain a State from the exercise of its taxing power on imports and exports; the same paramount character would seem to restrain, as it certainly may restrain, a State from such other exercise of this power, as is in its nature incompatible with, and repugnant to, the constitutional laws of the Union. A law, absolutely repugnant to another, as entirely repeals that other as if express terms of repeal were used.

On this ground the counsel for the bank place its claim to be exempted from the power of a State to tax its operations. There is no express provision for the case, but the claim has been sustained on a principle which so entirely pervades the constitution, is so intermixed with the materials which compose it, so interwoven with its web, so blended with its texture, as to be incapable of being separated from it, without rending it into shreds.

This great principle is, that the constitution and the laws made in pursuance thereof are supreme; that they control the constitution and laws of the respective States, and cannot be controlled by them. From this, which may be almost termed an axiom, other propositions are deduced as corollaries, on the truth or error of which, and on their application to this case, the cause has been supposed to depend. These are, 1st. that a power to create implies a power to preserve. 2nd. That a power to destroy, if wielded by a different hand, is hostile to, and incompatible with these powers to create and to preserve. 3d. That where this repugnancy exists, that authority which is supreme must control, not yield to that over which it is supreme.

*   *   *

That the power of taxing [the bank] by the States may be exercised so as to destroy it, is too obvious to be denied. But taxation is said to be an absolute power, which acknowledges no other limits than those expressly prescribed in the constitution, and like sovereign power of every other description, is trusted to the discretion of those who use it. But the very terms of this argument admit that the sovereignty of the State, in the article of taxation itself, is subordinate to, and may be controlled by the constitution of the United States. How far it has been controlled by that instrument must be a question of construction. In making this construction, no principle not declared, can be admissable, which would defeat the legitimate operations of a supreme government. It is of the very essence of supremacy to remove all obstacles to its action within its own sphere, and so to modify every power vested in subordinate governments, as to exempt its own operations from their own influence. This effect need not be stated in terms. It is so involved in the declaration of supremacy, so

necessarily implied in it, that the expression of it could not make it more certain. We must, therefore, keep it in view while construing the constitution.

The argument on the part of the State of Maryland, is, not that the States may directly resist a law of Congress, but that they may exercise their acknowledged powers upon it, and that the constitution leaves them this right in the confidence that they will not abuse it.

*   *   *

The sovereignty of a State extends to every thing which exists by its own authority, or is introduced by its permission; but does it extend to those means which are employed by Congress to carry into execution powers conferred on that body by the people of the United States? We think it demonstrable that it does not. Those powers are not given by the people of a single State. They are given by the people of the United States, to a government whose laws, made in pursuance of the constitution, are declared to be supreme. Consequently, the people of a single State cannot confer a sovereignty which will extend over them.

*   *   *

If we apply the principle for which the State of Maryland contends, to the constitution generally, we shall find it capable of changing totally the character of that instrument. We shall find it capable of arresting all the measures of the government, and of prostrating it at the foot of the States. The American people have declared their constitution, and the laws made in pursuance thereof, to be supreme; but this principle would transfer the supremacy, in fact, to the States.

If the States may tax one instrument, employed by the government in the execution of its powers, they may tax any and every other instrument. They may tax the mail; they may tax the mint; they may tax patent rights; they may tax the papers of the custom-house; they may tax judicial process; they may tax all the means employed by the government, to an excess which would defeat all the ends of government. This was not intended by the

American people. They did not design to make their government dependent on the States.

*   *   *

It has also been insisted, that, as the power of taxation in the general and State governments is acknowledged to be concurrent, every argument which would sustain the right of the general government to tax banks chartered by the States, will equally sustain the right of the States to tax banks chartered by the general government.

But the two cases are not on the same reason. The people of all the States have created the general government, and have conferred upon it the general power of taxation. The people of all the States, and the States themselves, are represented in Congress, and, by their representatives, exercise this power. When they tax the chartered institutions of the States, they tax their constituents; and these taxes must be uniform. But, when a State taxes the operations of the government of the United States, it acts upon institutions created, not by their own constituents, but by people over whom they claim no control. It acts upon the measures of a government created by others as well as themselves, for the benefit of others in common with themselves. The difference is that which always exists, and always must exist, between the action of the whole on a part, and the action of a part on the whole— between the laws of a government declared to be supreme, and those of a government which, when in opposition to those laws, is not supreme.

*   *   *

The Court has bestowed on this subject its most deliberate consideration. The result is a conviction that the States have no power, by taxation or otherwise, to retard, impede, burden, or in any manner control, the operations of the constitutional laws enacted by Congress to carry into execution the powers vested in the general government. This is, we think, the unavoidable consequence of that supremacy which the constitution has declared.

We are unanimously of opinion, that the law passed by the legislature of Maryland, imposing a tax on the Bank of the United States, is unconstitutional and void.

*   *   *

REVIEW QUESTIONS

1. What was Maryland's argument against the Second Bank of the United States?
2. What historical and legal precedents did Marshall, speaking for his court, use to refute that argument?
3. How did Marshall interpret the Constitution so as to bind the states to the general government?
4. Why did Marshall believe that most of the Constitution's framers intended that its provisions be loosely rather than strictly construed?

JOHN QUINCY ADAMS

The End of the "Era of Good Feelings" (1820)

By 1820 many Americans were no longer feeling "good." The flush of nationalistic spirit and enterprise that marked the postwar era was waning under the onslaught of personal and sectional ambition and misfortune. These rising problems were not enough to undermine Monroe's reelection in 1820, but they indicated trouble ahead

*for the coming decade. The Federalist Party was, at least on the national level, virtu-
ally dead, and the old Republican Party was being devoured by partisans within it.
Added to these difficulties was the national bellyache caused by economic woes. Secretary of State Adams, looking perhaps to his own as well as to his country's political
future, fretted over the causes and possible cures.*

From Allan Nevins, ed., *The Diary of John Quincy Adams, 1794–1845* (1928; New York:
Charles Scribner's Sons, 1951), pp. 223–24, 241–42. [Editorial insertions appear in square
brackets—*Ed.*]

*   *   *

Jan. 8, 1820.—One of the most remarkable features
of what I am witnessing every day is a perpetual
struggle in both Houses of Congress to control the
Executive—to make it dependent upon and subservient to them. They are continually attempting
to encroach upon the powers and authorities of the
President. As the old line of demarkation between
parties has been broken down, personal has taken
the place of principled opposition. The personal
friends of the President in the House are neither
so numerous, nor so active, nor so able as his opponents. Crawford's personal friends, instead of
befriending the Administration, operate as powerfully as they can, without exposing or avowing
their motives, against it. Every act and thought of
Crawford looks to the next Presidency. All his
springs of action work not upon the present, but
upon the future, and yet his path in the Department is now beset with thorns, from which he
shrinks, and which I think he will not ward off
with success. In short, as the first Presidential term
of Mr. Monroe's Administration has hitherto been
the period of the greatest national tranquillity enjoyed by this nation at any portion of its history, so
it appears to me scarcely avoidable that the second
term will be among the most stormy and violent. I
told him this day that I thought the difficulties before him were thickening and becoming hourly
more and more formidable. In our foreign relations, we stood upon terms with England as favorable as can ever be expected, but with a state of
things dissatisfactory for the present, and problem-
atical for the future, with regard to our commercial

intercourse with her American Colonies. With
France our situation was much less pleasing and
more unpromising. She is pressing absurd claims,
and refusing satisfaction for the most just and unequivocal claims on our part . . . [.]

A prospect thus dark and unpropitious abroad
is far more gloomy and threatening when we turn
our eyes homeward. The bank, the national currency, the stagnation of commerce, the depression
of manufactures, the restless turbulence and jealousies and insubordination of the State Legislatures, the Missouri slave question, the deficiencies
of the revenue to be supplied, the rankling passions
and ambitious projects of individuals, mingling
with everything, presented a prospect of the future
which I freely acknowledged was to me appalling.
I asked him whether these apprehensions were visionary, and, if not, whether he had contemplated
any distinct system of measures to be in preparation for the embarrassments which it was obvious
to foresee as inevitable at no distant day.

He said that, as to the Missouri question, he apprehended no great danger from that. He believed
a compromise would be found and agreed to,
which would be satisfactory to all parties.

*   *   *

May 17.—Ninian Edwards, the Senator from Illinois, and W. Lowndes, member of the House of
Representatives from South Carolina, called this
morning at my house to take leave. Edwards spoke
of the state of parties and of public affairs. At the
next session, he says, the great struggle will come
on. Edwards is first cousin to the Popes of Kentucky and Illinois, and therefore not in the interest

of Clay, of whom John Pope is the unsuccessful rival in Kentucky. But, as a Western man, Edwards feels himself to be rowing against the general current of Western feeling, and is uneasy under it. He remarks with anxiety the ascendency which Clay has been acquiring during the latter part of the session of Congress, and seems to dread that he will carry all before him. He supposes that he will resign his seat as Speaker, but not as member, of the House; that he will immediately engage extensively in the practice of the law, and will come next winter and attend at the same time the session of the Supreme Court and of Congress.

May 22.—I called upon Mr. Calhoun, and he went with me to Mr. Thomas Law's, in Prince George's County. On the ride we had much conversation upon various topics. I asked him whether he knew what was the occasion of the President's calling the cabinet meeting on Saturday. He said it was a letter that he had received from Mr. Jefferson, in which, though mentioning in terms of high commendation the Florida Treaty, he yet advises that its ratification should not now be accepted, but that we should look to the occupation of Texas. This explains to me what had been utterly unaccountable in the call of that meeting three days after my last note to Vivés and after the receipt of his answer. It reminded me of O'Brien's shrewd remark, that an old sea-captain never likes that his mate should make a better voyage than himself.

We conversed upon politics past, present, and future. Calhoun's anticipations are gloomy. He says there has been within these two years an immense revolution of fortunes in every part of the Union; enormous numbers of persons utterly ruined; multitudes in deep distress; and a general mass of disaffection to the Government, not concentrated in any particular direction, but ready to seize upon any event and looking out anywhere for a leader. The Missouri question and the debates on the tariff were merely incidental to this state of things. It

was a vague but wide-spread discontent, caused by the disordered circumstances of individuals, but resulting in a general impression that there was something radically wrong in the administration of the Government. These observations are undoubtedly well-founded. The disease is apparent, the remedy not discernible. The primary cause is that which has been the scourge of this country from its Colonial infancy—speculations in paper currency, now appearing in the shape of banks; the great multiplication, followed by the sudden and severe reduction, of fictitious capital; then the great falling off in the prices of all our principal articles of exportation, the competition of foreign manufactures carried on by starving workmen, with ours loaded with high wages, the diminution of commerce and the carrying trade, and the accumulation of debt as long as credit could be strained—all this, with ambitious and crafty and disappointed men on the watch for every misfortune and welcoming every disaster, together with the elated hopes, the dazzling promise, and the mortifying reverses of the Florida Treaty, accounts too well for the loss of popularity by the Administration within the last year.

*   *   *

REVIEW QUESTIONS

1. Who or what did Adams blame for undermining the government in general and the administration in particular?
2. Did he differentiate between new problems and older, long-standing ones?
3. Would such a differentiation have any significance for an understanding of change versus continuity in American history?
4. Did Adams provide an objective evaluation? Why or why not?

JAMES MONROE

FROM The *Monroe Doctrine* (1823)

The administration had to deal with increasingly complex foreign as well as domestic relations. In foreign affairs, however, it was particularly successful due to the diplomatic abilities of both president and secretary of state. Both Monroe and Adams were intent on securing the expanded borders of the United States and preserving the trade connections that were essential to economic growth. To accomplish these aims, they had to counter a number of challenges: the insurrections in colonial Spanish America that ended in newly independent Latin American countries desiring recognition from the United States; the possibility of European intervention in Latin America so as to gain or regain economic and territorial control; and the European, specifically Russian and British, claims to territory in North America. Adams opposed recognition of the new Latin American nations because he feared such an act could lead to direct involvement in their conflicts. He wished them well, but he did not want the United States to fight their battles. Monroe, however, wanted to extend recognition to show support for such independence and democratic movements and, more importantly, to forge beneficial economic ties. The two worked through their differences to produce a set of principles that eventually had a great impact on the definition and implementation of American foreign policy. Monroe presented the principles in his annual message to Congress in December 1823, which explains why they came to be known as the Monroe Doctrine, *but they were primarily the creation of Adams.*

From James D. Richardson, comp., *A Compilation of the Messages and Papers of the Presidents, 1789–1902*, vol. II (Bureau of National Literature and Art, 1904), pp. 207–20.

Seventh Annual Message

WASHINGTON, *December 2, 1823*
*Fellow-Citizens of the Senate and
House of Representatives:*

Many important subjects will claim your attention during the present session, of which I shall endeavor to give, in aid of your deliberations, a just idea in this communication. I undertake this duty with diffidence, from the vast extent of the interests on which I have to treat and of their great importance to every portion of our Union. I enter on it with zeal from a thorough conviction that there never was a period since the establishment of our Revolution when, regarding the condition of the civilized world and its bearing on us, there was

greater necessity for devotion in the public servants to their respective duties, or for virtue, patriotism, and union in our constituents.

Meeting in you a new Congress, I deem it proper to present this view of public affairs in greater detail than might otherwise be necessary. I do it, however, with peculiar satisfaction, from a knowledge that in this respect I shall comply more fully with the sound principles of our Government. The people being with us exclusively the sovereign, it is indispensable that full information be laid before them on all important subjects, to enable them to exercise that high power with complete effect. If kept in the dark, they must be incompetent to it. . . . Their interests in all vital questions are the same, and the bond, by sentiment as well as by interest, will be proportionably strengthened as they are better informed of the real state of public affairs, especially in difficult conjunctures. It is by such knowledge that local prejudices and jealousies are surmounted, and that a national policy, extending its fostering care and protection to all the great interests of our Union, is formed and steadily adhered to.

A precise knowledge of our relations with foreign powers as respects our negotiations and transactions with each is thought to be particularly necessary. Equally necessary is it that we should form a just estimate of our resources, revenue, and progress in every kind of improvement connected with the national prosperity and public defense. It is by rendering justice to other nations that we may expect it from them. It is by our ability to resent injuries and redress wrongs that we may avoid them.

The commissioners under the fifth article of the treaty of Ghent, having disagreed in their opinions respecting that portion of the boundary between the Territories of the United States and of Great Britain the establishment of which had been submitted to them, have made their respective reports in compliance with that article, that the same might be referred to the decision of a friendly power. It being manifest, however, that it would be difficult, if not impossible, for any power to perform that office without great delay and much inconvenience to itself, a proposal has been made by this Government, and acceded to by that of Great Britain, to endeavor to establish that boundary by amicable negotiation. It appearing from long experience that no satisfactory arrangement could be formed of the commercial intercourse between the United States and the British colonies in this hemisphere by legislative acts while each party pursued its own course without agreement or concert with the other, a proposal has been made to the British Government to regulate this commerce by treaty, as it has been to arrange in like manner the just claim of the citizens of the United States inhabiting the States and Territories bordering on the lakes and rivers which empty into the St. Lawrence to the navigation of that river to the ocean. For these and other objects of high importance to the interests of both parties a negotiation has been opened with the British Government which it is hoped will have a satisfactory result.

*　　*　　*

At the proposal of the Russian Imperial Government, made through the minister of the Emperor residing here, a full power and instructions have been transmitted to the minister of the United States at St. Petersburg to arrange by amicable negotiation the respective rights and interests of the two nations on the northwest coast of this continent. A similar proposal had been made by His Imperial Majesty to the Government of Great Britain, which has likewise been acceded to. The Government of the United States has been desirous by this friendly proceeding of manifesting the great value which they have invariably attached to the friendship of the Emperor and their solicitude to cultivate the best understanding with his Government. In the discussions to which this interest has given rise and in the arrangements by which they may terminate the occasion has been judged proper for asserting, as a principle in which the rights and interests of the United States are involved, that the American continents, by the free and independent condition which they have assumed and maintain, are henceforth not to be considered as subjects for future colonization by any European powers.

*　　*　　*

In compliance with a resolution of the House of Representatives adopted at their last session, instructions have been given to all the ministers of the United States accredited to the powers of Europe and America to propose the proscription of the African slave trade by classing it under the denomination, and inflicting on its perpetrators the punishment, of piracy. Should this proposal be acceded to, it is not doubted that this odious and criminal practice will be promptly and entirely suppressed. It is earnestly hoped that it will be acceded to, from the firm belief that it is the most effectual expedient that can be adopted for the purpose.

At the commencement of the recent war between France and Spain it was declared by the French Government that it would grant no commissions to privateers, and that neither the commerce of Spain herself nor of neutral nations should be molested by the naval force of France, except in the breach of a lawful blockade. This declaration, which appears to have been faithfully carried into effect, concurring with principles proclaimed and cherished by the United States from the first establishment of their independence, suggested the hope that the time had arrived when the proposal for adopting it as a permanent and invariable rule in all future maritime wars might meet the favorable consideration of the great European powers. Instructions have accordingly been given to our ministers with France, Russia, and Great Britain to make those proposals to their respective Governments, and when the friends of humanity reflect on the essential amelioration to the condition of the human race which would result from the abolition of private war on the sea and on the great facility by which it might be accomplished, requiring only the consent of a few sovereigns, an earnest hope is indulged that these overtures will meet with an attention animated by the spirit in which they were made, and that they will ultimately be successful.

*   *   *

The state of the Army in its organization and discipline has been gradually improving for several years, and has now attained a high degree of perfection. The military disbursements have been regularly made and the accounts regularly and promptly rendered for settlement. The supplies of various descriptions have been of good quality, and regularly issued at all of the posts. A system of economy and accountability has been introduced into every branch of the service which admits of little additional improvement. This desirable state has been attained by the act reorganizing the staff of the Army, passed on the 14th of April, 1818.

*   *   *

I transmit a return of the militia of the several States according to the last reports which have been made by the proper officers in each to the Department of War. By reference to this return it will be seen that it is not complete, although great exertions have been made to make it so. As the defense and even the liberties of the country must depend in times of imminent danger on the militia, it is of the highest importance that it be well organized, armed, and disciplined throughout the Union. . . .

*   *   *

The usual orders have been given to all our public ships to seize American vessels engaged in the slave trade and bring them in for adjudication, and I have the gratification to state that not one so employed has been discovered, and there is good reason to believe that our flag is now seldom, if at all, disgraced by that traffic.

It is a source of great satisfaction that we are always enabled to recur to the conduct of our Navy with pride and commendation. As a means of national defense it enjoys the public confidence, and is steadily assuming additional importance. It is submitted whether a more efficient and equally economical organization of it might not in several respects be effected. It is supposed that higher grades than now exist by law would be useful. They would afford well-merited rewards to those who have long and faithfully served their country, present the best incentives to good conduct, and the best means of insuring a proper discipline; destroy the inequality in that respect between military and naval services, and relieve our officers from many inconveniences and mortifications which occur when our vessels meet those of other nations, ours being the only service in which such grades do not exist.

*   *   *

Having communicated my views to Congress at the commencement of the last session respecting the encouragement which ought to be given to our manufactures and the principle on which it should be founded, I have only to add that those views remain unchanged, and that the present state of those countries with which we have the most immediate political relations and greatest commercial intercourse tends to confirm them. Under this impression I recommend a review of the tariff for the purpose of affording such additional protection to those articles which we are prepared to manufacture, or which are more immediately connected with the defense and independence of the country.

*   *   *

The sum which was appropriated at the last session for the repairs of the Cumberland road has been applied with good effect to that object. . . .

Many patriotic and enlightened citizens who have made the subject an object of particular investigation have suggested an improvement of still greater importance. They are of opinion that the waters of the Chesapeake and Ohio may be connected together by one continued canal, and at an expense far short of the value and importance of the object to be obtained. If this could be accomplished it is impossible to calculate the beneficial consequences which would result from it. A great portion of the produce of the very fertile country through which it would pass would find a market through that channel. Troops might be moved with great facility in war, with cannon and every kind of munition, and in either direction. Connecting the Atlantic with the Western country in a line passing through the seat of the National Government, it would contribute essentially to strengthen the bond of union itself. Believing as I do that Congress possess the right to appropriate money for such a national object (the jurisdiction remaining to the States through which the canal would pass), I submit it to your consideration whether it may not be advisable to authorize by an adequate appropriation the employment of a suitable number of the officers of the Corps of Engineers to examine the unexplored ground during the next season and to report their opinion thereon. It will likewise be proper to extend their examination to the several routes through which the waters of the Ohio may be connected by canals with those of Lake Erie.

As the Cumberland road will require annual repairs, and Congress have not thought it expedient to recommend to the States an amendment to the Constitution for the purpose of vesting in the United States a power to adopt and execute a system of internal improvement, it is also submitted to your consideration whether it may not be expedient to authorize the Executive to enter into an arrangement with the several States through which the road passes to establish tolls, each within its limits, for the purpose of defraying the expense of future repairs and of providing also by suitable penalties for its protection against future injuries.

*   *   *

It was stated at the commencement of the last session that a great effort was then making in Spain and Portugal to improve the condition of the people of those countries, and that it appeared to be conducted with extraordinary moderation. It need scarcely be remarked that the result has been so far very different from what was then anticipated. Of events in that quarter of the globe, with which we have so much intercourse and from which we derive our origin, we have always been anxious and interested spectators. The citizens of the United States cherish sentiments the most friendly in favor of the liberty and happiness of their fellow-men on that side of the Atlantic. In the wars of the European powers in matters relating to themselves we have never taken any part, nor does it comport with our policy so to do. It is only when our rights are invaded or seriously menaced that we resent injuries or make preparation for our defense. With the movements in this hemisphere we are of necessity more immediately connected, and by causes which must be obvious to all enlightened and impartial observers. The political system of the allied powers is essentially different in this respect from that of America. This difference proceeds from that which exists in their respective Governments; and to the defense of our own, which has been achieved by the loss of so much blood and treasure, and matured by the wisdom of their most enlightened citizens, and under which we have enjoyed unexampled felicity, this whole nation is devoted. We owe it, therefore, to candor and to the amicable relations existing between the United States and those powers to declare that we should consider any attempt on their part to extend their system to any portion of this hemisphere as dangerous to our peace and safety. With the existing colonies or dependencies of any European power we have not interfered and shall not interfere. But with the Governments who have declared their independence and maintained it, and whose independence we have, on great consideration and on just principles, acknowledged, we could not view any interposition for the purpose of oppressing them, or controlling in any other manner their destiny, by any European power in any other light than as the manifestation of an unfriendly disposition toward the United States. In the war between those new Governments and Spain we declared our neutrality at the time of their recognition, and to this we have adhered, and shall continue to adhere, provided no change shall occur which, in the judgment of the competent authorities of this Government, shall make a corresponding change on the part of the United States indispensable to their security.

The late events in Spain and Portugal shew that Europe is still unsettled. Of this important fact no stronger proof can be adduced than that the allied powers should have thought it proper, on any principle satisfactory to themselves, to have interposed by force in the internal concerns of Spain. To what extent such interposition may be carried, on the same principle, is a question in which all independent powers whose governments differ from theirs are interested, even those most remote, and surely none more so than the United States. Our policy in regard to Europe, which was adopted at an early stage of the wars which have so long agitated that quarter of the globe, nevertheless remains the same, which is, not to interfere in the internal concerns of any of its powers; to consider the government *de facto* as the legitimate government for us; to cultivate friendly relations with it, and to preserve those relations by a frank, firm, and manly policy, meeting in all instances the just claims of every power, submitting to injuries from none. But in regard to those continents circum-

stances are eminently and conspicuously different. It is impossible that the allied powers should extend their political system to any portion of either continent without endangering our peace and happiness; nor can anyone believe that our southern brethren, if left to themselves, would adopt it of their own accord. It is equally impossible, therefore, that we should behold such interposition in any form with indifference. If we look to the comparative strength and resources of Spain and those new Governments, and their distance from each other, it must be obvious that she can never subdue them. It is still the true policy of the United States to leave the parties to themselves, in the hope that other powers will pursue the same course.

If we compare the present condition of our Union with its actual state at the close of our Revolution, the history of the world furnishes no example of a progress in improvement in all the important circumstances which constitute the happiness of a nation which bears any resemblance to it. At the first epoch our population did not exceed 3,000,000. By the last census it amounted to about 10,000,000, and, what is more extraordinary, it is almost altogether native, for the immigration from other countries has been inconsiderable. At the first epoch half the territory within our acknowledged limits was uninhabited and a wilderness. Since then new territory has been acquired of vast extent, comprising within it many rivers, particularly the Mississippi, the navigation of which to the ocean was of the highest importance to the original States. Over this territory our population has expanded in every direction, and new States have been established almost equal in number to those which formed the first bond of our Union. This expansion of our population and accession of new States to our Union have had the happiest effect on all its highest interests. That it has eminently augmented our resources and added to our strength and respectability as a power is admitted by all. But it is not in these important circumstances only that this happy effect is felt. It is manifest that by enlarging the basis of our system and increasing the number of States the system itself has been greatly strengthened in both its branches. Consolidation and disunion have thereby been rendered equally impracticable. Each Government, confiding in its own strength, has less to apprehend from the other, and in consequence each, enjoying a greater freedom of action, is rendered more efficient for all the purposes for which it was instituted. It is unnecessary to treat here of the vast improvement made in the system itself by the adoption of this Constitution and of its happy effect in elevating the character and in protecting the rights of the nation as well as of individuals. To what, then, do we owe these blessings? It is known to all that we derive them from the excellence of our institutions. Ought we not, then, to adopt every measure which may be necessary to perpetuate them?

REVIEW QUESTIONS

1. How was Monroe's message both a plea and a program for national integrity?
2. What foreign policy principles did he present that succeeding generations have lumped together as the *Monroe Doctrine*?
3. How did he justify these principles? How did he propose to enforce them?
4. What were some of the other foreign and domestic issues that he deemed important?

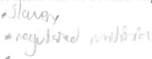

HENRY CLAY

On the Election, the Court, and Improvements (1823)

President Monroe may have been elected without opposition in 1820, but a number of individuals immediately began planning and politicking for the presidential election of 1824. One of those was Congressman Henry Clay from Kentucky. Clay was Speaker of the House in 1823, but he wanted to move into the executive branch. He thought that he had a solid shot at the presidency when the competition consisted of John Quincy Adams, Secretary of the Treasury William Crawford, and Secretary of War John C. Calhoun. Then General Andrew Jackson entered the fray and changed the dynamics of the contest. Even before Jackson officially entered the race, Clay realized that his interpretation of the Constitution *and national power, especially in his advocacy of certain programs, might alienate some voters.*

From James F. Hopkins, ed., *The Papers of Henry Clay*, vol. 3 (Lexington: University of Kentucky Press, 1963), pp. 477–81. [Editorial insertions appear in square brackets—*Ed.*]

To Francis T. Brooke

Lexington 28h. August 1823.

I received, my dear Sir, your very obliging letter of the 14h instant, and I pray you to believe that I do not place less value on your friendship because you have nothing to communicate "more favorable to my prospects." On the subject to which you allude I assure you most sincerely, I look with great calmness, and with a most perfect determination to acquiesce chearfully in whatever choice the Nation may make. It would be a poor compliment to our institutions to say that their solidity, or the public happiness, materially depended upon any selection that shall take place. I really think however that Virginia cannot justify herself to the Union for the apathy which you say prevails there on the question. Judging as I have done, at this distance, from the Enquirer [Richmond newspaper] and other Virginia prints I had supposed that great interest was felt and generally taken in its decision; and that there was even danger of her overstepping the line of cautious circumspection which her leading politicians were understood to have marked out for her.

This indifference, you say, arises from the absence of any pledge that the great interests of the people of Virginia will be taken care of by any of the competitors for the Chief Magistracy. If indeed no such pledge is to be found in the principles, integrity & character, as heretofore developed, of either of the Candidates, it is, I should think, quite too late in the day now for any pledge to be given or received. But, my dear Sir, what interests have Virginia and the South separate from the Union? You have mentioned a single subject only, that of the encroachments of the Federal Judiciary on State rights; and, as connected with this, the "broad doctrine now inculcated that Congress has the right to extend[,] not to regulate only[,] the jurisdiction of the Federal Courts." On that subject I am entirely at a loss to conceive any peculiar interest in the State of Virginia and the Southern States. All are equally concerned in the preservation of the State Sovereignties. All would be equally affected by Foederal usurpation. But I must confess that it

is the first time that I ever heard asserted such a doctrine as you say is now inculcated. The limit of the Federal Judiciary is to be found in the Constitution, and Congress can vest in it no power which is not there found. If such a doctrine as you state is really attempted to be inculcated you will find Kentucky now, as in the epoch of 1799, in spite of all your unkindness towards her, ready to co operate with you in opposing it. And no man in the Union will be more prompt than I shall be to second the opposition. I cannot suppose you to refer to the power which is claimed for the General Government to give effect to its laws through its own judiciary. For without that power; without Federal means to effectuate the constitutional resolves of the Federal will, there is an end to the General Government; there is inevitable if not instantaneous anarchy.

But, my dear Sir, on this subject of the Federal Judiciary and State rights I mean to say a few words to you, in the spirit of Virginia Independence, and in the frankness of sincere friendship. Has not Virginia exposed herself to the imputation of selfishness by the course of her conduct, or of that of many of her politicians? When, in the case of Cohens and Virginia, her authority was alone concerned, she made the most strenuous efforts against the exercise of power by the Supreme Court. But when the thunders of that Court were directed against poor Kentucky, in vain did she invoke Virginian aid. [Clay was probably referring to *Green v. Biddle* (1823), in which the Supreme Court declared unconstitutional Kentucky statutes on the disposition of land titles claimed by Kentucky settlers versus Virginia landowners (who had claimed the land before Kentucky separated from Virginia).] The Supreme Court it was imagined would decide on the side of supposed interests of Virginia. It has so decided; and, in effect, cripples the Sovereign power of the State of Kentucky noore [*sic*] than any other measure ever affected the Independence of any state in this Union, and not a Virginia voice is heard against the decision. The Supreme Court is viewed with complacency, and as a very different sort of tribunal, from that Supreme Court which decided Cohens s case. Again. Of all the irregular bodies none can be more so than a Congressional Caucus at Washington. None have a more consolodating tendency. Indeed it is espoused upon the principle of preventing the exercise of State or Federal rights through the medium of the H. of R. Yet the Virginia politicians (at least if we are to judge from the papers) warmly advocate the constitution of such a Caucus. Will it not be said that they are influenced by the consideration, not of preserving unimpaired State rights, but of giving to the State power of *Virginia* the utmost effect of which it is susceptible? Or that of securing the election of the alleged favorite of Virginia who, without the instrumentality of such an assemblage, is in danger of losing the election? [William H. Crawford] It is in vain to speak of the inconveniencies of a warmly contested election. They are incident to our system; and are happily provided for by it. And the transitions from a Congressional Caucus, to a Prætorian Cohort or Hereditary Monarchy, to escape from those vexations, are not so great as we might at first imagine.

I am aware that on two subjects I have the misfortune to differ with many of my Virginia friends—Internal Improvements and Home Manufactures. My opinion has been formed after much deliberation, and my best judgment yet tells me that I am right. I have not time nor would it be fitting as regards your comfort now to discuss the policy or the power of fostering those interests. I believe Virginia & the Southern States as much interested, directly or indirectly, as any other parts of the Union, in their encouragement. When this Government was first adopted, we had no interior. Our population was inclosed between the Sea and the Mountains which run parallel to it. Since then the West part of your State, the Western parts of N. York & Pennsa. & all the Western States have been settled. The Wars of Europe & the emigrants to the West consumed all the surplus produced on both sides of the Mountains. Those Wars have terminated; and emigration has ceased. We find ourselves annually in the possession of an immense surplus. There is no market for it abroad; there is none at home. If there were a foreign market, before we, in the interior, could reach it, the inter-

vening population would have supplied it. There can be no Foreign market adequate to the consumption of the vast & growing surplus of the produce of our Agriculture. We must then have a Home market. Some of us must cultivate; some fabricate. And we must have reasonable protection against the machinations of Foreign powers. On the Sea board you want a navy, fortifications, protection, foreign commerce. In the Interior we want Internal Improvements, Home Manufactures. You have what you want, and object to our getting what we want. Should not the interests of both parties be provided for?

It has appeared to me, in the administration of the General Government, to be a just principle, to enquire what great interests belong to each section of our Country, and to promote those interests as far as practicable consistently with the Constitution, having always an eye to the welfare of the whole. Assuming this principle, does any one doubt that if N. York, N. Jersey, Pennsa. Delaware Maryland & the Western States constituted an Independent Nation, it would immediately protect the two important interests in question? And is it not to be feared that, if protection is not to be found to vital interests, from the existing system, in great parts of the Confederacy, those parts will ultimately seek to establish a system that will afford the requisite protection? I would not, in the application of the principle indicated, give to the peculiar interests of great sections *all* the protection which they would probably receive if those sections constituted separate & independent States. I would however extend some protection & measure it by balancing the countervailing interests, if there be such, in other quarters of the Union.

I concur entirely with you in thinking that the North & East, but particularly New England, have laid in a great measure, the other parts of the Union under contribution. And of all the ill advised measures; of all the wasteful expenditures of public money, the Revolutionary pension list preeminently takes the lead. Never was there more public money spent with less practical benefit. But who proposed it? Your own Monroe [after Monroe pointed out that needy veterans of the Revolutionary war were not eligible for federal pensions, Congress enacted the pension law of 18 March 1818.]. I thought of it then as I think of it now; but opposition would have been silly & vain.

You will oppose my election I suppose in Virginia. I have no right to complain. Silence & Submission are my duty. You will oppose me because I think that the interests of all parts of the Union should be taken care of; in other words, that the interests of the Interior, on the two subjects mentioned, as well as those of the Maritime coast ought to be provided for. You will give your suffrages to Mr. Crawford or to Mr. Adams; and if Mr. Crawford or Mr. Adams be elected I venture to predict that we shall find either in his inaugural speech, or in his first message or speech (perhaps the latter mode of communication may be revived) to Congress, a recommendation of efficient encouragement to Domestic Manufactures & Internal improvements.

I am afraid that you will think me in a very bad humor. Far from it. I repeat, that I never enjoyed more perfect composure. My health, it is true, is extremely bad; and I am now confined at home by the endeavor to re establish it. But it neither affects my tranquillity nor gives me the spleen. In regard to the election, as to which I will make no professions of apathy or indifference, which I do not feel, my friends continue to be very confident; and my own opinion is that my prospects are not surpassed by those of either of the other gentlemen. Still I am not unaware that all things are uncertain. And I therefore continue resolved to preserve my philosophy, my principles & my conscience, be the event what it may.

*   *   *

REVIEW QUESTIONS

1. What part did Clay think state or regional interests should play in the presidential election?
2. Why did he criticize Virginia's interpretations and actions in regards to the powers of the federal judiciary?
3. Why did he criticize attempts to reinstitute a congressional caucus for the nomination of presidential candidates?
4. Why did he want the national government to take an active role in promoting internal improvements? How, according to Clay, would such action affect national and state interests?

11 ‍ THE JACKSONIAN IMPULSE

Tennessee militia soldiers, inspired by his toughness, had nicknamed Andrew Jackson "Old Hickory" during the War of 1812. Since that time, less inspired than aggravated, his political opponents called him quite a number of other names. Jackson probably deserved all of the monikers, good and bad, for he was a complex man whose personal and professional decisions produced conflicting reactions during his lifetime and thereafter. Although negative evaluations mounted in the late-twentieth century, Jackson was a hero to most of his contemporaries. He seemed to embody the image many Americans had, or wanted to have, of themselves. They embraced the image of the frontiersman, someone they saw as self-reliant, someone whose character was based in action not intellect: someone who used might to make right and who knew instinctively what right was. These Americans applauded him as a self-made man: he was an example to their sons that in America any boy through self determination, direction, and diligence could indeed become powerful. Jackson's opponents, however, pointed out that his conduct also demonstrated how action without full reflection could have negative repercussions. To them, his decisions showed why there had to be checks on the delegation and execution of power.

Jackson, over time, has come to epitomize the myth and reality of a new era in American democracy. The Jacksonian Age was a time when many Americans came to define democracy more inclusively and equality more broadly than the founders had. They accepted and celebrated greater participation by white men, no matter what their economic and social rank, in the political life of the nation. Yet in doing so, showing the complexity and contradictory nature of this age, they also expounded more fully on the ethnic and gendered limits to American democracy, equality, and opportunity. Some Americans did protest those restrictions, and would continue to protest them using the language of Revolutionary America and building upon the broader interpretations of Jacksonian America. During this period, women's suffrage and the abolition of slavery did not yet engage the nation's attention as they would later, but the issue of Native American rights and property certainly did.

Another issue of increasing concern was that of the allocation and exercise of power between national and state governments. This was a problem that was almost as old as the republic, but old compromises were fraying and new ones increasingly difficult to forge. In this new era of the common man there was no question of sovereignty remaining in the people, but there were many heated debates over which government—state or national—best protected that common man's rights and interests. When national and state legislation came into conflict, which one did citizens ultimately want to have precedence? Did they want the one that confirmed rule by the majority, or did they want those that protected minorities (state contingents) to have the power to check a possible tyranny by the majority? Some believed that the primacy of the national government had already been spelled out in the Constitution *and confirmed by Supreme Court decisions; others believed that the state governments, which were more closely tied to the people, better represented citizens' interests, and increasingly challenged the former.*

Jackson initially straddled the debate, but when put to the test during the nullification controversy, he came down firmly for the supremacy of the national government. Yet as a believer and practitioner in self-reliance, he also seemed to believe that the nation should not do what the state could do, nor should the state do what the individual could do. This showed in his constitutional scruples about national power in terms of internal improvements. As did Madison and Monroe before him, Jackson opposed federal support for local projects. Even so, Jackson was not a states-rights proponent; he only supported issues if they fit within his concept of national interests.

As a general and then as president, Jackson's duty was to execute national policy. In pursuing that end—ensuring the security and developing the strength of the country—Jackson assumed and exercised ever greater power, which sometimes got him into trouble. When he was a general, politicians accused him of exceeding his orders and delegated authority; and during his presidency, political opponents accused him of exceeding his constitutional authority. Operating within a rather expansive interpretation of executive limits, Jackson strengthened the power of the presidency through his use of appointments and the veto. While willing to work with the legislative branch, he refused to be ruled by it, just as he refused to allow the Supreme Court or the state governments to have the last say in national affairs. He believed that he knew what was best for the country and acted upon that belief. His popularity with the voters suggests that they agreed with him.

DANIEL WEBSTER

FROM Second Speech on Foot's Resolution (1830)

In the on-going tug of war between states and nation, the conflict over the 1828 tariff led to what has been called the nullification controversy. South Carolina was suffering from an agricultural depression when Congress passed what the state's citizens called the Tariff of Abominations. They believed that the tariff protected northern manufacturing at their expense. The tariff was another nail in the coffin of John Quincy Adams's presidency, a nail perhaps placed by John C. Calhoun of South Carolina, Adams's defecting vice president and Jackson's vice presidential candidate, who wrote, but published anonymously, the South Carolina Exposition and Protest. *Calhoun presented both the theory that the states could nullify national legislation they deemed unconstitutional as well as a procedure for such nullification. South Carolina did not immediately engage in this process, for with the election of Jackson and Calhoun, there was a pause in the action as the state waited for a new tariff policy to be drawn up by the incoming administration. Action on the tariff did not resume with the executive, however; it came in the legislature in January 1830. Senator Samuel A. Foot of Connecticut proposed a resolution to restrict the sale of public land in the West. After Thomas Hart Benton of Missouri denounced it as an attack on the West, Robert Y. Hayne of South Carolina stepped into the fray. He hoped that southern advocacy of a policy of cheap lands in the West would result in western support for the lower tariffs sought by the South. This sectional debate over land policy expanded quickly into one on national power as Hayne had to shift from promoting sectional interests to defending states' rights and the doctrine of nullification against the attacks of Daniel Webster of Massachusetts. Webster, a renowned orator and lawyer, had turned the tables on Hayne by moving from a defense of the East's motives to an offense against those who would put state or sectional interests above the national good. He resumed his argument on 26 January.*

From Daniel Webster, *The Writings and Speeches of Daniel Webster*, vol. VI (Boston: Little, Brown, & Co., 1903), pp. 50–51, 53–57, 60–69, 71–75. [Editorial insertions appear in square brackets—*Ed.*]

*   *   *

There yet remains to be performed, Mr. President, by far the most grave and important duty, which I feel to be devolved on me by this occasion. It is to state, and to defend, what I conceive to be the true principles of the Constitution under which we are here assembled. . . .

I understand the honorable gentleman from South Carolina to maintain, that it is a right of the State legislatures to interfere, whenever, in their judgment, this government transcends its constitutional limits, and to arrest the operation of its laws.

I understand him to maintain this right, as a right existing *under* the Constitution, not as a right to overthrow it on the ground of extreme necessity, such as would justify violent revolution.

I understand him to maintain an authority, on the part of the States, thus to interfere, for the purpose of correcting the exercise of power by the general government, of checking it, and of compelling it to conform to their opinion of the extent of its powers.

I understand him to maintain, that the ultimate power of judging of the constitutional extent of its own authority is not lodged exclusively in the general government, or any branch of it; but that, on the contrary, the States may lawfully decide for themselves, and each State for itself, whether, in a given case, the act of the general government transcends its power.

I understand him to insist, that, if the exigency of the case, in the opinion of any State government, require it, such State government may, by its own sovereign authority, annul an act of the general government which it deems plainly and palpably unconstitutional.

This is the sum of what I understand from him to be the South Carolina doctrine, and the doctrine which he maintains. I propose to consider it, and compare it with the Constitution. . . .

*   *   *

. . . I say, the right of a State to annul a law of Congress cannot be maintained, but on the ground of the inalienable right of man to resist oppression; that is to say, upon the ground of revolution. I admit that there is an ultimate violent remedy, above the Constitution and in defiance of the Constitution, which may be resorted to when a revolution is to be justified. But I do not admit, that, under the Constitution and in conformity with it, there is any mode in which a State government, as a member of the Union, can interfere and stop the progress of the general government, by force of her own laws, under any circumstances whatever.

*   *   *

There are other proceedings of public bodies which have already been alluded to, and to which I refer again, for the purpose of ascertaining more fully what is the length and breadth of that doctrine, denominated the Carolina doctrine, which the honorable member has now stood up on this floor to maintain. In one of them I find it resolved, that "the tariff of 1828, and every other tariff designed to promote one branch of industry at the expense of others, is contrary to the meaning and intention of the federal compact; and such a dangerous, palpable, and deliberate usurpation of power, by a determined majority, wielding the general government beyond the limits of its delegated powers, as calls upon the States which compose the suffering minority, in their sovereign capacity, to exercise the powers which, as sovereigns, necessarily devolve upon them, when their compact is violated."

Observe, Sir, that this resolution holds the tariff of 1828, and every other tariff designed to promote one branch of industry at the expense of another, to be such a dangerous, palpable, and deliberate usurpation of power, as calls upon the States, in their sovereign capacity, to interfere by their own authority. This denunciation, Mr. President, you will please to observe, includes our old tariff of 1816, as well as all others; because that was established to promote the interest of the manufacturers of cotton, to the manifest and admitted injury of the Calcutta cotton trade. . . . It so happens that, at the very moment when South Carolina resolves that the tariff laws are unconstitutional, Pennsylvania and Kentucky resolve exactly the reverse. *They* hold those laws to be both highly proper and strictly constitutional. And now, Sir, how does the honorable member propose to deal with this case? How does he relieve us from this difficulty, upon any principle of his? His construction gets us into it; how does he propose to get us out?

In Carolina, the tariff is a palpable, deliberate usurpation; Carolina, therefore, may nullify it, and refuse to pay the duties. In Pennsylvania, it is both clearly constitutional and highly expedient; and there the duties are to be paid. And yet we live under a government of uniform laws, and under a Constitution too, which contains an express provision, as it happens, that all duties shall be equal in all the States. Does not this approach absurdity?

If there be no power to settle such questions, independent of either of the States, is not the whole Union a rope of sand? Are we not thrown back again, precisely, upon the old Confederation?

It is too plain to be argued. Four-and-twenty interpreters of constitutional law, each with a power to decide for itself, and none with authority to bind any body else, and this constitutional law the only bond of their union! What is such a state of things but a mere connection during pleasure, or, to use the phraseology of the times, *during feeling*? And that feeling, too, not the feeling of the people, who established the Constitution, but the feeling of the State governments.

In another of the South Carolina addresses, . . . an attitude of open resistance to the laws of the Union is advised. Open resistance to the laws, then, is the constitutional remedy, the conservative power of the State, which the South Carolina doctrines teach for the redress of political evils, real or imaginary. And its authors further say, that, appealing with confidence to the Constitution itself, to justify their opinions, they cannot consent to try their accuracy by the courts of justice. In one sense, indeed, Sir, this is assuming an attitude of open resistance in favor of liberty. But what sort of liberty? The liberty of establishing their own opinions, in defiance of the opinions of all others; the liberty of judging and of deciding exclusively themselves, in a matter in which others have as much right to judge and decide as they; the liberty of placing their own opinions above the judgment of all others, above the laws, and above the Constitution. This is their liberty, and this is the fair result of the proposition contended for by the honorable gentleman. Or, it may be more properly said, it is identical with it, rather than a result from it.

*   *   *

No doubt, Sir, a great majority of the people of New England conscientiously believed the embargo law of 1807 unconstitutional; as conscientiously, certainly, as the people of South Carolina hold that opinion of the tariff. They reasoned thus: Congress has power to regulate commerce; but here is a law, they said, stopping all commerce, and stopping it indefinitely. The law is perpetual; that is, it is not limited in point of time, and must of course continue until it shall be repealed by some other law. It is as perpetual, therefore, as the law against treason or murder. Now, is this regulating commerce, or destroying it? Is it guiding, controlling, giving the rule to commerce, as a subsisting thing, or is it putting an end to it altogether? Nothing is more certain, than that a majority in New England deemed this law a violation of the Constitution. The very case required by the gentleman to justify State interference had then arisen. Massachusetts believed this law to be "a deliberate, palpable, and dangerous exercise of a power not granted by the Constitution." Deliberate it was, for it was long continued; palpable she thought it, as no words in the Constitution gave the power, and only a construction, in her opinion most violent, raised it; dangerous it was, since it threatened utter ruin to her most important interests. Here, then, was a Carolina case. How did Massachusetts deal with it? . . . Sir, she remonstrated, she memorialized, she addressed herself to the general government, not exactly "with the concentrated energy of passion," but with her own strong sense, and the energy of sober conviction. But she did not interpose the arm of her own power to arrest the law, and break the embargo. Far from it. Her principles bound her to two things; and she followed her principles, lead where they might. First, to submit to every constitutional law of Congress, and secondly, if the constitutional validity of the law be doubted, to refer that question to the decision of the proper tribunals. The first principle is vain and ineffectual without the second. A majority of us in New England believed the embargo law unconstitutional; but the great question was, and always will be in such cases, Who is to decide this? Who is to judge between the people and the government? And, Sir, it is quite plain, that the Constitution of the United States confers on the government itself, to be exercised by its appropriate department, and under its own responsibility to the people, this power of deciding ultimately and conclusively upon the just extent of its own authority. If this had not been done, we should not have advanced a single step beyond the old Confederation.

*   *   *

Mr. [Samuel] Dexter, . . . argued the New England cause. He put into his effort his whole heart, as well as all the powers of his understanding; for he had avowed, in the most public manner, his entire concurrence with his neighbors on the point in dispute. He argued the cause; it was lost, and New England submitted. The established tribunals pronounced the law constitutional, and New England acquiesced. Now, Sir, is not this the exact opposite of the doctrine of the gentleman from South Carolina? According to him, instead of referring to the judicial tribunals, we should have broken up the embargo by laws of our own; we should have repealed it, *quoad* New England; for we had a strong, palpable, and oppressive case. Sir, we believed the embargo unconstitutional; but still that was matter of opinion, and who was to decide it? We thought it a clear case; but, nevertheless, we did not take the law into our own hands, because we did not wish to bring about a revolution, nor to break up the Union; for I maintain, that between submission to the decision of the constituted tribunals, and revolution, or disunion, there is no middle ground; there is no ambiguous condition, half allegiance and half rebellion. . . .

Sir, the human mind is so constituted, that the merits of both sides of a controversy appear very clear, and very palpable, to those who respectively espouse them; and both sides usually grow clearer as the controversy advances. South Carolina sees unconstitutionality in the tariff; she sees oppression there also, and she sees danger. Pennsylvania, with a vision not less sharp, looks at the same tariff, and sees no such thing in it; she sees it all constitutional, all useful, all safe. The faith of South Carolina is strengthened by opposition, and she now not only sees, but *resolves*, that the tariff is palpably unconstitutional, oppressive, and dangerous; but Pennsylvania, not to be behind her neighbors, and equally willing to strengthen her own faith by a confident asseveration, *resolves*, also, and gives to every warm affirmative of South Carolina, a plain, downright, Pennsylvania negative. South Carolina, to show the strength and unity of her opinion,

brings her assembly to a unanimity, within seven voices; Pennsylvania, not to be outdone in this respect any more than in others, reduces her dissentient fraction to a single vote. Now, Sir, again, I ask the gentleman, What is to be done? . . . I was forcibly struck, Sir, with one reflection, as the gentleman went on in his speech. He quoted Mr. Madison's resolutions, to prove that a State may interfere, in a case of deliberate, palpable, and dangerous exercise of a power not granted. The honorable member supposes the tariff law to be such an exercise of power; and that consequently a case has arisen in which the State may, if it see fit, interfere by its own law. Now it so happens, nevertheless, that Mr. Madison deems this same tariff law quite constitutional. Instead of a clear and palpable violation, it is, in his judgment, no violation at all. So that, while they use his authority for a hypothetical case, they reject it in the very case before them. All this, Sir, shows the inherent futility, I had almost used a stronger word, of conceding this power of interference to the State, and then attempting to secure it from abuse by imposing qualifications of which the States themselves are to judge. One of two things is true; either the laws of the Union are beyond the discretion and beyond the control of the States; or else we have no constitution of general government, and are thrust back again to the days of the Confederation.

*   *   *

I wish now, Sir, to make a remark upon the Virginia resolutions of 1798. I cannot undertake to say how these resolutions were understood by those who passed them. Their language is not a little indefinite. In the case of the exercise by Congress of a dangerous power not granted to them, the resolutions assert the right, on the part of the State, to interfere and arrest the progress of the evil. This is susceptible of more than one interpretation. It may mean no more than that the States may interfere by complaint and remonstrance, or by proposing to the people an alteration of the Federal Constitution. This would all be quite unobjectionable. Or it may be that no more is meant than to assert the general right of revolution, as against all governments, in cases of intolerable oppression. This no one doubts, and this, in my opinion, is all that he who framed the resolutions could have meant by it; for I shall not readily believe that he was ever of opinion that a State, under the Constitution and in conformity with it, could, upon the ground of her own opinion of its unconstitutionality, however clear and palpable she might think the case, annul a law of Congress, so far as it should operate on herself, by her own legislative power.

I must now beg to ask, Sir, Whence is this supposed right of the States derived? Where do they find the power to interfere with the laws of the Union? Sir, the opinion which the honorable gentleman maintains is a notion founded in a total misapprehension, in my judgment, of the origin of this government, and of the foundation on which it stands. I hold it to be a popular government, erected by the people; those who administer it, responsible to the people; and itself capable of being amended and modified, just as the people may choose it should be. It is as popular, just as truly emanating from the people, as the State governments. It is created for one purpose; the State governments for another. It has its own powers; they have theirs. There is no more authority with them to arrest the operation of a law of Congress, than with Congress to arrest the operation of their laws. We are here to administer a Constitution emanating immediately from the people, and trusted by them to our administration. . . . Sir, the very chief end, the main design, for which the whole Constitution was framed and adopted, was to establish a government that should not be obliged to act through State agency, or depend on State opinion and State discretion. The people had had quite enough of that kind of government under the Confederation. Under that system, the legal action, the application of law to individuals, belonged exclusively to the States. Congress could only recommend; their acts were not of binding force, till the States had adopted and sanctioned them. Are we in that condition still? Are we yet at the mercy of State discretion and State construction? Sir, if we are,

then vain will be our attempt to maintain the Constitution under which we sit.

But, Sir, the people have wisely provided, in the Constitution itself, a proper, suitable mode and tribunal for settling questions of constitutional law. There are in the Constitution grants of powers to Congress, and restrictions on these powers. There are, also, prohibitions on the States. Some authority must, therefore, necessarily exist, having the ultimate jurisdiction to fix and ascertain the interpretation of these grants, restrictions, and prohibitions. The Constitution has itself pointed out, ordained, and established that authority. How has it accomplished this great and essential end? By declaring, Sir, that *"the Constitution, and the laws of the United States made in pursuance thereof, shall be the supreme law of the land, any thing in the constitution or laws of any State to the contrary notwithstanding."*

This, Sir, was the first great step. By this the supremacy of the Constitution and laws of the United States is declared. The people so will it. No State law is to be valid which comes in conflict with the Constitution, or any law of the United States passed in pursuance of it. But who shall decide this question of interference? To whom lies the last appeal? This, Sir, the Constitution itself decides also, by declaring, *"that the judicial power shall extend to all cases arising under the Constitution and laws of the United States."* These two provisions cover the whole ground. They are, in truth, the keystone of the arch! With these it is a government; without them it is a confederation. In pursuance of these clear and express provisions, Congress established, at its very first session, in the judicial act, a mode for carrying them into full effect, and for bringing all questions of constitutional power to the final decision of the Supreme Court. It then, Sir, became a government. It then had the means of self-protection; and but for this, it would, in all probability, have been now among things which are past. . . .

*   *   *

Direct collision, therefore, between force and force, is the unavoidable result of that remedy for the revision of unconstitutional laws which the gentleman contends for. . . . To resist by force the execution of a law, generally, is treason. Can the courts of the United States take notice of the indulgence of a State to commit treason? The common saying, that a State cannot commit treason herself, is nothing to the purpose. . . . Talk about it as we will, these doctrines go the length of revolution. They are incompatible with any peaceable administration of the government. They lead directly to disunion and civil commotion; and therefore it is, that at their commencement, when they are first found to be maintained by respectable men, and in a tangible form, I enter my public protest against them all.

The honorable gentleman argues, that if this government be the sole judge of the extent of its own powers, whether that right of judging be in Congress or the Supreme Court, it equally subverts State sovereignty. . . . The gentleman's opinion may be, that the right *ought not* to have been lodged with the general government; he may like better such a constitution as we should have under the right of State interference; but I ask him to meet me on the plain matter of fact. I ask him to meet me on the Constitution itself. I ask him if the power is not found there, clearly and visibly found there?

But, Sir, what is this danger, and what are the grounds of it? Let it be remembered, that the Constitution of the United States is not unalterable. It is to continue in its present form no longer than the people who established it shall choose to continue it. If they shall become convinced that they have made an injudicious or inexpedient partition and distribution of power between the State governments and the general government, they can alter that distribution at will.

* * *

. . . The people have preserved this, their own chosen Constitution, for forty years, and have seen their happiness, prosperity, and renown grow with its growth, and strengthen with its strength. They are now, generally, strongly attached to it. Overthrown by direct assault, it cannot be; evaded, undermined, NULLIFIED, it will not be, if we, and those who shall succeed us here, as agents and representatives of the people, shall conscientiously and vigilantly discharge the two great branches of our public trust, faithfully to preserve, and wisely to administer it.

* * *

I have not allowed myself, Sir, to look beyond the Union, to see what might lie hidden in the dark recess behind. I have not coolly weighed the chances of preserving liberty when the bonds that unite us together shall be broken asunder. I have not accustomed myself to hang over the precipice of disunion, to see whether, with my short sight, I can fathom the depth of the abyss below; nor could I regard him as a safe counsellor in the affairs of this government, whose thoughts should be mainly bent on considering, not how the Union may be best preserved, but how tolerable might be the condition of the people when it should be broken up and destroyed. While the Union lasts, we have high, exciting, gratifying prospects spread out before us, for us and our children. Beyond that I seek not to penetrate the veil. God grant that in my day, at least, that curtain may not rise! God grant that on my vision never may be opened what lies behind! When my eyes shall be turned to behold for the last time the sun in heaven, may I not see him shining on the broken and dishonored fragments of a once glorious Union; on States dissevered, discordant, belligerent; on a land rent with civil feuds, or drenched, it may be, in fraternal blood! Let their last feeble and lingering glance rather behold the gorgeous ensign of the republic, now known and honored throughout the earth, still full high advanced, its arms and trophies streaming in their original lustre, not a stripe erased or polluted, nor a single star obscured, bearing for its motto, no such miserable interrogatory as "What is all this worth?" nor those other words of delusion and folly, "Liberty first and Union afterwards"; but everywhere, spread all over in characters of living light, blazing on all its ample folds, as they float over the sea and over the land, and in every wind under the whole heavens, that other sentiment, dear to every true American heart,—Liberty *and* Union, now and for ever, one and inseparable!

REVIEW QUESTIONS

1. What were the main points of the doctrine of nullification as Webster summarized them?
2. What did Webster believe to be the flaws in Hayne's exposition of the doctrine of nullification?
3. Explain what Webster meant when he differentiated between constitutional, unconstitutional, and extraconstitutional means of redress or change.
4. How did Webster use historical precedents to support his position?
5. What did Webster fear would be the result of nullification?

South Carolina's Ordinance of Nullification (1832)

Webster did not quench the fires of nullification with his oratory; rather, his words further inflamed both sides of the controversy. Opponents and supporters in both national and state governments, executive and legislative branches, rallied their forces as they prepared to fight fire with fire. President Jackson split from Vice President Calhoun over the issue: the result was a new cabinet purged of Calhoun adherents and, in the next election, a new vice president, Martin Van Buren. Calhoun then moved into the Senate to promote and defend nullification there, as Hayne moved back to South Carolina to assume his gubernatorial duties. As governor, it was Hayne's responsibility to execute the will of the citizens of South Carolina as expressed not only by their representatives in the normal legislature but as presented in an ordinance passed on 24 November by a special convention. Despite some Congressional concessions—the lowering of duties in 1830 and then the passage of the Tariff of 1832 that reduced rates even further—South Carolina nullifiers were determined to turn their political theory into reality.

From *Statutes at Large of South Carolina*, vol. I (Columbia, SC: A. S. Johnston, 1836), p. 329ff. [Editorial insertions that appear in square brackets are from the 1836 edition—*Ed.*]

An Ordinance to Nullify certain acts of the Congress of the United States, purporting to be laws laying duties and imposts on the importation of foreign commodities.

Whereas the Congress of the United States, by various acts, purporting to be acts laying duties and imposts on foreign imports, but in reality intended for the protection of domestic manufactures, and the giving of bounties to classes and individuals engaged in particular employments, at the expense and to the injury and oppression of other classes and individuals, and by wholly exempting from taxation certain foreign commodities, such as are not produced or manufactured in the United States, to afford a pretext for imposing higher and excessive duties on articles similar to those intended to be protected, hath exceeded its just powers under the Constitution, which confers on it no authority to afford such protection, and hath violated the true meaning and intent of the Constitution, which provides for equality in imposing the burthens of taxation upon the several

States and portions of the Confederacy: *And whereas* the said Congress, exceeding its just power to impose taxes and collect revenue for the purpose of effecting and accomplishing the specific objects and purposes which the Constitution of the United States authorizes it to effect and accomplish, hath raised and collected unnecessary revenue for objects unauthorized by the Constitution:—

We, therefore, the people of the State of South Carolina in Convention assembled, do declare and ordain, . . . That the several acts and parts of acts of the Congress of the United States, purporting to be laws for the imposing of duties and imposts on the importation of foreign commodities, . . . and, more especially, . . . [the tariff acts of 1828 and 1832] . . . , are unauthorized by the Constitution of the United States, and violate the true meaning and intent thereof, and are null, void, and no law, nor binding upon this State, its officers or citizens; and all promises, contracts, and obligations, made or entered into, or to be made or entered into, with purpose to secure the duties imposed by the said acts, and all judicial proceedings which shall be hereafter had in affirmance thereof, are and shall be held utterly null and void.

And it is further Ordained, That it shall not be lawful for any of the constituted authorities, whether of this State or of the United States, to enforce the payment of duties imposed by the said acts within the limits of this State; but it shall be the duty of the Legislature to adopt such measures and pass such acts as may be necessary to give full effect to this Ordinance, and to prevent the enforcement and arrest the operation of the said acts and parts of acts of the Congress of the United States within the limits of this State, from and after the 1st day of February next, . . .

And it is further Ordained, That in no case of law or equity, decided in the courts of this State, wherein shall be drawn in question the authority of this ordinance, or the validity of such act or acts of the Legislature as may be passed for the purpose of giving effect thereto, or the validity of the aforesaid acts of Congress, imposing duties, shall any appeal be taken or allowed to the Supreme Court of the United States, nor shall any copy of the record be printed or allowed for that purpose; and if any such appeal shall be attempted to be taken, the courts of this State shall proceed to execute and enforce their judgments, according to the laws and usages of the State, without reference to such attempted appeal, and the person or persons attempting to take such appeal may be dealt with as for a contempt of the court.

And it is further Ordained, That all persons now holding any office of honor, profit, or trust, civil or military, under this State, (members of the Legislature excepted), shall, within such time, and in such manner as the Legislature shall prescribe, take an oath well and truly to obey, execute, and enforce, this Ordinance, and such act or acts of the Legislature as may be passed in pursuance thereof, according to the true intent and meaning of the same; and on the neglect or omission of any such person or persons so to do, his or their office or offices shall be forthwith vacated, . . . and no person hereafter elected to any office of honor, profit, or trust, civil or military, (members of the Legislature excepted), shall, until the Legislature shall otherwise provide and direct, enter on the execution of his office, . . . until he shall, in like manner, have taken a similar oath; and no juror shall be empannelled in any of the courts of this State, in any cause in which shall be in question this Ordinance, or any act of the Legislature passed in pursuance thereof, unless he shall first, in addition to the usual oath, have taken an oath that he will well and truly obey, execute, and enforce this Ordinance, and such act or acts of the Legislature as may be passed to carry the same into operation. . . .

And we, the People of South Carolina, to the end that it may be fully understood by the Government of the United States, and the people of the co-States, that we are determined to maintain this, our Ordinance and Declaration, at every hazard, *Do further Declare* that we will not submit to the application of force, on the part of the Federal Government, to reduce this State to obedience; but that we will consider the passage, by Congress, of any act . . . to coerce the State, shut up her ports, destroy or harass her commerce, or to enforce the acts hereby declared to be null and void, otherwise than through the civil tribunals of the country, as inconsistent with the longer continuance of South Carolina in the Union: and that the people of this State will thenceforth hold themselves absolved from all further obligation to maintain or preserve their political connexion with the people of the other States, and will forthwith proceed to organize a separate Government, and do all other acts and things which sovereign and independent States may of right to do.

REVIEW QUESTIONS

1. What justification was given for the act?
2. How was the state to implement nullification?
3. Which was given precedence: obedience to the state or to the nation?
4. Did this ordinance leave an opening for compromise? If so, how?

ANDREW JACKSON

FROM The President's Nullification Proclamation (1832)

President Jackson was not about to let South Carolina impose its interpretation of the Constitution upon the national government or to empower its sister states by example. The old duellist fired back at the state, first with a moderate charge in his annual message on 4 December 1832, and then with a full explosive charge in a proclamation on 10 December.

From James D. Richardson, comp., *A Compilation of the Messages and Papers of the Presidents, 1789–1902*, vol. II (Bureau of National Literature and Art, 1904), pp. 640–56. [Editorial insertions appear in square brackets—*Ed.*]

*   *   *

To preserve this bond of our political existence from destruction, to maintain inviolate this state of national honor and prosperity, and to justify the confidence my fellow-citizens have reposed in me, I, Andrew Jackson, President of the United States, have thought proper to issue this my proclamation, stating my views of the Constitution and laws applicable to the measures adopted by the convention of South Carolina and to the reasons they have put forth to sustain them, declaring the course which duty will require me to pursue, and, appealing to the understanding and patriotism of the people, warn them of the consequences that must in-

evitably result from an observance of the dictates of the convention.

*   *   *

The ordinance is founded, not on the indefeasible right of resisting acts which are plainly unconstitutional and too oppressive to be endured, but on the strange position that any one State may not only declare an act of Congress void, but prohibit its execution; that they may do this consistently with the Constitution; that the true construction of that instrument permits a State to retain its place in the Union and yet be bound by no other of its laws than those it may choose to consider as constitutional. It is true, they add, that to justify this abrogation of a law it must be palpably contrary to the Constitution: but it is evident that to give the right of resisting laws of that description, coupled with the uncontrolled right to decide what laws deserve that character, is to give the power of resisting all laws; for as by the theory there is no appeal, the reasons alleged by the State, good or bad, must prevail. If it should be said that public opinion is a sufficient check against the abuse of this power, it may be asked why it is not deemed a sufficient guard against the passage of an unconstitutional act by Congress? There is, however, a restraint in this last case which makes the assumed power of a State more indefensible, and which does not exist in the other. There are two appeals from an unconstitutional act passed by Congress—one to the judiciary, the other to the people and the States. There is no appeal from the State decision in theory, and the practical illustration shows that the courts are closed against an application to review it, both judges and jurors being sworn to decide in its favor. But reasoning on this subject is superfluous when our social compact, in express terms, declares that the laws of the United States, its Constitution, and treaties made under it are the supreme law of the land, and, for greater caution, adds "that the judges in every State shall be bound thereby, anything in the constitution or laws of any State to the contrary notwithstanding." . . .

*   *   *

. . . [T]he defects of the Confederation need not be detailed. Under its operation we could scarcely be called a nation. We had neither prosperity at home nor consideration abroad. This state of things could not be endured, and our present happy Constitution was formed, but formed in vain if this fatal doctrine prevails. It was formed for important objects that are announced in the preamble, made in the name and by the authority of the people of the United States, whose delegates framed and whose conventions approved it. The most important among these objects—that which is placed first in rank, on which all the others rest—is "*to form a more perfect union.*" Now, is it possible that even if there were no express provision giving su-

premacy to the Constitution and laws of the United States over those of the States, can it be conceived that an instrument made for the purpose of "*forming a more perfect union*" than that of the Confederation could be so constructed by the assembled wisdom of our country as to substitute for that Confederation a form of government dependent for its existence on the local interest, the party spirit, of a State, or of a prevailing faction in a State? Every man of plain, unsophisticated understanding who hears the question will give such an answer as will preserve the Union. Metaphysical subtlety, in pursuit of an impracticable theory, could alone have devised one that is calculated to destroy it.

I consider, then, the power to annul a law of the United States, assumed by one State, *incompatible with the existence of the Union, contradicted expressly by the letter of the Constitution, unauthorized by its spirit, inconsistent with every principle on which it was founded, and destructive of the great object for which it was formed.*

After this general view of the leading principle, we must examine the particular application of it which is made in the ordinance.

The preamble rests its justification on these grounds: It assumes as a fact that the obnoxious laws, although they purport to be laws for raising revenue, were in reality intended for the protection of manufactures, which purpose it asserts to be unconstitutional; that the operation of these laws is unequal; that the amount raised by them is greater than is required by the wants of the Government; and, finally, that the proceeds are to be applied to objects unauthorized by the Constitution. These are the only causes alleged to justify an open opposition to the laws of the country and a threat of seceding from the Union if any attempt should be made to enforce them. The first virtually acknowledges that the law in question was passed under a power expressly given by the Constitution to lay and collect imposts; but its constitutionality is drawn in question from the *motives* of those who passed it. However apparent this purpose may be in the present case, nothing can be more dangerous than to admit the position that an unconstitutional purpose entertained by the members who assent to a law enacted under a constitutional power shall make that law void. For how is that purpose to be ascertained? Who is to make the scrutiny? How often may bad purposes be falsely imputed, in how many cases are they concealed by false professions, in how many is no declaration of motive made? . . .

The next objection is that the laws in question operate unequally. This objection may be made with truth to every law that has been or can be passed. The wisdom of man never yet contrived a system of taxation that would operate with perfect equality. If the unequal operation of a law makes it unconstitutional, and if all laws of that description may be abrogated by any State for that cause, then, indeed, is the Federal Constitution unworthy of the slightest effort for its preservation. . . .

The two remaining objections made by the ordinance to these laws are that the sums intended to be raised by them are greater than are required and that the proceeds will be unconstitutionally employed.

The Constitution has given, expressly, to Congress the right of raising revenue and of determining the sum the public exigencies will require. The States have no control over the exercise of this right other than that which results from the power of changing the representatives who abuse it, and thus procure redress. Congress may undoubtedly abuse this discretionary power; but the same may be said of others with which they are vested. Yet the discretion must exist somewhere. The Constitution has given it to the representatives of all the people, checked by the representatives of the States and by the Executive power. The South Carolina construction gives it to the legislature or the convention of a single State, where neither the people of the different States, nor the States in their separate capacity, nor the Chief Magistrate elected by the people have any representation. . . .

The ordinance, with the same knowledge of the future that characterizes a former objection, tells you that the proceeds of the tax will be unconstitutionally applied. If this could be ascertained with certainty, the objection would with more propriety

be reserved for the law so applying the proceeds, but surely can not be urged against the laws levying the duty.

*   *   *

The Constitution declares that the judicial powers of the United States extend to cases arising under the laws of the United States, and that such laws, the Constitution, and treaties shall be paramount to the State constitutions and laws. The judiciary act prescribes the mode by which the case may be brought before a court of the United States by appeal when a State tribunal shall decide against this provision of the Constitution. The ordinance declares there shall be no appeal—makes the State law paramount to the Constitution and laws of the United States, forces judges and jurors to swear that they will disregard their provisions, and even makes it penal in a suitor to attempt relief by appeal. It further declares that it shall not be lawful for the authorities of the United States or of that State to enforce the payment of duties imposed by the revenue laws within its limits.

Here is a law of the United States, not even pretended to be unconstitutional, repealed by the authority of a small majority of the voters of a single State. Here is a provision of the Constitution which is solemnly abrogated by the same authority.

On such expositions and reasonings the ordinance grounds not only an assertion of the right to annul the laws of which it complains, but to enforce it by a threat of seceding from the Union if any attempt is made to execute them.

This right to secede is deduced from the nature of the Constitution, which, they say, is a compact between sovereign States who have preserved their whole sovereignty and therefore are subject to no superior; that because they made the compact they can break it when in their opinion it has been departed from by the other States. Fallacious as this course of reasoning is, it enlists State pride and finds advocates in the honest prejudices of those who have not studied the nature of our Government sufficiently to see the radical error on which it rests.

The people of the United States formed the Constitution, acting through the State legislatures in making the compact, to meet and discuss its provisions, and acting in separate conventions when they ratified those provisions; but the terms used in its construction show it to be a Government in which the people of all the States, collectively, are represented. We are *one people* in the choice of President and Vice-President. Here the States have no other agency than to direct the mode in which the votes shall be given. The candidates having the majority of all the votes are chosen. The electors of a majority of States may have given their votes for one candidate, and yet another may be chosen. The people, then, and not the States, are represented in the executive branch.

In the House of Representatives there is this difference, that the people of one State do not, as in the case of President and Vice-President, all vote for the same officers. The people of all the States do not vote for all the members, each State electing only its own representatives. But this creates no material distinction. When chosen, they are all representatives of the United States, not representatives of the particular State from which they come. They are paid by the United States, not by the State; nor are they accountable to it for any act done in the performance of their legislative functions; and however they may in practice, as it is their duty to do, consult and prefer the interests of their particular constituents when they come in conflict with any other partial or local interest, yet it is their first and highest duty, as representatives of the United States, to promote the general good.

The Constitution of the United States, then, forms a *government*, not a league; and whether it be formed by compact between the States or in any other manner, its character is the same. It is a Government in which all the people are represented, which operates directly on the people individually, not upon the States; they retained all the power they did not grant. But each State, having expressly parted with so many powers as to constitute, jointly with the other States, a single nation, can not, from that period, possess any right to secede, because such secession does not break a league, but

destroys the unity of a nation; and any injury to that unity is not only a breach which would result from the contravention of a compact, but it is an offense against the whole Union. To say that any State may at pleasure secede from the Union is to say that the United States are not a nation, because it would be a solecism to contend that any part of a nation might dissolve its connection with the other parts, to their injury or ruin, without committing any offense. Secession, like any other revolutionary act, may be morally justified by the extremity of oppression; but to call it a constitutional right is confounding the meaning of terms, and can only be done through gross error or to deceive those who are willing to assert a right, but would pause before they made a revolution or incur the penalties consequent on a failure.

Because the Union was formed by a compact, it is said the parties to that compact may, when they feel themselves aggrieved, depart from it; but it is precisely because it is a compact that they can not. A compact is an agreement or binding obligation. It may by its terms have a sanction or penalty for its breach, or it may not. If it contains no sanction, it may be broken with no other consequence than moral guilt; if it have a sanction, then the breach incurs the designated or implied penalty. A league between independent nations generally has no sanction other than a moral one; or if it should contain a penalty, as there is no common superior it can not be enforced. A government, on the contrary, always has a sanction, express or implied; and in our case it is both necessarily implied and expressly given. An attempt, by force of arms, to destroy a government is an offense, by whatever means the constitutional compact may have been formed; and such government has the right by the law of self-defense to pass acts for punishing the offender, unless that right is modified, restrained, or resumed by the constitutional act. In our system, although it is modified in the case of treason, yet authority is expressly given to pass all laws necessary to carry its powers into effect, and under this grant provision has been made for punishing acts which obstruct the due administration of the laws.

*   *   *

The States severally have not retained their entire sovereignty. It has been shown that in becoming parts of a nation, not members of a league, they surrendered many of their essential parts of sovereignty. The right to make treaties, declare war, levy taxes, exercise exclusive judicial and legislative powers, were all of them functions of sovereign power. The States, then, for all these important purposes were no longer sovereign. The allegiance of their citizens was transferred, in the first instance, to the Government of the United States; they became American citizens and owed obedience to the Constitution of the United States and to laws made in conformity with the powers it vested in Congress. This last position has not been and can not be denied. How, then, can that State be said to be sovereign and independent whose citizens owe obedience to laws not made by it and whose magistrates are sworn to disregard those laws when they come in conflict with those passed by another? What shows conclusively that the States can not be said to have reserved an undivided sovereignty is that they expressly ceded the right to punish treason—not treason against their separate power, but treason against the United States. Treason is an offense against *sovereignty*, and sovereignty must reside with the power to punish it. . . .

*   *   *

These are the alternatives that are presented by the convention—a repeal of all the acts for raising revenue, leaving the Government without the means of support, or an acquiescence in the dissolution of our Union by the secession of one of its members. When the first was proposed, it was known that it could not be listened to for a moment. It was known, if force was applied to oppose the execution of the laws, that it must be repelled by force; that Congress could not, without involving itself in disgrace and the country in ruin, accede to the proposition; and yet if this is not done in a given day, or if any attempt is made to execute the laws, the State is by the ordinance declared to be out of the Union. The majority of a convention assembled for the purpose have dictated these terms, or rather this rejection of all terms, in the name of the people of South Carolina. It is true that the governor of the State speaks of the submission of their grievances to a convention of all the States, which, he says, they "sincerely and anxiously seek and desire." Yet this obvious and constitutional mode of obtaining the sense of the other States on the construction of the federal compact, and amending it if necessary, has never been attempted by those who have urged the State on to this destructive measure. . . . If the legislature of South Carolina "anxiously desire" a general convention to consider their complaints, why have they not made application for it in the way the Constitution points out? The assertion that they "earnestly seek" it is completely negatived by the omission.

This, then, is the position in which we stand: A small majority of the citizens of one State in the Union have elected delegates to a State convention; that convention has ordained that all the revenue laws of the United States must be repealed, or that they are no longer a member of the Union. The governor of that State has recommended to the legislature the raising of an army to carry the secession into effect, and that he may be empowered to give clearances to vessels in the name of the State. No act of violent opposition to the laws has yet been committed, but such a state of things is hourly apprehended. And it is the intent of this instrument to *proclaim*, not only that the duty imposed on me by the Constitution "to take care that the laws be faithfully executed" shall be performed to the extent of the powers already vested in me by law, or of such others as the wisdom of Congress shall devise and intrust to me for that purpose, but to warn the citizens of South Carolina who have been deluded into an opposition to the laws of the danger they will incur by obedience to the illegal and disorganizing ordinance of the convention; to exhort those who have refused to support it to persevere in their determination to uphold the Constitution and laws of their country; and to point out to all the perilous situation into which the good people of that State have been led, and that the course they are urged to pursue is one of ruin and disgrace to the very State whose rights they affect to support.

*   *   *

I have urged you [South Carolinians] to look back to the means that were used to hurry you on to the position you have now assumed and forward to the consequences it will produce. Something more is necessary. Contemplate the condition of that country of which you still form an important part. Consider its Government, uniting in one bond of common interest and general protection so many different States, giving to all their inhabitants the proud title of *American citizen*, protecting their commerce, securing their literature and their arts, facilitating their intercommunication, defending their frontiers, and making their name respected in the remotest parts of the earth. . . . If your leaders could succeed in establishing a separation, what would be your situation? Are you united at home? Are you free from the apprehension of civil discord, with all its fearful consequences? Do our neighboring republics, every day suffering some new revolution or contending with some new insurrection, do they excite your envy? But the dictates of a high duty oblige me solemnly to announce that you can not succeed. The laws of the United States must be executed. I have no discretionary power on the subject; my duty is emphatically pronounced in the Constitution. Those who told you that you might peaceably prevent their execution deceived you; they could not have been deceived themselves. They know that a forcible opposition could alone prevent the execution of the laws, and they know that such opposition must be repelled. Their object is disunion. But be not deceived by names. Disunion by armed force is *treason*. Are you really ready to incur its guilt? If you are, on the heads of the instigators of the act be the dreadful consequences; on their heads be the dishonor, but on yours may fall the punishment. . . .

Fellow-citizens of the United States, the threat of unhallowed disunion, the names of those once respected by whom it is uttered, the array of military force to support it, denote the approach of a crisis in our affairs on which the continuance of our unexampled prosperity, our political existence, and perhaps that of all free governments may depend. . . . Having the fullest confidence in the justness of the legal and constitutional opinion of my duties which has been expressed, I rely with equal confidence on your undivided support in my determination to execute the laws, to preserve the Union by all constitutional means, to arrest, if possible, by moderate and firm measures the necessity of a recourse to force; and if it be the will of Heaven that the recurrence of its primeval curse on man for the shedding of a brother's blood should fall upon our land, that it be not called down by any offensive act on the part of the United States.

Fellow-citizens, the momentous case is before you. On your undivided support of your Government depends the decision of the great question it involves—whether your sacred Union will be preserved and the blessing it secures to us as one people shall be perpetuated. No one can doubt that the unanimity with which that decision will be expressed will be such as to inspire new confidence in republican institutions, and that the prudence, the wisdom, and the courage which it will bring to their defense will transmit them unimpaired and invigorated to our children.

May the Great Ruler of Nations grant that the signal blessings with which He has favored ours may not, by the madness of party or personal ambition, be disregarded and lost; and may His wise providence bring those who have produced this crisis to see the folly before they feel the misery of civil strife, and inspire a returning veneration for that Union which, if we may dare to penetrate His designs, He has chosen as the only means of attaining the high destinies to which we may reasonably aspire.

*   *   *

REVIEW QUESTIONS

1. Did Jackson's argument augment or simply echo Webster's? How so?
2. Did Jackson persuasively refute each of the points presented by the South Carolina nullificationists?
3. Why did Jackson believe that the interpretation of the Constitution as a state compact was incorrect? How did his perspective affect his view of secession?
4. Which branch of the national government did he indicate was the ultimate expression of the people's will? How does that help explain why he wielded the powers of his office as he did?

HEZEKIAH NILES

Indians within the United States (1827)

General Jackson combatted the Native Americans; President Jackson removed them. In doing so, he not only acted upon his own desires but those of many, probably most, though not all, United States citizens. As the new Americans filed into and filled out the states east of the Mississippi River, they butted up against independent Indians holding prime land. Presidents Monroe and Adams dealt with the mounting crisis by turning to an idea first proposed in the Jefferson administration—that of removal. Essentially, government officials tried to convince eastern tribes to exchange their lands voluntarily for new ones west of the Arkansas territory. The government, however, could not compel them to do so, for it had recognized tribal sovereignty under earlier treaties. As Hezekiah Niles reported in his newspaper, many American citizens believed that recognition, plus the idea of Native American assimilation, needed to be reexamined.

From "Indians within the United States," 29 December 1827, in Hezekiah Niles, ed., *Niles' Weekly Register* (Baltimore, MD). Bound originals in special collections, University of Pittsburgh Library. [Editorial insertions appear in square brackets—*Ed.*]

INDIANS WITHIN THE UNITED STATES. Among the documents from the war department transmitted to congress, are some highly interesting statements by colonel McKenney [Thomas McKenny directed Indian policy within the War Department], shewing the proceedings and result of his mission to the southern tribes, to effect their removal to the westward of the Mississippi. These people, long acquainted with the fidelity and devotion of the superintendant of Indian affairs, received him with great respect, and listened to him with the attention that they would have paid to a father and a friend. We expect to give the papers as soon as space shall be allowed for them—but the notice of a few particulars, with some passing remarks, may be useful at present. We have always felt a deep interest in the concerns of these poor people, and stand prepared to lend our feeble help to any reasonable project, bottomed upon the principle of establishing a *permanent* home for them—for we have been lately inclined to believe that they cannot be preserved, in a state of qualified sovereignty, when pressed upon all sides by a white population. Our wishes on this subject have nothing to do with events; and we should rather meet things as they are, than speculate upon them as we might wish that they should be.

The Chickasaws have agreed to remove—provided a favorable report is made of the lands to be assigned them, by persons appointed by themselves to examine the country. The number of this tribe is about 4,000, and somewhat increasing. The total value of their houses, mills, work shops, fences and stock, is put down at less than 300,000 dollars; and col. McKenney supposes that the whole cost of removal, paying them for their improvements, cannot exceed $494,750.

The Choctaws decidedly declined all propositions for an exchange of lands. The chiefs who attended the council seem to have been precommitted on that subject. They treated the colonel very kindly, and said to him, "It always gives us pain to disagree to a friend's talk." Col. McK. however, expresses an opinion that the Choctaws, as a people, are even now willing to adopt the offer made them, and thinks the way has been opened for their future acceptance of it.

With the Creeks a final and satisfactory arrangement was made, for giving up "all the lands claimed or owned by them within the chartered limits of Georgia."

The Cherokees were not visited; and we should suppose that any present attempt to effect their removal would rather retard than hasten it. They are just about to try the experiment of a regular government, and will not be diverted from it.

Col. McKenney speaks of the state of the Indians, especially the Creeks, as being very poor and wretched, indeed—being habitual drunkards, poverty and distress is visible every where. "I hold their recovery from it (drunkenness) and from its long train of miseries, while they retain their present relations to the states, to be hopeless," says the superintendant. And it is insisted upon by him, that emigration, only, beyond the limits of the present states and territories, can be productive of permanent good to this people. "Destruction lies before them;" and the colonel says that "humanity and justice unite in calling loudly upon the government as a parent, promptly to interfere and save them."

In regard to the Cherokees, the colonel declares, that "they ought not to be encouraged in forming a constitution and government *within* a state of the republic, to exist and operate independently of our laws." After considerable reflection on this proposition, we yield a rather unwilling assent to the justice of it, in the belief that conflicts would arise in which the Indians would be the sufferers, on several accounts and in various ways. We have hitherto been pleased with the progress of the Cherokees towards the formation of a government of written laws, and still most heartily wish them success in the project—but the exertion of those laws within the territory of a state, we now apprehend, would be followed by unhappy consequences—and, *as a people*, we have always thought that they could not exist in their present location—too many of their neighbors would shew but little respect to the laws of the Cherokees, though ready enough to put those of the United States in force against them.

The colonel suggests—1. the preparation of a *suitable* and *last home* for these unfortunate people; 2. the provision and means for their transportation and support—the taking of them "kindly, but *firmly*, by the hand, and telling them they *must go and enjoy it*;" 3. the forbidding all interference with their concerns—for which purpose the presence of a few troops would be necessary. He proposes, however, that reservations should be made, and the fee of the land be secured to those who might prefer to remain where they are.

These are subjects of much interest. It is a melancholy sight to behold these people continually harrassed and "driven from post to pillar"—now beset on the one side and then on the other, without security either in person or property; and, though the original proprietors of the soil, having only, as is now contended, a qualified right to enjoy it, and which we apprehend that they will be compelled to yield to force, if not given up by contract. On the whole, we fall into col. McKenney's views of their condition—reserving the right to revoke our present impressions on further reflection. But of this we are satisfied—that measures ought to be immediately taken, if not already operating, to secure for them a *permanent home* beyond the Mississippi, under the most solemn pledges possible, that they shall not be encroached upon or disturbed—it being understood that the country given to them shall be a wilderness forever, rather than *treated* for hereafter by the government of the U. States.

*   *   *

We are anxious that, by the public approbation of the work which he has published, col. McKenney may be encouraged to go on, and tell us all that he knows of the Indian character, habits and manners; that we ourselves may be instructed and our posterity profit by the knowledge of them. It has been said, "the proper study of mankind is man," and to the American people it must for ages to come be a matter of deep interest to understand who and what were the original possessors of the country over which the banner of their great republic waves; and it is important that the poor Indian should be described by the hand of a friend—not disposed to excuse his faults, but willing to render justice to his good qualities. We know the Indian chiefly as a savage warrior, crafty and reckless—but we desire to know him as a man, as a member of the great human family; that, when all his tribes shall disappear, (as we fear that they must in our land), a faithful history of him may remain for the use of posterity; and perchance, hand down something that will be creditable to our efforts to mete some small measure of justice to the rude and wild sons of the forest.

REVIEW QUESTIONS

1. Did Niles provide an objective report? Why or why not?
2. How did Superintendent McKenney describe the Indians' situation? How had that situation affected their condition?
3. How did McKenney propose to rectify their situation and thus reform their condition? Given this, was removal a reform movement?
4. Why did Niles express reservations about Cherokee progress after first commending it?
5. What did Niles believe was to be the ultimate fate of the Native Americans? What part were they to play in the history books?

ALEXIS DE TOCQUEVILLE

FROM A Letter to Countess de Tocqueville (1831)

Congress responded to the public's sentiments, the War Department's proposals, and the President's prodding, by passing the Indian Removal Act of 1830. While the act seemed to reiterate the voluntary nature of removal by stating that certain allocated western lands were for "such tribes or nations of Indians as may choose to exchange the lands where they now reside, and remove there," it actually empowered the executive branch to follow a more coercive policy. The Indian Removal Act facilitated the transfer of almost all of the remaining eastern Native American tribes. Although the Cherokees were among the last uprooted by the government and forced to make the journey west, their fight, first by legal means and then, for some, by arms, meant that most of the nation's attention was on them. This continued as they made the terrible trip across the South to reach their new lands across the Mississippi. Their mental and physical anguish marked their path; what became known as the Trail of Tears. They were not the only Indians to endure such travail. The Choctaws, Chickasaws, and Creeks blazed the way before them between 1830 and 1832. Their agonies did not go unremarked—indeed as word got back to the Cherokees that nation probably became all the more determined to resist—but they gained more sympathy from a foreign observer than from most Euro-Americans. Alexis de Tocqueville, a well-born Frenchman, traveled through the United States to observe and record the attitudes and actions of the new nation and its people in the early 1830s. As his 25 December 1831 letter to his mother shows, he was both fascinated and repelled by what he saw.

From Alexis de Tocqueville, *Selected Letters on Politics and Society*, ed. Roger Boesche; trans. James Toupin and Roger Boesche (Berkeley: University of California Press, 1985), pp. 68–73. Copyright © 1985 The Regents of the University of California. Reprinted by permission.

December 25, 1831,
on the Mississippi

Finally, finally, my dear mama, the signal is given; and here we are descending the Mississippi with all the swiftness that steam and current together can give to a vessel. We were beginning to despair of ever getting out of the wilderness in which we were confined. . . . Finally, one fine day, a little smoke was seen on the Mississippi, on the limits of the horizon; the cloud drew near little by little, and there emerged from it, neither a giant nor a dwarf as in fairy tales, but a huge steamboat, coming from New Orleans, and which, after parading before us for a quarter of an hour, as if to leave us in uncertainty as to whether it would stop or continue on its route, after spouting like a whale, finally headed toward us, broke through the ice with its huge framework and was tied to the bank. The entire population of our universe made its way to the riverside, which, as you know, then formed one of the furthest frontiers of our empire. The whole city of Memphis was in a flutter; no bells were rung because there are no bells, but people cried out hurrah! and the newcomers alighted on the bank in the manner of Christopher Columbus. We were not yet saved, however; the boat's destination was to go up the Mississippi to Louisville, and our purpose was to go to New Orleans. We

happily had about fifteen companions in adversity who desired no more than we did to make their winter quarters in Memphis. So we made a general *push* on the captain. . . . I am nevertheless of the conviction that he would not have turned in his tracks, without a fortunate event, to which we owe our not becoming citizens of Memphis. As we were thus debating on the bank, an infernal music resounded in the forest; it was a noise composed of drums, the neighing of horses, the barking of dogs. Finally a great troop of Indians, elderly people, women, children, baggage, all conducted by a European and heading toward the capital of our triangle. These Indians were the Chactas (or Choctaws), after the Indian pronunciation; . . . Be that as it may, you undoubtedly wish to know why these Indians had arrived there, and how they could be of use to us; patience, I beg you, now that I have time and paper, I want nothing to hurry me. You will thus know that the Americans of the United States, rational and unprejudiced people, moreover, great philanthropists, supposed, like the Spanish, that God had given them the new world and its inhabitants as complete property.

They have discovered, moreover, that, as it was proved (listen to this well) that a square mile could support ten times more civilized men than savage men, reason indicated that wherever civilized men could settle, it was necessary that the savages cede the place. You see what a fine thing logic is. Consequently, when the Indians begin to find themselves a little too near their brothers the whites, the President of the United States sends them a messenger, who represents to them that in their interest, properly understood, it would be good to draw back ever so little toward the West. The lands they have inhabited for centuries belong to them, undoubtedly: no one refuses them this incontestable right; but these lands, after all, are uncultivated wilderness, woods, swamps, truly poor property. On the other side of the Mississippi, by contrast, are magnificent regions, where the game has never been troubled by the noise of the pioneer's axe, where the Europeans will *never* reach. They are separated from it by more than a hundred leagues. Add to that gifts of inestimable price, ready to reward their compliance; casks of brandy, glass necklaces, pendant earrings and mirrors; all supported by the insinuation that if they refuse, people will perhaps see themselves as constrained to force them to move. What to do? The poor Indians take their old parents in their arms; the women load their children on their shoulders; the nation finally puts itself on the march, carrying with it its greatest riches. It abandons forever the soil on which, perhaps for a thousand years, its fathers have lived, in order to go settle in a wilderness where the whites will not leave them ten years in peace. Do you observe the results of a high civilization? The Spanish, truly brutal, loose their dogs on the Indians as on ferocious beasts; they kill, burn, massacre, pillage the new world as one would a city taken by assault, without pity as without discrimination. But one cannot destroy everything; fury has a limit. The rest of the Indian population ultimately becomes mixed with its conquerors, takes on their mores, their religion; it reigns today in several provinces over those who formerly conquered it. The Americans of the United States, more humane, more moderate, more respectful of law and legality, never bloodthirsty, are profoundly more destructive, and it is impossible to doubt that within a hundred years there will remain in North America, not a single nation, not even a single man belonging to the most remarkable of the Indian races. . . .

But I no longer know at all where I am in my story. It had to do, I think, with the Choctaws. The Choctaws formed a powerful nation that inhabited the frontier of the state of Alabama and that of Georgia. After long negotiations, they finally managed, this year, to persuade them to leave their country and to emigrate to the right bank of the Mississippi. Six to seven thousand Indians have already crossed the great river; those who arrived in Memphis came there with the aim of following their compatriots. The agent of the American government who accompanied them and was charged with paying for their passage, knowing that a steamboat had just arrived, hurried down to the bank. The price he offered for transporting the Indians sixty leagues down river managed to settle the shaken mind of the captain; the signal to depart was given. The prow was turned toward the south and we cheerfully climbed the ladder down which descended the poor passengers who, instead of going to Louisville, saw themselves forced to await the thaw in Memphis. So goes the world.

But we had not yet left; there was still the matter of embarking our exiled tribe, its horses and its dogs. Here began a scene which was something truly lamentable. The Indians came forward toward the shore with a despondent air; they first made the horses go, several of which, little accustomed to the forms of civilized life, took fright and threw themselves into the Mississippi, from which they could be pulled out only with difficulty. Then came the men, who, following their usual custom, carried nothing except their weapons; then the women, carrying their children attached to their backs or wrapped up in the blankets that covered them; they were, moreover, overburdened with loads that contained all their riches. Finally the old people were led on. There was among them a woman of a hundred and ten years of age. I have never seen a more frightening figure. She was naked, with the exception of a blanket that allowed one to see, in a thousand places, the most emaciated body that one can imagine. She was escorted by two or three generations of grandchildren. To leave her country at that age to go seek her fate in a strange land, what misery! There was, amidst the old people, a young girl who had broken her arm a week before; for want of care, the arm was frostbitten below the fracture. She nonetheless had to follow the common march. When all had gone by, the dogs advanced toward the bank; but they refused to enter the boat and took to making frightful howls. Their masters had to lead them by force.

There was, in the whole of this spectacle, an air of ruin and destruction, something that savored of a farewell that was final and with no return; no one could witness this without being sick at heart; the Indians were calm, but somber and taciturn. There was one of them who knew English and of whom I asked why the Choctaws were leaving their country —"To be free," he answered—I could never draw anything else out of him. We will deposit them tomorrow in the solitudes of Arkansas. It has to be confessed that this is a singular accident, that made us come to Memphis to witness the expulsion, one might say the dissolution, of one of the most celebrated and most ancient American nations.

*   *   *

REVIEW QUESTIONS

1. What is the tone of Tocqueville's letter?
2. Did he accept the American justification for removal?
3. How did the Americans compare with the Spanish?
4. If, as that one man said, the Choctaws were moving so as "to be free," why were they so desolate?

JOHN ROSS

FROM The Chief's Annual Message (1831)

Back East, both Jackson and Georgia wanted the Cherokees to move for a number of reasons: they desired Cherokee land, which encompassed not only rich soil for crops but deposits of gold as well; they deemed the Indians to be a threat to state and national security; and they believed the old "civilization" or assimilation program to have failed. In terms of the Cherokee Nation, the old program had not really failed, though it had not worked quite as the earlier administrations had planned. The Cherokee Nation had become what most white Americans recognized as a civilized tribe, but it had adopted and adapted facets of European-American civilization to suit its needs instead of simply assimilating into that engrossing culture. One of the concepts that the Cherokees adopted was that of constitutional government. In 1827 they wrote their own constitution which established a chief executive, a bicameral legislature, and a judiciary. John Ross, a man grown wealthy through his trade and agricultural enterprises and who had been active in Cherokee public affairs since 1816, became their first chief elected under this constitution. In this capacity he tried to get federal intervention on the behalf of his nation against the state of Georgia.

That state believed that it did, or should have, title to the Indian lands under the Compact of 1802. Upon that stand, Georgia passed legislation that ignored Cherokee tribal rights as part of a strategy to drive the Cherokees off their lands and, if possible, out of the state. Ross first appealed to the President and then to the Supreme Court in Cherokee Nation v. Georgia.

From Gary E. Moulton, ed., *The Papers of Chief John Ross*, vol. I (Norman: University of Oklahoma Press, 1985), pp. 224–30. © by the University of Oklahoma Press, Norman. [Editorial insertions that appear in square brackets are from Moulton's edition—*Ed.*]

Chattoga, Cher. Nation,
Oct. 24, 1831

Friends and Fellow Citizens

*　　*　　*

It will be recollected that the President of the United States [Andrew Jackson], at an early day after his induction into office, made us a declaratory and positive assurance that *so far as we had rights we should be protected in them,* and that "*an interference to the extent of affording protection to the Cherokees, and the occupancy of their soil, is what is demanded of the justice of the U.S. and will not be withheld;*" and that "*the intruders would be removed.*" After the promulgation of this assurance, detachments of the Federal troops were ordered within our territorial limits. This movement was hailed with joy and approbation on our part, under the sanguine hope that the *protection* which had so recently been promised us by Pres't Jackson was now to be afforded. But to our astonishment and disappointment the troops were soon found employed under the orders of their superiors, in preventing our citizens from working gold mines, belonging to this nation, and thereby treating them as trespassers upon their own soil. And on being requested by the Governor of Georgia [George R. Gilmer], with the assurance that "whatever measures may be adopted by the State of Georgia in relation to the Cherokees, the strongest desire will be felt to make them accord with the *policy* which has been *adopted by the present administration* of the General Government," the President ordered these troops to be withdrawn from our territory! Thus the military of the United States figured and decamped before our eyes without affording that protection which we had a right to expect, and which had so recently been pledged, leaving undisturbed the numerous intruders who have settled down upon our lands on the frontiers of Georgia and other adjacent states. Immediately after this, Georgia, under her own authority, levied a military force, which is known by the appelation of the "Georgia Guard," and stationed it in this nation, at the encampment which had been established and vacated by the United States troops.

The numerous subsisting treaties between the United States and this nation were negotiated, entered into, and constitutionally ratified on the part of the States by the competent authorities thereof; and they compose a part of "*the supreme law of the land,*" and "*the judges in every state shall be bound thereby, any thing in the constitution or laws of any state to the contrary notwithstanding.*" In reference to this clause of the Federal Constitution I may well borrow an expression of one of the most eminent Judges of Georgia, "can language be plainer or can words be stronger." Such was the language of an Honorable Judge in delivering an opinion from the bench in that state some years ago, in favor of some individuals who claimed title to land reserved to them by the treaty of 1819, between the United States and this nation, & against the title claimed under a grant from Georgia by certain citizens thereof.

The Judicial power extends to all cases in law & equity, arising under the constitution, the laws of the U. States, and treaties made, or which shall be made under their authority; and no state can enter into any treaty, alliance or confederation, or pass any law impairing the obligation of contracts; and

Congress alone possesses the power to regulate commerce with foreign nations, among the several states and with the Indian tribes. Here then, in the face of all these constitutional provisions, all the treaties made with the Cherokee Nation and the laws enacted by Congress in the spirit of those treaties for our protection, the present administration of the General Government, has tolerated Ga. in the recklessness of her own glory and reputation, to march across the line of her constitutional boundary to pass laws repugnant to those treaties and laws of the United States for the express object of perplexing and distressing our citizens by intolerable oppression, that we may be forced to surrender our lands for her benefit. Georgia has surveyed our country into districts—she has placed numerous intruders upon our soil, and in time of *profound peace* has levied *troops*, and still continues to keep them in service. Those troops without civil precepts have arrested our citizens at the point of the bayonet, marched them over the country with chains around their necks, and without trials have imprisoned them in a jail at their military station! Missionaries of the cross, who under the approbation of the authorities of the General Government were sent hither by the benevolence of religious associations, to instruct the Cherokees in the precepts of the Gospel and the arts of civilization, and who have met a welcome reception in this nation, and were successfully prosecuting the objects of their laudable and peaceful mission, have also been cruelly torn from their families and ministerial charge and similarly treated! Two of these worthy and inoffensive men [Samuel Worcester and Elizur Butler], who had been delivered over to the civil authority of Georgia, under the charge merely of *residing* in this Nation, and refusing to comply with a law of that state which goes to infringe upon the rights and liberties guaranteed to every free and loyal citizen under the constitution of the United States, have been sentenced by Judge [Augustin S.] Clayton to the penitentiary of Georgia, there to endure hard labor for the term of four years.

Being fully convinced that President [George] Washington and his successors well understood the constitutional powers of the General Government, and the rights of the individual states, as well as those belonging to the Indian Nations, and that the treaties made under their respective administrations with the Cherokee Nation were intended to be faithfully & honestly regarded on the part of the United States; and that the judicial power would extend to all cases of litigation that might arise under those treaties; it was determined on the expediency of employing legal Counsel to defend the rights of the Nation before the Courts of the United States. Finding, however, that the Courts of Georgia were disposed to prevent as far as possible any case from going up to the Supreme Court of the United States, our counsel advised the propriety of trying the original jurisdiction of the Court by applying, in the character of a *foreign state* for an injunction to restrain Georgia, her officers, citizens &c. from enforcing her laws within our territorial limits. Copies of the Bill for an injunction, and notice of the intended motion were accordingly served upon the Governor and Attorney General of that state. On the 5th of March last the motion was made by John Sergeant Esqr, who also delivered an able speech in favor of the application. William Wirt, Esqr, concluded with equal ability and force of argument on the same side. No counsel appeared on the part of Georgia but some of her representatives in Congress and other friends attended the Court and anxiously awaited the decision. The Court denied the injunction on the ground that the Cherokee Nation was not a *foreign state in the sense of the Constitution*. A majority, however, decided that "the Cherokees are a distinct political society, separate from others, capable of managing its own affairs and governing itself,["] and that the acts of the United States Government plainly recognized the Cherokee Nation as a *state* and the courts are bound by these acts. The Honorable Judges [Smith] Thompson and [Joseph] Story dissented from the majority—in a part of their opinion, and gave a very able and luminous opinion in favor of the jurisdiction of the Court and awarding the injunction. There can be no doubt that a majority of the Judges of the Supreme Court holds the law of Georgia extending jurisdiction within our limits to be unconstitutional, and whenever a case between proper parties can be brought before them, they will so decide . . .

*   *   *

By innumerable acts of injustice and oppression, the rights, liberties and lives our Citizens, have been threatened and jeopardized; and after placing our citizens almost in a state of duresse, the President has been induced by the urgent solicitations of Governor Gilmore [Gilmer], to send into the Nation special agents for the purpose of urging our Citizens to enroll their names for emigration west of the Mississippi river. These Agents are now in the Nation, and a part of them have been seen conversing with a few individuals at their houses, but with no success. By fair and honorable means there can be no danger as it regards the sentiments and disposition of our people on this subject. It is said their fears and credulity are to be operated upon— how far this may be true time will soon develope— at all events, by the admission of Governor Gilmer, the people are no longer *afraid of their chiefs,* nor under the influence of *white men,* and that they will *now* think and act for themselves by emigration. When this project fails it is not known to what cause the failure will be imputed, as our opponents seem determined not to believe the truth, that the opposition of the Cherokees is owing purely to a correct sense of their rights, and to their love of country.

Much has been said from time to time to make a false impression on the public mind in regard to our present controversy and difficulties with Georgia. There can be no subject easier understood than the true relationship between this Nation and the United States; nor the justness of any cause more obvious than ours when fairly investigated. The expediency of removing of our Nation west of the Mississippi has also been urged upon the incompatibility of permitting an independent Government to grow up within the limits of the United States. A correct understanding of our Treaties with the United States will show the absurdity of this argument and remove all fears of the possibility of any evil ever arising to any one of the States

from our present location. A weak defenceless community as we are, forming an alliance with, and placed in the heart of so powerful a Nation as the United States, and having surrendered a portion of our sovereignty, as a security for our protection, and our intercourse being confined exclusively with our protector, must necessarily produce that identity of interest and bond of friendship so natural to the ties of such an alliance. Something has also been said on the score of the public defence. It is true our population at present is small, but it is increasing as rapidly as could be expected. And have not the Cherokees at all times been ready to meet the common foe of the United States? Did they not sufficiently prove to the world their disposition on this subject during the last war? Did they not meet and fight the enemy as became warriors? Let the gallant commander, who now administers the affairs of the United States Government answer. Situated, therefore, as we are under the fostering care and protection of a magnanimous Government, there is every reason to cherish the hope that, under the auspices of a kind and generous administration, time would soon put to shame and lull to silence all the sophistry and unnatural clamour so boisterously paraded against our peaceful continuance upon the land of our fathers. By suitable encouragement and proper culture the arts and sciences would soon flourish in every section of our Nation, & the happy period be hastened when an incorporation into the great family of the American Republic would be greeted by every patriot, & posterity hail the event with grateful rejoicings. May such ever be the views and the prospects to guide us in our efforts to secure for our posterity the inestimable advantages and enjoyments, rights, and liberties, guarantied by treaties in our present location. On the other hand, by a removal West of the Mississippi, under the policy of the present administration of the General Government, to a barren and inhospitable region, we can flatter ourselves with no other prospect than the degradation, dispersion and ultimate extinction of our race.

*   *   *

REVIEW QUESTIONS

1. Did Ross charge Georgia with violations of the Cherokee or United States *Constitution*? What evidence did he present?
2. Of what did he accuse the United States government?

3. What measures did the Cherokee Nation take to protect and promote its interests?
4. Was Ross optimistic or pessimistic about his nation's chances for redress and the retention of their property? Explain.

FROM *Worcester v. Georgia* (1832)

In Cherokee Nation *v.* Georgia, *the Supreme Court refused to rule on the issue being disputed, that of the enforcement of state law within Cherokee territory, because, as Ross mentioned in his 1831 annual message, the Court did not deem the Cherokee Nation to be a foreign nation which could, as stated in the Constitution, bring a case before it. Chief Justice John Marshall referred to the Cherokee nation as a "domestic dependent nation." Yet even as that case closed, another opened. Georgia had required that whites living in Cherokee territory get a license to reside there and take an oath of allegiance to the state. In July the Georgia Guard arrested eleven missionaries who had refused to do so. Eventually nine of the missionaries either took the oath or left the state, but Samuel Worcester and Elizur Butler, who continued to refuse, were sentenced to four years of hard labor by a state court. They appealed their cases up to the Supreme Court, which in March 1832 ruled on the Worcester case and then extended its decision to Butler's.*

From Theda Perdue and Michael D. Green, eds., *The Cherokee Removal: A Brief History with Documents* (Boston: Bedford Books, 1995), pp. 70–75. [Editorial insertions appear in square brackets—*Ed.*]

March 1832

Mr. Chief Justice Marshall delivered the opinion of the Court.

This cause, in every point of view in which it can be placed, is of the deepest interest.

The defendant is a state, a member of the Union, which has exercised the powers of government over a people who deny its jurisdiction, and are under the protection of the United States.

The plaintiff is a citizen of the state of Vermont, condemned to hard labour for four years in the penitentiary of Georgia; under colour of an act which he alleges to be repugnant to the Constitution, laws, and treaties of the United States. . . .

The indictment charges the plaintiff in error, and others, being white persons, with the offence of "residing within the limits of the Cherokee nation without a license," and "without having taken the oath to support and defend the constitution and laws of the state of Georgia."

The defendant in the state Court appeared in proper person, and filed the following plea:

"And the said Samuel A. Worcester, in his own proper person, comes and says, that this Court ought not to take further cognisance of the action and prosecution aforesaid, because, he says, that, on the 15th day of July, in the year 1831, he was, and still is, a resident in the Cherokee nation; and that the said supposed crime or crimes, and each of them, were committed, if committed at all, at the town of New Echota, in the said Cherokee nation, out of the jurisdiction of this Court, and not in the county Gwinnett, or elsewhere, within the jurisdiction of this Court: and this defendant saith, that he is a citizen of the state of Vermont, one of the United States of America, and that he entered the aforesaid Cherokee nation in the capacity of a duly authorized missionary of the American Board of Commissioners for Foreign Missions, under the authority of the President of the United States, and has not since been required by him to leave it: that he was, at the time of his arrest, engaged in preaching the gospel to the Cherokee Indians, and in translating the sacred Scriptures into their language, with the permission and approval of the said Cherokee nation, and in accordance with the humane policy of the government of the United States for the civilization and improvement of the Indians; and that his residence there, for this purpose, is the residence charged in the aforesaid indictment: and this defendant further saith, that this prosecution the state of Georgia ought not to have or maintain, because, he saith, that several treaties have, from time to time, been entered into between the United States and the Cherokee nation of Indians. . . . all which treaties have been duly ratified by the Senate of the United States of America; and, by which treaties, the United States of America acknowledge the said Cherokee nation to be a sovereign nation, authorized to govern themselves, and all persons who have settled within their territory, free from any right of legislative interference by the several states composing the United States of America, in reference to acts done within their own territory; and, by which treaties, the whole of the territory now occupied by the Cherokee nation, on the east of the Mississippi, has been solemnly guarantied to them; all of which treaties are existing treaties at this day, and in full force. . . ."

This plea was overruled by the [state] Court.

And the prisoner being arraigned, plead not guilty. The jury found a verdict against him, and the Court sentenced him to hard labour, . . .

The indictment and plea in this case draw in question, we think, the validity of the treaties made by the United States with Cherokee Indians; if not so, their construction is certainly drawn in question; and the decision has been, if not against their validity, "against the right, privilege, or exemption, specially set up and claimed under them." They also draw into question the validity of a statute of the state of Georgia, "on the ground of its being repugnant to the Constitution, treaties, and laws of the United States, and the decision is in favour of its validity. . . ."

It has been said at the bar, that the acts of the legislature of Georgia seize on the whole Cherokee country, parcel it out among the neighbouring counties of the state, extend her code over the whole country, abolish its institutions and its laws, and annihilate its political existence.

If this be the general effect of the system, let us inquire into the effect of the particular statute and section on which the indictment is founded.

It enacts that "all white persons residing within the limits of the Cherokee nation on the 1st day of March next, or at any time thereafter, without a license or permit from his excellency the governor, or from such agent as his excellency the governor shall authorize to grant such permit or license, and who shall not have taken the oath hereinafter required, shall be guilty of a high misdemeanor, and, upon conviction thereof, shall be punished by confinement to the penitentiary, at hard labour, for a term not less than four years."

The eleventh section authorizes "the governor, should he deem it necessary for the protection of the mines, or the enforcement of the laws in force within the Cherokee nation, to raise and organize a guard," &c.

The thirteenth section enacts, "that the said guard or any member of them, shall be, and they are hereby authorized and empowered to arrest any person legally charged with or detected in a violation of the laws of this state, and to convey, as soon as practicable, the person so arrested, before a justice of the peace, judge of the Superior, or justice of inferior Court of this state, to be dealt with according to law."

The extra-territorial power of every legislature being limited in its action to its own citizens or subjects, the very passage of this act is an assertion of jurisdiction over the Cherokee nation, and of the rights and powers consequent on jurisdiction.

The first step, then, in the inquiry, which the Constitution and laws impose on this Court, is an examination of the rightfulness of this claim.

America, separated from Europe by a wide ocean, was inhabited by a distinct people, divided into separate nations, independent of each other and of the rest of the world, having institutions of their own, and governing themselves by their own laws. It is difficult to comprehend the proposition, that the inhabitants of either quarter of the globe could have rightful original claims of dominion over the inhabitants of the other, or over the lands they occupied; or that the discovery of either by the other should give the discoverer rights in the country discovered, which annulled the pre-existing right of its ancient possessors. . . .

The Indian nations had always been considered as distinct, independent political communities, retaining their original natural rights, as the undisputed possessors of the soil, from time immemorial, with the single exception of that imposed by irresistible power, which excluded them from intercourse with any other European potentate than the first discoverer of the coast of the particular region claimed; and this was a restriction which those European potentates imposed on themselves, as well as on the Indians. The very term "nation," so generally applied to them, means "a people distinct from others." The Constitution, by declaring treaties already made, as well as those to be made, to be the supreme law of the land, has adopted and sanctioned the previous treaties with the Indian nations, and consequently admits their rank among those powers who are capable of making treaties. The words "treaty" and "nation" are words of our own language, selected in our diplomatic and legislative proceedings, by ourselves, having each a definite and well understood mean-

ing. We have applied them to Indians, as we have applied them to the other nations of the earth. They are applied to all in the same sense.

Georgia, herself, has furnished conclusive evidence that her former opinions on this subject concurred with those entertained by her sister states, and by the government of the United States. Various acts of her legislature have been cited in the argument, including the contract of cession made in the year 1802, all tending to prove her acquiescence in the universal conviction that the Indian nations possessed a full right to the lands they occupied, until that right should be extinguished by the United States, with their consent: that their territory was separated from that of any state within whose chartered limits they might reside, by a boundary line, established by treaties: that, within their boundary, they possessed rights with which no state could interfere; and that the whole power of regulating the intercourse with them was vested in the United States. A review of these acts, on the part of Georgia, would occupy too much time, and is the less necessary, because they have been accurately detailed in the argument at the bar. Her new series of laws, manifesting her abandonment of these opinions, appears to have commenced in December, 1828.

In opposition to this original right, possessed by the undisputed occupants of every country; to this recognition of that right, which is evidenced by our history, in every change through which we have passed; is placed the charters granted by the monarch of a distant and distinct region, parcelling out a territory in possession of others whom he could not remove and did not attempt to remove, and the cession made of his claims by the treaty of peace.

The actual state of things at the time, and all history since, explain these charters; and the King of Great Britain, at the treaty of peace, could cede only what belonged to his crown. These newly asserted titles can derive no aid from the articles so often repeated in Indian treaties; extending to them, first, the protection of Great Britain, and afterwards that of the United States. These articles are associated with others, recognising their title to self-government. The very fact of repeated treaties with them recognises it; and the settled doctrine of the law of nations is, that a weaker power does not surrender its independence—its right to self-government, by associating with a stronger, and taking its protection. A weak state, in order to provide for its safety, may place itself under the protection of one more powerful, without stripping itself of the right of government, and ceasing to be a state. Examples of this kind are not wanting in Europe. "Tributary and feudatory states," says Vattel, "do not thereby cease to be sovereign and independent states, so long as self-government and sovereign and independent authority are left in the administration of the state." At the present day, more than one state may be considered as holding its right of self-government under the guarantee and protection of one or more allies.

The Cherokee nation, then, is a distinct community, occupying its own territory, with boundaries accurately described, in which the laws of Georgia can have no force, and which the citizens of Georgia have no right to enter, but with the assent of the Cherokees themselves, or in conformity with treaties, and with the acts of Congress. The whole intercourse between the United States and this nation, is, by our Constitution and laws, vested in the government of the United States.

The act of the state of Georgia, under which the plaintiff in error was prosecuted, is consequently void, and the judgment a nullity. Can this Court revise and reverse it?

If the objection to the system of legislation, lately adopted by the legislature of Georgia, in relation to the Cherokee nation, was confined to its extra-territorial operation, the objection, though complete, so far as respected mere right, would give this Court no power over the subject. But it goes much further. If the review which has been taken be correct, and we think it is, the acts of Georgia are repugnant to the Constitution, laws, and treaties of the United States.

They interfere forcibly with the relations established between the United States and the Cherokee nation, the regulation of which, according to the settled principles of our Constitution, are committed exclusively to the government of the Union.

They are in direct hostility with treaties, repeated in a succession of years, which mark out the boundary that separates the Cherokee country from Georgia; guaranty to them all the land within their boundary; solemnly pledge the faith of the United States to restrain their citizens from trespassing on it; and recognise the pre-existing power of the nation to govern itself.

They are in equal hostility with the acts of Congress for regulating this intercourse, and giving effect to the treaties.

The forcible seizure and abduction of the plaintiff in error, who was residing in the nation with its permission, and by authority of the President of the United States, is also a violation of the acts which authorize the chief magistrate to exercise this authority. . . .

It is the opinion of this Court that the judgment of the Superior Court for the county of Gwinnett, in the state of Georgia, condemning Samuel A. Worcester to hard labour in the penitentiary of the state of Georgia, for four years, was pronounced by that Court under colour of a law which is void, as being repugnant to the Constitution, treaties, and laws of the United States, and ought, therefore, to be reversed and annulled.

REVIEW QUESTIONS

1. What was Worcester's defense?
2. Did the Court believe that Georgia could rightfully claim jurisdiction over the Cherokee Nation on the basis of historical discovery and settlement? Why or why not?
3. Did the Court accept Georgia's contention that Indians had ceded their sovereignty in the charters or treaties they had made? Why or why not?
4. How did Marshall show that there were degrees of sovereignty—that this case was not predicated on a simple matter of having sovereignty or not having it?

WILSON LUMPKIN

FROM Georgia Governor's Annual Message (1832)

Cherokee resistance via the judiciary contributed to the tension between the national and state governments. The Supreme Court caused consternation and controversy as it ruled on the extent of state power over the Native Americans. Wilson Lumpkin, who became governor of Georgia in November 1831, had proclaimed that state jurisdiction over Cherokee territory was both constitutionally and morally justified in that it would prevent anarchy and bloodshed in that area. He said that "we cannot govern the country under consideration with honor to our character, and benefit and humanity to the Indians, until we have a settled, freehold, white population, planted on the unoccupied portion of that territory, under the influence of all the ordinary inducements of society, to maintain a good system of civil government."* Given that belief and desire, Governor Lumpkin was outraged by the decision in Worcester v. Georgia. *Although he dealt at length with the state's financial situation, the penitentiary system, the militia, and banking in his 1832 annual message, he began his address with a condemnation of the Court's decision and ended it with an examination of the nullification controversy and an acclamation of Georgia's sovereignty.*

From Wilson Lumpkin, *The Removal of the Cherokee Indians from Georgia, 1827–1841* (1907; New York: Augustus M. Kelly, Publishers, 1971), pp. 103–107, 119–25 *ibid pp. 95–96.

Executive Department, Georgia,
Milledgeville, November 6th, 1832.
Fellow Citizens:—

*　　*　　*

Our conflicts with Federal usurpation are not yet at an end. The events of the past year have afforded us new cause for distrust and dissatisfaction. Contrary to the enlightened opinions and just expectations of this and every other State in the Union, a majority of the judges of the Supreme Court of the United States have not only assumed jurisdiction in the cases of Worcester and Butler, but have, by their decision, attempted to overthrow that essential jurisdiction of the State, in criminal cases, which has been vested by our Constitution in the Superior Courts of our own State. In conformity with their decision, a mandate was issued to our

court, ordering a reversal of the decree under which those persons are imprisoned, thereby attempting and intending to prostrate the sovereignty of this State in the exercise of its constitutional criminal jurisdiction. These extraordinary proceedings of the Supreme Court have not been submitted to me officially, nor have they been brought before me in any manner which called for my official action. I have, however, been prepared to meet this usurpation of Federal power with the most prompt and determined resistence, in whatever form its enforcement might have been attempted by any branch of the Federal Government.

It has afforded me great satisfaction to find that our whole people, as with the voice of one man, have manifested a calm, but firm and determined resolution to sustain the authorities and sovereignty of their State against this unjust and unconstitutional encroachment of the Federal judiciary. The ingenuity of man might be challenged to show a single sentence in the Constitution of the United States giving power, either direct or implied, to the general government, or any of its departments, to nullify the laws of a State, enacted for the government of its own population, or coerce obedience, by force, to the mandates of the judiciary of the Union. . . .

*   *   *

Shortly after the adjournment of the Legislature, in December last, I communicated directly to the President of the United States the views of this State, as manifested by her legislation on the subject of our unoccupied lands lying in Cherokee County; and at the same time frankly communicated to him my views, especially as to the necessity and importance of an immediate survey, and perhaps occupancy, of these lands. The President has manifested equal solicitude with ourselves to effect an amicable and satisfactory adjustment of our territorial embarrassment. He has proposed to the Cherokee people terms of the most liberal character, with a view to induce them to emigrate to the West, &c., thereby to enable him to effect the great object of his solicitude, in permanently benefiting that unfortunate race, and at the same time to fulfil the long delayed obligation of the United States Government to Georgia, entered into by the compact of 1802.

Notwithstanding the extraordinary liberality of the proposition submitted to the Cherokees, and the kind spirit in which they were presented, the enemies of the President and of Georgia have so far succeeded as to prevent any satisfactory arrangement or treaty with them; and their reply to those liberal propositions evinces a most arrogant and uncompromising spirit.

*   *   *

. . . Nevertheless, amidst all these irregularities, strifes and disorders, there is much cause for sincere gratification, that the events of the year have produced nothing more seriously injurious to the interests and character of the State.

The survey of the County of Cherokee, in conformity with, and under the provisions of, the several acts of the Legislature, has been completed without any serious obstacle or difficulty, and, in the exercise of that discretion confided to me by law, I have not hesitated to move forward in that direct line which I deemed best calculated to ensure a speedy settlement of the unoccupied lands in Cherokee County. . . .

I deem it unnecessary at this time to enter upon an enlarged vindication of the policy which has been pursued by the authorities of Georgia on this subject. Suffice it to say that I have daily increased evidence that our policy has been founded in wisdom, justice and true benevolence, and will, ere long, terminate in the preservation of a remnant of these unfortunate Indians; and our State will be relieved from the libels and embarrassments of a thirty years' controversy.

It now becomes my duty to call the serious and deliberate attention of the Legislature to the subject of the present condition of the Cherokees who remain within our State. By our existing laws, their homes and improvements are secured to them, so long as they may choose to remain thereon; but these laws are by no means adapted to the security of their persons and property. Therefore, special and appropriate legislation is most earnestly recommended, whereby these objects will be secured to them, and their rights be as effectually shielded from violation as those of the white man. It is due to the character of the State that this dependent people should be protected by laws as liberal as may be consistent with their moral and intellectual condition. To afford them such protection, and to extend to them suitable privileges, without endangering the rights of our own citizens, will require the most careful deliberation and prudent forecast.

*   *   *

I might here close this communication, under the conviction of having submitted for the consideration of the Legislature the most important subjects which will require their attention during the present session; but at a time like the present, when our country is agitated from its centre to its circumference upon subjects of vital importance to the cause of liberty, and the perpetuation of our civil institutions, I deem it to be a duty attached to the trust which I occupy to give a free and frank avowal of my sentiments upon the exciting subjects before us regarding alone the interest of my country.

Upon all subjects relating to the usurpations of the Federal Government, and especially upon that of the protective tariff system, great unanimity of opinion prevails throughout this and the Southern States generally. They never will be reconciled to the present tariff, or the principles upon which it is based. They believe it to be contrary to the principles and spirit of the Federal Constitution, and the auxiliary measures by which this odious system of taxation is kept up and supported are no less objectionable than the tariff itself. The partial and extravagant appropriations of every succeeding Congress, since the introduction of this desolating and strife-stirring system, clearly evince an abandonment of those principles of economy and republican simplicity upon which our Federal system is based.

To preserve and perpetuate the blessings of our political institutions, it is indispensable that the Federal and State Governments should be kept within the limits of their constitutional spheres of action. Intolerable assumption and usurpations, which will not yield to the ordinary influence of reason and justice, must be checked by some means; and the power to accomplish this end must unquestionably reside in the respective Sovereignties. . . .

The people of this State have already, through their primary assemblies, as well as by their representatives in Congress, and the State Legislature, repeatedly remonstrated and protested against the protective tariff system, and declared their interminable hostility to it.

While the feelings of our people have been strong and urgent on this subject, they have, nevertheless, exercised a spirit of moderation and forbearance, under the prospect of relief being afforded before endurance would become intolerable.

We have looked to the final extinguishment of the public debt as the period when we should be relieved from the burthens of unequal taxation.

And our hopes have been strengthened and encouraged from the patriotic and independent course which has been pursued by the present Executive of the United States, in arresting, by his veto, unconstitutional measures of expenditure. This check upon the extravagant measures of Congress has been well calculated to strengthen the hope that the Federal Government might finally be brought back to the principles of the Constitution. . . . The proceedings of the late session of Congress were noted with intense interest and solicitude, and with a spirit and desire to find something in the proceedings of that body tending to harmony, founded upon acts of justice, and a more sacred regard to the principles of our Federal system. But each succeeding mail, during the late long session, did but strengthen my misgivings in longer looking to that body to save the country from the threatening evils of partial, oppressive and unconstitutional legislation. Yet justice requires the admission that in the passage of the Tariff act of the late session a majority of both branches of Congress did manifest something of a spirit of conciliation towards each other. This majority, too, manifested a spirit of co-operation with the Executive branch of the Federal Government, in sustaining this act, which (although by no means a satisfactory measure of compromise) has been calculated to allay present excitement, and to check the impetuosity of the rash and violent. This act was passed by the votes of members who did not approve its provisions, but sustained it as a choice of evils. They voted for its passage in preference to disunion, or the tariff act of 1828. While I consider the principles of the late act equally, if not more obnoxious than that of 1828, yet I am bound to admit that it relieves the whole people of the United States of a portion of the burthens of taxation; and, therefore, it may be considered as an effort, at least on the part of a portion of the friends of the protective system, to modify the law, so as to make it less obnoxious to our feelings. But unless this spirit of conciliation is followed by further concessions, they do but deceive themselves, if they suppose the South will ever become reconciled. . . .

If our opponents be capable of wise self-government, they must ere long be brought to see the justice of our cause, based as it is on principles no less essential to them than to us; at least, may we not hope that the common classes of the laboring people everywhere will yet be brought to unite with us against the whole system, as being designed to benefit an aristocratic few and to oppress the poor for the exclusive benefit of the wealthy. But should these, my best anticipations, be founded in error, and originate in weakness, I beseech my countrymen who are in favor of direct and immediate resistance to remember that they are required by every principle of sound philosophy, virtue and patriotism to exercise patience and long forbearance towards their brethren of the same faith and principles with themselves, in regard to the usurpations of the Federal Government. . . .

Principles of common courtesy must concede to the members of the same confederacy or co-partnership a right to participate in all councils where the subject under consideration, and the policy to be adopted, are equally interesting to each member. Whenever a case, however, shall arise wherein a single State shall be oppressed by the usurpations of Federal power, and that pressure shall be confined to her local interest alone, and consequently produce no identity of feeling or interest in the other States, then I would consider it the incumbent duty of the aggrieved State to judge and act for herself, independently of the advice and opinions of others.

It is due to the sovereign character of every State of the Union to maintain its territorial rights and policy over its own population.

These are rights which can never be surrendered by a free State, or submitted to the arbitration of others. But, upon the subject of the tariff, shall Georgia undertake to redress the grievances of the whole South? Shall we not hearken to the voice and movements of our sister States who agree with us in principle and feeling? Or shall we precipitately rush forward upon a novel and untried theory, which may disgust our sister States, end in

abortion, and prove to be worse than submission itself? The States which agree in principle must be brought to act in concert before they can reasonably hope to produce the consummation desired by the opponents of the protective system, as well as every true patriot and friend of the Federal Union. Separate action upon this subject is calculated to engender strife and disunion, anarchy and confusion among brethren of the same principles.

The mystical doctrine of nullification, as contended for by its advocates, has only tended to bewilder the minds of the people, inflame their passions, and prepare them for anarchy and revolution. Wherever it spreads, it engenders the most bitter strifes and animosities, and dissolves the most endearing relations of life. I believe nullification to be unsound, dangerous and delusive, in practice as well as theory. Its advocates have, with great ability, endeavored to make their theory harmonize with the principles and operations of our Federal and State systems of government. But in my opinion the very essence of their doctrine tends directly to destroy all harmony between the Federal and State governments, and must inevitably produce the most direct and vexatious conflict, whenever it may be attempted by a State to enforce the theory of nullification. I am unable to comprehend or conceive of a peaceable, constitutional harmony which would attend a measure emanating from one twenty-fourth part of the sovereign power of the Union; which measure should stop the revenue operations of the Federal Government. . . .

Georgia should not suffer herself to be deluded or flattered into the belief that her rights have heretofore been maintained upon the principle and doctrines of nullification, as contended for by the present advocates. It is true, we may look back with pride and pain on our past conflict with Federal usurpation. Upon several occasions we have been compelled to throw ourselves upon our reserved rights, and resist Federal encroachment; but we have never veiled ourselves in the flimsy garment of peaceable constitutional nullification. In these delicate and highly responsible acts, Georgia has always relied on her own population, the justice of her cause, and the virtue and intelligence of the people of the United States, to sustain her un-questionable constitutional rights. And hitherto our confidence has not been misplaced; we have had able friends and advocates in every part of the Union who have stood by us in times of the great-est peril. We are at present very improperly charged with nullifying the intercourse laws and Indian treaties of the United States, when, in fact, these laws and treaties were set aside, and had become measurably obsolete, by the acts and assumptions of the Cherokee Indians themselves; Georgia, by her course of policy, has only nullified the arrogant assumption of sovereign power, claimed and set up by a remnant of the aboriginal race within her ac-knowledged chartered limits.

Finally, fellow citizens, let us strive to be of one mind—let our measures be founded in wisdom,

justice and moderation—constantly bearing in mind the sacred truth, that a Nation or State "di-vided against itself, cannot stand."

REVIEW QUESTIONS

1. Did Lumpkin indicate that Georgia would de-sist in its attempts to extend its jurisdiction over the Cherokee people and obtain their territory?
2. How did he differentiate between Georgia's ar-guments and actions and those of South Car-olina?
3. Did he believe that both states were dealing with Federal usurpation of their rights?
4. What did he believe that the states should do to check federal power?

12 ❧ THE DYNAMICS OF GROWTH

Opportunity plus improvements equaled growth, and growth, to most Americans, meant progress and prosperity. Americans were fortunate in the natural riches of the land they claimed, claims that grew throughout the first half of the nineteenth century. Furthermore, as the nation grew physically, it encompassed more people who showed tremendous ingenuity in their energetic pursuit of individual and national improvements. Many of these people cultivated more and more land. Agriculture, however, blossomed not just because additional farmers worked on extensive, fertile homesteads, it flourished because other Americans, native born and immigrant, created better tools with which to work. Inventors devised mechanical aides, from the cotton gin that transformed the South to the mechanical seeders and reapers that, in the Old Northwest, helped turn sustenance farming into commercial agriculture.

The farmers, in turn, needed greater markets, and they had to be able to get their goods to them. Furthermore, as the farmers became markets for goods they could not easily or profitably produce, they needed to be supplied with such products. Well aware of the farmers' situation, Americans took a great interest in internal improvements—whether financed by the national or state governments.

While citizens wrangled over the type and sponsorship of improvements, their federal and local governments proceeded to build roadways and waterways. The National Road was the premier example of the former, and the numerous canals that gouged through the states, connecting rivers and lakes, cities and shipping terminals, established the latter. Yet these did not represent the greatest innovations in transportation. People had long used the power supplied by air, earth, and water, but in harnessing the power created by a combination of those elements—steam power—they revolutionized the ways by which people traveled. Steamships began to ply the country's rivers, lakes, and shorelines, and heralded the beginning of the end for the great ocean sailing ships. Steam-powered locomotives, engines on wheels that moved on tracks, also energized the movement of people and products.

The most dynamic element in this transformation was the human one. People invented machines to benefit people. Laborers used the machines to make the goods—including other mechanical devices—that the populace required. As demand for both workers and products grew, more and more people streamed in from the countryside as well as from other countries to work in the factories. The resulting confluence of cultures, with all its attendant turbulence and debris, was a mixed blessing for American society. While some Americans liked to see customs challenged by the new realities of industrialization and urbanization, many others found the process, and certainly the consequences, profoundly disturbing.

The growth of manufacturing expanded the ranks of landless laborers and contributed to social and economic stratification as Americans started to define the value of such workers and their work. Many, planted deep in the yeoman farmer tradition, did not understand those who chose to toil in factories rather than fields. While movement was an accepted part of the American experience when it included clearing new farms, the urban laborers' rootlessness was not. One result was that some Americans came to discriminate against industrial workers, especially when such laborers changed the face, figure, and speech of America's working class. When manufacturers readily hired women and children—indeed, they preferred them for certain tasks—people worried about them working outside family control (working within it had always been acceptable). While factory work was a positive in that it gave some women and families greater economic options, it also led to exploitation. Natives and immigrants like struggled with this and other dilemmas that were the byproducts of industrialization.

Immigrants were vital to American growth. The nation had natural resources in abundance, but while Americans were as energetic in populating the land as they were in planting crops, rail stakes, and factory foundations, they did not provide enough laborers. Fortunately for the nation—although some citizens believed that more misfortune than fortune attended their coming—immigrants flocked to these shores after 1820. Pushed from their motherlands by depression, famine, and political persecution, and pulled to America by images of prosperity, bountifulness, and tolerance, thousands upon thousands of peoples shipped off for the New World. Prominent among them were Germans and Irish, the two major European groups to migrate to the United States before 1860.

National power and prosperity benefitted from the interplay of land, people, and technology. Yet what many hailed as progress was not welcomed by all. Some feared that manufacturing and cities spelled not only the doom of the yeoman farmer, but of the political system created for him. Others decried the influence of *immigrants on American culture—a concept cynics may have choked on, but which boosters did not see as an oxymoron—and thus espoused nativism. Yet as much as nativists wanted to preserve an idealized past in their culture, American civilization was just as dynamic an invention as the mechanical ones, and just as susceptible to those who wanted to improve it.*

FROM *American Scenery* (1840)

Just as Americans today like to take pictures of their new cars, tout the speed and capacity of their computers, and look at images beamed from satellites, shuttles, and stations in space, Americans in the early nineteenth century delighted in recording their personal and public technological marvels. One of the new mechanical processes, as well as its product, was an early form of photography called the daguerreotype; but drawings, engravings, and paintings were easier and cheaper to reproduce for public consumption. Americans celebrated their growth and development by hanging such images in public buildings as well as private homes, and by publishing them in books, newspapers, and magazines. Interestingly, at the same time they so noted their technical progress, they also increasingly revered the depiction of nature in artwork.

From N. P. Willis, *American Scenery*. With 121 steelplate engravings from drawings by W. H. Bartlett. (Barre, MA: Imprint Society, 1971), pp. 133–36, 160–63. This was first published as *American Scenery; or, Land, Lake, and River: Illustrations of Transatlantic Nature* in 1840.

View of the Ferry at Brooklyn, New York

Brooklyn is as much a part of New York, for all purposes of residence and communication, as "the Borough" is of London. The steam ferry-boats cross the half-mile between it and the city every five minutes; and in less time than it usually takes to thread the press of vehicles on London Bridge, the elegant equipages of the wealthy cross to Long Island for the afternoon drive; morning visits are interchanged between the residents in both places—and, indeed, the east river is hardly more of a separation than the same distance in a street.

Brooklyn is the shire-town of King's County, and by this time, probably, is second in population only to New York. Land there, has risen in value to an enormous extent within the last few years; and it has become the fashion for business-men of New York to build and live on the fine and healthy heights above the river, where they are nearer their business, and much better situated than in the outskirts of the city itself. The town of Brooklyn is built on the summit and sides of an elevation springing directly from the bank of the river, and commanding some of the finest views in America. The prospect embraces a large part of East River, crowded with shipping, and tracked by an endless variety of steamers, flying through the channel in quick succession; of the city of New York, extending, as far as the eye can see, in closely piled masses

BROOKLYN FERRY

of architecture; of the Hudson, and the shore of Jersey, beyond; of the bay and its bright islands, and of a considerable part of Long and Staten Islands, and the Highlands of Neversink. A more comprehensive, lively, and interesting view is nowhere to be found.

*   *   *

Lockport—Erie Canal

This town, so suddenly sprung into existence, is about thirty miles from Lake Erie, and exhibits one of those wonders of enterprise which astonish calculation. The waters of Lake Erie, which have come thus far without much descent, are here let down sixty feet by five double locks and thence pursue a perfectly level course, sixty-five miles, to Rochester. The remarkable thing at Lockport, however, is a

deep cut from here to the Torenanta Creek, seven miles in length, and partly through solid rock, at an average depth of twenty feet. The canal boat glides through this flinty bed, with jagged precipices on each side; and the whole route has very much the effect of passing through an immense cavern.

*   *   *

View of the Railroad to Utica (taken at Little Falls)

Before the completion of the Railroad, when travellers to the West were contented with the philosophic pace of the canal-boat, one might take up a novel at Little Falls, and come fairly to the sequel by the time the steersman cried out "Bridge!" at

LOCKPORT—ERIE CANAL

RAILROAD TO UTICA

Utica. There were fifteen miles between them in those days; but now (to a man of indistinct ideas of geography, at least, and a traveller on the Rail-road) they are as nearly run together as two drops on the window-pane. The intermediate distance is, by all the usual measurements of wear and time, annihilated.

All this is very pleasant to people in a hurry; and as most people in our busy country come un-der that category, it is a very pleasant thing . . . altogether. . . .

REVIEW QUESTIONS

1. What do the scenes and their captions reveal about the state of transportation technology?
2. Do they indicate or imply that progress had a price? Was this deemed good or bad?
3. How are human and natural elements juxta-posed in these scenes?
4. What does a comparison of the three scenes re-veal about how transportation technology both met the demands of and made its own mark on the American landscape?

HEZEKIAH NILES

FROM Great National Interests (1826)

Transportation routes are lines of communication; thus, as travel was expedited so too was the dissemination of information. News—based in both fact and fiction, for ru-mors could travel as fast or faster than verified reports—traveled by way of ship, boat, wagon, and train. Almost every town had its newspaper, and if it was a big town or a city it had more than one. These papers performed essential services such as an-nouncing births, marriages, and deaths, and advertising everything from lost or found livestock, the newest medicinal elixirs, and jobs. They also published news that came in from out of town and in so doing served as a link between communities. Since most of these papers were not fully objective—they reflected the opinions of their pub-lishers and editors—large communities often had numerous ones printed by various interest groups. Smaller communities that did not have a newspaper or could not support more than one, could use the new transportation routes to bring in other pa-pers. When numerous papers were available, a reader had the opportunity to study conflicting accounts so as to form his or her own opinion. Hezekiah Niles, who edited and published Niles' Weekly Register *in Baltimore, tried for objectivity in reporting events and other peoples' opinions, but he also used his paper to support internal im-provements and promote manufacturing.*

From "Great National Interests," 21 October 1826, in Hezekiah Niles, ed., *Niles' Weekly Reg-ister* (Baltimore, MD). Bound originals in special collections, University of Pittsburgh Library. [Square brackets are from the original edition—*Ed.*]

Illustrative of the progress and present condition of manufactures in the United States, and concerning internal improvements, aiding and assisting every branch of the national industry.

The making of the New York canals did not really cost the people of the state the value of one cent, except so far as *foreign* materials may have been employed in the construction of them, or for that small portion of the profits on labor which the artists and laborers may have carried *out of the state*. On the contrary, they gave a large and wholesome circulation to money, and enriched many individuals; and the increased value of property, and of profit, resulting from them, must be supposed by counting up hundreds of millions of dollars, if, indeed, the benefits of them be within *supposition* at all! The rise in the value of lands and lots on their borders—at Albany, Troy, Rochester, Utica, Buffalo, and an hundred new and thrifty villages which have started into existence as if created by magic—the *new* employment of tens of thousands of persons—the *new* commodities transported to market, many of which, of great value, were hitherto as quiescent, or useless, because of the want of such market, with the *new* products of a teeming, busy, bustling and happy population—make up an aggregate of benefits that the mind cannot grasp with any degree of confidence in itself; and to all these should be added, the wealth and power caused by the increased inhabitants of the state on account of these things; perhaps directly and already, to the number of three or four hundred thousand persons! Such are the general effects of canals, roads and bridges. And besides, the revenue arising from tolls will not only pay the interest on the money expended, but speedily extinguish the debt, and then supply the chief part of all the funds required for the support of the government of New York! These canals cost $9,123,000, but the actual debt created was only 7,771,000, the interest payable on which was 419,000—but the tolls of the present year will amount to a million!—and the business of the canals will go *on, on, on*, and increase every year, for years to come, until the utmost shore of lake Superior teems with civilized men, and cities are located where the wolf has his home, and the bear takes up his winter-quarters.

Up to the 18th August last, and for the present season, about 9,000 tons of coal, 4,000 tons of wheat, 2,000 tons of iron ore, 1,500 tons of flour, and 4,000 tons of other articles, arrived at Philadelphia by the improved navigation of the Schuylkill—one hundred vessels laden with Schuylkill coal will have arrived at New York from Philadelphia, during the present season. What is the *new* profit, or value, of the products or employments caused by this comparatively small work, yet in the very infancy of its usefulness? What the amount of *new* capital put into useful operation? *Let it be calculated!*

Some particulars might be given about other canals; but these two cases have been referred to only to shew general results, and they speak a language that cannot be mistaken—to the glory of those who have supported INTERNAL IMPROVEMENTS, to the shame of some who have opposed them, and the [what shall I say?]—the *something* of others who were so much interested in *arguing* while others were employed in *digging*! But such will always be the difference between talking and doing—the talkers will become poorer and poorer, and the doers richer and richer. *One spade-full of earth removed in New York or Pennsylvania, has rendered more service, in either state, than a *ten-column essay* in the Richmond "Enquirer" has benefitted Virginia. The policy of the first, is to make even a small state a great one—of the other, to reduce a great state into a small one. Witness, Vermont and New York, and Maryland and Virginia. Population and power and wealth will centre where labor is honored, and business abounds. The little rough and rugged state of Vermont, has had as great an accession of citizens, since 1790, as the mighty state of Virginia—though the capital for increase in the latter was five times greater than the former had in the year just stated; and as to Maryland, Vermont *now* contains more of the people than she does, though the first numbered 208,000, and the last only 85,000, in 1790! These things speak in most intelligible language. Maryland has done nothing, (though we have talked much), in favor of internal improvements, or to encourage domestic industry, except through the public spirit of some private individuals located in Baltimore or Frederick—and, by a strange waywardness of policy, our representatives and delegates have generally, in fact, discouraged those who would have effected them, to increase the population and wealth of the state. A great field is open for improvement in Maryland—the Susquehannah and the Potomac, and the abundance of water-power adjacent to Baltimore, with our valuable mines and minerals, invite capital and enterprise—and they must be promptly exerted, or the state will retrogade yet further and further.

*   *   *

There are about 100 sail of coasters on the American side of lake Erie—500 will be required after the Ohio canal is finished, and fairly in use. Buffalo, a mere village before the war, has 5,000 inhabitants, and the number is *daily* increasing. One steam boat on the lake had not sufficient business two years since—six are now well employed. We shall soon have *ports* on Huron and Michigan. Green Bay will be an important point, and Michilimackinac the centre of a very extensive trade which will pass either to New York, Philadelphia, or New Orleans, by canals and river navigation, every foot of the way! A thousand miles of space has been reduced as if to fifty. Distance is subdued by science, supported by public spirit.

By means of the canals made, or making, the *coal* trade will be a mighty business, and the price of fuel be much reduced in those parts where wood is becoming scarce. It abounds in the immediate neighborhood of Pittsburg, and, in 1822, a million of bushels were used by 10,000 inhabitants, including the manufactories—1,500,000 bushels will probably be used in that city during the present year, because of the increased population and business. What then will the great cities require?

*   *   *

It is probable that the domestic consumption of cotton in the present year, [in 1816, 90,000 bales],

will amount to about or more than one hundred and fifty thousand bales—possibly, to 175,000. Next year, unless because of some unlooked-for events, to 200,000! Suppose this were thrown into the European market! The price of cotton, paid to our planters, by our own manufacturers, has been greater, on the average, than they have received of the British purchasers of their staple. About 30,000 bales annually arrive at Providence, R. I. for the mills in the neighborhood. Many single establishments at other places use 1,000—some 1,500, some 2,000! The consumption at Baltimore is 4,000.

*   *   *

There are between 50 and 60 cotton and woollen factories in New Hampshire, and it is supposed that they make 33,000,000 yards of cloth per annum. In 1810, the quantity made was only 4,274,185 yards. At Dover, 21,000 spindles and 750 power looms were lately at work, or preparing. At Salmon Falls, a village with 1,600 inhabitants has *jumped* up. Many mills are building with brick—one finished is 390 by 40, another 220 by 49, and six stories high! At New Market there is also a new village with 1,000 inhabitants—the capital of this last company is $600,000. This establishment now makes, or speedily will make, 3,600 yards of cloth, daily—though it has only just started, as it were. When the works are completed, a million and a half of yards of cloth will be made in a year, at New Market.

The capital vested in manufactures in Massachusetts, including the new works, may be estimated at between twenty-five and thirty millions of dollars—the factories, in 1824, were 161. At Lowell, 1,700,000 dollars have been recently employed. At Waltham, about the same sum; its stock has been sold at 40 per cent. above par. At Merrimack 1,200,000, all paid in; the Hamilton company has 600,000. At Taunton, 250 pieces of calico are made daily—employing 1,000, persons!—The furnaces at Wareham make 4,000 tons of metal annually, and there are two rolling and slitting mills and three forges at the same place, with large cotton mills, fulling mills, &c. Several villages, with with from 1,000 to 1,500 inhabitants have been built within a few years, all whose inhabitants were employed or subsisted by the factories. A busy, healthful population teems on spots over which a rabbit, a little while since, could hardly have made his way— . . .

The manufactories of Rhode Island, Connecticut and Vermont make up a large amount of capital—In Rhode Island there are about ninety cotton mills, and new ones are building! We venture to assert that the *surplus* product of the people of Rhode Island, aided as they are by scientific power, is of greater value than the surplus products of the whole state of Virginia, in which that power is not much used. By "surplus" I mean a value beyond what is required for the subsistence of the people. One person, assisted by machinery, is equal to from 100 to 200 without it. One hundred and fifty persons are employed in making lace at Newport, R.I. It is made at several other places, splendid, and as good, and at a less price than the imported. Providence is, perhaps, the richest town of its size in the world—and its population rapidly increases.

*   *   *

[Mr. Webster, at a late public dinner, gave the following appropriate and veritable sentiment:

"The mechanics and manufacturers of New England—Men who teach us how a little country is to be made a great one."

The females employed in the factories are remarkable for the propriety of their conduct—to be suspected of bad behaviour is to be dismissed.]

The cotton and woollen cloths made in New York are valued at from 15 to 18,000,000 dollars per ann. There are large manufactories of iron, wool, cotton, leather, glass, paper, &c. &c. One brewery at Newburg covers 7,500 square feet of ground. Hudson teems with manufacturing establishments, and the splendid cotton and woollen works at Matteawan are famous—they support a large population. Duchess, Oneida and many other counties, are *filled* with factories.

*   *   *

A grand display of manufactures has just been made at the Franklin Institute, Philadelphia. It was estimated that the rooms were visited by seven thousand persons in one day, and the crowd was great during the whole time of the exhibition. Cloths, cottons, glass-wares, porcelain, silks, works in wood, in metals, and of almost every description of materials, many of the very best and most beautiful kinds, were shewn and in astonishing variety and quantity. . . . All these things were, of course, of American manufacture.

*   *   *

Four thousand weavers find employment in Philadelphia—and several new villages of manufacturers have been built in the neighborhood. Among them Manyunk, with 2,000 inhabitants. The furnaces of Huntingdon county, only, make 6,000 tons of iron, annually. There are 165 hatters in the small town of Reading.

The city of Pittsburg contains 1,873 buildings and 12,796 inhabitants. One paper mill employs 190 persons—there are seven other paper mills in the city or its immediate neighborhood—seven rolling and slitting mills; eight air foundries, six steam engine factories, one large wire factory, seven glass works, &c. &c. Some of these are mighty establishments—one of them has two steam engines, of 100 and 120 horse power, to drive the machinery! *One* of the factories at Pittsburg makes glass to the value of 160,000 dollars a year—and others do nearly as much business. The whole glass manufacture in the United States is worth not less than three millions annually.

*   *   *

Delaware has many valuable cotton mills—several important woollen factories, and of paper, &c. The powder works of Mr. Dupont are said to be the largest in the world; and there are few more extensive establishments for making paper than one of those on the Brandywine.

In Maryland, there are various large and respectable factories in Cecil, Baltimore, Frederick and Washington counties—but we cannot give many particulars, just now.

*   *   *

Many extensive iron works are going into opera-tion in the northern part of *Ohio*, in consequence of the market about to be opened by the canals. There are large establishments of various kinds at Steubenville and Cincinnati, and respectable ones scattered through the country, and the flocks of sheep of Mr. Dickinson and others, are justly fa-mous. . . . In Jefferson county, in which Steu-benville is located, there are 25,000 sheep. Mr. Dickinson's flock is 8,000. At Steubenville, besides the great cloth manufactory, there are 2 steam flour mills, 2 do. cotton mills, 1 do. paper mill. 2 breweries, 2 copperas manufactories, 1 air foundry, 1 steam engine factory, 1 machine factory, 2 carding machines, &c. some of them very exten-sive. There are numerous valuable factories in Kentucky, Indiana and Tennessee—and some in western Virginia, North Carolina, &c. but we have little or not any particular information concerning them.

*   *   *

Before the perfect establishment of the cotton manufacture in the United States, those kind of goods which now sell for 12 cents, cost the con-sumers 25 cents! Cotton, for the last two or three years, has averaged a greater price for American consumption than it sold for in Europe! Let the planter look to this—it is true.

In 1815, in a congressional report, it was esti-mated that 200,000 persons were employed in the cotton and woollen manufactories of the United States! The present number engaged in *all* sorts of manufactories cannot be less than *two millions.* What a market do they *create.* We shall attempt to *calculate* it hereafter.

The hats, caps and bonnets, of straw or grass, manufactured in the United States, employ about 25,000 persons, chiefly females, and produce $825,000, in Massachusetts, only! The whole value of this manufacture is, probably, about a million and a half yearly.

The quantity of flannel now made in the United States is considerably greater than the whole importation ever amounted to—as reported at the custom houses.

Silk begins to be extensively cultivated in several of the states. The silk raised and manufactured in the town of Mansfield, Con. in 1825, was 3,000 lbs. worth $15,000, and in Windham county, in the same state, silk worth 54,000 dollars a year. We have seen fine specimens from North Carolina and one from Missouri. It is a very profitable cultivation, and nearly the whole business is done by women and children, who would otherwise be idle, and so it is pretty nearly a clear gain. One acre of land planted with mulberry trees, will feed as many worms as will make silk worth $200, in a good season.

*   *   *

There are probably not less than fifteen millions of sheep in the United States, and their numbers is in-creasing, though the price of woollen goods is very low—*too low.* But our farmers must raise less grain, and more of other articles than heretofore. Flax is exceedingly wanted—we import large quan-tities for our manufactories. It is abundantly proved in the neighborhood of Philadelphia and York, Pa. Georgetown, (Col.) Vevay, Indiana, &c. that the vine will flourish, and that excellent wine may be made in the United States; and 20,000 hands detached from the cultivation of wheat to that of the vine, would make a great difference in the general products of our agriculture. The olive begins to be cultivated as a crop in the south, and the Palma Christi grows bountifully. A moderate degree of attention to a few *new* articles of agricul-ture, would save us from five to eight millions of dollars a year, *and be so much of a clear gain.* The cultivation of the vine, especially in the neighbor-hood of cities, wherein the grapes may be sold, is wonderfully profitable. Half an acre of land, Mr. Carr's vineyard, near Philadelphia, produced 260 gallons of wine, the value of which, with that of the grapes sold, is estimated at $670, for the present year: *one* vine yielded 300 lbs. of fine grapes. . . .

*   *   *

It may generally be observed, that migrations from the eastern and middle Atlantic states to the west are not nearly so common as they were, except to particular sections. Employment and profit is found at home. The facts shewn at the next census will probably surprise even those who may have calculated the probable population of the several states.

* / * *

What then would be the state of our country, if our work-shops were in Europe? We should have, as it were, to live in caves and be clothed in skins. But we shall speak of these things hereafter—the whole intent of my present undertaking being to afford some faint idea of the importance of the manufacturing interest, and to show the people what has been done by the encouragement of the national industry, that they may more and more attend to the subject, and resolve that their public agents, whether of the general government or of the states, *shall* rather accelerate than impede the progress of things so indispensable to the general welfare—so

inseparably connected with the employment and profit of every citizen of the United States.

* * *

Review Questions

1. What evidence did Niles present to prove that manufacturing was a positive development for the country?
2. Did manufacturing appear to be a regional as well as a national issue?
3. What were the primary products being manufactured in the country at that time?
4. Did Niles note a connection between production, population, and prosperity?

JOSEPHINE L. BAKER

FROM *The Lowell Offering* (1845)

Niles only briefly mentioned Lowell, Massachusetts, yet that town garnered much attention for the factory system that operated there. Of interest to everyone was not just the system of production but the social system that the manufacturers, the Boston Associates, engineered to support it. Along with the numerous cotton mills that they erected in Lowell starting in 1822, these industrialists built boardinghouses for their workers, most of whom were single young women. The Boston Associates deliberately set out to attract such laborers by offering higher wages than women could make at the other legal occupations open to them, and by guaranteeing respectable living conditions that included educational opportunities. When word got out, as it quickly did, young women who needed to support themselves as well as those who wanted to work for a few years to build dowries or help their families financially flocked to the mills. The investment in wages and living as well as working conditions paid off: the manufacturers paid a reliable and generally biddable workforce with wages that, though high for women, were still lower than those for men. Initially many people hailed this system as more humane than labor practices elsewhere as well as an effective way of tapping underutilized human resources within the social order. As time went by, however, the physical plant of both factory and boardinghouse deteriorated. Supposedly benevolent paternalism turned into sometimes malevolent policing, especially when the mill workers protested, which they increasingly did. Their work and educational experiences so empowered some of the women that they were no longer as obedient or deferential as their managers wished. Josephine L. Baker revealed such sentiments when she described factory life in The Lowell Offering, *a magazine edited by and for women after 1842.*

From Benita Eisler, ed., *The Lowell Offering: Writings by New England Mill Women (1840– 1845)* (1977; New York: W. W. Norton & Co., Inc., 1998), pp. 77–82.

*   *   *

There is the "counting-room," a long, low, brick building, and opposite is the "store-house," built of the same material, after the same model. Between them, swings the ponderous gate that shuts the mills in from the world without. But, stop; we must get "a pass," ere we go through, or "the watchman will be after us." Having obtained this, we will stop on the slight elevation by the gate, and view the mills. The one to the left rears high its huge sides of brick and mortar, and the belfry, towering far above the rest, stands out in bold relief against the rosy sky. The almost innumerable windows glitter, like gems, in the morning sunlight. It is six and a half stories high, and, like the fabled monster of old, who guarded the sacred waters of Mars, it seems to guard its less aspiring sister to the right; that is five and a half stories high, and to it is attached the repair-shop. If you please, we will pass to the larger factory,—but be careful, or you will get lost in the mud, for this yard is not laid out in such beautiful order, as some of the factory yards are, nor can it be.

We will just look into the first room. It is used for cleaning cloth. You see the scrubbing and scouring machines are in full operation, and gigging and fulling are going on in full perfection. As it is very damp, and the labor is performed by the other half of creation, we will pass on, for fear of incurring their jealousy. But the very appearance might indicate that there are, occasionally, *fogs* and *clouds*; and not only fogs and clouds, but sometimes plentiful showers. In the second room the cloth is "*finished*," going through the various operations of burling, shearing, brushing, inking, fine-drawing, pressing, and packing for market. This is

the pleasantest room on the corporation, and consequently they are never in want of help. The shearing, brushing, pressing and packing is done by males, while the burling, inking, marking and fine-drawing is performed by females. We will pass to the third room, called the "cassimere weaving-room," where all kinds of cloths are woven, from plain to the most exquisite fancy. There are between eighty and ninety looms, and part of the dressing is also done here. The fourth is the "broad weaving-room," and contains between thirty and forty looms; and broad sure enough they are. Just see how lazily the lathe drags backward and forward, and the shuttle—how spitefully it hops from one end of it to the other. But we must not stop longer, or perchance it will hop at us. You look weary; but, never mind! there was an end to Jacob's ladder, and *so* there is a termination to these stairs. Now if you please we will go up to the next room, where the spinning is done. Here we have spinning jacks or jennies that dance merrily along whizzing and singing, as they spin out their "long yarns," and it seems but pleasure to watch their movements; but it is hard work, and requires good health and much strength. Do not go too near, as we shall find that they do not understand the established rules of *etiquette*, and might unceremoniously knock us over. We must not stop here longer, for it is twelve o'clock, and we have the "carding-room" to visit before dinner. There are between twenty and thirty set of cards located closely together, and I beg of you to be careful as we go amongst them, or you will get caught in the machinery. You walk as though you were afraid of getting blue. Please excuse me, if I ask you not to be afraid. 'Tis a wholesome color, and soap and water will wash it off.

The girls, you see, are partially guarded against it, by over-skirts and sleeves; but as it is not *fashionable* to wear masks, they cannot keep it from their faces. You appear surprised at the hurry and bustle now going on in the room, but your attention has been so engaged that you have forgotten the hour. Just look at the clock, and you will find that it wants but five minutes to "bell time." We will go to the door, and be ready to start when the others do; and now, while we are waiting, just cast your eyes to the stair-way, and you will see another flight of stairs, leading to another spinning-room; a picker is located somewhere in that region, but I cannot give you a description of it, as I have never had the courage to ascend more than five flight of stairs at a time. And—but the bell rings.

Now look out—not for the engine—but for the rush to the stair-way. O mercy! what a crowd. I do not wonder you gasp for breath; but, keep up courage; we shall soon be on terra firma again. Now, safely landed, I hope to be excused for taking you into such a crowd. Really, it would not be fair to let you see the factory girls and machinery for nothing. I shall be obliged to hurry you, as it is some way to the boarding-house, and we have but thirty minutes from the time the bell begins to ring till it is done ringing again; and then all are required to be at their work. There is a group of girls yonder, going our way; let us overtake them, and hear what they are talking about. Something unpleasant I dare say, from their earnest gestures and clouded brows.

"Well, I do think it is too bad," exclaims one.

"So do I," says another. "This cutting down wages *is not* what they cry it up to be. I wonder how they'd like to work as hard as we do, digging and drudging day after day, from morning till night, and then, every two or three years, have their wages reduced. I rather guess it wouldn't set very well."

"And, besides this, who ever heard, of such a thing as their being raised again," says the first speaker. "I confess that I never did, so long as I've worked in the mill, and that's been these ten years."

"Well, it is real provoking any how," returned the other, "for my part I should think they had made a clean sweep this time. I wonder what they'll do next."

"Listeners never hear any good of themselves" is a trite saying, and, for fear it may prove true in our case, we will leave this busy group, and get some dinner. There is an open door inviting us to enter. We will do so. You can hang your bonnet and shawl on one of those hooks, that extend the length of the entry for that purpose, or you can lay them on the banisters, as some do. Please to walk into the dining-room. Here are two large square tables, covered with checked clothes and loaded down with smoking viands, the odor of which is very inviting. But we will not stop here; there is the long table in the front room, at which ten or fifteen can be comfortably seated. You may place yourself at the head. Now do not be bashful or wait to be helped, but comply with the oft-made request, "help yourself" to whatever you like best; for you have but a few minutes allotted you to spend at the table. The reason why, is because you are a rational, intelligent, thinking being, and ought to know enough to swallow your food whole; whereas a horse or an ox, or any other dumb beast knows no better than to spend an hour in the *useless* process of mastication. The bell rings again, and the girls are hurrying to the mills; you, I suppose, have seen enough of them for one day, so we will walk up stairs and have a *tete-a-tete*.

You ask, if there are so many things objectionable, why we work in the mill. Well, simply for this reason,—every situation in life, has its trials which must be borne, and factory life has no more than any other. There are many things we do not like; many occurrences that send the warm blood mantling to the cheek when they must be borne in silence, and many harsh words and acts that are not called for. There are objections also to the number of hours we work, to the length of time allotted to our meals, and to the low wages allowed for labor; objections that must and will be answered; for the time has come when something, besides the clothing and feeding of the body is to be thought of; when the mind is to be clothed and fed; and this cannot be as it should be, with the present system of labor. Who, let me ask, can find that pleasure in life which they should, when it is spent in this way. Without time for the laborer's own work, and the improvement of the mind, save the few evening hours; and even then if the mind is enriched and stored with useful knowledge, it must be at the expense of health. And the feeling too, that comes over us (there is no use in denying it) when we hear the bell calling us away from repose that tired nature loudly claims—the feeling, that we are *obliged to go*. And these few hours, of which we have spoken, are far too short, three at the most at the close of day. Surely, methinks, every heart that lays claim to humanity will feel 'tis not enough. But this, we hope will, ere long, be done away with, and labor made what it should be; pleasant and inviting to every son and daughter of the human family.

There is a brighter side to this picture, over which we would not willingly pass without notice, and an answer to the question, why we work here? The time we *do* have is our own. The money we earn comes promptly; more so than in any other situation; and our work, though laborious is the same from day to day; we know what it is, and when finished we feel perfectly free, till it is time to commence it again.

Besides this, there are many pleasant associations connected with factory life, that are not to be found elsewhere.

There are lectures, evening schools and libraries, to which all may have access. The one thing needful here, is the time to improve them as we ought.

There is a class, of whom I would speak, that work in the mills, and will while they continue in operation. Namely, the many who have no home, and who come here to seek, in this busy, bustling "City of Spindles," a competency that shall enable them in after life, to live without being a burden to society,—the many who toil on, without a murmur, for the support of an aged mother or orphaned brother and sister. For the sake of them, we earnestly hope labor may be reformed; that the miserable, selfish spirit of competition, now in our midst, may be thrust from us and consigned to eternal oblivion.

There is one other thing that must be mentioned ere we part, that is the practice of sending agents through the country to decoy girls away from their homes with the promise of high wages, when the market is already stocked to overflowing. This is certainly wrong, for it lessens the value of labor, which should be ever held in high estimation, as the path marked out by the right hand of GOD, in which man should walk with dignity.

*   *   *

REVIEW QUESTIONS

1. Was there a moral to this story?
2. What criticisms did the author have about life and work in Lowell? What did she praise?
3. What were some of the different operations performed to manufacture cloth?
4. Which of the tasks was performed by the minority, the men, in this workforce?

ANNA MARIA KLINGER

Letters Home to Germany (1849–1850s)

Businessmen and families in need of laborers and servants often turned to immigrants. They could generally pay such workers less than they did native sons, and expend less worry about "protecting" them than they did native daughters. Although most of the immigrants could offer only unskilled or semi-skilled labor, there were artisans as well as professionals among them. Of the two major immigrant groups in the first half of the nineteenth century, the Germans, despite language problems, generally found greater acceptance than the Irish, mainly because there was already a strong German presence in America from the earlier colonial migrations, and because they were often better educated and financially prepared. Germans were also religiously diverse; although there were some Catholics and Jews, the majority belonged to Protestant sects. Furthermore, while many Germans settled in the eastern cities, many more moved west to establish new farms and communities there. Poor harvests, too-small farms, and mechanized industry drove many Germans to America, where, once settled, they wrote home to entice friends and family to join them. Anna Maria Klinger came from a poor, winegrowing family in Württemberg. She arrived in America in 1849 and immediately found work with the family of a German-American pharmacist. She soon married another immigrant, Franz Schano, who had deserted from the Bavarian army. They, in turn, helped five other Klingers emigrate during the 1850s.

From Walter D. Kamphoefner, Wolfgang Helbich, and Ulrike Sommer, eds., *News from the Land of Freedom: German Immigrants Write Home*, trans. Susan Carter Vogel (Ithaca: Cornell University Press, 1991), pp. 534, 536–39. Editorial insertions that appear in square brackets are from Kamphoefner's edition. Editorial insertions that appear in braces are by the editor of this Norton edition.—*Ed.*

Anna Maria Klinger

New Jork, March 18, 1849

Beloved parents and brothers and sisters,

Out of filial and sisterly love I feel obliged to inform you about my well-being in America. After a long and trying journey I arrived in New Jork safe and sound after all, and until now I have been quite well. . . . Now I want to tell you about my situation, that is that on the same day I arrived in New Jork, I went into service for a German family. I am content with my wages for now, compared to Germany, I make 4 dollars a month in our money [10] guilders, if you can speak English then it's considerably better, since the English pay a good wage, a servant gets 7 to 10 dollars a month, but if you can't speak or understand English you can't ask for so much pay. But I hope that things will get better, for it's always like that, no one really likes it at first, and especially if you are so lonely and forlorn in a foreign land like I am, no friends or relatives around. . . . The dear Lord is my shield and refuge. . . . I keep thinking you are fearful and worried about me because you have not received a letter for so long, first of all, we were at sea for one hundred and 5 days, 7 weeks we were docked at Blümuth [Plymouth] before our ship was done. You probably read in the letter I wrote to the mayor about the bad luck we had. From England to America things went well, we still had one big storm, but we suffered no more misfortune, there were 200 and 60 passengers on the ship. My journey from Stuttgart to Antwerben went well, I met up with those 3 girls who were also going from Stuttgart to America in Maintz, but they'd already met up with companions on the way, they started behaving so badly on the journey already, and at sea there were two tailor boys with those girls, I got annoyed because I couldn't stand such loose behavior, one of them went to Viladelfe [Philadelphia] and another in New Jork. . . .

The city of New Jork is the largest in America, it is so big you can't walk around it in one day, the religious institutions are like in Germany, there are 182 churches here, but belonging to different religions. Here you can find people from all corners of the world, there are about 4,000 German residents alone {actually, there were between fifty and sixty thousand}. I will be able to write more in the future when I have been here longer. But I do want to tell you this [that so many deserters] from the army have arrived here. . . . Gottlieb {her brother} should give my best to his cook where he was when I left, she only needs to come to America, it's very good for girls who have to work in service. I haven't regretted it yet. Write me, too, about what's happening in Stuttgart. Dear parents, my next letter will make you happier. . . .

Anna Maria Schano, née Klinger

[New York, probably mid-1850] [Beginning of letter missing] I've saved up to now in the time we've been married some 40 dollars in cash, not counting my clothes. Dear parents and brothers and sisters, I certainly don't want to tell you what to do, do what you want, for some like it here and some don't, but the only ones who don't like it here had it good in Germany, but I also think you would like it here since you never had anything good in Germany. I'm certainly glad not to be over there, and only those who don't want to work don't like it here, since in America you have to work if you want to amount to anything, you mustn't feel

ashamed, that's just how you amount to something, and so I want to tell you again to do what you want, since it can seem too trying on the journey and in America as well, and then you heap the most bitter reproaches on those who talked you into coming, since it all depends on whether you have good luck, just like in Germany. Dear parents, you wrote me that Daniel wants to come to America and doesn't have any money, that is certainly a problem. Now I want to give you my opinion, I've often thought about what could be done, I thought 1st if he could borrow the money over there, then when he has saved enough over here then he could send it back over, like a lot of people do, and secondly, I thought we would like to pay for him to come over, but right now we can't since it costs 28 dollars a person and I also want to tell you since my husband wrote to you, the money we want to send you, whether you want to use it to have one or two come over here or if you want to spend it on yourselves, you just have to let us know so we have an idea how much you still need, and you'll have to see to it that you have some more money, too, since we can't pay it all. [. . .] Things in Daniel's *Profesion* are not the best, he shouldn't count on that, it would be better if he were a tailor or shoemaker, but it doesn't matter, a lot of people don't work in their *Profesion* and learn others or other businesses, since you don't have to pay to learn a trade in America. Dear parents and brothers and sisters, if one of you comes over here and comes to stay with us we will certainly take care of you, since we are now well known, and you needn't be so afraid of America, when you come to America, just imagine you were moving to Stuttgart, that's how many Germans you can see here.

And as far as the Americans are concerned, whites and blacks, they won't harm you, since the blacks are very happy when you don't do anything to them, the only thing is the problem with the language. It's not as easy to learn as you think, even now I don't know much, and there are many people here who don't even learn it in 6 to 8 years, but if you start off working for Americans then you can learn in one year as much as in 10 years living with Germans. Dear parents and brothers and sisters, I'd like to be with you, you will surely be pleased to get the picture of us, to see me again, and I would also be so happy to see you again. In my dreams I've often been with you and also in my old job in Germany, but when I woke up, it wasn't true, but still I am happy in any case that I am in America. . . . We would have liked to have sent a few dollars along with this letter but at the moment we don't have much money, since I can well imagine you could use it now, but things go slowly the first few years, you have to take care of yourself, since the motto in America is help yourself. . . .

REVIEW QUESTIONS

1. What does Klinger reveal about the process of emigration/immigration?
2. How does she promote America to her relatives in Germany?
3. What does she believe to be the key(s) to doing well in America?

JOHN FRANCIS MAGUIRE

FROM *The Irish in America* (1867)

The Irish were weighed down by many woes in the nineteenth century, prime among them were British dominion and the famine wrought by the potato rot. The weight buried many at home and squeezed others out to find freedom and food abroad. These Irish immigrants, who by 1860 composed the largest foreign-born group in America, faced perhaps the greatest prejudice. John Francis Maguire, looking back on decades of Irish migration, tried to explain why to both Irish and American readers in his book, The Irish in America.

From John Francis Maguire, *The Irish in America*, 4th ed, (New York: D. & J. Sadlier & Company, 1867), pp. 215–19, 240, 252, 281–84, 333–37.

*   *   *

Irish emigrants of the peasant and labouring class were generally poor, and after defraying their first expenses on landing had little left to enable them to push their way into the country in search of such employment as was best suited to their knowledge and capacity: though had they known what was in store for too many of them and their children, they would have endured the severest privation and braved any hardship, in order to free themselves from the fatal spell in which the fasci-nation of a city life has meshed the souls of so many of their race. Either they brought little money with them, and were therefore unable to go on; or that little was plundered from them by those whose trade it was to prey upon the inexperience or credulity of the new-comer. Therefore, to them, the poor or the plundered Irish emigrants, the first and pressing necessity was employment; and so splendid seemed the result of that employment, even the rudest and most laborious kind, as compared with what they were able to earn in the old country, that it at once predisposed them in favour of a city life. . . . Then there were old friends and former companions or acquaintances to be met with at every street-corner; and there was news to give, and news to receive—too often, perhaps, in the liquor-store or dram-shop kept by a country-man—probably 'a neighbour's child,' or 'a decent boy from the next ploughland.' Then 'the chapel was handy,' and 'a Christian wouldn't be overtaken for want of a priest;' then there was 'the schooling convenient for the children, poor things,'—so the glorious chance was lost; and the simple, innocent countryman, to whom the trees of the virgin forest were nodding their branches in friendly invitation, and the blooming prairie expanded its fruitful bosom in vain, became the denizen of a city, for which he was unqualified by training, by habit, and by association. Possibly it was the mother's courage that failed her as she glanced at the flock of little ones who clustered around her, or timidly clung to her skirts, and she thought of the new dangers and further perils that awaited them; and it was her maternal influence that was flung into the trembling balance against the country and in favour of the city. Or employment was readily found for one of the girls, or one or two of the boys, and things looked so hopeful in the fine place that all thoughts of the fresh, breezy, healthful plain or hill-side were shut out at that supreme moment of the emigrant's destiny; though many a time after did he and they long for one breath of pure air, as they languished in the stifling heat of a summer in a tenement house. Or the pioneer of the family—most likely a young girl—had found good employment, and, with the fruits of her honest toil, had gradually brought out brothers and sisters, father and mother, for whose companionship her heart ever yearned; and possibly her affection was stronger than her prudence, or she knew nothing of the West and its limitless resources. Or sickness, that had followed the emigrant's family across the ocean, fastened upon some member of the group as they touched the soil for which they had so ardently prayed, and though the fever or the cholera did not destroy a precious life, it did the almost as precious opportunity of a better future! the spring of that energy which was sufficient to break asunder the

ties and habits of previous years—sufficient for flight from home and country—was broken, and those who faced America in high hope were thenceforth added to the teeming population of a city—to which class, it might be painful to speculate.

*   *   *

This headlong rushing into the great cities has the necessary effect of unduly adding to their population, thereby overtaxing their resources, however large or even extraordinary these resources may be, and of rudely disturbing the balance of supply and demand. The hands—the men, women, and children—thus become too many for the work to be done, as the work becomes too little for the hands willing and able to do it. What is worse, there are too many mouths for the bread of independence; and thus the bread of charity has to supplement the bread which is purchased with the sweat of the brow. Happy would it be for the poor in the towns of America, as elsewhere, if the bread of charity were the *only* bread with which the bread of independence is supplemented. But there is also the bread of degradation, and the bread of crime. And when the moral principle is blunted by abject misery, or weakened by disappointments and privation, there is but a narrow barrier between poverty and crime; and this, too frequently, is soon passed. For such labour as is thus recklessly poured into the great towns there is constant peril. It is true, there are seasons when there is a glut of work, when the demand exceeds the supply—when some gigantic industry or some sudden necessity clamours for additional hands; but there are also, and more frequently, seasons when work is slack, seasons of little employment, seasons of utter paralysis and stagnation. Cities are liable to occasional depressions of trade, resulting from over production, or the successful rivalry of foreign nations, or even portions of the same country; or there are smashings of banks, and commercial panics, and periods of general mistrust. Or, owing to the intense severity of certain seasons, there is a total cessation of employments of particular kinds, by which vast numbers of people are flung idle on the streets. . . .

The evil of overcrowding is magnified to a prodigious extent in New York, which, being *the* port of arrival—the Gate of the New World—receives a certain addition to its population from almost every ship-load of emigrants that passes through Castle Garden. There is scarcely any city in the world possessing greater resources than New York, but these resources have long since been strained to the very uttermost to meet the yearly increasing demands created by this continuous accession to its inhabitants; . . .

As in all cities growing in wealth and in population, the dwelling accommodation of the poor is yearly sacrificed to the increasing necessities or luxury of the rich. While spacious streets and grand mansions are on the increase, the portions of the city in which the working classes once found an economical residence, are being steadily encroached upon—just as the artisan and labouring population of the City of London are driven from their homes by the inexorable march of city improvements, and streets and courts and alleys are swallowed up by a great thoroughfare or a gigantic railway terminus. . . .

As stated on official authority, there are 16,000 tenement houses in New York, and in these there dwell more than half a million of people! This astounding fact is of itself so suggestive of misery and evil, that it scarcely requires to be enlarged upon; . . .

*   *   *

It is not at all necessary that an Irish immigrant should go West, whatever and how great the inducements it offers to the enterprising. There is land to be had, under certain circumstances and conditions, in almost every State in the Union. And there is no State in which the Irish peasant who is living from hand to mouth in one of the great cities as a day-labourer, may not improve his condition by betaking himself to his natural and legitimate avocation—the cultivation of the soil. Nor is the vast region of the South unfavourable to the laborious and energetic Irishman. On the contrary, there is no portion of the American continent in which he would receive a more cordial welcome, or

meet with more favourable terms. This would not have been so before the war, or the abolition of slavery, and the upset of the land system which was based upon the compulsory labour of the negro.

. . . The policy of the South is to increase and strengthen the white population, so as not to be, as the South yet is, too much dependent on the negro; and the planter who, ten years ago, would not sever a single acre from his estate of 2,000, or 10,000, or 20,000 acres, will now readily divide, if not all, at least a considerable portion of it, into saleable quantities, to suit the convenience of purchasers. . . .

*   *   *

Were I asked to say what I believed to be the most serious obstacle to the advancement of the Irish in America, I would unhesitatingly answer—*Drink*; meaning thereby the excessive use, or abuse, of that which, when taken in excess, intoxicates, deprives man of his reason, interferes with his industry, injures his health, damages his position, compromises his respectability, renders him unfit for the successful exercise of his trade, profession, or employment—which leads to quarrel, turbulence, violence, crime. I believe this fatal tendency to excessive indulgence to be the main cause of all the evils and miseries and disappointments that have strewed the great cities of America with those wrecks of Irish honour, Irish virtue, and Irish promise, which every lover of Ireland has had, one time or other, bitter cause to deplore. Differences of race and religion are but as a feather's weight in the balance; indeed these differences tend rather to add interest to the steady and self-respecting citizen. Were this belief, as to the tendency of the Irish to excess in the use of stimulants, based on the testimony of Americans, who might probably be somewhat prejudiced, and therefore inclined to judge unfavourably, or pronounce unsparingly, I should not venture to record it; but it was impressed upon me by Irishmen of every rank, class, and condition of life, wherever I went, North or South, East or West. It was openly deplored, or it was reluctantly admitted. I rarely heard an Irishman say that his country or his religion was an effectual barrier to his progress in the United States. . . .

The question here naturally arises,—do the Irish drink more than the people of any other nationality in America? The result of my observation and inquiries leads me to the conviction that *they do not*. How then comes it that the habit, if common to all is so pernicious to them? There are many and various reasons why this is so. In the first place, they are strangers, and, as such, more subject to observation and criticism than the natives of the country. They are, also, as a rule, of a faith different to that of the majority of the American people; and the fact that they are so does not render the observation less keen, nor does it render the criticism more gentle. Then, be it constitution, or temperament, or whatever else, excess seems to be more injurious to them than to others. They are genial, open-hearted, generous, and social in their tendencies; they love company, court excitement, and delight in affording pleasure or gratification to their friends. And not only are their very virtues leagued against them, but the prevailing custom of the country is a perpetual challenge to indulgence.

This prevailing custom or habit springs more from a spirit of kindness than from a craving for sensual gratification. Invitations to drink are universal, as to rank and station, time and place, hour and circumstance; they literally rain upon you. The Americans are perhaps about the most thoroughly wide-awake people in the world, yet they must have an 'eye-opener' in the morning. To prepare for meals, you are requested to fortify your stomach and stimulate your digestive powers with an 'appetizer.' To get along in the day, you are invited to accept the assistance of a 'pony.' If you are startled at the mention of 'a drink,' you find it difficult to refuse 'at least a nip.' And who but the most morose—and the Irishman is all geniality—can resist the influence of 'a smile?' Now a 'cocktail,' now a 'cobler'—here a 'julep,' there a 'smasher;' or if you shrink from the potency of the 'Bourbon,' you surely are not afraid of 'a single glass of lager beer!' To the generous, company-loving Irishman there is something like treason to friendship and death to good-fellowship in refusing these kindly-meant in-

vitations; but woe to the impulsive Irishman who becomes the victim of this custom of the country! The Americans drink, the Germans drink, the Scotch drink, the English drink—all drink with more or less injury to their health or circumstances; but whatever the injury to these, or any of these, it is far greater to the mercurial and light-hearted Irish than to races of hard head and lethargic temperament. . . .

It must be admitted that, in some cities of America—by no means in all, or anything like all—the Irish element figures unenviably in the police records, and before the inferior tribunals; and that in these cities the committals are more numerous than they should be in proportion to the numerical strength of the Irish population. . . . The deadly crimes—the secret poisonings, the deliberate murders, the deep-laid frauds, the cunningly-masked treachery, the dark villany, the spider-like preparation for the destruction of the unwary victim—these are not common to the Irish. Rows, riots, turbulence, acts of personal violence perpetrated in passion, are what are principally recorded of them in the newspapers; and in nine cases out of ten, these offences against the peace and order of the community, and which so deeply prejudice the public mind, not only against the perpetrators, but, what is far worse, against the ir-race and country, are attributable to one cause, and one cause alone—*drink*. . . .

*   *   *

. . . Whatever estimate Americans may form of their Irish fellow-citizens, be that estimate favourable or unfavourable, there is but one opinion as to the moral character of Irish women. Their reputation for purity does not rest on the boastful assertions of those who either regard all matters concerning their race or country from a favourable point of view, or who, to gratify a natural feeling, would wilfully exaggerate, or possibly misstate a fact: it is universally admitted. . . . Prejudices, strong prejudices, there are in the States, as in all countries in which diversity of race and religion exists; and where this diversity comprehends race and religion in the same individuals, these prejudices are certain to be the stronger and the more deeply rooted. The Irish Catholic has to contend against this double prejudice, which nevertheless is not powerful enough to interfere with the conviction, indeed admission, as to the moral character of the women of that country and that faith. The poor Irish emigrant girl may possibly be rude, undisciplined, awkward—just arrived in a strange land, with all the rugged simplicity of her peasant's training; but she is good and honest. Nor, as she rapidly acquires the refinement inseparable from an improved condition of life, and daily association with people of cultivated manners, does she catch the contagion of the vices of the great centres of wealth and luxury. Whatever her position,—and it is principally amongst the humble walks of life the mass of the Irish are still to be found,—she maintains this one noble characteristic: purity. In domestic service her merit is fully recognised. Once satisfied of the genuineness of her character, an American family will trust in her implicitly; and not only is there no locking up against her, but everything is left in her charge. Occasionally she may be hot tempered, difficult to be managed, perhaps a little 'turbulent'—especially when her country is sneered at, or her faith is wantonly ridiculed; but she is cheerful and laborious, virtuous and faithful.

An instance of very legitimate 'turbulence' occurred not long since in one of the most rising of the great Western cities. There lived, as a 'help,' in the house of a Protestant family, an intelligent and high-spirited Irish girl, remarkable for her exemplary conduct, and the zeal with which she discharged the duties of her position. Kate acted as a mother to a young brother and sister, whom she was bringing up with the greatest care; and a happy girl was Kate when she received good tidings of their progress in knowledge and piety. Kate, like many other people in the world, had her special torment, and that special torment was a playful-minded preacher who visited at the house, and who looked upon 'Bridget'—he *would* call her Bridget—as a fair butt for the exercise of his pleasant wit, of which he was justly proud. It was Kate's duty to attend table; and no sooner did she make

her appearance in the dining-room, than the playful preacher commenced his usual fun, which would be somewhat in this fashion: 'Well, Bridget, my girl! when did you pray last to the Virgin Mary? Tell me, Bridget, when were you with Father Pat? What did you give him, Bridget? What did the old fellow ask for the absolution this time? Now, I guess it was ten cents for the small sins, and $1 for the thumpers! Come now, Bridget, tell me what penance did that priest of yours give you?' Thus would the agreeable jester pelt the poor Irish girl with his generous pleasantries, to the amusement of the thoughtless, but to the serious annoyance of the fair-minded, who did not like to see her feelings so wantonly wounded. The mistress of the house mildly remonstrated with her servant's lively tormentor, though she did not herself admire 'Bridget's' form of prayer, and was willing to regard 'Father Pat's' absolution as a matter of bargain and sale. But the wit should have his way. 'Bridget' was a handsome girl, and the rogue liked to see the fire kindle in her grey eye, and the hot blood mantle over her fair round cheek; and then the laughter of his admirers was such delightful incense to his vanity, as peal after peal told how successfully the incorrigible wag 'roasted Bridget.' On one memorable day, however, his love of the humorous carried him just too far. A large company was assembled round the hospitable table of the mistress of the house. The preacher was present, and was brimming over with merriment. Kate entered the room, bearing a large tureen of steaming soup in her hands. 'Ho, ho, Bridget!—how are you, Bridget? Well, Bridget, what did you pay Father Pat for absolution this time? Come to me, Bridget, and I will give you as many dollars as will set you all straight with the old fellow for the next six months, and settle your account with purgatory too. Now, Bridget, tell us how many cents for each sin?' The girl had just reached the preacher as he finished his little joke; and if he wished to see the Irish eye flash out its light, and the Irish blood burn in the cheek, he had an excellent opportunity for enjoying that treat. It was Bridget's turn to be playful. Stopping next to his chair, and looking him steadily in his face, while she grasped the tureen of rich green-pea soup more firmly in her hands, she said: 'Now, sir, I often asked you to leave me alone, and not mind me, and not to insult me or my religion, what no real gentleman would do to a poor girl; and now, sir, as you want to know what I pay for absolution, here's my answer!' and, suiting the action to the word, she flung the hot steaming liquid over the face, neck, breast—entire person—of the playful preacher! . . . The sentiment—the generous American sentiment—was in Kate's favour, as she might have perceived in the manner of the guests. For the poor preacher, it may be said that the soup 'spoiled his dinner' for that day. He did not make his appearance again for some time; but when he did, it was as an altered and much-improved gentleman, who appeared to have lost all interest in the religious peculiarities of Kate, whom, strange to say, he never more called by the name of Bridget. The warm bath, so vigorously administered, had done him much service—Kate said, 'a power of good.'

*   *   *

REVIEW QUESTIONS

1. How was Maguire's book a commentary on American culture in general as well as on the Irish element within it in particular?
2. In combatting prejudice against the Irish, did Maguire perpetuate or even promote other biases?
3. What does this piece reveal about gender and class as well as ethnic relations and attitudes in the mid–nineteenth century?
4. What did the author believe most injured Irish interests and advancement in America? Did he say this was a problem of perception or practice?
5. Could this piece be used as a source on reform ideas and movements as well as on immigration? Explain.

SAMUEL F. B. MORSE

FROM *Imminent Dangers to the Free Institutions of the United States* (1835)

In another chapter of his book, John Maguire related the history of the Know-Nothing movement of the mid 1850s. He noted how adherents combined religious bigotry with nationalistic prejudice, all to the detriment of the Irish immigrant. He was quick to point out, however, that "there was nothing new in this Know-Nothingism. It was as old as the time of the Revolution, being Native Americanism under another name. Its animating spirit was hostility to the stranger—insane jealousy of the foreigner." While the elaborate organization and political power of the American (Know-Nothing) Party was a new development, Maguire had it right: this kind of intolerance was nothing new. Nativism grew as immigration increased. By the 1830s Americans fearful of possible immigrant power and cultural effects, including politicians and reformers, delivered impassioned arguments against unrestricted immigration. Prominent among them was Samuel F. B. Morse. Although he made a career of painting—an artist of some repute, he was chosen to paint a portrait of Lafayette for the city of

New York in 1825—Morse achieved lasting renown for inventing the telegraph. He was not the only one working on the concept, but his invention was the first to show itself practicable. With congressional support, Morse was able to build a line from Washington to Baltimore, and on 24 May 1844 he sent a passage from the Bible, "What hath God wrought," over the wire. Raised in a deeply religious, Protestant, home, Morse developed a strong antagonism against Catholicism, which became marked during his European tour in the early 1830s—the same tour that gave him some of the foundational ideas for the telegraph. On his return to a changing America he went public with his concerns, and found a ready audience.

From Samuel F. B. Morse, *Imminent Dangers to the Free Institutions of the United States through Foreign Immigration* . . . (1835; New York: Arno Press, Inc., 1969) pp. 6–15.

*   *   *

Our country, in the position it has given to foreigners who have made it their home, has pursued a course in relation to them, totally different from that of any other country in the world. This course, while it is liberal without example, subjects our institutions to peculiar dangers. In all other countries the foreigner, to whatever privileges he may be entitled by becoming a subject, can never be placed in a situation to be politically dangerous, for he has no share in the government of the country; . . .

. . . The writer believes, that since the time of the American Revolution, which gave the principles of Democratic liberty a home, those principles have never been in greater jeopardy than at the present moment. To his reasons for thus believing, he invites the unimpassioned investigation of every American citizen. If there is danger, let it arouse to defence. If it is a false alarm, let such explanations be given of most suspicious appearances as shall safely allay it. It is no *party* question, and the attempt to make it one, should be at once suspected. It concerns all of every party.

There is danger of re-action from Europe; and it is the part of common prudence to look for it, and to provide against it. The great political truth has recently been promulged at the capital of one of the principal courts of Europe, at Vienna, and by one of the profoundest scholars of Germany, (Frederick Schlegel, a devoted Roman Catholic, and one of the Austrian Cabinet,) the great truth,

clearly and unanswerably proved, that the *political revolutions to which European governments have been so long subjected, from the popular desires for liberty, are the natural effects of the Protestant Reformation.* That *Protestantism* favours *Republicanism*, while *Popery* as naturally supports *Monarchical* power. In these lectures, . . . there is a *most important* allusion to this country; and as it demonstrates one of the principal connecting points between European and American politics, and is the key to many of the mysterious doings that are in operation against American institutions under our own eyes, let Americans treasure it well in their memories. This is the passage:—"THE GREAT NURSERY *of these destructive principles,* (the principles of Democracy,) *the* GREAT REVOLUTIONARY SCHOOL *for* FRANCE *and* THE REST OF EUROPE, *is* NORTH AMERICA!" Yes, (I address Democratic Americans,) the influence of this Republican government, of your democratic system, is vitally felt by Austria. She confesses it. It is proscribed by the Austrian Cabinet. This country is designated directly to all her people, and to her allied despots, as the great *plague spot* of the world, the poisoned fountain whence flow all the deadly evils which threaten their own existence. . . . Is it wonderful after such an avowal in regard to America, that she should do something to rid herself and the world of such a tremendous evil? . . . But how shall she attack us? She cannot send her armies, they would be useless. She has told us by the mouth of her Counsellor of Legation, that Popery, while it is the natural antagonist to Protestantism, is opposed in its whole character to Republican liberty, and is the promoter and supporter of arbitrary power. How fitted then is Popery for her purpose! This she can send without alarming our fears, or, at least, only the fears of those "*miserable*," "*intolerant fanatics*," and "*pious bigots*," who affect to see danger to the liberties of the country in the mere introduction of a *religious system* opposed to their own, and whose cry of danger, be it ever so loud, will only be regarded as the result of "*sectarian fear*," and the plot ridiculed as a "*quixotic dream*." But is there any thing so irrational in such a scheme? Is it not the most natural and obvious act for Austria to do, with her views of the influence of Popery upon the form of government, its influence to pull down Republicanism, and build up monarchy; I say, is it not her most obvious act *to send Popery to this country if it is not here, or give it a fresh and vigorous impulse if it is already here*? At any rate *she is doing it*. She has set herself to work with all her activity to disseminate throughout the country the *Popish religion*. Immediately after the delivery of Schlegel's lectures, which was in the year 1828, a great society was formed in the Austrian capital, in Vienna, in 1829. The late Emperor, and Prince Metternich, and the Crown Prince, (now Emperor,) and all the civil and ecclesiastical officers of the empire, with the princes of Savoy and Piedmont, uniting in it, and calling it after the name of a canonized King, *St. Leopold*. This society is formed for a great and express purpose.... "*of promoting the greater activity of Catholic missions in America*;" these are the words of their own reports. Yes; these Foreign despots are suddenly stirred up to combine and promote the greater activity of Popery in this country; and this, too, just after they had been convinced of the truth, or, more properly speaking, had their memories quickened with it, that *Popery is utterly opposed to Republican liberty*. These are the facts in the case. Americans, explain them in your own way. If any choose to stretch their charity so far as to believe that these crowned gentlemen have combined in this Society solely for *religious* purposes; that they have organized a Society to collect moneys to be spent in this country,

and have sent Jesuits as their almoners, and shiploads of Roman Catholic emigrants, and for the sole purpose of converting us to the *religion* of Popery, and without any *political* design, credat Judæus Apella, non ego.

*   *   *

Let us examine the operations of this Austrian Society, for it is hard at work all around us; yes, here in this country, from one end to the other, at our very doors, in this city.... Its emissaries are here. And who are these emissaries? They are JESUITS. This society of men, after exerting their tyranny for upwards of 200 years, at length became so formidable to the world, threatening the entire subversion of all social order, that even the Pope, whose *devoted subjects* they are, and must be, by the vow of their society, was compelled to dissolve them. They had not been suppressed, however, for 50 years, before the waning influence of Popery and Despotism required their useful labours, to resist the spreading light of Democratic liberty, and the Pope, (Pius VII,) simultaneously with the formation of the Holy Alliance, revived the order of the Jesuits in all their power.... And do Americans need to be told what *Jesuits* are? If any are ignorant, let them inform themselves of their history without delay; no time is to be lost: their workings are before you in every day's events: they are a *secret* society, a sort of Masonic order, with superadded features of most revolting odiousness, and a thousand times more dangerous. They are not confined to one class in society; they are not merely priests, or priests of one religious creed, they are merchants, and lawyers, and editors, and men of any profession, and no profession, having no outward badge, (in this country,) by which to be recognised; they are about in all your society. They can assume any character, that of angels of light, or ministers of darkness, to accomplish their one great end, the *service* upon which they are sent, whatever that service may be. "They are all educated men, prepared, and sworn to *start at any moment, in any direction*, and for any service, commanded by the general of their order, bound to no family, community, or country, by the ordinary ties which bind men; and *sold for life* to the cause of the Roman Pontiff."

* * *

Is there no danger to the Democracy of the country from such formidable foes arrayed against it? Is Metternich its friend? Is the *Pope* its friend? Are his official documents, now daily put forth, *Democratic* in their character?

O there is no danger to the Democracy; for those most devoted to the Pope, the Roman Catholics, especially the Irish Catholics, are all on the side of Democracy. Yes; to be sure they are on the side of Democracy. They are just where I should look for them. Judas Iscariot joined with the true disciples. Jesuits are not fools. They would not startle our slumbering fears, by bolting out their monarchical designs directly in our teeth, and by joining the opposing ranks, *except so far as to cover their designs.* This is a Democratic country, and the Democratic party is and ever must be the strongest party, unless ruined by traitors and Jesuits in the camp. Yes; it is in the ranks of Democracy I should expect to find them, and for no good purpose be assured. Every measure of Democratic policy in the least exciting will be pushed to *ultraism,* so soon as it is introduced for discussion. Let every real Democrat guard against this common Jesuitical artifice of tyrants, an artifice which there is much evidence to believe is practising against them at this moment, an artifice *which if not heeded will surely be the ruin of Democracy*: it is founded on the well-known principle that "*extremes meet.*" The writer has seen it pass under his own eyes in Europe, in more than one instance. When in despotic governments popular discontent, arising from the intolerable oppressions of the tyrants of the people, has manifested itself by popular outbreakings, to such a degree as to endanger the throne, and the people seemed prepared to shove their masters from their horses, and are likely to mount, and seize the reins themselves; then, the popular movement, unmanageable any longer by resistance, is pushed to the extreme. The passions of the ignorant and vicious are excited to outrage by pretended friends of the people. Anarchy ensues; and then the mass of the people, who are always lovers of order and quiet, unite at once in support of the strong arm of force for protection; and despotism, perhaps, in another, but *preconcerted* shape, resumes its iron reign. Italy and Germany are furnishing examples every day. If an illustration is wanted on a larger scale, look at France in her late Republican revolution, and in her present relapse into despotism.

* * *

That Jesuits are at work upon the passions of the American community, managing in various ways to gain control, must be evident to all. They who have learned from history the general mode of proceeding of this crafty set of men, could easily infer that they were here, even were it not otherwise confirmed by unquestionable evidence in their correspondence with their foreign masters in Austria. There are some, perhaps, who are under the impression that the order of Jesuits is a purely religious Society for the dissemination of the Roman Catholic religion; and therefore comes within the protection of our laws, and must be tolerated. There cannot be a greater mistake. It was from the beginning a *political* organization, an absolute Monarchy masked by religion. It has been aptly styled "*tyranny by religion.*" . . .

* * *

. . . It becomes important to inquire, then, what are the *principal materials* in our society with which Jesuits can accomplish the political designs of the Foreign Despots embodied in the Leopold Foundation. And here let me make the passing remark, that there has been a great deal of mawkish sensitiveness on the subject of introducing any thing concerning religion into political discussions. This sensitiveness, as it is not merely foolish, arising from ignorance of the true line which separates political and theological matters, but also exposes the political interests of the country to manifest danger, I am glad to see is giving way to a proper feeling on the subject. Church and State must be for ever separated, but it is the height of folly to suppose, that in political discussions, *Religion* especially, the *political* character *of any and every religious creed* may not be publicly discussed. The absurdity of such a position is too manifest to dwell a moment upon it. And in considering the materials in our society adapted to the purposes of hostile attack upon our Institutions, we must of necessity notice the Roman Catholic religion. *It is this form of religion* that is most implicated in the conspiracy against our liberties. It is in this sect that the Jesuits are organized. It is this sect that is proclaimed by one of its own most brilliant and profound literary men to be *hostile in its very nature to republican liberty*; and it is the active extension of this sect that Austria is endeavouring to promote throughout this Republic. And Americans will not be cowed into silence by the cries of *persecution, intolerance, bigotry, fanaticism,* and such puerile catchwords, perpetually uttered against those who speak or write ever so calmly against the dangers of Popery. I can say, once for all, that no such outcry weighs a feather with me, nor does it weigh a feather with the mass of the American people. They have good sense enough to discriminate, especially in a subject of such vital importance to their safety, between *words* and *things*. I am not tenacious of *words*, except for convenience sake, the better to be understood, but if detestation of Jesuitism and tyranny, whether in a civil or ecclesiastical shape, is in future to be called *intolerance*, be it so; only let it be generally understood, and I will then glory in *intolerance*. When that which is now esteemed *virtue*, is to be known by general consent only by the name *vice*, why I will not be singular, but glory in *vice*, since the word is used to embody the *essential qualities of virtue*. I will just add, that those who are so fond of employing these epithets, forget that by so constantly, loosely, and indiscriminately using them, they cease to convey any meaning, or to excite any emotions but those of disgust towards those who use them.

To return to the subject; it is in the Roman Catholic ranks that we are principally to look for the materials to be employed by the Jesuits, and in what condition do we find this sect at present in

our country? We find it spreading itself into every nook and corner of the land; churches, chapels, colleges, nunneries and convents, are springing up as if by magic every where; an activity hitherto unknown among the Roman Catholics pervades all their ranks, and yet whence the means for all these efforts? Except here and there funds or favours collected from an inconsistent *Protestant*, (*so called* probably because born in a Protestant country, who is flattered or wheedled by some Jesuit artifice to give his aid to their cause,) the greatest part of the pecuniary means for all these works are from abroad. They are the contributions of his Majesty the Emperor of Austria, of Prince Metternich, of the late Charles X., and the other Despots combined in the Leopold Society. And who are the members of the Roman Catholic communion? What proportion are natives of this land, nurtured under our own institutions, and well versed in the nature of American liberty? Is it not notorious that the greater part are *Foreigners* from the various Catholic countries of Europe. Emigration has of late years been specially promoted among this class of Foreigners, and they have been in the proportion of three to one of all other emigrants arriving on our shores; they are from Ireland, Germany, Poland, and Belgium. From about the period of the formation of the Leopold Society, Catholic emigration increased in an amazing degree. Colonies of Emigrants, selected, perhaps, with a view to occupy particular places, (for, be it remembered, every portion of this country is as perfectly known at Vienna and Rome as in any part of our own country,) have been constantly arriving. The principal emigrants are from Ireland and Germany. We have lately been told by the captain of a lately arrived *Austrian vessel*, which, by the by, brought 70 emigrants from *Antwerp!* that a desire is suddenly manifested among the poorer class of the Belgian population, to emigrate to America. They are mostly, if not all, Roman Catholics, be it remarked, for Belgium is a Catholic country, and *Austrian vessels are bringing them here.* Whatever *the cause* of all this movement abroad to send to this country their poorer classes, the fact is certain, the class of emigrants is known, and the instrument, Austria, is seen in it—the same power that directs the Leopold Foundation.

*   *   *

I have shown what are the *Foreign materials* imported into the country, with which the Jesuits can work to accomplish their designs. Let us examine this point a little more minutely. These materials are the *varieties of Foreigners* of the same Creed, the Roman Catholic, over all of whom the Bishops or Vicars General hold, as a matter of course, ecclesiastical rule; and we well know what is the nature of Roman Catholic ecclesiastical rule,—it is the double refined spirit of despotism, which, after arrogating to itself the prerogatives of Deity, and so claiming to bind or loose the *soul* eternally, makes it, in the comparison, but a mere trifle to exercise absolute sway in all that relates to the body. The notorious ignorance in which the great mass of these emigrants have been all their lives sunk, until their minds are dead, makes them but senseless machines; they obey orders mechanically, for it is the habit of their education, in the despotic countries of their birth. And can it be for a moment supposed by any one that by the act of coming to this country, and being naturalized, their darkened intellects can suddenly be illuminated to discern the nice boundary where their *ecclesiastical obedience* to their priests *ends*, and their *civil independence* of them *begins*? The very supposition is absurd. They obey their priests as demigods, from the habit of their whole lives; they have been taught from infancy that their priests are infallible in the greatest matters, and can they, by mere importation to this country, be suddenly imbued with the knowledge that in civil matters their priests may err, and that they are not in these also their infallible guides? Who will teach them this? Will their priests? Let common sense answer this question. Must not the priests, as a matter almost of *certainty*, control the opinions of their ignorant flock in civil as well as religious matters? and do they not do it?

Mr. Jefferson, with that deep sagacity and foresight which distinguished him as a politician, foresaw, predicted, and issued his warning, on the great danger to the country of this introduction of foreigners. He doubted its policy, even when the advantages seemed to be greatest. He says, "The present desire of America, (in 1781,) is to produce rapid population by as great *importations of foreigners* as possible. *But is this founded in policy?*" * * * "Are there no *inconveniences* to be thrown into the scale against the advantage expected from a multiplication of numbers by the importation of foreigners? It is for the happiness of those united in society to harmonize as much as possible in matters which they must of necessity transact together."

*   *   *

What was dimly seen by the prophetic eye of Jefferson, is actually passing under our own eyes. Already have foreigners increased in the country to such a degree, that they justly give us alarm. They feel themselves so strong, as to organize themselves even as *foreigners* into *foreign bands*, and this for the purpose of influencing our elections. . . . That they are men who having *professed* to become Americans, by accepting our terms of naturalization, do yet, in direct contradiction to their professions, clan together as a separate interest, and retain their foreign appellation; that it is with such a separate foreign interest, organizing in the midst of us, that Jesuits in the pay of foreign powers are tampering; that it is this foreign corps of religionists that Americans of both parties have been for years in the habit of basely and traitorously encouraging to erect into an umpire of our political divisions, thus virtually surrendering the government into the hands of Despotic powers. In view of these facts, which every day's experience proves to be facts, is it not time, high time, that a true American spirit were roused to resist this alarming inroad of foreign influence upon our institutions, to avert dangers to which we have hitherto shut our eyes, and which if not remedied, and that immediately, will inevitably change the whole character of our government. I repeat what I first said, this is no party question, it concerns native Americans of all parties.

*   *   *

REVIEW QUESTIONS

1. Why did Morse believe that the massive immigration from Europe was part of a vast conspiracy against the United States?
2. Did he see this conspiracy as primarily religious or political in its means and its ends?
3. Was his conspiracy theory logical and his evidence supportable? In other words, did he prove his case?
4. Did he acknowledge and argue against his opponents or did he simply disparage them as he believed they disparaged nativists?
5. Was he against all immigrants?

ALEXIS DE TOCQUEVILLE

FROM Letters to Ernest de Chabrol and Louis de Kergorlay (1831)

As the United States grew so too did the paradoxes intrinsic to its society and culture. Not all Americans were aware of the incongruities, but both native and foreign observers who set out to examine the culture certainly were. Alexis de Tocqueville was one of the latter. Coming, as he was, out of post-revolutionary and post-Napoleonic France, he was deeply interested in the American experiment and how lessons learned on this continent could be applied to the European one. Tocqueville traveled through America at the same time that Morse was traveling through Europe: both made comparisons and came to conclusions about how Europe, in political and cultural matters, affected America and vice versa. Tocqueville recorded his initial reactions and analyses in numerous letters to his friends and family. Later, after much reflection, he wrote the influential Democracy in America.

From Alexis de Tocqueville, *Selected Letters on Politics and Society*, ed. Roger Boesche; trans. James Toupin and Roger Boesche (Berkeley: University of California Press, 1985) pp. 38–40, 45–56. [Editorial insertions appear in square brackets—*Ed.*]

To Ernest de Chabrol

New York, June 9, 1831

*   *   *

Imagine, my dear friend, if you can, a society formed of all the nations of the world: English, French, Germans . . . people having different languages, beliefs, opinions: in a word, a society without roots, without memories, without prejudices, without routines, without common ideas, without a national character, yet a hundred times happier than our own; more virtuous? I doubt it. That is the starting point: What serves as the link among such diverse elements? What makes all of this into one people? Interest. That is the secret. The private interest that breaks through at each moment, the interest that, moreover, appears openly and even proclaims itself as a social theory.

In this, we are quite far from the ancient republics, it must be admitted, and nonetheless this people is republican, and I do not doubt that it will be so for a long time yet. And for this people a republic is the best of governments.

I can explain this phenomenon only by thinking that America finds itself, for the present, in a physical situation so fortunate, that private interest is never contrary to the general interest, which is certainly not the case in Europe.

What generally inclines men to disturb the state? On the one hand, the desire to gain power; on the other, the difficulty of creating a happy existence for themselves by ordinary means.

Here, there is no public power, and, to tell the truth, there is no need for it. The territorial divisions are so limited; the states have no enemies, consequently no armies, no taxation, no central government; the executive power is nothing; it confers neither money nor power. As long as things remain this way, who will want to torment his life in order to attain power?

Now, looking at the other part of my assertion, one arrives at the same conclusion; because, if political careers are more or less closed, a thousand, ten thousand others are open to human activity. The whole world here seems a malleable material that man turns and fashions to his liking. An immense field, of which the smallest part has yet been traversed, is here open to industry. There is no man who cannot reasonably expect to attain the comforts of life: there is none who does not know that with love of work, his future is certain.

Thus, in this fortunate country, nothing attracts the restlessness of the human spirit toward political passions; everything, on the contrary, draws it toward activity that poses no danger to the state. I would wish that all of those who, in the name of America, dream of a republic for France, could come see for themselves what it is like here.

This last reason that I just gave you, to my mind the prime reason, explains equally well the only two outstanding characteristics that distinguish this people: its industrial spirit and the instability of its character.

Nothing is easier than becoming rich in America; naturally, the human spirit, which needs a dominant passion, in the end turns all its thoughts toward gain. As a result, at first sight this people seems to be a company of merchants joined together for trade, and as one digs deeper into the national character of the Americans, one sees that they have sought the value of everything in this world only in the answer to this single question: how much money will it bring in?

As for the instability of character, it breaks through in a thousand places; an American takes up, quits and takes up again ten trades in his lifetime; he changes his residence ceaselessly and continually forms new enterprises. Less than any other man in the world he fears jeopardizing a fortune once he has acquired it, because he knows with what ease he can acquire a new one.

Besides, change seems to him the natural state of man, and how could it be otherwise? Everything is ceaselessly astir around him—laws, opinions, public officials, fortunes—the earth itself here changes its face every day. In the midst of the universal movement that surrounds him, the American could not stay still.

One must not look here either for that family spirit, or for those ancient traditions of honor and virtue, that distinguish so eminently several of our old societies of Europe. A people that seems to live only to enrich itself could not be a virtuous people in the strict meaning of the word; but it is *well ordered*. All of the trifles that cling to idle riches it does not have: its habits are regular, there is little or no time to devote to women, and they seem to be valued only as mothers of families and managers of households. Mores are pure; this is incontestable. The *roué* of Europe is absolutely unknown in America; the passion for making a fortune carries away and dominates all others.

*   *   *

To Louis de Kergorlay

Yonkers, June 29, 1831,
20 miles from New York

*   *   *

You ask me in your last letter if there are *beliefs* here. I do not know what precise sense you attach to that word; what strikes me is that the immense majority of people are united in regard to certain *common opinions*. So far, that is what I have envied most about America. To begin with, I have not yet been able to overhear in a conversation with any-one, no matter to what rank in society they belong, the idea that a republic is not the best possible gov-ernment, and that a people does not have the right to give itself whatever government it pleases. The great majority understands republican principles in the most democratic sense, although among some one can see a certain aristocratic tendency piercing through that I will try to explain to you below. But that a republic is a good government, that it is nat-ural for human societies, no one seems to doubt— priests, magistrates, businessmen, artisans. That is an opinion that is so general and so little discussed, even in a country where freedom of speech is un-limited, that one could almost call it a belief. There is a second idea that seems to me to be of the same character; the immense majority has *faith* in hu-man wisdom and good sense, faith in the doctrine of human perfectibility. That is another point that finds little or no contradiction. That the majority can be fooled once, no one denies, but people think that necessarily in the long run the majority is right, that it is not only the sole legal judge of its interests but also the surest and most infallible judge. The re-sult of this idea is that enlightenment must be dif-fused widely among the people, that one cannot enlighten the people too much. You know how many times in France we have been anxious (we and a thousand others) to know if it is to be desir-able or fearful for education to penetrate through all the ranks of society. This question, which is so difficult for France to resolve, does not even seem to present itself here. I have already posed this ques-tion a hundred times to the most reflective men; I have seen, by the way they have answered it, that it has never given them pause, and to them even stat-ing the question had something shocking and ab-surd about it. Enlightenment, they say, is the sole guarantee we have against the mistakes of the mul-titude.

There you have, my dear friend, what I will call the *beliefs* of this country. They believe, in good faith, in the excellence of the government that rules them, they believe in the wisdom of the masses,

provided that they are enlightened, and they do not seem to suspect that there is some education that can never be shared by the masses and that none-theless can be necessary for governing a state.

As for what we generally understand by *beliefs*, ancient mores, ancient traditions, the power of memories, I have not seen any trace of these up to now. I even doubt that religious opinions have as great a power as one thinks at first sight. The state of religion among this people is perhaps the most curious thing to examine here. I will try to tell you what I know about this when I again pick up my letter, which I now have to interrupt, perhaps for several days.

Calwell, 45 miles from New York

My mind has been so stirred up since this morning by the beginning of my letter that I feel I have to take it up again without knowing just what I am going to say to you. I was speaking to you above about religion: one is struck on arriving here by the practical exactitude that accompanies the practice of religion. Sunday is observed Judaically, and I have seen streets blocked off in front of churches during the holy services. The law com-mands these things imperiously, and opinion, much stronger than the law, compels everyone to appear at church and to abstain from all amuse-ments. Nevertheless, either I am badly mistaken or there is a great store of doubt and indifference hid-den underneath these external forms. Political pas-sion is not mixed, as it is in our country, with irreligion, but even so religion does not have any more power. It is a very strong impulse that was given in days gone by and which now is expiring day by day. Faith is evidently inert; enter the churches (I mean the Protestant ones) and you hear them speak of morality; of dogma not a word, nothing that could in any way shock a neighbor, nothing that could reveal the hint of dissidence. The human spirit loves to plunge itself into ab-stractions of dogma, discussions which are espe-cially appropriate to a religious doctrine, whenever a belief has seized it strongly; the Americans them-selves were formerly like that. This so-called toler-ance, which, in my opinion, is nothing but a huge indifference, is pushed so far that in public establishments like prisons, the homes for juvenile delinquents . . . seven or eight ministers of different sects come to preach successively to the same inmates. But, I was saying, how those men and those children who belong to one sect find themselves listening to the ministry of another. The infallible response is this: the different preachers, because they occupy themselves only with treating the platitudes of morality, cannot do harm to one another. Besides, it is evident that here, generally speaking, religion does not move people deeply; in France those who believe demonstrate their belief by sacrifices of time, effort, and wealth. . . . It is an incredible thing to see the infinite subdivisions into which the sects have been divided in America. One might say they are circles successively drawn around the same point; each new one is a little more distant than the last. The Catholic faith is the immobile point from which each new sect distances itself a little more, while drawing nearer to pure deism. You feel that such a spectacle cannot fail to throw the mind of a thinking Protestant into inextricable doubt, and that indeed is the sentiment I think I see visibly ruling in the depths of almost everyone's soul. It seems clear to me that the reformed religion is a kind of compromise, a sort of *representative monarchy* in matters of religion. . . . I would like to have you see this curious spectacle; you would encounter here the struggle between two principles which divide the political world elsewhere. Protestants of all persuasions—Anglicans, Lutherans, Calvinists, Presbyterians, Anabaptists, Quakers, and a hundred other Christian sects—this is the core of the population. This church-going and indifferent population, which lives day to day, becomes used to a *milieu* which is hardly satisfying, but which is tranquil, and in which the *proprieties* are satisfied. . . . Above them is to be found a fistful of Catholics, who are making use of the tolerance of their ancient adversaries, but who are staying basically as intolerant as they have always been, as intolerant in a word as people who *believe*. For them there is only truth in a single point; on any line one side or another of this point: eternal damnation. They live in the midst of civil society, but they forbid themselves any rela-

tionship with the religious societies that surround them. It even seems to me that their dogma on liberty of conscience is pretty much the same as in Europe, and I am not sure that they would not be persecuting if they found themselves to be the strongest. These people are in general poor, but full of zeal, their priests are completely devoted to the religion of sacrifice they have embraced; they are not in effect businessmen of religion, as are the Protestant ministers. Everything I have observed to date leads me to think that Catholics are increasing in number in a prodigious manner. Many Europeans who are arriving strengthen their ranks; but conversions are numerous. New England and the Mississippi Basin are beginning to fill up with them. It is evident that all the naturally religious minds among the Protestants, serious and complete minds, which the uncertainties of Protestantism tire and which at the same time deeply feel the need for a religion, are abandoning the despair of seeking the truth and are throwing themselves anew under the empire of *authority*. Their reason is a burden that weighs on them and which they sacrifice with joy; they become Catholics. Catholicism, moreover, seizes the senses and the soul deeply and is better suited to the people than reformed religion; thus the greatest number of converts belongs to the working classes of the society. That is one of the ends of the chain; now we will pass to the other end. On the borders of Protestantism is a sect which is Christian only in name; these are the *Unitarians*. Among the Unitarians, which is to say among those who deny the Trinity and recognize only one God, there are some who see in Jesus Christ only an angel, others a prophet, finally others a philosopher like Socrates. These are pure deists; they speak of the Bible, because they do not want to shock opinion too strongly, as it is still completely *Christian*. They have a service on Sunday; I have been to one. There they read verses of Dryden or other English poets on the existence of God and the immortality of the soul. A speech on some point of morality is made, and the service is over. This sect is gaining proselytes in almost the same proportion as Catholicism, but it recruits in the upper ranks of society. It is growing rich, like Catholicism, from the losses of Protestantism. . . .

Thus you see: Protestantism, a mixture of authority and reason, is battered at the same time by the two absolute principles of *reason* and *authority*. Anyone who wants to look for it can see this spectacle to some extent everywhere; but here it is quite striking. . . . At a time that does not seem to me very far away, it seems certain that the two extremes will find themselves face to face. . . .

But to return to the current state of minds in America, one must not take what I have just said in too absolute a sense. I spoke to you of a *disposition* and not of accomplished facts. It is evident that there still remains here a larger foundation for Christian religion than in any other country in the world, to my knowledge, and I do not doubt that this disposition of minds still has influence on the political regime. It gives a moral and regular shape to ideas; it stops the deviations of the spirit of innovation; above all it makes very rare the disposition of the soul, so common among us, that compels people to rush over all obstacles *per fas et nefas* ["By fair means or foul."] toward the goal they have chosen. It is certain that a party, however it might desire to obtain a result, would still feel obliged to proceed toward it only by methods that have an appearance of morality and that do not openly shock religious beliefs, which are always more or less moral, even when they are false.

*   *   *

. . . I have heard it said in Europe that there was an aristocratic tendency in America. Those who say that are mistaken; this is one of the things that I would affirm most readily. Democracy is, on the contrary, either in full march in certain states or in its fullest imaginable extension in others. It is in the mores, in the laws, in the opinion of the majority. . . . The effects of a democratic government are visible elsewhere; that is, in a perpetual instability in men and in laws, an external equality pushed to its farthest point, a tone of manners and a uniformly common turn of ideas. . . . We ourselves are moving, my dear friend, toward a democracy without limits. I am not saying that this is a good thing; what I see in this country convinces me, on the contrary, that France will come

to terms with it badly; but we are being pushed toward it by an irresistible force. . . . In a word, from now on democracy seems to me a fact that a government can have the pretension of *regulating*, but of stopping, no. It is not without difficulty, I assure you, that I have surrendered to this idea; what I see in this country does not prove to me that, even in the most favorable circumstances, and they have existed here, the government of the multitude is an excellent thing. It is generally agreed that in the first days of the republic, the men of state, the members of the chambers, were much more distinguished than they are today. . . . Now the people no longer have *so fortunate a hand*. Their choices in general fall on those who flatter its passions and put themselves within its reach. This effect of democracy, together with the extreme instability in all things, with the absolute lack that one notices here of any spirit of continuation and duration, convinces me more every day that the most rational government is not that in which *all* the interested parties take part, but that which the most enlightened and most moral classes of the society direct. It cannot be concealed, however, that as a whole this country presents an admirable spectacle. . . .

*   *   *

REVIEW QUESTIONS

1. What kind of image did Tocqueville present of the growing America?
2. What did Tocqueville believe to be the outstanding characteristics of Americans? Why? Did Tocqueville present these as positive or negative traits?
3. What did he think were the ideological underpinnings of American society?
4. Did he see contradictions between what Americans professed and what they practiced?
5. How did his perception of Catholicism in America compare to Samuel Morse's?

13 ✑ AN AMERICAN RENAISSANCE: RELIGION, ROMANTICISM, AND REFORM

An English visitor, Frances Trollope, scathingly scribbled that "if the citizens of the United States were indeed the devoted patriots they call themselves, they would surely not thus encrust themselves in the hard, dry, stubborn persuasion, that they are the first and best of the human race, that nothing is to be learnt, but what they are able to teach, and that nothing is worth having, which they do not possess." She then clucked on about how such an attitude served as an antidote to—meaning it countered or prevented—improvement.

While it was true that Americans tended to crow like cocks on a dunghill, Trollope failed to recognize the concerns behind the cock-a-doodle-doos. True, there was bravado as well as bravery in American actions, qualms as well as convictions in their attitudes, but they were not about to reveal their doubts and weaknesses to an Englishwoman who represented what to many of them was still the enemy. Yes, Americans did generally believe that their nation and its citizens were the best in the world, an attitude distasteful to others who reserved that title for themselves, but many also thought that their society could and should be improved, and it was up to them—not a foreign observer—to determine what needed to be fixed and how it was to be done.

The 1830s and 1840s were thus years of great cultural as well as political ferment. The energetic, egalitarian spirit that marked Jacksonian democracy spilled over into a variety of reform crusades. A new generation of American moralists and thinkers saw themselves as inhabiting a nation of providential destiny and infinite potential, and they expressed an exuberant faith in the perfectibility of both individuals and society as a whole. As the poet-philosopher Ralph Waldo Emerson proclaimed in 1841, "the doctrine of Reform had never such scope as the present hour." Indeed, at mid-century the United States was awash in organized efforts to redress every social evil and conquer every personal failing.

Religious life during the decades before the Civil War took on a more optimistic and fervent tone as many Protestants adopted more inclusive visions of

God's grace and rejected the predestinarian tenets of orthodox Calvinism. Calvinists proclaimed the absolute sovereignty of God: God elected who was saved and who was damned. Ministers of the New Divinity theology, while accepting God's will, preached that people effected their own destiny by electing between good and evil. People of faith still believed in original sin, but more and more believers embraced the concept of a benevolent God who offered everyone the gift of salvation through the experience of spiritual conversion and a life of faith. Evangelical firebrands such as Charles G. Finney and the Methodist circuit rider Peter Cartwright were especially skilled at challenging orthodox theology and attracting throngs of believers to an emotional rather than reasoned piety. Finney's enthusiasm did not stop with conversion: he exhorted the converted to express their faith not only in church but through good works, including social reform.

In the midst of this so-called Second Great Awakening of the early nineteenth century, new religious denominations appeared which embraced people without regard to social standing or educational achievement. Such egalitarianism affected the status quo in other areas of culture and society as well, as Americans set out to correct their society's faults. The most profound version of reform idealism during this period was the peculiar romanticism practiced by the Transcendentalists, an eclectic coterie of New England poets and philosophers. A fluid group of geniuses and cranks, they included among their ranks people of genuine intellectual stature: clergymen such as Theodore Parker and Ralph Waldo Emerson; philosopher-writers such as Henry David Thoreau and Bronson Alcott; and such learned women as Elizabeth Peabody and Margaret Fuller.

The Transcendentalists exercised an influence on American thought that far exceeded their numbers. Full of burning enthusiasm and perfectionist illusions about the boundless possibilities of human nature and the American social experiment, they broke away from what Emerson called the cultural domination of "reverent and conservative minds" and the dry logic of Enlightenment rationalism. Celebrating the individual spirit over the collective state, intuitive over rational knowledge, they rejected the intellectual methodology that had established the republic as the proper way to reflect upon and reform its society.

These visionaries—and the authors and artists of the romantic movement they affected—gave free rein to their fertile imaginations so as to transcend the limits of reason and cultivate inner states of consciousness, for they believed that human existence encompassed more experiences than reason and logic could explain. Such philosophical idealism traced its roots to Plato and Kant and led the Transcendentalists to use the lamp of personal inspiration to illuminate changing states of consciousness and spirituality—and to wield the rod of personal revelation to beat upon the status quo.

The Transcendentalists emphasized self-reliance but also supported many of the organized efforts to reform social ills. Of course, many of the reform organizations were created to promote self-reliance as well as social responsibility. Ac-

tivists, many of whom were women, promoted the abolition of slavery, aid to the physically handicapped and mentally ill, prison improvements, state-supported public schools, temperance legislation, and women's rights.

Although this spirit of social reform was centered in New England and often fueled by an evangelical Protestant moralism, it penetrated all regions of the country and displayed quite secular motives as well. Burdened as well as bolstered by a naive optimism about human nature and the sufficiency of individual moral regeneration, the antebellum reform movements exercised a powerful influence on the country's culture and helped reveal to the young nation how much remained to be done to ensure the realization of the American dream.

CHARLES GRANDISON FINNEY

FROM *Lectures on Revivals of Religion* (1835, with 1868 revisions)

Charles Grandison Finney (1792–1875) was the most celebrated revivalist of the Second Great Awakening. Born in Connecticut, he was raised in various frontier towns in central New York, an area known as the "Burned-Over District" for the revivals that had swept through it. In 1821 Finney experienced a soul-wrenching conversion during which God told him "to plead his cause" to others, so he abandoned his legal career and became a celebrated converter of souls in upstate New York and New England. A man of imposing height, forceful appearance, and vibrant rhetoric, he mesmerized the thousands who flocked to hear him preach his appealing theology of conversion and redemption. Although initially ordained as a Presbyterian minister, Finney was not a Calvinist; indeed, he contributed to the breakdown of Calvinism in American religion. He insisted that sin was a voluntary act rather than a foreordained certainty, and therefore people could choose to be saved and elect to embrace a life of holiness. This focus on the individual—a religious belief shared by most middle-class churchgoers—shows how Finney was both a product and representative of the Jacksonian era. So too did his belief in progress. According to Finney, revivalism and reform went hand in hand, and he inspired many people to take up such causes as abolition and temperance.

From Charles Grandison Finney, *Lectures on Revivals of Religion*, ed. William G. McLoughlin, (Cambridge: The Belknap Press of Harvard University Press, 1960), pp. 9–12, 293–305. [Editorial insertions appear in square brackets unless otherwise noted—*Ed.*]

*   *   *

A "Revival of Religion" presupposes a declension. Almost all the religion in the world has been produced by revivals. God has found it necessary to take advantage of the excitability there is in mankind, to produce powerful excitements among them, before he can lead them to obey. Men are so [spiritually][1] sluggish, there are so many things to lead their minds off from religion, and to oppose the influence of the gospel, that it is necessary to raise an excitement among them, till the tide rises so high as to sweep away the opposing obstacles. They must be so excited that they will break over these counteracting influences, before they will obey God. [Not that excited feeling is religion, for it is not; but it is excited desire, appetite, and feeling that prevents religion. The will is, in a sense, enslaved by the carnal and worldly desires. Hence it is necessary to awaken men to a sense of guilt and danger, and thus produce an excitement of counter-feeling and desire which will break the power of carnal and worldly desire and leave the will free to obey God.][2]

*   *   *

There is so little *principle* in the church, so little firmness and stability of purpose, that [unless the religious feelings are awakened and kept excited, counter worldly feelings and excitements will prevail, and men will not obey God].[3] They have so little knowledge, and their principles are so weak, that unless they are excited, they will go back from the path of duty, and do nothing to promote the glory of God. The state of the world is still such, and probably will be till the millennium is fully come, that religion must be mainly promoted by these excitements. How long and how often has the experiment been tried, to bring the church to act steadily for God, without these periodical excitements! Many good men have supposed, and still suppose, that the best way to promote religion, is

to go along *uniformly*, and gather in the ungodly gradually, and without excitement. But however such reasoning may appear in the abstract, *facts* demonstrate its futility. If the church were far enough advanced in knowledge, and had stability of principle enough to *keep awake*, such a course would do; but the church is so little enlightened, and there are so many counteracting causes, that the church will not go steadily to work without a special excitement. . . .

. . . The great political, and other worldly excitements that agitate Christendom, are all unfriendly to religion, and divert the mind from the interests of the soul. Now these excitements can only be counteracted by *religious* excitements. And until there is religious principle in the world to put down irreligious excitements, it is in vain to try to promote religion, except by counteracting excitements. This is true in philosophy, and it is a historical fact.

It is altogether improbable that religion will ever make progress among *heathen* nations except through the influence of revivals. The attempt is now making to do it by education, and other cautious and gradual improvements. But so long as the laws of mind remain what they are, it cannot be done in this way. There must be excitement sufficient to wake up the dormant moral powers, and roll back the tide of degradation and sin. And precisely so far as our own land approximates to heathenism, it is impossible for God or man to promote religion in such a state of things but by powerful excitements. . . .

*   *   *

III. I proceed to mention some things *which ought to be done*, to continue this great and glorious revival of religion, which has been in progress for the last ten years.

1. *There should be great and deep repentings on the part of ministers.* WE, my brethren, must humble *ourselves* before God. It will not do for us to suppose that it is enough to call on the *people* to repent. We must repent, we must take the lead in repentance, and then call on the churches to follow.

---

[1] From the revised 1868 edition.
[2] From the revised 1868 edition.
[3] From the revised 1868 edition.

*   *   *

4. *The church must take right ground in regard to politics.* Do not suppose, now, that I am going to preach a political sermon, or that I wish to have you join and get up a *Christian party* in politics. No, I do not believe in that. But the time has come that Christians must vote for honest men, and take consistent ground in politics, or the Lord will curse them. They must be honest men themselves, and instead of voting for a man because he belongs to their party, Bank or Anti-Bank, Jackson, or Anti-Jackson, they must find out whether he is honest and upright, and fit to be trusted. They must let the world see that the church will uphold no man in office, who is known to be a knave, or an adulterer, or a Sabbath-breaker, or a gambler. Such is the spread of intelligence and the facility of communication in our country, that every man can know for whom he gives his vote. And if he will give his vote only for honest men, the country will be obliged to have upright rulers. . . . As on the subject of slavery and temperance, so on this subject, the church must act right or the country will be ruined. God cannot sustain this free and blessed country, which we love and pray for, unless the church will take right ground. Politics are a part of religion in such a country as this, and Christians must do their duty to the country as a part of their duty to God. It seems sometimes as if the foundations of the nation were becoming rotten, and Christians seem to act as if they thought God did not see what they do in politics. But I tell you, he does see it, and he will bless or curse this nation, according to the course they take.

5. *The churches must take right ground on the subject of slavery.* And here the question arises, what is right ground? And FIRST I will state some things that should be avoided.

(1.) First of all, *a bad spirit* should be avoided. Nothing is more calculated to injure religion, and to injure the slaves themselves, than for Christians to get into an angry controversy on the subject. It is a subject upon which there needs to be no angry controversy among Christians. Slave-holding professors, like rum-selling professors, may endeavor to justify themselves, and may be angry with those who press their consciences, and call upon them to give up their sins. Those proud professors of religion who think a man to blame, or think it is a shame to have a black skin, may allow their prejudices so far to prevail, as to shut their ears, and be disposed to quarrel with those who urge the subject upon them. But I repeat it, the subject of slavery is a subject upon which Christians, praying men, *need not* and *must not* differ.

(2.) Another thing to be avoided is *an attempt to take neutral ground* on this subject. Christians can no more take neutral ground on this subject, since it has come up for discussion, than they can take neutral ground on the subject of the sanctification of the Sabbath. It is a great national sin. It is a sin of the church. The churches by their silence, and by permitting slave-holders to belong to their communion, have been consenting to it. All denominations have been more or less guilty, although the Quakers have of late years washed their hands of it. It is in vain for the churches to pretend it is merely a political sin. I repeat it, it is the sin of the church, to which all denominations have consented. They have virtually declared that it is lawful. . . .

*   *   *

In the SECOND place, I will mention several things, that in my judgment the church are imperatively called upon to do, on this subject:

(1.) Christians of all denominations, should lay aside prejudice and *inform themselves* on this subject, without any delay. Vast multitudes of professors of religion have indulged prejudice to such a degree as to be unwilling to read and hear, and come to a right understanding of the subject. But Christians cannot pray in this state of mind. I defy any one to possess the spirit of prayer, while he is too prejudiced to examine this, or any other question of duty. . . .

(2.) Writings, containing temperate and judicious discussions on this subject, and such developments of facts as are before the public, should be quietly and extensively circulated, and should be carefully and prayerfully examined by the whole church. . . . [P]raying men should act judiciously, and that, as soon as sufficient information can be diffused through the community, the churches should meekly, but FIRMLY take decided ground on the subject, and express before the whole nation and the world, their abhorrence of this sin.

*   *   *

I believe the time has come, and although I am no prophet, I believe it will be found to have come, that the revival in the United States will continue and prevail, no farther and faster than the church take right ground upon this subject. The church are God's witnesses. The fact is that slavery is, preeminently, the *sin of the church*. It is the very fact that ministers and professors of religion of different denominations hold slaves, which sanctifies the whole abomination, in the eyes of ungodly men. Who does not know that on the subject of temperance, every drunkard in the land, will skulk behind some rum-selling deacon, or wine-drinking minister? It is the most common objection and refuge of the intemperate, and of moderate drinkers, that it is practised by professors of religion. It is *this* that creates the imperious necessity for excluding traffickers in ardent spirit, and rum-drinkers from the communion. Let the churches of all denominations speak out on the subject of temperance, let them close their doors against all who have any thing to do with the death-dealing abomination, and the cause of temperance is triumphant. A few years would annihilate the traffic. Just so with slavery.

It is the church that mainly supports this sin. Her united testimony upon this subject would settle the question. Let Christians of all denominations meekly but firmly come forth, and pronounce their verdict, let them clear their communions, and wash their hands of this thing, let them give forth and write on the head and front of this great abomination, SIN! and in three years, a public sentiment would be formed that would carry all before it, and there would not be a shack-led slave, nor a bristling, cruel slave-driver in this land.

*   *   *

6. If the church wishes to promote revivals, *she must sanctify the Sabbath*. There is a vast deal of Sabbath-breaking in the land. Merchants break it, travellers break it, the government breaks it. . . .

7. The church must take right ground on the subject of Temperance, and Moral Reform, and all the subject of practical morality which come up for decision from time to time.

There are those in the churches who are standing aloof from the subject of Moral Reform, and who are as much afraid to have any thing said in the pulpit against lewdness, as if a thousand devils had got up into the pulpit. On this subject, the church need not expect to be permitted to take neutral ground. In the providence of God, it is up for discussion. The evils have been exhibited, the call has been made for reform. . . .

*   *   *

REVIEW QUESTIONS

1. How did Finney justify his efforts to provoke an emotional state in his listeners?
2. What did Finney mean by "so little principle in the church"? Was he referring to a particular church?
3. Why did Finney promote political and social activism instead of calling for a withdrawal from such worldly concerns?
4. According to Finney, what role should the churches play in the abolition of slavery? In what sense did he charge that they had "consented" to the practice of slavery?
5. Did Finney perhaps underestimate the entrenchment of slavery and overestimate the power of converted Christians to effect change?

RALPH WALDO EMERSON

FROM Self-Reliance (1840)

Ralph Waldo Emerson (1801–1882) was the animating genius behind American Transcendentalism. He derived his outlook on life from a variety of sources—classical philosophy, German idealism, English romanticism, Oriental mysticism, and New England Puritanism—but he also learned much from his personal experiences. His minister father died in 1811, leaving his family destitute and dependent on their own ingenuity and frugality. Emerson later credited the "iron band of poverty, of necessity, of austerity" for steering him away from a life of material indulgence and pointing him toward "the grand, the beautiful, and the good." Family tradition initially led Emerson into the Unitarian ministry, but by 1832 he decided that conventional religion was too confining. So he retired from his Boston ministry, and, after an excursion to Europe, settled in Concord with his wife and mother. There he developed a scholarly routine of introspection, writing, lecturing, community service, and occasional preaching. In perhaps his most famous essay, "Self-Reliance," he urged his readers to believe in themselves and to choose transcendental nonconformity instead of simply following the conventional dictates of society.

From Ralph Waldo Emerson, *Essays: Second Series*, intro. Morse Peckham, (Columbus, OH: Charles E. Merrill Publishing Co., 1969), pp. 37–47, 60–63, 68.

. . . To believe your own thought, to believe that what is true for you in your private heart, is true for all men,—that is genius. . . . A man should learn to detect and watch that gleam of light which flashes across his mind from within, more than the lustre of the firmament of bards and sages. Yet he dismisses without notice his thought, because it is his. In every work of genius we recognise our own rejected thoughts: they come back to us with a certain alienated majesty. Great works of art have no more affecting lesson for us than this. They teach us to abide by our spontaneous impression with good humored inflexibility then most when the whole cry of voices is on the other side. Else, to-morrow a stranger will say with masterly good sense precisely what we have thought and felt all the time, and we shall be forced to take with shame our own opinion from another.

There is a time in every man's education when he arrives at the conviction that envy is ignorance; that imitation is suicide; that he must take himself for better, for worse, as his portion; that though the wide universe is full of good, no kernel of nourishing corn can come to him but through his toil bestowed on that plot of ground which is given to him to till. The power which resides in him is new in nature, and none but he knows what that is which he can do, nor does he know until he has tried. . . .

Trust thyself: every heart vibrates to that iron string. Accept the place the divine Providence has found for you; the society of your contemporaries, the connexion of events. Great men have always done so and confided themselves childlike to the genius of their age, betraying their perception that the Eternal was stirring at their heart, working through their hands, predominating in all their being. And we are now men, and must accept in the highest mind the same transcendent destiny; and not pinched in a corner, not cowards fleeing before a revolution, but redeemers and benefactors, pious aspirants to be noble clay plastic under the Almighty effort, let us advance and advance on Chaos and the Dark.

*   *   *

. . . Society everywhere is in conspiracy against the manhood of every one of its members. Society is a joint-stock company in which the members agree for the better securing of his bread to each shareholder, to surrender the liberty and culture of the eater. The virtue in most request is conformity. Self-reliance is its aversion. It loves not realities and creators, but names and customs.

Whoso would be a man must be a nonconformist. He who would gather immortal palms must not be hindered by the name of goodness, but must explore if it be goodness. Nothing is at last sacred but the integrity of our own mind. . . . I am ashamed to think how easily we capitulate to badges and names, to large societies and dead institutions. Every decent and well-spoken individual affects and sways me more than is right. I ought to go upright and vital, and speak the rude truth in all ways. If malice and vanity wear the coat of philanthropy, shall that pass? If an angry bigot assumes this bountiful cause of Abolition, and comes to me with his last news from Barbadoes, why should I not say to him, 'Go love thy infant; love thy wood-chopper: be good-natured and modest: have that grace; and never varnish your hard, uncharitable ambition with this incredible tenderness for black folk a thousand miles off. Thy love afar is spite at home.' Rough and graceless would be such greeting, but truth is handsomer than the affectation of love. Your goodness must have some edge to it—else it is none. . . .

Virtues are in the popular estimate rather the exception than the rule. There is the man *and* his virtues. Men do what is called a good action, as some piece of courage or charity, much as they would pay a fine in expiation of daily non-

appearance on parade. Their works are done as an apology or extenuation of their living in the world,—as invalids and the insane pay a high board. Their virtues are penances. I do not wish to expiate, but to live. My life is not an apology, but a life. It is for itself and not for a spectacle. I much prefer that it should be of a lower strain, so it be genuine and equal, than that it should be glittering and unsteady. . . . My life should be unique; it should be an alms, a battle, a conquest, a medicine. . . . I know that for myself it makes no difference whether I do or forbear those actions which are reckoned excellent. I cannot consent to pay for a privilege where I have intrinsic right. Few and mean as my gifts may be, I actually am, and do not need for my own assurance or the assurance of my fellows any secondary testimony.

What I must do, is all that concerns me, not what the people think. This rule, equally arduous in actual and in intellectual life, may serve for the whole distinction between greatness and meanness. It is the harder, because you will always find those who think they know what is your duty better than you know it. It is easy in the world to live after the world's opinion; it is easy in solitude to live after our own; but the great man is he who in the midst of the crowd keeps with perfect sweetness the independence of solitude.

*   *   *

For non-conformity the world whips you with its displeasure. And therefore a man must know how to estimate a sour face. The bystanders look askance on him in the public street or in the friend's parlor. If this aversation had its origin in contempt and resistance like his own, he might well go home with a sad countenance; but the sour faces of the multitude, like their sweet faces, have no deep cause,—disguise no god, but are put on and off as the wind blows, and a newspaper directs. Yet is the discontent of the multitude more formidable than that of the senate and the college. It is easy enough for a firm man who knows the world to brook the rage of the cultivated classes. Their rage is decorous and prudent, for they are timid as being very vulnerable themselves. But when to their feminine rage the indignation of the people is added, when the ignorant and the poor are aroused, when the unintelligent brute force that lies at the bottom of society is made to growl and mow, it needs the habit of magnanimity and religion to treat it godlike as a trifle of no concernment.

The other terror that scares us from self-trust is our consistency; a reverence for our past act or word, because the eyes of others have no other data for computing our orbit than our past acts, and we are loath to disappoint them.

*   *   *

A foolish consistency is the hobgoblin of little minds, adored by little statesmen and philosophers and divines. With consistency a great soul has simply nothing to do. He may as well concern himself with his shadow on the wall. Out upon your guarded lips! Sew them up with packthread, do. Else, if you would be a man, speak what you think to-day in words as hard as cannon balls, and to-morrow speak what to-morrow thinks in hard words again, though it contradict every thing you said to-day. Ah, then, exclaim the aged ladies, you shall be sure to be misunderstood. Misunderstood! It is a right fool's word. Is it so bad then to be misunderstood? Pythagoras was misunderstood, and Socrates, and Jesus, and Luther, and Copernicus, and Galileo, and Newton, and every pure and wise spirit that ever took flesh. To be great is to be misunderstood.

*   *   *

The populace think that your rejection of popular standards is a rejection of all standard, and mere antinomianism; and the bold sensualist will use the name of philosophy to gild his crimes. But the law of consciousness abides. There are two confessionals, in one or the other of which we must be shriven. You may fulfil your round of duties by clearing yourself in the *direct*, or, in the *reflex* way. Consider whether you have satisfied your relations to father, mother, cousin, neighbor, town, cat, and dog; whether any of these can upbraid you. But I may also neglect this reflex standard, and absolve me to myself. I have my own stern claims and perfect circle. It denies the name of duty to many offices that are called duties. But if I can discharge its debts, it enables me to dispense with the popular code. If any one imagines that this law is lax, let him keep its commandment one day.

And truly it demands something godlike in him who has cast off the common motives of humanity, and has ventured to trust himself for a task-master. High be his heart, faithful his will, clear his sight, that he may in good earnest be doctrine, society, law to himself, that a simple purpose may be to him as strong as iron necessity is to others.

If any man consider the present aspects of what is called by distinction *society*, he will see the need of these ethics. The sinew and heart of man seem to be drawn out, and we are become timorous desponding whimperers. We are afraid of truth, afraid of fortune, afraid of death, and afraid of each other. Our age yields no great and perfect persons. We want men and women who shall renovate life and our social state, but we see that most natures are insolvent; cannot satisfy their own wants, have an ambition out of all proportion to their practical force, and so do lean and beg day and night continually. Our housekeeping is mendicant, our arts, our occupations, our marriages, our religion we have not chosen, but society has chosen for us. We are parlor soldiers. The rugged battle of fate, where strength is born, we shun.

*   *   *

It is easy to see that a greater self-reliance,—a new respect for the divinity in man,—must work a revolution in all the offices and relations of men; in their religion; in their education; in their pursuits; their modes of living; their association; in their property; in their speculative views.

*   *   *

Insist on yourself; never imitate. Your own gift you can present every moment with the cumulative force of a whole life's cultivation; but of the adopted talent of another, you have only an extemporaneous, half possession. That which each can do best, none but his Maker can teach him. No man yet knows what it is, nor can, till that person has exhibited it. Where is the master who could have taught Shakspeare? Where is the master who could have instructed Franklin, or Washington, or Bacon, or Newton. Every great man is an unique. . . .

*   *   *

REVIEW QUESTIONS

1. How did Emerson define genius?
2. How was Emerson's promotion of nonconfor-

mity a refutation of the Enlightenment philosophy that was a foundation of the Republic (e.g., Locke's idea of social contract)?
3. Do you see any potential problems with Emerson's emphasis on absolute nonconformity to the ways of the world? Did he anticipate any such problems?
4. Why did Emerson consider consistency to be a vice rather than a virtue?
5. What does a comparison of Emerson's and Finney's works (and their followers) reveal about society in antebellum America?

HENRY DAVID THOREAU

FROM *Walden* (1854)

"I like people who can do things," Emerson said, and Henry David Thoreau (1817–1862) could do many things well, including carpentry, masonry, painting, surveying, sailing, and gardening. After graduating from Harvard and teaching school for several years, Thoreau decided to focus his energies on his true passions—nature study and poetry. The rebellious son of a pencil-maker father and abolitionist mother, Thoreau exuded a spirit of uncompromising integrity, manly vigor, self-reliant simplicity, and tart individuality. The short and sinewy Thoreau joyfully mastered the woodland arts. He loved to muck about in swamps and fields, communing with mud turtles and loons as well as his inner self. On 4 July 1845, Thoreau moved into a small cabin he had built on land owned by Emerson bordering Walden Pond, about two miles from Concord. Armed with jackknife, spyglass, diary, and pencil he found the woods and fields alive with fascinating sights, spiritual meaning, and elemental truths. During his twenty-six months at Walden Pond, Thoreau learned to simplify his material wants so as to "entertain the true problems of life." In Walden he offered readers a richly textured journal of his thoughts and activities while engaged in plain living and high thinking at Walden Pond. Although he returned to live in his family's household in 1847, Thoreau's heart remained in the woods.

From Henry David Thoreau, *The Writings of Henry David Thoreau*, vol. 2 (Boston: Houghton Mifflin & Co., 1906), pp. 8–10, 100–103, 108–109, 355–56.

*   *   *

The mass of men lead lives of quiet desperation. What is called resignation is confirmed desperation. From the desperate city you go into the desperate country, and have to console yourself with the bravery of minks and muskrats. A stereotyped but unconscious despair is concealed even under what are called the games and amusements of mankind. There is no play in them, for this comes after work. But it is a characteristic of wisdom not to do desperate things.

When we consider what, to use the words of the catechism, is the chief end of man, and what are the true necessaries and means of life, it appears as if men had deliberately chosen the common mode of living because they preferred it to any other. Yet they honestly think there is no choice left. But alert and healthy natures remember that the sun rose clear. It is never too late to give up our prejudices. No way of thinking or doing, however ancient, can be trusted without proof. What everybody echoes or in silence passes by as true to-day may turn out to be falsehood tomorrow, mere smoke of opinion, which some had trusted for a cloud that would sprinkle fertilizing rain on their fields. What old people say you cannot do, you try and find that you can. Old deeds for old people, and new deeds for new. . . . I have lived some thirty years on this planet, and I have yet to hear the first syllable of valuable or even earnest advice from my seniors. They have told me nothing, and probably cannot tell me anything to the purpose. Here is life, an experiment to a great extent untried by me; but it does not avail me that they have tried it. If I have any experience which I think valuable, I am sure to reflect that this my Mentors said nothing about.

*   *   *

I went to the woods because I wished to live deliberately, to front only the essential facts of life, and see if I could not learn what it had to teach, and not, when I came to die, discover that I had not lived. I did not wish to live what was not life, living is so dear; nor did I wish to practise resignation, unless it was quite necessary. I wanted to live

deep and suck out all the marrow of life, to live so sturdily and Spartan-like as to put to rout all that was not life, to cut a broad swath and shave close, to drive life into a corner, and reduce it to its lowest terms, and, if it proved to be mean, why then to get the whole and genuine meanness of it, and publish its meanness to the world; or if it were sublime, to know it by experience, and be able to give a true account of it in my next excursion. For most men, it appears to me, are in a strange uncertainty about it, whether it is of the devil or of God, and have *somewhat hastily* concluded that it is the chief end of man here to "glorify God and enjoy him forever."

Still we live meanly, like ants; though the fable tells us that we were long ago changed into men; . . . Our life is frittered away by detail. An honest man has hardly need to count more than his ten fingers, or in extreme cases he may add his ten toes, and lump the rest. Simplicity, simplicity, simplicity! I say, let your affairs be as two or three, and not a hundred or a thousand; instead of a million count half a dozen, and keep your accounts on your thumb-nail. In the midst of this chopping sea of civilized life, such are the clouds and storms and quicksands and thousand-and-one items to be allowed for, that a man has to live, if he would not founder and go to the bottom and not make his port at all, by dead reckoning, and he must be a great calculator indeed who succeeds. Simplify, simplify. Instead of three meals a day, if it be necessary eat but one; instead of a hundred dishes, five; and reduce other things in proportion. . . . The nation itself, with all its so-called internal improvements, which, by the way are all external and superficial, is just such an unwieldy and overgrown establishment, cluttered with furniture and tripped up by its own traps, ruined by luxury and heedless expense, by want of calculation and a worthy aim, as the million households in the land; and the only cure for it, as for them, is in a rigid economy, a stern and more than Spartan simplicity of life and elevation of purpose. It lives too fast. Men think that it is essential that the *Nation* have commerce, and export ice, and talk through a telegraph, and ride thirty miles an hour, without a doubt, whether *they* do or not; but whether we should live like ba-boons or like men, is a little uncertain. If we do not get out sleepers, and forge rails, and devote days and nights to the work, but go to tinkering upon our *lives* to improve *them*, who will build railroads? And if railroads are not built, how shall we get to heaven in season? But if we stay at home and mind our business, who will want railroads? We do not ride on the railroad; it rides upon us. Did you ever think what those sleepers are that underlie the rail-road? Each one is a man, an Irishman, or a Yankee man. The rails are laid on them, and they are cov-ered with sand, and the cars run smoothly over them. They are sound sleepers, I assure you. And every few years a new lot is laid down and run over; so that, if some have the pleasure of riding on a rail, others have the misfortune to be ridden upon. . . .

Why should we live with such hurry and waste of life? We are determined to be starved before we are hungry. Men say that a stitch in time saves nine, and so they take a thousand stitches to-day to save nine to-morrow. . . .

*   *   *

Let us spend one day as deliberately as Nature, and not be thrown off the track by every nutshell and mosquito's wing that falls on the rails. Let us rise early and fast, or break fast, gently and without perturbation; let company come and let company go, let the bells ring and the children cry,—deter-mined to make a day of it. Why should we knock under and go with the stream? Let us not be upset and overwhelmed in that terrible rapid and whirlpool called a dinner, situated in the meridian shallows. Weather this danger and you are safe, for the rest of the way is down hill. With unrelaxed nerves, with morning vigor, sail by it, looking an-other way, tied to the mast like Ulysses. If the en-gine whistles, let it whistle till it is hoarse for its pains. If the bell rings, why should we run? We will consider what kind of music they are like. Let us settle ourselves, and work and wedge our feet downward through the mud and slush of opinion, and prejudice, and tradition, and delusion, and ap-pearance, that alluvion which covers the globe,

through Paris and London, through New York and Boston and Concord, through Church and State, through poetry and philosophy and religion, till we come to a hard bottom and rocks in place, which we can call *reality*, . . . Be it life or death, we crave only reality. If we are really dying, let us hear the rattle in our throats and feel cold in the extremi-ties; if we are alive, let us go about our business.

*   *   *

I left the woods for as good a reason as I went there. Perhaps it seemed to me that I had several more lives to live, and could not spare any more time for that one. It is remarkable how easily and insensibly we fall into a particular route, and make a beaten track for ourselves. I had not lived there a week before my feet wore a path from my door to the pond-side; and though it is five or six years since I trod it, it is still quite distinct. It is true, I fear that others may have fallen into it, and so helped to keep it open. The surface of the earth is soft and impressible by the feet of men; and so with the paths which the mind travels. How worn and dusty, then, must be the highways of the world, how deep the ruts of tradition and con-formity! . . .

I learned this, at least, by my experiment; that if one advances confidently in the direction of his dreams, and endeavors to live the life which he has imagined, he will meet with a success unexpected in common hours. He will put some things behind, will pass an invisible boundary; new, universal, and more liberal laws will begin to establish themselves around and within him; or the old laws be ex-panded, and interpreted in his favor in a more lib-eral sense, and he will live with the license of a higher order of beings. In proportion as he simpli-fies his life, the laws of the universe will appear less complex, and solitude will not be solitude, nor poverty poverty, nor weakness weakness. If you have built castles in the air, your work need not be lost; that is where they should be. Now put the foundations under them.

*   *   *

REVIEW QUESTIONS

1. Why did Thoreau believe that most people led lives of "quiet desperation"? Was his experiment in simple living a response to that belief?
2. What was the significance of his comparing the nation's "establishment" with the "households" of its citizens?
3. How do his comments compare with those of Hezekiah Niles in Chapter 12? What does the result of this comparison reveal about the notion of improvement in antebellum American society?
4. What did Thoreau mean by his references to the "ruts of tradition" and "castles in the air"?

HENRY DAVID THOREAU

FROM **Resistance to Civil Government (1849)**

The United States went to war against Mexico in May 1846. That July, while living at Walden Pond, Thoreau refused to pay his poll tax as a protest against the conflict, for he saw the war as an effort to extend the realm of slavery. As a result, the local constable arrested him, and he spent the night in the Concord jail. The next day a relative—probably his aunt—paid the tax, and he was released. As Thoreau continued his study of the woods and himself, he also contemplated the nature of government and the citizen's connection to it: out of this came his statement explaining his act of protest. Published in 1849, his essay has since become the classic justification for acts of civil disobedience. Mohandas K. Gandhi was inspired by its message and adopted Thoreau's principles in his lifelong campaign to gain Indian independence from Great Britain. Thoreau's ideas also influenced Martin Luther King, Jr. in his campaign for racial equality in the 1950s and 1960s.

From Henry David Thoreau, *The Writings of Henry D. Thoreau: Reform Papers*, ed. Wendell Glick (Princeton: Princeton University Press, 1973), pp. 63–76, 86–90.

I heartily accept the motto,—"That government is best which governs least;" and I should like to see it acted up to more rapidly and systematically. Carried out, it finally amounts to this, which also I believe,—"That government is best which governs not at all;" and when men are prepared for it, that will be the kind of government which they will have. Government is at best but an expedient; but most governments are usually, and all governments are sometimes, inexpedient. . . .

This American government,—what is it but a tradition, though a recent one, endeavoring to transmit itself unimpaired to posterity; but each instant losing some of its integrity? It has not the vitality and force of a single living man; for a single man can bend it to his will. . . . *It* does not keep the country free. *It* does not settle the West. *It* does not educate. The character inherent in the American people has done all that has been accomplished; and it would have done somewhat more, if the government had not sometimes got in its way. For government is an expedient by which men would fain succeed in letting one another alone; and, as has been said, when it is most expedient, the governed are most let alone by it. . . .

But, to speak practically and as a citizen, unlike those who call themselves no-government men, I ask for, not at once no government, but *at once a better government*. Let every man make known what kind of government would command his respect, and that will be one step toward obtaining it.

After all, the practical reason why, when the power is once in the hands of the people, a majority are permitted, and for a long period continue, to rule, is not because they are most likely to be in the right, nor because this seems fairest to the minority, but because they are physically the strongest. But a government in which the majority rule in all cases cannot be based on justice, even as far as men understand it. . . . Must the citizen ever for a moment, or in the least degree, resign his conscience to the legislator? Why has every man a conscience, then? I think that we should be men first, and subjects afterward. It is not desirable to cultivate a respect for the law, so much as for the right. The only obligation which I have a right to assume, is to do at any time what I think right. . . .

*   *   *

How does it become a man to behave toward this American government to-day? I answer that he cannot without disgrace be associated with it. I cannot for an instant recognize that political organization as *my* government which is the *slave's* government also.

All men recognize the right of revolution; that is, the right to refuse allegiance to and to resist the government, when its tyranny or its inefficiency are great and unendurable. But almost all say that such is not the case now. . . . But when . . . oppression and robbery are organized, I say, let us not have such a machine any longer. In other words, when a sixth of the population of a nation which has undertaken to be the refuge of liberty are slaves, and a whole country is unjustly overrun and conquered by a foreign army, and subjected to military law, I think that it is not too soon for honest men to rebel and revolutionize. What makes this duty the more

urgent is the fact, that the country so overrun is not our own, but ours is the invading army.

*   *   *

. . . Practically speaking, the opponents to a reform in Massachusetts are not a hundred thousand politicians at the South, but a hundred thousand merchants and farmers here, who are more interested in commerce and agriculture than they are in humanity, and are not prepared to do justice to the slave and to Mexico, *cost what it may*. I quarrel not with far-off foes, but with those who, near at home, co-operate with, and do the bidding of those far away, and without whom the latter would be harmless. We are accustomed to say, that the mass of men are unprepared; but improvement is slow, because the few are not materially wiser or better than the many. It is not so important that many should be as good as you, as that there be some absolute goodness somewhere; for that will leaven the whole lump. There are thousands who are *in opinion* opposed to slavery and to the war, who yet in effect do nothing to put an end to them; who, esteeming themselves children of Washington and Franklin, sit down with their hands in their pockets, and say that they know not what to do, and do nothing; who even postpone the question of freedom to the question of free-trade, and quietly read the prices-current along with the latest advices from Mexico, after dinner, and, it may be, fall asleep over them both. . . .

*   *   *

Unjust laws exist: shall we be content to obey them, or shall we endeavor to amend them, and obey them until we have succeeded, or shall we transgress them at once? Men generally, under such a government as this, think that they ought to wait until they have persuaded the majority to alter them. They think that, if they should resist, the remedy would be worse than the evil. But it is the fault of the government itself that the remedy *is* worse than the evil. *It* makes it worse. Why is it not more apt to anticipate and provide for reform? Why does it not cherish its wise minority? Why does it cry and resist before it is hurt? Why does it not encourage its citizens to be on the alert to point out its faults, and *do* better than it would have them? Why does it always crucify Christ, and excommunicate Copernicus and Luther, and pronounce Washington and Franklin rebels?

*   *   *

As for adopting the ways which the State has provided for remedying the evil, I know not of such ways. They take too much time, and a man's life will be gone. I have other affairs to attend to. I came into this world, not chiefly to make this a good place to live in, but to live in it, be it good or bad. A man has not every thing to do, but something; and because he cannot do *every thing*, it is not necessary that he should do *something* wrong. It is not my business to be petitioning the governor or the legislature any more than it is theirs to petition me; and, if they should not hear my petition, what should I do then? But in this case the State has provided no way: its very Constitution is the evil. . . .

I do not hesitate to say, that those who call themselves abolitionists should at once effectually withdraw their support, both in person and property, from the government of Massachusetts, and not wait till they constitute a majority of one, before they suffer the right to prevail through them. I think that it is enough if they have God on their side, without waiting for that other one. Moreover, any man more right than his neighbors, constitutes a majority of one already.

*   *   *

Under a government which imprisons any unjustly, the true place for a just man is also a prison. The proper place to-day, the only place which Massachusetts has provided for her freer and less desponding spirits, is in her prisons, to be put out and locked out of the State by her own act, as they have already put themselves out by their principles. It is there that the fugitive slave, and the Mexican prisoner on parole, and the Indian come to plead the wrongs of his race, should find them; on that separate, but more free and honorable ground, where the State places those who are not *with* her

but *against* her,—the only house in a slave-state in which a free man can abide with honor. If any think that their influence would be lost there, and their voices no longer afflict the ear of the State, that they would not be as an enemy within its walls, they do not know by how much truth is stronger than error, nor how much more eloquently and effectively he can combat injustice who has experienced a little in his own person. Cast your whole vote, not a strip of paper merely, but your whole influence. A minority is powerless while it conforms to the majority; it is not even a minority then; but it is irresistible when it clogs by its whole weight. If the alternative is to keep all just men in prison, or give up war and slavery, the State will not hesitate which to choose. If a thousand men were not to pay their tax-bills this year, that would not be a violent and bloody measure, as it would be to pay them, and enable the State to commit violence and shed innocent blood. This is, in fact, the definition of a peaceable revolution, if any such is possible. . . .

*   *   *

I do not wish to quarrel with any man or nation. I do not wish to split hairs, to make fine distinctions, or set myself up as better than my neighbors. I seek rather, I may say, even an excuse for conforming to the laws of the land. I am but too ready to conform to them. . . . Seen from a lower point of view, the Constitution, with all its faults, is very good; the law and the courts are very respectable; even this State and this American government are, in many respects, very admirable and rare things, to be thankful for, such as a great many have described them; but seen from a point of view a little higher, they are what I have described them; seen from a higher still, and the highest, who shall say what they are, or that they are worth looking at or thinking of at all?

However, the government does not concern me much, and I shall bestow the fewest possible thoughts on it. It is not many moments that I live under a government, even in this world. . . .

*   *   *

The authority of government, even such as I am willing to submit to,—for I will cheerfully obey those who know and can do better than I, and in many things even those who neither know nor can do so well,—is still an impure one: to be strictly just, it must have the sanction and consent of the governed. It can have no pure right over my person and property but what I concede to it. The progress from an absolute to a limited monarchy, from a limited monarchy to a democracy, is a progress toward a true respect for the individual. Is a democracy, such as we know it, the last improvement possible in government? Is it not possible to take a step further towards recognizing and organizing the rights of man? There will never be a really free and enlightened State, until the State comes to recognize the individual as a higher and independent power, from which all its own power and authority are derived, and treats him accordingly. I please myself with imagining a State at last which can afford to be just to all men, and to treat the individual with respect as a neighbor; which even would not think it inconsistent with its own repose, if a few were to live aloof from it, not meddling with it, nor embraced by it, who fulfilled all the duties of neighbors and fellow-men. A State which bore this kind of fruit, and suffered it to drop off as fast as it ripened, would prepare the way for a still more perfect and glorious State, which also I have imagined, but not yet anywhere seen.

REVIEW QUESTIONS

1. Why did Thoreau believe that the best government is the one which governs least?
2. What governing principle did Thoreau want to substitute for the rule of the majority?
3. How did Thoreau use the *Declaration of Independence* and the *Constitution* to protest an "unjust" law?
4. How did his thoughts reflect and build upon those promoted by Emerson?
5. What do you think a person should do to change an "unjust" law?

HORACE MANN

The Condition of the Children of Laborers on Public Works (1840)

While some antebellum Americans studied Emerson's and Thoreau's works, many more avidly read the stories of such authors as Nathaniel Hawthorne, Washington Irving, Herman Melville, and Edgar Allan Poe. Americans were quite literate, and such literacy spoke well of parents' efforts to educate their children. Yet as the nation's society and economy became more complex, reformers called for changes in education so that the United States and its citizens could continue to prosper. Among the many reforms, none was more significant than the creation of a system of state-supported public schools. By the 1830s many social and political leaders had given up on the family as the primary agency of republican virtue and were exploring new ways to provide the external guidance and controls needed to manage a growing and increas-

ingly diverse population. Horace Mann (1796–1859) was the most prominent advocate of state-supported common schools. In 1837 he resigned his position as a state legislator and gave up his law practice in order to become the secretary of the first board of education established by the state of Massachusetts. For the next eleven years he championed universal free education. Mann believed such a system would benefit the nation both morally and materially. He presented his arguments in annual reports to the Massachusetts Board of Education, but he also began the Common School Journal *(from whence the following piece comes) in 1848 to instruct a wider audience on why and how to improve education.*

From Horace Mann, *Life and Works of Horace Mann*, vol. 5, *The Educational Writings of Horace Mann* (Boston: Lee and Shepard Publishers, 1891), pp. 193–96.

The Condition of the Children of Laborers on Public Works (1840).

. . . OUR country in general, and the State of Massachusetts in particular, owe a vast economical debt to that class of people, whose labor has been mainly instrumental in rearing the great material structures of which we so often boast. It is by the toil of that people, that these instruments of prosperity have been brought into being. In looking at the creative cause, their muscle bears a closer relation to the work, than our capital. They have materially changed the surface of the earth for our accommodation, and profit, and delight; building piers and wharves for our commerce, turning the bed of the ocean into dry land for the enlargement of our cities, cutting down the mountain and upheaving the valley, to smooth a pathway, by which distant and alien people might hold communion with each other. Were all considerations of social and Christian duty out of the question, an equitable and fair-minded people ought to blush, to receive such substantial benefits, without any other requital, than just enough of food and clothing for the laborers, to enable them to enlarge and prolong the benefits they are conferring. Allowing it to be ever so true, in point of fact, it would still be a low and unworthy view of the case, to regard them as ignorant, poor, and destitute of some of the elements of civilization, that belong to the age, and therefore to treat them as though their condition were remediless, or to refer the obligation of improvement to themselves. The only noble and worthy view is that which regards them as fellow-beings, capable of advancement, and suffering from the want of such aids, as it is in our power to render. It is impossible for us to pay them *in kind*; but there is a compensation, elevating both to the giver and the receiver, which we have the ability to bestow; there is a medium of payment, which we richly possess, and which they most of all need. We can confer the blessings of education upon their children. And the impulse of duty to do so may lawfully derive additional energy from the reflection, that every wise and humane measure, adopted for their welfare, directly promotes our own security. For, it must be manifest to every forecasting mind, that the children of this people will soon possess the rights of men, whether they possess the characters of men or not. There is a certainty about their future political and social powers, while there is a contingency, depending upon the education they receive, whether those powers shall be exercised for weal or woe. The idea of Burke, that education was the best preventive police, is a very just idea, and for his time, it was a very advanced one;—but, though a just idea, it is a very narrow one, because it is the noble office of education to do good positively, by refining the purest and elevating the highest blessings, as well as to do good negatively, by warding off evils. In that thought, Burke only declares, that education can save to the government the fees of jailers and hangmen, the expense of chains and halters;—he does not say, that education can convert the very materials, which go to make the felon and the traitor, into the strength and ornament of the State. It is obvious, that there may be people, who, from the very circumstances and condition of their birth, and therefore without fault of their own, may be so profoundly immersed in ignorance, as not to know how ignorant they are, and who, therefore, feel no discontent under their privations nor any aspirings after a more elevated existence. But for men, who have felt the enduring satisfactions of knowledge, who know the pleasure it confers, the pain it averts;—for such men to stand around their ignorant fellow-beings, and lift no hand to raise them from their debasement,—what is it, but for those who chance to be awake, to stand around the dwelling of their neighbors who are asleep, when that dwelling is on fire, and make no effort to extinguish the flames, nor to raise any cry of alarm, audible to the unconscious sleepers?

. . . There is another consideration pertaining to this subject, which we cannot express with half the energy that we feel. The children of the Irish are not infrequently brought into association with those of our native population, either at school, at work, or at play. On these occasions, the former are often treated with indignity and contempt by the latter. A garb less respectable, manners, in some respects, less proper, are made the subjects of scoff and ridicule. How unmanly, how ungenerous, how unjust, is this! No tattered garments, though rag is flapping farewell to rag,—no coarseness of man-

ners, though it descend to the very sty,—is half so shameful or so degrading, as the sneer with which pride insults misfortune. Children or men proclaim their own reproach, when their dress is better than their manners. Let parents and teachers see to this. Kindness and sympathy are due to those, whom circumstances have placed in an inferior condition; and the greater that inferiority, the greater should the kindness and sympathy be. Children should be early imbued, on this as well as on all other subjects, with the feelings, which they ought spontaneously to exercise when they become men; and no ignorance or rusticity is so disgraceful, as airs of superiority over those, who have enjoyed no opportunity for learning, and whose manners are the misfortune of birth, and not of their own choosing.

REVIEW QUESTIONS

1. According to Mann, why was the entire United States—not just individual businesses or families—indebted to laborers?
2. Why did Mann believe that material payment alone was not just recompense?
3. What did Mann mean when he wrote that "the children of this people will soon possess the rights of men, whether they possess the characters of men or not"? Why did he believe that should be a particular concern of the nation?
4. What did Mann believe to be the mission of education?

CATHARINE BEECHER

FROM *A Treatise on Domestic Economy* (1841)

Besides campaigning for public schooling, educational reformers called for changes in higher education and more consideration for the education of girls. While many Americans believed that girls should have elementary education, advanced training was another matter. Many believed that not only was higher education unnecessary given the woman's role in society, it would make a woman unsuitable for her station and perhaps weaken her constitution. There were many other Americans who disputed such notions, but they argued among themselves as to the proper nature of higher education for women. At the foundation of all of these arguments was the basic question: what was woman's role or sphere? Most believed that woman's role was a subordinate, domestic one. Catharine Beecher (1800–1878), the eldest daughter of the famous Presbyterian minister, revivalist, and reformer Lyman Beecher, accepted and advocated that role for women, but with a twist. As both teacher and author, Beecher inculcated the idea that women were to serve, indeed sacrifice themselves to, their families, but in doing so women became the saviors of society and thus, although subordinate, they exercised power. With this in mind, she promoted educational—mental, technical, and physical—reforms that would prepare women to be vigorously better homemakers and teachers.

From Catharine E. Beecher, *A Treatise on Domestic Economy* (Boston: Marsh, Capen, Lyon, and Webb, 1841), pp. 2–14. [Editorial insertions appear in square brackets—*Ed.*]

*   *   *

[I]n order that each individual may pursue and secure the highest degree of happiness within his reach, unimpeded by the selfish interests of others, a system of laws must be established, which sustain certain relations and dependencies in social and civil life. What these relations and their attending obligations shall be, are to be determined, not with reference to the wishes and interests of a few, but solely with reference to the general good of all; so that each individual shall have his own interest, as much as the public benefit, secured by them.

For this purpose, it is needful that certain relations be sustained, that involve the duties of subordination. There must be the magistrate and the subject, one of whom is the superior, and the other the inferior. There must be the relations of husband and wife, parent and child, teacher and pupil, employer and employed, each involving the relative duties of subordination. The superior in certain particulars is to direct, and the inferior is to yield obedience. Society could never go forward, harmoniously, nor could any craft or profession be successfully pursued, unless these superior and subordinate relations be instituted and sustained.

But who shall take the higher, and who the subordinate, stations in social and civil life? This matter, in the case of parents and children, is decided by the Creator. He has given children to the control of parents, as their superiors, and to them they remain subordinate, to a certain age, or so long as they are members of their household. And parents can delegate such a portion of their authority to teachers and employers, as the interests of their children require.

In most other cases, in a truly democratic state, each individual is allowed to choose for himself, who shall take the position of his superior. No woman is forced to obey any husband but the one she chooses for herself; nor is she obliged to take a husband, if she prefers to remain single. So every domestic, and every artisan or laborer, after passing from parental control, can choose the employer to whom he is to accord obedience, or, if he prefers to relinquish certain advantages, he can remain without taking a subordinate place to any employer.

Each subject, also, has equal power with every other, to decide who shall be his superior as a ruler. The weakest, the poorest, the most illiterate, has the same opportunity to determine this question, as the richest, the most learned, and the most exalted.

*   *   *

The tendencies of democratic institutions, in reference to the rights and interests of the female sex, have been fully developed in the United States; and it is in this aspect, that the subject is one of peculiar interest to American women. In this Country, it is established, both by opinion and by practice, that women have an equal interest in all social and civil concerns; and that no domestic, civil, or political, institution, is right, that sacrifices her interest to promote that of the other sex. But in order to secure her the more firmly in all these privileges, it is decided, that, in the domestic relation, she take a subordinate station, and that, in civil and political concerns, her interests be intrusted to the other sex, without her taking any part in voting, or in making and administering laws. The result of this order of things has been fairly tested, and is thus portrayed by M. De Tocqueville, a writer, who, for intelligence, fidelity, and ability, ranks second to none.

The following extracts present his views.

"There are people in Europe, who, confounding together the different characteristics of the sexes, would make of man and woman, beings not only equal, but alike. They would give to both the same functions, impose on both the same duties, and grant to both the same rights. They would mix them in all things,—their business, their occupations, their pleasures. It may readily be conceived, that, by *thus* attempting to make one sex equal to the other, both are degraded; and from so preposterous a medley of the works of Nature, nothing could ever result, but weak men and disorderly women.

"It is not thus that the Americans understand the species of democratic equality, which may be established between the sexes. They admit, that, as Nature has appointed such wide differences between the physical and moral constitutions of man and woman, her manifest design was, to give a distinct employment to their various faculties; and they hold, that improvement does not consist in making beings so dissimilar do pretty nearly the same things, but in getting each of them to fulfill their respective tasks, in the best possible manner.

The Americans have applied to the sexes the great principle of political economy, which governs the manufactories of our age, by carefully dividing the duties of man from those of woman, in order that the great work of society may be the better carried on.

*   *   *

"It is true, that the Americans rarely lavish upon women those eager attentions which are commonly paid them in Europe. But their conduct to women always implies, that they suppose them to be virtuous and refined; and such is the respect entertained for the moral freedom of the sex, that, in the presence of a woman, the most guarded language is used, lest her ear should be offended by an expression. In America, a young unmarried woman may, alone, and without fear, undertake a long journey.

"Thus the Americans do not think that man and woman have either the duty, or the right, to perform the same offices, but they show an equal regard for both their respective parts; and, though their lot is different, they consider both of them, as beings of equal value. . . . Thus, then, while they have allowed the social inferiority of woman to subsist, they have done all they could to raise her, morally and intellectually, to the level of man; and, in this respect, they appear to me to have excellently understood the true principle of democratic improvement.

"As for myself, I do not hesitate to avow, that, although the women of the United States are confined within the narrow circle of domestic life, and their situation is, in some respects, one of extreme dependence, I have nowhere seen women occupying a loftier position; and if I were asked, now I am drawing to the close of this work, in which I have spoken of so many important things done by the Americans, to what the singular prosperity and growing strength of that people ought mainly to be attributed, I should reply,—*to the superiority of their women.*"

This testimony of a foreigner, who has had abundant opportunities of making a comparison, is sanctioned by the assent of all candid and intelligent men, who have enjoyed similar opportunities.

It appears, then, that it is in America, alone, that women are raised to an equality with the other sex; and that, both in theory and practice, their interests are regarded as of equal value. They are made subordinate in station, only where a regard to their best interests demands it, while, as if in compensation for this, by custom and courtesy, they are always treated as superiors. Universally, in this Country, through every class of society, precedence is given to woman, in all the comforts, conveniences, and courtesies, of life.

In civil and political affairs, American women take no interest or concern, except so far as they sympathize with their family and personal friends; but in all cases, in which they do feel a concern, their opinions and feelings have a consideration, equal, or even superior, to that of the other sex.

In matters pertaining to the education of their children, in the selection and support of a clergyman, in all benevolent enterprises, and in all questions relating to morals or manners, they have a superior influence. In all such concerns, it would be impossible to carry a point, contrary to their judgement and feelings; while an enterprise, sustained by them, will seldom fail of success.

If those who are bewailing themselves over the fancied wrongs and injuries of women in this Nation, could only see things as they are, they would know, that, whatever remnants of a barbarous or aristocratic age may remain in our civil institutions, in reference to the interests of women, it is only because they are ignorant of it, or do not use their influence to have them rectified; for it is very certain that there is nothing reasonable which American women would unite in asking, that would not readily be bestowed.

The preceding remarks, then, illustrate the position, that the democratic institutions of this Country are in reality no other than the principles of Christianity carried into operation, and that they tend to place woman in her true position in society, as having equal rights with the other sex; and that, in fact, they have secured to American women a lofty and fortunate position, which, as yet, has been attained by the women of no other nation.

*   *   *

And this is the nation, which the Disposer of events designs shall go forth as the cynosure of nations, to guide them. . . . To us is committed the grand, the responsible privilege, of exhibiting to the world, the beneficent influences of Christianity, when carried into every social, civil, and political institution, and though we have, as yet, made such imperfect advances, already the light is streaming into the dark prison-house of despotic lands, while startled kings and sages, philosophers and statesmen, are watching us with that interest which a career so illustrious, and so involving their own destiny, is calculated to excite. They are studying our institutions, scrutinizing our experience, and watching for our mistakes, that they may learn whether "a social revolution, so irresistible, be advantageous or prejudicial to mankind."

There are persons, who regard these interesting truths merely as food for national vanity; but every reflecting and Christian mind, must consider it as an occasion for solemn and anxious reflection. Are we, then, a spectacle to the world? Has the Eternal Lawgiver appointed us to work out a problem involving the destiny of the whole earth? Are such momentous interests to be advanced or retarded, just in proportion as we are faithful to our high trust? "What manner of persons, then, ought we to be," in attempting to sustain so solemn, so glorious a responsibility?

But the part to be enacted by American women, in this great moral enterprise, is the point to which special attention should here be directed.

The success of democratic institutions, as is conceded by all, depends upon the intellectual and moral character of the mass of the people. If they are intelligent and virtuous, democracy is a blessing; but if they are ignorant and wicked, it is only a curse, and as much more dreadful than any other form of civil government, as a thousand tyrants are more to be dreaded than one. It is equally conceded, that the formation of the moral and intellectual character of the young is committed mainly to the female hand. The mother writes the character of the future man; the sister bends the fibres that hereafter are the forest tree; the wife sways the heart, whose energies may turn for good or for evil the destinies of a nation. Let the women of a country be made virtuous and intelligent, and the men will certainly be the same. The proper education of a man decides the welfare of an individual; but educate a woman, and the interests of a whole family are secured.

If this be so, as none will deny, then to American women, more than to any others on earth, is committed the exalted privilege of extending over the world those blessed influences, that are to renovate degraded man, and "clothe all climes with beauty."

No American woman, then, has any occasion for feeling that hers is an humble or insignificant lot. The value of what an individual accomplishes, is to be estimated by the importance of the enterprise achieved, and not by the particular position of the laborer. . . .

*   *   *

REVIEW QUESTIONS

1. What argument did Beecher present to show that hierarchy and democracy—in other words, subordination in an egalitarian society—were compatible?
2. How did she apply this concept to women?
3. Explain how being raised upon a pedestal was an act of subordination.
4. What power or influence did Beecher say women had on their society?
5. How was women's domesticity tied to national destiny?

MARGARET FULLER

FROM *Woman in the Nineteenth Century* (1845)

While Beecher defended a separate woman's sphere and tried to empower women within it, others, echoing American revolutionary and egalitarian sentiments, disputed such segregation and limitation. Some of these reformers concentrated on the passage of legislation that would protect a woman's rights in various situations, as in property settlements and divorce proceedings. Other reformers preferred to focus on the struggle for suffrage so as to have a public voice and power. Among the most radical of these reformers was Margaret Fuller (1810–1850). Educated by a father who believed that girls and boys were intellectually equal, Fuller (who later became an associate of the Transcendentalists) advocated the simple but disturbing doctrine of equal rights for women. She promoted this cause, along with her other artistic, literary, and social ideas, while she was the editor of the transcendentalist journal The Dial *in the early 1840s and then when she was a writer for the New York* Daily-Tribune. *The revolutionary sentiments in her book,* Woman in the Nineteenth*

Century, *shocked many Americans at the time, but she was not the first nor the last woman of her generation to argue against inequities based on gender.*

From Margaret Fuller, *Woman in the Nineteenth Century*, intro. Bernard Rosenthal (New York: W. W. Norton & Co., Inc., 1971), pp. 24–26, 28–30, 37–38, 93–96, 119–20.

*   *   *

It should be remarked that, as the principle of liberty is better understood, and more nobly interpreted, a broader protest is made in behalf of Woman. As men become aware that few men have had a fair chance, they are inclined to say that no women have had a fair chance. . . .

*   *   *

Though the national independence be blurred by the servility of individuals; though freedom and equality have been proclaimed only to leave room for a monstrous display of slave-dealing and slave-keeping; though the free American so often feels himself free, like the Roman, only to pamper his appetites and his indolence through the misery of his fellow-beings; still it is not in vain that the verbal statement has been made, "All men are born free and equal." There it stands, a golden certainty wherewith to encourage the good, to shame the bad. . . .

*   *   *

Of all its banners, none has been more steadily upheld, and under none have more valor and willingness for real sacrifices been shown, than that of the champions of the enslaved African. And this band it is, which, partly from a natural following out of principles, partly because many women have been prominent in that cause, makes, just now, the warmest appeal in behalf of Woman.

Though there has been a growing liberality on this subject, yet society at large is not so prepared for the demands of this party, but that its members are, and will be for some time, coldly regarded as the Jacobins of their day.

"Is it not enough," cries the irritated trader, "that you have done all you could to break up the national union, and thus destroy the prosperity of our country, but now you must be trying to break up family union, to take my wife away from the cradle and the kitchen-hearth to vote at polls, and preach from a pulpit? Of course, if she does such things, she cannot attend to those of her own sphere. She is happy enough as she is. She has more leisure than I have,—every means of improvement, every indulgence."

"Have you asked her whether she was satisfied with these *indulgences*?"

"No, but I know she is. She is too amiable to desire what would make me unhappy, and too judicious to wish to step beyond the sphere of her sex. I will never consent to have our peace disturbed by any such discussions."

" 'Consent—you?' it is not consent from you that is in question—it is assent from your wife."

"Am not I the head of my house?"

"You are not the head of your wife. God has given her a mind of her own."

"I am the head, and she the heart."

"God grant you play true to one another, then! I suppose I am to be grateful that you did not say she was only the hand. . . . But our doubt is whether the heart *does* consent with the head, or only obeys its decrees with a passiveness that precludes the exercise of its natural powers, or a repugnance that turns sweet qualities to bitter, or a doubt that lays waste the fair occasions of life. It is to ascertain the truth that we propose some liberating measures."

Thus vaguely are these questions proposed and discussed at present. But their being proposed at all implies much thought, and suggests more. Many women are considering within themselves what they need that they have not, and what they can have if they find they need it. Many men are considering whether women are capable of being and having more than they are and have, *and* whether, if so, it will be best to consent to improvement in their condition.

*   *   *

. . . We would have every arbitrary barrier thrown down. We would have every path laid open to Woman as freely as to Man. Were this done, and a slight temporary fermentation allowed to subside, we should see crystallizations more pure and of more various beauty. We believe the divine energy would pervade nature to a degree unknown in the history of former ages, and that no discordant collision, but a ravishing harmony of the spheres, would ensue.

Yet, then and only then will mankind be ripe for this, when inward and outward freedom for Woman as much as for Man shall be acknowledged as a *right*, not yielded as a concession. As the friend of the negro assumes that one man cannot by right hold another in bondage, so should the friend of Woman assume that Man cannot by right lay even well-meant restrictions on Woman. . . .

Were thought and feeling once so far elevated that Man should esteem himself the brother and friend, but nowise the lord and tutor, of Woman,— were he really bound with her in equal worship,— arrangements as to function and employment would be of no consequence. What Woman needs is not as a woman to act or rule, but as a nature to grow, as an intellect to discern, as a soul to live freely and unimpeded, to unfold such powers as were given her when we left our common home. If fewer talents were given her, yet if allowed the free and full employment of these, so that she may render back to the giver his own with usury, she will not complain; nay, I dare to say she will bless and rejoice in her earthly birth-place, her earthly lot. Let us consider what obstructions impede this good era, and what signs give reason to hope that it draws near.

*   *   *

Another sign of the times is furnished by the triumphs of Female Authorship. These have been great, and are constantly increasing. Women have taken possession of so many provinces for which men had pronounced them unfit, that, though these still declare there are some inaccessible to them, it is difficult to say just *where* they must stop.

*   *   *

The influence has been such, that the aim certainly is, now, in arranging school instruction for girls, to give them as fair a field as boys. As yet, indeed, these arrangements are made with little judgment or reflection; . . . Women are, often, at the head of these institutions; but they have, as yet, seldom been thinking women, capable of organizing a new whole for the wants of the time, and choosing persons to officiate in the departments. And when some portion of instruction of a good sort is got from the school, the far greater proportion which is infused from the general atmosphere of society contradicts its purport. Yet books and a little elementary instruction are not furnished in vain. Women are better aware how great and rich the universe is, not so easily blinded by narrowness or partial views of a home circle. "Her mother did so before her" is no longer a sufficient excuse. Indeed, it was never received as an excuse to mitigate the severity of censure, but was adduced as a reason, rather, why there should be no effort made for reformation.

Whether much or little has been done, or will be done,—whether women will add to the talent of narration the power of systematizing,—whether they will carve marble, as well as draw and paint,— is not important. But that it should be acknowledged that they have intellect which needs developing—that they should not be considered complete, if beings of affection and habit alone— is important.

Yet even this acknowledgment, rather conquered by Woman than proferred by Man, has been sullied by the usual selfishness. Too much is said of women being better educated, that they may become better companions and mothers *for men*. They should be fit for such companionship, and we have mentioned, with satisfaction, instances where it has been established. Earth knows no fairer, holier relation than that of a mother. It is one which, rightly understood, must both promote and require the highest attainments. But a being of infinite scope must not be treated with an exclusive view to any one relation. Give the soul free course, let the organization, both of body and mind, be freely developed, and the being will be fit for any and every relation to which it may be called. The intellect, no more than the sense of hearing, is to be cultivated merely that Woman may be a more valuable companion to Man, but because the Power who gave a power, by its mere existence signifies that it must be brought out toward perfection.

*   *   *

It is therefore that I would have Woman lay aside all thought, such as she habitually cherishes, of being taught and led by men. I would have her, like the Indian girl, dedicate herself to the Sun, the Sun of Truth, and go nowhere if his beams did not make clear the path. I would have her free from compromise, from complaisance, from helplessness, because I would have her good enough and strong enough to love one and all beings, from the fulness, not the poverty of being.

*   *   *

REVIEW QUESTIONS

1. Why did Fuller believe that the phrase "All men are born free and equal" was not made in vain?
2. Why were some people afraid of giving women equal rights?
3. How did Fuller's views on education for women compare to Beecher's?
4. Did Fuller believe that society had made some progress in gender issues?
5. How did her advocacy of woman's rights fit within the transcendentalist school?

WOMAN'S RIGHTS CONVENTION, SENECA FALLS

FROM *Declaration of Sentiments and Resolutions* (1848)

Margaret Fuller's voice was but one among many, thus when she left America for Europe in 1846 the call for woman's rights was far from extinguished. Elizabeth Cady Stanton (1815–1902) became active in woman's rights issues, as did many other women, by way of her involvement in the antislavery movement. After living in Boston in the mid 1840s and there enjoying the stimulating company of other reformers, the Stantons moved to Seneca Falls, New York, where husband Henry practiced law and Elizabeth continued her activism. Stanton wanted full legal equality as well as educational, political, and economic opportunities for women. In July 1848, Elizabeth Cady Stanton, Lucretia Mott, Jane Hunt, Mary McClintock, and Martha C. Wright organized a woman's rights convention that was held at the Wesleyan Methodist Church in Seneca Falls. On the agenda was a Declaration of Sentiments *and various resolutions calling for change. Stanton, who drafted the* Declaration of Sentiments *using another, earlier, and revered American declaration as her model, also submitted a resolution calling for suffrage—the vote—for women. The fight for suffrage and equal rights would continue beyond her lifetime.*

From Elizabeth Cady Stanton, Susan B. Anthony, and Matilda Joslyn Gage, eds., *History of Woman Suffrage*, vol. I (1881; New York: Arno Press and The New York Times, 1969), pp. 70–72.

Declaration of Sentiments

*   *   *

We hold these truths to be self-evident: that all men and women are created equal; that they are endowed by their Creator with certain inalienable rights; that among these are life, liberty, and the pursuit of happiness; that to secure these rights governments are instituted, deriving their just powers from the consent of the governed. . . . But when a long train of abuses and usurpations, pursuing invariably the same object evinces a design to reduce them under absolute despotism, it is their duty to throw off such government, and to provide new guards for their future security. Such has been the patient sufferance of the women under this government, and such is now the necessity which constrains them to demand the equal station to which they are entitled.

The history of mankind is a history of repeated injuries and usurpations on the part of man toward woman, having in direct object the establishment of an absolute tyranny over her. To prove this, let facts be submitted to a candid world.

He has never permitted her to exercise her inalienable right to the elective franchise.

He has compelled her to submit to laws, in the formation of which she had no voice.

He has withheld from her rights which are given to the most ignorant and degraded men— both natives and foreigners.

Having deprived her of this first right of a citizen, the elective franchise, thereby leaving her without representation in the halls of legislation, he has oppressed her on all sides.

He has made her, if married, in the eye of the law, civilly dead.

He has taken from her all right in property, even to the wages she earns.

He has made her, morally, an irresponsible being, as she can commit many crimes with impunity, provided they be done in the presence of her husband. In the covenant of marriage, she is compelled to promise obedience to her husband, he becoming, to all intents and purposes, her master—the law giving him power to deprive her of her liberty, and to administer chastisement.

He has so framed the laws of divorce, as to what shall be the proper causes, and in case of separation, to whom the guardianship of the children shall be given, as to be wholly regardless of the happiness of women—the law, in all cases, going upon a false supposition of the supremacy of man, and giving all power into his hands.

After depriving her of all rights as a married woman, if single, and the owner of property, he has taxed her to support a government which recognizes her only when her property can be made profitable to it.

He has monopolized nearly all the profitable employments, and from those she is permitted to follow, she receives but a scanty remuneration. He closes against her all the avenues to wealth and distinction which he considers most honorable to himself. As a teacher of theology, medicine, or law, she is not known.

He has denied her the facilities for obtaining a thorough education, all colleges being closed against her.

He allows her in Church, as well as State, but a subordinate position, claiming Apostolic authority for her exclusion from the ministry, and, with some exceptions, from any public participation in the affairs of the Church.

He has created a false public sentiment by giving to the world a different code of morals for men and women, by which moral delinquencies which exclude women from society, are not only tolerated, but deemed of little account in man.

He has usurped the prerogative of Jehovah himself, claiming it as his right to assign for her a sphere of action, when that belongs to her conscience and to her God.

He has endeavored, in every way that he could, to destroy her confidence in her own powers, to lessen her self-respect, and to make her willing to lead a dependent and abject life.

Now, in view of this entire disfranchisement of one-half the people of this country, their social and religious degradation—in view of the unjust laws above mentioned, and because women do feel themselves aggrieved, oppressed, and fraudulently deprived of their most sacred rights, we insist that they have immediate admission to all the rights and privileges which belong to them as citizens of the United States.

In entering upon the great work before us, we anticipate no small amount of misconception, misrepresentation, and ridicule; but we shall use every instrumentality within our power to effect our object. We shall employ agents, circulate tracts, petition the State and National legislatures, and endeavor to enlist the pulpit and the press in our behalf. We hope this Convention will be followed by a series of Conventions embracing every part of the country.

The following resolutions . . . were adopted:

*   *   *

Resolved, That such laws as conflict, in any way, with the true and substantial happiness of woman, are contrary to the great precept of nature and of no validity, for this is "superior in obligation to any other."

Resolved, That all laws which prevent woman from occupying such a station in society as her conscience shall dictate, or which place her in a po-

sition inferior to that of man, are contrary to the great precept of nature, and therefore of no force or authority.

Resolved, That woman is man's equal—was intended to be so by the Creator, and the highest good of the race demands that she should be recognized as such.

Resolved, That the women of this country ought to be enlightened in regard to the laws under which they live, that they may no longer publish their degradation by declaring themselves satisfied with their present position, nor their ignorance, by asserting that they have all the rights they want.

Resolved, That inasmuch as man, while claiming for himself intellectual superiority, does accord to woman moral superiority, it is pre-eminently his duty to encourage her to speak and teach, as she has an opportunity, in all religious assemblies.

Resolved, That the same amount of virtue, delicacy, and refinement of behavior that is required of woman in the social state, should also be required of man, and the same transgressions should be visited with equal severity on both man and woman.

Resolved, That the objection of indelicacy and impropriety, which is so often brought against woman when she addresses a public audience, comes with a very ill-grace from those who encourage, by their attendance, her appearance on the stage, in the concert, or in feats of the circus.

Resolved, That woman has too long rested satisfied in the circumscribed limits which corrupt customs and a perverted application of the Scriptures have marked out for her, and that it is time she should move in the enlarged sphere which her great Creator has assigned her.

Resolved, That it is the duty of the women of this country to secure to themselves their sacred right to the elective franchise.

Resolved, That the equality of human rights results necessarily from the fact of the identity of the race in capabilities and responsibilities.

Resolved, therefore, That, being invested by the Creator with the same capabilities, and the same consciousness of responsibility for their exercise, it is demonstrably the right and duty of woman, equally with man, to promote every righteous cause by every righteous means; and especially in regard to the great subjects of morals and religion, it is self-evidently her right to participate with her brother in teaching them, both in private and in public, by writing and by speaking, by any instrumentalities proper to be used, and in any assemblies proper to be held; and this being a self-evident truth growing out of the divinely implanted principles of human nature, any custom or authority adverse to it, whether modern or wearing the hoary sanction of antiquity, is to be regarded as a self-evident falsehood, and at war with mankind.

*   *   *

Resolved, That the speedy success of our cause depends upon the zealous and untiring efforts of both men and women, for the overthrow of the monopoly of the pulpit, and for the securing to woman an equal participation with men in the various trades, professions, and commerce.

REVIEW QUESTIONS

1. In what ways, according to the delegates who accepted this *Declaration*, were women treated unequally?
2. Although the *Declaration* states that man made woman "morally, an irresponsible being," a resolution states that man "does accord to woman moral superiority." Was this a contradiction? Explain.
3. Why did men see women as intellectually inferior?
4. Why were the sentiments expressed in the *Declaration* and resolutions revolutionary?
5. Were they more revolutionary than those stated in the Declaration of Independence?

SOJOURNER TRUTH

FROM Address to the Woman's Rights Convention, Akron, Ohio (1851)

Enslaved people, of course, had no rights, but among the free people of color, black women faced double discrimination based on race and gender. One black woman named Isabella (1797–1883), who was born a slave to a master of Dutch descent in the state of New York, served a number of masters before gaining her freedom in 1827. She then moved to New York City, worked as a house servant, and became involved in evangelical activities. In 1843 she experienced a mystical conversation with God in which she was told to "travel up and down the land" preaching the sins of slavery and the need for conversion. After changing her name to Sojourner Truth, she began crisscrossing the nation, exhorting audiences to be born again and take up the cause of abolitionism. Although unable to read or write, she was a woman of rare intelligence and uncommon courage. During the late 1840s she began promoting the woman's rights movement and in 1851 attended the convention in Akron, Ohio. There she discovered that many participants objected to her presence for fear that her abolitionist sentiments would deflect attention from women's issues. Hisses greeted the tall, gaunt woman as she rose to speak: "Woman's rights and niggers!" "Go it, darkey!" "Don't let her speak!" By the time she finished, however, the audience gave her a standing ovation.

From Frances D. Gage's reminiscences in *History of Woman Suffrage*, vol. I, Elizabeth Cady Stanton, Susan B. Anthony, and Matilda Joslyn Gage, eds. (1881; New York: Arno Press and The New York Times, 1969) p. 116.

*   *   *

"Wall, chilern, whar dar is so much racket dar must be somethin' out o' kilter. I tink dat 'twixt de niggers of de Souf and de womin at de Norf, all talkin' 'bout rights, de white men will be in a fix pretty soon. But what's all dis here talkin' 'bout?

"Dat man ober dar say dat womin needs to be helped into carriages, and lifted ober ditches, and to hab de best place everywhar. Nobody eber helps me into carriages, or ober mud-puddles, or gibs me any best place!" . . . "And a'n't I a woman? Look at me! Look at my arm! . . . I have ploughed, and planted, and gathered into barns, and no man could head me! And a'n't I a woman? I could work as much and eat as much as a man—when I could get it—and bear de lash as well! And a'n't I a woman? I have borne thirteen chilern, and seen 'em mos' all sold off to slavery, and when I cried out with my mother's grief, none but Jesus heard me! And a'n't I a woman?

"Den dey talks 'bout dis ting in de head; what dis dey call it?" ("Intellect," whispered some one near.) "Dat's it, honey. What's dat got to do wid womin's rights or nigger's rights? If my cup won't hold but a pint, and yourn holds a quart, wouldn't ye be mean not to let me have my little half-measure full?" And she pointed her significant finger, and sent a keen glance at the minister who had made the argument. The cheering was long and loud.

"Den dat little man in black dar, he say women can't have as much rights as men, 'cause Christ wan't a woman! Whar did your Christ come from?" Rolling thunder couldn't have stilled that crowd, as did those deep, wonderful tones, as she stood there with outstretched arms and eyes of fire. Raising her voice still louder, she repeated, "Whar did your Christ come from? From God and a woman! Man had nothin' to do wid Him." Oh, what a rebuke that was to that little man.

Turning again to another objector, she took up the defense of Mother Eve. I can not follow her through it all. It was pointed, and witty, and solemn; eliciting at almost every sentence deafening applause; and she ended by asserting: "If de fust woman God ever made was strong enough to turn de world upside down all alone, dese women togedder (and she glanced her eye over the platform) ought to be able to turn it back, and get it right side up again! And now dey is asking to do it, de men better let 'em." Long-continued cheering greeted this. " 'Bleeged to ye for hearin' on me, and now ole Sojourner han't got nothin' more to say."

*   *   *

REVIEW QUESTIONS

1. How did Truth equate the treatment of slaves with the treatment of women?
2. Did she suggest that laboring women, working-class women, had been ignored by the movement for women's rights?
3. How did she justify rights for women?
4. What factors made her presentation so effective?

14 ✍ MANIFEST DESTINY

By the 1830s many Americans may no longer have believed in predestination in a religious or spiritual sense, but a great many did espouse national predestination. They not only nodded in agreement when they read John Louis O'Sullivan's articles advocating expansion, they packed up and hied themselves out to the West. O'Sullivan, the editor of the United States Magazine and Democratic Review, *coined a now familiar term when in 1845 he wrote that "our manifest destiny is to overspread the continent allotted by Providence for the free development of our yearly multiplying millions." Both the idea of manifest destiny and the reality of expansion showed the nature of the American character and nation and profoundly influenced their continuing development.*

Contradictions abounded in the ideas supporting expansion, just as there were dichotomies between the ideas and their implementation. For instance, some citizens promoted expansion as a way of incorporating other peoples into American culture, while others used it to push them out. There were also regional variations to the arguments for and against expansion as northerners, southerners, and westerners pursued their own agendas. Some contemporaries noted these problems in their arguments against expansion. That opposition in itself also shows some of the complexity that was inherent to this issue. Opponents believed that expansion—either in its means or ends—would hurt, not help, the nation. The majority of Americans, however, supported such growth.

United States citizens generally celebrated their self-proclaimed manifest destiny; Native Americans, Mexicans, and Europeans who still had claims in the Western Hemisphere did not. As Americans moved west they trampled tribal lands, trespassed over territorial boundaries, and ignored international agreements. They saw themselves as an irresistible force and worried little about coming up against immoveable objects. Those confronting the Americans were seen simply as objects to be surmounted, removed, or destroyed rather than as peoples or nations with legitimate cultures and claims. Indians, such as the Cherokee, who had endured dispossession in the East found themselves under attack again in the West by white pioneers as well as those native to the areas in which they settled. Many of the peoples native to the West, such as the Apache, Comanche, Crow, and Sioux or Lakota, sharpened their combat skills to ensure their own survival and success in the maelstrom of competing ethnic and national groups. American movement also created conflict with neighboring countries. The Mexicans, who upon their independence in 1821 had claimed the Spanish possessions in North America, and the British in Canada, who via the Hudson Bay Company had established posts in the Northwest, struggled to contain the expansion of the United States.

The British eventually decided to compromise with the Americans over the Oregon territory. In accordance with the Buchanan-Pakenham Treaty of 1846, Britain accepted the lands north of the 49th parallel while the United States took those south of it. The Mexicans, however, did not see possession of the Texas territory as something open to compromise. As they were not willing to concede their claim, they fought two wars in attempts to retain it.

Mexico had initially encouraged American immigration into Texas, but when the government changed hands and the Americans outnumbered the Mexicans in the territory, the welcome withered. Upset by the newcomers who would not learn their language, respect their religion, or adhere to their laws (such as the abolition of slavery), the Mexicans under General Antonio López de Santa Anna tried to drive the Americans out of Texas in 1836. Although the Texans took a beating initially, they rallied to defeat the Mexicans at San Jacinto that April. The Texans established the Lone Star Republic and asked for annexation to the United States.

The American people and their Congress debated the annexation of Texas for nine years. They argued over whether its contributions to the nation's economy and security outweighed such effects as the probable extension of slavery as well as the possibility of war with Mexico. Finally, however, President John Tyler convinced Congress to annex Texas via a joint resolution in 1845. His successor, James K. Polk, immediately stepped into a crisis as Mexico protested the annexation of a state it claimed as its own territory. The Mexicans drew a line in the sand at the Nueces River over which they told the Americans not to step. First the Texans and then the Americans did: to the Rio Grande and beyond.

The United States immediately took the offensive in the Mexican War that started in May 1846. It pumped up its small regular army with tens of thousands of volunteers and then marched its forces into the California and New Mexico territories as well as into Mexico itself, all the way to the "halls of Montezuma": Mexico City. Mexican regular and guerilla forces fought back fiercely, but in the end the Mexican government signed the treaty of Guadalupe Hidalgo in February 1848 and thus relinquished Texas, New Mexico, and California.

Pioneering was a contributing factor in the movement to war; it was also a result of that war. Once the United States took possession of the lands it claimed via conquest, more and more Americans headed out to populate them. And while men may have won the West, women settled it. Neither the winning nor the settling was easy: both challenged the courage, convictions, and constitutions of white and black as well as American-born and immigrant pioneers. Whereas war tested the resolve of the nation, pioneering tested the resolve of individuals. Exploration and settlement was, as it had been for centuries, the great American adventure.

JOHN C. FRÉMONT

FROM *Report of the Exploring Expeditions to the Rocky Mountains* (1843–44)

Lewis and Clark had probed into the Northwest in their expedition of 1804–1806 to provide their president and nation with some vital information and a claim on the territory. By the 1840s Americans were ready to stake their individual claims just as their nation was set to confirm its possession. To facilitate these actions, John C. Frémont (1813–1890), an officer in the Corps of Topographical Engineers, had the job of adding to the earlier explorers' work. Frémont led expeditions in 1842 and 1843–44 to map out possible routes and settlement sites as well as record the flora, fauna, and humanity that inhabited the Rocky Mountain and Pacific Northwest. He did such a good job, and told such interesting stories in his reports (written with his wife's help), that he is best known as an explorer even though he also served his country as a soldier and politician.

From John Charles Frémont, *Report of the Exploring Expeditions to the Rocky Mountains*, March of America Facsimile Series, Number 79 (Ann Arbor, MI: University Microfilms, Inc., 1966), pp. 133–34, 143–46, 182–88, 191, 245–48. [Editorial insertions appear in square brackets —Ed.]

[*August 21, 1843*]

*   *   *

We continued our road down the river, and at night encamped with a family of emigrants—two men, women, and several children—who appeared to be bringing up the rear of the great caravan. I was struck with the fine appearance of their cattle, some six or eight yoke of oxen, which really looked as well as if they had been all the summer at work on some good farm. It was strange to see one small family travelling along through such a country, so remote from civilization. Some nine years since, such a security might have been a fatal one; but since their disastrous defeats in the country a little north, the Blackfeet have ceased to visit these waters. Indians, however, are very uncertain in their localities; and the friendly feelings, also, of those now inhabiting it may be changed.

According to barometrical observation at noon, the elevation of the valley was 6,400 feet above the sea; and our encampment at night in latitude 42° 03' 47", and longitude 111° 10' 53", by observation—the day's journey having been 26 miles. This encampment was therefore within the territorial limit of the United States; our travelling, from the time we entered the valley of the Green river, on the 15th of August, having been to the south of the 42d degree of north latitude, and consequently on Mexican territory; and this is the route all the emigrants now travel to Oregon.

The temperature at sunset was 65°; and at evening there was a distant thunder storm, with a light breeze from the north.

Antelope and elk were seen during the day on the opposite prairie; and there were ducks and geese in the river.

The next morning, in about three miles from our encampment, we reached Smith's fork, a stream of clear water, about 50 feet in breadth. It is timbered with cottonwood, willow, and aspen, and makes a beautiful debouchement through a pass about 600 yards wide, between remarkable mountain hills, rising abruptly on either side, and forming gigantic columns to the gate by which it enters Bear river valley. . . .

We made our halt at noon in a fertile bottom, where the common blue flax was growing abundantly, a few miles below the mouth of Thomas's fork, one of the larger tributaries of the river.

Crossing, in the afternoon, the point of a narrow spur, we descended into a beautiful bottom, formed by a lateral valley, which presented a picture of home beauty that went directly to our hearts. The edge of the wood, for several miles along the river, was dotted with the white covers of emigrant wagons, collected in groups at different camps, where the smokes were rising lazily from the fires, around which the women were occupied in preparing the evening meal, and the children playing in the grass; and herds of cattle, grazing about in the bottom, had an air of quiet security, and civilized comfort, that made a rare sight for the traveller in such a remote wilderness.

In common with all the emigration, they had been reposing for several days in this delightful valley, in order to recruit their animals on its luxuriant pasturage after their long journey, and prepare them for the hard travel along the comparatively sterile banks of the Upper Columbia. . . .

*   *   *

August 30.—We had constant thunder storms during the night, but in the morning the clouds were sinking to the horizon, and the air was clear and cold, with the thermometer at sunrise at 39°. Elevation by barometer 5,580 feet. We were in motion early, continuing up the little stream without encountering any ascent where a horse would not easily gallop, and, crossing a slight dividing ground at the summit, descended upon a small stream, along which we continued on the same excellent road. In riding through the pass, numerous cranes were seen; and prairie hens, or grouse, (*bonasia umbellus*,) which lately had been rare, were very abundant.

This little affluent brought us to a larger stream, down which we travelled through a more open bottom, on a level road, where heavily-laden wagons could pass without obstacle. The hills on the right grew lower, and, on entering a more open country, we discovered a Shoshonee village; and being desirous to obtain information, and purchase from them some roots and berries, we halted on the river, which was lightly wooded with cherry, willow, maple, service berry, and aspen. . . . A number of Indians came immediately over to visit us, and several men were sent to the village with goods, tobacco, knives, cloth, vermilion, and the usual trinkets, to exchange for provisions. But they had no game of any kind; and it was difficult to obtain any roots from them, as they were miserably poor, and had but little to spare from their winter stock of provisions. Several of the Indians drew aside their blankets, showing me their lean and bony figures; and I would not any longer tempt them with a display of our merchandise to part with their wretched subsistence, when they gave as a reason that it would expose them to temporary starvation. A great portion of the region inhabited by this nation formerly abounded in game; the buffalo ranging about in herds, as we had found them on the eastern waters, and the plains dotted with scattered bands of antelope; but so rapidly have they disappeared within a few years, that now, as we journeyed along, an occasional buffalo skull and a few wild antelope were all that remained of the abundance which had covered the country with animal life.

The extraordinary rapidity with which the buffalo is disappearing from our territories will not appear surprising when we remember the great scale on which their destruction is yearly carried on. With inconsiderable exceptions, the business of the American trading posts is carried on in their skins; every year the Indian villages make new lodges, for which the skin of the buffalo furnishes the material; and in that portion of the country where they are still found, the Indians derive their entire support from them, and slaughter them with a thoughtless and abominable extravagance. Like the Indians themselves, they have been a characteristic of the Great West; and as, like them, they are visibly diminishing, . . .

*   *   *

The extraordinary abundance of the buffalo on the east side of the Rocky mountains, and their extraordinary diminution, will be made clearly evident from the following statement: At any time between the years 1824 and 1836, a traveller might start from any given point south or north in the Rocky mountain range, journeying by the most direct route to the Missouri river; and, during the whole distance, his road would be always among large bands of buffalo, which would never be out of his view until he arrived almost within sight of the abodes of civilization.

At this time, the buffalo occupy but a very limited space, principally along the eastern base of the Rocky mountains, sometimes extending at their southern extremity to a considerable distance into the plains between the Platte and Arkansas rivers,

and along the eastern frontier of New Mexico as far south as Texas.

*   *   *

In 1842, I found the Sioux Indians of the Upper Platte *demontés*, as their French traders expressed it, with the failure of the buffalo; and in the following year, large villages from the Upper Missouri came over to the mountains at the heads of the Platte, in search of them. The rapidly progressive failure of their principal and almost their only means of subsistence has created great alarm among them; and at this time there are only two modes presented to them, by which they see a good prospect for escaping starvation: one of these is to rob the settlements along the frontier of the States; and the other is to form a league between the various tribes of the Sioux nation, the Cheyennes, and Arapahoes, and make war against the Crow nation, in order to take from them their country, which is now the best buffalo country in the west. This plan they now have in consideration; and it would probably be a war of extermination, as the Crows have long been advised of this state of affairs, and say that they are perfectly prepared. These are the best warriors in the Rocky mountains, and are now allied with the Snake Indians; and it is probable that their combination would extend itself to the Utahs, who have long been engaged in war against the Sioux. It is in this section of country that my observation formerly led me to recommend the establishment of a military post.

*   *   *

October 25.—The weather was pleasant, with a sunrise temperature of 36°. . . . We halted about three miles above the mouth, on account of grass; and the next morning arrived at the Nez Percé fort, one of the trading establishments of the Hudson Bay Company, a few hundred yards above the junction of the Walahwalah with the Columbia river. Here we had the first view of this river, and found it about 1,200 yards wide, and presenting the appearance of a fine navigable stream. We made our camp in a little grove of willows on the Walahwalah, which are the only trees to be seen in the neighborhood; but were obliged to send the animals back to the encampment we had left, as there was scarcely a blade of grass to be found. . . . The appearance of the post and country was without interest, except that we here saw, for the first time, the great river on which the course of events for the last half century has been directing attention and conferring historical fame. The river is, indeed, a noble object, and has here attained its full magnitude. About nine miles above, and in sight from the heights about the post, is the junction of the two great forks which constitute the main stream—that on which we had been travelling from Fort Hall, and known by the names of Lewis's fork, Shoshonee, and Snake river; and the North fork, which has retained the name of Columbia, as being the main stream.

We did not go up to the junction, being pressed for time; but the union of two large streams, coming one from the southeast, and the other from the northeast, and meeting in what may be treated as the geographical centre of the Oregon valley, thence doubling the volume of water to the ocean, while opening two great lines of communication with the interior continent, constitutes a feature in the map of the country which cannot be overlooked; and it was probably in reference to this junction of waters, and these lines of communication, that this post was established. They are important lines, and, from the structure of the country, must forever remain so—one of them leading to the South Pass, and to the valley of the Mississippi; the other to the pass at the head of the Athabasca river, and to the countries drained by the waters of the Hudson Bay. The British fur companies now use both lines; the Americans, in their emigration to Oregon, have begun to follow the one which leads towards the United States. Batteaus from tide water ascend to the junction, and thence high up the North fork, or Columbia. Land conveyance only is used upon the line of Lewis's fork. To the emigrants to Oregon, the Nez Percé is a point of interest, as being, to those who choose it, the termination of their overland journey. The broad expanse of the river here invites them to embark on its bosom;

and the lofty trees of the forest furnish the means of doing so.

*   *   *

[*March* 6, 1844. Continuing south before turning east.]

We made an acorn meal at noon, and hurried on; the valley being gay with flowers, and some of the banks being absolutely golden with the Californian poppy, (*eschscholtzia crocea.*) Here the grass was smooth and green, and the groves very open; the large oaks throwing a broad shade among sunny spots. Shortly afterwards we gave a shout at the appearance on a little bluff of a neatly built *adobe* house with glass windows. We rode up, but, to our disappointment, found only Indians. There was no appearance of cultivation, and we could see no cattle, and we supposed the place had been abandoned. We now pressed on more eagerly than ever; the river swept round in a large bend to the right; the hills lowered down entirely; and, gradually entering a broad valley, we came unexpectedly into a large Indian village, where the people looked clean, and wore cotton shirts and various other articles of dress. They immediately crowded around us, and we had the inexpressible delight to find one who spoke a little indifferent Spanish, but who at first confounded us by saying there were no whites in the country; but just then a well-dressed Indian came up, and made his salutations in very well spoken Spanish. In answer to our inquiries, he informed us that we were upon the *Rio de los Americanos*, (the river of the Americans,) and that it joined the Sacramento river about 10 miles below. Never did a name sound more sweetly! We felt ourselves among our countrymen; for the name of *American*, in these distant parts, is applied to the citizens of the United States. To our eager inquiries he answered, "I am a *vaquero* (cow herd) in the service of Capt. Sutter, and the people of this *rancheria* work for him." Our evident satisfaction made him communicative; and he went on to say that Capt. Sutter was a very rich man, and always glad to see his country people. We asked for his house. He answered, that it was just over the hill before us; and offered, if we would wait a moment, to take his horse and conduct us to it. We readily accepted his civil offer. In a short distance we came in sight of the fort; and, passing on the way the house of a settler on the opposite side, (a Mr. Sinclair,) we forded the river; and in a few miles were met a short distance from the fort by Capt. Sutter himself. He gave us a most frank and cordial reception—conducted us immediately to his residence—and under his hospitable roof we had a night of rest, enjoyment, and refreshment, which none but ourselves could appreciate. But the party left in the mountains with Mr. Fitzpatrick were to be attended to; and the next morning, supplied with fresh horses and provisions, I hurried off to meet them. On the second day we met, a few miles below the forks of the Rio de los Americanos; and a more forlorn and pitiable sight than they presented cannot well be imagined. They were all on foot—each man, weak and emaciated, leading a horse or mule as weak and emaciated as themselves. They had experienced great difficulty in descending the mountains, made slippery by rains and melting snows, and many horses fell over precipices, and were killed; and with some were lost the *packs* they carried. . . . We stopped and encamped as soon as we met; and a repast of good beef, excellent bread, and delicious salmon, which I had brought along, were their first relief from the sufferings of the Sierra, and their first introduction to the luxuries of the Sacramento. It required all our philosophy and forbearance to prevent *plenty* from becoming as hurtful to us now, as *scarcity* had been before.

The next day, March 8th, we encamped at the junction of the two rivers, the Sacramento and Americanos; and thus found the whole party in the beautiful valley of the Sacramento. It was a convenient place for the camp; and, among other things, was within reach of the wood necessary to make the pack saddles, which we should need on our long journey home, from which we were farther distant now than we were four months before, when from the Dalles of the Columbia we so cheerfully took up the homeward line of march.

Captain Sutter emigrated to this country from the western part of Missouri in 1838–'39, and formed the first settlement in the valley, on a large grant of land which he obtained from the Mexican Government. He had, at first, some trouble with the Indians; but, by the occasional exercise of well-timed authority, he has succeeded in converting them into a peaceable and industrious people. The ditches around his extensive wheat fields; the making of the sun-dried bricks, of which his fort is constructed; the ploughing, harrowing, and other agricultural operations, are entirely the work of these Indians, for which they receive a very moderate compensation—principally in shirts, blankets, and other articles of clothing. In the same manner, on application to the chief of a village, he readily obtains as many boys and girls as he has any use for. There were at this time a number of girls at the fort, in training for a future woollen factory; but they were now all busily engaged in constantly watering the gardens, which the unfavorable dryness of the season rendered necessary. The occasional dryness of some seasons, I understood to be the only complaint of the settlers in this fertile valley, as it sometimes renders the crops uncertain. Mr. Sutter was about making arrangements to irrigate his lands by means of the Rio de los Americanos. He had this year sown, and altogether by Indian labor, three hundred fanegas of wheat.

A few years since, the neighboring Russian establishment of Ross, being about to withdraw from the country, sold to him a large number of stock, with agricultural and other stores, with a number of pieces of artillery and other munitions of war; for these, a regular yearly payment is made in grain.

The fort is a quadrangular *adobe* structure, mounting 12 pieces of artillery, (two of them brass,) and capable of admitting a garrison of a thousand men; this, at present, consists of 40 Indians, in uniform—one of whom was always found on duty at the gate. As might naturally be expected, the pieces are not in very good order. The whites in the employment of Capt. Sutter, American, French and German, amount, perhaps, to 30 men. The inner wall is formed into buildings comprising the common quarters, with blacksmith and other workshops; the dwelling house, with a large distillery house, and other buildings, occupying more the centre of the area.

It is built upon a pond-like stream, at times a running creek communicating with the Rio de los Americanos, which enters the Sacramento about two miles below. The latter is here a noble river, about three hundred yards broad, deep and tranquil, with several fathoms of water in the channel, and its banks continuously timbered. There were two vessels belonging to Capt. Sutter at anchor near the landing—one a large two-masted lighter, and the other a schooner, which was shortly to proceed on a voyage to Fort Vancouver for a cargo of goods.

Since his arrival, several other persons, principally Americans, have established themselves in the valley. Mr. Sinclair, from whom I experienced much kindness during my stay, is settled a few miles distant, on the Rio de los Americanos. Mr. Coudrois, a gentleman from Germany, has established himself on Feather river, and is associated with Captain Sutter in agricultural pursuits. . . .

An impetus was given to the active little population by our arrival, as we were in want of every thing. Mules, horses, and cattle, were to be collected; the horse mill was at work day and night, to make sufficient flour; the blacksmith's shop was put in requisition for horse shoes and bridle bitts; and pack saddles, ropes, and bridles, and all the other little equipments of the camp, were again to be provided.

The delay thus occasioned was one of repose and enjoyment, which our situation required, and, anxious as we were to resume our homeward journey, was regretted by no one. In the mean time, I had the pleasure to meet with Mr. Chiles, who was residing at a farm on the other side of the river Sacramento, while engaged in the selection of a place for a settlement, for which he had received the necessary grant of land from the Mexican Government.

*　　*　　*

On the 22d we made a preparatory move, and encamped near the settlement of Mr. Sinclair, on the left bank of the Rio de los Americanos. I had dis-

charged five of the party: Neal, the blacksmith, (an excellent workman, and an unmarried man, who had done his duty faithfully, and had been of very great service to me,) desired to remain, as strong inducements were offered here to mechanics. Although at considerable inconvenience to myself, his good conduct induced me to comply with his request; and I obtained for him, from Captain Sutter, a present compensation of two dollars and a half per diem, with a promise that it should be increased to five, if he proved as good a workman as had been represented. He was more particularly an agricultural blacksmith. The other men were discharged with their own consent.

While we remained at this place, Derosier, one of our best men, whose steady good conduct had won my regard, wandered off from the camp, and never returned to it again; nor has he since been heard of.

March 24.—We resumed our journey with an ample stock of provisions and a large cavalcade of animals, consisting of 130 horses and mules, and about thirty head of cattle, five of which were milch cows. Mr. Sutter furnished us also with an Indian boy, who had been trained as a *vaquero*, and who would be serviceable in managing our cavalcade, great part of which were nearly as wild as buffalo; and who was, besides, very anxious to go along with us. Our direct course home was east; but the Sierra would force us south, above five hundred miles of travelling, to a pass at the head of the San Joaquin river. . . . From that pass we were to move southeastwardly, having the Sierra then on the right, and reach the "*Spanish trail,*" deviously traced from one watering place to another, which constituted the route of the caravans from *Puebla de los Angeles,* near the coast of the Pacific, to *Santa Fé* of New Mexico. . . . Following that trail through a desert, relieved by some fertile plains indicated by the recurrence of the term *vegas,* until it turned to the right to cross the Colorado, our course would be northeast until we regained the latitude we had lost in arriving at the Eutah lake, and thence to the Rocky mountains at the head of the Arkansas. This course of travelling, forced upon us by the structure of the country, would occupy a computed distance of two thousand miles before we reached the head of the Arkansas; not a settlement to be seen upon it; and the names of places along it, all being Spanish or Indian, indicated that it had been but little trod by *American* feet. Though long, and not free from hardships, this route presented some points of attraction, in tracing the Sierra Nevada— turning the Great Basin, perhaps crossing its rim on the south—completely solving the problem of any river, except the Colorado, from the Rocky mountains on that part of our continent—and seeing the southern extremity of the Great Salt lake, of which the northern part had been examined the year before.

* * *

REVIEW QUESTIONS

1. Most Americans were simply traveling through the Great Plains in the 1840s, and yet American expansion had already had a profound effect in this region. How so?
2. What kind of settlement had Captain Sutter established in California?
3. What kind of relationship did he have with the native peoples?
4. What did settlement along the *Rio de los Americanos* indicate about Mexican control of the area?

CATHERINE HAUN

A Pioneer Woman's Westward Journey (1849)

Although pioneering was usually initiated by men, they were by no means the only ones engaged in that endeavor. Many single men—and married men acting as temporary bachelors—seduced by the thought of rich lands and lodes, traveled west; but settlement was often contingent on the possibility of making and maintaining families there. Thousands of women, therefore, trudged the Overland Trail after 1840 when the great westward migration took off. Most of these women were married, and while some were forced to make the move, many others insisted on accompanying their men, for they were determined to maintain family unity despite the great potential risks to their health and safety. Some of the single women married on the trip or soon thereafter, while numerous married women were widowed. Many of these female pioneers had to deal with the rigors of the journey while pregnant or while caring for young children. Taken away from civilization, they were determined to take civilization with them. While the journey was liberating for a few, most battled the constant challenges to their feminine and domestic identities. Catherine Haun, young, newly married, and of the middle class, was one of the women who met the challenges with considerable strength and grace.

From Catherine Haun, "A Woman's Trip Across the Plains in 1849," in Lillian Schlissel, *Women's Diaries of the Westward Journey* (New York: Schocken Books, 1992), pp. 166–85. [Editorial insertions appear in square brackets—*Ed.*]

Early in January of 1849 we first thought of emigrating to California. It was a period of National hard times and we being financially involved in our business interests near Clinton, Iowa, longed to go to the new El Dorado and "pick up" gold enough with which to return and pay off our debts.

*   *   *

At that time the "gold fever" was contagious and few, old or young, escaped the malady. On the streets, in the fields, in the workshops and by the fireside, golden California was the chief topic of conversation. Who were going? How was best to "fix up" the "outfit"? What to take as food and clothing? Who would stay at home to care for the farm and womenfolks? Who would take wives and children along? Advice was handed out quite free of charge and often quite free of common sense. However, as two heads are better than one, all proffered ideas helped as a means to the end. The intended adventurers dilligently collected their belongings and after exchanging such articles as were not needed for others more suitable for the trip, begging, buying or borrowing what they could, with buoyant spirits started off.

Some half dozen families of our neighborhood joined us and probably about twenty-five persons constituted our little band.

*   *   *

. . . It was more than three months before we were thoroughly equipped and on April 24th, 1849 we left our comparatively comfortable homes—and the uncomfortable creditors—for the uncertain and dangerous trip, beyond which loomed up, in our mind's eye, castles of shining gold.

There was still snow upon the ground and the roads were bad, but in our eagerness to be off we ventured forth. This was a mistake as had we delayed for a couple of weeks the weather would have been more settled, the roads better and much of the discouragement and hardship of the first days of travel might have been avoided.

*   *   *

At the end of the month we reached Council Bluffs, having only travelled across the state of Iowa, a distance of about 350 miles every mile of which was beautifully green and well watered. . . .

As Council Bluffs was the last settlement on the route we made ready for the final plunge into the wilderness by looking over our wagons and disposing of whatever we could spare. . . .

*   *   *

The canvas covered schooners were supposed to be, as nearly as possible, constructed upon the principle of the "wonderful one-horse shay." It was very essential that the animals be sturdy, whether oxen, mules or horses. Oxen were preferred as they were less liable to stampede or be stolen by Indians and for long hauls held out better and though slower they were steady and in the long run performed the journey in an equally brief time. Besides, in an emergency they could be used as beef. When possible the provisions and ammunition were protected from water and dust by heavy canvas or rubber sheets.

Good health, and above all, not too large a proportion of women and children was also taken into consideration. The morning starts had to be made early—always before six o'clock—and it would be hard to get children ready by that hour. Later on experience taught the mothers that in order not to delay the trains it was best to allow the smaller children to sleep in the wagons until after several hours of travel when they were taken up for the day.

Our caravan had a good many women and children and although we were probably longer on the journey owing to their presence—they exerted a good influence, as the men did not take such risks with Indians and thereby avoided conflict; were more alert about the care of the teams and seldom had accidents; more attention was paid to cleanliness and sanitation and, lastly but not of less importance, the meals were more regular and better cooked thus preventing much sickness and there was less waste of food.

*   *   *

After a sufficient number of wagons and people were collected at this rendezvous we proceeded to draw up and agree upon a code of general regulations for train government and mutual protection—a necessary precaution when so many were to travel together. Each family was to be independent yet a part of the grand unit and every man was expected to do his individual share of general work and picket duty.

John Brophy was selected as Colonel. He was particularly eligible having served in the Black Hawk War and as much of his life had been spent along the frontier his experience with Indians was quite exceptional.

Each week seven Captains were appointed to serve on "Grand Duty." They were to protect the camps and animals at night. One served each night and in case of danger gave the alarm.

When going into camp the "leader wagon" was turned from the road to the right, the next wagon turned to the left, the others following close after and always alternating to right and left. In this way a large circle, or corral, was formed within which the tents were pitched and the oxen herded. The horses were picketed near by until bed time when they were tethered to the tongues of the wagons.

While the stock and wagons were being cared for, the tents erected and camp fires started by the side of the wagons outside the corral, the cooks busied themselves preparing the evening meal for the hungry, tired, impatient travelers.

When the camp ground was desirable enough to warrant it we did not travel on the Sabbath.

Although the men were generally busy mending wagons, harness, yokes, shoeing the animals etc., and the women washed clothes, boiled a big mess of beans, to be warmed over for several meals, or perhaps mended clothes or did other household straightening up, all felt somewhat rested on Monday morning, for the change of occupation had been refreshing.

*   *   *

During the entire trip Indians were a source of anxiety, we being never sure of their friendship. Se-cret dread and alert watchfulness seemed always necessary for after we left the prairies they were more treacherous and numerous being in the language of the pioneer trapper: "They wus the most onsartainest vermints alive."

One night after we had retired, some sleeping in blankets upon the ground, some in tents, a few under the wagons and others in the wagons, Colonel Brophy gave the men a practice drill. It was impromptu and a surprise. He called: "Indians, Indians!" We were thrown into great confusion and excitement but he was gratified at the promptness and courage with which the men responded. Each immediately seized his gun and made ready for the attack. The women had been instructed to seek shelter in the wagons at such times of danger, but some screamed, others fainted, a few crawled under the wagons and those sleeping in wagons generally followed their husbands out and all of us were nearly paralyzed with fear. Fortunately, we never had occasion to put into actual use this maneuver, but the drill was quite reassuring and certainly we womenfolk would have acted braver had the alarm ever again been sounded. . . .

*   *   *

Finally after a couple of weeks' travel the distant mountains of the west came into view.

This was the land of the buffalo. One day a herd came in our direction like a great black cloud, a threatening moving mountain, advancing towards us very swiftly and with wild snorts, noses almost to the ground and tails flying in midair. I haven't any idea how many there were but they seemed to be innumerable and made a deafening terrible noise As is their habit, when stampeding, they did not turn out of their course for anything. Some of our wagons were within their line of advance and in consequence one was completely demolished and two were overturned. Several persons were hurt, one child's shoulder being dislocated, but fortunately no one was killed.

Two of these buffaloes were shot and the humps and tongues furnished us with fine fresh meat. They happened to be buffalo cows and, in consequence, the meat was particularly good flavor and tender. It is believed that the cow can run faster than the bull. The large bone of the hind leg, after being stripped of the flesh, was buried in coals of buffalo chips and in an hour the baked marrow was served. I have never tasted such a rich, delicious food!

*   *   *

Buffalo chips, when dry, were very useful to us as fuel. On the barren plains when we were without wood we carried empty bags and each pedestrian "picked up chips" as he, or she, walked along. Indeed we could have hardly got along without thus useful animal, were always appropriating either his hump, tongue, marrowbone, tallow, skin or chips! . . .

*   *   *

Trudging along within the sight of the Platte, whose waters were now almost useless to us on account of the Alkali, we one day found a post with a cross board pointing to a branch road which seemed better than the one we were on. . . . We decided to take it but before many miles suddenly found ourselves in a desolate, rough country that proved to be the edge of the "Bad Lands" I shudder yet at the thought of the ugliness and danger of the territory. . . .

*   *   *

We saw nothing living but Indians, lizards and snakes. Trying, indeed, to feminine nerves. Surely Inferno can be no more horrible in formation. The pelting sun's rays reflected from the parched ground seemed a furnace heat by day and our campfires, as well as those of the Indians cast grotesque glares and terrifying shadows by night. The demen needed only horns and cloven feet to complete the soul stirring picture!

To add to the horrors of the surroundings one man was bitten on the ankle by a venemous snake. Although every available remedy was tried upon the wound, his limb had to be amputated with the aid of a common handsaw. Fortunately, for him, he

had a good, brave wife along who helped and cheered him into health and usefulness; for it was not long before he found much that he could do and was not considered a burden, although the woman had to do a man's work as they were alone. He was of a mechanical turn, and later on helped mend wagons, yokes and harness; and when the train was "on the move" sat in the wagon, gun by his side, and repaired boots and shoes. He was one of the most cheery members of the company and told good stories and sang at the campfire, putting to shame some of the able bodied who were given to complaining or selfishness. . . .

Finally after several days we got back onto the road and were entering the Black Hills Country. . . .

*   *   *

We had not traveled many miles in the Black Hills—the beginning of the Rocky Mountains—before we realized that our loads would have to be lightened as the animals were not able to draw the heavily laden wagons over the slippery steep roads. We were obliged to sacrifice most of our merchandise that was intended for our stock in trade in California and left it by the wayside; burying the barrels of alcohol least the Indians should drink it and frenzied thereby might follow and attack us. . . .

*   *   *

During the day we womenfolk visited from wagon to wagon or congenial friends spent an hour walking, ever westward, and talking over our home life back in "the states" telling of the loved ones left behind; voicing our hopes for the future in the far west and even whispering a little friendly gossip of emigrant life.

High teas were not popular but tatting, knitting, crocheting, exchanging recipes for cooking beans or dried apples or swapping food for the sake of variety kept us in practice of feminine occupations and diversions.

We did not keep late hours but when not too engrossed with fear of the red enemy or dread of impending danger we enjoyed the hour around the campfire. The menfolk lolling and smoking their pipes and guessing or maybe betting how many miles we had covered the day. We listened to readings, story telling, music and songs and the day often ended in laughter and merrymaking.

It was the fourth of July when we reached the beautiful Laramie River. Its sparkling, pure waters were full of myriads of fish that could be caught with scarcely an effort. It was necessary to build barges to cross the river and during the enforced delay our animals rested and we had one of our periodical "house cleanings." This general systematic re-adjustment always freshened up our wagon train very much, for after a few weeks of travel things got mixed up and untidy and often wagons had to be abandoned if too worn for repairs, and generally one or more animals had died or been stolen.

*   *   *

Cholera was prevalent on the plains at this time; the train preceding as well as the one following ours had one or more deaths, but fortunately we had not a single case of the disease. Often several graves together stood as silent proof of smallpox or cholera epidemic. The Indians spread the disease among themselves by digging up the bodies of the victims for the clothing. The majority of the Indians were badly pock-marked. . . .

*   *   *

It was with considerable apprehension that we started to traverse the treeless, alkali region of the Great Basin or Sink of the Humboldt. Our wagons were badly worn, the animals much the worse for wear, food and stock feed was getting low with no chance of replenishing the supply. During the month of transit we, like other trains, experienced the greatest privations of the whole trip. It was no unusual sight to see graves, carcasses of animals and abandoned wagons. In fact the latter furnished us with wood for the campfires as the sagebrush was scarce and unsatisfactory and buffalo chips were not as plentiful as on the plains east of the Rocky Mountains.

*   *   *

Across this drear country I used to ride horseback several hours of the day which was a great relief from the continual jolting of even our spring wagon. I also walked a great deal and this lightened the wagon. One day I walked fourteen miles and was not very fatigued.

. . . The men seemed more tired and hungry than were the women. Our only death on the journey occurred in this desert. The Canadian woman, Mrs. Lamore, suddenly sickened [after childbirth] and died, leaving her two little girls and grief stricken husband. We halted a day to bury her and the infant that had lived but an hour, in this weird, lonely spot on God's footstool away apparently from everywhere and everybody.

*   *   *

. . . we reached Sacramento on November 4, 1849, just six months and ten days after leaving Clinton, Iowa, we were all in pretty good condition. . . .

Although very tired of tent life many of us spent Thanksgiving and Christmas in our canvas houses. I do not remember ever having had happier holiday times. For Christmas dinner we had a grizzly bear steak for which we paid $2.50, one cabbage for $1.00 and—oh horrors—some *more* dried apples! And for a Christmas present the Sacramento river rose very high and flooded the whole town! . . . It was past the middle of January before we . . . reached Marysville—there were only a half dozen houses; all occupied at exorbitant prices. Some one was calling for the services of a lawyer to draw up a will and my husband offered to do it for which he charged $150.00.

This seemed a happy omen for success and he hung out his shingle, abandoning all thought of going to the mines. As we had lived in a tent and had been on the move for nine months, traveling 2400 miles we were glad to settle down and go housekeeping in a shed that was built in a day of lumber purchased with the first fee. . . .

*   *   *

REVIEW QUESTIONS

1. According to Haun's account, what did it take to be a successful pioneer?

2. What hazards did the pioneers face?
3. Did the journey have an effect on gender roles? Why or why not?
4. What does her story reveal about Haun herself?

JAMES P. BECKWOURTH AND T. D. BONNER

FROM *The Life and Adventures of James P. Beckwourth* (1856)

The story of the West is one bursting with color: vivid personalities, adventure tales galore, and magnificent scenery. Many celebrated individuals have had their stories told and retold in connection with westward expansion—Jim Bowie, Kit Carson, and Davy Crockett among them—but some frontiersmen whose contributions to settlement were as significant have not met with the same fame (or infamy, depending on the evaluator). James P. Beckwourth (1798–1866) had adventures that rivalled those of his more famous fellow frontiersmen, but although his story was published within his lifetime, he did not gain the national renown that his contemporaries did. One part of the problem was in the telling of his tale itself; while exaggeration was always part of frontier tales, Beckwourth was accused by some observers of outright lying. His account certainly was embellished, but some historians who have studied Beckwourth's story have found much of it essentially valid. The other part of the problem was that Beckwourth was an African American who did not fit within whitewashed frontier stories. Yet the proper story of the frontier is that of the contacts, conflicts, and cooperation among people of different ethnicities and cultures. Beckwourth lived, loved, worked, and fought with and among all of them. Adopted by the Crow, he performed warrior duties and married—many times—within the tribe. After he left the Crow he still continued to trade with them and other Native Americans as he moved in and out of Mexican-held territory. He also served the American military at various times.

From T. D. Bonner, *The Life and Adventures of James P. Beckwourth* (1856; New York: Arno Press and The New York Times, 1969), pp. 457–67, 472–76, 499, 506–507, 514–15, 519–20. [Editorial insertions appear in square brackets—*Ed.*]

*   *   *

[In the early 1840s Charles Towne and I] passed on into St. Fernandez, and found quite a number of American traders there, established in business, and supplying both mountaineers and Indians with goods. Here I encountered an old acquaintance, named Lee, with whom I entered into partnership. We purchased one hundred gallons of alcohol, and a stock of fancy articles, to return to the Indian country, and trade for robes and other peltry. We visited the Cheyennes on the South Fork of the Platte. We passed Bent's fort on our way thither. He hailed us, and inquired where we were going. I informed him that we were on our way to the Cheyenne village. He begged me not to go, as I valued my safety. . . . I replied to him that I anticipated no danger, and left him to pass on to their village.

The Indians were delighted at my arrival. I had heard that the hooping-cough was very prevalent among the children, and, as we happened to have several bushels of corn, and beans, and a large quantity of dried pumpkins, we could not have come at a more opportune moment. I told the Indians, in answer to their welcome, that I had come back to see them because I had heard their children were all sick. I called attention to my stock of vegetable esculents, as being best adapted for food for their children, and the best calculated to restore them to health. "Besides," I added, "I have brought a little whisky along, to put good life into your hearts."

*   *   *

I deposited my goods at Old Bark's lodge, who felt highly honored with the trust. The villagers collected round, and a dispute arose among them whether the whisky should be broached or not. Porcupine Bear objected, and Bob-tailed Horse, his brother-in-law, strongly advocated my opening the kegs. This led to a warm altercation between the two warriors, until the disputed question was to be decided by the arbitrament of battle. They both left the lodge to prepare for the combat, and returned in a few minutes fully armed and equipped.

Porcupine Bear argued his cause in the following strain: "Cheyennes, look at me, and listen well to my words. I am now about to fight my brother; I shall fight him, and shall kill him if I can. In doing this, I do not fight my brother, but I fight the greatest enemy of my people.

"Once we were a great and powerful nation: our hearts were proud, and our arms were strong. But a few winters ago all other tribes feared us; now the Pawnees dare to cross our hunting-grounds, and kill our buffalo. Once we could beat the Crows, and, unaided, destroyed their villages; now we call other villages to our assistance, and we can not defend ourselves from the assaults of the enemy. How is this, Cheyennes? The Crows drink no whisky. The earnings of their hunters and toils of their women are bartered to the white man for weapons and ammunition. This keeps them powerful and dreaded by their enemies. We kill buffalo by the thousand; our women's hands are sore with dressing the robes; and what do we part with them to the white trader for? We pay them for the white man's fire-water, which turns our brains upside down, which makes our hearts black, and renders our arms weak. It takes away our warriors' skill, and makes them shoot wrong in battle. Our enemies, who drink no whisky, when they shoot, always kill their foe. We have no ammunition to encounter our foes, and we have become as dogs, which have nothing but their teeth.

*   *   *

"I say, let us buy of the Crow what is useful and good, but his whisky we will not touch; let him take that away with him. I have spoken all I have to say, and if my brother wishes to kill me for it, I am ready to die. I will go and sit with my fathers in the spirit land, where I shall soon point down to the last expiring fire of the Cheyennes, and when they inquire the cause of this decline of their people, I will tell them with a straight tongue that it was the fire-water of the trader that put it out."

Old Bark then advanced between the two belligerents and thus spoke: "Cheyennes, I am your great chief; you know me. My word this day shall be obeyed. The Crow has come among us again, and has brought us good things that we need; he has also brought us a little whisky. He is poor, while we are yet strong, and we will buy all he has brought with him. This day we will drink; it will make us merry, and feel good to one another. We will all drink this once, but we will not act like fools; we will not quarrel and fight, and frighten our women and children. Now, warriors, give me your weapons."

This fiat admitted no appeal; it was law and gospel to his people; disobedience to his command subjected the offender to immediate death at the hands of the Dog Soldiers. The warriors delivered up their battle-axes, and the old chief handed them to me. "Crow," said he, "take these weapons that I have taken from my two children. Keep them until we have drunk up your whisky, and let no one have them till I bid you. Now, Crow, we are ready."

Slim Face and Gray Head, two Dog Soldiers, then harangued the village, and desired all who wished to trade to come and bring their robes and horses to Old Bark's lodge, and to remember that they were trading with the honest Crow, and not with white men, and that what they paid him was his.

They answered the summons in flocks, the women first, according to my established rule. My corn, beans, and pumpkins "exhaled like the dew," and I received in exchange their beautiful fancy robes. The women served, the men next came in for whisky. I sold on credit to some. When one wanted thus to deal, he would tell me what kind of a horse or mule he had: I would appeal to Old Bark for confirmation of the statement; if he verified it, I served the liquor. They all got drunk, Porcupine Bear, the temperance orator, with the rest; but there was not a single fight; all passed off harmoniously.

I received over four hundred splendid robes, besides moccasins and fancy articles. When I was ready to leave, thirty-eight horses and mules, a number corresponding to what I had marked, were brought forward. I packed up my peltry, and sent my partner on in advance with every thing except the horse I rode, telling him I would overtake him shortly.

*   *   *

When I passed Bent at his post he was perfectly confounded. He had seen one train pass belonging to me, and now I was conducting another, when, at the same time, he had supposed that there was not a robe in the village.

"Beckwourth," said he, "how you manage Indians as you do beats my understanding."

I told him that it was easily accounted for; that the Indians knew that the whites cheated them, and knew that they could believe what I said. Besides that, they naturally felt superior confidence in me on account of my supposed affinity of race. I had lived so much among them that I could enter into their feelings, and be in every respect one of themselves: this was an inducement which no acknowledged white trader could ever hope to hold out.

*   *   *

I arrived in Pueblo de Angeles (California) in January, 1844. There I indulged my new passion for trade, and did a very profitable business for several months. At the breaking out of the revolution in 1845, I took an active part against the mother country, . . .

*   *   *

The Upper Californians, on account of their great distance from the Mexican government, had long enjoyed the forms of an independent principality, although recognizing themselves as a portion of the Mexican Republic. They had for years past had the election of their own officers, their governor inclusive, and enjoyed comparative immunity from taxes and other political vexations. Under this abandonment, the inhabitants lived prosperous and contented; . . .

Two years prior to my arrival all this had been changed. President Santa Anna had appointed one of his creatures, Torrejon, governor, with absolute and tyrannical power; he arrived with an army of bandits to subject the defenseless inhabitants to every wrong that a debasing tyranny so readily indulges in. . . . The people's patience became at length exhausted, and they determined to die rather than submit to such inflictions. But they were ignorant how to shake off the yoke; they were unaccustomed to war, and knew nothing about political organizations. However, Providence finally raised up a man for the purpose, General José Castro, who had filled the office of commander under the former system, but who had been forced to retire into privacy at the inauguration of the reign of terror. He stepped boldly forth, and declared to the people his readiness to lead them to the warfare that should deliver their country from the scourge that afflicted them, he called upon them to second his exertions, and never desert his banner until California were purified of her present pollution. His patriotic appeal was responded to by all ranks. Hundreds flocked to his standard; the young and the old left their ranches and their cattle-grounds, and rallied round their well-tried chief.

There was at that time quite a number of Americans in the country, and, according to their interests and predilections, they ranged themselves upon opposing sides. . . .

*   *   *

After seeing the departure of the government troops, the rebel army returned to Pueblo, where they elected Colonel Pico governor; Colonel, now General Castro, commander of the forces; and filled other less important offices. Fandangoes, which were continued for a week, celebrated our success; and these festivities over, the insurgents returned to their various homes and occupations.

*   *   *

I now resumed my business, and dispatched my partner, Mr. Waters, after a fresh supply of goods; but, before he had time to return, fresh political commotions supervened. There still seemed to exist in the minds of the majority a strong hankering for the domination of Mexico, notwithstanding they had so recently sided with the Revolutionists in shaking off the yoke of the national government. Among other causes of excitement, too, the American adventurers resident there had raised the

"Bear Flag," and proclaimed their intention of establishing an independent government of their own. This caused us to be closely watched by the authorities, and matters seemed to be growing too warm to be pleasant.

In the midst of this gathering ferment, news reached us from Mazatlan of the declaration of war between the United States and Mexico, and I deemed it was fully time to leave. Colonel Fremont was at that juncture approaching from Oregon with a force, if combined with the Americans resident there, sufficient to conquer the whole country, and I would have liked exceedingly to join his forces, but to have proceeded toward him would have subjected me to mistrust, and consequent capture and imprisonment. If I looked south the same difficulties menaced me, and the west conducted me to the Pacific Ocean.

. . . My only retreat was eastward; so, considering all things fair in time of war, I, together with five trusty Americans, collected eighteen hundred stray horses we found roaming on the Californian ranchos, and started with our utmost speed from Pueblo de Angeles. . . .

General Kearney was just then on his march to Santa Fé. I took a drove of my horses, and proceeded down the Arkansas to meet him on his route; for it was probable there might be an opportunity of effecting some advantageous exchanges. The general came up, and found me in waiting with my stock; we had been acquainted for several years, and he gave me a very cordial reception.

*   *   *

I informed him that I was ready for service; and, accordingly, I sent all my remaining horses back to my plantation, and went on with the general to Santa Fé, which place submitted without firing a shot. The general sent me immediately back to Fort Leavenworth with dispatches. This was my service during the war. The occupation was a tolerably good one, and I never failed in getting my dispatches through. I enjoyed facilities superior to almost any other man, as I was known to almost all the Indians through whose country I passed.

*   *   *

The next spring [1850] I engaged in mining and prospecting in various parts of the gold region. I advanced as far as the American Valley, having one man in my company, and proceeded north into the Pitt River country, where we had a slight difficulty with the Indians. We had come upon a party who manifested the utmost friendship toward us; but I, knowing how far friendly appearances could be trusted to, cautioned my partner on no account to relinquish his gun, if the Indians should attempt to take it. They crowded round us, pretending to have the greatest interest in the pack that we carried, until they made a sudden spring, and seized our guns, and attempted to wrest them from our grasp. I jerked from them, and retreated a few steps; then, cocking my gun, I bade them, if they wished to fight, to come on. This produced a change in their feelings, and they were very friendly again, begging caps and ammunition of us, which, of course, we refused. We then walked backward for about one hundred and fifty yards, still keeping our pieces ready should they attempt further hostilities; but they did not deem it prudent to molest us again.

While on this excursion I discovered what is now known as "Beckwourth's Pass" in the Sierra Nevada. From some of the elevations over which we passed I remarked a place far away to the southward that seemed lower than any other. I made no mention of it to my companion, but thought that at some future time I would examine into it farther. . . .

In the spring of 1852 I established myself in Beckwourth Valley, and finally found myself transformed into a hotel-keeper and chief of a trading-post. My house is considered the emigrant's landing-place, as it is the first ranch he arrives at in the golden state, and is the only house between this point and Salt Lake. . . .

When I stand at my door, and watch the weary, way-worn travelers approach, their wagons holding together by a miracle, their stock in the last stage of emaciation, and themselves a perfect exaggeration of caricature, I frequently amuse myself with imagining the contrast they must offer to the *tout ensemble* and general appearance they presented to their admiring friends when they first set out upon their journey.

*   *   *

REVIEW QUESTIONS

1. What did Beckwourth reveal about the relationships and attitudes of the various peoples in the frontier West?
2. What did his words and actions reveal about his own attitudes?
3. Did the California Revolution help or hinder the American invasion that soon followed? How so?
4. Does Beckwourth epitomize the myth or image of the American frontiersman? Explain.

THOMAS J. GREEN

FROM *Reflections upon the Present Political and Probable Future Relations of Texas, Mexico, and the United States* (1845)

When Mexico cracked down on recalcitrant Texas settlers in 1836, the Texians—as General Thomas J. Green called them—responded with a declaration of independence. The resulting war ended on 21 April when General Sam Houston's forces beat the Mexicans at San Jacinto. Texas established itself as a republic and elected Houston as its first president; but it also proposed annexation to the United States. When that did not immediately happen, the new republic tried to chart an independent course, only to find that independence did not guarantee peace and prosperity. Disappointment in Houston's "peace policy" led to the election of the more militant General Mirabeau B. Lamar as president. Green was pleased when Texans repudiated Houston and elected Lamar in 1838. But when Lamar's strikes against the Indians and quasi-war with Mexico resulted in yet more debt and still no peace, Texans voted Houston back into office in 1841. Green was appalled. Green, who participated in the disastrous expedition against Mier (a Mexican town on the Rio Grande) in December, 1842, was an invective opponent of Mexico. He was also a critic of the United States when that nation failed to intervene to assure Texas's borders. This inveterate proponent of Texan independence advocated an aggressive, militaristic policy to secure the new republic and ensure its territorial and economic expansion.

From Thomas J. Green, *Journal of the Texian Expedition against Mier; . . . with Reflections upon the Present Political and Probable Future Relations of Texas, Mexico, and the United States* (New York: Harper & Brothers, Publishers, 1845), pp. 403–18, 432–35.

*   *   *

When the timid and weak-headed of our own, and the speculative and uninformed of other countries, have expressed doubts as to the ability of Texas to maintain herself against Mexico, these doubts were the offspring of ignorance and fear. A people like the bulk of the Texas population, born in and reared under the principles of free representative government, will not even entertain a question of change. That proposition which purposes to send them back to despotism can get no hold upon the popular thought, and the occasional recreant who would harbour it in his own bosom dare not utter it. Effeminacy, licentiousness, and corruption, after the slow and gradual inroads of ages, may undermine a nation's political morals, as will indulgence an individual's. . . . Thus it has been with those representative governments which have preceded us: the constituents had first to be corrupted one by one, and when all the members were affected, then the body sunk. Such may ultimately be the destiny of Texas; but, with the lights of the world before her, there can be no just fear that her course of freedom will be short of any nation which has gone before.

Can a nation born and raised in such principles long practise a *neighbourhood comity* with one whose principles are in such diametrical opposition?

*   *   *

Two nations so contiguous, so opposite in their policy, and every way so unlike each other, can never live in friendship with a border which invites both to its advantages. The Rio Grande, from its head to its source, from the forty-second to the twenty-fifth degree of north latitude, is capable of maintaining many millions of population, with a variety of product which no river upon the north continent can boast. This river, once settled with the enterprise and intelligence of the English race, will yearly send forth an agricultural export which it will require hundreds of steamers to transport to its delta, while its hides, wool, and metals may be increased to an estimate which would now appear chimerical.

If annexation of Texas to the United States of the North succeeds, this boundary can exist but for a short period; and though there seems to me to be a destiny in the womb of time which marks her southern boundary at the extremity of the north continent, where the two great oceans of the world will unite under a genial sun and a smooth navigation, yet her more *immediate* southern boundary must extend to the *Sierra Madre*, that great Chinese wall which separates the people of the Rio Grande from those of the more southern table-lands. Can this be considered a greedy desire upon the part of the mighty northern nation, when her facilities of communication with those people from her capital in twelve days are superior to their present means of communication with the capital of Mexico in thirty? We say not. This age has merged distance in time, and the people of the Rio Grande at present are as near neighbours to the capital of the United States as Boston was to Philadelphia at the promulgation of President Washington's inaugural message to the first Congress.

Should annexation not take place, this will be done, and sooner done by Texas. Both the government of the United States and Texas are founded upon the same political code. The same political sentiment enters into each. They have the same common origin—the same language, laws, and religion—the same pursuits and interests; and though they may remain independent of each other as to government, they are identified in weal and wo—they will flourish side by side *pari passu,*[1] and the blight which affects the one will surely reach the other. The unity of the Texian government, her immediate contiguity to Mexico, and her multiplied causes of quarrel therefrom, will cause her arms to extend south and west sooner than would those of the United States. In the later government of such a confederacy of republics there are many heads to consult and many interests to accommodate. These numerous sectional interests, whether real or fancied, must be accommodated, and by an action necessarily slower than that of Texas.

As I have said before, it was not my purpose to discuss, at present, the question of annexation. That has been often and ably done, and much has been said on both sides; but as a Texian, feeling a proper degree of pride in her nationality, and an absorbing interest in her welfare, whatever may be her destiny, duty requires me to deny a position which seems to have grown up with the argument, to wit, that most or all the advantages of union would result to Texas.

If Texas has been the applicant for this political copartnership, she has not been insensible to the fact that she would enter the firm as a junior partner, bringing with her into the concern more than her *pro rata*[2] of capital; she has not been insensible to the fact that she voluntarily abandons her own freedom to take a junior position in that mighty national confederation which will give her but a feeble voice in the general direction of affairs; she has not been blind to the fact that, by entering into the union, she makes herself a party to the many quarrels of conflicting interest which perpetually

---

[1] With equal step; together (French)—*Ed.*

[2] According to rate or proportion (Latin)—*Ed.*

excites that great national family; that by this step she voluntarily leaps into the questions of bank or no bank; of free trade, high tariff, and protection; of abolition and disunion; she is fully aware that she gives to the Northern States all the benefits of her carrying trade, to the injury of her own citizens, and taxes herself with northern manufactures at least thirty per cent. higher than she could procure like articles from other nations; she is not insensible to the fact that after this current year a ten per cent *ad valorem*[3] tariff, without direct taxation, will be ample for the support of her government, when, by coming into the Union, she voluntarily taxes herself four times that amount; she is not insensible to the fact that she offers to the confederacy four hundred miles of seacoast, with all the advantages of the rich valley of the Rio Grande, including sixteen degrees of latitude, from its source to its mouth, with more than one hundred millions of acres of public domain. And for what are these mighty surrenders made? Does Texas receive a *quid pro quo*[4] in having her coffers filled for the purpose of carrying on what ought to be her brilliant destiny even as one of the states? No! She receives just enough of the proceeds of her immense domain to pay a debt, not a tithe of its value. And to whom is this debt paid but to the citizens of the United States, most of whom have bought it upon speculation? Texas is none the better off for this, save in the protection of that national faith, which she prizes as an honest nation should. If this debt were paid to her own citizens, it would be that much towards her individual state wealth, whereas not one dollar in fifty comes to those citizens. It goes into the hands of foreign money-shavers and broker-gamblers, who care nothing beyond for her prosperity, because such people have no feelings except in the usury of coppers.

Thus it is that Texas would denude herself by abolishing her Constitution—by dismissing her foreign ministers—by cutting short her acquaintance with an enlightened world—by surrendering her separate independence, and committing national suicide—to submit to a high protective tariff, and resort to the grinding operation of a direct tax for the support of her state government, and then sink to an obscure corner in the constellation of states for that proud feeling which a majority of her citizens claim in their nativity. The United States can not, must not, therefore, view her as the only beneficiary to the contract.

*   *   *

Since the establishment of Texian independence, she cannot have viewed, but with regret and mortification, the rapid growth of principles in her fatherland, which no circumstances under annexation will cause her ever to submit to. At the establishment of Texian independence, a fanatical few preached the doctrine of universal equality between the white and black man, between the master and the slave. Then this few received the countenance of but few—then the many abhorred them as unprincipled disturbers in the large and happy household; no man of character gave countenance to the unnatural associations of such disgusting doctrines. How altered now the case? The contagion of fanaticism, however absurd, is like the contagion of physical maladies, which communicate by contiguity. It spread first to the ignorant, because they were in nearer contact. When it found a lodgment in the multitude, it met a response in the demagogue of higher standing; then found apologists in the Senate; next, advocates among the most talented, and now the election of President is bending to its influence. . . .

Are these all the advantages which would result to the United States by such a union? No, indeed! Many others might be enumerated; but, in connexion with the question of southern boundary, I will only notice two, which seems to have been overlooked by most writers upon the subject. 1st. The possession of the shortest and most practicable route to the settlements and commerce of the United States on the Pacific; and, 2dly. A boundary in connexion with the question of the amelioration and ultimate destiny of slavery in the United States. First, The annexation of Texas to the United States, with the Rio Grande as the consequent immediate

---

[3] According to the value (Latin)—*Ed.*
[4] One thing for another (Latin)—*Ed.*

southwestern boundary, would necessarily, by treaty or conquest, extend to the *Sierra Madre*, and, as a protection against the northern tribes of Indians, should cross to the Gulf of California about the 28th degree of north latitude. This would be the shortest and most expeditious route from the United States as well to her Oregon settlements as to her other numerous interests on the Pacific.

*   *   *

This short and expeditious route to the growing, and soon to be the important settlement of Oregon, and, at present, many other interests in the Pacific in the event of the acquisition of this country by the United States, would be the smallest reasons for the accomplishment of this route.

The most desirable portion of this continent lies between the 28th and 42d degrees of north latitude upon the Pacific. It presents more than a thousand miles of seacoast, with the important ports of Guaymas, San Diego, San Gabriel, Monterey, San Francisco, and many others, with a soil and climate of unsurpassed capability for grazing and agriculture, and a mineral wealth supposed to be equal, if not superior, to any in the world. This vast country of more than one million of square miles, lying due west of the settled portion of the United States, between the frozen regions of the north and the vertical sun of the south, between the gentle influences of the Pacific Ocean and the great backbone of the continent, capable of giving wealth and happiness to a hundred millions of souls, is now in possession of roaming tribes of unhoused Indians, and a few settlements of less than two hundred thousand Mexican subjects.

If Oregon is important to the United States, this country is a thousand times more so. . . . While it is due to the United States that she should not permit this important country to fall into European hands, it is equally due to her that she should possess it by any and every means necessary thereto.

Let the United States apply, if necessary, the usufruct doctrine of her possession of this country, which Old England and Old Spain practised towards the aborigines upon the discovery of this continent—a doctrine of common sense and sound reason—of human necessity and justice. If the Author of the universe intended the earth for the support of the few, to the exclusion of the greater number, the reverse of this doctrine is true, and then it is right and proper that a very few should hold this country, of which they can make no adequate use, to the exclusion of many millions in other portions of the earth, who may be dying for the want of space to live in. . . . For many wise reasons, the United States should extend her settlements over it; but should she, by a different policy, fail to do so, the all-seeing eye of Great Britain will not let slip such a golden opportunity in possessing herself of this desirable middle ground between home and her vast Eastern possessions. Besides, if the Oregon settlement is important to the United States, without a harbour sufficient for the entrance of her smallest vessels of war, the port of San Francisco, or some other port in the south, is absolutely necessary for her.

It may, however, well be questioned whether either Spain or the present government of Mexico has ever had any other than a nominal possession of this vast region; for only here and there, in a very few isolated spots, has she had a few people in real possession, and those few shut in by fortifications as protection against the aboriginal occupants. If, therefore, she has no power of absolutely possessing herself of this country, her declaration of ownership to it was arbitrary, and the act not justified by her means; and with the same propriety she might have claimed, to illimitable extent, that which she neither had the use of nor power of using, depriving millions of the earth's population of support and the proper uses thereof.

While I hold that it is both just and proper that any nation with an overgrown population may settle these vast wastes with her redundant people, I repeat again that it would be short-sighted policy in the United States to permit it. That nation, with her twenty millions of people, in the ordinary course of events, in fifty years, will have eighty to provide for, and a large country will be necessary for so many within the lifetime of numbers now busy in the politics of that country. . . . If it be wise policy, and the United States extends her dominions to the 28th degree upon the Pacific, then Texas becomes absolutely necessary to her. Then the *Texas wedge*, making into the centre of her square and compact surface, will appear obviously wrong. It would be a severance of her entirety, which few would be willing to reconcile; and without a union of the two countries, a conflict of interest would inevitably grow up between the separate nations, detrimental certainly to one, and probably to both. This conflict would beget countervailing laws, such as are at present in the bud, and would produce estrangement to the advantage of European powers, which would profit by the quarrel.

Secondly, This boundary, viewed with reference to the amelioration and ultimate destiny of the negro population of the United States.

Though I believe that so good a political institution does not exist in any nation for the government of its poorer or more dependant population as slavery in its general character in the south and southwestern portion of the United States and Texas; and while I believe that it is the reverse of either a "moral or political evil," viewed as it is at present, yet the day may come, and probably in the lifetime of that generation now coming into the world, when, either from individual interest or public policy, the white and black man can no longer occupy the same soil. Does it not, then, behoove the politicians of this day and time to cast about for the solution of that difficult problem before which all other questions of public policy must sink into utter insignificance? What is to be done with the black? is that difficult problem.

In the solution of this question, I hold it to be self-evident, that the abolition of slavery in the United States will not take place till it becomes the interest of the owner, and not then until there is a separate country to locate them upon.

*   *   *

... To provide these existing and forthcoming millions with a country accessible, and a climate suitable to that physical constitution which the great Author of the universe has given them, our southern boundary should extend to the twentieth de-

gree of north latitude, and nearly all will be accomplished which human wisdom can provide. Here is a country in soil, climate, and every other consideration far superior to the best portions of their native continent, within reach, and in the immediate direction of that great tide of emigration which is fast sweeping them from the ungenial and unprofitable North. By the immediate contiguity of this country to the United States, it will cost no greater outlay of means to transport them than the natural course of events will create and provide for.

If the object of the abolitionist is benevolence to the black race—if he wishes to avert this possible calamity and ruin—he should urge upon his government the acquisition of that which will most certainly effect it. Without professing to see farther in futurity than the lights which past experience will justify, it does appear to my mind that in seventy years, when the coloured population of the United States shall have increased to twenty, and the white, in their proportionate ratio, to one hundred and thirty millions, many, very many reasons teach that so many people, so differently marked by nature, cannot live in harmony within the present limits of that country. That in view of the case, whether their relative political condition shall remain as at present, or undergo the worst radical changes, the same good reasons urge this measure. . . .

*   *   *

Review Questions

1. Did Green have an extremist vision of expansion—of manifest destiny? Why or why not?
2. Did he promote annexation? Explain.
3. Why did he believe annexation would benefit the United States?
4. How could Green argue that annexation when coupled with expansion down to the twentieth latitude would—if the United States chose to pursue abolition—alleviate or even eliminate the slavery and race problems?

JAMES K. POLK

FROM The President's War Message to Congress (11 May 1846)

President John Tyler signed the Congressional resolution offering Texas annexation and statehood on 1 March 1845. He then left his successor, James K. Polk, to deal with the repercussions: one of the first was Mexico's dissolution of diplomatic relations. Mexico, which still disputed Texas's independence to the point that Texans such as General Green could talk about an ongoing quasi-war with that nation, was firmly set against the annexation. Polk, an ardent expansionist, proceeded to duel against Mexico with one hand and against Britain with the other. He was determined to secure Texas (the territory of which both he and the Texans defined rather broadly), plant the flag of the United States in the ranches, ports, and presidios of California, and take sole possession of the Oregon territory. He was able to accomplish the latter through diplomatic negotiations and compromise over the northern border at the 49th parallel, but to achieve the other two goals he had to go to war.

From James D. Richardson, comp., *A Compilation of the Messages and Papers of the Presidents*, vol. V (New York: Bureau of National Literature, Inc., 1897), pp. 2287–93. [Editorial insertions appear in square brackets—*Ed.*]

To the Senate and House of Representatives:

The existing state of the relations between the United States and Mexico renders it proper that I should bring the subject to the consideration of Congress. . . .

*   *   *

The strong desire to establish peace with Mexico on liberal and honorable terms, and the readiness of this Government to regulate and adjust our boundary and other causes of difference with that power on such fair and equitable principles as would lead to permanent relations of the most friendly nature, induced me in September last to seek the reopening of diplomatic relations between the two countries. Every measure adopted on our part had for its object the furtherance of these desired results. In communicating to Congress a succinct statement of the injuries which we had suffered from Mexico and which have been accumulating during a period of more than twenty years, every expression that could tend to inflame the people of Mexico or defeat or delay a pacific result was carefully avoided. An envoy of the United States repaired to Mexico with full powers to adjust every existing difference. But though present on the Mexican soil by agreement between the two Governments, invested with full powers, and bearing evidence of the most friendly dispositions, his mission has been unavailing. The Mexican Government not only refused to receive him or listen to his propositions, but after a long-continued series of menaces have at last invaded our territory and shed the blood of our fellow-citizens on our own soil.

It now becomes my duty to state more in detail the origin, progress, and failure of that mission. In pursuance of the instructions given in September last, an inquiry was made on the 13th of October, 1845, in the most friendly terms, through our consul in Mexico, of the minister for foreign affairs, whether the Mexican Government "would receive an envoy from the United States intrusted with full powers to adjust all the questions in dispute between the two Governments," with the assurance that "should the answer be in the affirmative such an envoy would be immediately dispatched to Mexico." The Mexican minister on the 15th of October gave an affirmative answer to this inquiry, requesting at the same time that our naval force at Vera Cruz might be withdrawn, lest its continued presence might assume the appearance of menace and coercion pending the negotiations. This force was immediately withdrawn. On the 10th of November, 1845, Mr. John Slidell, of Louisiana, was commissioned by me as envoy extraordinary and minister plenipotentiary of the United States to Mexico, and was intrusted with full powers to adjust both the questions of the Texas boundary and of indemnification to our citizens. The redress of the wrongs of our citizens naturally and inseparably blended itself with the question of boundary. The settlement of the one question in any correct view of the subject involves that of the other. I could not for a moment entertain the idea that the claims of our much-injured and long-suffering citizens, many of which had existed for more than twenty years, should be postponed or separated from the settlement of the boundary question.

Mr. Slidell arrived at Vera Cruz on the 30th of November, and was courteously received by the authorities of that city. But the Government of General Herrera was then tottering to its fall. The revolutionary party had seized upon the Texas question to effect or hasten its overthrow. Its determination to restore friendly relations with the United States, and to receive our minister to negotiate for the settlement of this question, was violently assailed, and was made the great theme of denunciation against it. The Government of General Herrera, there is good reason to believe, was sincerely desirous to receive our minister; but it yielded to the storm raised by its enemies, and on

the 21st of December refused to accredit Mr. Slidell upon the most frivolous pretexts. . . .

Five days after the date of Mr. Slidell's note [24 December] General Herrera yielded the Government to General Paredes without a struggle, and on the 30th of December resigned the Presidency. This revolution was accomplished solely by the army, the people having taken little part in the contest; and thus the supreme power in Mexico passed into the hands of a military leader.

Determined to leave no effort untried to effect an amicable adjustment with Mexico, I directed Mr. Slidell to present his credentials to the Government of General Paredes and ask to be officially received by him. . . .

Under these circumstances, Mr. Slidell, in obedience to my direction, addressed a note to the Mexican minister of foreign relations, under date of the 1st of March last, asking to be received by that Government in the diplomatic character to which he had been appointed. This minister in his reply, under date of the 12th of March, reiterated the arguments of his predecessor, and in terms that may be considered as giving just grounds of offense to the Government and people of the United States denied the application of Mr. Slidell. . . .

Thus the Government of Mexico, though solemnly pledged by official acts in October last to receive and accredit an American envoy, violated their plighted faith and refused the offer of a peaceful adjustment of our difficulties. . . .

In my message at the commencement of the present session I informed you that upon the earnest appeal both of the Congress and convention of Texas I had ordered an efficient military force to take a position "between the Nueces and the Del Norte." This had become necessary to meet a threatened invasion of Texas by the Mexican forces, for which extensive military preparations had been made. The invasion was threatened solely because Texas had determined, in accordance with a solemn resolution of the Congress of the United States, to annex herself to our Union, and under these circumstances it was plainly our duty to extend our protection over her citizens and soil.

This force was concentrated at Corpus Christi, and remained there until after I had received such information from Mexico as rendered it probable, if not certain, that the Mexican Government would refuse to receive our envoy.

Meantime Texas, by the final action of our Congress, had become an integral part of our Union. The Congress of Texas, by its act of December 19, 1836, had declared the Rio del Norte to be the boundary of that Republic. Its jurisdiction had been extended and exercised beyond the Nueces. The country between that river and the Del Norte had been represented in the Congress and in the convention of Texas, had thus taken part in the act of annexation itself, and is now included within one of our Congressional districts. Our own Congress had, moreover, with great unanimity, by the act approved December 31, 1845, recognized the country beyond the Nueces as a part of our territory by including it within our own revenue system, and a revenue officer to reside within that district has been appointed by and with the advice and consent of the Senate. It became, therefore, of urgent necessity to provide for the defense of that portion of our country. Accordingly, on the 13th of January last instructions were issued to the general in command of these troops to occupy the left bank of the Del Norte. This river, which is the southwestern boundary of the State of Texas, is an exposed frontier. From this quarter invasion was threatened; upon it and in its immediate vicinity, in the judgment of high military experience, are the proper stations for the protecting forces of the Government. . . .

The movement of the troops to the Del Norte was made by the commanding general under positive instructions to abstain from all aggressive acts toward Mexico or Mexican citizens and to regard the relations between that Republic and the United States as peaceful unless she should declare war or commit acts of hostility indicative of a state of war. He was specially directed to protect private property and respect personal rights.

The Army moved from Corpus Christi on the 11th of March, and on the 28th of that month arrived on the left bank of the Del Norte opposite to Matamoras, where it encamped on a commanding position, which has since been strengthened by the erection of fieldworks. A depot has also been established at Point Isabel, near the Brazos Santiago, 30 miles in rear of the encampment. The selection of his position was necessarily confided to the judgment of the general in command.

The Mexican forces at Matamoras assumed a belligerent attitude, and on the 12th of April General Ampudia, then in command, notified General Taylor to break up his camp within twenty-four hours and to retire beyond the Nueces River, and in the event of his failure to comply with these demands announced that arms, and arms alone, must decide the question. But no open act of hostility was committed until the 24th of April. On that day General Arista, who had succeeded to the command of the Mexican forces, communicated to General Taylor that "he considered hostilities commenced and should prosecute them." A party of dragoons of 63 men and officers were on the same day dispatched from the American camp up the Rio del Norte, on its left bank, to ascertain whether the Mexican troops had crossed or were preparing to cross the river, "became engaged with a large body of these troops, and after a short affair, in which some 16 were killed and wounded, appear to have been surrounded and compelled to surrender."

The grievous wrongs perpetrated by Mexico upon our citizens throughout a long period of years remain unredressed, and solemn treaties pledging her public faith for this redress have been disregarded. A government either unable or unwilling to enforce the execution of such treaties fails to perform one of its plainest duties.

Our commerce with Mexico has been almost annihilated. It was formerly highly beneficial to both nations, but our merchants have been deterred from prosecuting it by the system of outrage and extortion which the Mexican authorities have pursued against them, whilst their appeals through their own Government for indemnity have been made in vain. Our forbearance has gone to such an extreme as to be mistaken in its character. Had we acted with vigor in repelling the insults and redressing the injuries inflicted by Mexico at the commencement, we should doubtless have escaped all the difficulties in which we are now involved.

Instead of this, however, we have been exerting our best efforts to propitiate her good will. Upon the pretext that Texas, a nation as independent as herself, thought proper to unite its destinies with our own she has affected to believe that we have severed her rightful territory, and in official proclamations and manifestoes has repeatedly threatened to make war upon us for the purpose of reconquering Texas. In the meantime we have tried every effort at reconciliation. The cup of forbearance had been exhausted even before the recent information from the frontier of the Del Norte. But now, after reiterated menaces, Mexico has passed the boundary of the United States, has invaded our territory and shed American blood upon the American soil. She has proclaimed that hostilities have commenced, and that the two nations are now at war.

As war exists, and, notwithstanding all our efforts to avoid it, exists by the act of Mexico herself, we are called upon by every consideration of duty and patriotism to vindicate with decision the honor, the rights, and the interests of our country.

Anticipating the possibility of a crisis like that which has arrived, instructions were given in August last, "as a precautionary measure" against invasion or threatened invasion, authorizing General Taylor, if the emergency required, to accept volunteers, not from Texas only, but from the States of Louisiana, Alabama, Mississippi, Tennessee, and Kentucky, and corresponding letters were addressed to the respective governors of those States. . . .

In further vindication of our rights and defense of our territory, I invoke the prompt action of Congress to recognize the existence of the war, and to place at the disposition of the Executive the means of prosecuting the war with vigor, and thus hastening the restoration of peace. To this end I recommend that authority should be given to call into the public service a large body of volunteers to serve for not less than six or twelve months unless sooner discharged. A volunteer force is beyond question more efficient than any other description of citizen soldiers, and it is not to be doubted that a number far beyond that required would readily rush to the field upon the call of their country. I further recommend that a liberal provision be made for sustaining our entire military force and furnishing it with supplies and munitions of war.

The most energetic and prompt measures and the immediate appearance in arms of a large and overpowering force are recommended to Congress as the most certain and efficient means of bringing the existing collision with Mexico to a speedy and successful termination.

In making these recommendations I deem it proper to declare that it is my anxious desire not only to terminate hostilities speedily, but to bring all matters in dispute between this Government and Mexico to an early and amicable adjustment; and in this view I shall be prepared to renew negotiations whenever Mexico shall be ready to receive propositions or to make propositions of her own.

*   *   *

REVIEW QUESTIONS

1. Who provoked whom in the crisis between Mexico and the United States? Explain.
2. Did domestic issues play a role in the escalation of tensions between the two countries?
3. How did Polk try to resolve the issues causing conflict between the United States and Mexico?
4. Is there any indication in this message that the government's actions and attitudes may have hurt rather than helped its diplomatic efforts?
5. Was this call to arms in line with or a break from previously stated foreign policy aims (as in Washington's Farewell Address and the *Monroe Doctrine* for example)?

EPHRAIM KIRBY SMITH

Letters from the Front in the Mexican War (1845–47)

Ephraim Kirby Smith (1807–1847) was a career army officer from a military family. One of his grandfathers had fought at Bunker Hill; his father served in the War of 1812; while his uncle, Colonel Edmund Kirby, and his brother, Edmund Kirby Smith, participated in the Mexican War. His brother would survive the war and go on to serve in the Confederate Army while his son, Joseph Lee Kirby Smith, would graduate from West Point in 1857 and then die, fighting for the United States, during the Civil War. Kirby Smith (apparently he preferred his middle name) was a captain who had never engaged in battle until the Mexican War. The war was a learning experience in terms of combat and cultures. Even as Smith fulfilled his duties he took the time to observe his surroundings and study the people he encountered. He then recorded his thoughts in letters, many of which were written over many days or weeks, and sent them home to his wife.

From Ephraim Kirby Smith, *To Mexico with Scott: Letters of Captain E. Kirby Smith to His Wife*. Prepared by his daughter Emma Jerome Blackwood; intro. R. M. Johnston (Cambridge: Harvard University Press, 1917), pp. 17–19, 37–38, 57, 80–81, 93–94, 126–28, 138–40, 146, 151–56, 179–83, 188, 197–208, 211–12, 215–17. [Editorial insertions appear in square brackets—*Ed.*]

April 19. [1846. Camp near Matamoras] The aspect of Mexican and Oregon affairs changes more frequently than the moon. Perhaps one of them depends upon the other. If England and Uncle Sam settle the Oregon question, Mexico may be more readily induced to treat on the subject of Texas; but if John Bull and Brother Jonathan get by the ears, our yellow neighbors aided and sustained by English guineas will probably persist until, as they boast, their eagles are planted on the Sabine. . . .

Since I wrote last, matters have had a serious war-like tendency. General Ampudia who relieved General Mejia in command at Matamoras has sent a dispatch to General Taylor, requiring him to retreat in twenty-four hours, and adding that his refusal to do so would be considered a declaration of war. This, of course, was not acceded to by General Taylor, who replied that he had been sent here by his Government and should remain; that if Ampu-

dia chose to attack him, the consequences must rest on his own head and upon the Mexican nation. The next day, it is said, a courier arrived with orders superseding General Ampudia, and placing General Arista in command of the Northern army. So that General Ampudia has retired in disgust.

*   *   *

CAMP AT MATAMORAS,
June 2, 1846

A mixed command of volunteers and regulars is to be sent in a few days to Reynosa and Camargo from fifty to eighty miles up the river. I think they will have no fighting and the "Bloody Fifth" will not be sent. Major Belton is daily expected to arrive with some additional companies of artillery and we shall then have in the field a regular force of more than three thousand, and probably a volunteer force of ten thousand. I do not think from all I can learn from the most intelligent Mexicans here that the "magnanimous Mexican nation" will make peace on any terms, until they are dictated to her in the valley of Mexico. What long marches, bloody sieges, and dreadful battles are to be encountered before then cannot be foretold but that all will have to be met is most certain. . . . No news except the Second Infantry ordered here and a rumor that General Scott is coming to take command of the Army of Invasion.

* * *

[Monterey, Mexico, November 8, 1846] We are quite as much in the dark here with regard to the probable movements of the army as you can be. We are stationed on the salient point of our conquest, less than two thousand strong, entirely inactive, and so far as we know there are no troops of the enemy within two hundred miles of us. Santa Anna is recruiting, drilling, and equipping an army at San Luis Potosi already thirty thousand strong. He is casting all the church bells into cannon—I wish he had those that are deafening me at this moment—and says he will redeem the honor of the Mexican arms if we will pay him a visit at San Luis. He well knows it is almost impossible for an army drawing its supplies from the rear to march upon that place. . . . The intelligent portion of the Mexican population are of the opinion, and express it to us without reserve, that the war is *wicked* and aggressive on the part of the United States. They claim that Texas never extended farther than the Nueces, and say that it would have been yielded to that river without opposition. The inhabitants generally have not suffered by the war, but on the contrary have profited by it, while the army, it is said, are strong advocates for negotiation. If this war is to be protracted by the obstinacy of this people, I hope and expect to see the City of Mexico in another twelve months. . . .

* * *

CAMP PALO ALTO,
January 27, 1847

Our camp takes its name from the battle field which is but a few miles distant. Near us was the first pitched battle of the war; when, and where,

will be the *last*? *Quien sabe?* The better we have become acquainted with the people and the Mexican character, the more assured we all feel that the course pursued by our government is only calculated to protract the war. Proud, overbearing, ignorant, superstitious, and cruel in the extreme in their own wars, they do not in the least comprehend our temporizing forbearance. If, from the moment of invasion, instead of paying them two prices for everything our army wanted, we had laid waste their country, taking their horses, mules, herds, and crops, as they might have been required, leaving the sufferers to seek indemnification from their own government; if, instead of extending kindness and protection to the inhabitants, we had carried fire and sword into the heart of their country; if, instead of sending commissioners to treat asking for peace, and offering millions to make it, we had done all in our power to distress and harass them, treating them as a nation with contempt, they would not have thought as they now do, that we feared them; that the Whig party in our country were opposing the war, and about to leave the Executive without the means to prosecute it. They would have felt that they had no hope but in the successful operations of a campaign opposed to the entire strength of the United States. What their prospects would have been in such a case, their leaders and statesmen well know, and I believe that peace on advantageous terms would have been offered. *Now* we must fight it out with but little hope of a termination of the struggle in many years. . . .

* * *

CASTLE OF PEROTE,
April 29, 1847

I wrote you a few hastily penned pages from Jalapa in which I briefly noted our march from Tlacatalpin to Vera Cruz, and from that place to Jalapa. The entire route is full of interest, many points being the scenes of severe contests of Hernando Cortes, and besides the historical interest connected with every foot of the road, the scenery on every side is of the grandest character. The great national road from Vera Cruz to Mexico, which is an admirably constructed pavement, the work of the old Spaniards, winds up and down the sides of the huge hills now abruptly ascending, now pitching into some deep valley, where it crosses the ravine or dashing stream by a stone bridge whose beautiful construction puts to shame anything of the kind in the United States.

The entire distance after the traveler passes Jalapa is bordered with the luxuriant growth of tropical climes from the stately palm to the most diminutive cactus. The gorgeous flowers of this region are now in full bloom, and surpass anything in the vegetable kingdom of which I had before conceived. On the twenty-sixth, at two in the afternoon, our regiment marched out of Jalapa over the road of which I have been speaking. For about two miles it descended between beautiful pastures enclosed with good stone fences, and occasionally a corn or barley field all looking precisely like New England and lacking only its thriving population. The climate of this region cannot be surpassed, the soil is exceedingly rich and all the fruits in the world grow in it. If I could have my friends around me and a good government I should delight to pass my life in Jalapa. We halted at a little stream in the valley near a cotton factory, at the base of a rugged hill with an unwriteable Indian name, where Cortes fought one of his hardest battles. As soon as our train was in position we began the ascent of the eastern slope of the mountain, the road winding along its side and rising rapidly towards its summit. The afternoon was delightful, the air clear and bracing as on a November day in New York; the setting sun shone brilliantly on the snowy peak of Orizaba whose high crest was constantly in our view. At dark we reached the village of San Miguel. . . . This village most beautifully located in a kind of semisphere on the side of the mountain, with fine water, a glorious climate, and a productive soil, is a most miserable, filthy place.

*   *   *

May 1. . . . An order has been received from General Scott directing a forward movement of the whole army to commence as soon as the large provision train arrives. By this order it appears that he intends to abandon his rear and suffer his communications with the coast to be cut off. The army, therefore, is to depend upon the country for supplies which will probably be scanty enough—however, "Forward" is the word; the "Halls of the Montezumas" our destination, and I confidently think that we shall soon be in possession of the Capital, though I do *not* believe a "peace will be conquered." The guerilla system is already in operation. The train which is now coming up was attacked a few days since, and some killed and wounded on both sides, though the Mexicans were repulsed.

*   *   *

May 5.

*   *   *

My opinion of volunteers and the whole volunteer system is not changed in the least. They are expensive, unruly, and not to be relied upon in action. Their conduct towards the poor inhabitants has been horrible, and their coming is dreaded like death in every village in Mexico, while the regulars are met by the people almost as friends. A portion of them (the volunteers) have fled in every action in which they have been engaged and they can never succeed unless supported by the *line*. At Monterey, Buena Vista, and Cerro Gordo portions of them ran. General Taylor says in a letter that at Buena Vista, had they not been turned back by the enemy who had got to his rear, many more than did would have entirely fled the battle field. Pillow's Brigade of volunteers were defeated at Cerro Gordo, and he requested the General to send him a few regulars, if only one company, to support and set an example to his men. The first instance is yet to occur in this war in which a regular has abandoned his post or been defeated. Portions of the volunteers have fought most gallantly, but when they will fight, and when they won't, can only be determined by experiment. I am aware that these opinions would be considered almost treasonable in the United States, but here they are the sentiments of all the regulars and of a large number of the volunteer officers in the field.

*   *   *

May 6, Tepeyahualco (*correct spelling, pronounced Ta-pa-āh-wolko*). This was once a fine little town, most of it is now in ruins. It is between fifty and sixty miles from Puebla which is said to be the third city in Mexico. . . .

Some Mexican gentlemen came in this morning from Puebla. One of them, a very intelligent man, educated in Hartford, Connecticut, represents the country as in a most deplorable condition, the Government as utterly disorganized by the battle of Cerro Gordo, which he pronounces the most serious blow the Republic has ever received. The Government, he says, is not capable of carrying on the war or of making a peace. The roads are filled with bands of robbers under the name of guerillas, who are as ready to plunder and murder the Mexicans as they are to attack us. The city of Puebla has a deputation prepared to meet us before we reach its gates to escort us within its walls, and an officer ready to turn over the public property. From the best information there is not at this time more than four thousand Infantry of the enemy under arms in all this portion of Mexico. There are besides some three thousand cavalry under General Canalizo who escaped from the battle of Cerro Gordo, but they are of no account, and we neither know nor care where they are.

There is no middle class in this country. The upper "ten hundred" not "ten thousand" possess all the wealth and are continually quarreling about the control of affairs and creating constant revolutions. The millions are steeped in ignorance, vice, and poverty, abject to the priests and trampled to the dust by the wealthy. . . .

*   *   *

May 8. This is the anniversary of the battle of Palo Alto, my first fight, the first of the war, and perhaps the most important in its consequences. Little did we think, who were engaged in that contest, that in one year we would be in the heart of Mexico, and that a salute in honor of that victory would peal from the walls of San Juan D'Ulloa. Where shall we be a year hence? *Quien sabe?* perhaps in California, perhaps *at home*, which may God grant.

Seven regiments of volunteers are going home, their time having expired. This will reduce our force so much that it is doubtful whether General Scott will think it prudent to advance beyond Puebla. . . .

May 9. This is the anniversary of the battle of Resaca. How differently I feel now with regard to the war from what I did then! *Then* vague visions of glory and a speedy peace floated through my brain. *Now* I have learned in common with many other poor fellows that it is not he who patiently does his duty, or who in the hour of danger is in the front of the battle, who gains the laurel or the more vulgar reward of government patronage. It is too frequently the sycophant who flatters the foibles of his commanding officer, he who has political family influence, or whom some accident makes conspicuous, who reaps all the benefits of the exposure and labors of others. The long list of brevets, most outrageously unjust as they are, many of them double, is a register of evidence to the facts that success is a lottery and that government rewards are by no means dependent on merit. How tired and sick I am of a war to which I can see no probable termination! How readily would I exchange my profession for any honest, mechanical employment, were it possible to do so! How instantly would I resign if I saw any certainty of supporting my family in tolerable comfort or even decency in civil life! Why do I grumble or let you know how miserable I am? Think not I am always so. . . .

*   *   *

July 6. . . . Since my last writing the prospect of peace has much increased, the tone of the Mexican papers has altered in the last week—they have evidently endeavored to produce an impression on the public mind that peace is necessary, and as they are entirely controlled by those in authority it is evident that Santa Anna is trying to bring about a termination of the war. It matters not whether in this course of conduct he is swayed by the hope of getting hold of the "three million," or whether the fear of another defeat and the consequent loss of the Capital of the Aztecs weighs with him, certain it is that General Scott and Mr. Trist have received communications on this subject from the Mexican authorities, either through a secret agent sent to the city or through Mr. Bankhead the English resident minister—perhaps by both channels. Moreover we know that three commissioners have been nominated to meet those who have authority to act for our government. Nothing, however, can be done but by the authority of the Supreme Congress which commences its sessions day after tomorrow. If the peace party headed by the great One-legged can influence this turbulent popular assembly we may hope for favorable results. I am by no means sanguine in my hopes of a peace or even an armistice without much more bloodshed, and an entire change of policy in the conduct of the war. After every victory we are down upon our knees suing for peace, and as yet, although we have defeated their armies, the Mexican people have not felt the horrors of war,—but on the contrary have actually profited by it. Nothing but vague rumors are heard from the column advancing under General Pillow.

July 7. . . . Today all our fond anticipations are destroyed. Their Congress has dissolved without any definite action on the subject, and Santa Anna's proclamation for the defence of the city has reached us. Does the fool think he can keep ten thousand Yankees from entering it? . . .

*   *   *

TACUBAYA,
August 22, 1847

I hardly know how to commence a description of the events of the last three days. My brain is whirling from the long continued excitement and my body sore with bruises and fatigue—but I will try to get into my usual humdrum style and record things as they happened. . . . Early on the morning of the twentieth, the attack was made and the works carried at the point of the bayonet, scarcely a gun being fired. We took fifteen hundred prisoners and twenty-two pieces of artillery among which were the guns captured by Santa Anna at Buena Vista. As soon as the result was known to General

Worth, the Second Brigade of his division with our battalion were put in motion to endeavor to turn the position at San Antonio. For two hours we ran over the rocks moving by a flank, the enemy in a heavy column marching parallel to us and almost in gun shot, until the head of the Fifth Infantry pierced their line and the fight began at a quarter before twelve. . . . Our battalion when the firing began must have been near a half mile to the rear. The "double quick" was sounded and the whole advanced at a run. We soon reached the road and turned in hot pursuit. This road is a broad, stone causeway with corn fields and pastures on each side of it, divided by broad ditches filled with water from three to six feet deep,—the corn tall and very thick. It was soon seen as we rushed along the road that the enemy were only retreating to a fortified position which constituted their second line of defences at Churubusco. You will hear this called San Pablo and by another name which I cannot recall.

. . . We had advanced on the road less than a mile when we were ordered into the fields to assault the right of the enemy's position,—I am speaking of our battalion. We soon formed line in an open field behind the thick corn in our advance. The escopet balls were whistling over our heads, though at long range, and occasionally a cannon ball sang through the corn as it tore its path along in our front.

At this time the battle was fiercely contested on our left and front, but I did not, and do not now know what regiments were engaged. It must have been about half-past twelve. Immediately in front of us, at perhaps five hundred yards, the roll of the Mexican fire exceeded anything I have ever heard. The din was most horrible, the roar of cannon and musketry, the screams of the wounded, the awful cry of terrified horses and mules, and the yells of the fierce combatants all combined in a sound as hellish as can be conceived. We had not from our battalion as yet fired a gun, but now rapidly advanced, all apparently eager to bring the contest to a hand to hand combat in which we knew our superiority.

We could not tell what was before us—whether the enemy were in regular forts, behind breastworks, or delivering their fire from the cover afforded by the hedges and ditches which bordered the road and fields,—all was hidden by the tall corn.

We soon came out of it into a crossroad near some small houses, where we were exposed to a dreadful cross fire, which could scarcely be resisted. Many had fallen and the battalion was much scattered and broken. The grape round shot and musketry were sweeping over the ground in a storm which strewed it with the dead and dying. . . .

Up to this time we were not aware that the other divisions of the army were engaged, but we now learned that Twiggs and others were pressing them on the left and had been fighting them an hour or more. Before this we had discovered we were under the fire of two forts, one a bastion front *tête du pont* flanking, and being flanked by a larger work, built round an extensive convent. Now as the whole army shouted and rushed to the assault, the enemy gave way, retreating as best they could to Mexico. They were pursued by all, hundreds being shot down in the retreat, our Dragoons charging after them to the guns at the gate of the city, where they were stayed by a tremendous discharge from the battery covering the entrance. Three officers, Captains Kearney and McReynolds and Lieutenant Graham, were here wounded, and Major Mills of the Fifteenth Infantry killed.

As soon as the battle terminated and the pursuit ceased, I went back, tired and sore as I was, to collect the dead and dying of our battalion and did not return until night. The field presented an awful spectacle—the dead and the wounded were thickly sprinkled over the ground—the mangled bodies of the artillery horses and mules actually blocking up the road and filling the ditches. How sickening was the sight after all the excitement of the contest was past! . . .

The loss of the enemy must be immense. We have taken between two and three thousand prisoners, seven generals, and thirty-seven large guns. Their officers say, in killed, missing, and captured, they have lost over five thousand. They acknowl-

edge that they had twenty, some say thirty thousand, in the fight. It was a wonderful victory and undoubtedly the greatest battle our country has ever fought, and I hope will bring peace. At all events, the great city is at our mercy, and we could enter it at any hour.

*   *   *

On the twenty-third and twenty-fourth of August negotiations were going on, and finally on the twenty-fifth an armistice was concluded for the purpose of making a peace. By the armistice we are excluded from the city and either general can terminate it by giving forty-eight hours' notice. This I fear may be the result, though perhaps Santa Anna may be compelled to make a peace to save himself from his own countrymen who will certainly kill him if deserted by his troops, as he surely will be if we fight again. The money which he will receive from us may enable him to declare himself dictator and maintain a force with which he can defy all the Pronunciamentos in Mexico.

*   *   *

Commissioners were appointed on the twenty-sixth by Santa Anna, who met Mr. N. P. Trist on the evening of the twenty-seventh. Mr. Trist was accompanied by Major A. Van Buren whom, I presume, acted as his secretary. I am afraid Trist "has more cloth cut out than he can make up in his shop," but sincerely hope he may effect a treaty. At headquarters the utmost confidence is felt as to the result. They met last evening when the basis of the proposed treaty was submitted by Mr. Trist. They have met again today at some village a few miles from here. May God prosper and speed their consultations!

*   *   *

September 1. We are remaining quietly in our position here at Tacubaya, awaiting the result of the negotiations. Ex-President Herrara is the chief of the Mexican Commission, and none of the members are Santa Anna's political friends. This increases the chance of a favorable result, as it takes from

Santa Anna some of the responsibility, compelling the friends of these commissioners to unite with them in whatever course they may pursue. At headquarters the utmost confidence is felt that a peace will be made, and it surely will be if the Mexican president has sufficient power to effect it. The only fear is that he may not be able to overcome all the factions which are and will be opposed to him. His sincerity is sufficiently demonstrated by the fact that he has sent us, and is still sending us, all the supplies we require from the city. Over five hundred thousand dollars has already been received and more is still to come.

*   *   *

September 2. Everything remains *in statu quo* today. The commissioners are in session and so far as can be ascertained from the remarks of Mr. Trist and Major Van Buren last evening, after they had adjourned, everything is progressing favorably. We have many rumors from the Capital,—but they are so contradictory and sometimes so absurd that I scarcely listen to them. We are, however, certain that Santa Anna has collected from his scattered forces a large army and it is said has now over twenty thousand under arms in the city, keeping up a show of preparation for the war, which, however, gives us not the least uneasiness as we are confident of our ability to whip them at any time. Moreover, there will be no necessity of an assault as they will never suffer the Capital to be bombarded.

*   *   *

September 7. Since the second, until yesterday, nothing occurred worthy of note, though I thought there were abundant signs that Santa Anna was only "humbugging" us, indeed, as my journal shows, I have thought from the beginning that it was only a scheme on his part to keep us out of the city and to gain time. . . .

On the fifth it began to be rumored that the proffers made by Mr. Trist were rejected and the treaty violated; . . . On the evening of the sixth, however, General Scott declared the truce termi-

nated in consequence of the frequent violations of its articles by Santa Anna. We are now no more advanced than we were previous to the battle of the twentieth last. In the sixteen days during which he has been flattering us with the hopes of peace he has been actively collecting his scattered forces, and with all his energies preparing to renew the combat. He has now twenty-two thousand men under arms and the Capital placed in such a state of defence that the enemy loudly boasts we cannot take it. Fatal credulity! How awful are its consequences to us! By it, the fruits of our glorious and incomparable victory are entirely thrown away. In the sixteen days our provisions and forage have been almost entirely exhausted; eight hundred of our men are sick, which added to about the same number put *hors de combat*[1] by death and wounds leaves us nearly two thousand weaker than we were on the morning of the twentieth ultimo, and now, alas, we have all our fighting to do over again.

*   *   *

I have just learned that the plan of attack is arranged. A forlorn hope of five hundred men commanded by Major G. Wright is to carry the foundry and blow it up. At the same time an attack from our artillery, the rest of the first division and Cadwalader's Brigade is to be made upon their line and Chapultepec, our battalion forming the *reserve.* This operation is to commence at three in the morning. Tomorrow will be a day of slaughter. I firmly trust and pray that victory may crown our efforts though the odds are immense.

I am thankful that you do not know the peril we are in. Good night.

The writer fell mortally wounded early the next morning [at the battle of Molino del Rey].

REVIEW QUESTIONS

1. Did Smith believe that an invasion of Mexico was necessary to secure the annexation of Texas?

---

[1] Rendered unable to fight (French)—*Ed.*

2. Did he believe that military action against Mexico would be quick and easy? Were his forecasts accurate?

3. What was his opinion of Mexico and Mexicans? What did this reveal about him?

4. What did he reveal about the United States Army and the way it operated?

5. What did he think about the diplomatic negotiations that accompanied military actions?

HENRY CLAY

Speech about the Mexican War (1847)

After his unsuccessful run for the presidency in 1824, Henry Clay became John Quincy Adams's secretary of state. He then served in the United States Senate from 1831 to 1842 (and again from 1849 until his death in 1852). Clay had also tried for the presidency again in 1832 and 1844. While out of office, the dynamic orator continued to address public issues, propounding those he believed fostered a positive national destiny and arguing against those he believed would have a negative impact. Worried that it would have the latter effect, Clay opposed annexation of Texas in 1844. The next year he criticized President Tyler's method of annexation as unconstitutional and moaned that it would "totally change the peaceful character of the Republic, converting us in the end into a warlike, conquering Nation."* His fears were realized when war commenced after annexation and when expansion created further internal dissension. Initially, upon Texas's admission to the Union, Clay accepted the necessity of military action to defend the new state's borders. When, however, Polk and others started to wage a more ambitious campaign, Clay, the old "War Hawk" of 1812, began his own more offensive campaign against the war. There was also a personal dimension to Clay's opposition: he lost a son during the war, at Buena Vista in February 1847.

Henry Clay, *The Papers of Henry Clay*, vol. 10: *Candidate, Compromiser, Elder Statesman*, Melba Porter Hay, ed. (Lexington: University Press of Kentucky, 1991), pp. *219, 361–76.

Lexington, KY.

November 13, 1847

The day is dark and gloomy, unsettled and uncertain, like the condition of our country, in regard to the unnatural war with Mexico. The public mind is agitated and anxious, and is filled with serious apprehensions as to its indefinite continuance, and especially as to the consequences which its termination may bring forth, menacing the harmony, if not the existence, of our Union.

*   *   *

How did we unhappily get involved in this war? It was predicted as the consequence of the annexation of Texas to the United States. If we had not Texas, we should have no war. The people were told that if that event happened, war would ensue. They were told that the war between Texas and Mexico had not been terminated by a treaty of peace; that Mexico still claimed Texas as a revolted province: and that, if we received Texas in our Union, we took along with her, the war existing between her and Mexico. And the Minister of Mexico [Juan N. Almonte] formally announced to the Government at Washington, that his nation would consider the annexation of Texas to the United States as producing a state of war. But all this was denied by the partizans of annexation. They insisted we should have no war, and even imputed to those who foretold it, sinister motives for their groundless prediction.

But, notwithstanding a state of virtual war necessarily resulted from the fact of annexation of one of the belligerents to the United States, actual hostilities might have been probably averted by prudence, moderation and wise statesmanship. If General [Zachary] Taylor had been permitted to remain, where his own good sense prompted him to believe he ought to remain, at the point of Corpus Christi; and, if a negotiation had been opened with Mexico, in a true spirit of amity and conciliation, war possibly might have been prevented. But, instead of this pacific and moderate course, whilst Mr. [John] Slidell was bending [sic, wending] his way to Mexico with his diplomatic credentials, General Taylor was ordered to transport his cannon, and to plant them, in a warlike attitude, opposite to Matamoras, on the east bank of the Rio Bravo [Rio Grande]; within the very disputed territory, the adjustment of which was to be the object of Mr. Slidell's mission. What else could have transpired but a conflict of arms?

Thus the war commenced, and the President [James K. Polk] after having produced it, appealed to Congress. A bill was proposed to raise 50,000 volunteers, and in order to commit all who should vote for it, a preamble was inserted falsely attributing the commencement of the war to the act of Mexico. I have no doubt of the patriotic motives of those who, after struggling to divest the bill of that flagrant error, found themselves constrained to vote for it. . . .

The exceptionable conduct of the Federal party, during that last British War [of 1812], has excited an influence in the prosecution of the present war, and prevented a just discrimination between the two wars. That was a war of National defence, required for the vindication of the National rights and honor, and demanded by the indignant voice of the People. President [James] Madison himself, I know, at first, reluctantly and with great doubt and hesitation, brought himself to the conviction that it ought to be declared. . . . It was a just war, and its great object, as announced at the time, was "Free Trade and Sailors Rights," against the intolerable and oppressive acts of British power on the ocean. The justice of the war, far from being denied or controverted, was admitted by the Federal party, which only questioned it on considerations of policy. Being deliberately and constitutionally declared, it was, I think, their duty to have given to it their hearty co-operation. But the mass of them did not. They continued to oppose and thwart it, to discourage loans and enlistments, to deny the power of the General Government to march the militia beyond our limits, and to hold a Hartford Convention, which, whatever were its real objects, bore the aspect of seeking a dissolution of the Union itself. They lost and justly lost the public confidence.—But has not an apprehension of a similar fate, in a state of case widely different, repressed a fearless expression of their real sentiments in some of our public men?

How totally variant is the present war! This is no war of defence, but one unnecessary and of offensive aggression. It is Mexico that is defending her fire-sides, her castles and her altars, not we. And how different also is the conduct of the whig party of the present day from that of the major part of the federal party during the war of 1812! Far from interposing any obstacles to the prosecution of the war, if the Whigs in office are reproachable at all, it is for having lent too ready a facility to it, without careful examination into the objects of the war. And, out of office, who have rushed to the prosecution of the war with more ardor and alacrity than the Whigs? . . .

But the havoc of war is in progress, and the no less deplorable havoc of an inhospitable and pestilential climate. Without indulging in an unneccessary retrospect and useless reproaches on the past, all hearts and heads should unite in the patriotic endeavor to bring it to a satisfactory close. Is there no way that this can be done? . . .

A declaration of war is the highest and most awful exercise of sovereignty. . . . Whenever called upon to determine upon the solemn question of peace or war, Congress must consider and deliberate and decide upon the motives, objects and causes of the war. And, if a war be commenced without any previous declaration of its objects, as in the case of the existing war with Mexico, Congress must necessarily possess the authority, at any time, to declare for what purposes it shall be further prosecuted. If we suppose Congress does not possess the controlling authority attributed to it; if it be contended that a war having been once commenced, the President of the United States may direct it to the accomplishment of any objects he pleases, without consulting and without any regard to the will of Congress, the Convention will have utterly failed in guarding the nation against the abuses and ambition of a single individual. Either Congress, or the President, must have the right of determining upon the objects for which a war shall be prosecuted. There is no other alternative. If the President possess it and may prosecute it for objects against the will of Congress, where is the difference between our free government and that of any other nation which may be governed by an absolute Czar, Emperor, or King?

Congress may omit, as it has omitted in the present war, to proclaim the objects for which it was commenced or has been since prosecuted, and in cases of such omission the President, being charged with the employment and direction of the national force is, necessarily, left to his own judgment to decide upon the objects, to the attainment of which that force shall be applied. But, whenever Congress shall think proper to declare, by some authentic act, for what purposes a war shall be commenced or continued it is the duty of the President to apply the national force to the attainment of those purposes. In the instance of the last war with Great Britain, the act of Congress by which it was

declared was preceded by a message of President Madison enumerating the wrongs and injuries of which we complained against Great Britain. That message therefore, and without it the well known objects of the war, which was a war purely of defence, rendered it unnecessary that Congress should particularize, in the act, the specific objects for which it was proclaimed. The whole world knew that it was a war waged for Free Trade and Sailors' Rights.

It may be urged that the President and Senate possess the treaty making power, without any express limitation as to its exercise; that the natural and ordinary termination of a war is by a treaty of peace; and therefore, that the President and Senate must possess the power to decide what stipulations and conditions shall enter into such a treaty. But it is not more true that the President and Senate possess the treaty making power, without limitation, than that Congress possesses the war making power, without restriction. These two powers then ought to be so interpreted as to reconcile the one with the other; and, in expounding the constitution, we ought to keep constantly in view the nature and structure of our free government, and especially the great object of the Convention in taking the war-making power out of the hands of a single man and placing it in the safer custody of the representatives of the whole nation. The desirable reconciliation between the two powers is effected by attributing to Congress the right to declare what shall be the objects of war, and to the President the duty of endeavoring to obtain those objects by the direction of the national force and by diplomacy.

*   *   *

I conclude, therefore, Mr. President and Fellow-Citizens, with entire confidence, that Congress has the right either at the beginning or during the prosecution of any war, to decide the objects and purposes for which it was proclaimed, or for which it ought to be continued. And, I think, it is the duty of Congress, by some deliberate and authentic act, to declare for what objects the present war shall be longer prosecuted. . . . Let it resolve, simply, that the war shall, or shall not, be a war of conquest; and, if a war of conquest, what is to be conquered. Should a resolution pass, disclaiming the design of conquest, peace would follow, in less than sixty days, if the President would conform to his constitutional duty.

Here, fellow Citizens, I might pause, having indicated a mode by which the nation, through its accredited and legitimate representatives in Congress, can announce for what purposes and objects this war shall be longer prosecuted, and can thus let the whole people of the United States know for what end their blood is to be further shed and their treasure further expended, instead of the knowledge of it being locked up and concealed in the bosom of one man. . . . But I do not think it right to stop here. It is the privilege of the people, in their primitive assemblies, and of every private man, however humble, to express an opinion in regard to the purposes for which the war should be continued; and such an expression will receive just so much consideration and consequence as it is entitled to, and no more.

Shall this war be prosecuted for the purpose of conquering and annexing Mexico, in all its boundless extent, to the United States?

I will not attribute to the President of the United States any such design; but I confess that I have been shocked and alarmed by manifestations of it in various quarters[.] Of all the dangers and misfortunes which could befall this nation, I should regard that of its becoming a warlike and conquering power the most direful and fatal. History tells the mournful tale of conquering nations and conquerors. The three most celebrated conquerors, in the civilized world, were Alexander, Caesar and Napoleon. . . . Do you believe that the people of Macedon or Greece, of Rome, or France, were benefitted, individually or collectively, by the triumphs of their great Captains? Their sad lot was immense sacrifice of life, heavy and intolerable burdens, and the ultimate loss of liberty itself.

That the power of the United States is competent to the conquest of Mexico, is quite probable. But it could not be achieved without frightful carnage, dreadful sacrifices of human life, and the cre-

ation of an onerous national debt; nor could it be completely effected, in all probability, until after the lapse of many years. It would be necessary to occupy all its strongholds, to disarm its inhabitants, and to keep them in constant fear and subjection. To consummate the work, I presume that standing armies, not less than a hundred thousand men, would be necessary, to be kept perhaps always in the bosom of their country. These standing armies, revelling in a foreign land, and accustomed to trample upon the liberties of a foreign people, at some distant day, might be fit and ready instruments, under the lead of some daring and unprincipled chieftain, to return to their country and prostrate the public liberty.

Supposing the conquest to be once made, what is to be done with it? Is it to be governed, like Roman Provinces, by Proconsuls? Would it be compatible with the genius, character, and safety of our free institutions, to keep such a great country as Mexico, with a population of not less that nine millions, in a state of constant military subjection?

Shall it be annexed to the United States: Does any considerate man believe it possible that two such immense countries, with territories of nearly equal extent, with populations so incongruous, so different in race, in language, in religion and in laws, could be blended together in one harmonious mass, and happily governed by one common authority? Murmurs, discontent, insurrections, rebellion, would inevitably ensue, until the incompatible parts would be broken asunder, and possibly, in the frightful struggle, our present glorious Union itself would be dissevered or dissolved. We ought not to forget the warning voice of all history, which teaches the difficulty of combining and consolidating together, conquering and conquered nations. After the lapse of eight hundred years, during which the Moors held their conquest of Spain, the indomitable courage, perseverance and obstinacy of the Spanish race finally triumphed, and expelled the African invaders from the Peninsula. . . . And what has been the fact with poor, gallant, generous and oppressed Ireland? Centuries have passed away, since the overbearing Saxon overrun and subjugated the Emerald Isle. Rivers of

Irish blood have flowed, during the long and arduous contest. Insurrection and rebellion have been the order of the day; and yet, up to this time, Ireland remains alien in feeling, affection and sympathy, towards the power which has so long borne her down. Every Irishman hates, with a mortal hatred, his Saxon oppressor. Although there are great territorial differences between the condition of England and Ireland, as compared to that of the United States and Mexico, there are some points of striking resemblance between them. Both the Irish and the Mexicans are probably of the same Celtic race. Both the English and the Americans are of the same Saxon origin. The Catholic religion predominates in both the former, the Protestant among both the latter. Religion has been the fruitful cause of dissatisfaction and discontent between the Irish and the English nations[.] Is there not reason to apprehend that it would become so between the people of the United States and those of Mexico, if they were united together? Why should we seek to interfere with them, in their mode of worship of a common Saviour? We believe that they are wrong, especially in the exclusive character of their faith, and that we are right. They think that they are right and we wrong. What other rule can there be than to leave the followers of each religion to their own solemn convictions of conscientious duty towards God? Who, but the great Arbiter of the Universe, can judge in such a question? . . .

But I suppose it to be impossible that those who favor, if there be any who favor the annexation of Mexico to the United States, can think that it ought to be perpetually governed by military sway. Certainly no votary of human liberty could deem it right that a violation should be perpetrated of the great principles of our own revolution, according to which, laws ought not to be enacted and taxes ought not to be levied, without representation on the part of those who are to obey the one, and pay the other. Then, Mexico is to participate in our councils and equally share in our legislation and government. But, suppose she would not voluntarily choose representatives to the national Congress, is our soldiery to follow the electors to the ballot-box, and by force to compel them, at the point of the bayonet, to deposit their ballots? And how are the nine millions of Mexican people to be represented in the Congress of the United States of America and the Congress of the United States of the Republic of Mexico combined? Is every Mexican, without regard to color or caste, per capitum, to exercise the elective franchise? How is the quota of representation between the two Republics, to be fixed? Where is their Seat of Common Government to be established? And who can foresee or foretell, if Mexico, voluntarily or by force, were to share in the common government what would be the consequences to her or to us? . . . Those, whom God and Geography have pronounced should live asunder, could never be permanently and harmoniously united together.

Do we want for our own happiness or greatness the addition of Mexico to the the existing Union of our States? If our population was too dense for our territory, and there was a difficulty in obtaining honorably the means of subsistence, there might be some excuse for an attempt to enlarge our dominions. But we have no such apology. We have already, in our glorious country, a vast and almost boundless territory. . . . Ought we not to be profoundly thankful to the Giver of all good things for such a vast and bountiful land? Is it not the height of ingratitude to Him to seek, by war and conquest, indulging in a spirit of rapacity, to acquire other lands, the homes and habitations of a large portion of his common children? If we pursue the object of such a conquest, besides mortgaging the revenue and resources of this country for ages to come, in the form of an onerous national debt, we should have greatly to augment that debt, by an assumption of the sixty or seventy millions of the national debt of Mexico. For I take it that nothing is more certain than that, if we obtain, voluntarily or by conquest, a foreign nation we acquire it with all the incumbrances attached to it. . . .

Of all the possessions which appertain to man, in his collective or individual condition, none should be preserved and cherished, with more sedulous and unremitting care, than that of an unsullied character. It is impossible to estimate it too highly, in society, when attached to an individual, nor can it be exaggerated or too greatly magnified in a nation. Those who lose or are indifferent to it become just objects of scorn and contempt. . . . I am afraid that we do not now stand well in the opinion of other parts of christendom. Repudiation has brought upon us much reproach. All the nations, I apprehend, look upon us, in the prosecution of the present war, as being actuated by a spirit of rapacity, and an inordinate desire for territorial aggrandizement. Let us not forfeit altogether their good opinions. Let us command their applause by a noble exercise of forbearance and justice. In the elevated station which we hold, we can safely afford to practice the Godlike virtues of moderation and magnanimity. The long series of glorious triumphs, achieved by our gallant commanders and their brave armies, unattended by a single reverse, justify us, without the least danger of tarnishing the national honor, in disinterestedly holding out the olive branch of peace. . . .

*   *   *

But, it will be repeated, are we to have no indemnity for the expenses of this war? Mexico is utterly unable to make us any pecuniary indemnity, if the justice of the war on our part entitled us to demand it. Her country has been laid waste, her cities burned or occupied by our troops, her means so exhausted that she is unable to pay even her own armies. And every day's prosecution of the war, whilst it would augment the amount of our indemnity, would lessen the ability of Mexico to pay it.—We have seen, however, that there is another form in which we are to demand indemnity. It is to be territorial indemnity! I hope, for reasons already stated that that fire-brand will not be brought into our country.

Among the resolutions, which it is my intention to present for your consideration, at the conclusion of this address, one proposes, in your behalf and mine, to disavow, in the most positive manner, any desire, on our part, to acquire any foreign territory whatever, for the purpose of introducing slavery into it. I do not know that any citizen of the United States entertains such a wish.

But such a motive has been often imputed to the slave States, and I therefore think it necessary to notice it on this occasion. My opinions on the subject of slavery are well known. . . . I have ever regarded slavery as a great evil, a wrong, for the present, I fear, an irremediable wrong to its unfortunate victims. I should rejoice if not a single slave breathed the air or was within the limits of our country. But here they are, to be dealt with as well as we can, with a due consideration of all circumstances affecting the security, safety and happiness of both races. Every State has the supreme, uncontrolled and exclusive power to decide for itself whether slavery shall cease or continue within its limits, without any exterior intervention from any quarter. . . . In the State of Kentucky, near fifty years ago, I thought the proportion of slaves, in comparison with the whites, was so inconsiderable that we might safely adopt a system of gradual emancipation that would ultimately eradicate this evil in our State. That system was totally different from the immediate abolition of slavery for which the party of the Abolitionists of the present day contend. Whether they have intended it or not, it is my calm and deliberate belief, that they have done incalculable mischief even to the very cause which they have espoused, to say nothing of the discord which has been produced between different parts of the Union. According to the system, we attempted, near the close of the last century, all slaves in being were to remain such, but, all who might be born subsequent to a specified day, were to become free at the age of twenty-eight, and, during their service, were to be taught to read, write, and cypher. Thus, instead of being thrown upon the community, ignorant and unprepared, as would be the case by immediate emancipation, they would have entered upon the possession of their freedom, capable, in some degree, of enjoying it.—After a hard struggle, the system was defeated, and I regret it extremely, as, if it had been then adopted, our State would be now nearly rid of that reproach.

Since the epoch, a scheme of unmixed benevolence has sprung up, which, if it had existed at that time, would have obviated one of the greatest objections which was made to gradual emancipation, which was the continuance of the emancipated slaves to abide among us. That scheme is the American Colonization Society. About twenty-eight years ago, a few individuals, myself among them, met together in the city of Washington, and laid the foundations of that society. It has gone on, amidst extraordinary difficulties and trials, sustaining itself almost entirely, by spontaneous and voluntary contributions, from individual benevolence, without scarcely any aid from Government. The Colonies, planted under its auspices, are now well established communities, with churches, schools and other institutions appertaining to the civilized state. . . .

*   *   *

It may be argued, that, in admitting the injustice of slavery, I admit the necessity of an instantaneous reparation of that injustice. Unfortunately, however, it is not always safe, practicable or possible, in the great movements of States and public affairs of nations, to remedy or repair the infliction of previous injustice. In the inception of it, we may oppose and denounce it, by our most strenuous exertions, but, after its consummation, there is often no other alternative left us but to deplore its perpetration, and to acquiesce as the only alternative, in its existence, as a less evil that the frightful consequences which might ensue from the vain endeavor to repair it. Slavery is one of those unfortunate instances. . . . The case of the annexation of Texas to the United States is a recent and obvious one where, if it were wrong, it cannot now be repaired. Texas is now an integral part of our Union, with its own voluntary consent. Many of us opposed the annexation with honest zeal and most earnest exertions. But who would now think of perpetrating the folly of casting Texas out of the confederacy and throwing her back upon her own independence, or into the arms of Mexico? Who would now seek to divorce her from this Union? The Creeks and the Cherokee Indians were, by the most exceptionable means, driven from their country, and transported beyond the Mississippi river. Their lands have been fairly purchased and occupied by inhabitants of Georgia, Alabama, Missis-

sippi and Tennessee. Who would now conceive of the flagrant injustice of expelling those inhabitants and restoring the Indian country to the Cherokees and the Creeks, under color of repairing original injustice? During the war of our revolution, millions of paper money were issued by our ancestors, as the only currency with which they could achieve our liberties and independence.—Thousands and hundreds of thousands of families were stripped of their homes and their all and brought to ruin, by giving credit and confidence to that spurious currency. Stern necessity has prevented the reparation of that great national injustice.

*   *   *

I have embodied, Mr. President and fellow-citizens, the sentiments and opinions which I have endeavored to explain and enforce in a series of resolutions which I beg now to submit to your consideration and judgment. They are the following:

*   *   *

4. *Resolved*, as the further opinion of this meeting, that it is the right and duty of Congress to declare, by some authentic act, for what purposes and objects the existing war ought to be further prosecuted; that it is the duty of the President, in his official conduct, to conform to such a declaration of Congress; and that, if, after such declaration, the President should decline or refuse to endeavor, by all the means, civil, diplomatic, and military, in his power, to execute the announced will of Congress, and, in defiance of its authority, should continue to prosecute the war for purposes and objects other than those declared by that body, it would become the right and duty of Congress to adopt the most efficacious measures to arrest the further progress of the war, taking care to make ample provision for the honor, the safety and security of our armies in Mexico, in every contingency. And, if Mexico should decline or refuse to conclude a treaty with us, stipulating for the purposes and objects so declared by Congress, it would be the duty of the Government to prosecute the war with the utmost vigor, until they were attained by a treaty of peace.

5. *Resolved*, That we view with serious alarm, and are utterly opposed to any purpose of annexing Mexico to the United States, in any mode, and especially by conquest; that we believe the two nations could not be happily governed by one common authority, owing to their great difference of race, law, language and religion, and the vast extent of their respective territories, and large amount of their respective populations; that such a union, against the consent of the exasperated Mexican people, could only be effected and preserved by large standing armies, and the constant application of military force—in other words, by despotic sway exercised over the Mexican people, in the first instance, but which, there would be just cause to apprehend, might, in process of time, be extended over the people of the United States. That we deprecate, therefore, such a union, as wholly incompatible with the genius of our Government, and with the character of free and liberal institutions; and we anxiously hope that each nation may be left in the undisturbed possession of its own laws, language, cherished religion and territory, to pursue its own happiness, according to what it may deem best for itself.

6. *Resolved*, That, considering the series of splendid and brilliant victories achieved by our brave armies and their gallant commanders, during the war with Mexico, unattended by a single reverse, The United States, without any danger of their honor suffering the slightest tarnish, can practice the virtues of moderation and magnanimity towards their discomfited foe. We have no desire for the dismemberment of the United States of the Republic of Mexico, but wish only a just and proper fixation of the limits of Texas.

7. *Resolved*, That we do, positively and emphatically, disclaim and disavow any wish or desire, on our part, to acquire any foreign territory whatever, for the purpose of propagating slavery, or of introducing slaves from the United States, into such foreign territory.

8. *Resolved*, That we invite our fellow citizens of the United States, who are anxious for the restoration of the blessings of peace, or, if the existing war shall continue to be prosecuted, are desirous that its purpose and objects shall be defined and known; who are anxious to avert present and future perils and dangers, with which it may be fraught; and who are also anxious to produce contentment and satisfaction at home, and to elevate the national character abroad, to assemble together in their respective communities, and to express their views, feelings, and opinions.

Review Questions

1. How did Clay differentiate between the War of 1812 and the Mexican War?
2. How did he compare and contrast the Federalists during the former war and the Whigs during the latter one? Why did he do so?
3. What were his concerns about the war-making powers of the executive and legislative branches? What did he want the government to do?
4. Why did Clay believe the possible conquest and annexation of Mexico to be undesireable?
5. What does his argument reveal about him and his society?

15   THE OLD SOUTH

Southerners certainly wrote about their world, extolling their culture and defending their peculiar institution, but many other people—Northerners and foreign visitors—journeyed to the South to see it for themselves. To them such a trip was a combination of exotic adventure and reformist crusade, for southern lands and ways fascinated, confused, and in some instances, repelled them. The South embodied such powerful dichotomies under its strong sun and shielding shade trees—beauty versus ugliness, good against evil—that the stories about it, fictional and factual, could not help but reflect that.

The tales were many and varied as the witnesses to southern society and slavery each saw or experienced different aspects of the culture. Slaves, and many free blacks, looked at the South from the bottom up: from the bottom of the cotton and tobacco rows, the receiving end of the whip, and the rough floors of their quarters. Slaveowners saw it from quite a different perspective as they surveyed their fields from horseback or carriage, labored over the financial equation of provisions versus profits, and tried to establish or maintain comfortable, if not always gentile lifestyles. Their non-slaveowner neighbors wrestled with desire and distress: many desired to own their own laborers and thereupon build their estates, but some were distressed at the cost—both financial and moral. Visiting diarists and reporters often brought with them preconceived notions by which to interpret this southern scene, while the readers of their publications added their own interpretations. Thus, whether from different regions of America or from Europe, observers added their stories to that of the South.

That observers' accounts were published overseas as well as in the United States indicates that southern society and the growing conflict between North and South captivated and concerned foreign as well as domestic audiences. Slavery was an international issue. As the British and Foreign Anti-slavery Society noted in 1839, slavery existed in "British India, in the colonies of several of the nations of Europe, in the United States of America, in Texas, and in the Empire of Brazil."

Antislavery organizations attempted to end it in all of these places. Such international agitation and cooperation did serve to contain, though not eradicate, the trans-Atlantic slave trade in the early nineteenth century, but such activism faced greater resistance within nations. Although England abolished slavery in the British isles by the late eighteenth century and outlawed its slave trade in 1807, some in England did not want the issue to interfere with other strategic and economic interests. Across the ocean, in accordance with a constitutional provision, Congress abolished the external slave trade in America in 1808, but smuggling, often via Cuban traders, continued. Furthermore, when foreign reformers condemned the institution as it existed within the states, slavery proponents and even some abolitionists decried outside intervention in the country's internal affairs.

Antislavery sentiment had appeared with the introduction of slavery in the colonial era, but the creation of a formal organization against the institution did not occur until the Revolution. As Americans debated and fought for liberty and freedom, some saw the inherent contradiction of slavery. That perception, especially when added to certain religious beliefs, led to antislavery activism. Quakers founded the Pennsylvania Society for Promoting the Abolition of Slavery in 1775. The society was essentially inactive during the war years, but in 1785 and especially 1787 when constitutional debate led to hopes of reform, the society vigorously pushed for abolition. It did not get what it wanted in the new Constitution, but at that time, even in the South, many agreed that slavery's days were numbered; the fact that manumission was on the rise seemed to give proof to that. Due to no sense of urgency, abolitionism languished. But when planters moved out into the rich lands of the Old Southwest, and after the cotton gin made the processing of that crop easier, slavery grew—and that growth spurred the development of a new abolitionist movement.

Advocates on both sides of this great struggle presented their basic premises in the 1830s and then rehashed them again and again throughout the 1840s and 1850s until they threw away the words to pick up arms. Slavery may not have been the only cause of the Civil War, but as a physical presence and ideological issue it helped dig the grave of, if not bury, the early union. Attacked and defended culturally, socially, politically, and religiously, the South's peculiar institution became America's particular problem.

Many nations of the Atlantic world and beyond contended with the issue of slavery in the nineteenth century. As part of their internal reforms and international relations, these countries sometimes struggled to define and implement notions of citizenship and universal human rights. Yet although slavery was an international problem, it was a distinct American tragedy. In the United States, it contributed to a particularly bloody internal war and illuminated discrepancies between ideology and practice in the republic that was supposed to stand as an enlightened example to the rest of the world.

FRANCES ANNE KEMBLE

FROM A Woman's Account of Her Southern Sojourn (1838, 1863)

Fanny Kemble (1809–1893), born into an English theatrical family, sailed to America with her father and aunt in 1832. Even though the father-daughter team set the American stage alight with performances that were resoundingly applauded by audiences from Boston to Baltimore, Fanny Kemble disliked her profession. Escape came by way of marriage to Pierce Mease Butler in 1834. When she married, Kemble did not know that her wealthy Philadelphian bridegroom was also a Georgia planter. Upon finding out, primed as she was with English antislavery ideas and those of the minister William Ellery Channing, who preached that people opposed to slavery must make slaveowners aware of their sin, Kemble tried to prod her husband's conscience, a difficult task that became nearly impossible when they visited his plantations in 1838–39. Kemble found much to delight her senses but trouble her soul in the South, and she recorded both her pleasure and pain in a journal. She loved her husband, but her moral mission may have been one of the reasons why he eventually grew disenchanted with her and filed for the divorce which the Pennsylvania Court of Common Pleas granted in 1849. Kemble went back to acting and, after the Civil War began, to preparing her journal for publication. She published her journal in 1863 so that it would serve to convince English sympathizers of the South that the North's cause was just and thus Britain should not intervene—meaning it should not recognize or trade with the South—in the American struggle.

Frances Anne Kemble, *Journal of a Residence on a Georgian Plantation in 1838–1839*, ed. John A. Scott. (1961; New York: The New American Library, Inc., 1975), pp. 37–39.

*   *   *

In walking about Charleston, I was forcibly reminded of some of the older country towns in England—of Southampton a little. The appearance of the city is highly picturesque, a word which can apply to none other of the American towns; and although the place is certainly pervaded with an air of decay, it is a genteel infirmity, as might be that of a distressed elderly gentlewoman. It has none of the smug mercantile primness of the Northern cities, but a look of state, as of quondam wealth and importance, a little gone down in the world, yet remembering still its former dignity. The Northern towns, compared with it, are as the spruce citizen rattling by the faded splendors of an old family coach in his newfangled chariot—they certainly have got on before it. Charleston has an air of eccentricity, too, and peculiarity, which formerly were not deemed unbecoming the wellborn and well-bred gentlewoman, which her gentility itself sanctioned and warranted—none of the vulgar dread of vulgar opinion, forcing those who are possessed by it to conform to a general standard of manners, unable to conceive one peculiar to itself—this "what-'ll-Mrs.-Grundy-say" devotion to conformity in small things and great, which pervades the American body-social from the matter of churchgoing to the trimming of women's petticoats—this dread of singularity, which has eaten up all individuality amongst them, and makes their population like so many moral and mental lithographs, and their houses like so many thousand hideous brick twins.

I believe I am getting excited; but the fact is, that being politically the most free people on earth, the Americans are socially the least so; and it seems as though, ever since that little affair of establishing their independence among nations, which they managed so successfully, every American mother's son of them has been doing his best to divest himself of his own private share of that great public blessing, liberty.

But to return to Charleston. It is in this respect a far more aristocratic (should I not say democratic?) city than any I have yet seen in America, inasmuch as every house seems built to the owner's particular taste; and in one street you seem to be in an old English town, and in another in some continental city of France or Italy. This variety is extremely pleasing to the eye; not less so is the intermixture of trees with the buildings, almost every house being adorned, and gracefully screened, by the beautiful foliage of evergreen shrubs. These, like ministering angels, cloak with nature's kindly ornaments the ruins and decays of the mansions they surround; and the latter, time-mellowed (I will not say stained, and a painter knows the difference), harmonize in their forms and coloring with the trees, in a manner most delightful to an eye that knows how to appreciate this species of beauty.

There are several public buildings of considerable architectural pretensions in Charleston, all of them apparently of some antiquity (for the New World), except a very large and handsome edifice which is not yet completed, and which, upon inquiry, we found was intended for a guardhouse. Its very extensive dimensions excited our surprise; but a man who was at work about it, and who answered our questions with a good deal of intelligence, informed us that it was by no means larger than the necessities of the city required; for that they not unfrequently had between fifty and sixty persons (colored and white) brought in by the patrol in one night.

"But," objected we, "the colored people are not allowed to go out without passes after nine o'clock."

"Yes," replied our informant, "but they will do it, nevertheless; and every night numbers are brought in who have been caught endeavoring to evade the patrol."

This explained to me the meaning of a most ominous tolling of bells and beating of drums, which, on the first evening of my arrival in Charleston, made me almost fancy myself in one of the old fortified frontier towns of the Continent, where the tocsin is sounded, and the evening drum beaten, and the guard set as regularly every night as if an invasion were expected. In Charleston, however, it is not the dread of foreign invasion, but of domestic insurrection, which occasions these nightly precautions; and, for the first time since my residence in this free country, the curfew . . . recalled the associations of early feudal times, and the oppressive insecurity of our Norman conquerors. But truly it seemed rather anomalous hereabouts, and nowadays; though, of course, it is very necessary where a large class of persons exists in the very bosom of a community whose interests are known to be at variance and incompatible with those of its other members. And no doubt these daily and nightly precautions are but trifling drawbacks upon the manifold blessings of slavery . . . ; still I should prefer going to sleep without the apprehension of my servants' cutting my throat in my bed, even to having a guard provided to prevent their doing so. However, this peculiar prejudice of mine may spring from the fact of my having known many instances in which servants were the trusted and most trustworthy friends of their employers, and entertaining, besides, some odd notions of the reciprocal duties of *all* the members of families one towards the other.

*   *   *

REVIEW QUESTIONS

1. What fascinated Fanny Kemble about Charleston? Why?
2. What repelled her? Why?
3. Did she offer a commentary on American as well as southern culture in this entry? How so?
4. Does her account suggest that culture—not just the politics and economics of slavery—may have contributed to the schism between North and South?

FREDERICK DOUGLASS

FROM *Narrative of the Life of Frederick Douglass* (1845)

Whereas slaveowners feared the possible violence of slave retaliation, slaves faced the constant probability of violence against their persons. Frederick Douglass (1818–1895) wrote and spoke about the institution of slavery and southern culture based on his own youthful experiences as a slave in Maryland as well as on the stories of others. He could vividly describe how people lived within its constraints because he had suffered its blows. He constantly strove to make his audiences understand the inhumanity of the institution and the humanity of its victims so that the first would be abolished and the second accepted in American society. Douglass escaped from bondage, or as he liked to put it, stole himself from his master, when he was twenty years old. His accomplishment was due, at least in part, to the fact that, unlike most slaves, he had learned to read and had access to the wider world through his work in Baltimore. That education both in bondage and books served as the foundation for his success as an abolitionist, publisher, politician, and ultimately as the United States' consul general to Haiti.

From Michael Meyer, ed. *Frederick Douglass: The Narrative and Selected Writings* (New York: The Modern Library, 1984), pp. 24–30. [Editorial insertions appear in square brackets —*Ed.*]

. . . [Colonel Edward Lloyd's] plantation is about twelve miles north of Easton, in Talbot county, and is situated on the border of Miles River. The principal products raised upon it were tobacco, corn, and wheat. These were raised in great abundance; . . .

Colonel Lloyd kept from three to four hundred slaves on his home plantation, and owned a large number more on the neighboring farms belonging to him. . . . The overseers of these, and all the rest of the farms, numbering over twenty, received advice and direction from the managers of the home plantation. This was the great business place. It was the seat of government for the whole twenty farms. All disputes among the overseers were settled here. If a slave was convicted of any high misdemeanor, became unmanageable, or evinced a determination to run away, he was brought immediately here, severely whipped, put on board the sloop, carried to Baltimore, and sold to Austin Woolfolk, or some other slave-trader, as a warning to the slaves remaining.

Here, too, the slaves of all the other farms received their monthly allowance of food, and their yearly clothing. The men and women slaves received, as their monthly allowance of food, eight pounds of pork, or its equivalent in fish, and one bushel of corn meal. Their yearly clothing consisted of two coarse linen shirts, one pair of linen trousers, like the shirts, one jacket, one pair of trousers for winter, made of coarse negro cloth, one pair of stockings, and one pair of shoes; the whole of which could not have cost more than seven dollars. The allowance of the slave children was given to their mothers, or the old women having the care of them. The children unable to work in the field had neither shoes, stockings, jackets, nor trousers, given to them; their clothing consisted of two coarse linen shirts per year. When these failed them, they went naked until the next allowance-day. Children from seven to ten years old, of both sexes, almost naked, might be seen at all seasons of the year.

There were no beds given the slaves, unless one coarse blanket be considered such, and none but the men and women had these. This, however, is not considered a very great privation. They find less difficulty from the want of beds, than from the want of time to sleep; for when their day's work in the field is done, the most of them having their washing, mending, and cooking to do, and having few or none of the ordinary facilities for doing either of these, very many of their sleeping hours are consumed in preparing for the field the coming day; and when this is done, old and young, male and female, married and single, drop down side by side, on one common bed,—the cold, damp floor,—each covering himself or herself with their miserable blankets; and here they sleep till they are summoned to the field by the driver's horn. At the sound of this, all must rise, and be off to the field. There must be no halting; every one must be at his or her post; and woe betides them who hear not this morning summons to the field; for if they are not awakened by the sense of hearing, they are by the sense of feeling: no age nor sex finds any favor. Mr. Severe, the overseer, used to stand by the door of the quarter, armed with a large hickory stick and heavy cowskin, ready to whip any one who was so unfortunate as not to hear, or, from any other cause, was prevented from being ready to start for the field at the sound of the horn.

Mr. Severe was rightly named: he was a cruel man. I have seen him whip a woman, causing the blood to run half an hour at the time; and this, too, in the midst of her crying children, pleading for their mother's release. He seemed to take pleasure in manifesting his fiendish barbarity. Added to his cruelty, he was a profane swearer. . . . The field was the place to witness his cruelty and profanity. His presence made it both the field of blood and of blasphemy. From the rising till the going down of the sun, he was cursing, raving, cutting, and slashing among the slaves of the field, in the most frightful manner. His career was short. He died very soon after I went to Colonel Lloyd's; and he died as he lived, uttering, with his dying groans, bitter curses and horrid oaths. His death was regarded by the slaves as the result of a merciful providence.

Mr. Severe's place was filled by a Mr. Hopkins. He was a very different man. He was less cruel, less profane, and made less noise, than Mr. Severe. His course was characterized by no extraordinary demonstrations of cruelty. He whipped, but seemed to take no pleasure in it. He was called by the slaves a good overseer.

The home plantation of Colonel Lloyd wore the appearance of a country village. All the mechanical operations for all the farms were performed here. The shoemaking and mending, the blacksmithing, cartwrighting, coopering, weaving, and grain-grinding, were all performed by the slaves on the home plantation. The whole place wore a business-like aspect very unlike the neighboring farms. The number of houses, too, conspired to give it advantage over the neighboring farms. It was called by the slaves the *Great House Farm*. Few privileges were esteemed higher, by the slaves of the out-farms, than that of being selected to do errands at the Great House Farm. . . . He was called the smartest and most trusty fellow, who had this honor conferred upon him the most frequently. The competitors for this office sought as diligently to please their overseers, as the office-seekers in the political parties seek to please and deceive the people. The same traits of character might be seen in Colonel Lloyd's slaves, as are seen in the slaves of the political parties.

The slaves selected to go to the Great House Farm, for the monthly allowance for themselves and their fellow-slaves, were peculiarly enthusiastic. While on their way, they would make the dense old woods, for miles around, reverberate with their wild songs, revealing at once the highest joy and the deepest sadness. They would compose and sing as they went along, consulting neither time nor tune. . . . They would sometimes sing the most pathetic sentiment in the most rapturous tone, and the most rapturous sentiment in the most pathetic tone. . . . I have sometimes thought that the mere hearing of those songs would do more to impress some minds with the horrible character of slavery, than the reading of whole volumes of philosophy on the subject could do.

I did not, when a slave, understand the deep meaning of those rude and apparently incoherent songs. I was myself within the circle; so that I neither saw nor heard as those without might see and hear. They told a tale of woe which was then altogether beyond my feeble comprehension; they were tones loud, long, and deep; they breathed the prayer and complaint of souls boiling over with the bitterest anguish. Every tone was a testimony against slavery, and a prayer to God for deliverance from chains. The hearing of those wild notes always depressed my spirit, and filled me with ineffable sadness. I have frequently found myself in tears while hearing them. . . . To those songs I trace my first glimmering conception of the dehumanizing character of slavery. I can never get rid of that conception. Those songs still follow me, to deepen my hatred of slavery, and quicken my sympathies for my brethren in bonds. . . .

I have often been utterly astonished, since I came to the north, to find persons who could speak of the singing, among slaves, as evidence of their contentment and happiness. It is impossible to conceive of a greater mistake. Slaves sing most when they are most unhappy. The songs of the slave represent the sorrows of his heart; and he is relieved by them, only as an aching heart is relieved by its tears. At least, such is my experience. I have often sung to drown my sorrow, but seldom to express my happiness. Crying for joy, and singing for joy, were alike uncommon to me while in the jaws of slavery. The singing of a man cast away upon a desolate island might be as appropriately considered as evidence of contentment and happiness, as the singing of a slave; the songs of the one and of the other are prompted by the same emotion.

REVIEW QUESTIONS

1. Did Douglass describe Lloyd's plantation and its outlying farms as a microcosm of the larger southern society? Explain.
2. Were material rewards, or the lack thereof, part of the definition of slavery?
3. How did Douglass refute the prevailing southern—and, indeed, northern—perception of slave songs? Why was that important?
4. What was the difference between a bad overseer and a good one?

FREDERICK LAW OLMSTED

FROM Review of a First-Rate Cotton Plantation (1860)

Douglass described his life on a northern—Chesapeake region—plantation, but many people were especially interested in slave conditions on the cotton plantations of the Far South. Much of that area—especially the Deep South states of Alabama, Mississippi, Louisiana, Arkansas, and Texas—was just emerging from a frontier stage of development in the 1840s to the 1850s. There had been earlier European settlements in those regions, but the massive influx of Americans had only begun after the development of the cotton gin and after the United States had secured the area through wars and treaties. The area drew not only settlers but, especially with the rise of the slavery question, journalists as well. The New Englander Frederick Law Olmsted (1822–1903) proved to be one of the most acute of these observers. Olmsted had traveled to England and then through the American South, reporting on the natural and social landscapes. He became one of the founders of American landscape architecture, but in the years before the Civil War he concentrated on investigating the South, specifically the impact of slavery on its economy and society. In 1853–54 he journeyed down to Virginia, the Carolinas, and then west through to Texas, reporting back to the New York Daily Times *and compiling notes for his later books.*

From Frederick Law Olmsted, *The Slave States*, rev. and enl. ed., ed. Harvey Wish (New York: Capricorn Books, 1959), pp. 200–205. [Editorial insertions that appear in square brackets are from Wish's edition—*Ed.*]

We had a good breakfast in the morning, and immediately afterward mounted and rode to a very large cottonfield, where the whole field-force of the plantation was engaged.

It was a first-rate plantation. On the highest ground stood a large and handsome mansion, but it had not been occupied for several years, and it was more than two years since the overseer had seen the owner. He lived several hundred miles away, and the overseer would not believe that I did not know him, for he was a rich man and an honorable, and had several times been where I came from—New York.

The whole plantation, including the swamp land around it, and owned with it, covered several square miles. It was four miles from the settlement to the nearest neighbor's house. There were between thirteen and fourteen hundred acres under cultivation with cotton, corn, and other hoed crops, and two hundred hogs running at large in the swamp. It was the intention that corn and pork enough should be raised to keep the slaves and cattle. This year, however, it has been found necessary to purchase largely, and such was probably usually the case, though the overseer intimated the owner had been displeased, and he "did not mean to be caught so bad again."

There were 135 slaves, big and little, of which 67 went to field regularly—equal, the overseer thought, to 60 able-bodied hands. Beside the field-hands, there were 3 mechanics (blacksmith, carpenter and wheelwright), 2 seamstresses, 1 cook, 1 stable servant, 1 cattle-tender, 1 hog-tender,

1 teamster, 1 house servant (overseer's cook), and one midwife and nurse. These were all first-class hands; most of them would be worth more, if they were for sale, the overseer said, than the best of fieldhands. There was also a driver of the hoe-gang who did not labor personally, and a foreman of the plow-gang. These two acted as petty officers in the field, and alternately in the quarters.

There was a nursery for sucklings at the quarters, and twenty women at this time who left their work four times each day, for half an hour, to nurse their young ones, and whom the overseer counted as half-hands—that is, expected to do half an ordinary day's work.

Deserters and Detectives

He had no runaways out at this time, but had just sold a bad one to go to Texas. He was whipping the fellow, when he turned and tried to stab him—then broke from him and ran away. He had him caught almost immediately by the dogs. After catching him, he kept him in irons till he had a chance to sell him. His niggers did not very often run away, he said, because they were almost sure to be caught. As soon as he saw that one was gone he put the dogs on, and if rain had not just fallen, they would soon find him. Sometimes, though, they would outwit the dogs, but if they did they almost always kept in the neighborhood, because they did not like to go where they could not sometimes get back and see their families, and he would soon get wind of where they had been; they would come round their quarters to see their families and to get food, and as soon as he knew it, he would find their tracks and put the dogs on again. Two months was the longest time any of them ever kept out. They had dogs trained on purpose to run after niggers, and never let out for any thing else.

Driving

We found in the field thirty plows, moving together, turning the earth from the cotton plants, and from thirty to forty hoers, the latter mainly women, with a black driver walking about among them with a whip, which he often cracked at them, sometimes allowing the lash to fall lightly upon their shoulders. He was constantly urging them also with his voice. All worked very steadily, and though the presence of a stranger on the plantation must have been rare, I saw none raise or turn their heads to look at me. Each gang was attended by a "water-toter," that of the hoe-gang being a straight, sprightly, plump little black girl, whose picture, as she stood balancing the bucket upon her head, shading her bright eyes with one hand, and holding out a calabash with the other to maintain her poise, would have been a worthy study for Murillo.

Days and Hours of Labor

I asked at what time they began to work in the morning. "Well," said the overseer, "I do better by my niggers than most. I keep 'em right smart at their work while they do work, but I generally knock 'em off at 8 o'clock in the morning Saturdays, and give 'em all the rest of the day to themselves, and I always gives 'em Sundays, the whole day. Pickin' time, and when the crap's bad in grass, I sometimes keep 'em to it till about sunset, Saturdays, but I never work 'em Sundays."

"How early do you start them out in the morning, usually?"

"Well, I don't never start my niggers 'fore daylight except 'tis in pickin' time, then maybe I got 'em out a quarter of an hour before. But I keep 'em right smart to work through the day." He showed an evident pride in the vigilance of his driver, and called my attention to the large area of ground already hoed over that morning; well hoed, too, as he said.

"At what time do they eat?" I asked. They ate "their snacks" in their cabins, he said, before they came out in the morning (that is before daylight — the sun rising at this time at a little before five, and the day dawning, probably, an hour earlier); then at 12 o'clock their dinner was brought to them in a cart—one cart for the plow-gang and one for the hoe-gang. The hoe-gang ate its dinner in the field, and only stopped work long enough to eat it. The plow-gang drove its teams to the "weather houses"—open sheds erected for the purpose in different parts of the plantation, under which were cisterns filled with rain water, from which the water-toters carried drink to those at work. The mules were fed as much oats (in straw), corn and fodder as they would eat in two hours; this forage having been brought to the weather houses by another cart. The plowmen had nothing to do but eat their dinner in all this time. All worked as late as they could see to work well, and had no more food nor rest until they returned to their cabin. At half past nine o'clock the drivers, each on an alternate night, blew a horn, and at ten visited every cabin to see that its occupants were at rest, and not lurking about and spending their strength in fooleries, and that the fires were safe—a very unusual precaution; the negroes are generally at liberty after their day's work is done till they are called in the morning. When washing and patching were done, wood hauled and cut for the fires, corn ground, etc., I did not learn: probably all chores not of daily necessity, were reserved for Saturday. Custom varies in this respect. In general, with regard to fuel for the cabins, the negroes are left to look out for themselves, and they often have to go to "the swamp" for it, or at least, if it has been hauled, to cut it to a convenient size, after their day's work is done. The allowance of food was a peck of corn and four pounds of pork per week, each. When they could not get "greens" (any vegetables) he generally gave them five pounds of pork. They had gardens, and raised a good deal for themselves; they also had fowls, and usually plenty of eggs. He added, "the man who owns this plantation does more for his niggers than any other man I know. Every Christmas he sends me up a thousand or fifteen hundred dollars' [equal to eight or ten dollars each] worth of molasses and coffee, and tobacco, and calico, and Sunday tricks for 'em. Every family on this plantation gets a barrel of molasses at Christmas." (Not an uncommon practice in Mississippi, though the quantity is very rarely so generous. It is usually made somewhat proportionate to the value of the last crop sold.)

Beside which, the overseer added, they are able, if they choose, to buy certain comforts for themselves—tobacco for instance—with money earned by Saturday and Sunday work. Some of them went into the swamps on Sunday and made boards—"puncheons" made with the ax. One man sold last year as much as fifty dollars' worth.

* * *

This was the only large plantation that I had an opportunity of seeing at all closely, over which I was not chiefly conducted by an educated gentleman and slave owner, by whose habitual impressions and sentiments my own were probably somewhat influenced. From what I saw in passing, and from what I heard by chance of others, I suppose it to have been in no respect an unfavorable specimen of those plantations on which the owners do not reside. A merchant of the vicinity recently in New York tells me that he supposes it to be a fair enough sample of plantations of its class. There is nothing remarkable in its management that he had heard. When I asked about molasses and Christmas presents, he said he reckoned the overseer rather stretched that story, but the owner was a very good man. A magistrate of the district, who had often been on the plantation, said in answer to an inquiry from me, that the negroes were very well treated upon it, though not extraordinarily so. His comparison was with plantations in general. He also spoke well of the overseer. He had been a long time on this plantation—I think he said, ever since it had begun to be cultivated. This is very rare; it was the only case I met with in which an overseer had kept the same place ten years, and it was a strong evidence of his comparative excellence, that his employer had been so long satisfied with him. . . .

* * *

REVIEW QUESTIONS

1. How did Olmsted's account compare with Douglass' in both tone and content?

2. What was the difference between a first-class hand and a field-hand?

3. What were the working conditions on this plan-tation? Were there gender divisions in the labor?

4. What did the slaves do for themselves when they were "at liberty"?

FRANCES ANNE KEMBLE AND FREDERICK LAW OLMSTED

FROM Accounts about "Poor Whites" (1839, 1856)

The complexity of the southern social system was often hidden by superficial observations and stereotyping. One might argue that the common denominator was white against black, only to find that neither group was always united against the other. True, whites tended to claim an essential equality based on race, but that did not translate into social or economic equality among them. Wealthy planters were sometimes more disparaging of poor whites than they were of blacks. Some slaves picked up on this attitude and, assuming their owner's status as part of their identity, denigrated poor whites themselves. The poorer whites, in turn, were quick to remind blacks of their place in the social order. It was a world defined by relationships, "face" (one's honor, presence, and prestige), and place. While this world had a middle class of farmers, businessmen, and professionals that was comparable to the one in the North, observers seemed to be primarily interested in the extremes: the wealthy, the poor, and the enslaved. Frances Kemble and Frederick Olmsted, while living or visiting with the former and observing the latter, sought out information on those caught between the two.

From Frances Anne Kemble, *Journal of a Residence on a Georgian Plantation in 1838–1839*, ed. John A. Scott (1961; New York: The New American Library, Inc., 1975), pp. 110–12. From Frederick Law Olmsted, *The Slave States*, rev. and enl. ed., ed. Harvey Wish (New York: Capricorn Books, 1959), pp. 69–71. [Editorial insertions appear in square brackets unless otherwise indicated—*Ed.*]

*   *   *

After dinner I [Kemble] had a most interesting conversation with Mr. K[ing].[1] Among other subjects, he gave me a lively and curious description of the yeomanry of Georgia, more properly termed pinelanders. Have you visions now of well-to-do farmers with comfortable homesteads, decent

habits, industrious, intelligent, cheerful, and thrifty? Such, however, is not the yeomanry of Georgia. Labor being here the especial portion of slaves, it is thenceforth degraded, and considered unworthy of all but slaves. No white man, therefore, of any class puts hand to work of any kind soever. This is an exceedingly dignified way of proving their gentility for the lazy planters who prefer an idle life of semistarvation and barbarism to the degradation of doing anything themselves;

---

[1] Editorial insertion from Scott's edition.

but the effect on the poorer whites of the country is terrible. I speak now of the scattered white population, who, too poor to possess land or slaves, and having no means of living in the towns, squat (most appropriately is it so termed) either on other men's land or government districts—always here swamp or pine barren—and claim masterdom over the place they invade till ejected by the rightful proprietors. These wretched creatures will not, for they are whites (and labor belongs to blacks and slaves alone here), labor for their own subsistence. They are hardly protected from the weather by the rude shelters they frame for themselves in the midst of these dreary woods. Their food is chiefly supplied by shooting the wildfowl and venison, and stealing from the cultivated patches of the plantations nearest at hand. Their clothes hang about them in filthy tatters, and the combined squalor and fierceness of their appearance is really frightful.

This population is the direct growth of slavery. The planters are loud in their execrations of these miserable vagabonds; yet they do not see that so long as labor is considered the disgraceful portion of slaves, these free men will hold it nobler to starve or steal than till the earth, with none but the despised blacks for fellow laborers. The blacks themselves—such is the infinite power of custom—acquiesce in this notion, and, as I have told you, consider it the lowest degradation in a white to use any exertion. . . .

Talking of these pinelanders—gypsies, without any of the romantic associations that belong to the latter people—led us to the origin of such a population, slavery; and you may be sure I listened with infinite interest to the opinions of a man of uncommon shrewdness and sagacity, who was born in the very bosom of it, and has passed his whole life among slaves. If anyone is competent to judge of its effects, such a man is the one; and this was his verdict: "I hate slavery with all my heart; I consider it an absolute curse wherever it exists. It will keep those states where it does exist fifty years behind the others in improvement and prosperity."

Farther on in the conversation he made this most remarkable observation: "As for its being an irremediable evil—a thing not to be helped or got rid of—that's all nonsense; for, as soon as people become convinced that it is their interest to get rid of it, they will soon find the means to do so, depend upon it."

And undoubtedly this is true. This is not an age, nor yours a country, where a large mass of people will long endure what they perceive to be injurious to their fortunes and advancement. Blind as people often are to their highest and truest interests, your countryfolk have generally shown remarkable acuteness in finding out where their worldly progress suffered let or hindrance, and have removed it with laudable alacrity. Now the fact is not at all as we at the North are sometimes told, that the Southern slaveholders deprecate the evils of slavery quite as much as we do; that they see all its miseries; that, moreover, they are most anxious to get rid of the whole thing, but want the means to do so, and submit most unwillingly to a necessity from which they cannot extricate themselves. All this I thought might be true before I went to the South, and often has the charitable supposition checked the condemnation which was indignantly rising to my lips against these murderers of their brethren's peace. A little reflection, however, even without personal observation, might have convinced me that this could not be the case. If the majority of Southerners were satisfied that slavery was contrary to their worldly fortunes, slavery would be at an end from that very moment; but the fact is—and I have it not only from observation of my own, but from the distinct statement of some of the most intelligent Southern men that I have conversed with—the only obstacle to immediate abolition throughout the South is the immense value of the human property, and, to use the words of a very distinguished Carolinian, who thus ended a long discussion we had on the subject: "I'll tell you why abolition is impossible: because every healthy Negro can fetch a thousand dollars in the Charleston market at this moment." . . .

*   *   *

White Laboring People[2]

I [Olmsted] learned that there were no white laboring men here [Virginia] who hired themselves out by the month. The poor white people that had to labor for their living never would work steadily at any employment. "They mostly followed boating"—hiring as hands on the bateaus that navigate the small streams and canals, but never for a longer term at once than a single trip of a boat, whether that might be long or short. At the end of the trip they were paid by the day. Their wages were from fifty cents to a dollar, varying with the demand and individual capacities. They hardly ever worked on farms except in harvest, when they usually received a dollar a day, sometimes more. In harvest-time, most of the rural mechanics closed their shops and hired out to the farmers at a dollar a day, which would indicate that their ordinary earnings are considerably less than this. At other than harvest-time, the poor white people, who had no trade, would sometimes work for the farmers by the job, not often at any regular agricultural labor, but at getting rails or shingles, or clearing land.

He did not know that they were particular about working with negroes, but no white man would ever do certain kinds of work (such as taking care of cattle, or getting water or wood to be used in the house), and if you should ask a white man you had hired to do such things, he would get mad and tell you he wasn't a nigger. Poor white girls never hired out to do servants' work, but they would come and help another white woman about her sewing or quilting, and take wages for it. But these girls were not very respectable generally, and it was not agreeable to have them in your house, though there were some very respectable ladies that would go out to sew. Farmers depended almost entirely upon their negroes; it was only when they were hard pushed by their crops that they got white hands to help them any.

Negroes had commanded such high wages lately, to work on railroads and in tobacco-factories, that farmers were tempted to hire out too many of their people, and to undertake to do too much work with those they retained, and thus they were often driven to employ white men, and to give them very high wages by the day, when they found themselves getting much behind-hand with their crops. . . .

Of course, he did not see how white laborers were ever going to come into competition with negroes here, at all. You never could depend on white men, and you couldn't *drive* them any; they wouldn't stand it. Slaves were the only reliable laborers—you could command them and *make* them do what was right.

From the manner in which he always talked of the white laboring people, it was evident that, although he placed them in some sort on an equality with himself, and that in his intercourse with them he wouldn't think of asserting for himself any superior dignity, or even feel himself to be patronizing them in not doing so, yet he, all the time, recognized them as a distinct and a rather despicable class, and wanted to have as little to do with them as he conveniently could.

I have been once or twice told that the poor white people, meaning those, I suppose, who bring nothing to market to exchange for money but their labor, although they may own a cabin and a little furniture, and cultivate land enough to supply themselves with (maize) bread, are worse off in almost all respects than the slaves. They are said to be extremely ignorant and immoral, as well as indolent and unambitious. That their condition is not as unfortunate by any means as that of negroes, however, is most obvious, since from among them, men *sometimes* elevate themselves to positions and habits of usefulness, and respectability. They are said to "corrupt" the negroes, and to encourage them to steal, or to work for them at night and on Sundays, and to pay them with liquor, and also to constantly associate licentiously with them. They seem, nevertheless, more than any other portion of the community, to hate and despise the negroes.

*   *   *

[2] From Frederick Law Olmsted, *The Slave States*, pp. 69–71.

REVIEW QUESTIONS

1. Do the two accounts provide the same picture of the South's poor and/or laboring whites? Explain.

2. What do they reveal about white society?
3. What reason or reasons did the authors give for the condition of these white people?
4. Did they suggest that the abolition of slavery would benefit these southerners?

LYDIA MARIA CHILD

FROM Propositions Defining Slavery and Emancipation (1833)

Lydia Maria Child (1802–1880) was already a well-known writer when she took up the abolitionist cause. She had published novels, works on domestic management and child care, and founded a children's magazine. Promoting reform within the household was not enough for her, however; she wanted to help put the country's house in order by sweeping out slavery. In this desire and in her endeavors, she was at the forefront of the abolitionist movement that burst upon the national scene in the 1830s. Child was ostracized by some people and organizations because of her activism, and her outspoken advocacy adversely affected both the sales of her books and her magazine, but she remained a leader in the antislavery movement and then, after the Civil War, in endeavors to help the freed slaves and promote equality. In her book, An Appeal in Favor of that Class of Americans called Africans, *first published in 1833, she strove to make clear just what slavery was and what could and should be done about it.*

From Lydia Maria Child, *An Appeal in Favor of that Class of Americans called Africans* (1836; New York: Arno Press and The New York Times, 1968), pp. 41–42, 76–77, 82–83, 95–100. [Editorial insertions appear in square brackets—*Ed.*]

*   *   *

In order to show the true aspect of slavery among us, I will state distinct propositions, each supported by the evidence of actually existing laws.

1. *Slavery is hereditary and perpetual, to the last moment of the slave's earthly existence, and to all his descendants, to the latest posterity.*

2. *The labor of the slave is compulsory and uncompensated; while the kind of labor, the amount of* toil, and the time allowed for rest, are dictated solely by the master. No bargain is made, no wages given. A pure despotism governs the human brute; and even his covering and provender, both as to quantity and quality, depend entirely on the master's discretion.*

3. *The slave being considered a personal chattel, may be sold, or pledged, or leased, at the will of his master. He may be exchanged for marketable commodities, or taken in execution for the debts, or taxes, either of a living, or a deceased master. Sold at*

auction, "either individually, or in lots to suit the purchaser," he may remain with his family, or be separated from them for ever.

4. *Slaves can make no contracts, and have no legal right to any property, real or personal. Their own honest earnings, and the legacies of friends belong, in point of law, to their masters.*

5. *Neither a slave, nor free colored person, can be a witness against any white or free man, in a court of justice, however atrocious may have been the crimes they have seen him commit: but they may give testimony against a fellow-slave, or free colored man, even in cases affecting life.*

6. *The slave may be punished at his master's discretion—without trial—without any means of legal redress,—whether his offence be real, or imaginary: and the master can transfer the same despotic power to any person, or persons, he may choose to appoint.*

7. *The slave is not allowed to resist any free man under any circumstances: his only safety consists in the fact that his owner may bring suit, and recover, the price of his body, in case his life is taken, or his limbs rendered unfit for labor.*

8. *Slaves cannot redeem themselves, or obtain a change of masters, though cruel treatment may have rendered such a change necessary for their personal safety.*

9. *The slave is entirely unprotected in his domestic relations.*

10. *The laws greatly obstruct the manumission of slaves, even where the master is willing to enfranchise them.*

11. *The operation of the laws tends to deprive slaves of religious instruction and consolation.*

12. *The whole power of the laws is exerted to keep slaves in a state of the lowest ignorance.*

13. *There is in this country a monstrous inequality of law and right. What is a trifling fault in the white man, is considered highly criminal in the slave; the same offences which cost a white man a few dollars only, are punished in the negro with death.*

14. *The laws operate most oppressively upon free people of color.*

*   *   *

. . . [A] very brief glance will show that slavery is inconsistent with *economy*, whether domestic or political.

The slave is bought, sometimes at a very high price; in free labor there is no such investment of capital. When the slave is ill, a physician must be paid by the owner; the free laborer defrays his own expenses. The children of the slave must be supported by his master; the free man maintains his own. The slave is to be taken care of in his old age, which his previous habits render peculiarly helpless; the free laborer is hired when he is wanted, and then returns to his home. The slave does not care how slowly or carelessly he works; it is the free man's interest to do his business well and quickly. The slave is indifferent how many tools he spoils; the free man has a motive to be careful. The slave's clothing is indeed very cheap, but it is of no consequence to him how fast it is destroyed—his master *must* keep him covered, and that is all he is likely to do; the hired laborer pays more for his garments, but makes them last three times as long. The free man will be honest for reputation's sake; but reputation will make the slave none the richer, nor invest him with any of the privileges of a human being—while his poverty and sense of wrong both urge him to steal from his master. A salary must be paid to an overseer to compel the slave to work; the free man is impelled by the desire of increasing the comforts of himself and family. Two hired laborers will perform as much work as three slaves; by some it is supposed to be a more correct estimate that slaves perform only *half* as much labor as the same number of free laborers. Finally, *where* slaves are employed, manual industry is a degradation to white people, and indolence becomes the prevailing characteristic.

Slave-owners have indeed frequently shown great adroitness in defending this bad system; but, with few exceptions, they base their arguments upon the necessity of continuing slavery because it is already begun. Many of them have openly acknowledged that it was highly injurious to the prosperity of the State.

*   *   *

The inhabitants of free States are often told that they cannot argue fairly upon the subject of slavery because they know nothing about its actual operation; and any expression of their opinions and feelings with regard to the system, is attributed to ignorant enthusiasm, fanatical benevolence, or a wicked intention to do mischief.

But Mr. Clay, Mr. Brodnax, and Mr. Faulkner [from whom she had just quoted passages noting defects in the system] belong to slaveholding States; and the two former, if I mistake not, are slave-owners. *They* surely are qualified to judge of the system; and I might fill ten pages with other quotations from southern writers and speakers, who acknowledge that slavery is a great evil. . . . This system is so closely entwined with the apparent interests and convenience of individuals, that it will never want for able defenders, so long as it exists. But I believe I do not misrepresent the truth, when I say the prevailing opinion at the South is, that it would have been much better for those States, and for the country in general, if slavery had never been introduced.

*   *   *

But to return to the subject of emancipation. Nearly every one of the States north of Mason and Dixon's line once held slaves. These slaves were manumitted without bloodshed, and there was no trouble in making free colored laborers obey the laws.

I am aware that this desirable change must be attended with much more difficulty in the Southern States, simply because the evil has been suffered until it is fearfully overgrown; but it must not be forgotten that while they are using their ingenuity and strength to sustain it for the present, the mischief is increasing more and more rapidly. If this be not a good time to apply a remedy, when will be a better? They must annihilate slavery, or slavery will annihilate them.

It seems to be forgotten that emancipation from tyranny is not an emancipation from law; the negro, after he is made free, is restrained from the commission of crimes by the same laws which restrain other citizens: if he steals, he will be imprisoned: if he commits murder, he will be hung.

It will, perhaps, be said that the free people of color in the slave portions of *this* country are peculiarly ignorant, idle, and vicious? It may be so: for our laws and our influence are peculiarly calculated to make them bad members of society. But we trust the civil power to keep in order the great mass of ignorant and vicious foreigners continually pouring into the country; and if the laws are strong enough for this, may they not be trusted to restrain the free blacks?

In those countries where the slaves codes are mild, where emancipation is rendered easy, and inducements are offered to industry, insurrections are not feared, and free people of color form a valuable portion of the community. If we persist in acting in opposition to the established laws of nature and reason, how can we expect favorable results? But it is pronounced *unsafe* to change our policy. Every progressive improvement in the world has been resisted by despotism, on the ground that changes were dangerous. The Emperor of Austria thinks there is need of keeping his subjects ignorant, that good order may be preserved. But what he calls good order, is sacrificing the happiness of many to the advancement of a few; and no doubt knowledge *is* unfavorable to the continuation of such a state of things. It is precisely so with the slaveholder; he insists that the welfare of millions must be subordinate to his private interest, or else all good order is destroyed.

*   *   *

But if slaves were allowed to redeem themselves progressively, by purchasing one day of the week after another, as they can in the Spanish colonies, habits of industry would be gradually formed, and enterprise would be stimulated, by their successful efforts to acquire a little property. And if they afterward worked better as free laborers than they now do as slaves, it would surely benefit their masters as well as themselves.

*   *   *

It is commonly urged against emancipation that white men cannot possibly labor under the sultry climate of our most southerly States. This is a good reason for not sending the slaves out of the country, but it is no argument against making them free. No doubt we do need their labor; but we ought to pay for it. Why should their presence be any more disagreeable as hired laborers, than as slaves? In Boston, we continually meet colored people in the streets, and employ them in various ways, without being endangered or even incommoded. There is no moral impossibility in a perfectly kind and just relation between the two races.

If white men think otherwise, let *them* remove from climates which nature has made too hot for their constitutions. Wealth or pleasure often induces men to change their abode; an emigration for the sake of humanity would be an agreeable novelty. . . .

But the slaveholders try to stop all the efforts of benevolence, by vociferous complaints about infringing upon their *property*; and justice is so subordinate to self-interest, that the unrighteous claim is silently allowed, and even openly supported, by those who ought to blush for themselves, as Christians and as republicans. Let men *simplify* their arguments—let them confine themselves to one single question, "What right can a man have to compel his neighbor to toil without reward, and leave the same hopeless inheritance to his children, in order that *he* may live in luxury and indolence?" Let the doctrines of *expediency* return to the Father of Lies, who invented them, and gave them power to turn every way for evil. The Christian knows no appeal from the decisions of God, plainly uttered in his conscience.

*   *   *

. . . Personal freedom is the birthright of every human being. God himself made it the first great law of creation; and no human enactment can render it null and void. . . .

. . . Have the negroes no right to ask compensation for their years and years of unrewarded toil? It is true that they have food and clothing, of such kind, and in such quantities, as their masters think proper. But it is evident that this is not the worth of their labor; for the proprietors can give from one hundred to five and six hundred dollars for a slave, beside the expense of supporting those who are too old or too young to labor. They could not *afford* to do this, if the slave did not earn more than he receives in food and clothing. If the laws allowed the slave to redeem himself progressively, the owner would receive his money back again; and the negro's years of uncompensated toil would be more than lawful interest.

*   *   *

REVIEW QUESTIONS

1. How did Child define slavery? Was hers a complete definition?
2. Did she make emancipation sound like a rational as opposed to emotional proposition?
3. What argument did she make to convince her readers that emancipation would not lead to social disorder?
4. How did she propose to make emancipation economically viable?

WILLIAM LLOYD GARRISON

FROM *Declaration of Sentiments of the American Anti-Slavery Society* (1833)

In 1833, the same year that Lydia Maria Child published her appeal, a group of abolitionists gathered together to found the American Anti-Slavery Society. A number of the representatives had been involved in the creation of the New England Anti-Slavery Society in 1832 and the New York society that followed, but they believed that there should be a national organization. Prominent among them was William Lloyd Garrison (1805–1879). Garrison gave his first public address against slavery in 1829, and soon thereafter, in 1831, began publishing the Boston Liberator. *Over the next three decades he vigorously fought slavery with words even as he opposed violence to free the slaves. Besides his public speeches and Liberator editorials, Garrison helped to draft the New England society's constitution as well as the* Declaration of Sentiments *of the American Anti-Slavery Society. He also served as president of the latter society from 1843 to 1865.*

From *Selections from the Writings and Speeches of William Lloyd Garrison*. Orig. publ. in 1852 by R. F. Wallcut. (New York: Negro Universities Press, 1968), pp. 66–71.

The Convention assembled in the city of Philadelphia, to organize a National Anti-Slavery Society, promptly seize the opportunity to promulgate the following Declaration of Sentiments, as cherished by them in relation to the enslavement of one-sixth portion of the American people.

More than fifty-seven years have elapsed, since a band of patriots convened in this place, to devise measures for the deliverance of this country from a foreign yoke. The corner-stone upon which they founded the Temple of Freedom was broadly this—'that all men are created equal; that they are endowed by their Creator with certain inalienable rights; that among these are life, LIBERTY, and the pursuit of happiness.' . . .

We have met together for the achievement of an enterprise, without which that of our fathers is incomplete; and which, for its magnitude, solemnity, and probable results upon the destiny of the world, as far transcends theirs as moral truth does physical force.

*   *   *

Their principles led them to wage war against their oppressors, and to spill human blood like water, in order to be free. Ours forbid the doing of evil that good may come, and lead us to reject, and to entreat the oppressed to reject, the use of all carnal weapons for deliverance from bondage; relying solely upon those which are spiritual, and mighty through God to the pulling down of strong holds.

Their measures were physical resistance—the marshalling in arms—the hostile array—the mortal encounter. Ours shall be such only as the opposition of moral purity to moral corruption—he destruction of error by the potency of truth—the overthrow of prejudice by the power of love—and the abolition of slavery by the spirit of repentance.

Their grievances, great as they were, were trifling in comparison with the wrongs and sufferings of those for whom we plead. Our fathers were never slaves—never bought and sold like cattle—never shut out from the light of knowledge and religion—never subjected to the lash of brutal taskmasters.

But those, for whose emancipation we are striving—constituting at the present time at least one-sixth part of our countrymen—are recognized by law, and treated by their fellow-beings, as marketable commodities, as goods and chattels, as brute beasts; . . . For the crime of having a dark complexion, they suffer the pangs of hunger, the infliction of stripes, the ignominy of brutal servitude. They are kept in heathenish darkness by laws expressly enacted to make their instruction a criminal offence.

These are the prominent circumstances in the condition of more than two millions of our people, the proof of which may be found in thousands of indisputable facts, and in the laws of the slave-holding States.

Hence we maintain—that, in view of the civil and religious privileges of this nation, the guilt of its oppression is unequalled by any other on the face of the earth; and, therefore, that it is bound to repent instantly, to undo the heavy burdens, and to let the oppressed go free.

We further maintain—that no man has a right to enslave or imbrute his brother—to hold or acknowledge him, for one moment, as a piece of merchandize—to keep back his hire by fraud—or to brutalize his mind, by denying him the means of intellectual, social and moral improvement.

The right to enjoy liberty is inalienable. To invade it is to usurp the prerogative of Jehovah. Every man has a right to his own body—to the products of his own labor—to the protection of law—and to the common advantages of society. It is piracy to buy or steal a native African, and subject him to servitude. Surely, the sin is as great to enslave an American as an African.

Therefore we believe and affirm—that there is no difference, in principle, between the African slave trade and American slavery:

That every American citizen, who detains a human being in involuntary bondage as his property, is, according to Scripture, (Ex. xxi. 16,) a man-stealer:

That the slaves ought instantly to be set free, and brought under the protection of law:

That if they had lived from the time of Pharaoh down to the present period, and had been entailed through successive generations, their right to be free could never have been alienated, but their claims would have constantly risen in solemnity:

That all those laws which are now in force, admitting the right of slavery, are therefore, before God, utterly null and void; being an audacious usurpation of the Divine prerogative, a daring infringement on the law of nature, a base overthrow of the very foundations of the social compact, a complete extinction of all the relations, endearments and obligations of mankind, and a presumptuous transgression of all the holy commandments; and that therefore they ought instantly to be abrogated.

We further believe and affirm—that all persons of color, who possess the qualifications which are demanded of others, ought to be admitted forthwith to the enjoyment of the same privileges, and the exercise of the same prerogatives, as others; and that the paths of preferment, of wealth, and of intelligence, should be opened as widely to them as to persons of a white complexion.

We maintain that no compensation should be given to the planters emancipating their slaves:

Because it would be a surrender of the great fundamental principle, that man cannot hold property in man:

Because slavery is a crime, and therefore is not an article to be sold:

Because the holders of slaves are not the just proprietors of what they claim; freeing the slave is not depriving them of property, but restoring it to its rightful owner; it is not wronging the master, but righting the slave—restoring him to himself:

Because immediate and general emancipation would only destroy nominal, not real property; it would not amputate a limb or break a bone of the slaves, but by infusing motives into their breasts, would make them doubly valuable to the masters as free laborers; and

Because, if compensation is to be given at all, it should be given to the outraged and guiltless slaves, and not to those who have plundered and abused them.

We regard as delusive, cruel and dangerous, any scheme of expatriation which pretends to aid, either directly or indirectly, in the emancipation of the slaves, or to be a substitute for the immediate and total abolition of slavery.

We fully and unanimously recognise the sovereignty of each State, to legislate exclusively on the subject of the slavery which is tolerated within its limits; we concede that Congress, under the present national compact, has no right to interfere with any of the slave States, in relation to this momentous subject:

But we maintain that Congress has a right, and is solemnly bound, to suppress the domestic slave trade between the several States, and to abolish slavery in those portions of our territory which the Constitution has placed under its exclusive jurisdiction.

We also maintain that there are, at the present time, the highest obligations resting upon the people of the free States to remove slavery by moral and political action, as prescribed in the Constitution of the United States. They are now living under a pledge of their tremendous physical force, to fasten the galling fetters of tyranny upon the limbs of millions in the Southern States; they are liable to be called at any moment to suppress a general insurrection of the slaves; they authorize the slave owner to vote for three-fifths of his slaves as property, and thus enable him to perpetuate his oppression; they support a standing army at the South for its protection; and they seize the slave, who has escaped into their territories, and send him back to be tortured by an enraged master or a brutal driver. This relation to slavery is criminal, and full of danger: IT MUST BE BROKEN UP.

* * *

We shall organize Anti-Slavery S[...], ble, in every city, town and village i[...]

We shall send forth agents to lift up [...] of remonstrance, of warning, of entreaty, a[...] buke.

We shall circulate, unsparingly and extensively, antislavery tracts and periodicals.

We shall enlist the pulpit and the press in the cause of the suffering and the dumb.

We shall aim at a purification of the churches from all participation in the guilt of slavery.

We shall encourage the labor of freemen rather than that of slaves, by giving a preference to their productions: and

We shall spare no exertions nor means to bring the whole nation to speedy repentance.

Our trust for victory is solely in God. We may be personally defeated, but our principles never. Truth, Justice, Reason, Humanity, must and will gloriously triumph. . . .

* * *

Done at Philadelphia, December 6th, A.D. 1833

REVIEW QUESTIONS

1. Did the abolitionists at the convention believe that their work continued the Revolution? Did they think it of more value than the Revolution? Explain.
2. How do their sentiments illustrate both the romanticism and reform impulses of the time?
3. Given that other nations still had slavery, why did the abolitionists believe that the guilt for such oppression lay more heavily on the United States? And why did they accuse the national and free-state governments of aiding and abetting the southern states in the continuation of slavery?
4. What kind of emancipation program did they propose? Was it similar to the one suggested by Lydia Maria Child?

H. MANLY, PUBLISHER

Vindicated from the Treason and of the Northern Abolitionists (1836)

ntiments (1833)   473

ocieties, if possi-
our land.
the voice
d of re-

ther white southerners did not tamely endure such attacks on an w believed to be essential to both their economy and society.

Whereas many —though certainly not all—southerners of the late eighteenth century had accepted and even promoted the gradual end of slavery, their descendants had a change of heart as they pursued their fortunes. Some were initially rather apologetic about their continued use of slaves, explaining that necessity was a strict taskmaster; but as the attacks mounted and widened to include criticism of southern culture, Christianity, and honor, southerners rallied to the defense of their peculiar institution and, by extension, their way of life. They also counterattacked by pointing out the ties between the regional economies and the problems in northern society.

From *The South Vindicated from the Treason and Fanaticism of the Northern Abolitionists.* (1836; New York: Negro Universities Press, 1969), pp. 66–69, 71–72, 81–84, 93–94, 98, 109–14, 180–81, 288–90. [Editorial insertions appear in square brackets—*Ed.*]

Condition of Slaves in the United States

The extent of slavery in the different slave-holding states of this union, may be seen by the following table, digested from the census of 1830.

	Whites.	Free col'd.	Slaves.	Total col'd.	Total.
Maryland,	291,093	52,912	102,873	155,820	446,913
Virginia	694,270	47,348	469,757	517,105	1,211,375
North Carolina,	472,843	19,543	245,601	265,444	737,987
South Carolina,	275,863	7,921	315,401	323,322	518,185
Georgia,	296,806	2,486	217,531	220,017	516,823
Alabama, { North,	81,173	422	44,130	44,552	125,725
{ South,	109,233	1,150	73,419	74,569	183,802
Mississippi,	114,795	569	25,091	25,660	140,455
Kentucky,	517,787	4,917	165,213	170,130	687,917
Louisiana,	89,291	16,710	109,588	126,298	215,589
Tennessee,	535,748	4,555	141,603	146,158	681,906
Missouri,	114,795	569	25,091	25,660	140,455
District of Columbia,	27,647	6,093	6,058	12,151	39,868
——— Missouri,					
——— Arkansaw,	25,671	141	4,576	4,717	30,388
——— Florida,	18,375	844	15,501	16,345	34,720

The states in which slavery prevails, have been distinguished for their affluence. Notwithstanding the policy of the national government has borne heavily upon the South, notwithstanding the occasional depression of her staples, and the proverbially unfortunate pecuniary habits of her citizens, that portion of the union may still be regarded as peculiarly favoured. The slave-labour of the South has thus far practically disproved the theories of the North; and demonstrated that the institution of slavery, whatever objections may be alleged against it, is not calculated to diminish the national wealth, or retard the national prosperity. It will be seen hereafter, that the South pays nearly one-third of the revenue of the government; and of the one hundred millions of dollars annual exports sent from the country, *nine-tenths are raised by the South.* Of the productiveness of slave-labour, who can, after a knowledge of these facts, affect a doubt? The North, as well as the South, is enriched by that labour; and should any disastrous occurrences disturb the institutions of the South, not only the whites and negroes of the slave-holding states would sink into poverty and suffering, but the decayed manufactures, shrunken commerce, and ruined prosperity of the North, would show how near and vital is the connexion of the different sections of our common country.

Every country must have its labourers, men who are willing to be directed by the mind and capital of others, and to undergo, in consideration of support, the physical toil requisite for the attainment of the goods of life. In the North, this labour is done by the poor; in the South, by the negro. In both, the labourer is forced to endure the privations of his condition in life. In the North, not only is his toil severe, but poverty and anxiety attend him in his humble path in life. His family must be sustained; his wife attended in sickness; his children supported in youth. His means are often inadequate to his wants. He is bowed down by the consciousness of inequality, and haunted by the fear of the prison. Incertitude and anxiety are with him each hour of his life; and when sickness or age steals upon him, it often finds him without resources or hope. Thus is he dogged through life by poverty, fear, humiliation and oppression (for the title of freeman does not protect the poor from oppression) and dies with the unhappy consciousness that for his children is reserved the same lot of wretchedness. The labourer of the South knows none of these evils. He is scarcely acquainted with the meaning of the word care. He never suffers from inordinate labour—he never sickens from unwholesome food. No fear of want disturbs his slumbers. Hunger and cold are strangers to him; and in sickness or age he knows that he has a protector and a friend able and willing to shield him from suffering. His pleasures are such as his nature enjoys, and are unrestricted. He enjoys all the privileges which his simple heart craves, and which are wholesome for him. Thus protected from all the other has to fear, and secured in the enjoyment of all he desires—he is as happy as circumstances can render him.

We are aware that certain pseudo philanthropists affect great concern for the benighted state of the negro, and condemn the enactments which, in some of the states, discourage his education. We may be permitted to remark, that, but for the intrusive and intriguing interference of pragmatical fanatics, such precautionary enactments would never have been necessary. When such foes are abroad, industrious in scattering the seeds of insurrection, it becomes necessary to close every avenue by which they may operate upon the slaves. It becomes necessary to check or turn aside the stream, which instead of flowing healthfully upon the negro, is polluted and poisoned by the abolitionists, and rendered the source of discontent and excitement. Education, thus perverted, would become equally dangerous to the master and the slave: and while fanaticism continue, its war upon the South, the measures of necessary precaution and defence must be continued.

The situation of the slave is, in every particular, incompatible with the cultivation of his mind. It would not only unfit him for his station in life, and prepare him for insurrection, but would be found wholly impracticable in the performance of the duties of a labourer. . . .

*   *   *

The slaves of the South are protected from abuse or wrong by liberal laws, justly administered. Improper punishment, under-feeding or overworking, are prevented by enactments, which, should any master incur their penalties, effectually vindicate the cause of justice. The laws protect the slave as fully as the white man: they go further, and, as the slave is supposed to be completely dependent upon his master, they require that he should be supplied with the necessaries and comforts of his station, and treated with unvarying kindness. In some of the states it has, indeed, been necessary to pass rigid police laws to protect the country from insurrections; but these laws remain a dead letter, until the interference of insidious and evil men excites and stirs up the slaves, and renders caution and severity indispensable for the safety of the master. When abolitionists make the application of these laws necessary, it is they, and they alone, who are the authors of the restraint placed upon the slaves.

*   *   *

It should be distinctly understood, that while the South acknowledges no accountability to any power under heaven for her course or sentiments on the subject of slavery, she freely avows her conviction of her right to hold the negroes in bondage, and her persuasion that the domestic slavery of that section of our country, is not a moral or political evil. These sentiments are the result of a full and general investigation of the subject: and were the people of the North equally well acquainted with it, they would probably subscribe to the opinions of the South. The original importation of the African is regarded by us as a moral wrong, because associated with acts of violence and cruelty, which nothing can justify. But of the justice, necessity, and advantages of the institution, as now entailed upon the South, we cannot, after an examination of the subject, feel a doubt. To the negro himself, we consider it no calamity. He is happier here than on the shores of his own degraded, savage, and most unhappy country—or rather the country of his fathers. He is happier, also, as a slave, than he could be as a freeman. . . .

The abolitionists deny the right of the people of the South, under any circumstances, to hold their fellow men in bondage. Upon what grounds is this position assumed? . . . It is their duty to prove that an institution, which has existed almost from the creation of the world to the present time, which has been encouraged by the best men of the most enlightened ages, and which has met the sanction of the Highest—has become, since these moral luminaries arose upon the world, guilty and calamitous. It will be found difficult to obtain a direct and rational answer to so plain a demand. They deal wholly in rhetorical flourishes; and if they reply at all, will tell us that the negro slave should not be a slave, because "he was created free." The fact is exactly the reverse. He comes into the world a slave. . . . But they tell us—"it is the will of God that he should be free." It is somewhat strange, that the will of God, in this point, has never been

expressed until it came from the oracular mouths of the abolitionists. Such manifestations of the divine will never took place among the Jews, where slavery was universal, nor among the nations to which the disciples of our Saviour preached—nations which were overrun with slaves. The will and desire of God is the welfare of the species. If negro slavery in the South be inconsistent with the happiness of the human family, the argument may apply: but if, as we confidently assert, its existence is not at war with the well-being of the greatest number of those interested, it is wholly justifiable. And if, to go one step further, the measures of abolition, projected by the fanatics, are calculated to result in consequences calamitous to the race, they are, notwithstanding their ostentatious and obtrusive piety, guilty, in the face of heaven and earth, of crimes of the darkest and deepest crimson.

The phrase which occurs in the Declaration of American Independence—"all men are created free and equal"—is perpetually upon the lips of the abolitionist, to sanction his violation of the rights of the South. The following extract from a speech, delivered at the late public meeting in Philadelphia, by Mr. J. R. Burden, formerly Speaker of the Senate, and an early, fervent, and fearless advocate of the rights of the slave-holder, admirably illustrates the perversion and desecration of that celebrated sentence of Jefferson.

"On the 4th of July, 1776, in the immediate neighbourhood of this place, the Declaration of Independence was made. From it the advocates of black emancipation take their text, 'All men are created free and equal,' &c. The construction they put upon it is unlimited. Let us examine the subject carefully. Did the framers of the Declaration, the representatives of the people, intend to declare that domestic slavery was incompatible with the freedom of the colonies? If they did not, their words are of no use in the defence of negro emancipation. If they did, *why were not all the slaves then emancipated?*

*   *   *

"The people of the United States, in order to form a more perfect union and secure the blessings of liberty, established the constitution in 1787. Domestic slavery still existed. No constitution could have been formed, had emancipation been persisted in. No union could have been perfected, if theorists and dreamers had determined to deprive the slave-holding states of their property.

"The constitution was adopted; the union was established; the world looked on it with admiration; yet it did not prohibit domestic slavery. So far from it, one of its main features, that of representation, was based upon it. Further, it declared that the *traffic should not be prohibited* by Congress prior to the year 1808. Perhaps the framers of the constitution thought that, by that period, the increased population of the blacks, would supersede the necessity of importation.

"We hear, in our day, much prating about liberty and philanthropy. The signers of the Declaration of Independence, and the framers of the constitution, were quite as conversant with the rights of man, as the best of us; they had as much philanthropy; and, if you will have it, as much Christianity as we profess to have. They possessed the confidence of the people, and deserved it; they passed through the times that tried men's souls; and, without the fear, favour, or affection of power, but in the spirit of virtue, wisdom, and patriotism, perfected a union as imperishable as the globe we inhabit. Shall it be said that such men put a blot and a stain upon our country?—So much for the text of emancipation!"

*   *   *

At the period of the advent of Christ, slavery prevailed throughout the world. In that portion of Asia, in which Christianity was first preached, it existed in its severest form, and to a very great extent. Had it been regarded as an evil, it could not have escaped the animadversion, not only of Christ, but of all the holy men who became, at his departure, the preachers of his faith. A subject so nearly connected with the happiness of the mass of mankind, could not have escaped, and did not escape, their attention: and, had it not possessed their approbation, must have been condemned. Instead of this, however, we find the institution sanc-

tioned, slaveholders admitted into the bosom of the church, and slaves admonished to humility and obedience. . . .

*   *   *

[The abolitionists'] application of the "golden rule," strips it of its golden attributes, and makes it sanction all that it was intended to condemn. They insist that the maxim, as interpreted by them, requires that the authority of the master over the slave should be immediately relinquished. We may add that, it requires further, that the authority of the father over his child, of the master over his apprentice, of the tutor over his pupil, should also be given up. It requires that the ruler should not control the private citizen; that the judge should not sentence the convict, nor the jailor confine the thief. Neither the child, servant, nor scholar—the citizen, convict, nor thief are dealt with according to their desires; nor as those, in whose power they are placed, would desire, if their relative position were reversed. That rule which would require that their wishes should be regarded as rights, and conceded accordingly, would abrogate all law, would place the innocent at the mercy of the guilty, involve right and wrong in indistinguishable confusion, and render society a chaotic and jarring mass of wretchedness and crime.

*   *   *

It will be admitted, that one of the first and most essential requisites in the formation of republican character is intelligence. Without that, patriotism is blind and inefficient. Without it, a virtuous people may be readily deceived and betrayed, and lose their freedom before they dream that it is in peril. The slave-holder has, in this particular, the inestimable advantage of leisure. Relieved from the labour required for actual support, he is enabled to direct his attention to public affairs; to investigate political subjects, and exercise his privileges understandingly. This result has been fully attained at the south. In no population in the world is the same time devoted to political investigations; and nowhere are the rights of man so fully canvassed and understood by the mass of the citizens.

While we acknowledge that some of the noblest spirits which our race has boasted have been linked, through life, with poverty, and while we are proud to be enabled to boast that in no country are the poor more pure and virtuous than in our own, yet we must also admit that poverty has its temptations. Men who enter into politics, as do many in the north, for the purpose of making money, are but dangerous agents. . . . The institution of slavery, by forming the character of the citizen on a more elevated standard, by lifting him above the necessities and temptations of poverty, secures, to the councils of the country, men for whom, to repeat the words of Ferguson, "danger has no terror, interest no means to corrupt."

There is one result which has been accomplished by slavery, and which no other cause has hitherto completely effected—it has introduced a complete equality among the whites. Professor Dew thus describes the difference which prevails in the north and south in this particular. "The menial and low offices being all performed by the blacks, there is at once taken away the greatest cause of distinction and separation of the ranks of society. The man at the north will not shake hands familiarly with his servant, and converse and laugh, and dine with him, no matter how honest and respectable he may be. But go to the south, and you will find that no white man feels such inferiority of rank as to be unworthy of association with those around him. Colour alone is here the badge of distinction, the true mark of aristocracy, and all who are white are equal in spite of variety of occupation." . . .

*   *   *

The abolitionists, as another auxiliary in the attainment of their ends, have succeeded in enlisting female societies in their support. They sew for the cause; collect money for it; and render it all the aid which extraordinary zeal, combined with activity and leisure, can yield. When the most profound intellects in our country regard this exciting and momentous subject with awe, we cannot, without regret, see ladies rushing boldly into it. They forget that it is a political subject of the most important

character: and, easily led away by the religious appeals of the abolitionists and the gentle and generous, but in this case misguided, promptings of their own nature, they unreflectingly lend their aid to designs, the tendency and consequence of which they are incapable of understanding. Politics is not the sphere in which the sex is either useful or honored; and their interference with subjects of this character, if sufficiently important to have *any* influence, must have an evil one. It is peculiarly to be regretted, that the false eloquence of the abolition preachers could ever have attained such influence over them, as to render them forgetful of the situation of their fair and gentle sisters of the South. Have they studied the history of St. Domingo; and are they prepared to let loose upon the refined and innocent ladies of the South, the savage negro, incapable of restraint, and wild with ungovernable passions? Are they aware of the present apprehensions of the females of the slave-holding states; and are they willing to add another to the fears that now haunt their pillows? It is impossible that fanatacism can so far have perverted their sympathies, or steeled the holier charities of their nature. The *possibility* of insurrection and the negroes' saturnalia of blood and lust, should appal every female bosom, and deter them from a scheme of *benevolence* so dubious in its character, and so fearful in its consequences.

*   *   *

If the scheme of emancipation were entitled to our approbation and support, the manner in which it is urged, would be sufficient to excite just and general suspicion and alarm. A political cause that comes before the people, sustained on the one side by English influence, and on the other by an aspiring priesthood—may well be regarded, by republicans, with distrust and terror.

It is not difficult to divine the motives which induce Great Britain to encourage the incendiary efforts of the abolitionists. . . . Our ruined commerce and manufactures, would afford Great Britain a new and boundless source of affluence; while the destruction of a former foe and a present rival, would be regarded with feelings of malicious satisfaction. Many of her people also regard the example of republicanism in this country, as dangerous to the existing institutions of Europe, and would rejoice to see the fabric of our Union torn to pieces, and our land bleeding and groaning beneath the parricidal arms of her own infuriated children.

Such, we have every reason to believe, are the motives that have induced England to send her emissaries into this country, to aid the incendiary schemes of the emancipationists, to volunteer and contribute pecuniary support, in forwarding the same cause; and in short, to exercise every means in her power, to excite division and insurrection, and consummate the infamy of our people, and the downfall of our country. It is true, that she avows only motives of philanthropy. But why is that philanthropy directed hither? Why does it not turn to their brethren, the oppressed and starving people of Ireland, whose condition is so much worse than that of our slaves? Why does it overlook the perishing thousands, in the manufactories in England? Why is it not turned to the almost countless millions of slaves who groan beneath English tyranny in India? . . . It remains to be seen, whether British money will be allowed openly to circulate, in maintaining an opposition to our Union and our Constitution; and whether English emissaries will be permitted to go from state to state, preaching treason against those sacred rights, which were wrested from English tyranny, and established at the price of hundreds of thousands of American lives.

*   *   *

REVIEW QUESTIONS

1. What did the author offer as proof that man had the right "to hold his fellow-man in bondage"?
2. How could the author argue that the slave of the South was better off than the laborer of the North?
3. What were his arguments against educating slaves?
4. How effective was the argument that slavery had allowed southerners—rather than northerners—to embody more fully the virtues of the republic?
5. Was the author against the methods as well as the goal of abolitionism? Why?

LYDIA MARIA CHILD

FROM Prejudices Against People of Color (1836)

As slavery proponents shrewdly pointed out, many Americans, including some abolitionists, were racist. Given that, they asked their opponents whether freedom for the slaves was to mean equality. It was a tough question, for it required people to think beyond abolition itself, and to consider how they defined humanity. Child, Douglass, and others in the antislavery movement acknowledged the truth of the charge and the importance of the question. Child and others like her realized that they had a dual mission: to eradicate the spirit as well as the form of slavery. Some, including Douglass, hoped that abolition of the institution of slavery would erase the attitudes that had maintained it, for they believed slavery had created the prejudice against people of color. Others argued that differences between races—a perception that

*leads to racism—created slavery, and thus the solution would not be as simple
as abolition. These issues of cause, effect, and cure entangled reformers for
decades.*

From Lydia Maria Child, *An Appeal in Favor of that Class of Americans called Africans* (1836
edition; New York: Arno Press and The New York Times, 1968), pp. 195–99, 206–207.

WHILE we bestow our earnest disapprobation on the system of slavery, let us not
flatter ourselves that we are in reality any
better than our brethren of the South. Thanks to
our soil and climate, and the early exertions of the
excellent Society of Friends, the *form* of slavery
does not exist among us; but the very *spirit* of the
hateful and mischievous thing is here in all its
strength. The manner in which we use what power
we have, gives us ample reason to be grateful that
the nature of our institutions does not intrust us
with more. Our prejudice against colored people is
even more inveterate than it is at the South. The
planter is often attached to his negroes, and lav-
ishes caresses and kind words upon them, as he
would on a favorite hound: but our cold-hearted,
ignoble prejudice admits of no exception—no intermission.

The Southerners have long continued habit,
apparent interest and dreaded danger, to palliate
the wrong they do; but we stand without excuse.
They tell us that Northern ships and Northern capital have been engaged in this wicked business; and
the reproach is true. Several fortunes in this city
have been made by the sale of negro blood. If these
criminal transactions are still carried on, they are
done in silence and secrecy, because public opinion
has made them disgraceful. But if the free States
wished to cherish the system of slavery for ever,
they could not take a more direct course than they
now do. Those who are kind and liberal on all
other subjects, unite with the selfish and the proud
in their unrelenting efforts to keep the colored
population in the lowest state of degradation; and
the influence they unconsciously exert over children early infuses into their innocent minds the
same strong feelings of contempt.

The intelligent and well-informed have the
least share of this prejudice; and when their minds
can be brought to reflect upon it, I have generally
observed that they soon cease to have any at all. But
such a general apathy prevails and the subject is so
seldom brought into view, that few are really aware
how oppressively the influence of society is made
to bear upon this injured class of the community.
. . . In order that my readers may not be ignorant
of the extent of this tyrannical prejudice, I will as
briefly as possible state the evidence, and leave
them to judge of it, as their hearts and consciences
may dictate.

In the first place, an unjust law exists in this
Commonwealth, by which marriages between persons of different color is pronounced illegal. . . . In
the first place, the government ought not to be invested with power to control the affections, any
more than the consciences of citizens. A man has
at least as good a right to choose his wife, as he has
to choose his religion. His taste may not suit his
neighbors; but so long as his deportment is correct,
they have no right to interfere with his concerns. In
the second place, this law is a *useless* disgrace to
Massachusetts. Under existing circumstances, none
but those whose condition in life is too low to be
much affected by public opinion, will form such alliances; and they, when they choose to do so, *will*
make such marriages, in spite of the law. I know
two or three instances where women of the laboring class have been united to reputable, industrious colored men. These husbands regularly bring
home their wages, and are kind to their families. If
by some of the odd chances, which not unfrequently occur in the world, their wives should become heirs to any property, the children may be
wronged out of it, because the law pronounces
them illegitimate. And while this injustice exists
with regard to *honest*, industrious individuals, who

are merely guilty of differing from us in a matter of taste, neither the legislation nor customs of slaveholding States exert their influence against *immoral* connexions.

*   *   *

There is among the colored people an increasing desire for information, and laudable ambition to be respectable in manners and appearance. Are we not foolish as well as sinful, in trying to repress a tendency so salutary to themselves, and so beneficial to the community? Several individuals of this class are very desirous to have persons of their own color qualified to teach something more than mere reading and writing. But in the public schools, colored children are subject to many discouragements and difficulties; and into the private schools they cannot gain admission. . . .

In a town adjoining Boston, a well behaved colored boy was kept out of the public school more than a year, by vote of the trustees. His mother, having some information herself, knew the importance of knowledge, and was anxious to obtain it for her family. She wrote repeatedly and urgently; and the schoolmaster himself told me that the correctness of her spelling, and the neatness of her hand-writing, formed a curious contrast with the notes he received from many white parents. At last, this spirited woman appeared before the committee, and reminded them that her husband, having for many years paid taxes as a citizen, had a right to the privileges of a citizen; and if her claim were refused, or longer postponed, she declared her determination to seek justice from a higher source. The trustees were, of course, obliged to yield to the equality of the laws, with the best grace they could. The boy was admitted, and made good progress in his studies. Had his mother been too ignorant to know her rights, or too abject to demand them, the lad would have had a fair chance to get a living out of the State as the occupant of a workhouse, or penitentiary.

*   *   *

Will any candid person tell me why respectable colored people should not be allowed to make use of public conveyances, open to all who are able and willing to pay for the privilege? Those who enter a vessel, or a stage-coach, cannot expect to select their companions. If they can afford to take a carriage or boat for themselves, then, and then only, they have a right to be exclusive. I was lately talking with a young gentleman on this subject, who professed to have no prejudice against colored people, except so far as they were ignorant and vulgar; but still he could not tolerate the idea of allowing them to enter stages and steam-boats. "Yet, you allow the same privilege to vulgar and ignorant white men, without a murmur," I replied; "Pray give a good republican reason why a respectable colored citizen should be less favored." For want of a better argument, he said—(pardon me, fastidious reader)—he implied that the presence of colored persons was less agreeable than Otto of Rose, or Eau de Cologne; and this distinction, he urged was made by God himself. I answered, "Whoever takes his chance in a public vehicle, is liable to meet with uncleanly white passengers, whose breath may be redolent with the fumes of American cigars, or American gin. Neither of these articles have a fragrance peculiarly agreeable to nerves of delicate organization. Allowing your argument double the weight it deserves, it is utter nonsense to pretend that the inconvenience in the case I have supposed is not infinitely greater. But what is more to the point, do you dine in a fashionable hotel, do you sail in a fashionable steam-boat, do you sup at a fashionable house, without having negro servants behind your chair. Would they be any more disagreeable, as *passengers* seated in the corner of a stage, or a steam-boat, than as *waiters* in such immediate attendance upon your person?"

Stage-drivers are very much perplexed when they attempt to vindicate the present tyrannical customs; and they usually give up the point, by saying they themselves have no prejudice against colored people—they are merely afraid of the public. But stage-drivers should remember that in a popular government, they, in common with every other citizen, form a part and portion of the dreaded public.

The gold was never coined for which I would barter my individual freedom of acting and thinking upon any subject, or knowingly interfere with the rights of the meanest human being. The only true courage is that which impels us to do right without regard to consequences. To fear a populace is as servile as to fear an emperor. . . .

*   *   *

The state of public feeling not only makes it difficult for the Africans to obtain information, but it prevents them from making profitable use of what knowledge they have. A colored man, however intelligent, is not allowed to pursue any business more lucrative than that of a barber, a shoe-black, or a waiter. These, and all other employments, are truly respectable, whenever the duties connected with them are faithfully performed; but it is unjust that a man should, on account of his complexion, be prevented from performing more elevated uses in society. Every citizen ought to have a fair chance to try his fortune in any line of business, which he thinks he has ability to transact. Why should not colored men be employed in the manufactories of various kinds? If their ignorance is an objection, let them be enlightened, as speedily as possible. If their moral character is not sufficiently pure, remove the pressure of public scorn, and thus supply them with motives for being respectable.

All this can be done. It merely requires an earnest wish to overcome a prejudice, which has "grown with our growth and strengthened with our strength," but which is in fact opposed to the spirit of our religion, and contrary to the instinctive good feelings of our nature. When examined by the clear light of reason, it disappears. Prejudices of all kinds have their strongest holds in the minds of the vulgar and the ignorant. In a community so enlightened as our own, they must gradually melt away under the influence of public discussion. . . .

*   *   *

REVIEW QUESTIONS

1. What did Child mean when she wrote of the spirit of slavery? Do you agree with her definition?
2. How did the spirit of slavery manifest itself in the North?
3. What kind of social system did northerners appear to be implementing?
4. In arguing against racial bias, does Child reveal the existence of other biases?

16 ✒ THE CRISIS OF UNION

During the 1850s sectional interests and identities battered national ones. There was a contentiousness that threatened to tear the country apart, so many American politicians, reflecting the concerns of their constituents, proposed compromises to divert, if not stop, the conflicts. Unfortunately for the nation, however, compromise did not work as it had in the past: it now acted as a catalyst to crisis. Compromise worked when the parties involved were each willing to relinquish some demands to gain others, and when there was an underlying agreement on what issues were most important. Such a consensus had earlier existed when the majority of all the states' citizens held that maintaining the union took precedence over regional interests, but when that consensus crumbled there was but a weak foundation for a common, long-lasting solution.

The crisis had been building for some time. A few contemporaries traced its origins to the constitutional compromises, while others thought the first true signs of danger appeared in the nullification controversy of the 1830s. Certainly, many acknowledged that tempers had been roiling for quite a while as people argued over individuals' and states' rights—issues raised by the institution of slavery. Americans contested a person's right to property versus an individual's right to him—or herself. They debated whether the federal government could limit people's choices in the territories—as in the expansion of slavery—in ways it could not in the states. The Missouri Compromise had been an early effort to cap this volcano of public sentiment, the gag rule in Congress another, but as these measures were rescinded and new ones failed, Americans grappled with the possibility that there would be an eruption that could destroy the union.

Secession was not a new concept created in the 1850s, but receptivity to the idea had grown over the previous decades. In December 1844, for example, James Henry Hammond, a South Carolina planter and politician, wrote in his diary about his state's resolutions that denounced the repeal of the gag rule "as a flagrant outrage infringing on the Fed[eral] Compact" and which declared that congressional legislation restricting slavery would amount to a dissolution of the Union. Hammond believed the resolutions more openly threatened separation than any ever passed—harking back to the nullification controversy—before. He went on to pen, "Nothing in my opinion but Dis-union now or very shortly can [save us]. Those who are for delaying this event for the sake of peace are taking the surest steps to render war inevitable. If passions are excited and the thing is done in extreme heat, it will be done in blood." Almost six years later, in May 1850, he criticized Clay's compromise as presupposing "a desire on both sides to be at peace, when such is not the fact and, if it were, no compromise would be necessary." He thought the compromise would weaken the South while only temporarily suspending abolition agitation. He wanted the South to unite in its resistance to any and all limits on its rights and be ready for action. It took the South ten years.

Over that decade politicians tried various measures to stop the fissures that had appeared from becoming so wide and so deep that they split the nation apart. The first of these was the Compromise of 1850. Questions about the establishment of states and the expansion of slavery in the country's vast territories rocked the nation. While a few old masters, such as John C. Calhoun, and their accolytes, one being Jefferson Davis of Mississippi, argued that the only way to halt the widening schism was through an acknowledgement of southern rights, others, such as Henry Clay and Daniel Webster, sought to mend the rift through concessions to both sides of the divide. When Clay's package deal was defeated, a rising young leader in the Democratic Party, Stephen A. Douglas of Illinois, took on the task of getting the resolutions passed. He broke down Clay's program into five measures so that the lack of consensus on the sum of these issues would not prevent majorities from voting for each of them. Douglas's strategy worked: Congress admitted California as a free state, set the Texas state boundary and established the New Mexico territory, set up the Utah territory with (as in the New Mexico case) the issue of slavery left to the territorial legislatures, passed a new Fugitive Slave Act, and abolished the slave trade in the District of Columbia.

Most Americans accepted the compromise with relief if not joy. That relief was short-lived, for the question of slavery in the territories—and by extension, in the states—came up again when Douglas sought to organize the Nebraska territory and build a transcontinental railroad through it. To get southerners to vote for his bill, Douglas accommodated them on the slavery issue. He made "popular sovereignty," which enabled the people of the territories and new states to decide for themselves whether to include slavery, a part of his bill, and then supported the repeal of the Missouri Compromise's exclusion of slavery north of 36° 30'. He also agreed to organize two territories: Kansas and Nebraska. Douglas got what he wanted, but at great personal and national expense. He ruined his chances for the presidency and further undermined the union.

The controversy over Kansas became the conflict in Kansas, as settlers and their supporters battled one another over the inclusion or exclusion of slavery in their territory. As Kansans bled, other Americans continued to exchange verbal punches over the nation's great problem. They fought it out within and between the political parties. They argued over it within the judiciary. And they kept electing different presidents in their search for strong executive guidance. One thing followed another so rapidly that the union could not recover its equilibrium between blows. It reeled and staggered into war.

RALPH WALDO EMERSON

The Fugitive Slave Law (1854)

Many activists who had pushed for a variety of reforms in the 1830s and 1840s started to concentrate more on the slavery issue by the 1850s. Horace Mann, that champion of public schools, declared in 1848 that "before a man can be educated, he must be a free man." To work to that end, he shut down his Common School Journal *and took a seat in Congress. Ralph Waldo Emerson preferred intellectual to political activism, but the passage of the Fugitive Slave Law as part of the Compromise of 1850 and Douglas's Kansas-Nebraska Act in 1854 roused him to take a public stand. He urged his listeners and readers to examine their beliefs—which he trusted were against slavery and for liberty—and then act to ensure that political compromises did not undermine them.*

From Ralph Waldo Emerson, *The Selected Writings of Ralph Waldo Emerson*, ed. Brooks Atkinson (1940; New York: The Modern Library, Random House, 1950), pp. 861–76.

I DO not often speak to public questions—they are odious and hurtful, and it seems like meddling or leaving your work. . . . And then I see what havoc it makes with any good mind, a dissipated philanthropy. The one thing not to be forgiven to intellectual persons is, not to know their own task, or to take their ideas from others. . . .

My own habitual view is to the well-being of students or scholars. And it is only when the public event affects them, that it very seriously touches me. And what I have to say is to them. For every man speaks mainly to a class whom he works with and more or less fully represents. . . . And yet, when

I say the class of scholars or students—that is a class which comprises in some sort all mankind, comprises every man in the best hours of his life; and in these days not only virtually but actually. For who are the readers and thinkers of 1854? Owing to the silent revolution which the newspaper has wrought, this class has come in this country to take in all classes. Look into the morning trains which, from every suburb, carry the business men into the city to their shops, counting-rooms, work-yards and warehouses. With them enters the car—the newsboy, that humble priest of politics, finance, philosophy, and religion. He unfolds his magical sheets—twopence a head his bread of knowledge costs—and instantly the entire rectangular assembly, fresh from their breakfast, are bending as one man to their second breakfast. There is, no doubt, chaff enough in what he brings; but there is fact, thought, and wisdom in the crude mass, from all regions of the world.

I have lived all my life without suffering any known inconvenience from American Slavery. I never saw it; I never heard the whip; I never felt the check on my free speech and action, until, the other day, when Mr. Webster, by his personal influence, brought the Fugitive Slave Law on the country. I say Mr. Webster, for though the Bill was not his, it is yet notorious that he was the life and soul of it, that he gave it all he had: it cost him his life, and under the shadow of his great name inferior men sheltered themselves, threw their ballots for it and made the law. I say inferior men. There were all sorts of what are called brilliant men, accomplished men, men of high station, a President of the United States, Senators, men of eloquent speech, but men without self-respect, without character, and it was strange to see that office, age, fame, talent, even a repute for honesty, all count for nothing. They had no opinions, they had no memory for what they had been saying like the Lord's Prayer all their lifetime: they were only looking to what their great Captain did: if he jumped, they jumped, if he stood on his head, they did. In ordinary, the supposed sense of their district and State is their guide, and that holds them to the part of liberty and justice. But it is always a little difficult to decipher what this public sense is; and when a great man comes who knots up into himself the opinions and wishes of the people, it is so much easier to follow him as an exponent of this. He too is responsible; they will not be. It will always suffice to say—"I followed him."

*   *   *

In what I have to say of Mr. Webster I do not confound him with vulgar politicians before or since. There is always base ambition enough, men who calculate on the immense ignorance of the masses; . . . There are those too who have power

and inspiration only to do ill. Their talent or their faculty deserts them when they undertake anything right. Mr. Webster had a natural ascendancy of aspect and carriage which distinguished him over all his contemporaries. His countenance, his figure, and his manners were all in so grand a style, that he was, without effort, as superior to his most eminent rivals as they were to the humblest; . . .

*   *   *

The history of this country has given a disastrous importance to the defects of this great man's mind. Whether evil influences and the corruption of politics, or whether original infirmity, it was the misfortune of his country that with this large understanding he had not what is better than intellect, and the source of its health. It is a law of our nature that great thoughts come from the heart. If his moral sensibility had been proportioned to the force of his understanding, what limits could have been set to his genius and beneficent power? But he wanted that deep source of inspiration. . . .

Four years ago to-night, on one of those high critical moments in history when great issues are determined, when the powers of right and wrong are mustered for conflict, and it lies with one man to give a casting vote—Mr. Webster, most unexpectedly, threw his whole weight on the side of Slavery, and caused by his personal and official authority the passage of the Fugitive Slave Bill.

It is remarked of the Americans that they value dexterity too much, and honor too little; that they think they praise a man more by saying that he is "smart" than by saying that he is right. Whether the defect be national or not, it is the defect and calamity of Mr. Webster; and it is so far true of his countrymen, namely, that the appeal is sure to be made to his physical and mental ability when his character is assailed. . . .

*   *   *

But the question which History will ask is broader. In the final hour, when he was forced by the peremptory necessity of the closing armies to take a side—did he take the part of great principles, the side of humanity and justice, or the side of abuse and oppression and chaos?

Mr. Webster decided for Slavery, and that, when the aspect of the institution was no longer doubtful, no longer feeble and apologetic and proposing soon to end itself, but when it was strong, aggressive, and threatening an illimitable increase. He listened to State reasons and hopes, and left, with much complacency we are told, the testament of his speech to the astonished State of Massachusetts, *vera pro gratis*; a ghastly result of all those years of experience in affairs, this, that there was nothing better for the foremost American man to tell his countrymen than that Slavery was now at that strength that they must beat down their conscience and become kidnappers for it.

*   *   *

Here was the question, Are you for man and for the good of man; or are you for the hurt and harm of man? It was the question whether man shall be treated as leather? Whether the negro shall be, as the Indians were in Spanish America, a piece of money? Whether this system, which is a kind of mill or factory for converting men into monkeys, shall be upheld and enlarged? And Mr. Webster and the country went for the application to these poor men of quadruped law.

People were expecting a totally different course from Mr. Webster. If any man had in that hour possessed the weight with the country which he had acquired, he could have brought the whole country to its senses. But not a moment's pause was allowed. Angry parties went from bad to worse, and the decision of Webster was accompanied with everything offensive to freedom and good morals. . . . He told the people at Boston "they must conquer their prejudices"; that "agitation of the subject of Slavery must be suppressed." . . .

I said I had never in my life up to this time suffered from the Slave Institution. Slavery in Virginia or Carolina was like Slavery in Africa or the Feejees, for me. There was an old fugitive law, but it had become, or was fast becoming, a dead letter, and, by the genius and laws of Massachusetts, inoperative. The new Bill made it operative, required

me to hunt slaves, and it found citizens in Massachusetts willing to act as judges and captors. Moreover, it discloses the secret of the new times, that Slavery was no longer mendicant, but was become aggressive and dangerous.

The way in which the country was dragged to consent to this, and the disastrous defection (on the miserable cry of Union) of the men of letters, of the colleges, of educated men, nay, of some preachers of religion—was the darkest passage in the history. It showed that our prosperity had hurt us, and that we could not be shocked by crime. It showed that the old religion and the sense of the right had faded and gone out; that while we reckoned ourselves a highly cultivated nation, our bellies had run away with our brains, and the principles of culture and progress did not exist.

For I suppose that liberty is an accurate index, in men and nations, of general progress. The theory of personal liberty must always appeal to the most refined communities and to the men of the rarest perception and of delicate moral sense. For there are rights which rest on the finest sense of justice and, with every degree of civility, it will be more truly felt and defined. A barbarous tribe of good stock will, by means of their best heads, secure substantial liberty. But where there is any weakness in a race, and it becomes in a degree matter of concession and protection from their stronger neighbors, the incompatibility and offensiveness of the wrong will of course be most evident to the most cultivated. For it is—is it not?—the essence of courtesy, of politeness, of religion, of love, to prefer another, to postpone oneself, to protect another from oneself. That is the distinction of the gentleman, to defend the weak and redress the injured, as it is of the savage and the brutal to usurp and use others.

In Massachusetts, as we all know, there has always existed a predominant conservative spirit. We have more money and value of every kind than other people, and wish to keep them. The plea on which freedom was resisted was Union. I went to certain serious men, who had a little more reason than the rest, and inquired why they took this part? They answered that they had no confidence in their strength to resist the Democratic party; . . . and they stood stiffly on conservatism, and as near to monarchy as they could, only to moderate the velocity with which the car was running down the precipice. In short, their theory was despair; the Whig wisdom was only reprieve, a waiting to be last devoured. They side with Carolina, or with Arkansas, only to make a show of Whig strength, wherewith to resist a little longer this general ruin.

I have a respect for conservatism. I know how deeply founded it is in our nature, and how idle are all attempts to shake ourselves free from it. We are all conservatives, half Whig, half Democrat, in our essences: and might as well try to jump out of our skins as to escape from our Whiggery. There are two forces in Nature, by whose antagonism we exist; the power of Fate, Fortune, the laws of the world, the order of things, or however else we choose to phrase it, the material necessities, on the one hand—and Will or Duty or Freedom on the other.

May and Must, and the sense of right and duty, on the one hand, and the material necessities on the other: May and Must. In vulgar politics the Whig goes for what has been, for the old necessities—the Musts. The reformer goes for the Better, for the ideal good, for the Mays. But each of these parties must of necessity take in, in some measure, the principles of the other. Each wishes to cover the whole ground; to hold fast *and* to advance. Only, one lays the emphasis on keeping, and the other on advancing. I too think the *musts* are a safe company to follow, and even agreeable. But if we are Whigs, let us be Whigs of nature and science, and so for all the necessities. Let us know that, over and above all the *musts* of poverty and appetite, is the instinct of man to rise, and the instinct to love and help his brother.

* * *

The events of this month are teaching one thing plain and clear, the worthlessness of good tools to bad workmen; that official papers are of no use; resolutions of public meetings, platforms of conventions, no, nor laws, nor constitutions, any more. These are all declaratory of the will of the moment, and are passed with more levity and on grounds far less honorable than ordinary business transactions of the street.

You relied on the constitution. It has not the word *slave* in it; and very good argument has shown that it would not warrant the crimes that are done under it; that, with provisions so vague for an object not named, and which could not be availed of to claim a barrel of sugar or a barrel of corn, the robbing of a man and of all his posterity is effected. You relied on the Supreme Court. The law was right, excellent law for the lambs. But what if unhappily the judges were chosen from the wolves, and give to all the law a wolfish interpretation? You relied on the Missouri Compromise. That is ridden over. You relied on State sovereignty in the Free States to protect their citizens. They are driven with contempt out of the courts and out of the territory of the Slave States—if they are so happy as to get out with their lives—and now you relied on these dismal guaranties infamously made in 1850; and, before the body of Webster is yet crumbled, it is found that they have crumbled. This eternal monument of his fame and of the Union is rotten in four years. They are no guaranty to the free states. They are a guaranty to the slave states that, as they have hitherto met with no repulse, they shall meet with none.

I fear there is no reliance to be put on any kind or form of covenant, no, not on sacred forms, none on churches, none on bibles. For one would have said that a Christian would not keep slaves: but the Christians keep slaves. Of course they will not dare to read the Bible? Won't they? They quote the Bible, quote Paul, quote Christ, to justify slavery. If slavery is good, then is lying, theft, arson, homicide, each and all good, and to be maintained by Union societies.

These things show that no forms, neither constitutions, nor laws, nor covenants, nor churches, nor bibles, are of any use in themselves. The Devil nestles comfortably into them all. There is no help but in the head and heart and hamstrings of a man. Covenants are of no use without honest men to keep them; laws of none but with loyal citizens to obey them. . . . To make good the cause of Freedom, you must draw off from all foolish trust in others. You must be citadels and warriors yourselves, declarations of Independence, the charter, the battle and the victory. . . . And no man has a right to hope that the laws of New York will defend him from the contamination of slaves another day until he has made up his mind that he will not owe his protection to the laws of New York, but to his own sense and spirit. Then he protects New York. He only who is able to stand alone is qualified for society. And that I understand to be the end for which a soul exists in this world—to be himself the counterbalance of all falsehood and all wrong. . . .

*   *   *

Whenever a man has come to this mind, that there is no Church for him but his believing prayer; no Constitution but his dealing well and justly with his neighbor; no liberty but his invincible will to do right—then certain aids and allies will promptly appear: for the constitution of the Universe is on his side. It is of no use to vote down gravitation of morals. What is useful will last, whilst that which is hurtful to the world will sink beneath all the opposing forces which it must exasperate. . . . A man who commits a crime defeats the end of his existence. He was created for benefit, and he exists for harm; and as well-doing makes power and wisdom, ill-doing takes them away. A man who steals another man's labor steals away his own faculties; his integrity, his humanity is flowing away from him. The habit of oppression cuts out the moral eyes, and, though the intellect goes on simulating the moral as before, its sanity is gradually destroyed. . . .

I suppose in general this is allowed, that if you have a nice question of right and wrong, you would not go with it to Louis Napoleon, or to a political hack, or to a slave-driver. The habit of mind of traders in power would not be esteemed favorable to delicate moral perception. American slavery affords no exception to this rule. No excess of good nature or of tenderness in individuals has been able to give a new character to the system, to tear down the whipping-house. . . .

Slavery is disheartening; but Nature is not so helpless but it can rid itself at last of every wrong.

But the spasms of Nature are centuries and ages, and will tax the faith of short-lived men. Slowly, slowly the Avenger comes, but comes surely. The proverbs of the nations affirm these delays, but affirm the arrival. They say, "God may consent, but not forever. . . ."

These delays, you see them now in the temper of the times. The national spirit in this country is so drowsy, preoccupied with interest, deaf to principle. . . .

To faint hearts the times offer no invitation, and torpor exists here throughout the active classes on the subject of domestic slavery and its appalling aggressions. Yes, that is the stern edict of Providence, that liberty shall be no hasty fruit, but that event on event, population on population, age on age, shall cast itself into the opposite scale, and not until liberty has slowly accumulated weight enough to countervail and preponderate against all this, can the sufficient recoil come. All the great cities, all the refined circles, all the statesmen, Guizot, Palmerston, Webster, Calhoun, are sure to be found befriending liberty with their words, and crushing it with their votes. Liberty is never cheap. It is made difficult, because freedom is the accomplishment and perfectness of man. . . .

Whilst the inconsistency of slavery with the principles on which the world is built guarantees its downfall, I own that the patience it requires is almost too sublime for mortals, and seems to demand of us more than mere hoping. And when one sees how fast the rot spreads—it is growing serious—I think we demand of superior men that they be superior in this—that the mind and the virtue shall give their verdict in their day, and accelerate so far the progress of civilization. Possession is sure to throw its stupid strength for existing power, and appetite and ambition will go for that. Let the aid of virtue, intelligence and education be cast where they rightfully belong. They are organically ours. Let them be loyal to their own. I wish to see the instructed class here know their own flag, and not fire on their comrades. We should not forgive the clergy for taking on every issue the immoral side; nor the Bench, if it put itself on the side of the culprit; nor the Government, if it sustain the mob against the law.

It is a potent support and ally to a brave man standing single, or with a few, for the right, and out-voted and ostracized, to know that better men in other parts of the country appreciate the service and will rightly report him to his own and the next age. Without this assurance, he will sooner sink. He may well say, 'If my countrymen do not care to be defended, I too will decline the controversy, from which I only reap invectives and hatred.' Yet the lovers of liberty may with reason tax the coldness and indifferentism of scholars and literary men. They are lovers of liberty in Greece and Rome and in the English Commonwealth, but they are luke-warm lovers of the liberty of America in 1854. The universities are not, as in Hobbes's time, "the core of rebellion," no, but the seat of inertness. They have forgotten their allegiance to the Muse, and grown worldly and political. . . .

But I put it to every noble and generous spirit, to every poetic, every heroic, every religious heart, that not so is our learning, our education, our poetry, our worship to be declared. Liberty is aggressive, Liberty is the Crusade of all brave and conscientious men, the Epic Poetry, the new religion, the chivalry of all gentlemen. This is the oppressed Lady whom true knights on their oath and honor must rescue and save.

Now at last we are disenchanted and shall have no more false hopes. I respect the Anti-Slavery Society. It is the Cassandra that has foretold all that has befallen, fact for fact, years ago: foretold all, and no man laid it to heart. It seemed, as the Turks say, "Fate makes that a man should not believe his own eyes." But the Fugitive Law did much to unglue the eyes of men, and now the Nebraska Bill leaves us staring. The Anti-Slavery Society will add many members this year. The Whig Party will join it; the Democrats will join it. The population of the free states will join it. I doubt not, at last, the slave states will join it. But be that sooner or later, and whoever comes or stays away, I hope we have reached the end of our unbelief, have come to a belief that there is a divine Providence in the world, which will not save us but through our own cooperation.

REVIEW QUESTIONS

1. Daniel Webster was a renowned statesman who had worked to protect and strengthen the Union throughout his career. Emerson acknowledged that but condemned what Webster did in 1850. Why?

2. In censuring Webster and his adherents, Emerson provided a critique of leaders and followers and even, in reference to himself, those who had been somewhat disengaged in the growing crisis. What faults did Emerson see in both politicians and citizens?

3. What did Emerson want people to do? What did he want them to be?

4. How did sentiments such as Emerson's add to the crisis?

THE KNOW-NOTHING PARTY

The American Platform (1856)

In 1856 the nation's political parties met in conventions to decide on their platforms and presidential candidates. The delegates asserted their principles by reflecting upon the country's problems and presented their policies as solutions to its turmoil. The two major contenders in this campaign were the Democratic and Republican parties, but, reflecting national divisions, two other groups contested their priorities and programs. The Whig Party, which had been born in opposition to the Jacksonian Democratic Party and which was now dying due to the mortal wounds of sectional strife, offered more of a lament than a platform. The Whigs offered "no new principles" and "no new platform"; instead they declared that there was, "as a fundamental article of political faith, an absolute necessity for avoiding geographical parties. The danger, so clearly discerned by the Father of his Country, has now become fearfully apparent in the agitation now convulsing the nation, and must be arrested at once if we would preserve our constitution and our Union from dismemberment, and the name of America from being blotted out from the family of civilized nations."

The American or Know-Nothing Party was more vigorous in its assault on the nation's problems. It also took a different approach to them, for it did not think that the major threat to the American union and culture was slavery. When the party's delegates met in Philadelphia in February, they drafted a platform that proclaimed "Americans must rule America." While appealing to nativists throughout the country, they also specifically took aim at southern votes. Finally, they chose ex-President Millard Fillmore as their presidential candidate and Andrew Jackson Donelson of Tennessee as their vice-presidential nominee.

From Thomas V. Cooper, and Hector T. Fenton, *American Politics from the Beginning to Date* (Chicago: Charles R. Brodix, 1882), pp. 35–36.

1. An humble acknowledgment to the Supreme Being for His protecting care vouchsafed to our fathers in their successful revolutionary struggle, and hitherto manifested to us, their descendants, in the preservation of the liberties, the independence, and the union of these states.

2. The perpetuation of the Federal Union and constitution, as the palladium of our civil and religious liberties, and the only sure bulwarks of American independence.

3. *Americans must rule America;* and to this end *native*-born citizens should be selected for all state, federal, and municipal offices of government employment, in preference to all others. *Nevertheless,*

4. Persons born of American parents residing temporarily abroad, should be entitled to all the rights of native-born citizens.

5. No person should be selected for political station (whether of native or foreign birth), who recognizes any allegiance or obligation of any de-

scription to any foreign prince, potentate, or power, or who refuses to recognize the federal and state constitutions (each within its sphere) as paramount to all other laws, as rules of political action.

6. The unequaled recognition and maintenance of the reserved rights of the several states, and the cultivation of harmony and fraternal good-will between the citizens of the several states, and, to this end, non-interference by Congress with questions appertaining solely to the individual states, and non-intervention by each state with the affairs of any other state.

7. The recognition of the right of native-born and naturalized citizens of the United States, permanently residing in any territory thereof, to frame their constitution and laws, and to regulate their domestic and social affairs in their own mode, subject only to the provisions of the federal constitution, with the privilege of admission into the Union whenever they have the requisite population for one Representative in Congress: *Provided, always*, that none but those who are citizens of the United States under the constitution and laws thereof, and who have a fixed residence in any such territory, ought to participate in the formation of the constitution or in the enactment of laws for said territory or state.

8. An enforcement of the principles that no state or territory ought to admit others than citizens to the right of suffrage or of holding political offices of the United States.

9. A change in the laws of naturalization, making a continued residence of twenty-one years, of all not heretofore provided for, an indispensable requisite for citizenship hereafter, and excluding all paupers and persons convicted of crime from landing upon our shores; but no interference with the vested rights of foreigners.

10. Opposition to any union between church and state; no interference with religious faith or worship; and no test-oaths for office.

11. Free and thorough investigation into any and all alleged abuses of public functionaries, and a strict economy in public expenditures.

12. The maintenance and enforcement of all laws constitutionally enacted, until said laws shall be repealed, or shall be declared null and void by competent judicial authority.

13. Opposition to the reckless and unwise policy of the present administration in the general management of our national affairs, and more especially as shown in removing "Americans" (by designation) and conservatives in principle, from office, and placing foreigners and ultraists in their places; as shown in a truckling subserviency to the stronger, and an insolent and cowardly bravado towards the weaker powers; as shown in reopening sectional agitation, by the repeal of the Missouri Compromise; as shown in granting to unnaturalized foreigners the right of suffrage in Kansas and Nebraska; as shown in its vacillating course on the Kansas and Nebraska question; as shown in the corruptions which pervade some of the departments of the government; as shown in disgracing meritorious naval officers through prejudice or caprice; and as shown in the blundering mismanagement of our foreign relations.

14. Therefore, to remedy existing evils and prevent the disastrous consequences otherwise resulting therefrom, we would build up the "American Party" upon the principles hereinbefore stated.

*   *   *

REVIEW QUESTIONS

1. What did American Party adherents believe was the primary problem in the country?
2. How did they propose to correct that?
3. What was their position on states rights versus federal power?
4. What was their position on the establishment of territorial governments?

THE DEMOCRATIC PARTY

The Democratic Platform (1856)

While the Whig Party shattered under sectional pressures, the other major national party of the antebellum period, the Democratic Party, struggled to hold on to its partisans throughout the country. It tried to appeal to all its people both in its nominees for the executive offices and in the planks of its platform. The delegates at the Democratic convention in Cincinnati ultimately decided not to endorse the incumbent president, Franklin Pierce, or Stephen Douglas for president because the issues of the last few years, especially the Kansas-Nebraska situation, undermined their chances in a national election. After seventeen ballots, the Democrats chose James Buchanan of Pennsylvania for their presidential nominee; although a northerner, he was seen as willing to appease southern slaveowners. They nominated John Breckinridge of Kentucky for vice president. In their platform, the Democrats praised compromise and advocated limited federal government in domestic affairs and such traditional American concerns as freedom of the seas and free trade in foreign policy.

From Thomas V. Cooper, and Hector T. Fenton, *American Politics from the Beginning to Date* (Chicago: Charles R. Brodix, 1882), pp. 36–39.

Resolved, That the American democracy place their trust in the intelligence, the patriotism, and discriminating justice of the American people.

Resolved, That we regard this as a distinctive feature of our political creed, which we are proud to maintain before the world as a great moral element in a form of government springing from and upheld by the popular will; and we contrast it with the creed and practice of federalism, under whatever name or form, which seeks to palsy the will of the constituents, and which conceives no imposture too monstrous for the popular credulity.

Resolved, therefore, That entertaining these views, the Democratic party of this Union, through their delegates, assembled in general convention, coming together in a spirit of concord, of devotion to the doctrines and faith of a free representative government, and appealing to their fellow citizens for the rectitude of their intentions, renew and reassert, before the American people, the declaration of principles avowed by them, when, on former occasions, in general convention, they have presented their candidates for the popular suffrage.

1. That the Federal government is one of limited power, derived solely from the constitution, and the grants of power made therein ought to be strictly construed by all the departments and agents of the government, and that it is inexpedient and dangerous to exercise doubtful constitutional powers.

2. That the constitution does not confer upon the general government the power to commence and carry on a general system of internal improvements.

3. That the constitution does not confer authority upon the Federal government, directly or indirectly, to assume the debts of the several states, contracted for local and internal improvements or other state purposes; nor would such assumption be just or expedient.

4. That justice and sound policy forbid the Federal government to foster one branch of industry to the detriment of another, or to cherish the

interests of one portion of our common country; that every citizen and every section of the country has a right to demand and insist upon an equality of rights and privileges, and a complete and ample protection of persons and property from domestic violence and foreign aggression.

5. That it is the duty of every branch of the government to enforce and practice the most rigid economy in conducting our public affairs, and that no more revenue ought to be raised than is required to defray the necessary expenses of the government and gradual but certain extinction of the public debt.

6. That the proceeds of the public lands ought to be sacredly applied to the national objects specified in the constitution, and that we are opposed to any law for the distribution of such proceeds among the states, as alike inexpedient in policy and repugnant to the constitution.

7. That Congress has no power to charter a national bank; that we believe such an institution one of deadly hostility to the best interests of this country, dangerous to our republican institutions and the liberties of the people, and calculated to place the business of the country within the control of a concentrated money power and above the laws and will of the people; . . .

*   *   *

9. That we are decidedly opposed to taking from the President the qualified veto power, by which he is enabled, under restrictions and responsibilities amply sufficient to guard the public interests, to suspend the passage of a bill whose merits can not secure the approval of two-thirds of the Senate and House of Representatives, until the judgment of the people can be obtained thereon, and which has saved the American people from the corrupt and tyrannical dominion of the Bank of the United States and from a corrupting system of general internal improvements.

10. That the liberal principles embodied by Jefferson in the Declaration of Independence, and sanctioned in the Constitution, which makes ours the land of liberty and the asylum of the oppressed of every nation, have ever been cardinal principles

in the democratic faith; and every attempt to abridge the privilege of becoming citizens and owners of soil among us, ought to be resisted with the same spirit which swept the alien and sedition laws from our statute books.

And whereas, Since the foregoing declaration was uniformly adopted by our predecessors in national conventions, an adverse political and religious test has been secretly organized by a party claiming to be exclusively Americans, and it is proper that the American democracy should clearly define its relations thereto; and declare its determined opposition to all secret political societies, by whatever name they may be called—

Resolved, That the foundation of this union of states having been laid in, and its prosperity, expansion, and pre-eminent example in free government built upon, entire freedom of matters of religious concernment, and no respect of persons in regard to rank or place of birth, no party can justly be deemed national, constitutional, or in accordance with American principles, which bases its exclusive organization upon religious opinions and accidental birth-place. And hence a political crusade in the nineteenth century, and in the United States of America, against Catholics and foreign-born, is neither justified by the past history or future prospects of the country, nor in unison with the spirit of toleration and enlightened freedom which peculiarly distinguishes the American system of popular government.

Resolved, That we reiterate with renewed energy of purpose the well-considered declarations of former conventions upon the sectional issue of domestic slavery, and concerning the reserved rights of the states—

1. That Congress has no power under the constitution to interfere with or control the domestic institutions of the several states, and that all such states are the sole and proper judges of everything appertaining to their own affairs not prohibited by the constitution; that all efforts of the Abolitionists or others, made to induce Congress to interfere with questions of slavery, or to take incipient steps in relation thereto, are calculated to lead to the most alarming and dangerous consequences, and

that all such efforts have an inevitable tendency to diminish the happiness of the people and endanger the stability and permanency of the Union, and ought not to be countenanced by any friend of our political institutions.

2. That the foregoing proposition covers and was intended to embrace the whole subject of slavery agitation in Congress, and therefore the Democratic party of the Union, standing on this national platform, will abide by and adhere to a faithful execution of the acts known as the compromise measures, settled by the Congress of 1850—"the act for reclaiming fugitives from service or labor" included; which act, being designed to carry out an express provision of the constitution, can not, with fidelity thereto, be repealed, or so changed as to destroy or impair its efficiency.

3. That the Democratic party will resist all attempts at renewing in Congress, or out of it, the agitation of the slavery question, under whatever shape or color the attempt may be made.

4. That the Democratic party will faithfully abide by and uphold the principles laid down in the Kentucky and Virginia resolutions of 1792 and 1798, and in the report of Mr. Madison to the Virginia legislature in 1799; that it adopts these principles as constituting one of the main foundations of its political creed, and is resolved to carry them out in their obvious meaning and import.

And that we may more distinctly meet the issue on which a sectional party, subsisting exclusively on slavery agitation, now relies to test the fidelity of the people, north and south, to the constitution and the Union—

1. *Resolved*, That claiming fellowship with and desiring the co-operation of all who regard the preservation of the Union under the constitution as the paramount issue, and repudiating all sectional parties and platforms concerning domestic slavery which seek to embroil the states and incite to treason and armed resistance to law in the territories, and whose avowed purpose, if consummated, must end in civil war and disunion, the American democracy recognize and adopt the principles contained in the organic laws establishing the territories of Nebraska and Kansas, as embodying the only sound and safe solution of the slavery question, upon which the great national idea of the people of this whole country can repose in its determined conservation of the Union, and non-interference of Congress with slavery in the territories or in the District of Columbia.

2. That this was the basis of the compromise of 1850, confirmed by both the Democratic and Whig parties in national conventions, ratified by the people in the election of 1852, and rightly applied to the organization of the territories in 1854.

3. That by the uniform application of the Democratic principle to the organization of territories and the admission of new states, with or without domestic slavery, as they may elect, the equal rights of all the states will be preserved intact, the original compacts of the constitution maintained inviolate, and the perpetuity and expansion of the Union insured to its utmost capacity of embracing, in peace and harmony, every future American state that may be constituted or annexed with a republican form of government.

Resolved, That we recognize the right of the people of all the territories, including Kansas and Nebraska, acting through the legally and fairly expressed will of the majority of the actual residents, and whenever the number of their inhabitants justifies it, to form a constitution, with or without domestic slavery, and be admitted into the Union upon terms of perfect equality with the other states.

Resolved, finally, That in view of the condition of the popular institutions in the old world (and the dangerous tendencies of sectional agitation, combined with the attempt to enforce civil and religious disabilities against the rights of acquiring and enjoying citizenship in our own land), a high and sacred duty is devolved, with increased responsibility, upon the Democratic party of this country, as the party of the Union, to uphold and maintain the rights of every state, and thereby the union of the states, and to sustain and advance among us constitutional liberty, by continuing to resist all monopolies and exclusive legislation for the benefit of the few at the expense of the many, and by a vigilant and constant adherence to those principles and compromises of the constitution which are broad enough and strong enough to embrace and uphold the Union as it was, the Union as it is, and the Union as it shall be, in the full expression of the energies and capacity of this great and progressive people.

1. *Resolved*, That there are questions connected with the foreign policy of this country which are inferior to no domestic questions whatever. The time has come for the people of the United States to declare themselves in favor of free seas and progressive free trade throughout the world, and, by solemn manifestations, to place their moral influence at the side of their successful example.

2. *Resolved*, That our geographical and political position with reference to the other states of this continent, no less than the interest of our commerce and the development of our growing power, requires that we should hold sacred the principles involved in the Monroe doctrine. . . .

3. *Resolved*, That the great highway which nature, as well as the assent of states most immediately interested in its maintenance, has marked out for free communication between the Atlantic and Pacific oceans, constitutes one of the most important achievements realized by the spirit of modern times . . . ; and that result would be secured by a timely and efficient exertion of the control which we have the right to claim over it; and no power on earth should be suffered to impede or clog its progress by any interference with relations that may suit our policy to establish between our government and the governments of the states within whose dominions it lies; . . .

4. *Resolved*, That in view of so commanding an interest, the people of the United States cannot but sympathize with the efforts which are being made by the people of Central America to regenerate that portion of the continent which covers the passage across the inter-oceanic isthmus.

5. *Resolved*, That the Democratic party will expect of the next administration that every proper effort be made to insure our ascendency in the Gulf of Mexico, and to maintain permanent protection to the great outlets through which are emptied into its waters the products raised out of the soil and the commodities created by the industry of the people of our western valleys and of the Union at large.

6. *Resolved*, That the administration of Franklin Pierce has been true to Democratic principles, and, therefore, true to the great interests of the country; in the face of violent opposition, he has maintained the laws at home and vindicated the rights of American citizens abroad, and, therefore, we proclaim our unqualified admiration of his measures and policy.

REVIEW QUESTIONS

1. What did the Democrats indicate was the greatest threat to the American nation?
2. Did they agree with the American Party's assessment of the threat? Why or why not?
3. Did they address the slavery problem as a civil rights or states rights issue?
4. Why did they praise the legislative compromises of the early 1850s?
5. How did the Democratic Party promote itself at the expense of the Republican Party?

THE REPUBLICAN PARTY

The Republican Platform (1856)

The new Republican Party, accused of being a sectional rather than national organization by the Democrats, held its convention in Philadelphia. The party's emphasis on the containment of slavery, as well as the composition of its membership, did give some validity to the charge. Many of its members had been Whigs, and their influence was seen in the economic planks that advocated internal improvements financed by the federal government. Abolitionists and Free Soilers, coming from the Whig and Democratic parties, also influenced the creation of the party's platform and the nomination of candidates. The Republicans elected John Fremont of California, formerly a Free Soil Democrat, as their presidential candidate and William Dayton of New Jersey, a former Whig, as his running mate.

From Thomas V. Cooper, and Hector T. Fenton, *American Politics from the Beginning to Date* (Chicago: Charles R. Brodix, 1882), pp. 39–40.

This convention of delegates, assembled in pursuance of a call addressed to the people of the United States, without regard to past political differences or divisions, who are opposed to the repeal of the Missouri Compromise, to the policy of the present administration, to the extension of slavery into free territory; in favor of admitting Kansas as a free state, of restoring the action of the Federal government to the principles of Washington and Jefferson; and who purpose to unite in presenting candidates for the offices of President and Vice-President, do resolve as follows:

Resolved, That the maintenance of the principles promulgated in the Declaration of Independence, and embodied in the federal constitution, is essential to the preservation of our Republican institutions, and that the federal constitution, the rights of the states, and the union of the states, shall be preserved.

Resolved, That with our republican fathers we hold it to be a self-evident truth that all men are endowed with the inalienable rights to life, liberty, and the pursuit of happiness, and that the primary object and ulterior design of our Federal government were, to secure these rights to all persons within its exclusive jurisdiction; that as our republican fathers, when they had abolished slavery in all our national territory, ordained that no person should be deprived of life, liberty, or property, without due process of law, it becomes our duty to maintain this provision of the constitution against all attempts to violate it for the purpose of establishing slavery in any territory of the United States, by positive legislation, prohibiting its existence or extension therein. That we deny the authority of Congress, of a territorial legislature, of any individual or association of individuals, to give legal existence to slavery in any territory of the United States, while the present constitution shall be maintained.

Resolved, That the constitution confers upon Congress sovereign power over the territories of the United States for their government, and that in the exercise of this power it is both the right and the imperative duty of Congress to prohibit in the territories those twin relics of barbarism—polygamy and slavery.

Resolved, That while the constitution of the United States was ordained and established, in order to form a more perfect union, establish justice, insure domestic tranquillity, provide for the common defense, promote the general welfare, and secure the blessings of liberty, and contains ample provisions for the protection of the life, liberty, and property of every citizen, the dearest constitutional rights of the people of Kansas have been fraudulently and violently taken from them; their territory has been invaded by an armed force; spurious and pretended legislative, judicial, and executive officers have been set over them, by whose usurped authority, sustained by the military power of the government, tyrannical and unconstitutional laws have been enacted and enforced; the rights of the people to keep and bear arms have been infringed; test oaths of an extraordinary and entangling nature have been imposed, as a condition of exercising the right of suffrage and holding office; the right of an accused person to a speedy and public trial by an impartial jury has been denied; the right of the people to be secure in their persons, houses, papers, and effects against unreasonable searches and seizures, has been violated; they have been deprived of life, liberty, and property without due process of law; that the freedom of speech and of the press has been abridged; the right to choose their representatives has been made of no effect; murders, robberies, and arsons have been instigated or encouraged, and the offenders have been allowed to go unpunished; that all these things have been done with the knowledge, sanction, and procurement of the present national administration; and that for this high crime against the constitution, the Union, and humanity, we arraign the administration, the President, his advisers, agents, supporters, apologists, and accessories, either before or after the facts, before the country and before the world; and that it is our fixed purpose to bring the actual perpetrators of these atrocious outrages, and their accomplices, to a sure and condign punishment hereafter.

Resolved, That Kansas should be immediately admitted as a state of the Union with her present free constitution, as at once the most effectual way of securing to her citizens the enjoyment of the rights and privileges to which they are entitled, and of ending the civil strife now raging in her territory.

Resolved, That the highwayman's plea that "might makes right," embodied in the Ostend circular, was in every respect unworthy of American diplomacy, and would bring shame and dishonor upon any government or people that gave it their sanction.

Resolved, That a railroad to the Pacific ocean, by the most central and practicable route, is imperatively demanded by the interests of the whole country, and that the Federal government ought to render immediate and efficient aid in its construction, and, as an auxiliary thereto, the immediate construction of an emigrant route on the line of the railroad.

Resolved, That appropriations of Congress for the improvement of rivers and harbors of a national character, required for the accommodation and security of our existing commerce, are authorized by the constitution, and justified by the obligation of government to protect the lives and property of its citizens.

Resolved, That we invite the affiliation and cooperation of the men of all parties, however differing from us in other respects, in support of the principles herein declared; and believing that the spirit of our institutions, as well as the constitution of our country, guarantees liberty of conscience and equality of rights among citizens, we oppose all proscriptive legislation affecting their security.

REVIEW QUESTIONS

1. What did Republicans advocate in their platform? What did they condemn?
2. Did they answer the Democrats' charge that their endeavors would destroy the Union?
3. Was the Republican platform primarily an idealistic or pragmatic document?
4. How did it reflect the influence of the Declaration of Independence?
5. Was the focus on the Declaration as opposed to the Constitution significant? Explain.

FROM *Dred Scott v. Sandford* (1857)

James Buchanan, the Democratic candidate, won the presidency in 1856, but the joy of that success was soon buried under mounting troubles. As Buchanan tried to use his executive powers and political alliances to soothe the savage beasts of special and sectional interests, the Supreme Court stepped into the fray. It did so through the case of Dred Scott v. Sandford. *Scott, an African American, had brought suit in the state circuit court of St. Louis County, Missouri, in 1846 claiming that earlier residence in Illinois and the free territory of Wisconsin had made him free. The verdict and judgment were in his favor, but the state's supreme court later reversed them. In the meantime Scott sued his former master, John F. A. Sandford for assault against himself, his wife, and his two daughters. When the case came up in 1854, Sandford defended himself by arguing that Scott and his wife and daughters were his slaves and that "at the times mentioned in the plaintiff's declaration, the defendant, claiming to be owner as aforesaid, laid his hands upon said plaintiff, Harriet, Eliza, and Lizzie, and imprisoned them, doing in this respect, however, no more than what he might lawfully do, if they were of right his slaves at such times." The jury found for Sandford. Scott then filed a bill of exceptions against some of the proceedings of the court. That bill led to the Supreme Court case that was first argued in 1855 and then reargued at the 1856 December term. Chief Justice Roger B. Taney delivered the court's opinion in March 1857. In rendering its decision against Scott, the court also passed judgment on the constitutionality of the Missouri Compromise and challenged the concept of popular sovereignty.*

From *Report of the Decision of the Supreme Court . . . in the Case of Dred Scott versus John F. A. Sandford* (1857; New York: Da Capo Press, 1970), pp. 9–14, 16, 32–34, 36–38, 53–58. [Editorial insertions appear in square brackets—*Ed.*]

*   *   *

The question is simply this: Can a negro, whose ancestors were imported into this country, and sold as slaves, become a member of the political community formed and brought into existence by the Constitution of the United States, and as such become entitled to all the rights, and privileges, and immunities, guarantied by that instrument to the citizen? One of which rights is the privilege of suing in a court of the United States in the cases specified in the Constitution.

It will be observed, that the plea applies to that class of persons only whose ancestors were negroes of the African race, and imported into this country, and sold and held as slaves. The only matter in issue before the court, therefore, is, whether the descendants of such slaves, when they shall be emancipated, or who are born of parents who had become free before their birth, are citizens of a State, in the sense in which the word citizen is used in the Constitution of the United States. . . .

The situation of this population was altogether unlike that of the Indian race. The latter, it is true, formed no part of the colonial communities, and never amalgamated with them in social connections or in government. But although they were uncivilized, they were yet a free and independent people, associated together in nations or tribes, and governed by their own laws. Many of these political communities were situated in territories to which the white race claimed the ultimate right of dominion. But that claim was acknowledged to be subject to the right of the Indians to occupy it as long as they thought proper, and neither the English nor colonial Governments claimed or exercised any dominion over the tribe or nation by whom it was occupied, nor claimed the right to the possession of the territory, until the tribe or nation consented to cede it. These Indian Governments were regarded and treated as foreign Governments, . . . Treaties have been negotiated with them, and their alliance sought for in war; and the people who compose these Indian political communities have always been treated as foreigners not living under our Government. It is true that the course of events has brought the Indian tribes within the limits of the United States under subjection to the white race; and it has been found necessary, for their sake as well as our own, to regard them as in a state of pupilage, and to legislate to a certain extent over them and the territory they occupy. But they may, without doubt, like the subjects of any other foreign Government, be naturalized by the authority of Congress, and become citizens of a State, and of the United States; and if an individual should leave his nation or tribe, and take up his abode among the white population, he would be entitled to all the rights and privileges which would belong to an emigrant from any other foreign people.

We proceed to examine the case as presented by the pleadings.

The words "people of the United States" and "citizens" are synonymous terms, and mean the same thing. They both describe the political body who, according to our republican institutions, form the sovereignty, and who hold the power and conduct the Government through their representatives. They are what we familiarly call the "sovereign people," and every citizen is one of this people, and a constituent member of this sovereignty. The question before us is, whether the class of persons described in the plea in abatement compose a portion of this people, and are constituent members of this sovereignty? We think they are not, and that they are not included, and were not intended to be included, under the word "citizens" in the Constitution, and can therefore claim none of the rights and privileges which that instrument provides for and secures to citizens of the United States. On the contrary, they were at that time considered as a subordinate and inferior class of beings, who had been subjugated by the dominant race, and, whether emancipated or not, yet remained subject to their authority, and had no rights or privileges but such as those who held the power and the Government might choose to grant them.

It is not the province of the court to decide upon the justice or injustice, the policy or impolicy, of these laws. The decision of that question belonged to the political or law-making power; to those who formed the sovereignty and framed the Constitution. The duty of the court is, to interpret the instrument they have framed, . . .

In discussing this question, we must not confound the rights of citizenship which a State may confer within its own limits, and the rights of citizenship as a member of the Union. It does not by any means follow, because he has all the rights and privileges of a citizen of a State, that he must be a citizen of the United States. He may have all of the rights and privileges of the citizen of a State, and yet not be entitled to the rights and privileges of a citizen in any other State. For, previous to the adoption of the Constitution of the United States, every State had the undoubted right to confer on whomsoever it pleased the character of citizen, and to endow him with all its rights. But this character of course was confined to the boundaries of the State, and gave him no rights or privileges in other States beyond those secured to him by the laws of nations and the comity of States. Nor have the several States surrendered the power of conferring these rights and privileges by adopting the Constitution of the United States. Each State may still confer them upon an alien, or any one it thinks proper, or upon any class or description of persons; yet he would not be a citizen in the sense in which that word is used in the Constitution of the

United States, nor entitled to sue as such in one of its courts, nor to the privileges and immunities of a citizen in the other States. The rights which he would acquire would be restricted to the State which gave them. The Constitution has conferred on Congress the right to establish an uniform rule of naturalization, and this right is evidently exclusive, and has always been held by this court to be so. Consequently, no State, since the adoption of the Constitution, can by naturalizing an alien invest him with the rights and privileges secured to a citizen of a State under the Federal Government, . . .

*   *   *

The question then arises, whether the provisions of the Constitution, in relation to the personal rights and privileges to which the citizen of a State should be entitled, embraced the negro African race, at that time in this country, or who might afterwards be imported, who had then or should afterwards be made free in any State; and to put it in the power of a single State to make him a citizen of the United States, and endue him with the full rights of citizenship in every other State without their consent? Does the Constitution of the United States act upon him whenever he shall be made free under the laws of a State, and raised there to the rank of a citizen, and immediately clothe him with all the privileges of a citizen in every other State, and in its own courts?

The court think the affirmative of these propositions cannot be maintained. And if it cannot, the plaintiff in error could not be a citizen of the State of Missouri, within the meaning of the Constitution of the United States, and, consequently, was not entitled to sue in its courts.

It is true, every person, and every class and description of persons, who were at the time of the adoption of the Constitution recognised as citizens in the several States, became also citizens of this new political body; but none other; it was formed by them, and for them and their posterity, but for no one else. . . .

*   *   *

In the opinion of the court, the legislation and histories of the times, and the language used in the Declaration of Independence, show, that neither the class of persons who had been imported as slaves, nor their descendants, whether they had become free or not, were then acknowledged as a part of the people, nor intended to be included in the general words used in that memorable instrument.

It is difficult at this day to realize the state of public opinion in relation to that unfortunate race, which prevailed in the civilized and enlightened portions of the world at the time of the Declaration of Independence, and when the Constitution of the United States was framed and adopted. But the public history of every European nation displays it in a manner too plain to be mistaken.

They had for more than a century before been regarded as beings of an inferior order, and altogether unfit to associate with the white race, either in social or political relations; and so far inferior, that they had no rights which the white man was bound to respect; and that the negro might justly and lawfully be reduced to slavery for his benefit. . . .

*   *   *

The opinion thus entertained and acted upon in England was naturally impressed upon the colonies they founded on this side of the Atlantic. And, accordingly, a negro of the African race was regarded by them as an article of property, and held, and bought and sold as such, in every one of the thirteen colonies which united in the Declaration of Independence, and afterwards formed the Constitution of the United States. The slaves were more or less numerous in the different colonies, as slave labor was found more or less profitable. But no one seems to have doubted the correctness of the prevailing opinion of the time.

*   *   *

[The Declaration of Independence] proceeds to say: "We hold these truths to be self-evident: that all men are created equal; that they are endowed by their Creator with certain unalienable rights; that among them is life, liberty, and the pursuit of happiness; that to secure these rights, Governments are instituted, deriving their just powers from the consent of the governed."

The general words above quoted would seem to embrace the whole human family, and if they were used in a similar instrument at this day would be so understood. But it is too clear for dispute, that the enslaved African race were not intended to be included, and formed no part of the people who framed and adopted this declaration; for if the language, as understood in that day, would embrace them, the conduct of the distinguished men who framed the Declaration of Independence would have been utterly and flagrantly inconsistent with the principles they asserted; and instead of the sympathy of mankind, to which they so confidently appealed, they would have deserved and received universal rebuke and reprobation.

Yet the men who framed this declaration were great men—high in literary acquirements—high in their sense of honor, and incapable of asserting principles inconsistent with those on which they were acting. They perfectly understood the meaning of the language they used, and how it would be understood by others; and they knew that it would not in any part of the civilized world be supposed to embrace the negro race, which, by common consent, had been excluded from civilized Governments and the family of nations, and doomed to slavery. They spoke and acted according to the then established doctrines and principles, and in the ordinary language of the day, and no one misunderstood them. . . .

This state of public opinion had undergone no change when the Constitution was adopted, as is equally evident from its provisions and language.

*   *   *

No one, we presume, supposes that any change in public opinion or feeling, in relation to this unfortunate race, in the civilized nations of Europe or in this country, should induce the court to give to the words of the Constitution a more liberal construction in their favor than they were intended to bear when the instrument was framed and adopted.

Such an argument would be altogether inadmissible in any tribunal called on to interpret it. If any of its provisions are deemed unjust, there is a mode prescribed in the instrument itself by which it may be amended; but while it remains unaltered, it must be construed now as it was understood at the time of its adoption. . . . Any other rule of construction would abrogate the judicial character of this court, and make it the mere reflex of the popular opinion or passion of the day. This court was not created by the Constitution for such purposes. Higher and graver trusts have been confided to it, and it must not falter in the path of duty.

What the construction was at that time, we think can hardly admit of doubt. We have the language of the Declaration of Independence and of the Articles of Confederation, in addition to the plain words of the Constitution itself; we have the legislation of the different States, before, about the time, and since, the Constitution was adopted; we have the legislation of Congress, from the time of its adoption to a recent period; and we have the constant and uniform action of the Executive Department, all concurring together, and leading to the same result. And if anything in relation to the construction of the Constitution can be regarded as settled, it is that which we now give to the word "citizen" and the word "people."

And upon a full and careful consideration of the subject, the court is of opinion, that, upon the facts stated in the plea in abatement, Dred Scott was not a citizen of Missouri within the meaning of the Constitution of the United States, and not entitled as such to sue in its courts; and, consequently, that the Circuit Court had no jurisdiction of the case, and that the judgment on the plea in abatement is erroneous.

. . . [T]he question as to the jurisdiction of the Circuit Court is presented on the face of the bill of exception itself, taken by the plaintiff at the trial; for he admits that he and his wife were born slaves, but endeavors to make out his title to freedom and citizenship by showing that they were taken by their owner to certain places, hereinafter mentioned, where slavery could not by law exist, and that they thereby became free, and upon their return to Missouri became citizens of that State.

Now, if the removal of which he speaks did not give them their freedom, then by his own admission he is still a slave; and whatever opinions may be entertained in favor of the citizenship of a free person of the African race, no one supposes that a slave is a citizen of the State or of the United States. If, therefore, the acts done by his owner did not make them free persons, he is still a slave, and certainly incapable of suing in the character of a citizen.

The principle of law is too well settled to be disputed, that a court can give no judgment for either party, where it has no jurisdiction; and if, upon the showing of Scott himself, it appeared that he was still a slave, the case ought to have been dismissed, and the judgment against him and in favor of the defendant for costs, is, like that on the plea in abatement, erroneous, and the suit ought to have been dismissed by the Circuit Court for want of jurisdiction in that court.

*   *   *

... [I]n this case it *does appear* that the plaintiff was born a slave; and if the facts upon which he relies have not made him free, then it appears affirmatively on the record that he is not a citizen, and consequently his suit against Sandford was not a suit between citizens of different States, and the court had no authority to pass any judgment between the parties. The suit ought, in this view of it, to have been dismissed by the Circuit Court, and its judgment in favor of Sandford is erroneous, and must be reversed.

*   *   *

We proceed, therefore, to inquire whether the facts relied on by the plaintiff entitled him to his freedom.

The case, as he himself states it, on the record brought here by his writ of error, is this:

The plaintiff was a negro slave, belonging to Dr. Emerson, who was a surgeon in the army of the United States. In the year 1834, he took the plaintiff from the State of Missouri to the military post at Rock Island, in the State of Illinois, and held him

there as a slave until the month of April or May, 1836. At the time last mentioned, said Dr. Emerson removed the plaintiff from said military post at Rock Island to the military post at Fort Snelling, situate on the west bank of the Mississippi river, in the Territory known as Upper Louisiana, acquired by the United States of France, and situate north of the latitude of thirty-six degrees thirty minutes north, and north of the State of Missouri. Said Dr. Emerson held the plaintiff in slavery at said Fort Snelling, from said last-mentioned date until the year 1838.

In the year 1835, Harriet, who is named in the second count of the plaintiff's declaration, was the negro slave of Major Taliaferro, who belonged to the army of the United States. In that year, 1835, said Major Taliaferro took said Harriet to said Fort Snelling, a military post, situated as hereinbefore stated, and kept her there as a slave until the year 1836, and then sold and delivered her as a slave, at said Fort Snelling, unto the said Dr. Emerson hereinbefore named. Said Dr. Emerson held said Harriet in slavery at said Fort Snelling until the year 1838.

In the year 1836, the plaintiff and Harriet intermarried, at Fort Snelling, with the consent of Dr. Emerson, who then claimed to be their master and owner. Eliza and Lizzie, named in the third count of the plaintiff's declaration, are the fruit of that marriage. . . .

In the year 1838, said Dr. Emerson removed the plaintiff and said Harriet, and their said daughter Eliza, from said Fort Snelling to the State of Missouri, where they have ever since resided.

Before the commencement of this suit, said Dr. Emerson sold and conveyed the plaintiff, and Harriet, Eliza, and Lizzie, to the defendant, as slaves, and the defendant has ever since claimed to hold them, and each of them, as slaves.

In considering this part of the controversy, two questions arise: 1. Was he, together with his family, free in Missouri by reason of the stay in the territory of the United States hereinbefore mentioned? And 2. If they were not, is Scott himself free by reason of his removal to Rock Island, in the State of Illinois, as stated in the above admissions?

We proceed to examine the first question.

The act of Congress, upon which the plaintiff relies, declares that slavery and involuntary servitude, except as a punishment for crime, shall be forever prohibited in all that part of the territory ceded by France, under the name of Louisiana, which lies north of thirty-six degrees thirty minutes north latitude, and not included within the limits of Missouri. And the difficulty which meets us at the threshold of this part of the inquiry is, whether Congress was authorized to pass this law under any of the powers granted to it by the Constitution; for if the authority is not given by that instrument, it is the duty of this court to declare it void and inoperative, and incapable of conferring freedom upon any one who is held as a slave under the laws of any one of the States.

The counsel for the plaintiff has laid much stress upon that article in the Constitution which confers on Congress the power "to dispose of and make all needful rules and regulations respecting the territory or other property belonging to the United States;" but, in the judgment of the court, that provision has no bearing on the present controversy, and the power there given, whatever it may be, is confined, and was intended to be confined, to the territory which at that time belonged to, or was claimed by, the United States, and was within their boundaries as settled by the treaty with Great Britain, and can have no influence upon a territory afterwards acquired from a foreign Government. It was a special provision for a known and particular territory, and to meet a present emergency, and nothing more.

*   *   *

. . . The power to expand the territory of the United States by the admission of new States is plainly given [to Congress]; and in the construction of this power by all the departments of the Government, it has been held to authorize the acquisition of territory, not fit for admission at the time, but to be admitted as soon as its population and situation would entitle it to admission. It is acquired to become a State, and not to be held as a colony and governed by Congress with absolute authority; . . .

All we mean to say on this point is, that, as there is no express regulation in the Constitution defining the power which the General Government may exercise over the person or property of a citizen in a Territory thus acquired, the court must necessarily look to the provisions and principles of the Constitution, and its distribution of powers, for the rules and principles by which its decision must be governed.

Taking this rule to guide us, it may be safely assumed that citizens of the United States who migrate to a Territory belonging to the people of the United States, cannot be ruled as mere colonists, dependent upon the will of the General Government, and to be governed by any laws it may think proper to impose. The principle upon which our Governments rest, and upon which alone they continue to exist, is the union of States, sovereign and independent within their own limits in their internal and domestic concerns, and bound together as one people by a General Government, possessing certain enumerated and restricted powers, . . . A power, therefore, in the General Government to obtain and hold colonies and dependent territories, over which they might legislate without restriction, would be inconsistent with its own existence in its present form. Whatever it acquires, it acquires for the benefit of the people of the several States who created it. It is their trustee acting for them, and charged with the duty of promoting the interests of the whole people of the Union in the exercise of the powers specifically granted.

*   *   *

. . . The power to acquire necessarily carries with it the power to preserve and apply to the purposes for which it was acquired. The form of government to be established necessarily rested in the discretion of Congress. . . . [T]he choice of the mode must depend upon the exercise of a discretionary power by Congress, acting within the scope of its constitutional authority, and not infringing upon the rights of person or rights of property of the citizen who might go there to reside, or for any other lawful purpose. It was acquired by the exercise of this discretion, and it must be held and governed in like manner, until it is fitted to be a State.

But the power of Congress over the person or property of a citizen can never be a mere discretionary power under our Constitution and form of Government. The powers of the Government and the rights and privileges of the citizen are regulated and plainly defined by the Constitution itself. And when the Territory becomes a part of the United States, the Federal Government enters into possession in the character impressed upon it by those who created it. It enters upon it with its powers over the citizen strictly defined, and limited by the Constitution, from which it derives its own existence, and by virtue of which alone it continues to exist and act as a Government and sovereignty. It has no power of any kind beyond it; and it cannot, when it enters a Territory of the United States, put off its character, and assume discretionary or despotic powers which the Constitution has denied to it. It cannot create for itself a new character separated from the citizens of the United States, and the duties it owes them under the provisions of the Constitution. The Territory being a part of the United States, the Government and the citizen both enter it under the authority of the Constitution, with their respective rights defined and marked out; and the Federal Government can exercise no power over his person or property, beyond what that instrument confers, nor lawfully deny any right which it has reserved.

A reference to a few of the provisions of the Constitution will illustrate this proposition.

For example, no one, we presume, will contend that Congress can make any law in a Territory respecting the establishment of religion, or the free exercise thereof, or abridging the freedom of speech or of the press, or the right of the people of the Territory peaceably to assemble, and to petition the Government for the redress of grievances.

*   *   *

These powers, and others, in relation to rights of person, which it is not necessary here to enumerate, are, in express and positive terms, denied to the General Government; and the rights of private property have been guarded with equal care. Thus the rights of property are united with the rights of person, and placed on the same ground by the fifth amendment to the Constitution, which provides that no person shall be deprived of life, liberty, and property, without due process of law. And an act of Congress which deprives a citizen of the United States of his liberty or property, merely because he came himself or brought his property into a particular Territory of the United States, and who had committed no offence against the laws, could hardly be dignified with the name of due process of law.

*   *   *

It seems, however, to be supposed, that there is a difference between property in a slave and other property, and that different rules may be applied to it in expounding the Constitution of the United States. . . .

*   *   *

Now, as we have already said in an earlier part of this opinion, upon a different point, the right of property in a slave is distinctly and expressly affirmed in the Constitution. The right to traffic in it, like an ordinary article of merchandise and property, was guarantied to the citizens of the United States, in every State that might desire it, for twenty years. And the Government in express terms is pledged to protect it in all future time, if the slave escapes from his owner. This is done in plain words—too plain to be misunderstood. And no word can be found in the Constitution which gives Congress a greater power over slave property, or which entitles property of that kind to less protection than property of any other description. The only power conferred is the power coupled with the duty of guarding and protecting the owner in his rights.

Upon these considerations, it is the opinion of the court that the act of Congress which prohibited a citizen from holding and owning property of this kind in the territory of the United States north of the line therein mentioned, is not warranted by the

Constitution, and is therefore void; and that neither Dred Scott himself, nor any of his family, were made free by being carried into this territory; even if they had been carried there by the owner, with the intention of becoming a permanent resident.

*   *   *

REVIEW QUESTIONS

1. Why did Chief Justice Taney note that African Americans did not hold the same status before the court as Native Americans?

2. Why did he make a distinction between state and national citizenship?
3. Was he completely accurate in his presentation of historical precedents to support the Court's contention that African Americans could not be citizens? Did historical precedents alone inform the decision of the Court?
4. What argument did he present to show that the Missouri Compromise was unconstitutional?
5. How did Chief Justice Taney's interpretation of the *Constitution* compare to Marshall's in earlier cases (see Chapters 9 and 10)?

ABRAHAM LINCOLN AND STEPHEN DOUGLAS

FROM The Lincoln-Douglas Debates (1858)

Abraham Lincoln was practicing rather than making law at the beginning of the decade, but as acts he considered dangerous were passed, he left the courtroom for convention floors and speakers' platforms. Lincoln had served before in the Illinois legislature and for one term in Congress as a Whig. He was still a Whig in 1854 when he again entered the public arena to oppose the Kansas-Nebraska Act. In 1856, however, Lincoln left the weakened Whigs to help found the Republican Party of Illinois and, by extension, the national Republican Party. In June 1858 the Republican Party endorsed him for the Senate seat then held by Stephen Douglas. Once Lincoln had the Republican nomination he began following Douglas through the state of Illinois in order to hear and refute his opponent's charges more effectively. It was also a way to pressure Douglas into agreeing to public debates. Lincoln and Douglas debated seven times—21 and 27 August, 15 and 18 September, and 7, 13, and 15 October—at seven different places—Ottawa, Freeport, Jonesboro, Charleston, Galesburg, Quincy, and Alton—in Illinois. All except the Jonesboro debate drew audiences of over 10,000 people. The debates were set up so that one candidate would lead off, the other would answer, and then the first would have a short rejoinder. Lincoln and Douglas took turns on the lead position. In all of these debates they covered much of the same material, but the emphasis of each man's argument shifted a bit each time as he answered issues raised in the previous debate as well as any intervening speeches.

From Abraham Lincoln, *Speeches and Writings, 1832–1858* (New York: The Library of America, 1989), pp. 774–81, 785–86, 788–95, 797–98, 800–808, 810–12, 814–15, 818–19.

Seventh Lincoln-Douglas Debate, Alton, Illinois

Seventh, and last joint debate. October 15. 1858. Douglas as reported in the Chicago Times. Lincoln as reported in the Press & Tribune.

Senator Douglas' Speech

*   *   *

LADIES AND GENTLEMEN: It is now nearly four months since the canvass between Mr. Lincoln and myself commenced. On the 16th of June the Republican Convention assembled at Springfield and nominated Mr. Lincoln as their candidate for the U.S. Senate, and he, on that occasion, delivered a speech in which he laid down what he understood to be the Republican creed and the platform on which he proposed to stand during the contest. The principal points in that speech of Mr. Lincoln's were: First, that this government could not endure permanently divided into free and slave States, as our fathers made it; that they must all become free or all become slave; all become one thing or all become the other, otherwise this Union could not continue to exist. . . . His second proposition was a crusade against the Supreme court of the United States because of the Dred Scott decision; urging as an especial reason for his opposition to that decision that it deprived the negroes of the rights and benefits of that clause in the Constitution of the United States which guarantees to the citizens of each State, all the rights, privileges, and immunities of the citizens of the several States. On the 10th of July I returned home, and delivered a speech to the people of Chicago, in which I announced it to be my purpose to appeal to the people of Illinois to sustain the course I had pursued in Congress. In that speech I joined issue with Mr. Lincoln on the points which he had presented. Thus there was an issue clear and distinct made up between us on these two propositions laid down in the speech of Mr. Lincoln at Springfield, and controverted by me in my reply to him at Chicago. On the next day, the 11th of July, Mr. Lincoln replied to me at Chicago, explaining at some length, and re-affirming the positions which he had taken in his Springfield speech. In that Chicago speech he even went further than he had before, and uttered sentiments in regard to the negro being on an equality with the white man. (That's so.) He adopted in support of this position the argument which Lovejoy and Codding, and other Abolition lecturers had made familiar in the northern and central portions of the State, to wit: that the Declaration of Independence having declared all men free and equal, by Divine law, also that negro equality was an inalienable right, of which they could not be deprived. . . .

The issue thus being made up between Mr. Lincoln and myself on three points, we went before the people of the State. . . . I took up Mr. Lincoln's three propositions in my several speeches, analyzed them, and pointed out what I believed to be the radical errors contained in them. First, in regard to his doctrine that this government was in violation of the law of God which says, that a house divided against itself cannot stand, I repudiated it as a slander upon the immortal framers of our constitution. I then said, have often repeated, and now again assert, that in my opinion this government can endure forever, (good) divided into free and slave States as our fathers made it,—each State having the right to prohibit, abolish or sustain slavery just as it pleases. ("Good," "right," and cheers.) This government was made upon the great basis of the sovereignty of the States, the right of each State to regulate its own domestic institutions to suit itself, and that right was conferred with understanding and expectation that inasmuch as each locality had separate interests, each locality must have different and distinct local and domestic institutions, corresponding to its wants and interests. Our fathers knew when they made the government, that the laws and institutions which were well adapted to the green mountains of Vermont, were unsuited to the rice plantations of South Carolina. . . . They knew that in a Republic as broad as this, having such a variety of soil, climate and interest, there must necessarily be a corresponding variety of local laws—the policy and institutions of each State adapted to its condition and wants. For this reason this Union was established on the right of each State to do as it pleased on the question of slavery, and every other question; and the various States were not allowed to complain of, much less interfere, with the policy of their neighbors. ("That's good doctrine," "that's the doctrine," and cheers.)

*   *   *

. . . Why can he not say whether he is willing to allow the people of each State to have slavery or not as they please, and to come into the Union when they have the requisite population as a slave or a free State as they decide? I have no trouble in answering the question. I have said everywhere, and now repeat it to you, that if the people of Kansas want a slave State they have a right, under the constitution of the United States, to form such a State, and I will let them come into the Union with slavery or without, as they determine. ("That's right," "good," "hurrah for Douglas all the time," and cheers.) If the people of any other territory desire slavery let them have it. If they do not want it let them prohibit it. It is their business not mine. ("That's the doctrine.") It is none of your business in Missouri whether Kansas shall adopt slavery or reject it. It is the business of her people and none of yours. The people of Kansas has as much right to decide that question for themselves as you have in Missouri to decide it for yourselves, or we in Illinois to decide it for ourselves. ("That's what we believe," "We stand by that," and cheers.)

*   *   *

My friends, there never was a time when it was as important for the Democratic party, for all national men, to rally and stand together as it is today. We find all sectional men giving up past differences and continuing the one question of slavery, and when we find sectional men thus uniting, we should unite to resist them and their treasonable designs. Such was the case in 1850, when Clay left the quiet and peace of his home, and again entered upon public life to quell agitation

and restore peace to a distracted Union. Then we Democrats, with Cass at our head, welcomed Henry Clay, whom the whole nation regarded as having been preserved by God for the times. He became our leader in that great fight, and we rallied around him the same as the Whigs rallied around old Hickory in 1832, to put down nullification. (Cheers.) Thus you see that whilst Whigs and Democrats fought fearlessly in old times about banks, the tariff, distribution, the specie circular, and the sub-treasury, all united as a band of brothers when the peace, harmony, or integrity of the Union was imperiled. (Tremendous applause.) It was so in 1850, when abolitionism had even so far divided this country, North and South, as to endanger the peace of the Union; Whigs and Democrats united in establishing the compromise measures of that year, and restoring tranquillity and good feeling. These measures passed on the joint action of the two parties. They rested on the great principle that the people of each State and each territory should be left perfectly free to form and regulate their domestic institutions to suit themselves. You Whigs and we Democrats justified them in that principle. In 1854, when it became necessary to organize the territories of Kansas and Nebraska, I brought forward the bill on the same principle. In the Kansas-Nebraska bill you find it declared to be the true intent and meaning of the act not to legislate slavery into any State or territory, nor to exclude it therefrom, but to leave the people thereof perfectly free to form and regulate their domestic institutions in their own way. ("That's so," and cheers.) I stand on that same platform in 1858 that I did in 1850, 1854, and 1856. . . .

*   *   *

. . . The whole South are rallying to the support of the doctrine that if the people of a Territory want slavery they have a right to have it, and if they do not want it that no power on earth can force it upon them. I hold that there is no principle on earth more sacred to all the friends of freedom than that which says that no institution, no law, no constitution, should be forced on an unwilling people contrary to their wishes; and I assert that the Kansas and Nebraska bill contains that principle. . . . I say to you that there is but one hope, one safety for this country, and that is to stand immovably by that principle which declares the right of each State and each territory to decide these questions for themselves. (Hear him, hear him.) This government was founded on that principle, and must be administered in the same sense in which it was founded.

But the Abolition party really think that under the Declaration of Independence the negro is equal to the white man, and that negro equality is an inalienable right conferred by the Almighty, and hence, that all human laws in violation of it are null and void. With such men it is no use for me to argue. I hold that the signers of the Declaration of Independence had no reference to negroes at all when they declared all men to be created equal. They did not mean negro, nor the savage Indians, nor the Fejee Islanders, nor any other barbarous race. They were speaking of white men. . . . But it does not follow, by any means, that merely because the negro is not a citizen, and merely because he is not our equal, that, therefore, he should be a slave. On the contrary, it does follow, that we ought to extend to the negro race, and to all other dependent races all the rights, all the privileges, and all the immunities which they can exercise consistently with the safety of society. Humanity requires that we should give them all these privileges; christianity commands that we should extend those privileges to them. The question then arises what are those privileges, and what is the nature and extent of them. My answer is that that is a question which each State must answer for itself. We in Illinois have decided it for ourselves. We tried slavery, kept it up for twelve years, and finding that it was not profitable we abolished it for that reason, and became a free State. We adopted in its stead the policy that a negro in this State shall not be a slave and shall not be a citizen. We have a right to adopt that policy. For my part I think it is a wise and sound policy for us. You in Missouri must judge for yourselves whether it is a wise policy for you. If you choose to follow our example, very good; if

you reject it, still well, it is your business, not ours. . . . If the people of all the States will act on that great principle, and each State mind its own business, attend to its own affairs, take care of its own negroes and not meddle with its neighbors, then there will be peace between the North and the South, the East and the West, throughout the whole Union. (Cheers.) Why can we not thus have peace? Why should we thus allow a sectional party to agitate this country, to array the North against the South, and convert us into enemies instead of friends, merely that a few ambitious men may ride into power on a sectional hobby? . . .

Mr. Lincoln's Reply

On being introduced to the audience, after the cheering had subsided Mr. Lincoln said:

LADIES AND GENTLEMEN: . . .

*   *   *

. . . I have heard the Judge state two or three times what he has stated to day—that in a speech which I made at Springfield, Illinois, I had in a very especial manner, complained that the Supreme Court in the Dred Scott case had decided that a negro could never be a citizen of the United States. I have omitted by some accident heretofore to analyze this statement, and it is required of me to notice it now. In point of fact it is *untrue*. I never have complained *especially* of the Dred Scott decision because it held that a negro could not be a citizen, and the Judge is always wrong when he says I ever did so complain of it. I have the speech here, and I will thank him or any of his friends to show where I said that a negro should be a citizen, and complained especially of the Dred Scott decision because it declared he could not be one. I have done no such thing, . . . I spoke of the Dred Scott decision . . . endeavoring to prove that the Dred Scott decision was a portion of a system or scheme to make slavery national in this country. I pointed out what things had been decided by the court. I mentioned as a fact that they had decided that a negro could not be a citizen—that they had done so, as I supposed, to deprive the negro, under all circumstances, of the remotest possibility of ever becoming a citizen and claiming the rights of a citizen of the United States under a certain clause of the Constitution. I stated that, without making any complaint of it at all. I then went on and stated the other points decided in the case, . . .

Out of this, Judge Douglas builds up his beautiful fabrication—of my purpose to introduce a perfect, social, and political equality between the white and black races. His assertion that I made an "especial objection" (that is his exact language) to the decision on this account, is untrue in point of fact.

*   *   *

You have heard him frequently allude to my controversy with him in regard to the Declaration of Independence. I confess that I have had a struggle with Judge Douglas on that matter, and I will try briefly to place myself right in regard to it on this occasion. I said— . . .

It may be argued that there are certain conditions that make necessities and impose them upon us, and to the extent that a necessity is imposed upon a man he must submit to it. I think that was the condition in which we found ourselves when we established this government. We had slaves among us, we could not get our Constitution unless we permitted them to remain in slavery, we could not secure the good we did secure if we grasped for more; and having by necessity submitted to that much, it does not destroy the principle that is the charter of our liberties. Let that charter remain as our standard.

Now I have upon all occasions declared as strongly as Judge Douglas against the disposition to interfere with the existing institution of slavery. You hear me read it from the same speech from which he takes garbled extracts for the purpose of proving upon me a disposition to interfere with the institution of slavery, and establish a perfect social and political equality between negroes and white people.

Allow me while upon this subject briefly to present one other extract from a speech of mine, more than a year ago, at Springfield, in discussing this very same question, soon after Judge Douglas took his ground that negroes were not included in the Declaration of Independence:

I think the authors of that notable instrument intended to include *all* men, but they did not mean to declare all men equal *in all respects*. They did not mean to say all men were equal in color, size, intellect, moral development or social capacity. They defined with tolerable distinctness in what they did consider all men created equal—equal in certain inalienable rights, among which are life, liberty and the pursuit of happiness. This they said, and this they meant. They did not mean to assert the obvious untruth, that all were then actually enjoying that equality, nor yet, that they were about to confer it immediately upon them. In fact they had no power to confer such a boon. They meant simply to declare the *right* so that the *enforcement* of it might follow as fast as circumstances should permit.

They meant to set up a standard maxim for free society which should be familiar to all: constantly looked to, constantly labored for, and even though never perfectly attained, constantly approximated and thereby constantly spreading and deepening its influence and augmenting the happiness and value of life to all people, of all colors, everywhere.

There again are the sentiments I have expressed in regard to the Declaration of Independence upon a former occasion—sentiments which have been put in print and read wherever anybody cared to know what so humble an individual as myself chose to say in regard to it.

*   *   *

The principle upon which I have insisted in this canvass, is in relation to laying the foundations of new societies. I have never sought to apply these principles to the old States for the purpose of abolishing slavery in those States. It is nothing but a miserable perversion of what I *have* said, to assume that I have declared Missouri, or any other slave State shall emancipate her slaves. I have proposed no such thing. . . .

*   *   *

. . . I have said, and I repeat, my wish is that the further spread of it may be arrested, and that it may be placed where the public mind shall rest in the belief that it is in the course of ultimate extinction. [Great applause.] . . . I entertain the opinion upon evidence sufficient to my mind, that the fathers of this Government placed that institution where the public mind *did* rest in the belief that it was in the course of ultimate extinction. Let me ask why they made provision that the source of slavery—the African slave trade—should be cut off at the end of twenty years? Why did they make provision that in all the new territory we owned at that time slavery should be forever inhibited? Why stop its spread in one direction and cut off its source in another, if they did not look to its being placed in the course of ultimate extinction?

Again; the institution of slavery is only mentioned in the Constitution of the United States two or three times, and in neither of these cases does the word "slavery" or "negro race" occur; but covert language is used each time, and for a purpose full of significance. . . .

*   *   *

. . . I understand the contemporaneous history of those times to be that covert language was used with a purpose, and that purpose was that in our Constitution, which it was hoped and is still hoped will endure forever—when it should be read by intelligent and patriotic men, after the institution of slavery had passed from among us—there should be nothing on the face of the great charter of liberty suggesting that such a thing as negro slavery had ever existed among us. [Enthusiastic applause.] This is part of the evidence that the fathers of the Government expected and intended the institution of slavery to come to an end. . . .

. . . I have not only made the declaration that I do not *mean* to produce a conflict between the States, but I have tried to show by fair reasoning, and I think I have shown to the minds of fair men, that I propose nothing but what has a most peaceful tendency. The quotation that I happened to make in that Springfield speech, that "a house divided against itself cannot stand," and which has proved so offensive to the Judge, was part and parcel of the same thing. He tries to show that variety in the domestic institutions of the different States is necessary and indispensable. I do not dispute it. I have no controversy with Judge Douglas about that. . . . I understand, I hope, quite as well as Judge Douglas or anybody else, that the variety in the soil and climate and face of the country, and consequent variety in the industrial pursuits and productions of a country, require systems of law conforming to this variety in the natural features of the country. I understand quite as well as Judge Douglas, that if we here raise a barrel of flour more than we want, and the Louisianians raise a barrel of sugar more than they want, it is of mutual advantage to exchange. That produces commerce, brings us together, and makes us better friends. We like one another the more for it. And I understand as well as Judge Douglas, or anybody else, that these mutual accommodations are the cements which bind together the different parts of this Union—that instead of being a thing to "divide the house"—figuratively expressing the Union,—they tend to sustain it; they are the props of the house tending always to hold it up.

But when I have admitted all this, I ask if there is any parallel between these things and this institution of slavery? I do not see that there is any parallel at all between them. . . . You may say and Judge Douglas has intimated the same thing, that all this difficulty in regard to the institution of slavery is the mere agitation of office seekers and ambitious Northern politicians. He thinks we want to get "his place," I suppose. [Cheers and laughter.] I agree that there are office seekers amongst us. The Bible says somewhere that we are desperately selfish. I think we would have discovered that fact without the Bible. I do not claim that I am any less so than the average of men, but I do claim that I am not more selfish than Judge Douglas. [Roars of laughter and applause.]

But is it true that all the difficulty and agitation we have in regard to this institution of slavery springs from office seeking—from the mere ambition of politicians? Is that the truth? How many times have we had danger from this question? Go back to the day of the Missouri Compromise. Go back to the Nullification question, at the bottom of which lay this same slavery question. Go back to the time of the Annexation of Texas. Go back to the troubles that led to the Compromise of 1850. You will find that every time, with the single exception of the Nullification question, they sprung from an endeavor to spread this institution. There never was a party in the history of this country, and there probably never will be of sufficient strength to disturb the general peace of the country. Parties themselves may be divided and quarrel on minor questions, yet it extends not beyond the parties themselves. But does *not* this question make a disturbance outside of political circles? Does it not enter into the churches and rend them asunder? . . . Is it not this same mighty, deep seated power that somehow operates on the minds of men, exciting and stirring them up in every avenue of society—in politics, in religion, in literature, in morals, in all the manifold relations of life? [Applause.] Is this the work of politicians? Is that irresistible power which for fifty years has shaken the government and agitated the people to be stilled and subdued by pretending that it is an exceedingly simple thing, and we ought not to talk about it? [Great cheers and laughter.] . . .

The Judge alludes very often in the course of his remarks to the exclusive right which the States have to decide the whole thing for themselves. I agree with him very readily that the different States have that right. He is but fighting a man of straw when he assumes that I am contending against the right of the States to do as they please about it. Our controversy with him is in regard to the new Territories. We agree that when the States come in as States they have the right and the power to do as they please. We have no power as citizens of the free States or in our federal capacity as members of the Federal Union through the general government, to disturb slavery in the States where it exists. We profess constantly that we have no more inclination than belief in the power of the Government to disturb it; yet we are driven constantly to defend ourselves from the assumption that we are

warring upon the rights of the *States*. What I insist upon is, that the new Territories shall be kept free from it while in the Territorial condition. Judge Douglas assumes that we have no interest in them—that we have no right whatever to interfere. I think we have some interest. I think that as white men we have. Do we not wish for an outlet for our surplus population, if I may so express myself? Do we not feel an interest in getting to that outlet with such institutions as we would like to have prevail there? . . .

Now irrespective of the moral aspect of this question as to whether there is a right or wrong in enslaving a negro, I am still in favor of our new Territories being in such a condition that white men may find a home—may find some spot where they can better their condition—where they can settle upon new soil and better their condition in life. [Great and continued cheering.] I am in favor of this not merely, (I must say it here as I have elsewhere,) for our own people who are born amongst us, but as an outlet for *free white people everywhere*, the world over—in which Hans and Baptiste and Patrick, and all other men from all the world, may find new homes and better their conditions in life. [Loud and long continued applause.]

. . . The real issue in this controversy—the one pressing upon every mind—is the sentiment on the part of one class that looks upon the institution of slavery *as a wrong*, and of another class that *does not* look upon it as a wrong. The sentiment that contemplates the institution of slavery in this country as a wrong is the sentiment of the Republican party. It is the sentiment around which all their actions—all their arguments circle—from which all their propositions radiate. They look upon it as being a moral, social and political wrong; and while they contemplate it as such, they nevertheless have due regard for its actual existence among us, and the difficulties of getting rid of it in any satisfactory way and to all the constitutional obligations thrown about it. Yet having a due regard for these, they desire a policy in regard to it that looks to its not creating any more danger. They insist that it should as far as may be, *be treated* as a wrong, and one of the methods of treating it as a wrong is to *make provision that it shall grow no larger.* [Loud applause.] . . .

On this subject of treating it as a wrong, and limiting its spread, let me say a word. Has any thing ever threatened the existence of this Union save and except this very institution of Slavery? What is it that we hold most dear amongst us? Our own liberty and prosperity. What has ever threatened our liberty and prosperity save and except this institution of Slavery? . . .

That is the real issue. . . . It is the eternal struggle between these two principles—right and wrong—throughout the world. They are the two principles that have stood face to face from the beginning of time; and will ever continue to struggle. The one is the common right of humanity and the other the divine right of kings. It is the same principle in whatever shape it develops itself. It is the same spirit that says, "You work and toil and earn bread, and I'll eat it." [Loud applause.] No matter in what shape it comes, whether from the mouth of a king who seeks to bestride the people of his own nation and live by the fruit of their labor, or from one race of men as an apology for enslaving another race, it is the same tyrannical principle. . . . Whenever the issue can be distinctly made, and all extraneous matter thrown out so that men can fairly see the real difference between the parties, this controversy will soon be settled, and it will be done peaceably too. There will be no war, no violence. It will be placed again where the wisest and best men of the world, placed it. Brooks of South Carolina once declared that when this Constitution was framed, its framers did not look to the institution existing until this day. When he said this, I think he stated a fact that is fully borne out by the history of the times. But he also said they were better and wiser men than the men of these days; yet the men of these days had experience which they had not, and by the invention of the cotton gin it became a necessity in this country that slavery should be perpetual. I now say that willingly or unwillingly, purposely or without purpose, Judge Douglas has been the most prominent instrument in changing the position of the institution of slavery which the fathers of the government expected to come to an end ere this—*and putting it upon Brooks' cotton gin basis,* [Great applause,]—placing it where he openly confesses he has no desire there shall ever be an end of it. [Renewed applause.]

*   *   *

Mr. Douglas' Reply

*   *   *

His first criticism upon me is the expression of his hope that the war of the administration will be prosecuted against me and the Democratic party of his State with vigor. He wants that war prosecuted with vigor; I have no doubt of it. His hopes of success, and the hopes of his party depend solely upon it. They have no chance of destroying the Democracy of this State except by the aid of federal patronage. . . . There is something really refreshing in the thought that Mr. Lincoln is in favor of prosecuting one war vigorously. (Roars of laughter.) It is the first war I ever knew him to be in favor of prosecuting. (Renewed laughter.) It is the first war that I ever knew him to believe to be just or constitutional. (Laughter and cheers.) When the Mexican war was being waged, and the American army was surrounded by the enemy in Mexico, he thought that war was unconstitutional, unnecessary and unjust. ("That's so," "you've got him," "he voted against it," &c.) He thought it was not commenced on the right *spot.* (Laughter.)

*   *   *

. . . Mr. Lincoln told you that the slavery question was the only thing that ever disturbed the peace and harmony of the Union. Did not nullification once raise its head and disturb the peace of this Union in 1832? Was that the slavery question, Mr. Lincoln? Did not disunion raise its monster head during the last war with Great Britain? Was that the slavery question, Mr. Lincoln? The peace of this country has been disturbed three times, once during the war with Great Britain, once on the tariff question, and once on the slavery question. ("Three cheers for Douglas.") His argument, therefore, that slavery is the only question that has ever created dissension in the Union falls to the ground. It is true that agitators are enabled now to use this slavery question for the purpose of sectional strife. ("That's so.") He admits that in regard to all things else, the principle that I advocate, making each State and territory free to decide for itself ought to prevail. . . . I say that all these laws are local and domestic, and that local and domestic concerns should be left to each State and each territory to manage for itself. If agitators would acquiesce in that principle, there never would be any danger to the peace and harmony of this Union. ("That's so," and cheers.)

Mr. Lincoln tries to avoid the main issue by attacking the truth of my proposition, that our fathers made this government divided into free and slave States, recognizing the right of each to decide all its local questions for itself. Did they not thus make it? . . . He says that he looks forward to a time when slavery shall be abolished everywhere. I look forward to a time when each State shall be allowed to do as it pleases. . . . Hence, I say, let us maintain this government on the principles that our fathers made it, recognizing the right of each State to keep slavery as long as its people determine, or to abolish it when they please. (Cheers.) But Mr. Lincoln says that when our fathers made this government they did not look forward to the state of things now existing; and therefore he thinks the doctrine was wrong; and he quotes Brooks, of South Carolina, to prove that our fathers then thought that probably slavery would be abolished, by each State acting for itself before this time. Suppose they did; suppose they did not foresee what has occurred,— does that change the principles of our government?

They did not probably foresee the telegraph that transmits intelligence by lightning, nor did they foresee the railroads that now form the bonds of union between the different States, or the thousand mechanical inventions that have elevated mankind. But do these things change the principles of the government? Our fathers, I say, made this government on the principle of the right of each State to do as it pleases in its own domestic affairs, subject to the constitution, and allowed the people of each to apply to every new change of circumstance such remedy as they may see fit to improve their condition. This right they have for all time to come. (Cheers.)

*   *   *

REVIEW QUESTIONS

1. How did Douglas refute Lincoln's contention that the nation could not remain divided?
2. How did Douglas describe popular sovereignty to the audience?
3. What specific charges did he level against the Republican Party (and, by extension, against Lincoln)?
4. How did Lincoln answer those charges?
5. What do you think of Lincoln's interpretation of the *Constitution* and the Founders' intentions in terms of slavery? Why did he make the argument that he did?
6. Lincoln stated that slavery is the root of all dissension and disunion; Douglas rejected that interpretation. With whom do you agree? Why?

HINTON ROWAN HELPER

FROM *The Impending Crisis of the South* (1857)

Hinton Rowan Helper (1829–1909) was born in Rowan County, North Carolina. It was a region of small farmers, many of whom were of German descent, and one with a substantial Quaker element. Thus, due to economic, ethnic, and religious blocks, slavery had not rooted deeply there. That may partly explain Helper's later antislavery stand. Another reason he may have argued against it was his upbringing, along with the fact that as a poor boy he could not succeed in the South because of the way slavery skewed its economy and society. He left the South in his search for fame and fortune, first moving to New York, and then journeying west during an attack of gold fever. When that fever soon abated in failure, Helper returned to the East, and wrote The Land of Gold *(1855) to debunk the image of California as the promised land. He then wrote scathing critiques of the South that focused on the incompatibility of slavery and economic progress. Citing statistic after statistic he presented a strong, even if exaggerated, case that continued investment in land and slaves prevented the South from having a strong, diversified, and balanced economy. Helper also argued that slavery chained down white non-slaveholders. Abolitionists embraced his arguments as southerners raged against this betrayal by one of their own. Yet Helper had never been a true southern agrarian: he was essentially a capitalist deriding a precapitalist economy, and as such he argued against the institution of slavery, not for the people in slavery. Helper was also a vehement racist, though he toned that down in this book—perhaps in consideration of the audience he wanted to attract. In later years Helper endeavored to exclude blacks from America, not give them equality within it.*

From Hinton Rowan Helper, *The Impending Crisis of the South: How to Meet It*, intro. George M. Fredrickson (1857: Cambridge: The Belknap Press of Harvard University Press, 1968), pp. 21–26, 28, 42–45, 120–21.

The Free and the Slave States

It is a fact well known to every intelligent Southerner that we are compelled to go to the North for almost every article of utility and adornment, from matches, shoepegs and paintings up to cotton-mills, steamships and statuary; that we have no foreign trade, no princely merchants, nor respectable artists; that, in comparison with the free states, we contribute nothing to the literature, polite arts and inventions of the age; that, for want of profitable employment at home, large numbers of our native population find themselves necessitated to emi-grate to the West, whilst the free states retain not only the larger proportion of those born within their own limits, but induce, annually, hundreds of thousands of foreigners to settle and remain amongst them; that almost everything produced at the North meets with ready sale, while, at the same time, there is no demand, even among our own citizens, for the productions of Southern industry; that, owing to the absence of a proper system of business amongst us, the North becomes, in one way or another, the proprietor and dispenser of all our floating wealth, and that we are dependent on Northern capitalists for the means necessary to build our railroads, canals and other public improvements; that if we want to visit a foreign country, even though it may lie directly South of us, we find no convenient way of getting there except by taking passage through a Northern port; and that nearly all the profits arising from the exchange of commodities, from insurance and shipping offices, and from the thousand and one industrial pursuits of the country, accrue to the North, and are there invested in the erection of those magnificent cities and stupendous works of art which dazzle the eyes of the South, and attest the superiority of free institutions!

The North is the Mecca of our merchants, and to it they must and do make two pilgrimages per annum—one in the spring and one in the fall. All our commercial, mechanical, manufactural, and literary supplies come from there. We want Bibles, brooms, buckets and books, and we go to the North; . . . we want toys, primers, school books, fashionable apparel, machinery, medicines, tombstones, and a thousand other things, and we go to the North for them all. Instead of keeping our money in circulation at home, by patronizing our own mechanics, manufacturers, and laborers, we send it all away to the North, and there it remains; it never falls into our hands again.

In one way or another we are more or less subservient to the North every day of our lives. In infancy we are swaddled in Northern muslin; in childhood we are humored with Northern gewgaws; in youth we are instructed out of Northern books; at the age of maturity we sow our "wild oats" on Northern soil; in middle-life we exhaust our wealth, energies and talents in the dishonorable vocation of entailing our dependence on our children and on our children's children, and, to the neglect of our own interests and the interests of those around us, in giving aid and succor to every department of Northern power; in the decline of life we remedy our eye-sight with Northern spectacles, and support our infirmities with Northern canes; in old age we are drugged with Northern physic; and, finally, when we die, our inanimate bodies, shrouded in Northern cambric, are stretched upon the bier, borne to the grave in a

Northern carriage, entombed with a Northern spade, and memorized with a Northern slab!

*   *   *

And now to the point. In our opinion, . . . the causes which have impeded the progress and prosperity of the South, which have dwindled our commerce, and other similar pursuits, into the most contemptible insignificance; sunk a large majority of our people in galling poverty and ignorance, rendered a small minority conceited and tyrannical, and driven the rest away from their homes; entailed upon us a humiliating dependence on the Free States; disgraced us in the recesses of our own souls, and brought us under reproach in the eyes of all civilized and enlightened nations—may all be traced to one common source, and there find solution in the most hateful and horrible word, that was ever incorporated into the vocabulary of human economy—*Slavery!*

Reared amidst the institution of slavery, believing it to be wrong both in principle and in practice, and having seen and felt its evil influences upon individuals, communities and states, we deem it a duty, no less than a privilege, to enter our protest against it, and to use our most strenuous efforts to overturn and abolish it! Then we are an abolitionist? Yes! not merely a freesoiler, but an abolitionist, in the fullest sense of the term. We are not only in favor of keeping slavery out of the territories, but, carrying our opposition to the institution a step further, we here unhesitatingly declare ourself in favor of its immediate and unconditional abolition, in every state in this confederacy, where it now exists! Patriotism makes us a freesoiler; state pride makes us an emancipationist; a profound sense of duty to the South makes us an abolitionist; a reasonable degree of fellow feeling for the negro, makes us a colonizationist. . . .

*   *   *

. . . Nothing short of the complete abolition of slavery can save the South from falling into the vortex of utter ruin. Too long have we yielded a submissive obedience to the tyrannical domination of an inflated oligarchy; too long have we tolerated their arrogance and self-conceit; too long have we tolerated their arrogance and self-conceit; too long have we submitted to their unjust and savage exactions. Let us now wrest from them the sceptre of power, establish liberty and equal rights throughout the land, and henceforth and forever guard our legislative halls from the pollutions and usurpations of proslavery demagogues.

*   *   *

. . . Notwithstanding the fact that the white non-slaveholders of the South, are in the majority, as five to one, they have never yet had any part or lot in framing the laws under which they live. There is no legislation except for the benefit of slavery, and slaveholders. As a general rule, poor white persons are regarded with less esteem and attention than negroes, and though the condition of the latter is wretched beyond description, vast numbers of the former are infinitely worse off. A cunningly devised mockery of freedom is guarantied to them, and that is all. To all intents and purposes they are disfranchised, and outlawed, and the only privilege extended to them, is a shallow and circumscribed participation in the political movements that usher slaveholders into office.

*   *   *

The lords of the lash are not only absolute masters of the blacks, who are bought and sold, and driven about like so many cattle, but they are also the oracles and arbiters of all non-slaveholding whites, whose freedom is merely nominal, and whose unparalleled illiteracy and degradation is purposely and fiendishly perpetuated. How little the "poor white trash," the great majority of the Southern people, know of the real condition of the country is, indeed, sadly astonishing. The truth is, they know nothing of public measures, and little of private affairs, except what their imperious masters, the slave-drivers, condescend to tell, and that is but precious little, and even that little, always garbled and one-sided, is never told except in public harangues; for the haughty cavaliers of shackles

and handcuffs will not degrade themselves by holding private converse with those who have neither dimes nor hereditary rights in human flesh.

Whenever it pleases, and to the extent it pleases, a slaveholder to become communicative, poor whites may hear with fear and trembling, but not speak. . . . If they dare to think for themselves, their thoughts must be forever concealed. The expression of any sentiment at all conflicting with the gospel of slavery, dooms them at once in the community in which they live, and then, whether willing or unwilling, they are obliged to become heroes, martyrs, or exiles. . . . Non-slaveholders are not only kept in ignorance of what is transpiring at the North, but they are continually misinformed of what is going on even in the South. Never were the poorer classes of a people, and those classes so largely in the majority, and all inhabiting the same country, so basely duped, so adroitly swindled, or so damnably outraged.

It is expected that the stupid and sequacious masses, the white victims of slavery, will believe, and, as a general thing, they do believe, whatever the slaveholders tell them; and thus it is that they are cajoled into the notion that they are the freest, happiest and most intelligent people in the world, and are taught to look with prejudice and disapprobation upon every new principle or progressive movement. Thus it is that the South, woefully inert and inventionless, has lagged behind the North, and is now weltering in the cesspool of ignorance and degradation.

*   *   *

Non-slaveholders of the South! farmers, mechanics and workingmen, we take this occasion to assure you that the slaveholders, the arrogant demagogues whom you have elected to offices of honor and profit, have hoodwinked you, trifled with you, and used you as mere tools for the consummation of their wicked designs. They have purposely kept you in ignorance, and have, by moulding your passions and prejudices to suit themselves, induced you to act in direct opposition to your dearest rights and interests. By a system of the grossest subterfuge and misrepresentation, and in order to avert, for a season, the vengeance that will most assuredly overtake them ere long, they have taught you to hate the abolitionists, who are your best and only true friends. Now, as one of your own number, we appeal to you to join us in our patriotic endeavors to rescue the generous soil of the South from the usurped and desolating control of these political vampires. Once and forever, at least so far as this country is concerned, the infernal question of slavery must be disposed of; a speedy and perfect abolishment of the whole institution is the true policy of the South—and this is the policy which we propose to pursue. Will you aid us, will you assist us, will you be freemen, or will you be slaves? These are questions of vital importance; weigh them well in your minds; come to a prudent and firm decision, and hold yourselves in readiness to act in accordance therewith. You must either be for us or against us—anti-slavery or pro-slavery; it is impossible for you to occupy a neutral ground; it is as certain as fate itself, that if you do not voluntarily oppose the usurpations and outrages of the slavocrats, they will force you into involuntary compliance with their infamous measures. Consider

well the aggressive, fraudulent and despotic power which they have exercised in the affairs of Kanzas; and remember that, if, by adhering to erroneous principles of neutrality or non-resistance, you allow them to force the curse of slavery on that vast and fertile field, the broad area of all the surrounding States and Territories—the whole nation, in fact—will soon fall a prey to their diabolical intrigues and machinations. Thus, if you are not vigilant, will they take advantage of your neutrality, and make you and others the victims of their inhuman despotism. Do not reserve the strength of your arms until you shall have been rendered powerless to strike; . . .

*   *   *

REVIEW QUESTIONS

1. Did Helper essentially argue that slavery had enslaved the South? How so?
2. Was he worried about the morality of slavery?
3. Why did Helper's attack enrage, and perhaps frighten, southerners more than Lincoln's did?

JOHN BROWN

Harper's Ferry, Virginia (1859)

Lincoln and Helper angered slaveowners; John Brown (1800–1859) terrified them. They had decried Brown as a dangerous fanatic for his free-soil activities in the territory of Kansas, but verbal condemnation was not enough when Brown moved against their persons and peculiar institution in the established state of Virginia. On 16 October 1859, a Sunday night, Brown set out with a group of approximately nineteen men, including at least five African Americans, in a raid on the federal arsenal in Harper's Ferry. His plan to free and arm slaves embodied the slaveowner's greatest fear: a black uprising. Southerners moved quickly and decisively to stop him, and they soon received military support to do so because he had attacked a federal installation and threatened domestic insurrection. The Virginia militia surrounded the engine house in which Brown's force had holed up on the seventeenth; on the next day,

United States marines commanded by Lieutenant Colonel Robert E. Lee and led by Lieutenant J. E. B. Stuart broke through the doors of the structure and took Brown and his surviving men prisoners. On 26 October, a grand jury delivered a bill of indictment against each prisoner for conspiring with blacks to cause an insurrection, for committing treason against the Commonwealth of Virginia, and for murder. Brown's trial began the following day and ended on Monday 31 October with his conviction. On Wednesday evening Brown, still recovering from the wounds he had received upon his surrender, walked with difficulty into the courtroom to make a statement and receive his sentence.

From Louis Ruchames, ed., *A John Brown Reader* (London: Abelard-Schuman, 1959), pp. 125–27, 159.

John Brown's Last Speech to the Court, November 2, 1859

I have, may it please the Court, a few words to say.

In the first place, I deny everything but what I have all along admitted,—the design on my part to free the slaves. I intended certainly to have made a clean thing of that matter, as I did last winter, when I went into Missouri and there took slaves without the snapping of a gun on either side, moved them through the country, and finally left them in Canada. I designed to have done the same thing again, on a larger scale. That was all I intended. I never did intend murder, or treason, or the destruction of property, or to excite or incite slaves to rebellion, or to make insurrection.

I have another objection; and that is, it is unjust that I should suffer such a penalty. Had I interfered in the manner which I admit, and which I admit has been fairly proved (for I admire the truthfulness and candor of the greater portion of the witnesses who have testified in this case),—had I so interfered in behalf of the rich, the powerful, the intelligent, the so-called great, or in behalf of any of their friends,—either father, mother, brother, sister, wife, or children, or any of that class,—and suffered and sacrificed what I have in this interference, it would have been all right; and every man in this court would have deemed it an act worthy of reward rather than punishment.

This court acknowledges, as I suppose, the validity of the law of God. I see a book kissed here which I suppose to be the Bible, or at least the New Testament. That teaches me that all things whatsoever I would that men should do to me, I should do even so to them. It teaches me, further, to "remember them that are in bonds, as bound with them." I endeavored to act up to that instruction. I say, I am yet too young to understand that God is any respecter of persons. I believe that to have interfered as I have done—as I have always freely admitted I have done—in behalf of His despised poor, was not wrong, but right. Now, if it is deemed necessary that I should forfeit my life for the furtherance of the ends of justice, and mingle my blood further with the blood of my children and with the blood of millions in this slave country whose rights are disregarded by wicked, cruel, and unjust enactments,—I submit; so let it be done!

Let me say one word further.

I feel entirely satisfied with the treatment I have received on my trial. Considering all the circumstances, it has been more generous than I expected. But I feel no consciousness of guilt. I have stated from the first what was my intention, and what was not. I never have had any design against the life of any person, nor any disposition to commit treason, or excite slaves to rebel, or make any general insurrection. I never encouraged any man to do so, but always discouraged any idea of that kind.

Let me say, also, a word in regard to the statements made by some of those connected with me. I hear it has been stated by some of them that I have induced them to join me. But the contrary is true. I do not say this to injure them, but as regretting their weakness. There is not one of them but joined me of his own accord, and the greater part of them at their own expense. A number of them I never saw, and never had a word of conversation with, till the day they came to me; and that was for the purpose I have stated.

Now I have done.

This sentence was handed by Brown to one of his guards on the morning of his execution.

Charlestown, Va, 2d, December, 1859. I John Brown am now quite *certain* that the crimes of this *guilty, land: will* never be purged *away*; but with Blood. I had *as I now think: vainly* flattered myself that without *verry much* bloodshed; it might be done.

REVIEW QUESTIONS

1. Did Brown accept the charges of treason, murder, and inciting insurrection?
2. What did he say had been his plan?
3. Did he have a defense or justification for what actually happened?
4. Brown knew Ralph Waldo Emerson. Was there perhaps a connection between the actions of the former and the words of the latter? Did Brown illustrate the extremes to which Emerson's sentiments could be applied, or did he in fact go beyond them?

FROM South Carolina's Ordinance of Secession and Declaration of Independence (1860)

Brown's actions and Lincoln's election made the split between North and South a chasm. Fearing that Brown was a harbinger of other such physical assaults and that Lincoln would use his office to abolish slavery, many southern leaders believed that they could no longer rely on political or polemic defenses within the union. They decided that the only way they could defend their peculiar institution, particular way of life, and political sentiments was to secede. They had to move quickly to mobilize support, for not every person, nor every state, in the South was ready for such action when Lincoln won the presidential election in November 1860. "Secessionitis" was particularly strong in South Carolina, and that state consequently took the lead in disunion. On 20 December a special state convention unanimously passed an Ordinance of Secession; a few days later it justified its actions in its own Declaration of Independence (what has also been called a Declaration of the Causes of Secession). Copies were sent to the other southern states, which, already predisposed to "secessionitis," soon passed their own ordinances.

From Howard W. Preston, ed., *Documents Illustrative of American History, 1606–1863* (New York: G. P. Putnam's Sons, 1886), pp. 305–12.

Ordinance of Secession

An ordinance to dissolve the Union between the State of South Carolina and other States united with her under the compact entitled "The Constitution of the United States of America."

We, the People of the State of South Carolina, in Convention assembled, do declare and ordain, and it is hereby declared and ordained, that the Ordinance adopted by us in Convention, on the Twenty-third of May, in the year of our Lord one thousand seven hundred and eighty-eight, whereby the Constitution of the United States was ratified, and also all other Acts and parts of Acts of the General Assembly of the State ratifying amendments of the said Constitution, are hereby repealed, and the Union now subsisting between South Carolina and other States, under the name of the United States of America, is hereby dissolved.

South Carolina Declaration of Independence

The State of South Carolina, having determined to resume her separate and equal place among nations, deems it due to herself, to the remaining United States of America, and to the nations of the world, that she should declare the causes which have led to this act.

In the year 1765, that portion of the British empire embracing Great Britain, undertook to make laws for the government of that portion composed of the thirteen American colonies. A struggle for the right of self-government ensued, which resulted, on the 4th of July, 1776, in a declaration by the colonies, "that they are, and of right ought to be, free and independent states, . . ."

They further solemnly declared, that whenever any "form of government becomes destructive of the ends for which it was established, it is the right of that people to alter or abolish it, and to institute a new government." . . .

In pursuance of this declaration of independence, each of the thirteen states proceeded to exercise its separate sovereignty; adopted for itself a constitution, and appointed officers for the administration of government in all its departments—legislative, executive, and judicial. For purpose of defense, they united their arms and their counsels; and, in 1778, they united in a league, known as the articles of confederation, whereby they agreed to intrust the administration of their external relations to a common agent, known as the Congress of the United States, expressly declaring in the first article, "that each state retains its sovereignty, freedom, and independence, and every power, jurisdiction, and right which is not, by this confederation, expressly delegated to the United States in Congress assembled."

Under this consideration the war of the Revolution was carried on, and on the 3d of September, 1783, the contest ended, and a definite treaty was signed by Great Britain, in which she acknowledged the independence of the colonies in the following terms:

Article I. His Britannic Majesty acknowledges the said United States, viz.: New Hampshire, Massachusetts Bay, Rhode Island and Providence Plantation, Connecticut, New York, New Jersey, Pennsylvania, Delaware, Maryland, Virginia, North Carolina, South Carolina, and Georgia, to be free, sovereign, and independent states; that he treats them as such; and for himself, his heirs, and successors, relinquishes all claim to the government, proprietary and territorial rights of the same, and every part thereof.

Thus was established the two great principles asserted by the colonies, namely, the right of a state to govern itself, and the right of a people to abolish a government when it becomes destructive of the ends for which it was instituted. And concurrent with the establishment of these principles was the fact, that each colony became and was recognized by the mother country as a free, sovereign, and independent state.

In 1787, deputies were appointed by the states to revise the articles of confederation, and on September 17th, 1787, the deputies recommended for the adoption of the states the articles of union known as the constitution of the United States.

The parties to whom the constitution was submitted were the several sovereign states; they were to agree or disagree, and when nine of them agreed, the compact was to take effect among those concurring; and the general government, as the common agent, was then to be invested with their authority.

*   *   *

By this constitution, certain duties were charged on the several states, and the exercise of certain of their powers not delegated to the United States by the constitution, nor prohibited by it to the states, are reserved to the states respectively, or to the people. On the 23d of May, 1788, South Carolina, by a convention of people, passed an ordinance assenting to this constitution, and afterwards altering her own constitution to conform herself to the obligation she had undertaken.

Thus was established, by compact between the states, a government with defined objects and powers, limited to the express words of the grant, and to so much more only as was necessary to execute the power granted. The limitations left the whole remaining mass of power subject to the clause reserving it to the state or to the people, and rendered unnecessary any specification of reserved powers.

We hold that the government thus established is subject to the two great principles asserted in the declaration of independence, and we hold further that the mode of its formation subjects it to a third fundamental principle, namely—the law of compact. We maintain that in every compact between two or more parties, the obligation is mutual—that the failure of one of the contracting parties to perform a material part of the agreement entirely released the obligation of the other, and that, where no arbiter is appointed, each party is remitted to his own judgment to determine the fact of failure with all its consequences.

In the present case that fact is established with certainty. We assert that fifteen of the states have deliberately refused for years past to fulfil their constitutional obligation, and we refer to their own statutes for the proof.

The constitution of the United States, in its fourth article, provides as follows:

"No person held to service or labor in one state, under the laws thereof, escaping into another, shall, in consequence of any law or regulation therein, be discharged from any service or labor, but shall be delivered up, on claim of party to whom such service or labor may be due."

This stipulation was so material to the compact that without it that compact would not have been made. . . .

The same article of the constitution stipulates also for the sedition by the several states of fugitives from justice from the other states.

The general government, as the common agent, passed laws to carry into effect these stipulations of the states. For many years these laws were executed. But an increasing hostility on the part of the northern states to the institution of slavery has led to a disregard of their obligations, and the laws of the general government have ceased to effect the objects of the constitution. The states of Maine, New Hampshire, Vermont, Massachusetts, Connecticut, Rhode Island, New York, Pennsylvania, Illinois, Indiana, Ohio, Michigan, Wisconsin, and Iowa have enacted laws which either nullify the acts of Congress, or render useless any attempt to execute them. In many of these states the fugitive is discharged from the service of labor claimed, and in none of them has the state government complied with the stipulation made in the constitution. . . . In the state of New York even the right of transit for a slave has been denied by her tribunals, and the states of Ohio and Iowa have refused to surrender to justice fugitives charged with murder and inciting servile insurrection in the state of Virginia. Thus the constitutional compact has been deliberately broken and disregarded by the nonslaveholding states, and the consequence follows that South Carolina is released from its obligation.

The ends for which this constitution was framed are declared by itself to be "to form a more perfect union, establish justice, insure domestic tranquillity, provide for the common defence, protect the general welfare, and secure the blessings of liberty to ourselves and posterity."

These ends it endeavored to accomplish by a federal government, in which each state was recognized as an equal, and had separate control over its own institutions. The right of property in slaves was recognized by giving to free persons distinct political rights; by giving them the right to represent, and burdening them with direct taxes for three-fifths of their slaves; by authorizing the importation of slaves for twenty years, and by stipulating for the rendition of fugitives from labor.

We affirm that these ends for which this government was instituted have been defeated, and the government itself has been made destructive of them by the action of the non-slaveholding state. These states have assumed the right of deciding upon the propriety of our domestic institutions, and have denied the rights of property established in fifteen of the states and recognized by the constitution; they have denounced as sinful the institution of slavery; they have permitted the open establishment among them of societies whose avowed object is to disturb the peace and claim the property of the citizens of other states. They have encouraged and assisted thousands of our slaves to leave their homes, and those who remain have been incited by emissaries, books, and pictures to servile insurrection.

For twenty-five years this agitation has been steadily increasing, until it has now secured to its aid the power of the common government. Observing the forms of the constitution, a sectional party has found within that article establishing the executive department the means of subverting the constitution itself. A geographical line has been drawn across the Union, and all the states north of that line have united in the election of a man to the high office of President of the United States, whose opinions and purposes are hostile to slavery. He is to be entrusted with the administration of the common government, because he has declared that that "government cannot endure permanently half slave, half free," and that the public mind must rest in the belief that slavery is in the course of ultimate extinction.

This sectional combination for the subversion of the constitution has been aided in some of the states by elevating to citizenship persons who, by the supreme law of the land, are incapable of becoming citizens, and their votes have been used to inaugurate a new policy hostile to the south, and destructive of its peace and safety.

On the 4th of March next, this party will take possession of the government. It has announced that the south shall be excluded from the common territory; that the judicial tribunals shall be made sectional, and that a war must be waged against slavery until it shall cease throughout the United States.

The guarantees of the constitution will then no longer exist; the equal rights of the states will be lost. The slaveholding states will no longer have the power of self-government or self-protection, and the federal government will have become their enemies.

Sectional interest and animosity will deepen the irritation, and all hope of remedy is rendered vain by the fact that public opinion at the north has invested a great political error with the sanctions of a more erroneous religious belief.

We, therefore, the people of South Carolina, by our delegates in convention assembled, appealing to the Supreme Judge of the world for the rectitude of our intentions, have solemnly declared that the union heretofore existing between this state and the other states of North America is dissolved, and that the state of South Carolina has resumed her position among the nations of the world as a free, sovereign, and independent state, with full power to levy war, conclude peace, contract alliances, establish commerce, and to do all other acts and things which independent states may, of right, do.

And, for the support of this declaration, with a firm reliance on the protection of Divine Providence, we mutually pledge to each other, our lives, our fortunes, and our sacred honor.

REVIEW QUESTIONS

1. Did South Carolina believe that secession was a legal or constitutional act?
2. What were the three great rights or principles upon which South Carolina was basing its actions?
3. What specific charges did it levy against the northern states? Were they, not the southern states, to blame for the disintegration of the union?
4. Did South Carolina essentially argue that secession was the last step in disunion, not the first?

17 ✍ THE WAR OF THE UNION

Rebellion—Civil War—War between the States—War of Northern Aggression:
the words referred to the same event, but as seen from different perspectives.
These titles at first simply gave a name to the climax of the nation's crisis, but
later they came to define and be defined by the terrible toll of four years of bloody
conflict. Although often talked about as a war between North and South and a
war between brothers, this cataclysm engulfed all of America's regions and peoples
as it devastated farms and families, strained resources, killed millions, and even
scorched the nation's connections with other countries.

The war began with declarations and proclamations as adversaries justified
their stands and toed lines in the sand. Then they called in their friends to stand
with them as they dared their opponents to step over those lines. The southern
states challenged the federal government with their declarations of secession and
by arming and drilling their swelling militias. The new president of the United
States, Abraham Lincoln, first responded with requests for dialogue and calm de-
liberation, but when South Carolina, taking the initiative again, fired on Fort
Sumter in Charleston harbor on 12 April 1861, Lincoln fired back. On the 15th
he issued a call for military volunteers from the loyal states, and then on the
19th, "with a view . . . to the protection of the public peace, and the lives and
property of quiet and orderly citizens pursuing their lawful occupations," he pro-
claimed a blockade against the southern ports. Lincoln hoped that the use of such
a naval blanket would suffocate the flames of rebellion; instead, it fanned them.

More southern states seceded and joined the compact that had been formal-
ized between their sister states in March. The government of the Confederate
States of America raised armies for defense and appointed ministers to pursue its
interests abroad. The Confederacy wanted foreign powers to recognize its inde-
pendence, for that acknowledgment would undermine the Union's contention that
the war was an internal insurrection—a civil war—not a war between states or
nations. Recognition was also a prerequisite to indispensable trade connections

and perhaps military alliances. The United States government, by employing the diplomatic connections it had established over the years, wielding its economic might, and threatening war against those who intervened, countered the Confederacy abroad by warning other nations away from recognition and intervention. Foreign nations deliberated upon the enticements of the South and demands of the North, and then made their decisions based on their own best interests, not America's. The fact that some nations, especially Britain, contemplated recognition instead of dismissing the southern suit, was another powerful lesson on vulnerability for the United States.

While United States and Confederate ministers skirmished abroad, their governments and citizens focused on the vital, vicious battles being waged on American soil. Initially, many men (and a few women in disguise) flocked to enlist in their state regiments. They were eager to fight in what they were sure would be a short but glorious war. As the war lengthened and its toll—human casualties, property destruction, social disruption—mounted, however, Americans everywhere began to question the causes and costs. The war, a time of extermination, began a period of self-examination.

Southerners said that they fought so that they, using the words of 1776, would not be slaves. They, even less so than the founders, failed to see the irony in that. Charles T. O'Ferrall, a cavalry officer in the Army of Northern Virginia who later became a congressman for and then governor of the state of Virginia, reflected back on southerners' justifications when he published his memoirs in 1904. O'Ferrall wrote, "in spite of charters, compacts, and constitutions, a people who conscientiously believe they have been oppressed and wronged and can secure no redress have the inborn right to throw off the yoke that galls and strike for their liberties." While he declared, years after the war, that there was "no longer a spirit of revolt or rebellion" in his "bosom," he also said that he was proud to have been a rebel who stood "upon the eternal principles of the Declaration of Independence." If George Washington and his compatriots gloried in the term rebel, then O'Ferrall thought, so should the followers of Jefferson Davis and Robert E. Lee.

Northerners also declared that they fought for the ideas and fruits of the Revolution. As Lincoln intoned on 19 November 1863 at Gettysburg:

> Four score and seven years ago our fathers brought forth on this continent, a new nation, conceived in Liberty, and dedicated to the proposition that all men are created equal.
>
> Now we are engaged in a great civil war, testing whether that nation, or any nation so conceived and so dedicated, can long endure. . . .
>
> . . . It is for us the living, . . . to be dedicated here to the unfinished work which they who fought here have thus far so nobly advanced. . . . that this nation, under God, shall have a new birth of freedom—and that government of the people, by the people, for the people, shall not perish from the earth.

FREDERICK DOUGLASS

FROM **The Reasons for Our Troubles (1862)**

Was slavery truly the cause, or just the catalyst, of the cataclysm? That question, in turn, begs another: If the crisis was about slavery, was the war about it? Since neither side initially recruited and rallied its troops specifically for or against slavery, such questions engaged contemporaries of the war as well as later historians. Frederick Douglass was appalled by the avoidance of the issue, for he believed that "the mission of the war was the liberation of the slave as well as the salvation of the Union." He argued that the two parts of the mission were inseparable, contradicting others who not only separated them but made the former subordinate to the latter. Douglass refused to let the war distract Americans from the abolition of slavery and the emancipation of the slaves. He traveled through the northern states on extensive lecture tours in 1861 and the winter of 1862, urging his audiences to send petitions and delegations to Washington, D.C., so as to convince the administration to establish a policy in support of freedom. He presented his case to a Philadelphia audience at National Hall on 14 January 1862 and then published his speech in his journal, Douglass' Monthly, *the following month.*

From Frederick Douglass, *The Life and Writings of Frederick Douglass*, vol. III, ed. Philip S. Foner (New York: International Publishers, 1952), pp. 198–208.

*   *   *

To-day, all is changed. The face of every loyal citizen is sicklied over with the pale cast of thought. Every pillar in the national temple is shaken. The nation itself has fallen asunder in the centre. A million of armed men confront each other. Hostile flags wave defiance in sight of the National Capital during a period of six long and anxious months. Our riches take wings. Credit is disturbed, business is interrupted, national debt—the mill-stone on the neck of nations—and heavy taxation, which breaks the back of loyalty, loom in the distance. As the war progresses, property is wantonly destroyed, the wires are broken down, bridges demolished, railroads are pulled up and barricaded by fallen trees; still more and worse, the great writ of *habeas corpus* is suspended from necessity, liberty of speech and of the press have ceased to exist. An order from Richmond or Washington—one stroke of the pen from Davis or Lincoln sends any citizen to prison, . . . A hateful system of espionage is in process of formation, while war and blood mantles the whole land as with the shadow of death. We speak and write now by the forbearance of our rulers, not by the sacredness of our rights. I speak this not in complaint; I admit the necessity, while I lament it. The scene need not be further portrayed. It is dismal and terrible beyond all description. . . .

The spoilers of the Republic have dealt with the nation as burglars—stealing all they could carry away, and burning the residue.—They have emptied your treasury, plundered your arsenals, scattered your navy, corrupted your army, seduced your officers, seized your forts, covered the sea with pirates, "heated your enemies, cooled your friends," insulted your flag, defied your Government, converted the national defences into instruments of national destruction, and have invited hostile armies of foreign nations to unite with them in completing the national ruin. All this, and more, has been done by the very men whom you have honored, paid and trusted, and that, too, while they were solemnly sworn to protect, support and defend your Constitution and Government against all foes at home and abroad.

To what cause may we trace our present sad and deplorable condition? A man of flighty brain and flippant tongue will tell you that the cause of all our national troubles lies solely in the election of Abraham Lincoln to the President of the Republic. To the superficial this is final. Before Lincoln there was peace; after Lincoln there was rebellion. It stands to reason that Lincoln and rebellion are related as cause and effect. Such is their argument; such is their explanation. I hardly need waste your time in showing the folly and falsehood of either. Beyond all question, the facts show that this rebellion was planned and prepared long before the name of Abraham Lincoln was mentioned in connection with the office he now holds, and that though the catastrophe might have been postponed, it could not have been prevented, nor long delayed. The worst of our condition is not to be sought in our disaster on flood or field.—It is to be found rather in the character which contact with slavery has developed in every part of the country, so that at last there seems to be no truth, no candor left within us. We have faithfully copied all the cunning of the serpent without any of the harmlessness of the dove, or the boldness of the lion.

In dealing with the causes of our present troubles we find in quarters, high and low, the most painful evidences of dishonesty. It would seem, in the language of Isaiah, that the whole head is sick, and the whole heart is faint, that there is no soundness in it.—After-coming generations will remark with astonishment this feature in this dark chapter in our national history. They will find in no public document emanating from the loyal Government, anything like a frank and full statement of the real causes which have plunged us in the whirlpool of civil war. On the other hand, they will find the

most studied and absurd attempts at concealment. Jefferson Davis is reticent. He seems ashamed to tell the world just what he is fighting for. Abraham Lincoln seems equally so, and is ashamed to tell the world what he is fighting against.

If we turn from the heads of the Government to the heads of the several Departments, we are equally befogged. The attempt is made to conceal the real facts of the case.—Our astute Secretary of State is careful to enjoin it upon our foreign ministers to remain dumb in respect to the real causes of the rebellion. They are to say nothing of the moral differences existing between the two sections of the country. There must be no calling things by their right names—no going straight to any point which can be reached by a crooked path. When slaves are referred to, they must be called persons held to service or labor. When in the hands of the Federal Governments, they are called contrabands—a name that will apply better to a pistol, than to a person. The preservation of slavery is called the preservation of the rights of the South under the Constitution. This concealment is one of the most contemptible features of the crisis. Every cause for the rebellion but the right one is pointed out and dwelt upon. Some make it geographical; others make it ethnographical.

*   *   *

But even this cause does not hold true.—There is no geographical reason for national division. Every stream is bridged, and every mountain is tunnelled. All our rivers and mountains point to union, not division—to oneness, not to warfare. There is no earthly reason why the corn fields of Pennsylvania should quarrel with the cotton fields of South Carolina. The physical and climatic differences bind them together, instead of putting them asunder.

A very large class of persons charge all our national calamities upon the busy tongues and pens of the Abolitionists. Thus we accord to a handful of men and women, everywhere despised, a power superior to all other classes in the country. . . .

Others still explain the whole matter, by telling us that it is the work of defeated and disappointed politicians at the South. I shall waste no time upon either. The cause of this rebellion is deeper down than either Southern politicians or Northern Abolitionists. . . . The Southern politicians and the Northern Abolitionists are the fruits, not the trees. They indicate, but are not original causes. The trouble is deeper down, and is fundamental; there is nothing strange about it. The conflict is in every way natural.—"How can two walk together except they be agreed?" . . . It is something of a feat to ride two horses going the same way, and at the same pace, but a still greater feat when going in opposite directions.

Just here lies a true explanation of our troubles. . . . We have attempted to maintain our Union in utter defiance of the moral chemistry of the universe. We have endeavored to join together things which in their nature stand eternally asunder. We have sought to bind the chains of slavery on the limbs of the black man, without thinking that at last we should find the other end of that hateful chain about our own necks.

A glance at the history of the settlement of the two sections of this country will show that the causes which produced the present rebellion, reach back to the dawn of civilization on this continent. In the same year that the Mayflower landed her liberty-seeking passengers on the bleak New England shore, a Dutch galliot landed a company of African slaves on the banks of the James river, Virginia. The Mayflower planted liberty at the North, and the Dutch galliot slavery at the South.—There is the fire, and there is the gunpowder. Contact has produced the explosion. What has followed might have been easily predicted. Great men saw it from the beginning, but no great men were found great enough to prevent it.

The statesmanship of the last half century has been mainly taxed to perpetuate the American Union. A system of compromise and concessions has been adopted. A double-dealing policy—a facing-both-ways statesmanship, naturally sprung up, and became fashionable—so that political success was often made to depend upon political cheating. One section or the other must be deceived. Before railroads and electric wires were spread over the country, this trickery and fraud had a chance of success. The lighting made deception more difficult, and the Union by compromise impossible. Our Union is killed by lightning.

In order to have union, either in the family, in the church, or in the State, there must be unity of idea and sentiment in all essential interests. Find a man's treasure, and you have found his heart. Now, in the North, freedom is the grand and all-comprehensive condition of comfort, prosperity and happiness. All our ideas and sentiments grow out of this free element. Free speech, free soil, free men, free schools, free inquiry, free suffrage, equality before the law, are the natural outgrowths of freedom. Freedom is the centre of our Northern social system. It warms into life every other interest, and makes it beautiful in our eyes. Liberty is our treasure, and our hearts dwell with it, and receives its actuating motives from it.

What freedom is to the North as a generator of sentiment and ideas, *that* slavery is to the South. It is the treasure to which the Southern heart is fastened. It fashions all their ideas, and moulds all their sentiments.—Politics, education, literature, morals and religion in the South, all bear the bloody image and superscription of slavery. Here, then, are two direct, point-blank and irreconcilable antagonisms under the same form of government. The marvel is not that civil war has come, but that it did not come sooner. But the evil is now upon us, and the question as to the causes which produced it, is of less consequence than the question as to how it ought to be, and can be thrown off. How shall the civil war be ended?

It can be ended for a time in one of two ways. One by recognizing the complete independence of the Southern Confederacy, and indemnifying the traitors and rebels for all the expense to which they have been put, in carrying out this tremendous slaveholding rebellion; and the second is by receiving the slaveholding States back into the Union with such guarantees for slavery as they may demand for the better security and preservation of slavery. In either of these two ways it may be put down for a time; but God forbid that any such methods of obtaining peace shall be adopted; for neither the one nor the other could bring any permanent peace.

I take it that these United States are to remain united. National honor requires national unity. To abandon that idea would be a disgraceful, scandalous and cowardly surrender of the majority to a rebellious minority—the capitulation of twenty million loyal men to six million rebels—and would draw after it a train of disasters such as would heap curses on the very graves of the present generation. As to giving the slave States new guarantees for the safety of slavery, that I take to be entirely out of the question. The South does not want them, and the North could not give them if the South could accept them. To concede anything to these slave-holding traitors and rebels in arms, after all their atrocious crimes against justice, humanity, and every sentiment of loyalty, would be tantamount to the nation's defeat, and would substitute in the future the bayonet for the ballot, and cannon balls for Congress, revolution and anarchy for government, and the pronunciamentoes of rebel chiefs for regulating enacted laws.

There is therefore no escape. The only road to national honor, and permanent peace to us, is to meet, fight, dislodge, drive back, conquer and subdue the rebels. . . .

We have bought Florida, waged war with friendly Seminoles, purchased Louisiana, annexed Texas, fought Mexico, trampled on the right of petition, abridged the freedom of debate, paid ten million to Texas upon a fraudulent claim, mobbed the Abolitionists, repealed the Missouri Compromise, winked at the accursed slave trade, helped to extend slavery, given slave-holders a larger share of all the offices and honors than we claimed for ourselves, paid their postage, supported the Government, persecuted free Negroes, refused to recognize Haiti and Liberia, stained our souls by repeated compromises, borne with Southern bluster, allowed our ships to be robbed of their hardy sailors, defeated a central road to the Pacific, and have descended to the meanness and degradation of Negro dogs, and hunted down the panting slave escaping from his tyrant master—all to make the South love us; and yet how stand our relations?

At this hour there is everywhere at the South, nursed and cherished, the most deadly hate towards every man and woman of Northern birth. We, here at the North, do not begin to understand the strength and bitter intensity of this slaveholding malice. Mingled with it is a supercilious sense of superiority—a scornful contempt—the strutting pride of the turkey, with the cunning and poison of the rattlesnake. I say again, we must meet them, defeat them, and conquer them. Do I hear you say that this is more easily said than done? I admit it. . . .

*   *   *

But how shall the rebellion be put down? I will tell you; but before I do so, you must allow me to say that the plan thus far pursued does not correspond with my humble notion of fitness. Thus far, it must be confessed, we have struck wide of the mark, and very feebly withal. The temper of our steel has proved much better than the temper of our minds. While I do not charge, as some have done, that the Government at Washington is conducting the war upon peace principles, it is very plain that the war is not being conducted on war principles.

We are fighting the rebels with only one hand, when we ought to be fighting them with both. We are recruiting our troops in the towns and villages of the North, when we ought to be recruiting them on the plantations of the South. We are striking the guilty rebels with our soft, white hand, when we should be striking with the iron hand of the black man, which we keep chained behind us. We have been catching slaves, instead of arming them. We have thus far repelled our natural friends to win the worthless and faithless friendship of our unnatural enemies. We have been endeavoring to heal over the rotten cancer of slavery, instead of cutting out its death-dealing roots and fibres. We pay more attention to the advice of the half-rebel State of Kentucky, than to any suggestion coming from the loyal North. We have shouldered all the burdens of slavery, and given the slaveholders and traitors all its benefits; and robbed our cause of half its dignity in the eyes of an onlooking world.

I say here and now, that if this nation is destroyed—if the Government, shall, after all, be broken to pieces, and degraded in the eyes of the world—if the Union shall be shattered into fragments, it will neither be for the want of men, nor of money, nor even physical courage, for we have all these in abundance; but it will be solely owing to the want of moral courage and wise statesmanship in dealing with slavery, the *cause* and motive of the rebellion.

*   *   *

I have been often asked since this war began, why I am not at the South battling for freedom. My answer is with the Government. The Washington Government wants men for its army, but thus far, it has not had the boldness to recognize the manhood of the race to which I belong. It only sees in the slave an article of commerce—a contraband. I do not wish to say aught against our Government, for good or bad; it is all we have to save us from anarchy and ruin; but I owe it to my race, in view of the cruel aspersions cast upon it, to affirm that, in denying them the privileges to fight for their country, they have been most deeply and grievously wronged. Neither in the Revolution, nor in the last war did any such narrow and contemptible policy obtain. It shows the deep degeneracy of our times—the height from which we have fallen—that, while Washington, in 1776, and Jackson, in 1814, could fight side by side with Negroes, now, not even the best of our generals are willing so to fight. Is McClellan better than Washington? Is Halleck better than Jackson?

*   *   *

Thus far we have shown no lack of force. A call for men is answered by half a million. A call for money brings down a hundred million. A call for prayers brings a nation to its altars. But still the rebellion rages.—Washington is menaced. The Potomac is blockaded. Jeff Davis is still proud and defiant, and the rebels are looking forward hopefully to a recognition of their independence, the breaking of the blockade, and their final severance from the North.

Now, what is the remedy for all this? The answer is ready. Have done at once and forever with the wild and guilty phantasy that any one man can have a right of property in the body and soul of another man. Have done with the now exploded idea that the old Union, which has hobbled along through seventy years upon the crutches of compromise, is either desirable or possible, now, or in the future. Accept the incontestible truth of the "irrepressible conflict." It was spoken when temptations to compromise were less strong than now. Banish from your political dreams the last lingering adumbration that this great American nation can ever rest firmly and securely upon a mixed basis, part of iron, part of clay, part free, and part slave. . . .

To let this occasion pass unimproved, for getting rid of slavery, would be a sin against unborn generations. The cup of slave-holding iniquity is full and running over; now let it be disposed of and finished forever. Reason, common sense, justice, and humanity alike concur with this necessary step for the national safety. But it is contended that the nation at large has no right to interfere with slavery in the States—that the Constitution gives no power to abolish slavery. This pretext is flung at us at every corner, by the same men who, a few months ago, told us we had no Constitutional right to coerce a seceded State—no right to collect revenue in the harbors of such States—no right to subjugate such States—and it is part and parcel of the same nonsense.

In the first place, slavery has no Constitutional existence in the country. There is not a provision of that instrument which would be contravened by its abolition. But if every line and syllable of the Constitution contained an explicit prohibition of the abolition of slavery, the right of the nation to abolish it would still remain in full force. In virtue of a principle underlying all government—that of national self-preservation—the nation can no more be bound to disregard this, than a man can be bound to commit suicide. This law of self preservation is the great end and object of all Governments and Constitutions. The means can never be superior to the end. But will our Government ever arrive at this conclusion? That will depend upon two very opposite elements.

First, it will depend upon the sum of Northern virtue.

Secondly, upon the extent of Southern villainy.

Now, I have much confidence in Northern virtue, but much more in Southern villainy.— Events are greater than either party to the conflict. We are fighting not only a wicked and determined foe, but a maddened and desperate foe. We are not fighting serviles, but our masters—men who have ruled over us for fifty years. If hard pushed, we may expect them to break through all the restraints of civilized warfare.

I am still hopeful that the Government will take direct and powerful abolition measures. That hope is founded on the fact that the Government has already traveled further in that direction than it promised. . . . No President, no Cabinet, no army can withstand the mighty current of events, or the surging billows of the popular will. The first flash of rebel gunpowder, ten months ago, pouring shot and shell upon the starving handful of men at Sumter, instantly changed the whole policy of the nation. Until then, the ever hopeful North, of all parties, was still dreaming of compromise. The heavens were black, the thunder rattled, the air was heavy, and vivid lightning flashed all around; but our sages were telling us there would be no rain. But all at once, down came the storm of hail and fire.

*   *   *

Nothing stands to-day where it stood yesterday. Humanity sweeps onward. To-night with saints and angels, surrounded with the glorious army of martyrs and confessors, of whom our guilty world was not worthy, the brave spirit of old John Brown serenely looks down from his eternal rest, beholding his guilty murderers in torments of their own kindling, and the faith for which he nobly died steadily becoming the saving faith of the nation. . . .

We have seen great changes—everybody has changed—the North has changed—Republicans have changed—and even the Garrisonians, of whom it has been said that repentance is not among their virtues, even they have changed; and from being the stern advocates of a dissolution of the Union, they have become the uncompromising advocates of the perpetuity of the Union. I believed ten years ago that liberty was safer in the Union than out of the Union; but my Garrisonian friends could not then so see it, and of consequence dealt me some heavy blows. My crime was in being ten years in advance of them. But whether the Government shall directly abolish slavery or not, the war is essentially an abolition war. When the storm clouds of this rebellion shall be lifted from the land, the slave power, broken and humbled, will be revealed. Slavery will be a conquered power in the land. I am, therefore, for the war, for the Government, for the Union, for the Constitution in any and every event.

Douglass' Monthly, February, 1862

REVIEW QUESTIONS

1. Douglass listed numerous causes of the war—as presented by his contemporaries. What were they?
2. Did Douglass trace the nation's calamity to its politics or its character? Why did he make that distinction?
3. What were some of the alternatives for ending the war? Did he advocate the more peaceful solutions? Why or why not?
4. How did he propose to strengthen the Union's military fitness? Would this also strengthen the nation's moral fiber?
5. Did he present a case for seeing the war as a fight for northern instead of southern independence?

ABRAHAM LINCOLN

Letter for Springfield Rally (1863)

To do as Douglass demanded, to make this a war against slavery, was difficult for Lincoln. Adopting emancipation meant abandoning the possibility of reconciliation through compromise and introduced the possibility of not just greater southern resistance but northern opposition as well. Overall, however, Lincoln came to believe that positive results—in both foreign and domestic relations—would outweigh negative ones. Lincoln, therefore, using the war powers of the presidency, proclaimed the emancipation of the slaves on 1 January 1863. Most northerners applauded the proclamation, but some criticized it, along with some of his other political and military strategies. Lincoln addressed such criticisms in a letter that he sent to his old friend James C. Conkling (a lawyer active in the Illinois Republican party) to be read before the crowd at the Springfield rally on 3 September 1863.

From Abraham Lincoln, *Speeches and Writings, 1859–1865* (New York: The Library of America, 1989), pp. 495–99. [Editorial insertions appear in square brackets—*Ed.*]

My Dear Sir.   Washington, August 26, 1863.

Your letter inviting me to attend a mass-meeting of unconditional Union-men, to be held at the Capital of Illinois, on the 3d day of September, has been received.

It would be very agreeable to me, to thus meet my old friends, at my own home; but I can not, just now, be absent from here, so long as a visit there, would require.

The meeting is to be of all those who maintain unconditional devotion to the Union; and I am sure my old political friends will thank me for tendering, as I do, the nation's gratitude to those other noble men, whom no partizan malice, or partizan hope, can make false to the nation's life.

There are those who are dissatisfied with me. To such I would say: You desire peace; and you blame me that we do not have it. But how can we attain it? There are but three conceivable ways. First, to suppress the rebellion by force of arms. This, I am trying to do. Are you for it? If you are, so far we are agreed. If you are not for it, a second way is, to give up the Union. I am against this. Are you for it? If you are, you should say so plainly. If you are not for *force*, nor yet for *dissolution*, there only remains some imaginable *compromise*. I do not believe any compromise, embracing the maintenance of the Union, is now possible. All I learn, leads to a directly opposite belief. The strength of the rebellion, is its military—its army. That army dominates all the country, and all the people, within its range. Any offer of terms made by any man or men within that range, in opposition to that army, is simply nothing for the present; because such man or men, have no power whatever to enforce their side of a compromise, if one were made with them. To illustrate—Suppose refugees from the South, and peace men of the North, get together in convention, and frame and proclaim a compromise embracing a restoration of the Union; in what way can that compromise be used to keep Lee's army out of Pennsylvania? Meade's army can keep Lee's army out of Pennsylvania; and, I think, can ultimately drive it out of existence. But no paper compromise, to which the controllers of Lee's army are not agreed, can, at all, affect that army. In an effort at such compromise we should waste time, which the enemy would improve to our disadvantage; and that would be all. A compromise, to be effective, must be made either with those who control the rebel army, or with the people first liberated from the domination of that army, by the success of our own army. Now allow me to assure you, that no word or intimation, from that rebel army, or from any of the men controlling it, in relation to any peace compromise, has ever come to my knowledge or belief. All charges and insinuations to the contrary, are deceptive and groundless. And I promise you, that if any such proposition shall hereafter come, it shall not be rejected, and kept a secret from you. I freely acknowledge myself the servant of the people, according to the bond of service—the United States constitution; and that, as such, I am responsible to them.

But, to be plain, you are dissatisfied with me about the negro. Quite likely there is a difference of opinion between you and myself upon that subject. I certainly wish that all men could be free, while I suppose you do not. Yet I have neither adopted, nor proposed any measure, which is not consistent with even your view, provided you are for the Union. I suggested compensated emancipation; to which you replied you wished not to be taxed to buy negroes. But I had not asked you to be taxed to buy negroes, except in such way, as to save you from greater taxation to save the Union exclusively by other means.

You dislike the emancipation proclamation; and, perhaps, would have it retracted. You say it is unconstitutional—I think differently. I think the constitution invests its commander-in-chief, with the law of war, in time of war. The most that can be said, if so much, is, that slaves are property. Is there—has there ever been—any question that by the law of war, property, both of enemies and friends, may be taken when needed? And is it not needed whenever taking it, helps us, or hurts the enemy? Armies, the world over, destroy enemies' property when they can not use it; and even destroy their own to keep it from the enemy. Civilized belligerents do all in their power to help themselves, or hurt the enemy, except a few things re-

garded as barbarous or cruel. Among the exceptions are the massacre of vanquished foes, and non-combatants, male and female.

But the proclamation, as law, either is valid, or is not valid. If it is not valid, it needs no retraction. If it is valid, it can not be retracted, any more than the dead can be brought to life. Some of you profess to think its retraction would operate favorably for the Union. Why better *after* the retraction, than *before* the issue? There was more than a year and a half of trial to suppress the rebellion before the proclamation issued, the last one hundred days of which passed under an explicit notice that it was coming, unless averted by those in revolt, returning to their allegiance. The war has certainly progressed as favorably for us, since the issue of the proclamation as before. I know as fully as one can know the opinions of others, that some of the commanders of our armies in the field who have given us our most important successes, believe the emancipation policy, and the use of colored troops, constitute the heaviest blow yet dealt to the rebellion; and that, at least one of those important successes, could not have been achieved when it was, but for the aid of black soldiers. Among the commanders holding these views are some who have never had any affinity with what is called abolitionism, or with republican party politics; but who hold them purely as military opinions. I submit these opinions as being entitled to some weight against the objections, often urged, that emancipation, and arming the blacks, are unwise as military measures, and were not adopted, as such, in good faith.

You say you will not fight to free negroes. Some of them seem willing to fight for you; but, no matter. Fight you, then, exclusively to save the Union. I issued the proclamation on purpose to aid you in saving the Union. Whenever you shall have conquered all resistance to the Union, if I shall urge you to continue fighting, it will be an apt time, then, for you to declare you will not fight to free negroes.

I thought that in your struggle for the Union, to whatever extent the negroes should cease helping the enemy, to that extent it weakened the enemy in his resistance to you. Do you think differently? I thought that whatever negroes can be got to do as soldiers, leaves just so much less for white soldiers to do, in saving the Union. Does it appear otherwise to you? But negroes, like other people, act upon motives. Why should they do any thing for us, if we will do nothing for them? If they stake their lives for us, they must be prompted by the strongest motive—even the promise of freedom. And the promise being made, must be kept.

The signs look better. . . . And while those who have cleared the great river [the Mississippi] may well be proud, even that is not all. It is hard to say that anything has been more bravely, and well done, than at Antietam, Murfreesboro, Gettysburg, and on many fields of lesser note. Nor must Uncle Sam's Web-feet be forgotten. At all the watery margins they have been present. Not only on the deep sea, the broad bay, and the rapid river, but also up the narrow muddy bayou, and wherever the ground was a little damp, they have been, and made their tracks. Thanks to all. For the great republic—for the principle it lives by, and keeps alive—for man's vast future,—thanks to all.

Peace does not appear so distant as it did. I hope it will come soon, and come to stay; and so come as to be worth the keeping in all future time.

It will then have been proved that, among free men, there can be no successful appeal from the ballot to the bullet; and that they who take such appeal are sure to lose their case, and pay the cost. And then, there will be some black men who can remember that, with silent tongue, and clenched teeth, and steady eye, and well-poised bayonet, they have helped mankind on to this great consummation; while, I fear, there will be some white ones, unable to forget that, with malignant heart, and deceitful speech, they have strove to hinder it.

Still let us not be over-sanguine of a speedy final triumph. Let us be quite sober. Let us diligently apply the means, never doubting that a just God, in his own good time, will give us the rightful result.

REVIEW QUESTIONS

1. What were the three ways to attain peace that Lincoln listed?
2. Which one did he advocate? Why?
3. How did he defend the *Emancipation Proclamation*?
4. What does his defense reveal about his reasons for issuing it? What does it reveal about public opinion?

SUSIE KING TAYLOR

FROM *Reminiscences of My Life in Camp* (1902)

Susie King Taylor, "born under the slave law in Georgia, in 1848," was brought up by her grandmother in Savannah. Her grandmother, by Taylor's description, appears to have been free, or if a slave, one who was allowed a great deal of freedom. This grandmother saw to it that Taylor learned to read and write at a clandestine school. Taylor's accomplishments served her well when Union troops took possession of the sea islands off of Georgia's coast in the spring of 1862, for upon her fleeing to their lines with her uncle's family, she was put in charge of a school for the children of St. Simon's Island. While there she met her first husband, Edward King. Together with her husband, who was made a sergeant, and some of her relatives, Taylor became part of the First South Carolina Volunteers (later known as the 33rd United States Colored Troops or 33rd United States Colored Infantry), the first black regiment organized by the Union Army. There was still opposition to the recruitment of black troops in the North, but necessity and some white officers challenged the prejudices and fears behind that opposition as they filled their regiments in the South. Taylor later wrote of her experiences to "show how much service and good we can do to each other, and what sacrifices we can make for our liberty and rights, and that there were 'loyal women,' as well as men, in those days, who did not fear shell or shot, who cared for the sick and dying; women who camped and fared as the boys did, and who are still caring for the comrades in their declining years."

From Susie King Taylor, *Reminiscences of My Life in Camp* (1902; New York: Arno Press and The New York Times, 1968), pp. 15–17, 22–27, 29–30, 42–44, 50–51.

*   *   *

The latter part of August, 1862, Captain C. T. Trowbridge, with his brother John and Lieutenant Walker, came to St. Simon's Island from Hilton Head, by order of General Hunter, to get all the men possible to finish filling his regiment which he had organized in March, 1862. He had heard of the skirmish on this island, and was very much pleased at the bravery shown by these men. He found me at Gaston Bluff teaching my little school, and was much interested in it. When I knew him better I found him to be a thorough gentleman and a staunch friend to my race.

Captain Trowbridge remained with us until October, when the order was received to evacuate, and so we boarded the Ben-De-Ford, a transport, for Beaufort, S. C. When we arrived in Beaufort, Captain Trowbridge and the men he had enlisted went to camp at Old Fort, which they named "Camp Saxton." I was enrolled as laundress.

*   *   *

The first colored troops did not receive any pay for eighteen months, and the men had to depend wholly on what they received from the commissary, established by General Saxton. A great many of these men had large families, and as they had no money to give them, their wives were obliged to support themselves and children by washing for the officers of the gunboats and the soldiers, and making cakes and pies which they sold to the boys in camp. Finally, in 1863, the government decided to give them half pay, but the men would not accept this. They wanted "full pay" or nothing. They preferred rather to give their services to the state, which they did until 1864, when the government granted them full pay, with all the back pay due.

I remember hearing Captain Heasley telling his company, one day, "Boys, stand up for your full pay! I am with you, and so are all the officers." This captain was from Pennsylvania, and was a very good man; all the men liked him. . . .

I had a number of relatives in this regiment,— several uncles, some cousins, and a husband in Company E, and a number of cousins in other companies. Major Strong, of this regiment, started home on a furlough, but the vessel he was aboard was lost, and he never reached his home. He was one of the best officers we had. After his death, Captain C. T. Trowbridge was promoted major, August, 1863, and filled Major Strong's place until December, 1864, when he was promoted lieutenant-colonel, which he remained until he was mustered out, February 6, 1866.

*   *   *

March 10, 1863, we were ordered to Jacksonville, Florida. Leaving Camp Saxton between four and five o'clock, we arrived at Jacksonville about eight o'clock next morning, accompanied by three or four gunboats. When the rebels saw these boats, they ran out of the city, leaving the women behind, and we found out afterwards that they thought we had a much larger fleet than we really had. Our regiment was kept out of sight until we made fast at the wharf where it landed, and while the gunboats were shelling up the river and as far inland as possible, the regiment landed and marched up the street, where they spied the rebels who had fled from the city. They were hiding behind a house about a mile or so away, their faces blackened to disguise themselves as negroes, and our boys, as they advanced toward them, halted a second, saying, "They are black men! Let them come to us, or we will make them know who we are." With this, the firing was opened and several of our men were wounded and killed. The rebels had a number wounded and killed. It was through this way the discovery was made that they were white men. Our men drove them some distance in retreat and then threw out their pickets.

While the fighting was on, a friend, Lizzie Lancaster, and I stopped at several of the rebel homes, and after talking with some of the women and children we asked them if they had any food. They claimed to have only some hard-tack, and evidently did not care to give us anything to eat, but this was not surprising. They were bitterly against our people and had no mercy or sympathy for us.

The second day, our boys were reinforced by a regiment of white soldiers, a Maine regiment, and by cavalry, and had quite a fight. On the third day, Edward Herron, who was a fine gunner on the steamer John Adams, came on shore, bringing a small cannon, which the men pulled along for more than five miles. This cannon was the only piece for shelling. On coming upon the enemy, all secured their places, and they had a lively fight, which lasted several hours, and our boys were nearly captured by the Confederates; but the Union boys carried out all their plans that day, and succeeded in driving the enemy back. . . .

*   *   *

We remained here a few weeks longer, when, about April first, the regiment was ordered back to Camp Saxton, where it stayed a week, when the order came to go to Port Royal Ferry on picket duty. . . . We arrived at Seabrooke at about four o'clock, where our tents were pitched and the men put on duty. We were here a few weeks, when Company E was ordered to Barnwell plantation for picket duty.

Some mornings I would go along the picket line, and I could see the rebels on the opposite side of the river. Sometimes as they were changing pickets they would call over to our men and ask for something to eat, or for tobacco, and our men would tell them to come over. Sometimes one or two would desert to us, saying, they "had no negroes to fight for." Others would shoot across at our picket, but as the river was so wide there was never any damage done, and the Confederates never attempted to shell us while we were there.

I learned to handle a musket very well while in the regiment, and could shoot straight and often hit the target. I assisted in cleaning the guns and used to fire them off, to see if the cartridges were dry, before cleaning and reloading, each day. I thought this great fun. I was also able to take a gun all apart, and put it together again.

*   *   *

One night, Companies K and E, on their way to Pocotaligo to destroy a battery that was situated down the river, captured several prisoners. The rebels nearly captured Sergeant King, who, as he sprang and caught a "reb," fell over an embankment. In falling he did not release his hold on his prisoner. Although his hip was severely injured, he held fast until some of his comrades came to his aid and pulled them up. These expeditions were very dangerous. Sometimes the men had to go five or ten miles during the night over on the rebel side and capture or destroy whatever they could find.

*   *   *

. . . We had fresh beef once in a while, and we would have soup, and the vegetables they put in this soup were dried and pressed. They looked like hops. Salt beef was our stand-by. Sometimes the men would have what we called slap-jacks. This was flour, made into bread and spread thin on the bottom of the mess-pan to cook. Each man had one of them, with a pint of tea, for his supper, or a pint of tea and five or six hard-tack. I often got my own meals, and would fix some dishes for the non-commissioned officers also.

Mrs. Chamberlain, our quartermaster's wife, was with us here. She was a beautiful woman; I can see her pleasant face before me now, as she, with Captain Trowbridge, would sit and converse with me in my tent two or three hours at a time. She was also with me on Cole Island, and I think we were the only women with the regiment while there. I remember well how, when she first came into camp, Captain Trowbridge brought her to my tent and introduced her to me. I found her then, as she remained ever after, a lovely person, and I always admired her cordial and friendly ways.

Our boys would say to me sometimes, "Mrs. King, why is it you are so kind to us? you treat us just as you do the boys in your own company." I replied, "Well, you know, all the boys in other companies are the same to me as those in my Company E; you are all doing the same duty, and I will do just the same for you." "Yes," they would say, "we know that, because you were the first woman we saw when we came into camp, and you took an interest in us boys ever since we have been here, and we are very grateful for all you do for us."

When at Camp Shaw, I visited the hospital in Beaufort, where I met Clara Barton. There were a number of sick and wounded soldiers there, and I went often to see the comrades. Miss Barton was always very cordial toward me, and I honored her for her devotion and care of those men.

*   *   *

On February 28, 1865, the remainder of the regiment were ordered to Charleston, as there were signs of the rebels evacuating that city. Leaving Cole Island, we arrived in Charleston between nine and ten o'clock in the morning, and found the "rebs" had set fire to the city and fled, leaving women and children behind to suffer and perish in the flames. The fire had been burning fiercely for a day and night. When we landed, under a flag of truce, our regiment went to work assisting the citizens in subduing the flames. It was a terrible scene. For three or four days the men fought the fire, saving the property and effects of the people, yet these white men and women could not tolerate our black Union soldiers, for many of them had formerly been their slaves; and although these brave men risked life and limb to assist them in their distress, men and even women would sneer and molest them whenever they met them.

I had quarters assigned me at a residence on South Battery Street, one of the most aristocratic parts of the city, where I assisted in caring for the sick and injured comrades. After getting the fire under control, the regiment marched out to the race track, where they camped until March 12, when we were ordered to Savannah, Ga. We arrived there on the 13th, about eight o'clock in the evening, and marched out to Fairlong, near the A. & G. R. R., where we remained about ten days, when we were ordered to Augusta, Ga., where Captain Alexander Heasley, of Co. E, was shot and killed by a Confederate. After his death Lieutenant Parker was made captain of the company, and was with us until the regiment was mustered out. . . .

The regiment remained in Augusta for thirty days, when it was ordered to Hamburg, S. C., and then on to Charleston. It was while on their march through the country, to the latter city, that they came in contact with the bushwhackers (as the rebels were called), who hid in the bushes and would shoot the Union boys every chance they got. Other times they would conceal themselves in the cars used to transfer our soldiers, and when our boys, worn out and tired, would fall asleep, these men would come out from their hiding places and cut their throats. Several of our men were killed in this way, but it could not be found out who was committing these murders until one night one of the rebels was caught in the act, trying to cut the throat of a sleeping soldier. He was put under guard, court-martialed, and shot at Wall Hollow.

*   *   *

REVIEW QUESTIONS

3. How did Confederate soldiers and civilians react to these troops?

1. How were African-American troops treated by the United States government? How were they treated by their officers?

4. What was life like for Taylor within camp?

5. What was her contribution to the war?

2. What kind of military operations did these troops engage in?

JAMES B. GRIFFIN

Letters from a Confederate Officer (1862)

James B. Griffin (1825–1881) was not one of the towering figures of the Confederacy, nor was he simply a soldier in the ranks: he was a southern gentleman, like many others, who went to war to defend his rights and to liberate the South from the North's attempts to subjugate her. He did not specifically state that he fought to preserve slavery, but among the rights he fought for was the right to continue his way of life. Griffin, as one of the wealthiest men in the Edgefield District of South Carolina, belonged to his society's elite class. He was, however, not rich enough, nor powerful enough to be part of its aristocracy. He did hold leadership positions in his community and state, the most prestigious being brigadier general in the South Carolina militia, but he generally preferred to focus on planting rather than politics. Griffin owned 61 slaves and 1,500 acres of land in 1860 and used both primarily in cotton production. When war threatened his world in 1861, he was primed to act. That spring Wade Hampton III of South Carolina created a special regiment, a legion that combined the three arms—infantry, cavalry, and artillery—of the military. Hampton appointed Griffin to the post of major of the cavalry. When the Legion's second in command was killed at Manassas (the cavalry missed the engagement as they had been left behind to continue their training), Griffin was promoted to lieutenant colonel. While fulfilling his duties on the Virginia front (attended by two slaves, Ned and Abram), he wrote regularly to his wife, Eliza, nicknamed Leila. Griffin remained with the Legion until June of 1862 when, after it was reorganized and the field officer ranks were opened up to elections, he lost his position to another officer and resigned.

From Judith N. McArthur and Orville Vernon Burton, eds., *"A Gentleman and an Officer": A Military and Social History of James B. Griffin's Civil War* (New York: Oxford University Press, 1996), pp. 132–37, 141–48, 159–65. [Editorial insertions that appear in square brackets are from the McArthur and Burton edition—*Ed.*]

Head Qrs. Legion Camp Wigfall
Sunday night January 5th 1862

My Darling Wife

. . . Camp life is so monotonous, so much of a sameness, that it is really trying to one's patience at times. This frequently accounts for the fact that Soldiers grow extremely eager for a fight. They want something to relieve the dull monotony of the camp life. This is the case, at this time with our troops. I believe they would, almost to a man, be delighted if the Enemy would come along. . . . Col Hampton had another regiment sent to him to day, he now has under his command, besides the Legion, three Regiments and a field battery. He will now be able to give the Yanks a warm reception, wherever they may choose to try to cross the Occoquan. It looked a little squally day before yesterday evening. There was a succession of fires apparently signal fires, from away up the lines near Alexandria, down the Potomac. I dont know what was the meaning of them—It may have been their signal for an advance, but if so they were deterred by a sleet which fell that night. . . . It is now exceedingly cold, but I dont suffer from the cold. A good many of our men have been skating for the last day or two. One poor fellow from the Ga Regiment, was drowned yesterday. Two men were skating when the ice broke and they both went down. This Georgian jumped in and saved them—And afterwards went back to show how he saved them, when the ice broke with him, he went down and drowned before they could get him out. I wrote to you in my last that Maj'r Butler was sick. I am happy to inform you that he is convalescent—I saw him to day—I hope soon to see him again in the saddle. We have a good many Commissioned Officers now sick—On that account we are in bad condition for a fight—So far as the men are concerned we are in very good fighting condition. I am satisfied that the condition of our army would not be improved, by going into winter quarters, without an engagement. I feel the army would be a good deal demoralized, by such an event. I dont know what to think, whether they will attack us or not. I am fully confident if they do come that we will *lick* them. And if we give them a thorough licking, in their present shattered condition, I think they will begin to think about giving it up. I wish they would quit their foolishness[.] For I tell you, I would much prefer being at home with my Wife and Children—I am delighted to hear that the citizens of old South Carolina, and old Edgefield especially, have come up to the mark—without being drafted. It would have been an everlasting disgrace to have drafted the men when the Enemy were on our own soil. . . .

*   *   *

Head Qrs Legion
Camp Near Occoquan Jany 10th
1862

My Darling Leila

. . . Oh, My Darling what a comfort to me it is, to know that you and the dear Children although separated from me, are well, and appear to be getting along so well. I am also delighted to hear that the Negroes are behaving so well—Do say to them that I hear with pleasure of their good behaviour, and hope they will continue to behave well—tell them they shall not loose anything by keeping it up. I hope also from what you and Willie both write, that our new overseer may do well. Tell him, I have entire confidence in him although a Stranger, from what I have heard of him, and he must do his best. Do ask him if he has a good stand of wheat and oats, and how they look. Has he fed away all the pea vines yet, and how does he get along with his business generally. Tell him to be economical with the corn, I think there is no doubt but he will have plenty, but still it is safest to be economical. Do tell him to see himself to measuring the corn when they go to the mill, and see that no more is sent than is necessary, and that it all comes back. Dont forget sometimes to have the wheat sunned. My Darling I do think you are getting to be a *first rate* manager. And whilst I hope that the time is not near at hand for you, Still, I believe you would make a right managing Widdow. But excuse me—My Darling that is too serious a subject to joke about just now. I am pleased to hear that you have your garden in such fine order. I hope to enjoy some of your nice vegetables this year. Dont forget the Watermelon patch when the proper time arrives. Tell your man Peter, that he knows my plan for planting, and he must pursue it just as if I were there to attend to it. Tell him to make some hills next month, dig the holes deep and put the manure low down, that is the secret of success. If you have an early Spring he might plant a few hills as early as the 10th of March and then keep on planting all the time after that, every week or two. By the way you have never written me how much cotton you and Peter made last year. . . . I really am at a loss to conjecture what is the programme of the Enemy. It was said when the weather was so fine that they were waiting for *hard* weather. Now we have had that and they still tarry. I am thoroughly satisfied, that McClelland [*sic*] doesnt want to come at all. It has been said by some that he has feigned sickness to give him an excuse for not advancing. It seems that Public opinion would force him to move, as they are already speaking of one who is to supercede him. My opinion is that his reputation now hangs upon a rather slender thread. If he advances, and gets whipped, his reputation is gone—and if he does not advance, it appears as if they will call in another. I hear that he has pledged to advance by the 15th of this month. And I dont believe now he can do so if he wishes. The rains have made the roads so soft, that I dont believe Artillery can be carried over them. But as the Frenchman said, "we shall see what we shall see". My Darling I am really afraid that my letters are not very interesting to you but you must bear in mind that I have nothing else to write about. Tell Willie I am obliged to him for his letter, tell him he doesnt improve as much in writing as I would wish, but to keep trying, he will learn after awhile. Tell him to write to me every week. Give my love to all the Children and kiss them for me. Also remember me to all my friends and relatives. Abram and Ned beg to be remembered to all. Good night, My Love—

Your Jimmie

You asked me if I would like to have a pair of pants. Why, certainly I would be proud to wear them— spun[,] wove and made by your own direction.

JBG

Head Qrs of the Legion
Jany 30th 1862

My Dear Leila

. . . My Darling this is another gloomy day, been raining all day. Yesterday was a very pretty day, it seems as if we cant have more than one pretty day, and then pay for it by having three or four rainy ones. The sun hasnt shone, I dont think more than three or four days this whole month. I have been closely engaged to day, My Darling, examining the Commissary's quarterly report. It was an exceedingly tedious job. And consequently I feel rather tired. I should have written you last night, but for the fact that I didnt sleep much the night before, and was quite sleepy. I said, I didnt sleep much, night before last—It was quite an eventful night. Let me give you an account of it. In the first place a lot of young men from the "Washington Light Infantry" (Citizens of Charleston) took it into their heads to give a concert. They accordingly went to the village of Occoquan, distant from the camp about two miles, and about four from the camp of the Enemy. Just think of that, the idea of having an entertainment of that kind almost within gun shot of the Enemy's lines. But then we had the river Occoquan between us. I knew nothing of the affair until the arrangement was all completed. In the morning before the night of the concert—they asked through their Capt, permission to have it. I consented on condition that they would preserve good order, conduct themselves properly, and not report anything about it in the newspapers. They invited our Field and Staff and said it was gotten up for our express benefit. So that we all concluded to go. Col Hampton being in Richmond. I left the camp in charge of Capt Gary and went down. When I arrived, I found the audience already in attendance. The room was a very nice one, small, and pretty well filled. The crowd consisted mostly of Officers and about a dozen Ladies. I assure you I was surprised to see, in this country, such a collection of the "Fair Sex." True they were not so pretty but they were so dignified and Lady like. The Boys had erected a stage in one end of the house, and had one corner canvassed off for the performers to retire in. This canvass consisted of a very large and handsome quilt, which I suppose they had borrowed for the occasion, and a couple of Soldiers blankets. The curtain which was used to expose the Stage was made of the fly of a tent. They didnt have gas light, but good old *tallow candles*, with a wick about the size of your little finger. So you may imagine that the light wasnt very brilliant. The Performers were all blacked, and sung various songs, and performed beautifully on several instruments. They had the piano, two violins, a tamborine and one fellow played the banjo and another beat the bones. The music was really exquisite, and the whole affair passed off very pleasantly indeed. They closed about eleven oclock and we set out for camp—We had ridden about a mile when my ear caught the sound of a rifle, in the direction of Colchester. The very place we are guarding and where we always keep a picket. In a few seconds I heard another, and then another, and then a volley. I was riding my fine mare "Belle Tucker". I gave her the spur and she soon carried me to the ferry where our Picket was stationed. I was accompanied by Adjt Barker. I found after seeing the Picket that the firing was over the river, in an old house just across the ferry. It had by this time all ceased. But I could distinctly hear the moaning and groaning of some one who was undoubtedly wounded. I immediately suspected the cause. We have for a long time had eight or ten Texians over the river who have been acting as scouts for us. They have harrassed the Enemy a great deal and they the Enemy have made many fruitless attempts to catch them. It turned out as I suspected[.] The Texians were all in this old house (there were eight of them in all[)], and had all gone to bed, leaving no watch at all. The Enemy were doubtless piloted to the house, and the first thing the Texians knew, the Enemy were trying to break the door down. The house was a two story one with several rooms in it—they separated some in each room, and the firing commenced. The night was exceedingly dark—and the Texians couldnt tell how many they were fighting. Certainly a pretty large crowd. The firing lasted only a few minutes, and the Cowardly rascals ran off—leaving two of their men dead and one badly wounded (died that night) in the yard. One of the Texians was wounded but not seriously. I ordered more men down to the river, and awaited to see what would turn up—It wasnt long before I heard a whistle across the river—I answered, and the Texians asked for a boat—I sent over and had them brought over and the wounded man attended to—He is now doing very well. Those Texians are number one men, and their conduct on that occasion was as gallant and brave as any thing that has occurred in this war. Just think of their cool courage, to be suddenly surprised by an Enemy, from whom they had no reason to expect any quarter—Surrounded in the night by these rascals, in an old house, which was but a shell—and see them separating themselves each man with his rifle in hand slipping to a window and firing at their opponents—who were also pouring the bullets into the old House. Just think, I say of this conduct and compare it to the dastardly cowardice of the Enemy who had at last found the very men whom of all others they wanted to find—they had them completely surrounded and one would suppose just where they would like to have them. They also from the sign, next day, had a large force—And notwithstanding all this as soon as their men began to fall they actually ran off—The Texians say they carried off several wounded, they could distinctly hear them complaining and groaning as they went off. But they left one wounded man on the ground who hallooed and begged them to come back after him. I suppose he was the one I heard crying after I got down. The Texians came out after the Enemy were gone, and found this wounded man and two dead ones—They carried the wounded man in the house—built up a fire for him, gave him some water—took the arms of the three men, and then brought their own wounded man down to the river—When I sent for them as I have already told you. The next morning they went over and decently buried them. I didnt get back to camp that night until near three O Clock—and that is the reason I was so sleepy last night. Dont you think it was quite an adventerous night? . . .

*   *   *

Head Quarters of the Legion
Camp near Occoquan Feby 2nd
1862

My Dearest Wife

. . . This is the *rainiest—snowiest—muddiest* and with all, the most disagreeable country I ever met up with. This has been a clear sunny day—and now, (ten O Clock at night) it is raining—Night before last it snowed—Yesterday it thawed, and it seems that every thing combines to keep the earth saturated with water. The roads, being traveled over every day by wagons, of course continue to grow worse. I havent travelled over them but from accounts, and from what I see around here, I know they are awful. I have been trying for the last two weeks—to have some new batteries built—but owing to the dreadful weather, get along very slowly. We never have two days in succession in which we can work. I never was so heartily tired of mud and water in my life. Col Hampton has not yet returned from Richmond—He has been gone a week—I am expecting him every day.

My Darling, you have no idea how proud I felt, yesterday while reading one of your very dear letters to find that you felt that you had reason (as you thought) to be proud of your Husband. It done me a *power* of good. For while I dont expect much from the cold Charity of the world— And indeed ask for little, It is really charming and enspiriting to feel that you are appreciated by one who loves you and one who is prompted by no deceitful motives, to bestow praise on you. But My Darling, let me say, while I thank you for the compliment, I have so far done nothing to merit it—Except perhaps, in showing a willingness to do, whenever an opportunity may offer. I have so far, never had the fortune (whether good or bad) to be engaged with the Enemy—I hope however, if it shall ever be my fortune to be engaged with them, that my conduct will be such, that if I do not merit your praise, will not cause you to feel ashamed—I, like every man, of course would not like the idea of being even wounded in battle—But I would dislike very much to go out of this Campaign without going through at least one battle—More especially as most of the officers of

the Legion have had that good fortune. I assure you that the dangers of a battle, are not near so great as one, who is unacquainted, would suppose. I do not expect any fighting of consequence, in this army before Spring—But I think it will come then pretty heavy, if there is no change.

I honestly believe that the battle itself is about the least of dangers, to which the Soldier is exposed. Sickness is much more dangerous, caused from necessary exposure. The health of our Command is very good, at this time considering the quantity of bad weather we have had. My own health continues very good—I wouldnt have believed that I could have gone through what I have. But it doesnt hurt me at all. I have entire command of the Legion, during the Col's absence and flatter myself that we get along very well. I cant tell whether the men like me or not—they are very respectful to me, but that they are obliged to be— Military authority is the most powerful known to man. But doesnt do harm unless abused—I think the officers generally like me and most of the men two [*sic*] but some of them I reckon do not—An Officer, as a general rule, who does his duty is apt to make some Enemies.

*   *   *

Head Qrs of the Legion
February 19th 1862

My Dear Leila

Well, my Darling, I have at last received my trunk, it came to day—Just four weeks from the time you started it. My Darling you just tried yourself to see how many nice things you could send. I opened the trunk to day (it came about twelve O Clock) and had a regular party. Invited the whole mess and Capt Gary, Lieut Tompkins and Ball from Laurens, a member of Gary's company. I cut one of the cakes, which was beautiful and very nice, and opened the apple cordial. All agreed in pronouncing it *splendid*. You were very highly complimented, while the cake & cordial was rapidly consumed. Every thing came perfectly safe and sound, notwithstanding the length of time it had been coming. The sausages were somewhat moulded, but I dont think are at all damaged, at least I hope not, for I am really *longing* for some. We also sampled the nice brandy peaches, I told the party that they were put up by your own fair hands, and four years ago at that. They were really very nice. Col Hampton is laid up in his tent with the mumps. (I tell him he is the largest case of mumps, I ever saw) So that he could not participate in the feast. I, sent him, however, a share of the good things. My darling every thing you sent is really a treat, but I believe I appreciate more than any thing else, the nice butter. I can eat it with a relish, and have the satisfaction of knowing it is *clean* and nice. We had such a nice lunch and enjoyed it so much, that we didnt have dinner until five O Clock, and it being a dark evening we had to have a candle lit. I suppose you will think that we are quite aristocratic. And so we are. Our usual meal hours are as follows, Breakfast from nine to ten (Dark rainy mornings from ten to eleven.[)] Dinner from three to four, *tea* from eight to nine. Dont you think that is rather aristocratic. We sampled, at dinner, your catsup—it is splendid. Every thing is nice *very nice*, ham[,] biscuit and all. For all of which my Darling will please accept the sincere thanks of her husband, and also of the whole mess. I am also obliged to you for the clothing you sent. I didnt need any thing except the towels and handkerchiefs, I have lost some that I had. The shirts you sent are very pretty, I will wear them after the cold weather is gone. I wear nothing now but the calicoe. . . . My Darling the Mail has just come and the papers bring the unwelcome news of the capture of Fort Donnelson [*sic*] by the Federals. Our reverses have been frequent of late— It seems that we fought gallantly at the Fort—but the full particulars I havent seen. Our defeat at Roanoke was really disgraceful. Well, I hope the day of triumph is not far distant. I have no other news to write—It has been raining all day as usual.

Do remember me kindly to your Father and family, also to all friends. Give my love to all the Children, and accept for yourself the warmest love of your devoted

Jimmie

Camp of the Legion
February 26th 1862

My Darling Leila

I am delighted, my Darling to learn by your last letter that Minnie has at last "Come through". And I am also pleased, and tender my congratulations that she has another Boy. Notwithstanding you all were anxious for her to have a daughter. I really think she should be proud that she has another Boy. This is the time, above all others, that *men* should be raised. And this too, is the time above all others when females deserve sympathy. I assure you, I feel, far more anxiety about my dear little daughters, than I do about my Boys. For while men can manage to work for themselves, and can fight the battles of their Country if necessary, Females are very dependent. True, they too can do a great deal, and, 'tis true that our Southern Ladies have done and are still acting a conspicuous part in this war[.] In many instances (to the shame of our Sex be it said) a much bolder and more *manly* part than many men. But still, when it comes to the physical test, of course, they are helpless. It is on this account, that I think the Parents should congratulate themselves on the birth of a son rather than a daughter. We cannot see, My Darling, into the future, but I trust & have confidance in our people to believe, that if the unprincipled North shall persist in her policy of Subjugating the South, that we, who are able to resist them, will continue to do so, until we grow old and worn out in the service, and that then, our Sons will take the arms from our hands, and spend their lives, if necessary, in battling for Liberty and independence. As for my part, If this trouble should not be settled satisfactorily to us sooner—I would be proud of the thought that our youngest Boy—Yes Darling little Jimmie, will after awhile be able and I trust willing to take his Father's place in the field, and fight until he dies, rather than, be a Slave, *Yea* worse than a Slave to Yankee Masters—Have you ever anticipated, My Darling, what would be our probable condition, if we should be conquered in this war? The picture is really too horrible to contemplate. In the first place, the tremendous war tax, which will have accumulated, on the northern Government, would be paid entirely and exclusively by the property belonging to the Southerners. And more than this we would be an humbled, down trodden and disgraced, people. Not entitled to the respect of any body, and have no respect for ourselves. In fact we would be the most wretched and abject people on the face of the Earth. Just be what our Northern Masters say we may be. Would you, My Darling, desire to live, if this was the case? would you be willing to leave your Children under such a government? No—I know you would sacrifice every comfort on earth, rather than submit to it. Excuse me, My Darling, I didnt intend to, run off in this strain. You might think, from my painting this horrid picture to you, that I had some doubts as to whether we might not have to experience it. But No, I havent the most remote idea that we will. I think our people will arouse themselves, shake off the lethargy, which seems now to have possession of them, and will meet the issue like *men*. We must see that we have *all*—Yes our all—staked upon the result—And we are obliged to succeed and we will do it. Just at this time the Enemy appears to have advantage of us. But this is no more than we have, all along, had of him, until lately. He did not succombe and give up for it—and shall we, Who have so much more to fight for than he has, do so? I am completely surprised and mortified at the feeling manifested by our people at this time. But they will soon rally and come with redoubled energy. Our Soldiers too, or rather our Generals have got to learn to fight better. The idea, of a Genl surrendering with 12000 men under his command,[1] is a species of bravery and Generalship, which I do not understand. I wish Congress would pass a law breaking an officer of his commission who surrenders. . . . My Darling tell Spradley, not to commence planting corn early[.] My land will not admit of early planting, of either corn or cotton. I generally, commence planting corn from the 15th to the 20th of March, and cotton about the same time in april. I see that Congress is about passing a bill, to impose a heavy tax on cotton raised this year[.] If they pass it—I wish no land planted in cotton except the new ground, and the field next to the overseers house, all the ballance planted in corn. I will write you, however in time. My Darling, Now is the time to bring out all your courage—Do not become despondent—Dont matter what *alarmists* and Croakers may say—take advice from him whom you *know* will advise you for the best. Keep up your spirits and your courage, and the clouds will soon pass away, and sun shine will return—My sheet is full—and I will close by begging to be remembered to all—My love to My Children and my Darling Leila

from your Husband

REVIEW QUESTIONS

1. What kind of tone did Griffin take with his wife? What does that reveal about him and about their relationship?
2. Was there any evidence in the letters that the war affected gender roles and relations?
3. What did Griffin reveal about camp life near the enemy line?
4. What opinions did he hold of the North and northerners?
5. What did he think about southern attitudes and actions at that time? Why did he believe the South would ultimately prevail?

---

[1] Brigadier General Simon B. Buckner surrendered the garrison at Fort Donelson.

ELISHA HUNT RHODES

FROM The Diary of a Union Soldier (1862)

Elisha Hunt Rhodes (1842–1917) was a boy when he enlisted as a private in the 2nd Rhode Island Volunteers; he was a man and the colonel in charge of the regiment when it was disbanded in July 1865. His story shows how the war and the Union Army offered opportunities for advancement to able—and lucky, for many an able man died—young men who could face, survive, and grow through adversity. Rhodes's pluck, intelligence, and sense of responsibility showed at an early age. When his father died, the sixteen-year-old boy left school and became a clerk for a mill supplier so he could support his mother and two brothers. Because his family needed him, he resisted enlisting in the first regiment raised by Rhode Island, but when the call went out to form the second one, he could not contain his desire to join the army. After obtaining his mother's consent, he marched off to war.

From Robert Hunt Rhodes, ed., *All for the Union: The Civil War Diary and Letters of Elisha Hunt Rhodes* (1985: New York: Orion Books, 1991) pp. 60–61, 64–65, 73–79, 81–85, 92–93. [Editorial insertions appear in square brackets—*Ed.*]

*   *   *

March 21/62—I am twenty years of age today. The past year has been an eventful one to me, and I thank God for all his mercies to me. I trust my life in the future may be spent in his service. When I look back to March 21/61 I am amazed at what has transpired. Then I was a peaceful clerk in Frederick Miller's office. Today I am a soldier anxious to move. I feel to thank God that he has kept me within his fold while so many have gone astray, and trust that he will give me Grace to continue to serve Him and my country faithfully. I have now been in service ten months and feel like a veteran. Sleeping on the ground is fun, and a bed of pine boughs better than one of feathers. We are still waiting for orders which must come very soon. Many of the men are broken down by the late march, but I am stronger than ever.

*   *   *

Camp Brightwood, Tuesday morning, March 25/62, One o'clock—We are to leave Camp at 7 A.M. to take steamer, destination unknown. So Goodbye old Camp Brightwood where we have had lots of fun and learned a soldier's duty. May God bless and prosper us.

*   *   *

Newport News, Va., March 29/62—We are now at Newport News where the Union Army can be found. The next place is Yorktown where the Rebels will be found.

March 31/62—Our tents have come, and we are in comfort again. Plenty of beef, pork, ham, bacon, etc. Yesterday I had a beefsteak and sweet potatoes. Very good living for a soldier. I called at General Keyes' Headquarters yesterday. I am well and contented as usual. Camp life agrees with me.

*   *   *

Battlefield of Williamsburg, Va., May 7th 1862—Sunday last we received news of the evacuation of Yorktown, and we were ordered to leave our camp at Young's Farm and join the main Army. We crossed the river at Lee's Mills and then followed the line of forts and rifle pits until midnight when we encamped in a deserted Rebel camp. Everything denoted the haste in which the Rebels left their works. It rained hard all night, and we lay in the mud and water but felt happy, for now it was our turn to chase and the Rebels to run. Early Monday morning we moved towards Williamsburg, and about noon we began to hear the roar of cannon and rattle of musketry. We pushed on through mud that caused teams to be mired and batteries to halt, but by taking advantage of the woods and fields where the ground was not so soft or cut up, our Division arrived under fire at 4 P.M. Here we were placed in the reserves and remained until nearly dark when our Brigade was pushed to the front and took position in the edge of a piece of woods about six hundred yards in front of Fort Magruder. Until dark we could see the Rebel gunners load and fire the cannon from the fort, and we had to stand it, for we were ordered for some reason not to fire. All night the shells continued to burst over our heads, and in the mud and discomfort we prayed for daylight. Sometime after midnight we could hear the rumble of teams in the direction of Williamsburg, and just as day began to break Major Nelson Viall and myself crawled towards the fort. After approaching quite near and not seeing anyone we arose and walked up the glacis and looked into an embrasure. Behold, the fort was deserted. We hurried around to the rear and entered the gate. The ground was covered with dead men and horses. I found in one of the tents left standing some documents that gave the number of the garrison. While we were in the fort the 10th Mass. charged across the open space and entered the fort. They were surprised to find two Rhode Island soldiers already in possession. Both General Couch and Gen. Charles Devens who commands our Brigade made speeches to our Regiment and thanked the men for their coolness under fire. The field presented a horrible appearance, and in one small spot I counted sixty dead bodies. The Rebels threw away much of their baggage, and the road is filled with broken teams and gun carriages. Our Cavalry are now in pursuit, and many prisoners are being sent to the rear. Thank God for this victory and may we have many more and so end the war.

May 8th 1862—Monday night orders were received for a Light Brigade under command of General George Stoneman to be formed and follow the retreating Rebels. The 2nd R.I. Vols, Col. Frank Wheaton; the 98th Penn. Vols, Col. John F. Ballier; the 6th U.S. Cavalry; the 8th Illinois Cavalry, Col. Farnsworth Robertson's and Tidball's regular Batteries were detailed for this duty. Colonel Wheaton commands the two Infantry Regiments and Lt. Colonel Steere the 2nd R.I. We are now fifteen miles from Williamsburg on the road to Richmond, and we pick up prisoners every mile. The bugle has just sounded the advance and we must move.

Camp near Pamunkey River, Va., May 11/62— Friday our Cavalry came up with the Rebels and charged through the lines, and falling into an ambush, turned and came back. The Cavalry lost three killed and several wounded but brought back a number of prisoners. The Rebels opened with skill and we were ordered to move up. Our Artillery replied and the Rebel rear guard moved on. We followed to this place and are now waiting orders. Food is scarce, and all that we have to eat is the cattle killed by the way. No bread or salt in the Regiment and I am most starved. But it is all for the Union and we do not complain.

May 12th 1862—Left camp in the evening and marched to White House Landing on the Pamunkey River. Here we found three gun boats, and we feel more comfortable. In the evening we attended an outdoor jubilee meeting held by the Negroes. One of them preached a sermon. He tried to prove from the Bible that truth that every man must seek his own salvation. . . .

*   *   *

Malvern Hill July 1/62—O the horrors of this day's work, but at last we have stopped the Rebel advance, and instead of following us they are fleeing to Richmond. The battle of today is beyond description. The enemy advanced through fields of grain and attacked our lines posted upon a long range of hills. Our gun boat threw shell over our heads and into the Rebel lines. All attempts to drive us from our position failed and at night the Rebels retired. Our Regiment supported the Batteries of our camps and did not suffer much, but saw the whole of the grand fight.

Harrison's Landing, James River, July 3/62— We left Malvern Hill last night and in the midst of a pouring rain marched to this place where we arrived early this morning. O how tired and sleepy I am. We have had no rest since June 24th, and we are nearly dead. The first thing I noticed in the river was the steamer *Canonicus* of Providence. It made me think of home. We stacked arms and the men laid down in the rain and went to sleep. Lieutenant-Colonel Viall threw a piece of canvas over a bush and putting some straw upon the ground invited me to share it with him. We had just gone to sleep when a Rebel Battery opened and sent their shells over our heads. We turned out in a hurry and just in time, too, for a shot or shell struck in the straw that we had just left. This shot covered Colonel Viall's horse with mud. We were ordered to leave our knapsacks and go after this Rebel Battery. But our men could hardly move, and after going a short distance we halted and other troops went on in pursuit. Battery "E" 1st R.I. Artillery sent out some guns and I hear that one of the Rebel guns was captured. We returned to our knapsacks and the men are trying to sleep.

July 4th 1862— This morning all the troops were put to work upon the line of forts that have been laid out. As I was going to the spring I met General McClellan who said good morning pleasantly and told our party that as soon as the forts were finished we should have rest. He took a drink of water from a canteen and lighted a cigar from one of the men's pipes. At Malvern Hill he rode in front of our Regiment and was loudly cheered. I have been down to the river. I rode the Adjutant's horse and enjoyed the sight of the vessels. Gun boats and transports are anchored in the stream. Rest is what we want now, and I hope we shall get it. I could sleep for a week. The weather is very hot, but we have moved our camp to a wood where we get the shade. This is a queer 4th of July, but we have not forgotten that it is our national birthday,

and a salute has been fired. We expect to have something to eat before long. Soldiering is not fun, but duty keeps us in the ranks. Well, the war must end some time, and the Union will be restored. I wonder what our next move will be. I hope it will be more successful than our last.

Harrison's Landing, Va., July 9/62— The weather is extremely hot, and as the men are at work on the forts they suffer much. The Army is full of sick men, but so far our Regiment seems to have escaped. The swamp in which we lived while in front of Richmond caused chills and fever. I have been very well, in fact not sick at all. Lt. Col. Nelson Viall of our Regiment is now in command of the 10th Mass. Vols., their field officers being all sick or wounded. Fred Arnold is in the hospital in Washington. Last night President Lincoln made a visit to the Army. As he passed along the lines salutes were fired, and the men turned out and cheered. We see General McClellan nearly every day, and he often speaks to the men. How I should like to see my home. In God's own time we shall meet on earth or in Heaven. I have been busy all day preparing muster and pay rolls. We hope to get some money some day.

*   *   *

Harrison's Landing Sunday July 27/62— We are having a fine day and commenced regular camp duties the same as at Camp Brightwood. After "Guard Mount" the Regiment was paraded in front of Colonel Wheaton's quarters and we had church service. The men were seated in the form of a hollow square, and the Chaplain preached from the centre. Some of the men are very much interested, while others are totally indifferent to what is going on. The band is now playing in front of the Colonel's tent, and crowds of soldiers are listening to the music. The Colonel has returned from his visit to Mrs. Wheaton at Fortress Monroe. The Sloop of War *Dacotah* has arrived. Lieut. Wm. Ames' brother is an officer on board of her. Some of the Rhode Island Artillery boys paid me a visit today.

July 31/62— I have been quite sick for a few days but am all right again now. Col Wheaton has recommended me for promotion to Second Lieutenant, for as the letter reads: "Good conduct in the different engagements on the Peninsular." I suppose my commission will come soon. Hurrah. Yesterday the Army was under arms as it was reported that the Rebel iron clad *Merrimac* was coming. Well let her come, and bring the Rebel Army with her. We can take care of them now. I have received a box. The cake was spoiled, but the other things were all right.

Harrison's Landing, Va. Aug. 2nd 1862—Today we moved our camp back into a pine grove. Shelter tents have been issued to the men. Each man has one piece about six feet long and four feet wide. Two men button these pieces together, and by throwing it over a ridge pole, supported at each end, a shelter is formed. It is open at each end and serves to shield from the sun, but makes a regular shower bath when it rains. The men carry each a piece of tent in their knapsacks. We have a fine camp with regular company streets. Tonight we had a fine dress parade followed by Divine Service. We have a large open field near our camp which we use for parades and drills. It is rumored that we are to move. I hope it will be towards Richmond.

Aug. 3/62—Thursday morning about 1 o'clock a gun was heard followed by the bursting of a shell near our camp. This was repeated, and soon the gunboats joined in with the heavy shots and we had music. We found that a Rebel Light Battery had taken position on the south side of the James and opened upon our fleet of transports, some of the shells coming over to the camps. The gunboats drove the enemy away, and the next morning troops crossed the river and burned the houses that gave the enemy shelter. We are looking for recruits, but so far in vain. If men are not patriotic enough to volunteer to save the country I hope a draft will be ordered.

*   *   *

Camp near Yorktown, Va., Aug. 24/62—Sunday night again and I fear we are no nearer the end of the war than we were when we first landed at Fortress Monroe five months ago. But then we have learned some things, and now I hope we shall go ahead and capture Richmond. We have moved our camp from near the river to a hill where we get plenty of pure water from a spring. This is a great luxury, for in most of our camps we have been obliged to go long distances for water. This hill was occupied by General Fitz-John Porter's Corps during the late siege, and we occasionally find shot and shell lying about. Each company has a wide street, and we have a parade ground in front of the camp. It looks now as if our Corps (Keyes 4th) would remain on the Peninsular, as most of the other troops have been sent away. I was much surprised at the appearance of Yorktown. We entered town through a gate in a fort built upon a bluff. There are not more than twenty houses in the village and some of these must have been built before the Revolutionary War for they are of the gamble roof style and all tumbling down. Passing through the main street we saw the old forts built by the British Army when it was beseiged by Washington in 1781. Some of these forts were used by the Rebels. Still further on we saw the Rebel works built of bags of sand covered with earth. Some of them were on high bluffs with deep ravines in front. Some of the Rebel guns are still mounted, while others lay upon the ground dismounted by our fire. Passing through another gate we came to the open plain which separated Yorktown from our batteries. Here we halted for a short time, and I visited a large lot enclosed by a rail fence over the entrance to which were the words: "Union Cemetery." . . . We marched on to our old lines where we saw the Batteries for heavy guns and mortars. A darkey said that the shell from our guns "played a tune like a fiddle." We passed through the old camps and encamped near the river. I visited with Levi Carr in one of our bayonet earthworks. It is in the yard of a plantation. The owner told me that he moved away when the fight began, but he might have remained in safety for not one Rebel shot struck his house. He said that he owned hundreds of acres of land, but could only raise two and a half dollars in money, and that he got from our people. The people are very poor indeed. They are reaping their reward. . . .

*   *   *

Sunday Aug. 31/62—We arrived at Alexandria this morning after a pleasant sail from Yorktown. Here we learned that a battle had been fought at, or near, Manassas. We landed and marched in the direction of the old Bull Run ground where we understand our forces have met the enemy.

Sept. 1st 1862—Today we passed through Fairfax Court House and formed line of battle at Germantown with a battle going on two miles in our front. It rained in torrents, and I never in all my life ever heard such thunder or saw such lightning. It seemed as if Nature was trying to outdo man in the way of noise, for all the time the cannon roared and muskets rattled while the air was filled with flying missiles. But Nature won, and the battle ceased. We camped on the field for the night amid the dead and dying.

Sept. 2nd 1862—This morning we found the entire Army retreating and our Division was left to protect and cover the rear. As soon as our lines were formed our troops that had been fighting the day before passed through to the rear. As the Rebels came in sight we too moved off with the gallant 1st Rhode Island Cavalry with us. The Rebels shelled us lively, but we did not stop and reached Alexandria all right about midnight.

Sept. 3/62—Today we took a steamer at Alexandria and went up the Potomac past Washington, through the draw at Long Bridge and landed at Georgetown. From here we marched up the river and crossed Chain Bridge into Virginia again. It is hard to have reached the point we started from last March, and Richmond is still the Rebel Capital.

Camp near Chain Bridge, Va., Sept. 5/62—Last Wednesday after landing at Alexandria, Levi Carr and myself procured a quart of milk, and as we had only one cup and one spoon sat down to take turns in enjoying our feast. As we were eating Colonel Wheaton called: "Lieutenant Rhodes!" I went across the railroad track to where he was standing where he took me by the hand and congratulated me on my promotion. Well, I am proud, and I think I have a right to be, for thirteen months ago I enlisted as a private and I am now an officer. I am grateful to God for all his mercies to me.

*   *   *

Near Williamsport, Md., Sept. 23/62— . . . [On] the 17th, we saw the Battle of Antietam fought almost at our feet. We could see the long lines of battle, both Union and Rebel and hear the roar as it came from the field. The Rebel trains of waggons were moving all day towards the river. At dark we marched down the mountain and started for the battlefield where we arrived and went into camp. The next morning we were put in the front lines. I have never in my soldier life seen such a sight. The dead and wounded covered the ground. In one spot a Rebel officer and twenty men lay near a wreck of a Battery. It is said Battery "A" 1st R.I. Artillery did this work. The Rebel sharpshooters and skirmishers were still at work and the bullets whizzed merrily. At noon the Rebels asked and received permission to bury their dead, and the firing ceased for awhile but commenced again in the afternoon. The 2nd R.I. was ordered forward and we charged up a hill and driving the enemy away took possession. Here we lay all night with the bullets flying over us most of the time.

The next morning the enemy shelled our Regiment, but it was their last shots, for as we moved forward they retired, and we entered Sharpsburg. The town is all battered to pieces and is not worth much. Here we remained until midnight of the 19th when we moved to Williamsport. It was reported that the Rebels were here in force. After forming our lines the entire Division moved on the town with flags flying. It was a grand sight to see our long lines extending through fields and woods, hills and dales, make this advance. Picket or skirmish firing was going on in front, but after marching some distance we halted. Several were killed in the Division and many wounded. Sunday morning we found that the enemy had recrossed the river. O, why did we not attack them and drive them into the river? I do not understand these things. But then I am only a boy.

*   *   *

Near Downsville, Md., Tuesday Sept. 30th 1862— Still in Maryland with all sorts of rumors about our next move. The days are hot and the nights cold, and just now we are having beautiful weather with moonlight nights, which makes guard duty very pleasant. I suppose that we shall be looking for winter quarters soon.

We have a mess composed of the following officers: Capt. Samuel B. M. Read and Lieut. Benjamin B. Manchester of Co. "I," Lieut. Edward A. Russell commanding Co. "C" and Captain Stephen H. Brown and Lieut. Elisha H. Rhodes of Co. "D." We have attached to our mess three servants to carry our blankets, shelter tents and a few simple cooking utensils. When we halt the servants put up our shelter tents and find us straw if possible. They do our cooking and look after things generally. Near our present camp there lives an old lady who supplies our mess with soft bread. On the march salt pork toasted on a stick with hard bread and coffee is our principal diet. . . . Sunday last a soldier of Co. "A" died and was buried with military honors. It was not an unusual scene for us, yet it is always solemn. First came the muffled drums playing the "Dead March" then the usual escort for a private. Eight privates, commanded by a corporal, with arms reversed. Then an ambulance with the body in a common board coffin covered with the Stars and Stripes. Co. "A" with side arms only followed while the Company officers brought up the rear. On arriving at the grave the Chaplain offered prayer and made some remarks. The coffin was then lowered into the grave, and three volleys were fired by the guard, and then the grave was filled up. The procession returned to camp with the drums playing a "Quick March." Everything went on as usual in camp as if nothing had happened, for death is so common that little sentiment is wasted. It is not like death at home. May God prepare us all for this event which must sooner or later come to all of us.

*   *   *

Oct. 8/62— . . . The people in Maryland appear as a rule to be loyal to our government and have suffered much during the past few weeks. The nights are cold, and, as our shelter tents furnish poor protection, the men spend a good deal of the night about huge camp fires. But we do not complain, as it is all for the Union. The war will not end until the North wakes up. As it is now conducted it seems to me to be a grand farce. When certain politicians, Army contractors and traitors North are put out of the way, we shall succeed. General McClellan is popular with the Army, and we feel that he has not had a fair chance.[1]

*   *   *

Near Downsville, Oct. 10th 1862—Mrs. Wheaton, the wife of our Colonel, is in camp. She is very kind to the officers and men and is a great favorite with all. Gen. Charles Devens is now in command of our Division and Colonel Wheaton commands the Brigade. Lt. William Ames is sick in Washington. It is reported that he is to be made Major of the 12th R.I. Vols. Well, he will make a good one. The weather is very fine and we have had no rain for a long time. Orders have come for us to move and we are all ready, but know nothing of our destination. Virginia probably.

Camp near Downsville, Md., Oct. 15th 1862— For the past four days it has been cloudy and very cold and as the men have no overcoats they suffer some. We are, however, expecting new clothing very soon. We are very much ashamed that the Rebels were allowed to make their late raid into Pennsylvania. If this Army cannot protect the loyal states we had better *sell out* and go home. I ought not to complain, but I am mortified to think that we did not catch some of the Rebel raiders. We are all ready for a move. Let me describe the camp after marching orders are received. We see an orderly or staff officer dash into camp with his horse covered with foam, and he says: "Colonel Wheaton, your Regiment will move in fifteen minutes." The orders are sent around to the Captains, and down comes the shelter tents, blankets are packed up and haversacks filled with rations. Perhaps, and it

---

[1]Since I wrote the above as a boy, I have changed my mind in regard to Gen. McClellan. I now honestly believe that while he was a good organizer of Armies, yet he lacked the skill to plan campaigns or handle large bodies of troops. [E. Hunt Rhodes, 1885]

usually happens, all the straw is burned, when another orderly rides leisurely into camp and says: "The order to move is countermanded." Then we go to work, set up our shelters and get ready to live again. Some of the men will be quite glad while the growlers who always find fault say: "It is always so, and we never shall leave this camp." The same men will want to get back after marching a few miles. I am acting Adjutant for a few days.

*   *   *

Dec. 31/62—Well, the year 1862 is drawing to a close. As I look back I am bewildered when I think of the hundreds of miles I have tramped, the thousands of dead and wounded that I have seen, and the many strange sights that I have witnessed. I can truly thank God for his preserving care over me and the many blessings I have received. One year ago tonight I was an enlisted man and stood cap in hand asking for a furlough. Tonight I am an officer and men ask the same favor of me. It seems to me right that officers should rise from the ranks, for only such can sympathize with the private soldiers. The year has not amounted to much as far as the War is concerned, but we hope for the best and feel sure that in the end the Union will be restored. Good bye, 1862.

REVIEW QUESTIONS

1. What did Rhodes reveal about camp life?
2. How does his description compare to Griffin's?
3. Did he provide realistic or romantic portrayals of camp and combat?
4. In his evaluations of northern attitudes and actions, what did he criticize?
5. How did Rhodes change between March and December 1862? What accounts for that change?

LOUISA MAY ALCOTT

FROM *Hospital Sketches* (1863)

Women were active participants in the Civil War. Most, on both sides of the conflict, like Eliza "Leila" Griffin, added farm and business duties to their domestic ones after they waved their menfolk off to war. Some women preferred to march with the men. A few did so as soldiers—Sarah Rosetta Wakeman, for instance, enlisted as Private Lyons Wakeman in the 153rd Regiment, New York State Volunteers—but numerous others, Susie King Taylor being one, became camp followers and served as laundresses, servants, and on occasion as regimental nurses. Many other women served cause and country by nursing in military hospitals. In the Union, most of these nurses worked under the aegis of the United States Sanitary Commission. The Commission's job was to improve camp and hospital cooking, centralize the supply system, and reform medical care. It, along with Dorothea Dix who became the Supervisor of Nurses, helped create the Women's Department for nursing in the military hospitals. Those who wished to serve as nurses were supposed to be between the ages of 30 and 50, display strong constitutions and moral character, and be "matronly persons of experience, good conduct, or superior education and serious disposition." Not all who nursed demonstrated these characteristics, but one who did (though she was partial to levity) was Louisa May Alcott (1832–1888). Alcott would later become nationally renowned as the author of Little Women, *but in 1862 the budding writer was a former teacher and governess burning to contribute to the war effort. She reported for duty at a hospital in Washington, D.C., on 14 December, just in time to deal with the influx of wounded from the battle of Fredericksburg. Alcott soon contracted typhoid fever and was invalided home, but she recorded her experiences as "Nurse Tribulation Periwinkle" in* Hospital Sketches.

From Louisa May Alcott, *Hospital Sketches* (1863; Cambridge: The Belknap Press of Harvard University Press, 1960), pp. 27–39. [Editorial insertions appear in square brackets—*Ed.*]

A Day

"They've come! they've come! hurry up, ladies—you're wanted."

"Who have come? the rebels?"

This sudden summons in the gray dawn was somewhat startling to a three days' nurse like myself, and, as the thundering knock came at our door, I sprang up in my bed, prepared

> "To gird my woman's form,
> And on the ramparts die,"

if necessary, but my room-mate took it more coolly, and, as she began a rapid toilet, answered my bewildered question,—

"Bless you, no child; it's the wounded from Fredericksburg; forty ambulances are at the door, and we shall have our hands full in fifteen minutes."

"What shall we have to do?"

"Wash, dress, feed, warm and nurse them for the next three months, I dare say. Eighty beds are ready, and we were getting impatient for the men to come. Now you will begin to see hospital life in earnest, for you won't probably find time to sit down all day, and may think yourself fortunate if you get to bed by midnight. Come to me in the ball-room when you are ready; the worst cases are always carried there, and I shall need your help."

So saying, the energetic little woman twirled her hair into a button at the back of her head, in a "cleared for action" sort of style, and vanished, wrestling her way into a feminine kind of pea-jacket as she went.

I am free to confess that I had a realizing sense of the fact that my hospital bed was not a bed of roses just then, or the prospect before me one of unmingled rapture. My three days' experiences had begun with a death, and, owing to the defalcation of another nurse, a somewhat abrupt plunge into the superintendence of a ward containing forty beds, where I spent my shining hours washing faces, serving rations, giving medicine, and sitting in a very hard chair, with pneumonia on one side, diptheria on the other, five typhoids on the opposite, and a dozen dilapidated patriots, hopping, lying, and lounging about, all staring more or less at the new "nuss," who suffered untold agonies, but concealed them under as matronly an aspect as a spinster could assume, and blundered through her trying labors with a Spartan firmness, which I hope they appreciated, but am afraid they didn't. Having a taste for "ghastliness," I had rather longed for the wounded to arrive, for rheumatism wasn't heroic, neither was liver complaint, or measles; even fever had lost its charms since "bathing burning brows" had been used up in romances, real and ideal; but when I peeped into the dusky street lined with what I at first had innocently called market carts, now unloading their sad freight at our door, I recalled sundry reminiscences I had heard from nurses of longer standing, my ardor experienced a sudden chill, and I indulged in a most unpatriotic wish that I was safe at home again, with a quiet day before me, and no necessity for being hustled up, as if I were a hen and had only to hop off my roost, give my plumage a peck, and be ready for action. . . .

*   *   *

The first thing I met was a regiment of the vilest odors that ever assaulted the human nose, and took it by storm. . . . [T]he worst of this affliction was, every one had assured me that it was a chronic weakness of all hospitals, and I must bear it. I did, armed with lavender water, with which I so besprinkled myself and premises, that, like my friend, Sairy, I was soon known among my patients as "the nurse with the bottle." Having been run over by three excited surgeons, bumped against by migratory coal-hods, water-pails, and small boys; nearly scalded by an avalanche of newly-filled tea-pots, and hopelessly entangled in a knot of colored sisters coming to wash, I progressed by slow stages up stairs and down, till the main hall was reached, and I paused to take breath and a survey. There they were! "our brave boys," as the papers justly call them, for cowards could hardly have been so riddled with shot and shell, so torn and shattered, nor have borne suffering for which we have no name, with an uncomplaining fortitude, which made one glad to cherish each as a brother. In they came, some on stretchers, some in men's arms, some feebly staggering along propped on rude crutches, and one lay stark and still with covered face, as a comrade gave his name to be recorded before they carried him away to the dead house. . . .

The sight of several stretchers, each with its legless, armless, or desperately wounded occupant, entering my ward, admonished me that I was there to work, not to wonder or weep; so I corked up my feelings, and returned to the path of duty, which was rather "a hard road to travel" just then. The house had been a hotel before hospitals were needed, and many of the doors still bore their old names; some not so inappropriate as might be imagined, for my ward was in truth a *ball-room*, if gun-shot wounds could christen it. Forty beds were prepared, many already tenanted by tired men who fell down anywhere, and drowsed till the smell of food roused them. Round the great stove was gathered the dreariest group I ever saw—ragged, gaunt and pale, mud to the knees, with bloody bandages untouched since put on days before; many bundled

up in blankets, coats being lost or useless; and all wearing that disheartened look which proclaimed defeat, more plainly than any telegram of the Burnside blunder. I pitied them so much, I dared not speak to them, though, remembering all they had been through since the route at Fredericksburg, I yearned to serve the dreariest of them all. Presently, Miss Blank tore me from my refuge behind piles of one-sleeved shirts, odd socks, bandages and lint; put basin, sponge, towels, and a block of brown soap into my hands, with these appalling directions:

"Come, my dear, begin to wash as fast as you can. Tell them to take off socks, coats and shirts, scrub them well, put on clean shirts, and the attendants will finish them off, and lay them in bed."

If she had requested me to shave them all, or dance a hornpipe on the stove funnel, I should have been less staggered; but to scrub some dozen lords of creation at a moment's notice, was really—really—. However, there was no time for nonsense, and, having resolved when I came to do everything I was bid, I drowned my scruples in my washbowl, clutched my soap manfully, and, assuming a businesslike air, made a dab at the first dirty specimen I saw, bent on performing my task *vi et armis* [by force] if necessary. I chanced to light on a withered old Irishman, wounded in the head, which caused that portion of his frame to be tastefully laid out like a garden, the bandages being the walks, his hair the shrubbery. He was so overpowered by the honor of having a lady wash him, as he expressed it, that he did nothing but roll up his eyes, and bless me, in an irresistible style which was too much for my sense of the ludicrous; so we laughed together, and when I knelt down to take off his shoes, he "flopped" also and wouldn't hear of my touching "them dirty craters. May your bed above be aisy darlin', for the day's work ye are doon!—Woosh! there ye are, and bedad, it's hard tellin' which is the dirtiest, the fut or the shoe." It was; and if he hadn't been to the fore, I should have gone on pulling, under the impression that the "fut" was a boot, for trousers, socks, shoes and legs were a mass of mud. . . .

*   *   *

Another, with a gun-shot wound through the cheek, asked for a looking-glass, and when I brought one, regarded his swollen face with a dolorous expression, as he muttered—

"I vow to gosh, that's too bad! I warn't a bad looking chap before, and now I'm done for; won't there be a thunderin' scar? and what on earth will Josephine Skinner say?"

He looked up at me with his one eye so appealingly, that I controlled my risibles, and assured him that if Josephine was a girl of sense, she would admire the honorable scar, as a lasting proof that he had faced the enemy, for all women thought a wound the best decoration a brave soldier could wear. I hope Miss Skinner verified the good opinion I so rashly expressed of her, but I shall never know.

The next scrubbee was a nice looking lad, with a curly brown mane, and a budding trace of gingerbread over the lip, which he called his beard, and defended stoutly, when the barber jocosely suggested its immolation. He lay on a bed, with one leg gone, and the right arm so shattered that it must evidently follow; yet the little Sergeant was as merry as if his afflictions were not worth lamenting over, and when a drop or two of salt water mingled with my suds at the sight of this strong young body, so marred and maimed, the boy looked up, with a brave smile, though there was a little quiver of the lips, as he said,

"Now don't you fret yourself about me, miss; I'm first rate here, for it's nuts to lie still on this bed, after knocking about in those confounded ambulances, that shake what there is left of a fellow to jelly. I never was in one of these places before, and think this cleaning up a jolly thing for us, though I'm afraid it isn't for you ladies."

"Is this your first battle, Sergeant?"

"No, miss; I've been in six scrimmages, and never got a scratch till this last one; but it's done the business pretty thoroughly for me, I should say. Lord! what a scramble there'll be for arms and legs, when we old boys come out of our graves, on the Judgment Day: wonder if we shall get our own

again? If we do, my leg will have to tramp from Fredericksburg, my arm from here, I suppose, and meet my body, wherever it may be."

The fancy seemed to tickle him mightily, for he laughed blithely, and so did I; which, no doubt, caused the new nurse to be regarded as a light-minded sinner by the Chaplain, who roamed vaguely about, informing the men that they were all worms, corrupt of heart, with perishable bodies, and souls only to be saved by a diligent perusal of certain tracts, and other equally cheering bits of spiritual consolation, when spirituous ditto would have been preferred.

"I say, Mrs.!" called a voice behind me; and, turning, I saw a rough Michigander, with an arm blown off at the shoulder, and two or three bullets still in him—as he afterwards mentioned, as carelessly as if gentlemen were in the habit of carrying such trifles about with them. I went to him, and, while administering a dose of soap and water, he whispered, irefully:

"That red-headed devil, over yonder, is a reb, damn him! You'll agree to that, I'll bet? He's got shet of a foot, or he'd a cut like the rest of the lot. Don't you wash him, nor feed him, but jest let him holler till he's tired. It's a blasted shame to fetch them fellers in here, along side of us; and so I'll tell the chap that bosses this concern; cuss me if I don't."

I regret to say that I did not deliver a moral sermon upon the duty of forgiving our enemies, and the sin of profanity, then and there; but, being a red-hot Abolitionist, stared fixedly at the tall rebel, who was a copperhead, in every sense of the word, and privately resolved to put soap in his eyes, rub his nose the wrong way, and excoriate his cuticle generally, if I had the washing of him.

My amiable intentions, however, were frustrated; for, when I approached, with as Christian an expression as my principles would allow, and asked the question—"Shall I try to make you more comfortable, sir?" all I got for my pains was a gruff—

"No; I'll do it myself."

"Here's your Southern chivalry, with a witness," thought I, dumping the basin down before him, thereby quenching a strong desire to give him a summary baptism, in return for his ungraciousness; for my angry passions rose, at this rebuff, in a way that would have scandalized good Dr. Watts. He was a disappointment in all respects, (the rebel, not the blessed Doctor,) for he was neither fiendish, romantic, pathetic, or anything interesting; but a long, fat man, with a head like a burning bush, and a perfectly expressionless face: so I could hate him without the slightest drawback, and ignored his existence from that day forth. . . .

Having done up our human wash, and laid it out to dry, the second syllable of our version of the word war-fare was enacted with much success. Great trays of bread, meat, soup and coffee appeared; and both nurses and attendants turned waiters, serving bountiful rations to all who could eat. I can call my pinafore to testify to my good will in the work, for in ten minutes it was reduced to a perambulating bill of fare, presenting samples of all the refreshments going or gone. It was a lively scene; the long room lined with rows of beds, each filled by an occupant, whom water, shears, and clean raiment, had transformed from a dismal ragamuffin into a recumbent hero, with a cropped head. To and fro rushed matrons, maids, and convalescent "boys," skirmishing with knives and forks; retreating with empty plates; marching and counter-marching, with unvaried success, while the clash of busy spoons made most inspiring music for the charge of our Light Brigade: . . .

Very welcome seemed the generous meal, after a week of suffering, exposure, and short commons; soon the brown faces began to smile, as food, warmth, and rest, did their pleasant work; and the grateful "Thankee's" were followed by more graphic accounts of the battle and retreat, than any paid reporter could have given us. Curious contrasts of the tragic and comic met one everywhere; and some touching as well as ludicrous episodes, might have been recorded that day. A six foot New Hampshire man, with a leg broken and perforated by a piece of shell, so large that, had I not seen the wound, I should have regarded the story as a Munchausenism, beckoned me to come and help him, as he could not sit up, and both his bed and beard were getting plentifully anointed with soup. As I fed my big nestling with corresponding mouthfuls, I asked him how he felt during the battle.

"Well, 'twas my fust, you see, so I aint ashamed to say I was a trifle flustered in the beginnin', there was such an all-fired racket; for ef there's anything I do spleen agin, it's noise. But when my mate, Eph Sylvester, caved, with a bullet through his head, I got mad, and pitched in, lickety cut. Our part of the fight didn't last long; so a lot of us larked round Fredericksburg, and give some of them houses a pretty consid'able of a rummage, till we was ordered out of the mess. Some of our fellows cut like time; but I warn't a-goin to run for nobody; and, fust thing I knew, a shell bust, right in front of us, and I keeled over, feelin' as if I was blowed higher'n a kite. I sung out, and the boys come back for me, double quick; but the way they chucked me over them fences was a caution, I tell you. . . ."

*　　*　　*

Observing that the man next him had left his meal untouched, I offered the same service I had performed for his neighbor, but he shook his head.

"Thank you, ma'am; I don't think I'll ever eat again, for I'm shot in the stomach. But I'd like a drink of water, if you aint too busy.["]

I rushed away, but the water-pails were gone to be refilled, and it was some time before they reappeared. I did not forget my patient patient, meanwhile, and, with the first mugful, hurried back to him. He seemed asleep; but something in the tired white face caused me to listen at his lips for a breath. None came. I touched his forehead; it was cold: and then I knew that, while he waited, a better nurse than I had given him a cooler draught, and healed him with a touch. I laid the sheet over the quiet sleeper, whom no noise could now disturb; and, half an hour later, the bed was empty. . . .

All having eaten, drank, and rested, the surgeons began their rounds; and I took my first lesson in the art of dressing wounds. It wasn't a festive scene, by any means; for Dr. P., whose Aid I constituted myself, fell to work with a vigor which soon convinced me that I was a weaker vessel, though nothing would have induced me to confess it then. He had served in the Crimea, and seemed to regard a dilapidated body very much as I should have regarded a damaged garment; and, turning up his cuffs, whipped out a very unpleasant looking housewife, cutting, sawing, patching and piecing, with the enthusiasm of an accomplished surgical seamstress; explaining the process, in scientific terms, to the patient, meantime; which, of course, was immensely cheering and comfortable. There was an uncanny sort of fascination in watching him, as he peered and probed into the mechanism of those wonderful bodies, whose mysteries he understood so well. The more intricate the wound, the better he liked it. A poor private, with both legs off, and shot through the lungs, possessed more attractions for him than a dozen generals, slightly scratched in some "masterly retreat;" and had any one appeared in small pieces, requesting to be put together again, he would have considered it a special dispensation.

The amputations were reserved till the morrow, and the merciful magic of ether was not thought necessary that day, so the poor souls had to bear their pains as best they might. It is all very well to talk of the patience of woman; and far be it from me to pluck that feather from her cap, for, heaven knows, she isn't allowed to wear many; but the patient endurance of these men, under trials of the flesh, was truly wonderful; their fortitude seemed contagious, and scarcely a cry escaped them, though I often longed to groan for them, when pride kept their white lips shut, while great drops stood upon their foreheads, and the bed shook with the irrepressible tremor of their tortured bodies. One or two Irishmen anathematized the doctors with the frankness of their nation, and ordered the Virgin to stand by them, as if she had been the wedded Biddy to whom they could administer the poker, if she didn't; but, as a general thing, the work went on in silence, broken only by some quiet request for roller, instruments, or plaster, a sigh from the patient, or a sympathizing murmur from the nurse.

It was long past noon before these repairs were even partially made; and, having got the bodies of my boys into something like order, the next task was to minister to their minds, by writing letters to the anxious souls at home; answering questions, reading papers, taking possession of money and valuables; for the eighth commandment was reduced to a very fragmentary condition, both by the blacks and whites, who ornamented our hospital with their presence. Pocket books, purses, miniatures, and watches, were sealed up, labelled, and handed over to the matron, till such times as the owners thereof were ready to depart homeward or campward again. . . .

* * *

REVIEW QUESTIONS

1. What were a nurse's duties?
2. Did Alcott's hospital appear to be professionally run and organized?
3. Did gender or class issues affect treatment?
4. Did prisoners receive medical assistance?
5. Did Alcott's use of humor disguise or illuminate the pathos and tragedy of war? Was her story an example of literary romanticism?

ROBERT E. LEE

Appomattox, Virginia (1865)

*As 1865 dawned, the Confederacy set. General William T. Sherman, who had com-
pleted a Union strategy of splitting the South into isolated and vulnerable sections
with his destructive "March to the Sea" from Atlanta to Savannah in December 1864,
began mowing through the Carolinas in February. That month Vice President
Alexander Stephens of the Confederacy met with President Lincoln aboard a Union
ship about ending the war, but although the meeting was evidence of a faltering
South, Stephens still refused to surrender unless the Union recognized southern independence. Once again the politicians could not solve the conflict, so the military had
to end it. The contest devolved upon the forces of General Ulysses S. Grant
(1822–1885), the commanding general of the Union Army, and those of General
Robert E. Lee (1807–1870), commander of the Army of Northern Virginia. Grant was
an 1843 West Point graduate who had served with distinction in the Mexican War
but had become a particularly undistinguished civilian until the Civil War resur-
rected him as a bold and successful military leader. Lee, an 1829 graduate of West
Point, had been one of the ablest and most respected officers in the United States
Army before the war. He had been offered command of the federal forces when the
war began, but turned down the job and the country: he resigned his commission.
Soon thereafter he took command of Virginia's army. The last days of the war commenced with Lee's abandonment of Petersburg and Richmond on 2 April. In the hope
that he could get around Grant and move south to join General Joseph E. Johnston's
troops in North Carolina, he started his troops westward toward Lynchburg. They
never arrived, for the Union forces soon had them surrounded. On 9 April 1865 Lee
surrendered to Grant at Appomatox Court House.*

From Clifford Dowdey, ed., *The Wartime Papers of R. E. Lee* (Boston: Little, Brown, and Co.,
1961), pp. 934–39.

General Order, No. 9

Headquarters, Army of Northern Virginia
April 10, 1865

After four years of arduous service, marked by
unsurpassed courage and fortitude, the Army of
Northern Virginia has been compelled to yield to
overwhelming numbers and resources.

I need not tell the brave survivors of so many
hard fought battles, who have remained steadfast
to the last, that I have consented to the result from
no distrust of them.

But feeling that valor and devotion could accomplish nothing that would compensate for the
loss that must have attended the continuance of
the contest, I determined to avoid the useless sacrifice of those whose past services have endeared
them to their countrymen.

By the terms of the agreement officers and men
can return to their homes and remain until exchanged. You will take with you the satisfaction

that proceeds from the consciousness of duty faithfully performed, and I earnestly pray that a Merciful God will extend to you His blessing and protection.

With an increasing admiration of your constancy and devotion to your country, and a grateful remembrance of your kind and generous considerations for myself, I bid you all an affectionate farewell.

R. E. LEE
Genl

*   *   *

To Jefferson Davis

Near Appomattox Court House, Virginia
April 12, 1865

Mr. President:

It is with pain that I announce to Your Excellency the surrender of the Army of Northern Virginia. The operations which preceded this result will be reported in full. I will therefore only now state that upon arriving at Amelia Court House on the morning of the 4th with the advance of the army, on its retreat from the lines in front of Richmond and Petersburg, and not finding the supplies ordered to be placed there, nearly twenty-four hours were lost in endeavoring to collect in the country subsistence for men and horses. This delay was fatal, and could not be retrieved. The troops, wearied by continued fighting and marching for several days and nights, obtained neither rest nor refreshment; and on moving on the 5th on the Richmond and Danville Railroad, I found at Jetersville the enemy's cavalry, and learned the approach of his infantry and the general advance of his army towards Burkeville. This deprived us of the use of the railroad, and rendered it impracticable to procure from Danville the supplies ordered to meet us at points of our march. Nothing could be obtained from the adjacent country. Our route to the Roanoke was therefore changed, and the march directed upon Farmville, where supplies were ordered from Lynchburg. The change of route threw the troops on the roads pursued by the ar-

tillery and wagon trains west of the railroad, which impeded our advance and embarrassed our movements. On the morning of the 6th Genl Longstreet's corps reached Rice's Station on the Lynchburg Railroad. It was followed by the commands of Genls R. H. Anderson, Ewell, and Gordon, with orders to close upon it as fast as the progress of the trains would permit or as they could be directed (diverted) on roads farther west. Genl Anderson, commanding Pickett's and B. R. Johnson's divisions, became disconnected with Mahone's division, forming the rear of Longstreet. The enemy's cavalry penetrated the line of march through the interval thus left and attacked the wagon train moving towards Farmville. This caused serious delay in the march of the center and rear of the column, and enabled the enemy to mass upon their flank. After successive attacks Anderson's and Ewell's corps were captured or driven from their position. The latter general, with both of his division commanders, Kershaw and Custis Lee, and his brigadiers, were taken prisoners. Gordon, who all the morning, aided by Genl W. H. F. Lee's cavalry, had checked the advance of the enemy on the road from Amelia Springs and protected the trains, became exposed to his combined assaults, which he bravely resisted and twice repulsed; but the cavalry having been withdrawn to another part of the line of march, and the enemy massing heavily on his front and both flanks, renewed the attack about 6 p.m., and drove him from the field in much confusion. The army continued its march during the night, and every effort was made to reorganize the divisions which had been shattered by the day's operations. But the men depressed by fatigue and hunger, many threw away their arms, while others followed the wagon trains and embarrassed their progress. On the morning of the 7th rations were issued to the troops as they passed Farmville, but the safety of the trains requiring their removal upon the approach of the enemy, all could not be supplied. The army reduced to two corps under Longstreet and Gordon, moved steadily on the road to Appomattox Court House. Thence its march was ordered by Campbell Court House through Pittsylvania towards Danville. The roads were wretched and the progress of the trains slow. By great efforts the head of the column reached Appomattox Court House on the evening of the 8th, and the troops were halted for rest. The march was ordered to be resumed at one (1) a.m. on the 9th. Fitz Lee with the cavalry, supported by Gordon, was ordered to drive the enemy from his front, wheel to the left, and cover the passage of the trains, while Longstreet, who from Rice's Station had formed the rear guard, should close up and hold the position. Two battalions of artillery and the ammunition wagons were directed to accompany the army. The rest of the artillery and wagons to move towards Lynchburg. In the early part of the night the enemy attacked Walker's artillery train near Appomattox Station on the Lynchburg Railroad, and were repelled. Shortly afterwards their cavalry dashed towards the Court House till halted by our line. During the night there were indications of a large force massing on our left and front. Fitz Lee was directed to ascertain its strength, and to suspend his advance till daylight if necessary. About five (5) a.m. on the 9th, with Gordon on his left, he moved forward and opened the way. A heavy force of the enemy was discovered opposite Gordon's right, which, moving in the direction of Appomattox Court House, drove back the left of the cavalry and threatened to cut off Gordon from Longstreet. His cavalry at the same time threatening to envelop his left flank, Gordon withdrew across the Appomattox River, and the cavalry advanced on the Lynchburg road and became separated from the army. Learning the condition of affairs on the lines, where I had gone under the expectation of meeting Genl Grant to learn definitely the terms he proposed in a communication received from him on the 8th, in the event of the surrender of the army, I requested a suspension of hostilities until these terms could be arranged. In the interview which occurred with Genl Grant in compliance with my request, terms having been agreed on, I surrendered that portion of the Army of Northern Virginia which was on the field, with its arms, artillery, and wagon trains; the officers and men to be paroled, retaining their side arms and private effects. I deemed this course the best

under all the circumstances by which we were surrounded. On the morning of the 9th, according to the reports of the ordnance officers, there were seven thousand eight hundred and ninety-two (7892) organized infantry with arms, with an average of seventy-five (75) rounds of ammunition per man. The artillery, though reduced to sixty-three (63) pieces, with ninety-three (93) rounds of ammunition, was sufficient. These comprised all the supplies of ordnance that could be relied on in the State of Virginia. I have no accurate report of the cavalry, but believe it did not exceed two thousand and one hundred (2100) effective men. The enemy was more than five times our numbers. If we could have forced our way one day longer it would have been at a great sacrifice of life; at its end, I did not see how a surrender could have been avoided. We had no subsistence for man or horse, and it could not be gathered in the country. The supplies ordered to Pamplin's Station from Lynchburg could not reach us, and the men deprived of food and sleep for many days, were worn out and exhausted.

With great respect, yr obdt svt
R. E. LEE
Genl

To Jefferson Davis

Richmond, Virginia
April 20, 1865

Mr. President:

The apprehensions I expressed during the winter, of the moral condition of the Army of Northern Virginia, have been realized. The operations which occurred while the troops were in the entrenchments in front of Richmond and Petersburg were not marked by the boldness and decision which formerly characterized them. Except in particular instances, they were feeble; and a want of confidence seemed to possess officers and men. This condition, I think, was produced by the state of feeling in the country, and the communications received by the men from their homes, urging their return and the abandonment of the field. The movement of the enemy on the 30th March to Dinwiddie Court House was consequently not as strongly met as similar ones had been. Advantages were gained by him which discouraged the troops, so that on the morning of the 2d April, when our lines between the Appomattox and Hatcher's Run were assaulted, the resistance was not effectual: several points were penetrated and large captures made. At the commencement of the withdrawal of the army from the lines on the night of the 2d, it began to disintegrate, and straggling from the ranks increased up to the surrender on the 9th. On that day, as previously reported, there were only seven thousand eight hundred and ninety-two (7892) effective infantry. During the night, when the surrender became known, more than ten thousand men came in, as reported to me by the Chief Commissary of the Army. During the succeeding days stragglers continued to give themselves up, so that on the 12th April, according to the rolls of those paroled, twenty-six thousand and eighteen (26,018) officers and men had surrendered. Men who had left the ranks on the march, and crossed James River, returned and gave themselves up, and many have since come to Richmond and surrendered. I have given these details that Your Excellency might know the state of feeling which existed in the army, and judge of that in the country. From what I have seen and learned, I believe an army

cannot be organized or supported in Virginia, and as far as I know the condition of affairs, the country east of the Mississippi is morally and physically unable to maintain the contest unaided with any hope of ultimate success. A partisan war may be continued, and hostilities protracted, causing individual suffering and the devastation of the country, but I see no prospect by that means of achieving a separate independence. It is for Your Excellency to decide, should you agree with me in opinion, what is proper to be done. To save useless effusion of blood, I would recommend measures be taken for suspension of hostilities and the restoration of peace.

I am with great respect, yr obdt svt
R. E. Lee
Genl

Review Questions

1. Was defeat the result of one particular factor or a concourse of circumstances?
2. Did Lee blame his soldiers for the defeat?
3. What were some of the terms of the surrender?
4. Why did Lee recommend a cessation of all hostilities and acceptance of reunion?

INTERPRETING VISUAL SOURCES: PICTURING THE CIVIL WAR

MATHEW BRADY AND ASSOCIATES

The Civil War was the first "modern" war in American history. People have described it as such because of who and what were involved in the conflict and how many people participated in or were affected by it. The majority of Americans of both sexes, all ethnic groups, and from the various regions either participated in or felt the impact of this "total war"—a term denoting warfare extending beyond battlefields and military forces to encompass, batter, and even destroy civilian persons, property, and societies.

Technology contributed to the totality of this war. Modern military weapons were more powerful, more accurate, and more plentiful due to new manufacturing processes and the multiplying factories and factory workers producing them. These weapons were used not only on the battlefields but against civilian communities. Those "under the gun" certainly felt the impact of the technology, but even those away from the camps, communities, and battlefields of war could see and thus feel the impact through the product of another new mechanical and chemical marvel: the camera.

A number of photographers and combat artists, most associated with the Union forces, headed into camps and combat to record the war. Mathew B. Brady (1822–1896) was one of the most distinguished and, at least at the beginning of the conflict, perhaps most prolific of the group. In 1861 Brady not only set out to photograph the war himself, he assembled the material and human resources needed to cover more than one army or battlefield at a time. Over the following years, some of his associates, such as Alexander Gardner, Timothy H. O'Sullivan, and James F. Gibson, left his employ and continued their work independently. Brady, on the other hand, became more dependent on assistants over time as his eyesight failed; even so, whether he was operating the cameras, supervising shoots, or putting on gallery shows, Brady provided the public with some remarkable images of the war.

Brady's work reflected his constant desire to perfect his craft and his strong drive to preserve the images of the people and events of his era for posterity. Soon after the photographic process invented by Louis Jacques Mandé Daguerre became public knowledge in 1839, Brady set out to master it. He experimented with everything from preparing the photographic plates, modifying and maneuvering the camera boxes and lenses as needed, seating a subject or finding the best place to record a scene, to mixing the chemicals and developing the plates with them. He soon became a very successful professional photographer and established studios in both Washington, D.C., and New York City.

While many people commissioned him to take their pictures, Brady sought out America's leading figures in politics, the sciences, and the arts. Between 1845 and 1861 he managed to seat or stand many of these leaders before his cameras. In doing so Brady was already forging a connection between photography and the historical record, a link that grew during the war when Brady and other photographers headed out to record military scenes.

After receiving permission from President Lincoln to work within the Union Army's camps and accompany it in combat, Brady set up a black, hooded wagon that became known as the "What-is-it" wagon. He designed it to transport and shield not only his cameras but the exposed wet plates from which he and his people would develop their photographs. Troops may have questioned what it was at first, but Brady, his assistants, his competitors, and their equipment soon became familiar sights.

The photographers set up their big cameras—and they were huge contraptions balanced on long legs and draped in dark cloth—in camps, where they could safely photograph soldiers at their everyday tasks and officers in meetings, but they also hazarded themselves and their equipment on battlefields. These cameramen did manage to produce a few action shots, but the fact that there were not many was due more to the limitations of the equipment rather than any unwillingness on the part of the photographers to take them. Moving objects only produced blurs in photographs, and the lighting conditions had to be just right for anything to develop on the plates then in use. The photographers may not have taken many shots of the armies in action, but they made up for that in the numerous photographs they produced of the dead and destroyed at battles' end. Gardner, in particular, seemed especially interested in recording the human toll.

Brady was prolific in taking photographs, but he was even better at disseminating them. The master photographer showed and sold his work and that of his assistants at his galleries. In fact, his promotion of their work under his name may have been what drove some of them out of his employ (it also made proper attribution difficult for later historians). Most Americans then, however, were interested in the products, not the producers. Those who visited Brady's gallery shows, purchased copies of the photographs, or saw the woodcut illustrations based on his images in newspapers, could examine the scenes and see the faces of war as they had never seen them before. Brady and his fellow photographers thus helped strip away some of the glory of war as they exposed both the humanity and inhumanity of camp and combat.

Yorktown Fortifications (1862)

1862 Photograph of Entrenchments and Heavy Artillery at Yorktown, VA
From Roy Meredith, *Mr. Lincoln's Camera Man: Mathew Brady*, rev. ed. (1946; New York:
Dover Publications, Inc., 1974), p. 105.

*1861, the first year of the war, was actually rather quiet in terms of army operations.
Both sides had to recruit soldiers, stockpile supplies, decide on strategies, and then
move their troops into place. In 1862 fierce fighting in the West led to Union victories
at Fort Henry, Fort Donnelson, and Shiloh. The morale and expectations raised by
success in the West were, however, soon leveled by lost opportunities and defeat in the
East. The Peninsular Campaign, for instance, which was supposed to have climaxed
with Union forces marching into Richmond, ended with the troops pulling out and
heading north to defend against Confederate invasions there. General George B.
McClellan actually built the Army of the Potomac into a very strong, disciplined
force, which showed in the siege of Yorktown between 5 April and 4 May. He did not
use it to advantage, however, in the following battles.*

*For much of the siege the weather hindered photographic operations, but when-
ever the rain lifted and the clouds blew away, Brady and his assistant operators were
out in camp and on the fortifications. Their photographs revealed the combination of
old and new in this war: how McClellan built up massive fortifications (modified
from older military engineering traditions) to house modern weaponry—their new,
very heavy artillery pieces. As it turned out, the Confederates decided not to challenge
those pieces—they abandoned their works instead. McClellan would have to leave the
safe haven of his fortifications and pursue them, not something at which this cautious
general excelled. When he had still not taken Richmond by July, Lincoln packed the
general off to Washington.*

Antietam/Sharpsburg (1862)

Troops Deployed: Union Forces
From Roy Meredith, *Mr. Lincoln's Camera Man: Mathew Brady*, rev. ed. (1946; New York: Dover Publications, Inc., 1974) p. 125.

Lincoln gave McClellan a chance to redeem himself against the Confederate forces, now under command of General Robert E. Lee, that invaded western Maryland in September. McClellan, with the advantage of having received critical intelligence about the disposition of Lee's troops, should have moved to the attack right away, but instead he waited (courageous about his own safety, he was perhaps overly careful of his soldiers) for sixteen hours before moving forward. McClellan thus lost the chance to strike a truly decisive if not fatal blow against the Confederate forces. The Union forces did win the battle of Antietam (called Sharpsburg by the Confederates) on 17 September, but victory came at a horrendous cost: over 2,000 Union soldiers died and more than 10,000 others were pronounced wounded or missing, while Lee's dead, wounded, and missing combined to a total of over 10,000. When McClellan failed to pursue that weakened Confederate army and prevent it from reaching safety (and the chance to fight again another day), the disgusted Lincoln removed him from command and commenced a search for a more aggressive general.

Two of Brady's operators, Gardner and Gibson, trekked after the Union forces to the village of Sharpsburg and from there out into the battlefields that had once been cornfields between the Antietam and Potomac rivers. There is some uncertainty

TROOPS DEAD: SOUTHERN CASUALTIES AT THE SUNKEN ROAD
From Roy Meredith, *Mr. Lincoln's Camera Man: Mathew Brady*, rev. ed. (1946; New York: Dover Publications, Inc., 1974) p. 125.

as to whether the photographers arrived on the day of battle or the day thereafter, thus it was either on the 17th or 18th when they first set up their camera behind McClellan's headquarters. If it was on the 17th, as Gardner noted (with an eye to later public viewing, he may have taken dramatic license), then the photographers may have caught Sumner's Second Army Corps beginning to move against D. H. Hill's Confederate division. If the scene was shot on the 18th, then they actually recorded a reserve artillery unit that had moved up to replace the troops that had been active the day before.

On the day of the battle, the Confederates were pushed back to the Sunken Road, but they fought every step of the way. Once they were entrenched in the road, they repelled attack after attack by the federal forces until, finally, they had to leave it in the hands of their dead and dying. On the 19th, after the Union troops confirmed their possession of the field, Gardner and Gibson headed out to capture the carnage on their plates. Although a few European photographers had taken pictures of the victims of their mid-nineteenth-century wars, this was apparently the first time American photographers had been able or willing to set up their equipment before all the dead were buried. The resulting images of bloated, contorted corpses morbidly fascinated the American viewing public.

Fredericksburg (1862–63)

AFTER THE BOMBARDMENT, DECEMBER 1862
From Roy Meredith, *Mr. Lincoln's Camera Man: Mathew Brady*, rev. ed. (1946; New York: Dover Publications, Inc., 1974), p. 143.

In December 1862 Union forces struck Confederate troops at Fredericksburg in northern Virginia. General Ambrose E. Burnside was determined to cross the Rappahannock River and dislodge the southern forces that held the town on the river's west bank. On 11 December, federal engineers struggled to construct a bridge as southern sharpshooters took aim to stop them. Burnside's solution to that threat was an artillery barrage that not only knocked out the snipers but destroyed a good bit of the town. Then General Joseph Hooker sent over two regiments to cover the bridge builders by fighting through the town. Nightfall brought a pause in the combat, but the next day, once pontoon bridges were in place, the Federal army crossed the river. In the midst of vicious street fighting, Union soldiers sacked the town.

Brady, assisted by O'Sullivan, drove the "What-is-it" wagon across one of the bridges and quickly set up a camera to photograph the destroyed town. As it turned out, they only had that one day. On the 13th the two forces renewed the battle, and this time the southern troops won.

Brady returned to Fredericksburg in the spring of 1863 when once again Union and Confederate forces were facing off there. General Hooker, who had replaced Burnside, decided to leave a decoy force in place to deceive the southerners and move the main part of his army to Chancellorsville to attack Lee's left flank. It was a good plan, but Lee managed to move his troops quickly enough to counter the threat. While the two primary forces clashed at Chancellorsville between 2–4 May, the remaining troops, with Brady driving his wagon in their wake, fought for Fredericksburg. The Union troops took the latter, but the Confederates won the former. Soldiers were wounded, as Brady showed, and killed at both.

UNION WOUNDED, MAY 1863
From Roy Meredith, *Mr. Lincoln's Camera Man: Mathew Brady*, rev. ed. (1946; New York: Dover Publications, Inc., 1974), p. 158.

Gettysburg (1863)

DEAD CONFEDERATE SOLDIER, DEVIL'S DEN, 6 JULY 1863
From William A. Frassanito, *Gettysburg: A Journey in Time* (New York: Charles Scribner's Sons, 1975), p. 188.

DEAD CONFEDERATE SOLDIER, DEVIL'S DEN
From William A. Frassanito, *Gettysburg: A Journey in Time* (New York: Charles Scribner's Sons, 1975), p. 189.

*Brady arrived at the Gettysburg, Pennsylvania, battlefield too late to record the hu-
man remains of that three-day engagement in July 1863. When he did arrive, he directed his assistants to photograph the landscape and landmarks of the area. The first
photographers to reach the battlefield and record the carnage were Brady's former associates, Gardner, O'Sullivan, and Gibson. Gardner, the leader of the group, apparently made it his mission to preserve the toll of war on his plates. This could have
been a statement about the destructiveness of war, but it was also a marketing ploy:
people paid to be horrified. Gardner and his crew took pictures of the dead on the 5th
and 6th of July. Their subjects were primarily Confederates, perhaps because the
Union Army buried its dead first, perhaps because northern audiences may have
found pictures of enemy dead more acceptable or palatable than such photographs of
their own soldiers.*

*The Gardner contingent did not merely record the fallen where they found them.
These cameramen, like others, moved their cameras around their subjects in attempts
to capture compelling photographic compositions. In a few instances they also moved
props—weapons and equipment—and even bodies so that they could create stronger
pictorial stories. Gardner and O'Sullivan did this when they found the body of a
young Confederate soldier amidst the boulders and stone walls of Devil's Den.*

DEAD CONFEDERATE SOLDIER IN NEW POSITION
From William A. Frassanito, *Gettysburg: A Journey in Time* (New York: Charles Scribner's
Sons, 1975), p. 190.

Freedman's Camp (1865)

RICHMOND, VIRGINIA: FREEDMAN'S ENCAMPMENT
From Roy Meredith, *Mr. Lincoln's Camera Man: Mathew Brady*, rev. ed. (1946; New York: Dover Publications, Inc., 1974), p. 198.

During the war many slaves fled to the Union Army. Called "contrabands," some served as laborers and servants, while others eventually became soldiers. Once the war was over, many, though certainly not all, ex-slaves continued to move away from their former masters and homes. Some moved north or west, heading for the areas they had long heard described as free or full of opportunities. Many more freedmen, as they were titled, gathered where there were federal military forces and government officials. The Bureau of Refugees, Freedmen, and Abandoned Lands attempted to care for their immediate needs and assist them in gaining the support and skills they required to help themselves. It could offer, however, only temporary solutions—as temporary as the tents in a Freedman's camp, such as this one within sight of Richmond, Virginia—to some of the very difficult problems of Reconstruction.

REVIEW QUESTIONS

1. In what ways do these photographs reveal aspects of modern warfare and total war?
2. What do they reveal about the people, including the photographers themselves, involved in or affected by armed conflict?

3. Do these photographs illuminate the reality of war? Do they romanticize war?
4. How could a photographic record of a scene affect someone's interpretation of an historical event?

18 ⚘ RECONSTRUCTION: NORTH AND SOUTH

The assassination of Abraham Lincoln in April 1865 brought Vice President Andrew Johnson into the White House. A Tennessee Democrat who served two terms as governor before being elected to the Senate in 1857, he was an ardent Unionist who blamed the slaveholding planter elite for secession and the Civil War. Johnson was the only southern senator who refused to embrace the Confederacy in 1861. Such credentials help explain why Lincoln invited him to be his running mate in 1864.

The Radical Republicans hoped that President Johnson would embrace their comprehensive effort to reconstruct the defeated South. Johnson shared their disdain for the former Confederate leaders and for the planter class, but he also cherished states' rights and feared any effort to expand federal authority. He also retained many of the racial prejudices of his native region. "White men alone must manage the South," Johnson told a journalist. Unlike the Radical Republicans, he balked at putting freed blacks in control of southern politics.

Like Lincoln, Andrew Johnson hoped that middle-class white southern Unionists, along with repentant ex-Confederates, would take control of restoring the South to the Union. He required that the new state constitutional conventions formally abolish slavery, renounce secession, and void all war debts that the state had incurred. The states then could hold elections and officially return to the Union. By April 1866 all of the southern states had fulfilled these requirements, albeit grudgingly, and had formed new governments. At the same time, they steadfastly refused to allow blacks to vote. Johnson, however, was dismayed that the new political leaders were more often former Confederates than southern Unionists.

The Union victory in the Civil War and the official end of slavery created excited expectations among the freed slaves. Some adopted new names to express their new identity and to make a new beginning. Others discarded the clothes provided by their masters and took up new modes of dress. Many freed people left the plantations and migrated to neighboring towns and cities, where federal troops offered protection.

But freedom itself did not provide security or the resources necessary for meaningful lives. In March 1865 Congress created the Freedmen's Bureau, an agency administered by the War Department, to provide the former slaves with emergency supplies and to help them find employment, procure land, and pursue educational opportunities. By 1870 the Bureau was supervising more than 4,000 schools.

Yet for all of its heroic efforts, the Freedmen's Bureau could help only a small percentage of former slaves. Few freed people were able to acquire land of their own. Most of them were forced to become wage laborers, or sharecroppers or tenant farmers contracting with white landowners to work their land in exchange for food, tools, clothing, and a place to live. This agrarian system, however necessary in the face of the social and economic realities confronting the region, soon placed the freed slaves in a dependent relationship reminiscent of slavery itself.

As the new "lily-white" state governments coalesced in 1865 and 1866, most of them drafted "Black Codes" limiting the rights and freedoms of African Americans. These laws varied from state to state, but all of them restricted the independence of blacks and channeled them into the service of the white-dominated social and economic order.

Some whites decided that such restrictive laws did not sufficiently impress upon blacks their subordinate status. In an effort to promote white supremacy they founded secret organizations such as the Ku Klux Klan. The Klan, organized by former Confederate soldiers, used violence and terror to intimidate blacks and to disrupt the efforts of Radical Republicans from "reconstructing" the South. During one campaign season in Louisiana, over 200 blacks were killed in one parish alone. Congress passed laws intended to suppress the Klan, but to little avail.

Reconstruction officially ended in 1877 with the withdrawal of the last federal troops from the South. African Americans in the region retained certain constitutional rights, but in practice white supremacy had been reestablished through force and terror. With the loss of federal protection, blacks found themselves not only at the mercy of the southern political elite but also locked into a dependent economic relationship through the sharecrop system as well.

NEW YORK TIMES

FROM The Late Convention of Colored Men (1865)

Many former slaves knew that freedom did not bring them security after the Civil War. They were no longer slaves, but they had no property, no money, and little education. In each state, groups of former slaves met to share their concerns and to request assistance from the federal government. The following message was sent from a convention of freedmen in Alexandria, Virginia, in 1865.

From "The Late Convention of Colored Men," *The New York Times*, 13 August 1865.

We, the undersigned members of a convention of colored citizens of the State of Virginia, would respectfully represent that, although we have been held as slaves, and denied all recognition as a constituent of your nationality for almost the entire period of the duration of your government, and that by your permission we have been denied either home or country, and deprived of the dearest rights of human nature; yet when you and our immediate oppressors met in deadly conflict upon the field of battle, the one to destroy and the other to save your government and nationality, we, with scarce an exception, in our inmost souls espoused your cause, and watched, and prayed, and waited, and labored for your success.

When the contest waxed long, and the result hung doubtfully, you appealed to us for help, and how well we answered is written in the rosters of the two hundred thousand colored troops now enrolled in your service; and as to our undying devotion to your cause, let the uniform acclamation of escaped prisoners, "Whenever we saw a black face we felt sure of a friend," answer.

Well, the war is over, the rebellion is "put down," and we are declared free! Four-fifths of our enemies are paroled or amnestied, and the other fifth are being pardoned, and the President has, in his efforts at the reconstruction of the civil government of the States, late in rebellion, left us entirely at the mercy of these subjugated but unconverted rebels, in everything save the privilege of bringing us, our wives and little ones, to the auction block. He has, so far as we can understand the tendency and bearing of his action in the case, remitted us for all our civil rights, to men, a majority of whom regard our devotions to your cause and flag as that which decided the contest against them! This we regard as destructive of all we hold dear, and in the name of God, of justice, of humanity, of good faith, of truth and righteousness, we do most solemnly and earnestly protest. Men and brethren, in the hour of your peril you called upon us, and despite all time-honored interpretation of constitutional obligations, we came at your call and you are saved—and now we beg, we pray, we entreat you not to desert us in this the hour of our peril!

We know these men—know them well—and we assure you that, with the majority of them, loyalty is only "lip deep," and that their professions of loyalty are used as a cover to the cherished design of getting restored to their former relation with the Federal Government, and then, by all sorts of "unfriendly legislation," to render the freedom you have given us more intolerable than the slavery they intended for us.

We warn you in time that our only safety is in keeping them under Governors of the military persuasion until you have so amended the Federal

Constitution that it will prohibit the States from making any distinction between citizens on account of race or color. In one word, the only salvation for us besides the power of the Government, is in the possession of the ballot. Give us this, and we will protect ourselves. No class of men relatively as numerous as we were ever oppressed when armed with the ballot. But, 'tis said we are ignorant. Admit it. Yet who denies we know a traitor from a loyal man, a gentleman from a rowdy, a friend from an enemy?

. . . All we ask is an equal chance with the white traitors varnished and japanned with the oath of amnesty. Can you deny us this and still keep faith with us? "But," say some, "the blacks will be overreached by the superior knowledge and cunning of the whites." Trust us for that. We will never be deceived a second time. "But," they continue, "the planters and landowners will have them in their power, and dictate the way their votes shall be cast." We did not know before that we were to be left to the tender mercies of these landed rebels for employment. Verily, we thought the Freedmen's Bureau was organized and clothed with power to protect us from this very thing, by compelling those for whom we labored to pay us, whether they liked our political opinions or not! . . .

We are "sheep in the midst of wolves," and nothing but the military arm of the Government-prevents us and all the truly loyal white men from being driven from the land of our birth. Do not then, we beseech you, give to one of these "wayward sisters" the rights they abandoned and forfeited when they rebelled until you have secured our rights by the aforementioned amendment to the Constitution.

Let your action in our behalf be thus clear and emphatic, and our respected President, who, we feel confident, desires only to know your will, to act in harmony therewith, will give you his most earnest and cordial cooperation; and the Southern States, through your enlightened and just legislation, will speedily award us our rights. Thus not only will the arms of the rebellion be surrendered, but the ideas also.

REVIEW QUESTIONS

1. What service had former slaves performed that they believed entitled them to the protection of the federal government?
2. What did the petitioners mean when they said that the southerner was "subjugated but unconverted"?
3. What two steps did the freed blacks claim would ensure that their own rights would be guaranteed?

CHARLES SOULE

To the Freed People of Orangeburg (1865)

In helping former slaves adapt to their new conditions, the Freedmen's Bureau sent civilian and military officials throughout the South. In rural Orangeburg, South Carolina, Union army captain Charles Soule sternly advised the "freed people" how to behave.

From Records of the Commissioner, Bureau of Refugees, Freedmen and Abandoned Lands Record Group 105, National Archives, Washington, D.C.

You have heard many stories about your condition as freemen. You do not know what to believe: you are talking too much; waiting too much; asking for too much. If you can find out the truth about this matter, you will settle down quietly to your work. Listen, then, and try to understand just how you are situated.

You are now free, but you must know that the only difference you can feel yet, between slavery and freedom, is that neither you nor your children can be bought or sold. You may have a harder time this year than you have ever had before; it will be the price you pay for your freedom. You will have to work hard, and get very little to eat, and very few clothes to wear.

If you get through this year alive and well, you should be thankful. Do not expect to save up anything, or to have much corn or provisions ahead at the end of the year. You must not ask for more pay than free people get at the North. There, a field hand is paid in money, but has to spend all his pay every week, in buying food and clothes for his family and in paying rent for his house. You cannot be paid in money,—for there is no good money in the District,—nothing but Confederate paper. Then, what can you be paid with? Why, with food, with clothes, with the free use of your little houses and lots. You do not own a cent's worth except yourselves. The plantation you live on is not yours, nor the houses, nor the cattle, mules and horses; the seed you planted with was not yours, and the ploughs and hoes do not belong to you.

Now you must get something to eat and something to wear, and houses to live in. How can you get these things? By hard work—and nothing else, and it will be a good thing for you if you get them until next year, for yourselves and for your families. You must remember that your children, your old people, and the cripples, belong to you to support now, and all that is given to them is so much pay to you for your work.

If you ask for anything more; if you ask for a half of the crop, or even a third, you ask too much; you wish to get more than you could get if you had been free all your lives. Do not ask for Saturday either: free people everywhere else work Saturday, and you have no more right to the day than they have. If your employer is willing to give you part of the day, or to set a task that you can finish early, be thankful for the kindness, but do not think it is something you must have.

When you work, work hard. Begin early at sunrise, and do not take more than two hours at noon. Do not think, because you are free you can choose your own kind of work. Every man must work under orders. The soldiers, who are free, work under officers, the officers under the general, and the general under the president. There must be a head man everywhere, and on a plantation the head man, who gives all the orders, is the owner of the place. Whatever he tells you to do you must do at once, and cheerfully. Never give him a cross word or an impudent answer.

If the work is hard, do not stop to talk about it, but do it first and rest afterwards. If you are told to go into the field and hoe, see who can go first and lead the row. If you are told to build a fence, build it better than any fence you know of. If you are told to drive the carriage Sunday, or to mind the cattle, do it, for necessary work must be done even on the Sabbath. Whatever the order is, try and obey it without a word [of resistance][1] . . . .

You do not understand why some of the whites who used to own you, do not have to work in the field. It is because they are rich. If every man were poor, and worked in his own field, there would be no big farms, and very little cotton or corn raised to sell; there would be no money, and nothing to buy. Some people must be rich, to pay the others, and they have the right to do no work except to look out after their property. It is so everywhere, and perhaps by hard work some of you may by-and-by become rich yourselves.

Remember that all your working time belongs to the man who hires you: therefore you must not leave work without his leave not even to nurse a child, or to go and visit a wife or husband. When you wish to go off the place, get a pass as you used

---

[1] Editorial insertion.

to, and then you will run no danger of being taken up by our soldiers. . . .

Do not think of leaving the plantation where you belong. If you try to go to Charleston, or any other city, you will find no work to do, and nothing to eat. You will starve, or fall sick and die. Stay where you are, in your own homes, even if you are suffering. There is no better place for you anywhere else. . . .

In every set of men there are some bad men and some fools; who have to be looked after and punished where they go wrong. The Government will punish grown people now, and punish them severely, if they steal, lie idle, or hang around a man's place when he does not want them there, or if they are impudent. You ought to be civil to one another, and to the men you work for. Watch folks who have always been free, and you will see that the best people are the most civil.

The children have to be punished more than those who are grown, for they are full of mischief. Fathers and mothers should punish their own children, but if they happen to off,[2] or if a child is caught stealing or behaving badly about the big house, the owner of the plantation must switch him, just as he should his own children.

---

[2] Away from home.

Do not grumble if you cannot get as much pay on your place as someone else. One man can afford to pay more than another. Make the best of everything, and if there is anything which you think is wrong, or hard to bear, try to reason it: if you cannot, ask leave to send one man to town to see an officer. Never stop work on any account, for the whole crop must be raised and got in, or we shall starve. . . .

In short, do just about as the good men among you have always done. Remember that even if you are badly off, no one can buy or sell you: remember that if you help yourselves, *God* will help you, and trust hopefully that next year and the year after will bring some new blessing to you.

REVIEW QUESTIONS

1. Why did Soule tell the freed slaves that they might have a "harder time this year than they have ever had before"?
2. Would Soule have delivered much the same message to poor whites? Why or why not?
3. Given Soule's advice, would the lives of the freed slaves differ greatly from that of slaves? Explain.

MARY AMES

From a New England Woman's Diary in Dixie in 1865

Nothing was more exasperating to freed slaves than the difficulty of acquiring land in the postwar South—even if they had the money to purchase it. The following letter to President Andrew Johnson (from a group of freedmen on Edisto Island off the coast of South Carolina) poignantly reveals the angry frustration of newly freed slaves seeing their land returned to the former white planters who were judged to hold "legal" title.

From Mary Ames, *From a New England Woman's Diary in Dixie in 1865* (Springfield, MA: Plimpton, 1906), pp. 101–02.

Edisto Island S.C. Oct. 28th, 1865
To the President of these United States:

We the freedmen Of Edisto Island South Carolina have learned From you through Major General O O Howard commissioner of the Freedman's Bureau. with deep sorrow and Painful hearts of the possibility of government restoring These lands to the former owners. We are well aware Of the many perplexing and trying questions that burden Your mind. and do therefore pray to god (the preserver of all. and who has through our Late and beloved President[1] proclamation and the war made Us A free people) that he may guide you in making Your decisions. and give you that wisdom that Cometh from above to settle these great and Important Questions for the best interests of the country and the Colored race: Here is where secession was born and Nurtured. Here is were we have toiled nearly all Our lives as slaves and were treated like dumb Driven cattle. This is our home, we have made These lands what they are. we were the only true and Loyal people that were found in possession of these Lands. we have been always ready to strike for Liberty and humanity yea to fight if needs be To preserve this glorious union. Shall not we who Are freedman

and have been always true to this Union have the same rights as are enjoyed by Others? Have we broken any Law of these United States? have we forfeited our rights of property In Land?—If not then! are not our rights as A free people and good citizens of these United States To be considered before the rights of those who were Found in rebellion against this good and just Government (and now being conquered) come (as they Seem) with penitent hearts and beg forgiveness For past offences and also ask if their lands Cannot be restored to them are these rebellious Spirits to be reinstated in their *possessions* And we who have been abused and oppressed For many long years not to be allowed the Privilige of purchasing land But be subject To the will of these large Land owners? God forbid. Land monopoly is injurious to the advancement of the course of freedom, and if Government Does not make some provision by which we as Freedmen can obtain A Homestead, we have Not bettered our condition.

We have been encouraged by Government to take Up these lands in small tracts, receiving Certificates of the same—we have thus far Taken Sixteen thousand (16,000) acres of Land here on This Island. We are ready to pay for this land When Government calls for it. and now after What has been done will the good and just government take

[1]Abraham Lincoln (1809–1865).

from us all this right and make us Subject to the will of those who have cheated and Oppressed us for many years God Forbid!

We the freedmen of this Island and of the State of South Carolina—Do therefore petition to you as the President of these United States, that some provisions be made by which Every colored man can purchase land. and Hold it as his own. We wish to have A home if It be but A few acres. without some provision is Made our future is sad to look upon. yess our Situation is dangerous. we therefore look to you In this trying hour as A true friend of the poor and Neglected race. for protection and Equal Rights. with the privilege of purchasing A Homestead—A Homestead right here in the Heart of South Carolina.

We pray that God will direct your heart in Making such provision for us as freedmen which Will tend to unite these states together stronger Than ever before—May God bless you in the Administration of your duties as the President Of these United States is the humble prayer Of us all.—

In behalf of the Freedmen
Henry Bram
Committee Ishamel. Moultrie.
yates. Sampson

REVIEW QUESTIONS

1. What arguments did the freed slaves offer to support their claim to the land?
2. How might the former white owners have responded to the slaves' claims?
3. How do you think Andrew Johnson would have responded to the petition had the freed slaves been white? Explain.

Black Codes of Mississippi (1865)

The so-called Black Codes were enacted by the newly reconstituted southern state legislatures to address the legal status of the freed slaves. Some of the codes, such as Georgia's, were lenient; others, such as those of Louisiana and Mississippi, were efforts to restore slavery in all but name. Most of the Black Codes were suspended by the federal military governors of the reconstructed states; and both the Civil Rights Act of 1866 and the Fourteenth Amendment were prompted in part as a response to these attempts at suppressing the rights of blacks. The following sections from the Mississippi code deal with civil rights, apprenticeship, vagrancy, and penal crimes.

From *Laws of the State of Mississippi*, 1865 (Jackson, MS, 1866), pp. 82–90, 165.

1. Civil Rights of Freedmen in Mississippi

Sec. 1. *Be it enacted,* . . . That all freedmen, free negroes, and mulattoes may sue and be sued, implead and be impleaded, in all the courts of law and equity of this State, and may acquire personal property . . . by descent or purchase, and may dispose of the same in the same manner and to the same extent that white persons may: *Provided,* That the provisions of this section shall not be so construed as to allow any freedman, free negro, or mulatto to rent or lease any lands or tenements except in incorporated cities or towns, in which places the corporate authorities shall control the same. . . .

Sec. 3. . . . All freedmen, free negroes, or mulattoes who do now and have herebefore lived and cohabited together as husband and wife shall be taken and held in law as legally married, and the issue shall be taken and held as legitimate for all purposes: that it shall not be lawful for any freedman, free negro, or mulatto to intermarry with any white person; nor for any white person to intermarry with any freedman, free negro, or mulatto: and any person who shall so intermarry, shall be deemed guilty of felony, and on conviction thereof shall be confined in the State penitentiary for life; and those shall be deemed freedmen, free negroes, and mulattoes who are of pure negro blood, and those descended from a negro to the third generation, inclusive, though one ancestor in each generation may have been a white person.

Sec. 4. . . . In addition to cases in which freedmen, free negroes, and mulattoes are now by law competent witnesses, freedmen, free negroes, or mulattoes shall be competent in civil cases, when a party or parties to the suit, either plaintiff or plaintiffs, defendant or defendants, and a white person or white persons, is or are the opposing party or parties, plaintiff or plaintiffs, defendant or defendants. They shall also be competent witnesses in all criminal prosecutions where the crime charged is alleged to have been committed by a white person upon or against the person or property of a freedman, free negro, or mulatto: *Provided*, that in all cases said witnesses shall be examined in open court, on the stand; except, however, they may be examined before the grand jury, and shall in all cases be subject to the rules and tests of the common law as to competency and credibility. . . .

Sec. 6. . . . All contracts for labor made with freedmen, free negroes, and mulattoes for a longer period than one month shall be in writing, and in duplicate, attested and read to said freedman, free negro, or mulatto by a beat, city or county officer, or two disinterested white persons of the county in which the labor is to be performed, of which each party shall have one; and said contracts shall be taken and held as entire contracts, and if the laborer shall quit the service of the employer before the expiration of his term of service, without good

cause, he shall forfeit his wages for that year up to the time of quitting.

Sec. 7. . . . Every civil officer shall, and every person may, arrest and carry back to his or her legal employer any freedman, free negro, or mulatto who shall have quit the service of his or her employer before the expiration of his or her term of service without good cause; and said officer and person shall be entitled to receive for arresting and carrying back every deserting employee aforesaid the sum of five dollars, and ten cents per mile from the place of arrest to the place of delivery; and the same shall be paid by the employer, and held as a set-off for so much against the wages of said deserting employee: *Provided*, that said arrested party, after being so returned, may appeal to the justice of the peace or member of the board of police of the county, who, on notice to the alleged employer, shall try summarily whether said appellant is legally employed by the alleged employer, and has good cause to quit said employer; either party shall have the right of appeal to the county court, pending which the alleged deserter shall be remanded to the alleged employer or otherwise disposed of, as shall be right and just; and the decision of the county court shall be final. . . .

Sec. 9. . . . If any person shall persuade or attempt to persuade, entice, or cause any freedman, free negro, or mulatto to desert from the legal employment of any person before the expiration of his or her term of service, or shall knowingly employ any such deserting freedman, free negro, or mulatto, or shall knowingly give or sell to any such deserting freedman, free negro, or mulatto, any food, raiment, or other thing, he or she shall be guilty of a misdemeanor, and, upon conviction, shall be fined not less than twenty-five dollars and not more than two hundred dollars and the costs; and if said fine and costs shall not be immediately paid, the court shall sentence said convict to not exceeding two months' imprisonment in the county jail, and he or she shall moreover be liable to the party injured in damages: *Provided*, if any person shall, or shall attempt to, persuade, entice, or cause any freedman, free negro, or mulatto to desert from any legal employment of any person, with the view to employ said freedman, free negro, or mulatto without the limits of this State, such person, on conviction, shall be fined not less than fifty dollars, and not more than five hundred dollars and costs; and if said fine and costs shall not be immediately paid, the court shall sentence said convict to not exceeding six months imprisonment in the county jail.

*   *   *

Mississippi Vagrant Law

Sec. 1. *Be it enacted, etc.,* . . . That all rogues and vagabonds, idle and dissipated persons, beggars, jugglers, or persons practicing unlawful games or plays, runaways, common drunkards, common night-walkers, pilferers, lewd, wanton, or lascivious persons, in speech or behavior, common railers and brawlers, persons who neglect their calling or employment, misspend what they earn, or do not provide for the support of themselves or their families, or dependents, and all other idle and disorderly persons, including all who neglect all lawful business, habitually misspend their time by frequenting houses of ill-fame, gaming-houses, or tippling shops, shall be deemed and considered vagrants, under the provisions of this act, and upon conviction thereof shall be fined not exceeding one hundred dollars, with all accruing costs, and be imprisoned at the discretion of the court, not exceeding ten days.

Sec. 2. . . . All freedmen, free negroes and mulattoes in this State, over the age of eighteen years, found on the second Monday in January, 1866, or thereafter, with no lawful employment or business, or found unlawfully assembling themselves together, either in the day or night time, and all white persons so assembling themselves with freedmen, free negroes or mulattoes, or usually associating with freedmen, free negroes or mulattoes, on terms of equality, or living in adultery or fornication with a freed woman, free negro or mulatto, shall be deemed vagrants, and on conviction thereof shall be fined in a sum not exceeding, in the case of a

freedman, free negro or mulatto, fifty dollars, and a white man two hundred dollars, and imprisoned at the discretion of the court, the free negro not exceeding ten days, and the white man not exceeding six months. . . .

Sec. 7. . . . If any freedman, free negro, or mulatto shall fail or refuse to pay any tax levied according to the provisions of the sixth section of this act, it shall be *prima facie* evidence of vagrancy, and it shall be the duty of the sheriff to arrest such freedman, free negro, or mulatto or such person refusing or neglecting to pay such tax, and proceed at once to hire for the shortest time such delinquent tax-payer to any one who will pay the said tax, with accruing costs, giving preference to the employer, if there be one.

*   *   *

4. Penal Laws of Mississippi

Sec. 1. *Be it enacted,* . . . That no freedman, free negro or mulatto, not in the military service of the United States government, and not licensed so to do by the board of police of his or her county, shall keep or carry fire-arms of any kind, or any ammunition, dirk or bowie knife, and on conviction thereof in the county court shall be punished by fine, not exceeding ten dollars, and pay the costs of such proceedings, and all such arms or ammunition shall be forfeited to the informer; and it shall be the duty of every civil and military officer to arrest any freedman, free negro, or mulatto found with any such arms or ammunition, and cause him or her to be committed to trial in default of bail.

Sec. 2. . . . Any freedman, free negro, or mulatto committing riots, routs, affrays,[1] trespasses, malicious mischief, cruel treatment to animals, seditious speeches, insulting gestures, language, or acts, or assaults on any person, disturbance of the peace, exercising the function of a minister of the Gospel without a license from some regularly organized church, vending spirituous or intoxicating liquors,

---

[1] Brawls.

or committing any other misdemeanor, the punishment of which is not specifically provided for by law, shall, upon conviction thereof in the county court, be fined not less than ten dollars, and not more than one hundred dollars, and may be imprisoned at the discretion of the court, not exceeding thirty days.

Sec. 3. . . . If any white person shall sell, lend, or give to any freedman, free negro, or mulatto any fire-arms, dirk or bowie knife, or ammunition, or any spirituous or intoxicating liquors, such person or persons so offending, upon conviction thereof in the county court of his or her county, shall be fined not exceeding fifty dollars, and may be imprisoned, at the discretion of the court, not exceeding thirty days. . . .

Sec. 5. . . . If any freedman, free negro, or mulatto, convicted of any of the misdemeanors provided against in this act, shall fail or refuse for the space of five days, after conviction, to pay the fine and costs imposed, such person shall be hired out by the sheriff or other officer, at public outcry, to any white person who will pay said fine and all costs, and take said convict for the shortest time.

REVIEW QUESTIONS

1. Which crime carried the harshest penalty? Why?
2. Summarize the regulations related to employment of freed slaves. How did they represent a form of slavery?
3. The Black Codes were criticized for their vagueness. Cite an example of such vagueness, and note ways in which the codes could be interpreted or manipulated.

HOWELL COBB

An Unreconstructed Southerner (1868)

Many former Confederates resented and resisted the presence of federal troops in the South after the Civil War and the efforts of the Congress to "reconstruct" the region's political, social, and economic life. Howell Cobb (1815–1868) was a prominent Georgia attorney and Democratic politician who served as the Speaker of the United States House of Representatives, governor of Georgia, secretary of treasury under President James Buchanan, and as a major general in the Confederate army. In this letter to the federal commander of the third military district, which included Georgia, he expresses the bitter feelings of many white southerners.

From Howell Cobb to J. D. Hoover, 4 January 1868, in *The Correspondence of Robert Toombs, Alexander H. Stephens, and Howell Cobb*, ed. U. B. Phillips (Washington, D.C., 1913), pp. 690–94.

. . . We of the ill-fated South realize only the mournful present whose lesson teaches us to prepare for a still gloomier future. . . . The people of the south, conquered, ruined, impoverished, and oppressed, bear up with patient fortitude under the heavy weight of their burdens. Disarmed and reduced to poverty, they are powerless to protect themselves against wrong and injustice; and can only await with broken spirits that destiny which the future has in store for them. At the bidding of their more powerful conquerors they laid down their arms, abandoned a hopeless struggle, and returned to their quiet homes under the plighted faith of a soldier's honor that they should be protected so long as they observed the obligations imposed upon them of peaceful law-abiding citizens.

Despite the bitter charges and accusations brought against our people, I hesitate not to say that since that hour their bearing and conduct have been marked by a dignified and honorable submission which should command the respect of their bitterest enemy and challenge the admiration of the civilized world. Deprived of our property and ruined in our estates by the results of the war, we have accepted the situation and given the pledge of a faith never yet broken to abide it. Our conquerors seem to think we should accompany our acquiescence with some exhibition of gratitude for the ruin which they have brought upon us. We cannot see it in that light.

Since the close of the war they have taken our property of various kinds, sometimes by seizure, and sometimes by purchase,—and when we have asked for remuneration have been informed that the claims of rebels are never recognized by the Government. To this decision necessity compels us to submit; but our conquerors express surprise that we do not see in such ruling the evidence of their kindness and forgiving spirit.

They have imposed upon us in our hour of distress and ruin a heavy and burdensome tax, peculiar and limited to our impoverished section. Against such legislation we have ventured to utter an earnest appeal, which to many of their leading spirits indicates a spirit of insubordination which calls for additional burdens. They have deprived us of the protection afforded by our state constitutions and laws, and put life, liberty and property at the disposal of absolute military power. Against this violation of plighted faith and constitutional right we have earnestly and solemnly protested, and our protests have been denounced as insolent;—and our restlessness under the wrong and oppression which have followed these acts has been

construed into a rebellious spirit, demanding further and more stringent restrictions of civil and constitutional rights. They have arrested the wheels of State government, paralyzed the arm of industry, engendered a spirit of bitter antagonism on the part of our negro population towards the white people with whom it is the interest of both races they should maintain kind and friendly relations, and are now struggling by all the means in their power both legal and illegal, constitutional and unconstitutional, to make our former slaves *our masters*, bringing these Southern states under the power of *negro supremacy*.

To these efforts we have opposed appeals, protests, and every other means of resistance in our power, and shall continue to do so to the bitter end. If the South is to be made a pandemonium and a howling wilderness, the responsibility shall not rest upon our heads.

Our conquerors regard these efforts on our part to save ourselves and posterity from the terrible results of their policy and conduct as a new rebellion against the constitution of our country, and profess to be amazed that in all this we have failed to see the evidence of their great magnanimity and exceeding generosity. Standing today in the midst of the gloom and suffering which meets the eye in every direction, we can but feel that we are the victims of cruel legislation and the harsh enforcement of unjust laws. . . .

We regarded the close of the war as ending the relationship of enemies and the beginning of a new national brotherhood, and in the light of that conviction felt and spoke of constitutional equality. . . .

We claimed that the result of the war left us a state in the Union, and therefore under the protection of the constitution, rendering in return cheerful obedience to its requirements and bearing in common with the other states of the Union the burdens of government, submitting even as we were compelled to do to *taxation without representation*; but they tell us that a successful war to keep us in the Union left us out of the Union and that the pretension we put up for constitutional protection evidences bad temper on our part and a want of appreciation of the generous spirit which declares that the constitution is not over us for the purposes of protection. . . .

In such reasoning is found a justification of the policy which seeks to put the South under negro supremacy. Better, they say, to hazard the consequences of negro supremacy in the south with its sure and inevitable results upon Northern prosperity than to put faith in the people of the south who though overwhelmed and conquered have ever showed themselves a brave and generous people, true to their plighted faith in peace and in war, in adversity as in prosperity. . . .

*   *   *

With an Executive[1] who manifests a resolute purpose to defend with all his power the constitution of his country from further aggression, and a Judiciary whose unspotted record has never yet been tarnished with a base subserviency to the unholy demands of passion and hatred, let us indulge the hope that the hour of the country's redemption is at hand, and that even in the wronged and ruined South there is a fair prospect for better days and happier hours when our people can unite again in celebrating the national festivals as in the olden time.

REVIEW QUESTIONS

1. How are white southerners portrayed in this excerpt?
2. What do you think Cobb meant when he said that "property of various kinds" had been stolen?
3. According to Cobb, what was the motive behind the supposed attempt to create "negro supremacy" in the South?

---

[1] President Andrew Johnson (1808–1875).

Organization and Principles of The Ku Klux Klan (1868)

The Ku Klux Klan was the largest of several white supremacist societies that emerged in the post–Civil War era. Founded in Pulaski, Tennessee, in 1865, it grew rapidly among Confederate veterans across the South. General Nathan Bedford Forrest was the first Grand Wizard. The Klan used terror and violence to defy the efforts of Radical Republicans to "reconstruct" southern society. The following is an early statement of the Klan's principles.

From W. L. Fleming, ed., *The Ku Klux Klan: Its Origin, Growth and Disbandment*, by J. C. Lester and D. L. Wilson (New York: Neale, 1905), pp. 154ff.

Creed

We, the Order of the * * *, reverentially acknowledge the majesty and supremacy of the Divine Being, and recognize the goodness and providence of the same. And we recognize our relation to the United States Government, the supremacy of the Constitution, the Constitutional Laws thereof, and the Union of States thereunder.

Character and Objects of the Order

This is an institution of Chivalry, Humanity, Mercy, and Patriotism; embodying in its genius and its principles all that is chivalric in conduct, noble in sentiment, generous in manhood, and patriotic in purpose; its peculiar objects being

First: To protect the weak, the innocent, and the defenseless, from the indignities, wrongs, and outrages of the lawless, the violent, and the brutal; to relieve the injured and oppressed; to succor the suffering and unfortunate, and especially the widows and orphans of Confederate soldiers.

Second: To protect and defend the Constitution of the United States, and all laws passed in conformity thereto, and to protect the States and the people thereof from all invasion from any source whatever.

Third: To aid and assist in the execution of all constitutional laws, and to protect the people from unlawful seizure, and from trial except by their peers in conformity to the laws of the land.

Titles

Sec. 1. The officers of this Order shall consist of a Grand Wizard of the Empire, and his ten Genii; a Grand Dragon of the Realm, and his eight Hydras; a Grand Titan of the Dominion, and his six Furies; a Grand Giant of the Province, and his four Goblins; a Grand Cyclops of the Den, and his two Night Hawks; a Grand Magi, a Grand Monk, a Grand Scribe, a Grand Exchequer, a Grand Turk, and a Grand Sentinel.

Sec. 2. The body politic of this Order shall be known and designated as "Ghouls."

Territory and its Divisions

Sec. 1. The territory embraced within the jurisdiction of this Order shall be coterminous with the States of Maryland, Virginia, North Carolina, South Carolina, Georgia, Florida, Alabama, Mississippi, Louisiana, Texas, Arkansas, Missouri, Kentucky, and Tennessee; all combined constituting the Empire.

Sec. 2. The Empire shall be divided into four departments, the first to be styled the Realm, and coterminous with the boundaries of the several States; the second to be styled the Dominion, and to be coterminous with such counties as the Grand Dragons of the several Realms may assign to the charge of the Grand Titan. The third to be styled the Province, and to be coterminous with the several counties; *Provided* the Grand Titan may, when he deems it necessary, assign two Grand Giants to one Province, prescribing, at the same time, the jurisdiction of each. The fourth department to be styled the Den, and shall embrace such part of a Province as the Grand Giant shall assign to the charge of a Grand Cyclops. . . .

Interrogations to be asked

1st. Have you ever been rejected, upon application for membership in the * * *, or have you ever been expelled from the same?

2d. Are you now, or have you ever been, a member of the Radical Republican party, or either of the organizations known as the "Loyal League" and the "Grand Army of the Republic?"

3d. Are you opposed to the principles and policy of the Radical party, and to the Loyal League, and the Grand Army of the Republic, so far as you are informed of the character and purposes of those organizations?

4th. Did you belong to the Federal army during the late war, and fight against the South during the existence of the same?

5th. Are you opposed to negro equality, both social and political?

6th. Are you in favor of a white man's government in this country?

7th. Are you in favor of Constitutional liberty, and a Government of equitable laws instead of a Government of violence and oppression?

8th. Are you in favor of maintaining the Constitutional rights of the South?

9th. Are you in favor of the re-enfranchisement and emancipation of the white men of the South, and the restitution of the Southern people to all their rights, alike proprietary, civil, and political?

10th. Do you believe in the inalienable right of self-preservation of the people against the exercise of arbitrary and unlicensed power? . . .

REVIEW QUESTIONS

1. How could the Klan express such reverence for the Constitution while castigating Union army veterans?
2. Why would poor whites have been attracted to the Klan?
3. How would freed slaves have reacted to the Klan's principles?

LEE GUIDON

FROM *Lay My Burden Down*

During the 1930s historians interviewed hundreds of former slaves. Their oral testimonies have provided a rich source of information about life in the South during Reconstruction. The following account of black culture and Klan activity was given by Lee Guidon, born a slave in upstate South Carolina.

From B. A. Botkin, ed., *Lay My Burden Down: A Folk History of Slavery* (Chicago: University of Chicago Press, 1945), pp. 223–24. Copyright 1989 by Curtis Brown, Ltd.

. . . After freedom a heap of people say they was going to name theirselves over. They named theirselves big names, then went roaming round like wild, hunting cities. They changed up so it was hard to tell who or where anybody was. Heap of 'em died, and you didn't know when you hear about it if he was your folks hardly. Some of the names was Abraham, and some called theirselves Lincum. Any big name 'cepting their master's name. It was the fashion. I heard 'em talking 'bout it one evening, and my pa say, "Fine folks raise us and we gonna hold to our own names." That settled it with all of us. . . .

I reckon I do know 'bout the Ku Kluck. I knowed a man named Alfred Owens. He seemed all right, but he was a Republican. He said he was not afraid. He run a tanyard[1] and kept a heap of guns in a big room. They all loaded. He married a Southern woman. Her husband either died or was killed. She had a son living with them. The Ku

---

[1] A place where hides are turned into leather.

Kluck was called Upper League. They get this boy to unload all the guns. Then the white men went there. The white man give up and said, "I ain't got no gun to defend myself with. The guns all unloaded, and I ain't got no powder and shot." But the Ku Kluck shot in the houses and shot him up like lacework. He sold fine harness, saddles, bridles—all sorts of leather things. The Ku Kluck sure run them outen their country. They say they not going to have them round, and they sure run them out, back where they came from. . . .

For them what stayed on like they were, Reconstruction times 'bout like times before that 'cepting the Yankee stole out and tore up a scandalous heap. They tell the black folks to do something, and then come white folks you live with and say Ku Kluck whup you. They say leave, and white folks say better not listen to them old Yankees. They'll git you too far off to come back, and you freeze. They done give you all the use they got for you. How they do? All sorts of ways. Some stayed at their cabins glad to have one to live in and farmed on. Some running round begging, some hunting work for money, and nobody had no money 'cepting the Yankees, and they had no homes or land and mighty little work for you to do. No work to live on. Some going every day to the city. That winter I heard 'bout them starving and freezing by the wagon loads.

I never heard nothing 'bout voting till freedom. I don't think I ever voted till I come to Mississippi. I votes Republican. That's the party of my color, and I stick to them as long as they do right. I don't dabble in white folks' business, and that white folks' voting is their business. If I vote, I go do it and go on home.

I been plowing all my life, and in the hot days I cuts and saws wood. Then when I gets outa cotton-picking, I put each boy on a load of wood and we sell wood. The last years we got $3 a cord. Then we clear land till next spring. I don't find no time to be loafing. I never missed a year farming till I got the Bright's disease[2] and it hurt me to do

hard work. Farming is the best life there is when you are able. . . .

When I owned most, I had six head mules and five head horses. I rented 140 acres of land. I bought this house and some other land about. The anthrax killed nearly all my horses and mules. I got one big fine mule yet. Its mate died. I lost my house. My son give me one room, and he paying the debt off now. It's hard for colored folks to keep anything. Somebody gets it from 'em if they don't mind.

The present times is hard. Timber is scarce. Game is about all gone. Prices higher. Old folks cannot work. Times is hard for younger folks too. They go to town too much and go to shows. They going to a tent show now. Circus coming, they say. They spending too much money for foolishness. It's a fast time. Folks too restless. Some of the colored folks work hard as folks ever did. They spends too much. Some folks is lazy. Always been that way.

I signed up to the government, but they ain't give me nothing 'cepting powdered milk and rice what wasn't fit to eat. It cracked up and had black something in it. A lady said she would give me some shirts that was her husband's. I went to get them, but she wasn't home. These heavy shirts give me heat. They won't give me the pension, and I don't know why. It would help me buy my salts and pills and the other medicines like Swamp Root. They won't give it to me.

REVIEW QUESTIONS

1. Why do you think some slaves changed their names after Emancipation?
2. What was the greatest challenge for ex-slaves? Explain.
3. According to this account, which problems were shared by former slaves and poor whites?

---

[2] A kidney ailment.

Klan Terrorism in South Carolina

During the early 1870s the Congress held hearings to investigate reports that the Ku Klux Klan was engaging in widespread intimidation and violence against blacks in the South. The following three documents relate to a series of racial incidents in York County, South Carolina in 1871. Throughout the South, where Radical Reconstruction was being implemented, blacks were joining Union Leagues, Republican organizations that also had secret rituals. The first document is an article from the Yorkville Enquirer *describing the rash of violence in the community. The second document is the courtroom testimony of a black woman,* Harriet Postle, *whose family was assaulted by Klansmen. The third document is the testimony of Lawson B. Davis, a white Klansman accused of such terrorism.*

From U.S. Congress, *Report of the Joint Select Committee to Inquire into the Condition of Affairs in the Late Insurrectionary States* (Washington, D.C., 1872), 3:1540–41; 1951–52; 1943–44.

Whipping and House-Burning.

The state of things which exists in many sections of our country is alarming. Scarcely a night passes but some outrage is perpetrated against the welfare of some community. Houses are burned, persons are whipped, and in some instances killed, by parties unknown, and for causes which no one can decipher. These things are not right; they are not prudent. They are grave crimes against God and the best interest of the country.

By common consent, the house-burning is charged upon the colored race, and the whipping and killing upon the so-called Ku-Klux. This is not certainly known to be the case, but the probability is that the supposition with regard to the perpetrators of these deeds is correct. One thing must be evident to every observing man: there is concert of action both in the house-burning and in the whipping and killing.

For some years there has been, and still is, we are informed by one who claims to know, an organization known as the Union League. Of this we know nothing, save what we have learned by observing its workings. From what we have been able to learn, we are convinced that the Union League is a secret political organization, and on this ground alone, if we knew nothing about its operations and results, we would condemn it. We take the broad ground that all secret political organizations are nothing but conspiracies against the established government of a country, and as such are ruinous to the peace and quiet and prosperity of the people.

Of the Ku-Klux we know even less than we do of the Union League. Sometimes we are disposed to believe that there is no such organization; at other times we think differently. Recent developments rather indicate that there is such an organization, and it is made of no mean material. This is mere conjecture on our part. We do not know one single individual who holds connection with the Ku-Klux. It is evident, however, that there is some sort of complicity of action in the whipping and killing that has recently been perpetrated in this country, and which is going on at present all over the State, and, in fact, all over the South.

We do not believe, from what we know of the political party which is opposed to the Union League and the political tenets of the dominant party in South Carolina, that the Ku-Klux is a political organization, in the strict sense of that term.

Whatever may be its object, we are convinced that the Ku-Klux is doing much harm. To be honest and frank, we charge the Union League with the shameful state of things which now exists. It has placed its members in a predicament which is anything but enviable. The ostensible purpose for which the thing was organized was, we suppose, to protect the freedman; the real purpose, however, was, as is acknowledged by some of its members, to consolidate the votes of the freedman, that designing men might be elevated to positions of honor and profit. There is no doubt but the Union League has done the colored people a great injury. It has been the means of arraying them in hostility against the white man, and the result always has been that in every conflict between the white man and the colored man, the condition of the latter has been materially injured. We do not blame the colored people for joining the League; but we do blame those designing white men who enticed them into this snare of destruction.

However much we may reprobate the Union League, this does not cause us to love or approve of the Ku-Klux. Two wrongs never can make one right. Both the Union League and the Ku-Klux are founded upon dangerous principles, and are working the ruin of this county. We have no disposition to make prediction, especially while so unsettled a state of things continues as exists in this county at present; but we will venture to say that if this house-burning and whipping does not stop soon, it will culminate in a conflict which will be fatal to some party.

What is the duty of every good citizen, under existing circumstances? It is the duty, we believe, of the leading colored people to influence their race to abandon the League and to refrain from acts of violence. On the other hand, it is the duty of the white people, especially the old men, to advise the young men not to engage in whipping and murdering the colored people. So long as the present state of things exists, no one is safe. The minds of the white people are filled with anxiety lest their houses may be burned down at any time, and no doubt the minds of the colored people are filled with dread lest they be dragged from their beds

and taken to the forest and whipped, or, perchance, shot. We have no party purposes to subserve by what we say. All we desire is to assist in restoring peace and quiet to our county. These outrages must stop now, or worse will come. If a few more houses are burned, the public mind will be so exasperated that, in all probability, something will be done that will be very injurious to the public good. It is the imperative duty of every good citizen to discourage house-burning and whipping. We must be permitted to say that it is our impression that, so long as the Union League exists, some kind of an opposing party will also exist. The sooner all such organizations cease to exist, the better it will be for all parties.

Testimony of Harriet Postle.

Examination by Mr. CORBIN:

I live in the eastern part of York County, about four miles from Rock Hill, on Mr. James Smith's plantation; I am about thirty years old; my husband is a preacher; I have a family of six children; the oldest is about fourteen; the Ku-Klux visited me last spring; it was some time in March; I was asleep when they came; they made a great noise and waked me up, and called out for Postle; my husband heard them and jumped up, and I thought he was putting on his clothes, but when I got up I found he was gone; they kept on hallooing for Postle and knocking at the door; I was trying to get on my clothes, but I was so frightened I did not get on my clothes at all; it looked like they were going to knock the door down; then the rest of them began to come into the house, and my oldest child got out and ran under the bed; one of them saw him and said, "There he is; I see him;" and with that three of them pointed their pistols under the bed; I then cried out, "It is my child;" they told him to come out; when my child came out from under the bed, one of them said, "Put it on his neck;" and the child commenced hallooing and crying, and I begged them not to hurt my child; the man did not hurt it, but one of them ran the child back against the wall, and ground a piece of skin off as big as my hand; I then took a chair and sat it back upon a loose plank, and sat down upon it; one of the men stepped up; seeing the plank loose, he just jerked the chair and threw me over, while my babe was in my arms, and I fell with my babe to the floor, when one of them clapped his foot upon the child, and another had his foot on me; I begged him, for the Lord's sake, to save my child; I went and picked up my babe, and when I opened the door and looked I saw they had formed a line; they asked me if Postle was there; I said no; they told me to make up a light, but I was so frightened I could not do it well, and I asked my child to make it up for me; then they asked me where my husband was; I told them he was gone; they said, "He is here somewhere;" I told them he was gone for some meal; they said he was there somewhere, and they called me a damned liar; one of them said: "He is under the house;" then one of them comes to me and says: "I am going to have the truth tonight; you are a damned, lying bitch, and you are telling a lie;" and he had a line, and commenced putting it over my neck; said he: "You are telling a lie; I know it; he is here;" I told them again he was gone; when he had the rope round my head he said, "I want you to tell where your husband is;" and, said he, "The truth I've got to have;" I commenced hallooing, and says he: "We are men of peace, but you are telling me a damned lie, and you are not to tell me any lies to-night;" and the one who had his foot on my body mashed me badly, but not so badly as he might have done, for I was seven or eight months gone in travail; then I got outside of the house and sat down, with my back against the house, and I called the little ones to me, for they were all dreadfully frightened; they said my husband was there, and they would shoot into every crack; and they did shoot all over the place, and there are bullet-holes there and bullet-marks on the hearth yet; at this time there were some in the house and some outside, and says they to me: "We're going to have the truth out of you, you damned, lying bitch; he is somewhere about here;" said I: "He is gone;" with that he clapped his hands on my neck, and with one hand put the line over my neck; and he says again: "We're going to have

the truth out of you, you damned bitch;" and with that he beat my head against the side of the house till I had no sense hardly left; but I still had hold of my babe.

Mr. CORBIN:

Question. Did you recognize anybody?

Answer. Yes, sir; I did; I recognized the first man that came into the house; it was Dr. Avery, [pointing to the accused.] I recognized him by his performance, and when he was entangling the line round my neck; as I lifted my hand to keep the rope off my neck, I caught his lame hand; it was his left hand that I caught, his crippled hand; I felt it in my hand, and I said to myself right then, "I knows you;" and I knew Joe Castle and James Matthews—the old man's son; I didn't know any one else; I suppose there was about a dozen altogether there; Dr. Avery had on a red gown with a blue face, with red about his mouth, and he had two horns on his cap about a foot long; the line that he tried to put over my neck was a buggy-line, not quite so wide as three fingers, but wider than two; they said to me that they rode thirty-eight miles that night to see old Abe Broomfield and preacher Postle; they said that they had heard that preacher Postle had been preaching up fire and corruption; they afterward found my husband under the house, but I had gone to the big house with my children to take them out of the cold, and I did not see them pull him out from the house.

*   *   *

Testimony of Lawson B. Davis,

Witness for the prosecution:

I reside in York County, and have lived there two years. I was initiated as a member of the Ku-Klux Klan. I took the oath at my own house. Three persons were initiated at the same time. I attended one meeting and heard the constitution and by-laws. That was in last January. The contents of the oath, as near as I can remember, were that female friends, widows, and orphans were to be objects of our protection, and that we were to support the Constitution as it was bequeathed to us by our forefathers; and there was to be opposition to the thirteenth, fourteenth, and fifteenth amendments.[1] The fourteenth was particularly specified in the oath I took. The oath was repeated, and I repeated it after them. There was no written document present. The penalty for divulging its secrets was death.

The constitution and by-laws were here handed to the witness by Mr. Corbin.

The witness continued: That is the same oath that I took except the second section, which, as repeated to me, was "opposition to the thirteenth, fourteenth, and fifteenth amendments." The organization, when I joined it, was called the Invisible Empire of the South. After I joined I found it was the asme as the Ku-Klux organization. When I found that I determined to leave them. The first meeting I attended there were eight or ten persons sworn in, and a proposition was brought forward to make a raid upon such and such persons. I inquired the reason, and they said they were prominently connected with the Union League. Their object was to discountenance people from joining the League. I heard this from the members. They said that those who belonged to the League were to be visited and warned; that they must discontinue their connection with the League. If they did not, on the second visit they were to leave the country, and if they didn't leave they were to be whipped; and if after this they did not leave, they were to be killed. I know this was how the purposes of the order were to be carried out. I have known of instances of raiding for guns.

They made one raid upon Jerry Adams; Charley Byers told me they had whipped him; he was to be chief of the Klan; he said they had scared the boy very badly—they had fired several guns at him, but didn't mean to hit him. The only charge I ever heard against Jerry Adams was that he was a

radical. He was a republican and a colored man. Charley Good, who was whipped very badly by the Klan, came to my house two or three days afterwards. He was a blacksmith, and a very good workman—the best in that part. Charley Good was whipped so badly that he could not follow his trade for several days. Two or three weeks after that he was killed.

Wesley Smith, and William Smith, and William White were among those who killed Charley Good. Smith said he was a member of Smarr's Klan, and some members of that Klan assisted in putting Charley Good's body out of the way. The two Smiths, I know, were members of the Klan. Charley Good was killed because he was a republican. He told me, in the presence of some other persons, that he knew who had whipped him. I told him it would be better for him to keep that to himself. Wesley Smith gave, as the reason for killing him, that Charley Good knew some of the party who had whipped him. I was ordered to assist in disposing of the body of Charley Good. I did not, till then, know that he was missing. They came and summoned me and Mr. Howard to go and secrete the body, which was lying near to where he was murdered.

Wesley Smith said that all who were members of the organization were required to assist, so that they might be connected with it, and that the matter might not get out. I told him that I did not want to go, but he said that all the members had to go. We were ordered to meet at the gate about a quarter of a mile from his house. I left about 9 o'clock and went up to Mr. Howard's, and Wesley Smith had given him the same instructions. He did not feel willing to go, and I said those were my feelings exactly. We waited until the hour had passed, and then when we left we met some ten or fifteen of the party. It was a dark night, and I only recognized Thomas L. Berry, Pinckney Caldwell, Wesley Smith, and Madison Smarr. He is said to be the chief of the Klan. Madison Smarr said I had escaped a scouring. He said the body was very heavy to carry. And Pinckney Caldwell told me that "Charley Good is now at the bottom of the river. The body would not sink, and I jumped in upon

---

[1] Amendments to the U.S. Constitution associated with the Civil War. The Thirteenth, ratified in 1865, abolished slavery; the Fourteenth (1866) provided "equal protection under the law"; and the Fifteenth (1870) granted the right to vote to black males.

him," he said, "and fastened him there, as well as I could, with a stake."

Charley Good was at one time a member of a militia company, and, being told it was not to his interest, he left it and returned his gun. He was regarded as a man of republican principles, and was considered a person of some influence in that neighborhood. I never heard him charged with being a member of the Union League.

*   *   *

REVIEW QUESTIONS

1. Based on these testimonies, characterize the methods used by the Klan to intimidate blacks.
2. According to these excerpts, why did the KKK harass certain blacks?
3. How did blacks react to this kind of continuous treatment? What choices did they have?